MW01132394

The Cassville Affairs

Also by Robert D. Jenkins, Sr.

The Battle of Peach Tree Creek: Hood's First Sortie, 20 July 1864 (2013)

To the Gates of Atlanta: From Kennesaw Mountain to Peach Tree Creek, 1–19 July 1864 (2015)

MERCER UNIVERSITY PRESS

Endowed by

TOM WATSON BROWN

and

THE WATSON-BROWN FOUNDATION, INC.

THE CASSVILLE AFFAIRS

Johnston, Hood, and the Failed Confederate Strategy in the Atlanta Campaign, 19 May 1864

Robert D. Jenkins, Sr.

MERCER UNIVERSITY PRESS
Macon, Georgia

MUP/ H1044

© 2024 by Mercer University Press
Published by Mercer University Press
1501 Mercer University Drive
Macon, Georgia 31207
All rights reserved. This book may not be reproduced in whole or in part, including illustrations, in any form (beyond that copying permitted by Sections 107 and 108 of the U.S. Copyright Law and except by reviewers for the public press), without written permission from the publisher.

28 27 26 25 24 5 4 3 2 1

Books published by Mercer University Press are printed on acid-free paper that meets the requirements of the American National Standard for Information Sciences—Permanence of Paper for Printed Library Materials.

Printed and bound in Canada.

This book is set in Adobe Caslon.

Cover/jacket design by Burt&Burt.

ISBN 978-0-88146-931-8
Cataloging-in-Publication Data is available from the Library of Congress

The sketch on the dust jacket depicts the Federal Cavalry charge at Cassville on the afternoon of 19 May 1864. While the artist is unknown, the sketch appeared in Homer Mead, *The Eighth Iowa Cavalry in the Civil War, Autobiography and Personal Recollections of Homer Mead, M.D., Augusta, Illinois* (Carthage, IL: S. C. Davidson,1925). Dr. Mead participated in the attack with the Iowa regiment and lost his horse in the charge.

to Shari Ann…

Acknowledgments

As I write this note from my "laughin' place," my Civil War library in the basement of our home atop Rocky Face Ridge, where I have the privilege of looking out across Dogwood Valley and at Taylor's Ridge—the same ridge that McPherson's Army of the Tennessee used to flank Dalton and the Confederate Army of Tennessee under General Joseph E. Johnston—I am reminded of all of the people who have helped me along the Cassville journey, people who have kept me from getting lost in the proverbial "briar patch" that is the Gravelly Plateau, or "Cassville Triangle," as I have chosen to name it.

From our home, which I affectionately call "Buzzard's Roost," much to the dismay of my beautiful and loving wife, Shari Ann, I am also reminded of all the places, both geographic and virtual, that this journey has taken me. With the advent of internet, online access to libraries, and friends and colleagues who communicate via email and other social media, discovering new sources, and reconsidering old sources, has never been more convenient. I have also been fortunate to be just forty-five minutes away, or a "lunch hour after court," from Cassville. During my trips to the battlefield, I have found multiple routes to reach Cassville from the north, much like Sherman and Hooker and Schofield and McCook and Stoneman did on a warm, no hot, Thursday, 19 May 1864. I have often wondered how the Confederate high command got things so mixed up there. That set me to thinking...and questioning....

I am grateful to Mercer University Press, editor Marc Jolley, and to the wonderful staff, Marsha Luttrell, Regenia Toole, and Mary Beth Kosowski, for your support, encouragement, and friendship, and for providing me with the latitude to develop this paper in both a historiographic and narrative form. Thank you, Marc, Marsha, Jenny, and Mary Beth! I am grateful!

I am also indebted to my friend and mentor, Dr. Elizabeth (Betsy) Hoole McArthur, for her wisdom, encouragement, and keen eye in editing this work, both for content and grammar. Betsy's father, Dr. William Stanley Hoole, was a founding member of the Alabama Historical Society and the editor-in-chief of its journal, the *Alabama Review*, from 1948 to 1967. Betsy has carried forward his mantle of historic literary excellence with wonderful scholarship. I am humbled by her continued support, advice, critique, encouragement, and friendship.

Thank you also to my friend and mentor, Charlie Crawford, for his review and advice and for catching many embarrassing errors. Thank you for your leadership in battlefield preservation in Georgia, for your support of Save the Dalton Battlefields, LLC, and the preservation of Potato Hill Park and other sites in Dalton and Whitfield County, and north Georgia. I am also so very thankful for your encouragement, wisdom, knowledge, and advice on my writing projects from Peach Tree Creek to Dalton to Cassville.

I am also grateful to a number of colleagues who have offered their assistance and have shared primary source materials. I am particularly indebted to my friends, historians Gary Ecelbarger of Alexandria, Virginia, and Dave Powell of Chicago, Illinois, who have graciously shared multiple sources with me and who have allowed me to banter and bounce theories and original (sometimes off-the-wall) ideas about Adairsville and Cassville when I needed a sounding board. Gary, your books on the battles of Atlanta and Ezra Church remain the best, most accurate works. I will be happy when you return to chase more battles in Georgia. Thank you also, Dave, for your advice on this project. Your magnum opus on the campaign promises to be epic! Thank you for letting me join along on the ride.

Thank you also to Chief Historian James (Jim) Ogden, Chickamauga and Chattanooga National Military Park, Fort Oglethorpe, Georgia, for your inspiration and direction, and for giving of your time from your ridiculously busy schedule to point me in the right direction on multiple occasions. It was Jim Ogden's suggestion that I try to determine the locations of Major General Joseph Wheeler and his cavalry that unlocked many of the mysteries of the Cassville conundrum. Once I was able to uncover the confusing road names, locations, and usages, and then place Wheeler's cavalrymen on the map, everything else began to fall into place. Thank you, Jim, for your wisdom, leadership, encouragement, and friendship, and for being available. Nobody knows the subject of the American Civil War better, and you share your knowledge so richly and freely. Your support is humbling, and I am grateful.

There are certain people you come across in life that, no matter what the circumstances, they will be there for you and will help you to get out of the ditch—the kind of giver that you cannot outgive. My friend T. D. (Dave) Helton is one of those people for me. Dave has tirelessly helped me both with this book project and with writing projects and Whitfield County parks projects in designing historic markers, images, and maps over the decades. Your expertise in graphic design and map-making is second to none. Thank you, Dave, both for your cartography work and for your friendship, and for letting me sing bad songs and tell silly jokes over the years. I am truly grateful and humbled by your friendship.

I am indebted to prior research by the late historians Wilbur G. Kurtz and William R. Scaife, who shed much light on the Atlanta Campaign and from whom much valuable information has been obtained over the years. The Kurtz papers at the Keenan Research Center, Atlanta History Center, remain one of the most important troves of treasure on the campaign.

I am also indebted to Professor Richard McMurry for your scholarship on the Atlanta Campaign and for your mentorship. Thank you, Richard, for your wit, your wisdom, your humor, your insights, your compassion, and your friendship. Thank you also for devoting time with me to challenge me with insights throughout this project, to sharpen my focus, and to point me to obscure sources. Thank you also for penning a foreword for this book. I am both grateful and humbled.

I am grateful, as well, for the friendship and advice from Dr. Steve Davis, who encouraged me to write an article on Cassville that ultimately led to this book. Bowden Hall, also known as the History Building at Emory University's History Department, has produced no finer historians of the Civil War than Richard and Steve. Bell Irvin Wiley would have been proud. Even a brief visit with either of you turns into an erudite discussion from your sagacious and eloquent sharing of knowledge and insights. I often run to Webster's and Roget's following such an encounter. I have been richly blessed by a network of historians and friends, and I am humbled by and grateful to both of you.

Thank you also to Larry Daniel for sharing your insights and manuscript on Adairsville for an upcoming series of essays on the Atlanta Campaign that, at the time my manuscript was delivered to the press, was yet to be published. Thank you to Dr. Keith Bohannon of the University of West Georgia for your support and for providing primary source materials freely over the years. Today's world of collaboration among Civil War historians is truly an exciting, rewarding, and enjoyable time, and the opportunities for correcting past errors in historiography by mutual sharing of primary sources and ideas have never been greater.

I am indebted to Mr. Trey Gaines, director of the Bartow County History Museum, and his staff for your support and access to the many maps, files, and primary materials located therein, including the 1949 Kurtz map that opened up the possibility of an error in the location of the Spring Place Road in previous studies.

I am indebted to historians and enthusiasts Matthew Beard, Stewart Bennett, Greg Biggs, Dale Black, James (Bo) Blalock, Brad Butkovich, Robert Carter, Chris Cash, Daniel Cone, Jerry Holmes, Stephen (Sam) Hood, Norman Dasinger Sr., Norman Dasinger Jr., Michael Hitt, Ken Padgett,

Tony Patton, Brad Quinlin, Blake Scoggins, Bradley Shumpert, Marvin Sowder, Brad Stephens, Lee White, Robert White, Wayne Willingham, Jeff Wright, and others who have shared information, maps, or articles, or identified and preserved the oral history of the area. The names and locations of such sites as Five Forks, the Spring Place Road, Crow Springs, Iron Mountain, Copper Mine Road, Dewey's Crossroads, and Wofford's (not Warford's) Crossroads hopefully will remain alive and correctly identified for future historians to hopefully find their way through the Cassville Triangle (Gravelly Plateau) successfully, thanks to the collective efforts of shared knowledge. Thank you, Norman, as well, for pointing me in the right direction at Rome and concerning the Henry Clayton Papers at ADAH.

I am especially grateful for all of the deep internet research and findings of Tony Patton, who has a unique talent for finding rare or overlooked manuscripts and maps, including many previously unpublished maps and documents from the National Archives and other government and university libraries and collections. Thank you, Tony. You are the best "rabbit hole" hunter, and your exceptional critical reasoning skills continue to unmask many lost or unknown facts, particularly at the Battle of Resaca and the events in northwest Georgia.

I am also thankful to Michael and Andrea Surcey, Matthew Beard, and to Huey Murphy for their hospitality and graciousness in allowing me to explore their property. Nothing beats being on the grounds of the place where important historic events happened. Thank you for opening up your homes and lands to allow me to explore! I am grateful to each of you.

As I am approaching the completion of six decades of spinning around the sun, I become increasingly aware of and grateful for the loving care, encouragement, and support provided to me by my family. I am grateful to my late father, Bob Jenkins; Aunt Elaine McIntyre; Uncle Ben and Aunt Sara Jenkins; Aunt "T" Aileen Beazley Hawkins; Aunt June Anderson; and grandparents Robert D. McRae and Marguerite McRae, who loved and encouraged me throughout their lives. I am also thankful for the love, support, encouragement, and friendship of my mother, Joy Jenkins. Thank you, Mom, Mama, Grampster, for being the perfect mother!

I am reminded that all things come from God, and that He is the Alpha and Omega, the Great Provider, and the source of all wisdom. I am humbled and thankful that God has richly blessed me with a loving wife and soulmate, Shari Ann Jenkins; two children, Katie Beth Jenkins and Robert Jenkins Jr.; two stepchildren, Joshua Halliburton and Anna Halliburton; longtime workmate and friend, Amy Harris; and a law practice where hopefully God has used our office to help other people during a time of need in their lives. Any success that I have achieved is due to the grace and gift of God.

Finally, thank you to my wife, Shari. During much of my life, I often wondered what having a soulmate looked and felt like. I am so very humbled and grateful to God that Shari came into my life. Thank you for the countless hours that you have endured as I shared the newest revelation about Cassville on so many occasions. Thank you for your wisdom, advice, patience, sacrifice, support, and encouragement. In you, I have found my love, my life mate, my soulmate, the keeper of my heart, and my best friend. Thank you for loving me. Thank you for choosing me. Thank you for being my heart. I dedicate this book to you.

Always,
Bobby Jenkins
Buzzard's Roost, Georgia
2 May 2023

Foreword

People who study American history attach much importance to certain dates: 4 July 1776 (the Declaration of Independence); 6 April 1917 (the United States enters World War I); and 7 December 1941 (the attack on Pearl Harbor). Civil War historians also point to several especially consequential days: 12 April 1861 (the firing on Fort Sumter); 1 January 1863 (the Emancipation Proclamation takes effect); and 14 April 1865 (Abraham Lincoln is shot at Ford's Theater).

Those of us who happily spend our time trying to understand the Civil War as it unfolded in the all-important area between the Appalachian Mountains and the Mississippi River can also point to crucial days on which key events occurred: 6 April 1862 (the death of Albert Sidney Johnston at Shiloh); 4 July 1863 (the surrender of Vicksburg); 29 November 1864 (the Confederate fiasco at Spring Hill); and 19 May 1864....

What in the world happened 19 May 1864? The better question is what did *not* happen then? The even better question is *why* didn't it happen? In this important book Robert Jenkins attempts to answer these questions.

I'll not spoil the suspense by giving you the answers here. Suffice it to say for now that if Bob's thesis holds up under the cross-examination that is sure to come (as a lawyer, he will appreciate the analogy), it will go far to enhance our understanding of the war in the West. It will also have an impact on the way we think about some important Confederates.

Richard M. McMurry
Dalton, Georgia
1 May 2023

CONTENTS

APPENDICES

Index of Exhibits

*Note: Only a section of these maps is shown. The actual maps are much larger, and a full-sized would be unreadable. Most of these maps are available from the National Archives, and the URL for each available full-size map is included.

**Appears at the end of the Index of Maps

Index of Maps

*Note- the placement of the divisions and corps, and most of the brigades, for each of the Federal and Confederate units on the maps provided are based on primary sources discovered by the author. A few of the Confederate brigade placements are based upon the author's interpretation when no definitive source is available. In these instances, the author has provided this clarification and his explanation in the body of the text.

Road Number Key to Maps[1]

No.	Name
1	Adairsville-Cassville Road (today US 41, Ga. 3, Joe Frank Harris Hwy.)
2	Copper Mine Road, Ironton Road, Old Spring Place Road (1820s–1840s) (today, south to north, Kimsey Circle, Janice Lane, Cedar Creek Road)
2a	Mosteller's Mill Road
2b	Section of Ironton (Iron Mountain) Road (no longer in existence)
2c	By-Road (Wheeler) (no longer in existence)
2d	Unnamed cut-off road from "the forks in the road" (Hooker's term) (today Manning Mill Road)
2e	Section of Ironton (Iron Mountain) Road (no longer in existence)
3	Spring Place Road (since about 1851)
3a	"Country Road" (Johnston's term); it connected with the new Spring Place Road (Road 3) (today Brown Loop Road)
4	Pine Log Road, also Fairmount Road (today Cass-White Road)
5	Canton Road (today Old Cass-White Road)
6	Tennessee Road, also Jackson Military Road (1825), also Old Federal Road (today US 411, Ga. 61)
7	Adairsville-Pine Log-Canton Road (today Ga. 140)
8	Adairsville-Kingston Road (today, Hall Station Road)
9	Kingston-Cassville Road (today Kingston Hwy, Ga. 293, Fire Tower Road)
10	Cartersville Road (today, Mac Johnson Road)

[1] Key to maps prepared by Robert Jenkins and T. D. Helton.

PART 1

THE MORNING AFFAIR: THE FAILED CONFEDERATE OFFENSIVE

Introduction

The events of 19 May 1864, at and around Cassville, Georgia, remain two of the most confusing and misunderstood controversies of the war. In what has come to be known as the Cassville Affair, the Confederate Army of Tennessee, commanded by General Joseph E. Johnston, planned a surprise attack on the pursuing Federal forces led by Major General William T. Sherman. Instead of launching an offensive against the Northerners, however, or digging in to repel the bluecoats the following day, Johnston reluctantly withdrew his army overnight.

While it is called the Cassville Affair, there were two controversies, or affairs, at Cassville that led to the Southern withdrawal from the village without compelling a fight. The first one was the inability of the Confederate army to initiate its surprise attack on the *morning* of 19 May. The second, which occurred on the *evening* of that day, was the failure of the Southern forces to maintain a defensive position at Cassville, or Manassas, as the city had come to be named in honor of the Confederate victory at the Battle of First Manassas.

After realizing that his opportunity for striking a blow against a portion of the pursuing Federals had passed, Johnston moved his army from a range of hills north and west of Cassville to a line of hills south and east of the town where he had his men entrench. There, he expected to receive and repel an attack by Sherman's legions the following day. Instead, following a dispute with two of his corps commanders, lieutenant generals John Bell Hood and Leonidas Polk, Johnston reluctantly withdrew his army south of the Etowah River to fight another day. The first, or Morning Cassville Affair, is the subject of part 1, while the events of the Evening Cassville Affair or controversy, is covered in part 2.

The organization for this book is unconventional. First, the two Cassville affairs, the Morning Offensive and the Evening Defensive, have been separated into two parts to dissect and discuss each more effectively. The two "affairs" were clearly separate events that required different decisions by the Confederate leaders, the first whether to attack, and the second, whether to remain and defend. Over time, and through the tangled historiography of the Cassville events, historians and students have merged the two into one subject, or "affair," as they struggled to determine whether Johnston or Hood was telling the truth about what happened while they each defended their reputation. By exploring the two events and the command decisions separately, the two dilemmas that the Southern leaders faced can be better understood. Also, a timeline of events, as well as a better understanding of the location of troops at given times, can be developed.

The other unconventional organization in this book is that it contains a mixture of both a historiographic and narrative form. What has been previously published on Cassville has been based on false or inaccurate records contained in *The War of the Rebellion: A Compilation of the Official Records of the Union and Confederate Armies* (or, *Official Records*, cited as *OR*), or on a faulty understanding of the road structure, or on a leader's statement, which was often self-serving or misleading, without testing the validity of each claim. Thus, a considerable amount of inaccurate history has been published, even after the most careful efforts by previous scholars. The subject is complex. The events were confusing, the roads were not understood (then or now), and the available accounts were sparse. Certain chapters are therefore devoted to explaining (and correcting) events as they were previously understood while other chapters flow more freely in narrative form to tell the story of what did occur.

The rural road structure between Adairsville and Cassville, and the land to the east of these small towns, has never been fully explored or explained in previous writings. This area is known locally as the Gravelly Plateau. The region is a densely forested, rugged, and hilly range across which there were a handful of winding roads and wagon trails with various names that have not been clarified by previous studies. Unfortunately, some historians have incorrectly labeled some of these roads based on inaccurate assumptions or false or misleading documents. I am hopeful this book will correct these mistakes and fill some of the gaps in our knowledge and understanding of both the region and the roads across the Gravelly Plateau. For clarity, I will call this area the Cassville Triangle, denoting the space between Cassville, Adairsville, and Pine Log. It is southeast of Adairsville and northeast of Cassville, forming a triangle of towns that lie ten to twelve miles from each other. Chapter 5 provides an in-depth study of the road network across the Gravelly Plateau where the Confederate army made plans to attack a part of Sherman's legions as they traveled to Cassville.

After untangling the elusive road names, locations, and usages, tracing the troop movements of the various forces on a timeline becomes paramount, but any analysis of troop movements or timelines without a clear and accurate picture of the terrain and road structure would be speculative. Therefore, a series of maps showing the locations of units, North and South, at various times during the events leading up to and including the clash at Cassville, have been included, together with a detailed key identifying each of the roads and the names used to describe each road.

The maps I created were made in conjunction with the outstanding mapmaking and computer graphics skills of my friend and colleague, T. D. (Dave) Helton.[1] The 1891 topographic base map was selected for several important reasons.

First, the base map strikes a balance between being closest to the Civil War time frame while taking advantage of the more modern surveying and mapmaking advances that occurred in the late 1800s. Second, it was created before the advent of bulldozers and other large earth-moving equipment and before the creation of several major highways and accompanying commercial developments. The base map has been overlayed with the data collected from the other maps and studies provided herein to provide as much detail—including homesteads, road locations, and the Civil War era topography—as possible. Because this study involves a number of maps, each map is identified either by the name of its creator or by the name of the officer for whom it was prepared. Maps that were created by others, including the military engineers,

---

[1] The base map we used is derived from multiple sources: an 1891 topographical map prepared by the United States Geological Survey Department, J. W. Powell, director (scale 1:125000). It includes descriptions and references from the maps of the Atlanta Campaign, Second Epoch, compiled by Edward Ruger, superintendent, Topographical Engineer Office, Army of the Cumberland, and T.B. Van Horne, published in 1875 and amended 1877 to include surveys made by J. T. Dodge and captured Confederate maps as preserved in the Library of Congress, and as published in the *Atlas to Accompany the Official Records of the Union and Confederate Armies, 1891–1895*, Plate 58, Map 1, commonly referred to as "The Second Epoch" (hereafter the "Ruger Map"). The author's maps also include references from hand-drawn maps by Captain W.E. Merrill, chief topographical engineer for the Army of the Cumberland and used by the Federal forces in the Atlanta Campaign; Captain Edward A. Bennett, topographical engineer for the Army of the Cumberland's XX Corps, 18–23 May 1864, *Official Atlas*, Plate 101, Map 11 (hereafter the "Merrill Map"); G. W. Blakeslee, Map of Route of Harrison's [Ward's] Brigade from Adairsville to Euharlee, 17–23 May 1864 (hereafter the "Blakeslee Map"); Captain Wilbur S. Foster, Confederate engineer (hereafter the "Foster Map"); Major General Will. T. Martin, "Maps of Adairsville, Cassville, Cartersville and vicinity," prepared by John M. Stewart, engineer, and J.S. Tyner, assistant engineer for Major General Will. T. Martin (hereafter the "Martin Map"); and Major General Jos. Wheeler, Copy of a Rebel Map Received from War Department Showing Georgia, produced in 1864 (hereafter the "Wheeler Map").

officers and participants, and previous historians, are included in the index of exhibits. Maps I created with the technical assistance of T. D. Helton are in the index of maps. The base map, called the "Jenkins and Helton Base Map" (Map 1), contains a number designation for each of the relevant roads in our study, which can be located in the key and referenced throughout the text.[2]

Next, unraveling the plan of the attack (and the difference between Johnston's understanding of the battle plan versus Hood's understanding of it) is vital. What was the plan? When, where, and how was the surprise attack to be launched, and what happened to disrupt the plan? A comparison of the two leaders' battle plans, or explanations, is covered in chapters 6 and 7. Johnston's and Hood's battle plans for the Cassville Offensive were different, and only through the prism of a study of the roads, official reports and journals (the original manuscripts and the published *Official Records* versions), letters, diaries, postwar writings by the men and officers, as well as previous historical

---

[2] See Wheeler's report, *OR*, ser. 1, vol. 38, pt. 3, 946. Compare the Confederate Foster, Martin, and Wheeler maps with the maps prepared by Merrill and Ruger.

Additional sources consulted for the base map include Wilbur G. Kurtz's 1949 hand-drawn map prepared for Colonel Thomas Spencer, published in the *Cartersville (GA) Daily Tribune News*, 8 November 1949 (hereafter the "Kurtz Map 2"). An earlier map prepared by Wilbur G. Kurtz for Bartow County appeared in Cunyus, *History of Bartow County*, 233 (hereafter the "Kurtz Map 1"). Importantly, in this 1933 work, Kurtz drew only four roads on the Adairsville–Canton arc, and he included a reference to a Spring Place Road in a location (up the road to Mosteller's Mill and shown as Road 2 and 2a). But in his map of 1949, Kurtz did not include this reference, and he added a fifth road in the correct location for the Spring Place Road northeast of Cassville, connecting it with the Pine Log Road at the Five Forks intersection.

Also consulted was a map prepared by Captain Walter J. Morris, chief engineer, Confederate Army of Mississippi, 19 May 1864, *Official Atlas*, Plate 62, Map 7 (hereafter the "Morris Map"). This map features prominently in the Evening Cassville Controversy concerning the Confederate defensive operations at Cassville during the evening of 19 May 1864.

Also consulted were the maps prepared by William R. Scaife, one each for the Morning (hereafter the "Scaife Map 1") and Evening (hereafter the "Scaife Map 2") Affairs (Scaife, *Campaign for Atlanta*, 48e; "Waltz between the Rivers," 284a).

I discovered a map published in the *New Orleans Times Picayune*, Sunday, 22 October 1893. It was prepared by Joseph E. Johnston in 1874 (hereafter the "Johnston Map"). This map is important because it provides insight into Johnston's understanding of the location of the "country road" that he referred to in his memoirs, and it also provides specific geographic references that can be identified today. See Johnston to Johnsen, 19 June 1874, 319; also, *New Orleans Times Picayune*, 22 October 1893.

analyses, can the mysteries of the Morning Cassville Affair be solved and the origins of misunderstandings and misstatements be traced.[3]

Also, a thorough review of the Federal perspective is warranted. Virtually all previous articles on Cassville have focused on the dispute between Johnston and Hood, and understandably so, as it is integral to the issue. To properly place the Northern troops on the map and follow the sequence of their movements on 18 and 19 May across the Gravelly Plateau, or Cassville Triangle, research of primary source material, both North and South, is imperative. Neither placing Federal soldiers on an imaginary map based on where or when Johnston or Hood believed or expected them to be, nor assuming (or even guessing) which soldiers were on which roads, is adequate.

The events at Cassville did not happen in a vacuum. Like all events, what happens immediately before necessarily affects the events that follow, regardless of preparation. Thus, the events following the evacuation of Resaca by the Confederate forces and their pursuit by the Federals—including the action at Adairsville, Rome, and Kingston—are covered in chapters 2 and 3.

One unique advantage in a study of the Cassville Affairs is that after 19 May both sides separated their forces a few miles away and took a three-day respite (Friday, 20 May–Monday, 23 May), after which Sherman renewed his offensive with another flanking movement into the woods and dense underbrush of Paulding County. This maneuver would lead to the battles around New Hope Church, which soldiers called the "Hell Hole." It was during this lull that a considerable volume of letters and diary entries were written. Students of Cassville can glean much about what happened during the first three weeks of the campaign for Georgia through these largely untapped sources.

Drawing on all available primary material, chapter 9 provides a narrative of the events that occurred on the morning of 19 May. This section explains how the events unfolded on the morning of 19 May around Cassville and allows readers and students to follow the correct courses of the Federal units into town, distinguish between Hood's battle plan and Johnston's battle plan (or Johnston's understanding of it), and put to rest any remaining doubt about the location of Major General Daniel Butterfield's division as it approached Cassville from the northwest around the same time that McCook's troopers arrived from the northeast. At the start of this project, I thought that part of Butterfield's Division had wandered east into Hood's troops, but detailed research into both primary materials and road structures has corrected that impression. I hope it will correct the readers' beliefs, as well.

[3] Resources devoted to Cassville are listed in the bibliography.

During the Civil War there was no standard measurement of time. Critical to a study of events during a battle, however, is the sequence of events and the relationship of events with each other. For example, *when* something occurs helps to explain *why* certain leaders and soldiers acted or reacted in the ways that they did. The times provided in the text are derived from the participants. While they may not have all used the same standard measurement of time or accurately recorded the time of their participation, they provide a reference from which a timeline of the events can be determined. Ironically, each time given by the participants throughout the day can be corroborated by multiple contemporaneous sources, and each time posted matches within a reasonable timeframe the many other events as they occurred across the battlefield.

Finally, some of the original or primary source materials concerning the events at Cassville have been altered. Two critical discrepancies have been found between the original manuscripts and the accounts that were published in the *Official Records*, a source that most Civil War historians have come to rely upon as infallible. Published between 1880 and 1901, these records are a massive collection of reports, dispatches, correspondence, and orders bundled together into 128 volumes. The collection was intended to be as complete a set of accounts on the events, campaigns, and battles of the war as possible. In large part, it has accomplished its mission—so much so that its accuracy has rarely been challenged. However, at least two errors need to be examined to correct the previously misunderstood and mis-told story of Cassville. These will be covered in chapter 4.

Hopefully, with new revelations presented here, readers will be able to see the past errors in Cassville's historiography and begin to imagine the scenes of 19 May through the prism of the new materials and new perspectives. So, from Buzzard's Roost, the site of the beginning of the Georgia Campaign (Atlanta Campaign for the traditionalists), the campaign that decided the fate of the war (for my Eastern Theater-centric friends), I hope that this book will both challenge and inspire you to reexamine the controversial events at Cassville and the Confederate leadership during this decisive campaign.

Chapter 1

Johnston's Campaign Strategy

Following the crossing of the Oostanaula River by Brigadier General Thomas M. Sweeny's Federal division at Lay's Ferry on 15 May 1864, Johnston's outnumbered Confederate troops fell back from Resaca, first to Calhoun on Monday, 16 May, and then to Adairsville on Tuesday, 17 May.[1] Sherman continued to apply pressure by spreading his forces along a wide arc, hoping to force battle between the Oostanaula River and the Etowah River, some thirty-five miles to the south. Sherman believed that Johnston would try to retreat below the Etowah River to seek safety in the Allatoona Mountains where the Western & Atlantic Railroad, the lifeline for both armies, ran through a strongly fortified pass. Sherman wanted to attack Johnston between the two rivers, where the open ground was devoid of the rugged mountain ridges that existed north of the Oostanaula River between Dalton and Chattanooga, or south of the Etowah River around the Allatoona Mountains.

Johnston believed that Dalton, where his army had encamped for the winter, was indefensible, despite the long Rocky Face Ridge mountain range that protected this "Gateway to Georgia," as Dalton has been called. The Confederate leader reasoned that Dalton could be flanked by a Federal force moving from Chattanooga to Rome, where the Northern invaders could then strike east to Kingston to cut his line of supply and communication with Atlanta. Instead, Sherman's men surprised Johnston by slipping through Snake Creek Gap and striking Resaca, where they found the gap, in the words of historian Richard McMurry, "unoccupied, unguarded, unobstructed, and unobserved."[2] The Gateway into Georgia had been opened via the back door!

However, on 8 May 1864, Brigadier General James Cantey, who was at Resaca, informed Johnston that Federals were traveling through Snake Creek Gap. Cantey had learned the news from Confederate scouts who were patrolling the gap. When he learned of the threat, Johnston immediately dispatched Colonel Warren Grigsby's Kentucky cavalry brigade. Grigsby's Kentucky

---

[1] Reports of Major General Grenville M. Dodge and Brigadier General John M. Corse, *OR*, ser. 1, vol. 38, pt. 3, 378, 400; Major General Sherman, correspondence with Major General Henry W. Halleck and with Corse, *OR*, ser. 1, vol. 38, pt. 4, 189, 196–98.

[2] McMurry, *Atlanta 1864*, 63.

troopers were the same ones who had alerted Johnston to the Federal threat at Dug Gap Mountain. Also, together with the 1st and 2nd Arkansas Mounted Rifles (dismounted), Grigsby's men fought a severe battle for three hours against Brigadier General John W. Geary's division between 4 p.m. and 7 p.m. While resting and fixing a late dinner that evening, they received Johnston's order to ride to Sugar Valley at the southern end of Snake Creek Gap and confront the second threatening Federal force.[3]

Johnston reportedly told Colonel Ellison Capers of the 24th South Carolina Infantry Regiment (Gist's Brigade) during the winter encampment at Dalton, that "a mountainous country is bad fighting ground, and a mountain line a bad line to defend, as the mountains are curtains behind which the enemy can mass his troops unseen, and by sudden flank movements take his adversary by disadvantage."[4]

In contrast, Major General Daniel E. Sickles, who had been sent by President Abraham Lincoln to observe and advise him on the progress of Sherman's campaign into Georgia, reported to Lincoln following the Battle of Resaca, "I have accompanied General Sherman's army in the successful campaign from Chattanooga to Resaca, witnessing the retreat of the enemy from successive lines of fortified positions through forty miles of mountains. *If Georgia cannot be defended on its northern frontier it cannot be defended anywhere.*"[5]

Johnston claimed in his postwar apology, published ten years afterward, that he wanted to give battle at Calhoun, but upon arrival he discovered two things: 1) there was no suitable location from which he could cover and defend the multiple roads and fords that lay south of the Oostanaula River between Snake Creek Gap and Resaca, and 2) "a large creek, the Oothcalooga [Oothkalooga Creek], which must have divided any position taken, would have been a great impediment."[6]

However, in Johnston's official report of the campaign, written shortly after his removal from command and the fall of Atlanta, he explained that his

---

[3] Tell, "Special Correspondence from Cantey's Brigade," *Montgomery Weekly Advertiser*, 8 June 1864; Cantey to Brigadier General William W. Mackall, chief of staff, *OR*, ser. 1, vol. 38, pt. 4, 678; Mackall original journal (hereafter Mackall Journal, "A" sample).

[4] Capers, *Soldier-Bishop Ellison Capers*, 79.

[5] Sickles to Lincoln, 16 May 1864, *OR*, ser. 1, vol. 38, pt. 4, 215–16, and authority affirmed by Sherman at p. 11. Emphasis added.

[6] Johnston, *Narrative of Military Operations*, 319.

reason for not fighting at Calhoun was that he had not yet consolidated all of the reinforcements from Lieutenant General Leonidas Polk's Army of Mississippi.[7] In fairness, Johnston had not yet received Major General Samuel French's division of some forty-seven hundred effective infantry, which was still trying to join him from Alabama before the Federals closed the door on Rome on 17 and 18 May.[8] Brigadier General William H. Jackson's Confederate cavalry division with at least thirty-seven hundred troopers also arrived during this time.[9] With these additions, Johnston would have as many as seventy-four thousand men of all arms at and around Cassville.[10]

Johnston's army strength during the Atlanta Campaign has been difficult to navigate and verify, in part because Confederate reinforcements arrived piecemeal throughout May 1864 as conditions in Georgia rapidly changed with the Federal advance. Another variable was the way most Confederate reports calculated troop strength. For example, in the "Return for Johnston's

---

[7] Johnston's report, *OR*, ser. 1, vol. 38, pt. 3, 615.

[8] This number includes French's Division of Cockrell's Missouri (1,490), Ector's North Carolina and Texas (1,165), and Sears' Mississippi (2,110) Brigades (see *OR*, ser. 1, vol. 32, pt. 3, 862). When these troops arrived at Cassville, however, a request was made for six thousand rations to feed French's Division (see *OR*, ser. 1, vol. 38, pt. 4, 725). Additionally, the balance of Polk's artillery arrived with French with another three hundred artillerists and twelve guns. With the addition of these men, together with the noncombatants or slightly sick men, French's Division on 10 June numbered 5,666 present, a figure tallied after the loss of casualties from Cassville through the New Hope Church battles (see *OR*, ser. 1, vol. 38, pt. 3, 677).

[9] Jackson's Division, which includes Armstrong's Mississippi, Ferguson's Alabama/Mississippi, and Ross's Texas cavalry brigades, on 10 June had an effective total of 4,747, and an aggregate present of 6,056 (see *OR*, ser. 1, vol. 38, pt. 3, 677). However, Johnston claimed that Jackson came with only 3,700 troopers. (See Johnston, "Opposing Sherman's Advance to Atlanta," 267.)

[10] In a letter to his wife, Nellie, dated 25 June 1864, trooper William L. Nugent of Ferguson's Cavalry Brigade pointed out the failure of the Confederate forces to consolidate until they reached the vicinity of Marietta. Believing that if the Southern army had come together north of the Oostanaula River, then the great battle could have been fought at or near Resaca. "I do not know who is to blame for all this, nor that any one is censurable," he concluded. "At Resaca the Yankees detached a whole army corps [just Davis's Division] and sent it to Rome beyond supporting distance. If Johnston, at this opportune moment, could have had Polk's army and all the troops he now has, Sherman would have been crushed. As it was, he was compelled to fall back to secure his left flank & protect the communications" (Cash and Howorth, eds., *My Dear Nellie*, 184–85).

Army of Tennessee," dated 30 April 1864, which is the last report for Johnston's army while located in Dalton, Johnston claimed to have an "effective total," of 43,887 men in and around Dalton and northwest Georgia (an area that included Rome, Calhoun, and Resaca). The "effective total" is the number of infantrymen carrying a rifle, or artillerists ready to man a gun, or cavalrymen with a healthy horse ready to take to the field. It excluded officers of all branches of service. However, Johnston reported a total of 63,777 officers and men present in all branches (including the sick or infirm and noncombatants) in the same area as of 30 April 1864, a week prior to the opening of the Atlanta Campaign.[11]

In espousing the Fabian Policy,[12] expanded on by nineteenth-century American officer Dennis Hart Mahan, Johnston believed in the "active

---

[11] By 9 May 1864, when McPherson's forces advanced out of Snake Creek Gap to threaten Resaca, Johnston had some 65,464 men available to him. These included the addition of 400 men from the 37th Mississippi Infantry of Cantey's Brigade that arrived in Resaca prior to the action, plus 927 men from the 63rd Georgia Infantry who had joined Mercer's Brigade at Dalton, and another 360 men of the 1st and 2nd Arkansas mounted Infantry, Dismounted, who had arrived in time to repel Geary's Division assault on Dug Gap Mountain on 8 May (see Mackall Journal, "A" sample, 8 May 1864; *OR*, ser. 1, vol. 38, pt. 3, 676).

By 13 May 1864, when the battle opened at Resaca, with the addition of 6,208 officers and men of all branches in Loring's Division from west Alabama (though, since not all of Loring's regiments had arrived yet in Georgia, this figure must be reduced by perhaps 1,500 men), and the balance of General Daniel H. Reynolds's brigade, which included the 4th and 25th Arkansas infantry regiments and the 39th North Carolina Infantry Regiment, totaling approximately another 800 men, it is possible that Johnston had as many as 70,862 men of all arms at Resaca, including officers and noncombatants (*OR*, ser. 1, vol. 38, pt. 3, 676, *OR*, ser. 1, vol. 32, pt. 3, 862).

With French's Division of infantry and artillery, and Jackson's Division of cavalry added at Cassville, Johnston had, at least in theory, more than 80,000 (82,584) soldiers available, and well over 70,000 "combat-ready" men. It is reasonable, therefore, to conclude that while Johnston had only 40,000 to 45,000 "effective" (present for duty) men at Dalton during the first week of May, he had between 60,000 to 65,000 men at Resaca the following week, and 70,000 to 75,000 men a few days later at Cassville. For an excellent discussion of the Confederate troop strength during the Atlanta Campaign, see McMurry, *Atlanta 1864*, 194–97, and Newton, *Lost for the Cause*, 89–129.

[12] The Fabian policy derives its name from the Roman leader Quintus Fabius Maximus Verrucosus, who was called the "Cunctator," meaning the "Delayer."

defensive" strategy. Mahan, a 1824 graduate of West Point, studied at the French School of Application for Artillery and Engineering at Metz, France, from 1825 to 1830. Mahan believed that the common American citizen-soldier could best be used by acting on the defensive first from behind field fortifications. In his "active defensive" scheme, Mahan reasoned that if the Americans could entice the enemy to strike at him first while acting on the defensive, that he could weaken the enemy, and then counterstrike to his advantage. Mahan believed that because America had a much smaller standing army than the European powers of the time (France, England, and Prussia, who each fielded large, professional armies), this concept was more suited for the young nation.[13]

Mahan's "active defensive" strategy was rejected by virtually all nineteenth-century American military leaders in favor of the more popular theory of war advanced by Antoine Henri Jomini. Jomini advocated the "direct approach, or massing of troops for frontal attacks," as explained by historian Earl Hess, who wrote, "Jomini and others even believed the spirited offensive could be successful against field fortifications."[14]

The origins of our traditional understanding of the events at Adairsville and Cassville can be traced to early historians Matthew Forney Steele and Thomas Robson Hay. In 1909, Steele, a major in the Second United States Cavalry (later commissioned as colonel), and, between 1903 and 1909, an instructor at the US Army War College in Fort Leavenworth, Kansas, was a native of Huntsville, Alabama. Born in 1861, Steele was raised by his mother, steeped in the postwar nostalgia and Southern sentiment, which supported popular heroes, including Johnston. Steele became a United States officer with an excellent reputation for his knowledge of military history and tactics.

In 1909, Steele published *American Campaigns*, one of the first serious studies of American military campaigns from the Colonial Wars (pre-Revolutionary War) to the Spanish-American War. In his work, which included twenty of twenty-seven chapters on Civil War campaigns, one of which was devoted to the Atlanta Campaign, Steele, citing Johnston's published statements in his *Narrative of Military Operations* and his article in *Battles and*

During the Second Punic War (218–201 BCE), when the numerically superior North African army (led by Hannibal) invaded Rome, Fabius successfully delayed his enemy for eighteen years until he was finally able to subdue him ("Quintus Fabius Maximus Verrucosus").

[13] Hess, *Field Armies and Fortifications*, 5–7.

[14] Ibid.

Leaders, espoused Johnston's positions about the Confederate command decisions at Adairsville and Cassville. As for supporting primary sources, Steele relied upon the "O" sample "Journal" by T. B. Mackall, and the "Memoranda" of William Mackall. Critically, neither of these two sources provides any support for Johnston's claim that he devised a battle plan at Adairsville. Both Mackall documents will be examined in detail in this text. Concerning Johnston's claims relative to the "Evening Cassville Affair," Steele again relied on Johnston's claims from his postwar writings in accepting his position and supported it with the diary of Samuel G. French and a journal of Major Henry Hampton. Both of these sources will be examined, as well, in Part II.[15]

Beginning with articles in 1923 and 1924, historian Thomas Robson Hay, a native of Philadelphia and graduate of Pennsylvania State College (now Penn State University), advanced Johnston's position in a series of academic journals. After receiving an electrical engineering degree and developing a career as an editor of trade journals, Hay pursued his passion in the study of the Civil War. Bringing an academic and scientific mind to the subject, and one that was not affected by any preconceived Southern loyalties or bias, Hay also believed Johnston's version of the events at Adairsville and Cassville, and other than citing a letter from Johnston to veteran Charles Johnsen of the Washington Artillery of New Orleans, written in 1874, the same year that Johnston's *Narrative of Military Operations* was published, Hay produced no new or primary sources. Hay cited Johnston, Steele, and the string citations from Steele's 1909 work in each of his first two published articles, which appeared in the *Georgia Historical Quarterly* in March 1923 and June 1924. Steele lived to be ninety-one and died in 1953 in Fargo, North Dakota, while Hay lived until 1972 and passed at the age of eighty-five in Glen Cove, Long Island, New York.[16]

With these two pillars, a Southern-born army officer and instructor in the United States military, and a Northern-born academic, writer, editor, and historian, both of whom strongly supported Johnston's position against President Davis and collaterally as it related to John Bell Hood, the military

---

[15] Steele, *American Campaigns*, 1:539–40; Johnston, *Narrative of Military Operations*, T. B. Mackall Journal, "O" sample, in *OR*, ser. 1, vol. 38, pt. 3, 978–91, W. W. Mackall, "Memoranda of the Operations at Cassville on May 19, 1864," *OR*, ser. 1, vol. 38, pt. 3, 621–22; French, *Two Wars*; Major Henry Hampton, "Itinerary of Hardee's Army Corps May 15–June 14," *OR*, ser. 1, vol. 38, pt. 3, 704–708.

[16] Thomas Robson Hay, "The Atlanta Campaign," 23–24; Hay, "The Davis-Hood-Johnston Controversy of 1864," 69.

reputation of Joseph E. Johnston, the veracity of his statements—and the validity of his positions relative to the Atlanta Campaign—was secured. Over the past one-hundred-plus years, various historians have chipped away at this position as newly discovered primary sources have emerged and new studies have been performed. Each of these historians who dared to question the veracity of Johnston's claims, however, have faced substantial criticism and even ridicule in the courts of public opinion and among traditional historians who have not been curious enough to look behind the pillars of Hay and Steele or the stories of Johnston. The first post-1900 historian to question the traditional view was Alfred P. James.[17]

In 1927, Alfred P. James questioned the veracity of Johnston's *Narrative*, claiming that "[i]ts unreliability is evident from even a casual reading."[18] James quoted Harvard lawyer and historian Francis W. Palfrey, who served as an officer in the United States Army during the war: "The more I study Johnston's writings, the more cause I find to distrust them. I like to believe in him; but I cannot do so absolutely, for I find he permits himself great freedom in asserting what he does not know to be true, and what proves with fuller knowledge not to be true."[19]

James pointed out Johnston's powerful political and familial connections; many of Johnston's relatives came from "prominent and influential families in the South." Comparing the two Virginians, Johnston and Robert E. Lee, James noted that Lee was the pride of the Tidewater Virginia aristocracy while Johnston came from the Up-County Virginia aristocratic society. In other words, both men were "untouchable" in Southern postwar view. If

---

[17] A good example of the confusion caused by Johnston's untruthful assertions relative to Adairsville and Cassville in his *Narrative*, and on Hay's and Steele's reliance on them, can be found in the biography of William J. Hardee by the excellent historian Nathaniel Cheairs Hughes Jr. Hughes correctly deduced the purpose of Johnston's 17 May council as being about how to withdraw from Adairsville safely, but then, in reliance on Hay's 1923 article, mistakenly assumed that Johnston planned an attack at Cassville on the evening of 18 May in a second war council (see Hughes Jr., *William Joseph Hardee*, 351).

[18] James, "General Joseph Eggleston Johnston," 342.

[19] James, quoting Francis W. Palfrey, *Military Historical Society of Massachusetts*, 1:197. James added, "This allegation is true even of some of Johnston's official military reports, notably of the one on the battle of Seven Pines. On this particular report, see G. W. Smith, *Confederate War Papers* (New York, 1884), Part I, passim, and *The Battle of Seven Pines* (New York, 1891); also, E. P. Alexander, *Military Memoirs of a Confederate* (New York, 1907)" (1:197n4).

Robert E. Lee's reputation has been hewn from marble as has been popularly coined, then that of Johnston has been carved out of granite and cast in bronze.[20]

A statue and monument in tribute to Johnston stands in Dalton, Georgia, a place that Johnston believed was indefensible. Rocky Face Ridge, which protected Dalton, served as a screen for the Federals to move around its left flank, he said. "The position of Dalton had little to recommend it as a defensive one. It had neither intrinsic strength nor strategic advantage," explained the Virginian. "It neither fully covered its own communications nor threatened those of the enemy."[21]

In contrast, Hood believed that the Atlanta Campaign was lost by the failure to use the mountain passes and gaps around Dalton. "Great ranges of mountains running across the line of march and deep rivers are stands from which a well-directed army is not easily driven or turned," he advanced in his official report.[22] In his postwar *Advance and Retreat*, Hood expounded on his position about Dalton: "Between the two armies arose, I might say, a high wall of stone, as the name Rocky-faced Ridge indicates. The Confederate position was one of the strongest to be desired; it was necessary to hold but two gaps in the mountains: Mill Creek and Snake Creek." Hood explained that if those two gaps were held with small detachments, then much of the Southern army could have struck Sherman's forces in flank in Crow Valley and at Tunnel Hill, forcing Sherman either to retreat to Chattanooga or to be defeated in detail.[23]

Perhaps the most revealing statement from Johnston concerning his strategy for waging war during the Atlanta Campaign comes from Johnston's own words found in both his official report and his *Narrative*, in which he

---

[20] James, "General Joseph Eggleston Johnston," 342–59. There are no statues of John Bell Hood in Dalton, Georgia, or anywhere, for that matter, where the Confederate Army of Tennessee fought or traveled. However, a larger-than-life bronze statue sits atop a four-piece granite monument of Joseph E. Johnston at the Huff House in Dalton, Georgia, the site of his headquarters during the winter 1863–1864 encampment. Whatever your opinion of monuments of former Confederate soldiers, the statue is a work of art. Commissioned by the Bryan M. Thomas (now the Private Drewry R. Smith) Chapter of the United Daughters of the Confederacy, it was designed by Nashville, Tennessee, native Belle Kinney and sculpted under the direction of Kinney at the Tiffany's Studio in New York City. It was dedicated on 24 October 1912 (McArthur, "Tribute to General Joseph E. Johnston," 263–66).

[21] Johnston, *Narrative of Military Operations*, 277.

[22] Hood's report, *OR*, ser. 1, vol. 38, pt. 3, 628.

[23] Hood, *Advance and Retreat*, 83–87.

espoused Mahan's "active defense" strategy. Explaining that he believed that he was greatly outnumbered and that Polk's army had not yet consolidated with him, Johnston said, "I, therefore, determined to fall back slowly until circumstances should put the chances of battle in our favor, keeping so near the US army as to prevent its sending re-enforcements to Grant, and hoping, by taking advantage of positions and opportunities, to reduce the odds against us by partial engagements." He then added, "I also expected it [the Federal army opposing him] to be materially reduced before the end of June by the expiration of the terms of service of many of the regiments which had not re-enlisted. In this way we fell back to Cassville in two marches." Submitted on 20 October 1864, just four months after the events at Adairsville and Cassville, the report includes no mention by Johnston about devising any master plan to divide and conquer Sherman while meeting with his subordinates at Adairsville.[24]

In his *Narrative*, Johnston repeated his defense of his "active defensive" strategy. "I therefore thought it our policy to stand on the defensive, to spare the blood of our soldiers by fighting under cover habitually, and to attack only when bad position or division of the enemy's forces might give us advantages counter-balancing that of superior numbers." Johnston also repeated his logic about anticipating a substantial reduction in Sherman's force in June due to enlistment term expirations among many veteran Federal regiments.[25]

Mahan's "active defensive" strategy theory was therefore Johnston's chosen strategy for the campaign. Given the circumstances Johnston faced, whether one agrees or disagrees with his Fabian Policy is a source of healthy debate. However, after yielding the truth of his defensive mindset, implementing a strategy to not commit to a general engagement before late June, and attempting to reduce Sherman's strength through defensive tactics, Johnston then added a series of excuses concerning his conduct at Calhoun, Adairsville, and Cassville. While poring over a map at Adairsville, he would subsequently claim that he devised his master counterstrike. In reality, Johnston wrote a tale about planning a surprise attack at Cassville. It is a claim he would subsequently make that he devised his master counterstrike. In reality, without support from any contemporaneous account, but it has been bolstered through more than a century and a half of unchallenged repetition.

---

[24] Johnston's report, *OR*, ser. 1, vol. 38, pt. 3, 615.
[25] Johnston, *Narrative of Military Operations*, 318.

Chapter 2

The Adairsville Affair

Following his withdrawal from Calhoun on 16 May, Johnston next made a stand at Adairsville. In what has come to be known as "The Adairsville Affair," Johnston claimed that he wanted to entrench and give battle on 17 May just north of the town. He explained that his engineers had told him that there was a plain between two ridges in which he could place his army, and, with both flanks secured by the ridges, offer battle. But, upon arrival, he found that "the breadth of the valley here exceeded so much the front of our army properly formed for battle [in a double line of defenders], that we could obtain no advantage of ground; so, after resting about eighteen hours, the troops were ordered to move to Cassville."[1]

Lieutenant General William J. Hardee's corps was tasked with supporting portions of Major General Joseph "War Baby" or "War Child" Wheeler's cavalry, which had been covering the retreat from Calhoun. Soon, Federal columns approached the Confederate infantry lines where Hardee had deployed his men. Major General Benjamin Cheatham's all-Tennessee division covered the Calhoun-Adairsville Road, with Cleburne's Division in support on the left flank and rear. Brigadier General Frank C. Armstrong's newly arrived Mississippi cavalry brigade from Jackson's Division was hurried to the east to cover and defend the right flank. Armstrong's Brigade included the 1st, 2nd, 28th, and Ballentine's Mississippi cavalry regiments. When the approaching blue-clad soldiers began to deploy and extend their line to the west and across the Oothkalooga Creek, Bate's Division was sent to extend Cleburne's left, and Hindman's Division of Hood's Corps moved to extend Cheatham's right.[2]

Hindman's Division was placed on a high ridge that commanded the entire area (along the east side of today's I-75 from exit 310 north to the rest

---

[1] Johnston, *Narrative of Military Operations*, 319–20.

[2] Wheeler was often referred to as the "War Child" due to his young age and appearance (see Collier, *"War Child's Children,"* 95); he was also referred to as "War Baby Wheeler" by George Knox Miller in a letter to his wife, Celestine McCann Miller, 14 April 1864, Tunnel Hill, Georgia (see McMurry, ed., *Uncompromising Secessionist*, 191). Cleburne's report, *OR*, ser. 1, vol. 38, pt. 3, 723; Bate's report, *OR Supp.*, pt. 1, vol. 7, 93. Wheeler's men were augmented by Brigadier General Frank C. Armstrong's newly arrived Mississippi cavalry brigade from Jackson's Division.

area). The anchor of that ridge is Iron Mountain (today, Vulcan Mine located to the southeast of I-75 and Georgia Highway 140). Beyond Hindman's right, advancing Federal cavalry threatened the Confederate eastern flank at Mosteller's Mill.[3] Brigadier General Zacharias Deas and his Alabama Brigade from Hindman's Division was rushed over to cover the road leading to the mill.

One veteran from Ballentine's cavalry regiment remembered that it "was engaged with the enemy [for] several hours" at Adairsville. During the clash with Federal troopers, the 1st Mississippi Cavalry, commanded by Colonel R. A. Pinson, lost one killed and three wounded while 2nd Mississippi Cavalry, led by Major John J. Perry, lost four men wounded. In all, Armstrong's Brigade sustained thirty-one casualties in the action with most of the casualties occurring in the 28th Mississippi Cavalry under Colonel Peter B. Starke.[4]

Brigadier General John Newton's second division of Major General Oliver O. Howard's IV Corps led the Federal parry south of Calhoun. Colonel Francis T. Sherman's First Brigade was in front. Colonel Sherman's men had been skirmishing with Wheeler's Cavalry throughout the day until catching up with Johnston's main body by late afternoon. General William Sherman, who thought that there was only a brigade of mounted infantry opposing Colonel Sherman, pressed Howard and his brigade commander to move more quickly. Colonel Sherman rode back to Howard to explain that he had met greater resistance in the form of the main body of Confederate infantry. General Sherman was finally convinced when shell fire began to spray a little too close for comfort for him and his staff, who had ridden forward to examine the situation.[5]

---

[3] At the time of the Civil War, Berryman F. Mosteller and his family ran a sash-saw mill and a corn and wheat mill that was called Mosteller's Mill. After the war, additional mills were added to the community, which began to be called Mosteller's Mills. However, I have used the singular, "Mosteller's Mill," to reflect its name during the Civil War. (See Cunyus, *History of Bartow County*, where the author of the chapter on the Civil War period, Wilbur Kurtz, uses the singular "Mill," at 223–24, and compare the chapter on manufactories by Cunyus who uses the plural "Mills," at 264–65.)

[4] Lindsley, *Military Annals of Tennessee, Confederate*, 2:760; Rowland, *Mississippi*, 376, 406, 450; *Jackson (MS) Clarion-Ledger*, 9 June 1864; Montgomery, *Reminiscences of a Mississippian*, 164, 168.

[5] Howard's report, *OR*, ser. 1, vol. 38, pt. 1, 191; Newton's report, *OR*, ser. 1, vol. 38, pt. 1, 293–94; Castel, *Decision in the West*, 193–94; Sherman, *Memoirs*, 2:37.

As the Federals came within range of the Confederate lines, Newton deployed Brigadier General Charles G. Harker's third brigade to the left of Sherman's Brigade, and Brigadier General George D. Wagner's second brigade to the right and rear of Sherman. With the Thirty-Sixth, Forty-Fourth, Seventy-Third, Seventy-Fourth, and Eighty-Eighth Illinois, together with the Fifteenth Missouri and the Twenty-Fourth Wisconsin (now under the command of Major Arthur McArthur, Jr., Lieutenant Colonel Theodore S. West having been wounded on 14 May at Resaca), Colonel Sherman's men slowly and steadily advanced, until encountering a hailstorm of bullets from Cheatham's veterans that stopped the Federal advance cold. Some Northern soldiers' accounts would later call this action the Battle of Pleasant Hill though they had experienced nothing pleasant at that hill that day.[6]

Howard reported that he lost about two hundred men in the brief action. The casualties sustained in Colonel Sherman's brigade included the following: the Thirty-six Illinois lost one officer and twelve men killed and wounded (while serving as skirmishers throughout the morning), the Forty-Fourth Illinois lost four killed and thirty-two wounded, the Seventy-Fourth Illinois lost one officer wounded, one man killed, and twenty-nine men wounded, and the Twenty-Fourth Wisconsin lost five killed, including Lieutenant Thomas T. Keith, and twelve wounded, including Lieutenant George Allanson. Brigadier General George D. Wagner reported twenty-six men killed and wounded in his brigade, which had supported Colonel Sherman's attack on the right, with half of his casualties sustained by the Twenty-Sixth Ohio (thirteen wounded, two mortally).[7]

On the Confederate side, Brigadier General George E. Maney's brigade held the center of Cheatham's Division, while the other three Tennessee brigades lengthened the lines on both sides of Maney's regiments. The 1st and 27th Tennessee, led by Colonel Hume R. Field of Maney's Brigade, bore the brunt of the Federal assault. The 1st and 27th Tennessee held a part of the line that jutted out from the main line on the grounds of the Robert C. Saxon house, a rock, octagonal-shaped structure that made for an ideal defensive position. Called "Oak Grove" by Saxon, the unusual house and its outbuildings were located just north of the Gordon-Cass (now Bartow) County line, on a knoll east of the Calhoun-Adairsville Road. In the action, Field lost

[6] Estabrook, *Wisconsin Losses in the Civil War*, 121–23.

[7] *OR*, ser. 1, vol. 38, pt. 1, 191; *OR*, ser. 1, vol. 38, pt. 1, 313, 315, 318, 328; Quiner, *Military History of Wisconsin*, 729–30; Estabrook, *Wisconsin Losses in the Civil War*, 121–23; *OR*, ser. 1, vol. 38, pt. 1, 332 and 350.

thirty men killed and wounded in his consolidated regiment.[8] Meanwhile, in Cleburne's Division, soldier R. W. Colville of the 3rd Confederate regiment of Govan's Brigade, reported two killed and nine wounded in the action.

Trooper Thomas H. Williams of the 1st Tennessee Cavalry in Colonel Henry M. Ashby's Tennessee brigade recorded that the Federals drove Wheeler's Cavalry back eight miles that day. O. P. Hargis of the 1st Georgia Cavalry in Brigadier General Alfred Iverson's brigade witnessed an intense artillery duel between the two sides. "We lay there the balance of the evening under a heavy fire of artillery. We had many killed and wounded," explained Hargis. All told, Wheeler lost 120 men killed and wounded in the day's action. "That evening I thought the sun would never go down," continued Hargis. "About half an hour before the sun [set] we were ordered back to our horses and went into camp that night."[9]

During the brief defensive stand just north of Adairsville, Johnston considered his options. While Cheatham's Tennesseans held back Howard's men at the Saxon house, Johnston pored over a map of the region with his chief of staff, William W. Mackall. As Johnston and Mackall looked at the map, firing could be heard at Rome.[10]

According to Johnston, he summoned engineer Lieutenant Andrew H. Buchanan, who "was questioned minutely over the map as to the character of the ground, in the presence of Lieutenant-Generals Polk and Hood, who had been informed of my object." Johnston explained that Buchanan had surveyed the section between Adairsville, Kingston, and Cassville, and that Buchanan "described the country on the direct road [the Adairsville-Cassville Road] as open, and unusually favorable for attack." Johnston further stated that "it was evident, from the map, that the distance between the two Federal columns

---

[8] *Athens (GA) Southern Banner*, 9 July 1864, 1, copied from a Northern account that originally appeared in the *New York Tribune*. The Saxon house, used by Federals as a hospital following the battle and subsequent Confederate withdrawal, was destroyed by Union soldiers afterward (Castel, *Decision in the West*, 193–94; Watkins, *"Co. Aytch,"* 151); R. W. Colville, letter to father Captain W. E. Colville, 22 May 1864, vertical files, Confederate TN-1, Kennesaw Mountain NMP.

[9] Cater, "Civil War Papers of John Bell Hamilton," 119; Hargis Journal, 38; Lindsley, *Military Annals of Tennessee, Confederate*, 2:86.

[10] Mackall Journal, "O" sample, in *OR*, ser. 1, vol. 38, pt. 3, 982. Colonel Taylor Beattie, who served as an attaché during Hood's planned attack on 19 May, called William Mackall, the "owl of the army." Beattie noted in his diary that William Mackall was always opposed to fighting—always predicting disaster" (Taylor Beatie diary, 25 July 1864, Southern Historical Collection, UNC Chapel Hill).

would be greatest when that [road] following the railroad [the Adairsville-Kingston Road] should be near Kingston." Buchanan thought, according to Johnston, "that the communications between the columns at this part of their march would be eight or nine miles, by narrow and crooked country roads."[11]

The only source for Johnston's version of events, in which he claimed that he devised a surprise attack at Cassville as he pored over a map with the lieutenant generals and his chief of staff on the evening of 17 May at Adairsville, is Johnston's own memoirs, written ten years afterward. Johnston's *Narrative of Military Operations*, written in 1874, provides the first time in recorded history that I have found the claim that Johnston planned a surprise attack while meeting with his subordinates at Adairsville.[12]

In his official report, completed 20 October 1864, Johnston wrote,

> I, therefore, determined to fall back slowly until circumstances should put the chances of battle in our favor, keeping so near the U. S. army as to prevent its sending re-enforcements to Grant, and hoping, by taking advantage of positions and opportunities, to reduce the odds against us by partial engagements. I also expected it to be materially reduced before the end of June by the expiration of the terms of service of many of the regiments which had not re-enlisted. In this way we fell back to Cassville in two marches.
>
> At Adairsville (about midway), on the 17th, Polk's cavalry, under Brigadier-General Jackson, met the army, and Hardee after severe skirmishing checked the enemy. At this point, on the 18th, Polk's and Hood's corps took the direct road to Cassville, Hardee's that by Kingston. About half the Federal army took each road. French's division having joined Polk's corps on the 18th, on the morning of the 19th, when half the Federal army was near Kingston, the two corps at Cassville were ordered to advance against the troops that had followed them from Adairsville, Hood's leading on the right.[13]

There is nothing in Johnston's report to confirm or deny that he made any plan for offensive operations while he was at Adairsville on 17 May. While he explained that he ordered an attack on the morning of 19 May, there is nothing in his claims to support the assertion that he planned

[11] Johnston, *Narrative of Military Operations*, 320. See also Castel, *Decision in the West*, 195, 589n93.

[12] Johnston, *Narrative of Military Operations*, 320.

[13] Johnston's report, *OR*, ser. 1, vol. 38, pt. 3, 615.

anything ahead of time other than the justification for the attack on the belief that Sherman had divided his forces in pursuit.

The only other contemporaneous account by Johnston is found in his response to President Davis's 18 May telegram to him following news of Johnston's retreat over the Oostanaula River. Davis wrote, "Your dispatch of [May] 16th received; read with disappointment. I hope the re-enforcements sent will enable you to achieve important results."[14] In reply, Johnston explained that he tried to make an attack at Resaca and another one at Cassville. However, there is no mention that he planned or ordered the Cassville attack prior to 19 May. Johnston's telegram to President Davis read,

> ETOWAH, May 20, 1864.
> His Excellency President DAVIS:
> In the last eight days the enemy have pressed us back to this place, thirty-two miles. We kept near him to prevent his detaching to Virginia, as you directed, and have repulsed every attack he has made. On the 12th [of May] at Resaca my arrangements for an attack were defeated by his crossing a column at Calhoun close to my communications, and yesterday, having ordered a general attack, while the officer charged with the lead was advancing he was deceived by a false report that a heavy column of the enemy had turned our right and was close upon him, and took a defensive position. When the mistake was discovered, it was too late to resume the movements.
> J. E. JOHNSTON,
> General.[15]

Historians have never questioned the veracity of Johnston's story that he planned the Cassville attack two days earlier while at Adairsville, but there are no contemporaneous accounts either to corroborate or to refute it. There are only a few accounts of the meeting, two by Johnston supporters, William and T. B. Mackall, but neither of these accounts mention anything about a

---

[14] Davis to Johnston, *OR*, ser. 1, vol. 38, pt. 4, 725.

[15] Johnston to Davis, *OR*, ser. 1, vol. 38, pt. 4, 728. The reference to 12 May was in error. T. B. Mackall, who apparently wrote Johnston's reply, thought that Johnston had asked him to put the date of the army's withdrawal from Dalton, not the date of the withdrawal from Resaca on 15 May. (See Mackall Journal, "O" sample, in *OR*, ser. 1, vol. 38, pt. 3, 985, where he recorded, "President's dispatch of 18th answered and misstatement of dates in General J[ohnston's] previous dispatch corrected. (Mistake owing to my giving date of leaving Dalton instead of Resaca, which I understood was asked.)"

planned offensive strike. One is a letter from William Mackall to his wife, which details Johnston's baptism afterward but does not say anything about planning a surprise attack. The other is the published version of the T. B. Mackall Journal (hereafter "O" sample, for the *Official Records* version).[16]

Lieutenant T. B. Mackall, a young cousin to Chief of Staff William Mackall and an aide-de-camp, maintained a personal and unofficial journal during the first part of the Atlanta Campaign. In his published journal, the "O" sample, the following is recorded concerning the meeting: "I [was] sent after General P[olk] about 6 p.m. All in council. Can the army be withdrawn when so many roads into Calhoun? Carry a dispatch in room; General W. W. [Mackall] and J[ohnston] looking at map. Latter traces road from here to Cassville; asks how long will it take all to go down one road?" Mackall's journal continued, "[Hood] says it can't be done. [Hardee] said we will have to fight. [Hood] has been anxious to get from this place south of Etowah."[17]

Over the years, historians have taken these words, and Johnston's explanation as given in his *Narrative*, as proof of Johnston's claim that he had devised a battle plan that evening to divide his forces, induce Sherman into likewise dividing his columns, and then strike the blue column that proceeded southeast down the Adairsville-Cassville Road (Road 1) when it was isolated from the support of the other Federal column marching due south down the Adairsville-Kingston Road (Road 8).[18]

In the Mackall Journal, "O" sample, the version most favorable to Johnston's position, the additional entries for 17 May include references to Federal advances toward Rome to the west, to within six miles of Cartersville to the southeast, and west of the Oothkalooga Creek, to the immediate west of Johnston's army. Mackall recorded, "Enemy reported on west of Oothkalo[o]ga Creek," and in response to this discovery, "Bate sent over," meaning that Bate's Division was moved to the left of Hardee's line to meet the Northern threat.[19]

At the same time, it was reported that Federal cavalry had roamed far to the southeast, around the right of the Confederate army, and appeared to be headed for the Western & Atlantic Railroad bridge over the Etowah River

---

[16] Johnston, *Narrative of Military Operations*, 320; William Mackall to Aminta Mackall, 18 May 1864, Johnston Papers; *OR*, ser. 1, vol. 38, pt. 3, 982. There are five versions of the Mackall Journal, which will be discussed at length in chapter 4.

[17] *OR*, ser. 1, vol. 38, pt. 3, 982.

[18] Johnston, *Narrative of Military Operations*, 320.

[19] *OR*, ser. 1, vol. 38, pt. 3, 982.

known as Hightower Bridge. T. B. Mackall noted, "Cavalry reported six miles of Cartersville. Pontoons at Cassville." In response to this threat, Mackall next wrote, "Jackson's division cavalry ordered back. One brigade had no corn for three days. (Pontoons ordered to Etowah.)"[20]

Concerning the threat to Rome, T. B. Mackall recorded, "Firing heard at Rome, while all this going on [referring to the first two Federal threats, left of the Oothkalooga Creek and the railroad bridge over the Etowah River near Cartersville]. Telegram from Lieutenant-Colonel Steever, Rome, saying enemy in force, shelling town."[21]

It was in this context then, after recording the three specific Federal threats above, that T. B. Mackall was then sent at about 6 p.m. to get General Polk and bring him to Johnston's headquarters to discuss, along with lieutenant generals Hardee and Hood, what their course of action should be. T. B. Mackall's journal then continued with "All in council," and the all-important question of the evening, "Can the army be withdrawn…?" Johnston then traced on the map the direct route from Adairsville to Cassville and asked, "How long will it take all to go down one road?"[22]

It is in response to this question that Hood replied that it "can't be done." Clearly, Hood understood that Johnston's army at Adairsville, which had grown to about seventy-four thousand men by that point, could not withdraw down a single road without risking disaster because of the time required to move such a large number by one route. But, if multiple routes were available, then the army could fall back much more quickly and safely. Safe retreat from Adairsville, then, was the purpose for the meeting on the evening of 17 May, and not any epiphany reached by Johnston to devise a strategy of "divide and conquer" that he did not describe until a decade later.[23]

Aside from Johnston, Hood, Polk, Hardee, William Mackall, and T. B. Mackall, one other key individual was present in the room during the meeting: thirty-five-year-old Lieutenant Andrew H. Buchanan, the Confederate engineer whom Johnston had summoned to provide information and review a map of the area south of Adairsville. Prior to the war, Buchanan had been a

---

[20] Ibid.

[21] Ibid. Lt. Colonel West Steever was a staff officer for Gen. Polk. (Evans, 592).

[22] Ibid.

[23] Ibid.; Johnston, *Narrative of Military Operations*, 319–20. Historian Larry Daniel is also skeptical about Johnston's claim that he devised a "divide and conquer" plan for Sherman at Cassville on 17 May at Adairsville (telephone conversation by the author with Larry Daniel, 4 March 2023). See also Daniel, "Adairsville."

mathematics and engineering assistant professor at Cumberland University under Major General Alexander Peter Stewart. Buchanan claimed that Johnston had relied on Buchanan's maps to plan battles. He also used them to plan retreats. After the war, Buchanan would return to his profession, and, while he continued to praise his old chieftain, including writing a tribute to Johnston in the *Confederate Veteran* magazine, he never wrote about Johnston's claims about the evening at Adairsville. Perhaps Buchanan simply believed Johnston, as did many of his soldiers and postwar followers.[24]

T. B. Mackall recorded that at "7:10 p.m., [Major Thomas Benton] Roy and [Lieutenant Colonel Edward H.] Cunningham have just been called for. In waiting." Roy was Hardee's chief of staff, and Cunningham served as Hood's assistant inspector general. These two men were summoned to make preparations for the army's withdrawal from Adairsville and to coordinate the routes that each corps would take. Neither Roy nor Cunningham recorded anything about a plan for an impending attack or battle plan.[25]

T. B. Roy issued a circular (meaning to all division commanders) order at 8:15 p.m. on behalf of General Hardee for the evacuation of Adairsville of his corps via the Adairsville-Kingston Road (Road 8). "All artillery and ordnance trains will be immediately placed on the Adairsville and Kingston road," the circular read, "and will receive orders from Major General Bate. Colonel Smith, chief of artillery, and Major Riley, chief of ordnance, will see that the artillery and ordnance, respectively, report promptly as above-directed."[26]

General Polk's staff officer and son-in-law, William Gale, recorded in his diary for 17 May: "About dark, Genl. Johnston sent for General Polk in haste. The enemy appeared in front of Rome, and had a fight with French's command. The cavl. [cavalry] lost 100 men killed & wounded. Rome was evacuated by us and occupied by the enemy." Gale did not mention making plans for an attack, and his next diary entry referred to Johnston's baptism ceremony that evening, which filled the balance of his recordings for 17 May.[27]

General Leonidas Polk wrote his wife on 21 May 1864, his first opportunity to write her during the Atlanta Campaign. In his letter, Bishop Polk wrote, "When General Johnston will offer battle I do not know, but think that it cannot be many days hence." Had Johnston devised a battle plan four

---

[24] Buchanan, "From Engineer for Army of Tennessee," 369–71.

[25] *OR*, ser. 1, vol. 38, pt. 3, 982.

[26] *OR*, ser. 1, vol. 38, pt. 4, 724–25.

[27] Gale diary, 17 May entry.

days earlier on 17 May at Adairsville, the same evening that Polk baptized him, or had Johnston formulated the battle plan that Hood requested on the morning of 19 May at Cassville, surely Bishop Polk would have included it in his letter of 21 May. But he did not because he had not heard of any such plan on 17 May or order on 19 May by Johnston; he had only been aware of Hood's plan.[28]

T. B. Mackall made several additional entries to his journal, including a cipher that had been received on 16 May but was not translatable, and after requesting that it be resent, a "repetition received on [May] 17th, at night. Forrest will start on [May] 20th from Corinth to cross Tennessee at Florence with 3,500 picked men and 2 batteries." Mackall also noted an additional entry concerning the events at Rome. "Colonel [Benjamin] Hill reported on authority of [a] scout that [the] enemy were moving down toward Rome, on Calhoun and Rome road, Palmer's corps in advance, wagon trains along, and one brigade [of] cavalry. Did not learn whether any other force was behind."[29]

Thus, while much detail was recorded in several contemporaneous accounts about Federal threats toward Rome, threats toward Cartersville and the railroad crossing at the Etowah River bridge, a threat west of the Calhoun-Adairsville Road across the Oothkalooga Creek, Johnston's baptism, and of using multiple roads to evacuate the army from Adairsville, no contemporaneous records exist to support Johnston's claim that he had devised an offensive plan of attack during the 17 May evening meeting at Adairsville. Looking at the contemporaneous sources critically, it appears that the chief, and perhaps sole, concern was evacuation and whether it could be safely made on one road or not.

There were three other officers from Hardee's staff who were either witnesses to the events at Johnston's headquarters that evening, or who were close to Hardee shortly afterward. These were Lieutenant William L. Trask, Major Henry Hampton, and Captain John W. Greene, an engineer.

Lieutenant William Trask wrote in his journal on 17 May,

> I now felt sure the long expected battle was to come off.... We were doomed to disappointment again. Night found all our generals in close consultation. Johnston, Polk, Hardee, and Hood were all exchanging views and it was determined to move farther south. Shortly after dark a thick fog

[28] Polk, letter to wife, 21 May 1864, Altoona Station, Ga., in Polk, *Leonidas Polk, Bishop and General*, 2:363.

[29] "O sample," *OR*, ser. 1, vol. 38, pt. 3, 982.

> covered the earth and the army began to retreat, again, moving very quietly from the field.

Trask continued, "The troops now began to realize for the first time that we were retreating from the enemy and their faces denoted disappointment and gloom. They marched sullenly along, occasionally giving vent to their feelings by a slur at some general passing by." He explained, "Up to now all thought Johnston was either flanking the enemy or making some strategic move by which he would be defeated. Every move Johnston made was looked upon as one of strategy, to compel the enemy to fight at a disadvantage."[30]

"They now begin to think Johnston is being outgeneraled and that Sherman is beating him at a game he was thought to be the champion of," Trask added. "They think if the battle could be fought before the hundred day men can be placed in the field we will have no trouble in defeating the enemy." Lieutenant Trask worried that delay in fighting would only serve to strengthen the enemy while weakening the Southern cause when he wrote, "but if the fight is put off a while longer we will have at least fifty thousand more men to fight than we now have, and the war will continue no telling how long." Trask also recorded signs of desertion that evening: "I notice many men demoralized and disheartened. Several of the Kentuckians [from the famous "Orphan Brigade"], no doubt disgusted with the prospect, threw their guns into the bushes as they marched along and no doubt sought the first opportunity to fall out and hide themselves for the purpose of falling into the enemy's hands and getting a chance to go home."[31]

Major Henry Hampton recorded the events of the 17 May meeting in his *Itinerary of Hardee's Army Corps,* as

> in this council it was understood that General Hardee advocated giving battle to the enemy in the position we then held in front of Adairsville, information having been received that McPherson's corps [*sic*] of the enemy were in the neighborhood of Rome and another had gone to Virginia, which would have given us greatly the advantage of the enemy, as we had our whole army massed at Adairsville.

From this account, Hardee's justification in wanting to stand and fight above Adairsville is evident, for he apparently reasoned that, if McPherson's force was near Rome and another Federal corps had gone to Virginia, Sherman's force in front of Johnston above Adairsville would only be as large as

---

[30] Hafendorfer, *Civil War Journal of William L. Trask*, 144–45.
[31] Ibid.

the Southern army, or perhaps considerably smaller. Therefore, he likely determined, why not make a stand and try to beat the Northern force when the relative size of each force was nearly the same?[32]

Two days later, on the evening of 19 May after Johnston's General Order had been read to all of the Southern soldiers, Captain Greene wrote a letter to his mother from Cassville. In it he explained that "our army has been steadily falling back since you left [from Calhoun]." (His family lived on part of the Resaca battlefield property.) Greene wrote, "The enemy have shown every disposition to force Gen. J[ohnston] to battle and tho' his army is a splendid one—all think to seem he did perfectly right to retire sufficiently far from the mountain passes—when in case of victory for us (which we all count as sure tho' outnumbered)." Greene continued, "the enemy will pay a heavy price for his temerity. I believe a *stand* will be made in this neighborhood, and if the enemy continue to press on as boldly as they have—a general engagement cannot be long delayed." It is clear that Greene had only that afternoon heard Johnston's General Order, which contained nothing about any specific battle plan or call for an offensive—merely a call to stand and face the enemy—and he was simply relaying this information and his belief to his mother.[33]

None of Hardee's staff officers recorded any suggestion that Johnston had devised or related a grand strategy to trap Sherman. Each of them, as well as all the other contemporaneous accounts, recorded details about how the army could safely retreat from Adairsville using multiple roads, and several of the accounts recorded Hardee's desire to remain and fight north of the village. If Johnston had made any comment about making a surprise attack, someone most certainly would have recorded it. But no one did.

There are no claims that Johnston had devised a plan to divide and conquer Sherman while looking a map at Adairsville from any period newspapers, at least none that I have discovered. Recently published studies of notable newspapers that covered the Atlanta Campaign reveal that the editors relied on secondary sources or Johnston's *Narrative of Military Operations* concerning their coverage of the events at Adairsville and Cassville instead of quoting from any contemporaneous article or edition. In B. G. Ellis's fine work, *The Moving Appeal*, which chronicles the war's coverage by the *Memphis Appeal*, Ellis mistakenly dates the publication of Johnston's "General Order" as being on 18 May, the same order that Johnston did not write until between 7:00

---

[32] Major Henry Hampton, "Itinerary of Hardee's Army Corps," *OR*, ser. 1, vol. 38, pt. 3, 402.

[33] John W. Greene to Mother, 18 May 1864, Cassville, Georgia.

a.m. and 8:00 a.m. on 19 May at Cassville. Ellis compounds the error by adding that Johnston somehow got a printer at Adairsville to print his order, thirty-six hours after he had evacuated Adairsville. Ellis's confusion originates from two sources: a reliance on Johnston's *Narrative* and a misstatement in Sherman's *Memoirs* where Sherman mistakenly recalled receiving at Adairsville a copy of Johnston's "General Order" a day or two *after* the Confederates had abandoned Cassville, i.e., 20 or 21 May. The only contemporaneous account that Ellis produced came from a reporter known as Thrasher, who inaccurately wrote on 18 May for the *Appeal* that he believed that "a major battle was shaping up" in the Oothcaloga Valley, west of Cassville." The Oothcaloga Valley is north of Adairsville and was the site of the Battle of Adairsville on the afternoon of 17 May.[34]

Similarly, in Stephen Davis's and Bill Hendrick's outstanding new book, *The Atlanta Daily Intelligencer Covers the Civil War*, the authors also rely on Johnston's *Narrative* and on Ellis's sources in *The Moving Appeal* concerning the events at Adairsville and Cassville. Davis and Hendrick quoted from a copy of Johnston's order published on 20 May in the *Atlanta Daily Intelligencer*, adding the erroneous assumption "that on the evening of May 18, he [Johnston] had a bellicose order drawn up to be read to the troops." However, as may be found in the *Official Records*, Johnston's order was dated 19 May, not May 18, and from "Cassville, Ga.," not Adairsville.[35] In sharp contrast, the *Atlanta Intelligencer's* coverage of the events of 18 May, not only failed to include anything about a planned attack by Johnston, but instead opined that the Confederate army would fall back again to the line of the Etowah River. The newspaper reporter, writing from Cartersville, claimed "I learn from a reliable source that the army will fall back to the Etowah River two miles south of Cartersville, where a stand, temporary, I expect, is likely to be made." The writer added that "Gen. Johnston's Headquarters, is at Cassville tonight [evening of 18 May], about seven miles from this place [Cartersville]. What the intentions of the General are, no one knows, as he keeps his own counsel, and is not very apt to inform any one of his plans."[36]

---

[34] Ellis, *The Moving Appeal*, 291.

[35] Johnston's General Orders, *OR*, ser. 1, vol. 38, pt. 4, 728.

[36] Davis and Hendrick, *Atlanta Daily Intelligencer Covers the Civil War*, 383–84; Johnston's General Orders, *OR*, ser. 1, vol. 38, pt. 4, 728; compare "General Johnston's Address to the Army, May 20, Cassville, Ga.," *Columbus (Georgia) Daily Sun*, 24 May 1864, 1, https://gahistoricnewspapers.galileo.usg.edu/lccn/sn82014939/1864-05-24/ed-1/seq-1/ (accessed 24 July 2023);

Notably absent from early postwar publications by pro-Johnston sympathizers and veterans are any claims that Johnston planned a surprise attack while at Adairsville. Edward A. Pollard, editor of the *Richmond Examiner*, wrote *The Lost Cause* in 1867, just two years following the war's closure. In it, Pollard accepted Johnston's position about the Cassville events as Pollard understood it at that time. Arguably a Johnston apologist as well as a critic of President Davis, Pollard wrote in a light most favorable to Johnston about the Cassville subject. He included details about the dispute that occurred between Johnston, and Hood and Polk during the evening of 19 May, and Pollard quoted from Johnston's official report that the subsequent withdrawal was "a step which I [Johnston] have regretted ever since." However, Pollard's account does not mention anything about any offensive plan by Johnston at Cassville, or of any plans for a surprise attack while holding a council of war at Adairsville. In fact, Adairsville is not even mentioned by Pollard, who boasts proudly of the skill of Johnston's retreat from Resaca, from which he claimed Johnston "took up at leisure his line of retrograde movement in the direction of the Etowah River, passing through Kingston and Cassville."[37]

Former Georgia cavalry leader Colonel Isaac W. Avery, who led the 4th Georgia Cavalry during the campaign, wrote *The History of Georgia from 1850 to 1881* (1881), which is regarded as a treatise on Georgia history. Colonel Avery emphasized his close relationship to Johnston and bragged about being privy to Johnston's strategic plans during the Atlanta Campaign. Notably absent from Avery's work are any comments about a plan for a surprise attack by Johnston during his council on 17 May at Adairsville. In fact, Avery skipped from describing the events at Calhoun on 16 May to the events at Cassville on 19 May, as he apparently found nothing of interest to cover about Adairsville. Avery next discussed with pride and in some detail about the positive effect of Johnston's "ringing battle order—a model of terse, fiery rhetoric" which he claimed that he read to his brigade (Iverson's), "in the falling twilight [of 19 May], in an old field environed by solemn woods. The men called for a speech," added the colonel, "and in common with others, the writer made a few words of deep-felt appeal from a convenient stump." Avery's treatise, written seven years after the release of *Johnston's Narrative of Military Operations*, instead focused on the effect of Johnston's battle order

"Special Correspondence to the Atlanta Intelligencer, May 18, 1864, Cartersville, Ga.," *Columbus (Georgia) Times*, 21 May 1864, 2, https://gahistoricnewspapers.galileo.usg.edu/lccn/sn86053047/1864-05-21/ed-1/seq-2/ (accessed 24 July 242023).

[37] Pollard, *Lost Cause*, 541.

relative to the anticipation of a battle on 20 May, *the next day*. Avery added that "Gen. Johnston thereafter traveled with the writer in the fall of 1864, from Macon to Charlotte (North Carolina), and that the battle [planned at Cassville for 20 May] was renounced [claimed Johnston to Avery] by him at the urgent entreaty of generals Hood and Polk, two of his corps commanders, who said they could not hold their positions.[38]

If Johnston had indeed formulated a plan of battle to divide and conquer Sherman during the evening meeting on 17 May at Adairsville, someone would have recorded it. But not a single diarist, journalist, letter-writer, official report writer, or early postwar writer put it to pen because it did not happen. If it had, someone would have written about it, and it would have been front-page news in any number of the five newspapers operating at the time in Atlanta, or the two papers in Augusta, the two in Columbus, and the ones in Macon. The complete absence of any newspaper account on the subject speaks volumes as to its fiction. T. B. Mackall would surely not have missed it in his journal, nor would William Mackall have forgotten it in his memoranda written on 22 September 1864, strictly for the purpose of supporting Johnston.

Greatest of all, Johnston would have told us in his "Official Report" that he had devised a master plan two days prior to Cassville. The Confederate commander would surely not have missed an opportunity to educate President Davis and the Confederate government of his brilliant idea, or brag to Colonel Avery that same fall, or to Sherman a year later if he had concocted such a plan. Instead, Johnston simply said, "on the morning of the [May] 19th, when half the Federal army was near Kingston, the two corps at Cassville were ordered to advance against the troops that had followed them from Adairsville, Hood's leading on the right," a claim Hood sharply denied in his report both as to the originator of the plan and to the details of it. Moreover, in his 20 October 1864 report, Johnston did not claim that he planned a defensive at Calhoun or Adairsville, or that he planned an offensive while at Adairsville, all assertions that would not appear in print until his *Narrative* a decade later.[39]

One final piece of evidence to consider in determining whether Johnston planned a battle of "divide and conquer" on the evening of 17 May at Adairsville comes from an unlikely source: William Tecumseh Sherman. Following the war, in autumn 1865, Sherman had a chance meeting with

---

[38] Avery, *History of the State of Georgia*, 276

[39] Johnston's report, *OR*, ser. 1, vol. 38, pt. 3, 615.

Johnston while the two were traveling on a Mississippi riverboat between Memphis, Tennessee, and Cairo, Illinois. The two, who were also joined by former XVII Corps commander Major General Francis P. Blair, had a cordial visit where they, according to Sherman, "talked over our battles again, played cards, and questioned each other as to particular parts of our mutual conduct in the game of war. I told Johnston that I had seen his order of preparation, in the nature of an address to his army, announcing his purpose to retreat no more, but to accept battle at Cassville."[40] Sherman asked Johnston what he meant by the order.

Johnston then recited his intent to remain and fight, *defensively*, the next day, but that Hood and Polk argued against it due to their lines being subject to enfilade fire by the Federal artillery. Johnston explained that he ultimately relented. However, Sherman recorded no statement or suggestion from Johnston about any claim that he had planned an *offensive*, either on 17 May at Adairsville, or the morning of 19 May at Cassville. Sherman's meeting with Johnston, as well as a subsequent meeting with Hood, will be discussed further in Part 2.[41]

No mention was apparently made or lamentation given by Johnston to either Avery or Sherman about any failed strike on the morning of 19 May.

---

[40] Sherman, *Memoirs*, 2:39–40. On the top of page 39, Sherman included, "I procured the copy of an order which Johnston had made at Adairsville, in which he recited that he had retreated as far as strategy required, and his army must be prepared for battle at Cassville." While this statement might be considered to give support to Johnston's claim that he had devised his "master plan" at Adairsville, this theory must be defeated for three reasons: 1. The order was not prepared at Adairsville, but instead was written on 19 May between 7 a.m. and 8 a.m. at Cassville; 2. At the time Sherman wrote his *Memoirs*, published in 1875, he had read Johnston's *Narrative of Military Operations*, published the year before, so Johnston's position that he had devised a plan at Adairsville two days earlier, was fresh on Sherman's mind. Sherman referred to Johnston's *Narrative* in his book (see Sherman, *Memoirs*, 2:49, where Sherman disagreed with Johnston's estimate of the relative casualties of both sides on page 357 of Johnston's *Narrative*); and 3. When Sherman questioned Johnston about what he meant by his "General Order" during the fall 1865 meeting on the riverboat, Johnston's response was solely about the disagreement between him and Hood and Polk during the evening meeting. In other words, Johnston's reply to Sherman about what he meant by issuing his "General Order" was that he intended to remain and defend the following morning (See Sherman, *Memoirs*, 2:40). A full transcription of Sherman's meeting with Johnston and of a subsequent meeting with Hood is provided in chapter 18.

[41] Ibid.

Johnston's complaint to Avery and Sherman about Cassville centered on not being able to remain in a defensive stand the following morning due to Hood and Polk's remonstrations, according to both Avery and Sherman. These two statements by Johnston, made much more contemporaneously with the events during the Atlanta Campaign, are substantially the same, make no mention of the planning for a battle two days earlier at Adairsville, and concentrate on the events during the evening of 19 May and the failure to remain and defend on 20 May. Johnston's claims that he planned to divide and conquer Sherman while looking at a map on 17 May at Adairsville will not be seen until the release of his *Narrative of Military Operations*, a decade after he has had an opportunity to bolster his story and his military reputation.

The truth is that the Confederates were caught off guard by the rapid movement of the Federal armies toward them and around them, and they could have become trapped at Adairsville had they chosen to remain and fight as Hardee suggested. Hood was correct to recommend withdrawal until they could find a more suitable position where they could regroup and then either defend or attack.

As for Johnston's claim that he had planned to stand and fight at Adairsville, Trask's journal entry belies him:

> Tuesday Morning, May 17th—This morning at 2 AM, the entire army left Calhoun and before noon it arrived at Adairsville where we stopped to rest a few hours, thinking we would not be troubled with the Federals for a time. We were much mistaken for while General Hardee and the rest of us were quietly lying on the grass in the shade intending to take a nap, General Wheeler, who with his cavalry was bringing up the rear, was rapidly driven back until the enemy was directly upon us.

Hardee and his staff quickly mounted and galloped at full speed to General Cleburne to order his troops into line to support Cheatham's Division, which was also rapidly preparing to receive the unexpected Federal advance. Trask's entries revealed nothing that resembled a planned defensive at Adairsville: "The Yankees were upon us before the lines were formed and we lost quite a number of officers and men before the excitement simmered down....Soon, however, our lines were formed, several of Cheatham's regiments [were] ordered forward and the enemy speedily driven back."[42]

In the foggy predawn hours of 18 May, Johnston would send Hardee's Corps and the wagon train south on the straighter and flatter road that ran along the railroad to Kingston, where they would turn east and proceed to

---

[42] Hafendorfer, *Civil War Journal of William L. Trask*, 144.

Cassville. There, Hardee would link up with the balance of the Southern force. Conversely, Johnston would send Polk's and Hood's corps directly southeast to Cassville. In his memoirs, the Southern commander explained that Sherman would divide his forces by sending half of his men toward Kingston following Hardee and the other half toward Cassville following Polk and Hood. Johnston said that there were only two roads from Adairsville south that would reach Kingston and Cassville, and that Sherman would follow him on those two routes while splitting his forces.[43]

However, there were several routes to Cassville that could be used by Federal forces at Adairsville, and not just one route as suggested by Johnston. This point concerning the confusing roads across the Gravelly Plateau region between Adairsville and Cassville will be discussed in detail in chapter 5. Also, Sherman did not divide his forces, as Johnston would later write, but instead directed all his infantry units to aim toward Kingston, thereby providing mutual support for each marching column, and at the same time ordered his cavalry divisions to strike the railroad on each flank.[44]

During the stormy Tuesday evening at Adairsville, following Johnston's baptism by Bishop-General Polk, General Hood slept in Johnston's headquarters tent as a dense fog rolled in and a steady rain fell. They would be on the road by 4 a.m.[45]

Until this point in the campaign, and continuing well into June, Johnston's relationship with Hood remained friendly, so much so that there were indications Hardee was becoming somewhat jealous of it. Hardee was disturbed that Johnston did not seek his counsel when Johnston took command of the army at Dalton on 27 December 1863, and that, later, when Hood arrived in Dalton in late February 1864, Johnston repeatedly sought Hood's advice. Hardee apparently was initially acquiescent, but by the third week of June, he complained to his new wife that "I found Hood with him [Johnston] when I arrived & I left him there.... Hood, I think, is helping the General to

---

[43] *OR*, ser. 1, vol. 38, pt. 3, 615–16; Johnston, *Narrative of Military Operations*, 320.

[44] Sherman to Schofield, 18 May, 10:30 p.m., *OR*, ser. 1, vol. 38, pt. 4, 242–43. Dave Powell makes this point in his new volume on the Atlanta Campaign (see Powell, "Atlanta Campaign," vol. 1).

[45] Mackall Journal, "A" sample, 5 May–31 July 1864. Weather report found in typewritten copy of Trask diary (staff officer for General Hardee), 13.

do the strategy, and from what I can see is doing most of it. I only hope it may be well done."[46]

Sherman had spread his forces much wider than Johnston realized, which might have led to even greater opportunities for Johnston had he been in an offensive mindset instead of merely looking to withdraw from Adairsville and consolidate his army at Cassville with his escape route to the Etowah River via Hightower Bridge covered. Following the Confederate evacuation of Resaca, Sherman sent Brigadier General Jefferson C. Davis's second division of the XIV Corps to sweep the west bank of the Oostanaula River in the direction of Rome to look for a suitable crossing. Acting on his own initiative, Davis continued his movement to threaten and then take Rome, a move that nearly cut off French's Division from joining Johnston's forces at Cassville.

On the morning of 18 May, after the head of McPherson's Army of the Tennessee joined the van of Thomas's Army of the Cumberland at Adairsville, Sherman sent Major General James B. McPherson's two corps, the XV and XVI Corps, to the southwest toward Woodlands (today known as Barnsley Gardens), some eight miles west of Adairsville. McPherson's veterans reached Woodlands by 6:30 p.m. At the same time, the Federal commander ordered Howard's IV Corps to continue to press south along the main wagon road and railroad toward Kingston while the remaining two divisions of Major General John M. Palmer's XIV Corps followed Howard.[47]

To the east of Adairsville, Major General Joseph Hooker's XX Corps trailed the IV Corps as its long wagon train passed the town. Hooker and his division commanders looked for alternative routes to the southeast to avoid the traffic. Following Hooker was the Army of the Ohio's XXIII Corps, led by Major General John M. Schofield. Schofield's column halted on the evening of 18 May at Mosteller's Mill (called Marsteller's or Marstellar's Mill by most Union accounts) located about five miles east of Adairsville on the road toward Pine Log. Hooker and Schofield would be poised to reach Cassville the next day.

[46] Hughes, Jr., *General William J. Hardee*, 211; Symonds, *Joseph E. Johnston*, 250–51, 310.

[47] *OR*, ser. 1, vol. 38, pt. 3, 33; *OR*, ser. 1, vol. 38, pt. 4, 233, 244.

Chapter 3

The Fight for Rome

The Oostanaula and Etowah Rivers converge at Rome to form the Coosa River that flows west into Alabama and then south until it merges with the Tallapoosa and forms the Alabama River just south of Wetumpka, Alabama, at Fort Jackson. Before the advent of rail transportation, steamboats were the most effective and common means of both passenger travel and shipping. The area around the beginning of Coosa River was originally inhabited by an Upper Creek tribe called the Abihka, who eventually moved west toward the present city of Gadsden, Alabama. The headwaters of the Coosa River were next inhabited by the Cherokee people in the mid-1700s. The Iroquoian-speaking Cherokees named the settlement "Etowah," which meant "the head of the Coosa," or beginning of the river.[1]

When European-American settlers began to arrive in the region following the Native American removal from northwest Georgia, they called it "Rome" because the seven hills that line the three rivers reminded them of the ancient city of Rome, Italy, which is also ringed by seven hills. Founded in 1834 by War of 1812 veterans, Cherokees who remained, land speculators, and farmers, Rome, Georgia, quickly became the center of the region's commerce and transportation due to its river connection with central and south Alabama and the Gulf Coast although it was a cumbersome route. Passengers and goods from Rome could take a river steamboat west as far as Greensport, Alabama, then disembark and transfer to wagons that could travel to Blue Mountain, Alabama. Next, passengers and goods could take a train at Blue Mountain and be transported to Selma, Alabama, then board or be loaded on a steamboat and sent down the Alabama River to Mobile and the Gulf Coast.

Following the construction of the Western & Atlantic Railroad in the 1840s, a spur line was built linking Rome to Kingston, Georgia. This new line made transportation and shipping for Rome's inhabitants much easier. Originally called the Memphis Branch Railroad and Steamboat Company of Georgia, the spur line became the Rome Railroad and began operation in 1848. By 1860, Rome had grown to a population of 4,010, as compared to

---

[1] Waselkov and Smith, "Upper Creek Archaeology," 244–45; Ethridge, *Creek Country*, 27; "Cherokee County Historical Maps," Digital Library of Georgia; "Original Cherokee County Divided," Digital Library of Georgia.

Dalton's population of 2,700 and Chattanooga's of 2,400 residents at that time.[2]

During the war, Rome produced war materials, including cannon, mechanical devices and tools, industrial materials, cartridge boxes, bayonet scabbards, haversacks, pistol belts, and buckets. Rome was home to the Noble Brothers Foundry, Howe and Rich's, H. K. Shackleford's, and John O'Neal's factories, all of which contributed significantly to the Southern war effort. The loss of the "City of Seven Hills" would be a significant blow to the Confederacy.[3]

May 1864 was a harrowing time for the defenders at Rome. Before the arrival of Federal troops at the gates of Rome, the only Confederate forces in the city were some washed up troopers from Major General William T. Martin's cavalry division. They were unfit to take to the field with the rest of their comrades when Martin was ordered on 7 May to move from Rome to Calhoun. This contingent of unfit-for-duty cavalrymen was led by Brigadier General Henry Brevard Davidson. They numbered about 150 men, just about enough to put down a rebellion in the city, should Rome fall from within, but not enough to defend against one.[4]

As if the Rome garrison were not ill-equipped enough, its commander, General Davidson, had just been released from arrest by Johnston on Sunday, 8 May, as Federal troops were preparing to attack Dug Gap Mountain in Dalton. He had been recommended by his old friend and previous employer, William Mackall. Earlier in the war, while serving on Mackall's staff as a colonel, they had both been captured at Island No. 10 on 7 April 1862. Davidson had been relieved of duty and placed under arrest by Wheeler for nonfeasance of orders on 13 February 1864 while Davidson had been tasked with scouting north and west of Tunnel Hill.[5]

---

[2] City manager's office, RomeFloyd.com, Governments of Floyd County and City of Rome, Georgia; Rome City Commission, RomeFloyd.com, Governments of Floyd County and City of Rome, Georgia; United States Census Bureau; United States Geological Survey, 25 October 2007.

[3] Slay, "Playing a Sinking Piano," 483–504; Fort Attaway Preservation Society records.

[4] *OR*, ser. 1, vol. 38, pt. 4, 674.

[5] Davidson appeared to be a good candidate for promotion when he was commissioned brigadier general on 18 August 1863, by Secretary of War James A. Seddon. The Tennessee-born soldier had served with distinction in the Mexican War and graduated from West Point in the same class as John Bell Hood and John Schofield. But something was unsatisfactory about Davidson, and those who served

with him were apparently aware of his inadequacies. R. H. Chilton served with Davidson at Staunton, Virginia. Upon learning of the news of Davidson's promotion and reassignment to command a cavalry brigade under Major General Nathan Bedford Forrest, Chilton wrote gleefully on 17 August 1863 that Davidson has been relieved "at last," and he asked for assistance in shipping a trunk to expedite his departure (Chilton to "HdQrs ANVa," 17 August 1863, General Henry Brevard Davidson [unpublished, private collection, transcribed copy of summary in my possession]).

Arriving in Georgia on the eve of the Chickamauga battle, Davidson's presence was hardly felt when Brigadier General John Pegram, who had been promoted to command a cavalry division, continued to lead his old brigade personally, now assigned to Davidson. Following Chickamauga, Davidson was assigned to Wheeler, who found little use for him. By November 1863, Wheeler had effectively stripped Davidson of his brigade by ordering Brigadier General W. Y. C. Humes to command most of Davidson's troopers, a novel way to get action without relieving the ineffective general (*OR*, ser. 1, vol. 31, pt. 3, 721).

General Braxton Bragg had also observed and complained to Richmond about Davidson. On 19 November 1863, the same day that Wheeler reassigned Humes, Bragg wrote adjutant and inspector general Samuel Cooper. He stated that, while Davidson was a loyal Tennessean who had attained the rank of general, it did not necessarily follow that his leadership would be efficient. Nevertheless, Bragg, after noting that Wheeler had managed to circumvent Davidson, asked his cavalry commander what he intended to do with the negligent Tennessee general. Writing from his headquarters on Missionary Ridge on 21 November 1863, Bragg asked Wheeler, "You have forgotten General Davidson was assigned in the order of organizations to the Tennessee River, near Dalton. What disposition will you make of him?" (*OR*, ser. 1, vol. 31, pt. 3, 716, 721, 728).

By February 1864, Wheeler's use of Davidson was finally exhausted when the insolent Tennessee general quipped over the chain-of-command concerning reports from scouts who were supposed to be reconnoitering between Tunnel Hill, Ringgold, and Nickajack Gap. Writing from his headquarters in Tunnel Hill, Wheeler told Davidson, "It is with extreme regret that I am forced to take the action embodied in the Special Orders No. 23. Since our first association, manifestations of great indifference, or rather an apparently studied apathy, have forced me to the conviction that a proper interest was wanting on your part, in sustaining me by a proper observance of orders and a preservation of subordination in your command.... Our constant intercourse has increased my conviction that you are determined to seize every opportunity to show contempt for my instructions" (Wheeler to Davidson, 13 February 1864, Special Orders No. 23, Davidson letters).

In an effort to advise Davidson on his court-martial defense, Mackall first asked what he had said to upset Wheeler. Then, after learning of the details, Mackall followed with a second note to his friend, suggesting that he "just state simply your own

When the May 1864 crisis in Georgia began in earnest and Johnston needed someone to manage the situation at Rome, Mackall reminded him of Davidson. Quickly, after receiving Johnston's consent on 8 May, Mackall sent a dispatch to Davidson, who was in Rome awaiting his court-martial. "You are released from arrest. General Johnston gives you command of Rome and expects you to organize the troops left there. Get them in order. Get all information and secure the place till [Major General William W.] Loring arrives." It was expected that Loring's lead brigade under Colonel Thomas M. Scott would be arriving in Rome on the same day. However, Loring and each of his three brigades from Polk's Army of Mississippi would be hurried forward to join the Confederate forces at Resaca, leaving the fate of Rome, once again, to the hands of Davidson and 150 mounted men.[6]

The other Confederate force in and around Rome during the first ten days of May 1864 was the cavalry division of Major General William T. Martin, who was ordered on 5 May to Rome from Cartersville, where his troopers had been foraging their horses. Martin was ordered to patrol the river crossings between Rome and Resaca and to perform reconnaissance as far north of Rome as Lafayette as the Federal offensive began. Martin's Division consisted of two cavalry brigades, Brigadier General John T. Morgan's brigade that contained the 1st, 3rd, 4th, 7th, and 51st Alabama Cavalry, the 12th Alabama Cavalry Battalion, and Brigadier General Alfred Iverson's brigade, which included the 1st, 2nd, 3rd, 4th, and 6th Georgia Cavalry. However, by 7 May, all of Martin's troopers were posted at various fords and crossings along the

---

case and make no comment about the conduct of others" (Mackall, no place or date, Davidson letters).

[6] William Mackall to Davidson, Dalton, Georgia, 8 May 1864, *OR*, ser. 1, vol. 38, pt. 4, 680; Scott stated to Johnston that he was "on march four miles south of Jacksonville, AL, May 8, 1864" (*OR*, ser. 1, vol. 38, pt. 4, 679).

After Davidson's service in the defense of Rome was completed, Johnston had no further use for him, and after Davidson pressed his friend for an explanation, Mackall replied, "The General released you to take command of Rome, because he thought your courage and energy would be useful there but he does not think it for the interest of the service that you should again serve with Wheeler" (Mackall to Davidson, 21 May 1864, Davidson letters).

The maligned Davidson was finally vindicated when he received a letter from President Davis after Secretary of War James Seddon interceded for him. Writing to George Day, he announced that "the President has acted upon my case. I am honorably restored to duty" (Davidson to George W. Day, Richmond, 22 September 1864, Davidson letters).

east bank of the Oostanaula River north of Rome and extending to Resaca, except for a few scattered patrols that were operating in the Armuchee Valley, north of Rome and on the west bank of the river.[7]

Farmer's Bridge

While the Battle of Resaca was underway on the morning of Saturday, 14 May 1864, Sherman sent Brigadier General Kenner Garrard with his division of cavalry to the southwest, along the west bank of the Oostanaula River. Garrard was ordered to cross the river and destroy the track of the Western & Atlantic Railroad north of Kingston. If he was unable to cross, then Garrard and his troopers were ordered to "threaten Rome, and the Coosa [River] below Rome, [so] that the enemy may not receive provisions, forage, or reinforcements from that direction."[8]

At 11 a.m. on 14 May, Garrard responded unconvincingly, "Your dispatch of to-day, 8 a.m., is just received. I will move at once and do the best I can." By 2 p.m., Garrard and his two available brigades, the First Brigade led by Colonel Robert H.G. Minty, a very capable commander, and the Third Mounted Infantry under the brave and proven Colonel John T. Wilder, were on the move toward Rome, "about 36 miles distant," according to Sergeant Benjamin F. Magee of Company I, Seventy-Second Indiana Mounted Infantry. Minty's Brigade consisted of the Fourth Michigan Cavalry, the Seventh Pennsylvania Cavalry, and the Fourth US Cavalry, while Wilder's Brigade included the Ninety-Eighth Illinois Mounted Infantry and the Seventeenth and Seventy-Second Indiana Mounted Infantry units.[9]

Wilder's Brigade was in the lead on 14 May, moving cautiously toward Rome. They went into camp by 10 p.m., having gone about halfway to Rome. The next morning, Minty's Brigade took the lead, as Garrard's troopers moved more slowly. Instead of finding a passable ford or ferry over the river, the blue-coat cavalrymen found Confederate troopers on their front, and Minty's men skirmished with them throughout the morning.

---

[7] *OR*, ser. 1, vol. 38, pt. 4, 664, 674; *OR Supp.*, pt. 2, vol. 5, 434.

[8] *OR*, ser. 1, vol. 38, pt. 4, 187.

[9] Ibid.; Magee, *History of the 72nd Indiana Volunteer Infantry*, 297; Scaife, *Campaign for Atlanta*, 170–71. The 123rd Illinois Mounted Infantry, with its Spencer rifles, though attached to Wilder's Brigade, does not appear to have participated in the expedition to Rome (*OR*, ser. 1, vol. 38, pt. 1, 102; Connolly, *Three Years in the Army of the Cumberland*, 195, 208–209).

Opposing the Federal cavalry parry was the 12th Alabama Cavalry Battalion under the command of Colonel Warren Stone Reese. These troopers were a part of Morgan's Brigade who, as part of Martin's Division, had been ordered to guard the crossings of the Oostanaula River south of Calhoun to Rome, while Iverson's Georgia Cavalry Brigade was covering the river crossings around Calhoun to Resaca. Company G of the 12th Alabama Battalion was ordered to guard Farmer's Bridge (at Old Summerville Road) over Armuchee Creek, a tributary that flowed into the Oostanaula River about five miles north of Rome.[10]

Garrard's horsemen were on the move at 5 a.m. Sunday, 15 May. By about 8 a.m., Minty later recalled, "my advance struck the enemy's pickets near Farmer's Bridge, or Armuchee creek, and drove in the advance videttes, and a few of my scouts charged over the bridge, but the advance guard halted to allow the column to close up." Minty's report continued, "They were not supported, and consequently were driven back with one man and four horses wounded. On my arrival at the bridge, I sent scouts to examine the creek to the right and left. Bad fords were reported both above and below the bridge." The Federal brigade commander quickly ordered his regiments into action. "I crossed two companies of the 4th Michigan below and six companies of that regiment above, together with the 4th US Cavalry. I then crossed the bridge with one battalion 4th Michigan Cavalry [four companies], followed by the 7th Pennsylvania Cavalry and the one gun of the Chicago Board of Trade Battery."[11]

One Alabama trooper's recollections were later published in a Columbus, Georgia, newspaper. He recalled that, "at nine o/clock Sunday morning the enemy attacked our picket post at Farmer's bridge, on the Summerville Road, eight miles from Rome. They approached by the Floy[d] Springs Road, and numbered, as counted by one of Colonel Cameron's scouts, 2,200." He explained that "the post was guarded by Company G, 12th Ala. Cav. Battalion, Capt. Wm. Lokey commanding. Capt. L[okey] and his brave men behaved most gallantly, holding the enemy in check two hours, or until a courier could be sent to Rome and return *without reinforcements* [emphasis original]."[12]

Sergeant Magee recorded in his diary that Minty's men killed "a rebel Captain, wounding four or five privates, and taking a few prisoners." Upon reaching Armuchee Creek and Farmer's Bridge, Magee remembered, "we

---

[10] *OR Supp.*, pt. 2, vol. 1, 101–103.

[11] Robertson, *Michigan in the War*, 639, 661; *OR Supp.*, pt. 2, vol 29, 818.

[12] "Battle of Farmer's Bridge," *Columbus (Georgia) Times*, 21 May 1864, 2.

found the chances for a fight first rate, the cavalry having been repulsed [referring to Minty's Brigade of cavalry as opposed to Wilder's Brigade of mounted infantry]." According to Minty, Captain Lokey, 12th Alabama Cavalry, was mortally wounded, and nine men killed. "We took six prisoners," he added.[13]

Captain Lokey of Company G was killed, together with nine of his men, while another ten were captured. Unable to hold back the overwhelming Federal force any longer, the survivors fell back toward Rome. Upon reaching the Southern pickets at Farmer's Bridge, Garrard ordered Minty's Brigade to "drive them in, which he did," according to Minty, "and pursued the enemy to within sight of Rome, where he developed a force too large to engage." Minty reported that he sent the Fourth Michigan Cavalry forward and, "after a sharp skirmish," as he later explained, "the Fourth Michigan carried the position by a charge, killing 1 captain and 9 men, and capturing 6 men."[14]

Minty's Brigade continued to pursue the retreating Confederates "to within two miles of Rome," Minty continued, "where I found Jackson's division of cavalry in position supported by a division of infantry." The only infantry left at Rome on Sunday, 15 May, was Davidson's 150-man garrison, who together with Brigadier General Lawrence S. (Sul) Ross's Texas Cavalry brigade, some 1,009 Texans, prepared to receive Minty. Also, Captain Almaria L. Huggins's Tennessee battery was placed at Fort Attaway on the Old Summerville Road to repel the Northern invaders. Garrard's force was double the size of the Rome defenders, but Garrard only sent Minty to probe toward the Georgia city while he and Wilder's Brigade split off in search of a ford over the Oostanaula River.[15]

After arriving in Rome on 14 May, Jackson rushed Captain Edward Croft's Columbus Georgia battery of "Flying Artillery," four three-inch ordnance rifled guns and the balance of his three brigades, to Rome. Jackson had received an urgent message from Polk during the night of 14 May to hurry his division to Calhoun, twenty-one miles to the northeast, because Johnston

[13] Magee, *History of the 72nd Indiana Volunteer Infantry, 297;* Robertson, *Michigan in the War*, 661.

[14] Brewer, *Alabama*, 688; "Battle of Farmer's Bridge," *Columbus (Georgia) Times*, 21 May 1864, 2; Garrard's report, *OR*, ser. 1, vol. 38, pt. 2, 803; Minty's report, *OR*, ser. 1, vol. 38, pt. 2, 811; French, *Two Wars*, 193–94; Forbes, *Haulin' Brass*, 187–88.

[15] Minty's report, *OR*, ser. 1, vol. 38, pt. 2, 811; French, *Two Wars*, 193–94; Forbes, *Haulin' Brass*, 187–88; Lindsley, *Military Annals of Tennessee, Confederate*, 2:803.

had learned that the Federals had crossed the river at Lay's Ferry. Taking Ferguson's and Armstrong's brigades with him, Jackson prudently left Ross's Texas brigade and Croft's battery at Rome to augment Davidson's meager defense garrison.[16]

Huggins's Battery, already in place northwest of Rome, likely was located at Fort Attaway on the west side of the Summerville Road (today's US 27) while Croft's Battery, which arrived just before the action, was placed on the hill to the right, or east, of the Summerville Road in a newly prepared position where a crude gun battery was quickly erected to complement the rifle pits already dug by portions of Davidson's 150-man demi-brigade. When the Rome garrison was warned by a dispatch rider from Captain Lokey at Farmer's Bridge, it seems at least a section of Huggins's Battery, together with Croft's Battery was moved to an advance position on the Summerville Road in support of the 9th Texas Legion, which had just arrived and been ordered to dismount and advance in a skirmish line. As will be seen, it seems Ross planned to use the guns and the 9th Texas Legion on the Summerville Road to lure the Federals into the valley formed by Dry Run Creek and then strike the unsuspecting Northerners from the west with the balance of his mounted brigade.

Minty received a warm reception from the defenders as he approached Rome. Wilder's Brigade was supposed to cross the river and support Minty's attack with a matching probe on the southeast side of the river. According to Garrard, "an examination of the Oosentaula [*sic*] River proved that a crossing was impracticable, as there were neither fords nor bridges between Rome and Resaca." An unnamed Southern observer witnessed the scene: "the enemy leaving about half of their force advanced—pressing our pickets to A. R. Smith's place two and half miles from town. They planted a battery on the hill where Rev. Mr. Hillyer formerly lives, now owned by Mr. A. Maupin." The Federal battery was the Chicago Board of Trade's artillery under Lieutenant George I. Robinson. "Our cavalry—and it may not be prudent," continued the Confederate witness, "in extreme caution, to say how many or what command—went out to meet them."[17]

As Minty's force neared Rome, Ross's Texans and Davidson's contingent rode out to meet them. "They dismounted and formed about a half mile this

---

[16] *OR*, ser. 1, vol. 38, pt. 4, 710, 714.

[17] *OR*, ser. 1, vol. 38, pt. 2, 853; "Battle of Farmer's Bridge," *Columbus (Georgia) Times*, 21 May 1864, 2.

side of Mr. Smith's place, at right angles with the road," the Southern observer explained. He continued,

> A battery was put in position and some dozen shots fired at the enemy. Our skirmishers also exchanged a few musket shots with those of the Abolitionists, but there were no casualties on our side after the skirmish at the bridge. The enemy continued in line about an hour and then withdrew, falling back, pursued by our men, to Farmer's Bridge, where they were up to a late hour Sunday night.[18]

Minty reported that, after pushing back Company G of the 12th Alabama Cavalry from Farmer's Bridge, he "pushed forward rapidly to within three miles of Rome, where the enemy in considerable force, and holding a strong position, made a stand, showing four pieces of artillery. They at the same time moved strong columns on both my flanks." Minty wisely moved back. "Immediately in my rear the Dallas road,[19] came in on the road on which I advanced [US Highway 27]. I therefore fell back to a position north of the junction of the road," Minty continued. "Here Lieutenant Colonel [Josiah B.] Park, commanding the 4th Michigan Cavalry, reported that a column of infantry was moving around my left, and at the same time Smith's [Ross's] brigade of cavalry was discovered on my right."[20]

The column of infantry that was moving around on Minty's left, or east, was the 9th Texas Legion of Ross's Brigade, led by Colonel Dudley W. Jones. Ross ordered the 9th Texas to dismount and sent them forward to skirmish with the oncoming Federals and lure them into range of the balance of the brigade and Southern artillery. The column that was flanking Minty to the west, or right, was the balance of Ross's Brigade.[21]

---

[18] "Battle of Farmer's Bridge," *Columbus (Georgia) Times*, 21 May 1864, 2; Kerr, *Griscom*, 142; Forbes, *Haulin' Brass*, 188.

[19] The Old Dallas Road and the Redmond Gap Road both approached Rome from the west and northwest, respectively, across the campus of today's Berry College, and merged into one road near Hermann Hall at Berry College. There, they continued southeast as one road and across US Highway 27, then across the Oostanaula River and to the southwest of today's Rome Braves Stadium and continuing into town, eventually becoming Chantillon Road NE and North Avenue. The Old Dallas Road passed through Rome to the southeast and eventually led to the Etowah Native American Mounds, Euharlee, and Dallas (additional research on old roads around Rome provided by Norman Dasinger Jr.).

[20] Robertson, *Michigan in the War*, 661.

[21] Crabb, *All Afire to Fight*, 213; Kerr, ed., *Fighting with Ross' Texas Cavalry Brigade*, 142; Forbes, *Haulin' Brass*, 188.

After Croft's guns fired a couple of rounds into the path of the Fourth Michigan, the Federal troopers turned and fell back quickly. Jones and his 9th Texas Legion then remounted and pursed the blue-clad horsemen. Four times Jones and his regiment charged Minty's men as they steadily withdrew. The Federals continued to withdraw fighting until they reached Farmer's Bridge then waited on Garrard for reinforcements and orders. According to Magee of the Seventy-Second Indiana of Wilder's Brigade, Minty lost four men wounded during the action. On the Southern side, Davidson's contingency lost two men while Jones's 9th Texas Legion lost one scout and captured one Federal trooper. Also, during the action, Private James A. Neeld, of Fayetteville, Tennessee, in Captain Almaria L. Huggins's Tennessee battery, was killed by a saber-thrust from a member of the Fourth US Regular Cavalry.[22]

After repelling the first Federal threat on the "City of Seven Hills," the citizens breathed a collective sigh of relief on the evening of Sunday, 15 May. Ten Alabama soldiers had paid the price with their lives at Farmer's Bridge to buy valuable time before the city was occupied. They were buried in a small cemetery on a hill overlooking Armuchee Creek near where they fell. In Rome, two of the three churches continued their services. But there was considerable excitement in town. Throughout the day, many of the ladies gathered on Court House Hill (also called Neely Hill or Clock Tower Hill today) to witness the anticipated battle. It never came. For the moment, Rome was still in Confederate hands.[23]

Rome

After learning of Garrard's failure to either effect a crossing over the Oostanaula River and damage the railroad, or capture Rome, Sherman did not hide his disappointment: "I regret exceedingly you did not avail yourself of the chance I gave you to cut the railroad. At the time you reached the bridge, Martin's cavalry was all that was on that flank, and they widely scattered." In response to Garrard's claim that cavalry from Forrest and/or Roddy in Mississippi or Alabama was at Rome, he quipped,

---

[22] Robertson, *Michigan in the War*, 661; Magee, *History of the 72nd Indiana Volunteer Infantry*, 297; Kerr, ed., *Fighting with Ross' Texas Cavalry Brigade*, 142; Lindsley, *Military Annals of Tennessee, Confederate*, 2:803.

[23] Georgia's Rome Office of Tourism, Farmer's Bridge, Civil War History, Greater Rome CVB https://romegeorgia.org/; "Battle of Farmer's Bridge," *Columbus (Georgia) Times*, 21 May 1864, 2.

> Forrest on the 6th [of May] was retreating before Sam. Sturgis, in Mississippi, toward Tupelo. In person he may be at Rome, but if his horses are there they can outmarch ours. Roddy on the 11th was at Tuscumbia. Now Martin's and Wheeler's divisions are covering the retreat of Johnston for Allatoona, and I want you to dash in and strike the retreating masses in flank and all around.

The frustrated Federal commander continued, "Leave your artillery at the bridge, or better still, throw it into the Oostenaula [*sic*], and operate rapidly against the enemy retreating by all roads for Atlanta via Allatoona." Sherman added that he would send a division to assist. "Now, do not spare horseflesh, but strike boldly on the flank of the retreating columns." Clearly Sherman wanted action, and clearly Garrard was not the man for it.[24]

The division that would be given the task of joining Garrard on the west bank was the Second Division of the XIV Corps, Army of the Cumberland, commanded by Brigadier General Jefferson C. Davis.[25] In sharp contrast to Garrard, Davis was a man of action. Davis and his division moved southwest toward Rome, via today's Georgia Highway 156, Floyd Springs Road, and the Old Summerville Road, on the morning of Monday, 16 May. They marched fifteen miles before darkness halted their advance a few miles from Armuchee Creek at Floyd Springs, where they camped for the evening. Davis's Division included three brigades, led by Brigadier General James D. Morgan, Colonel John G. Mitchell, and Colonel Daniel McCook of the "Tribe of Dan" as they have been called in the famous "Fighting McCooks."[26]

During the night, as Davis reported, Garrard and his troopers "passed through my camp en route for Lay's Ferry, near Resaca. General Garrard

---

[24] Sherman to Garrard, 15 May [probably written on 16 May] 1864, *OR*, ser. 1, vol. 38, pt. 4, 197–98. Sherman's comments about Forrest were likely in response to Colonel Robert H. G. Minty's report where Minty related news that Major General Nathan B. Forrest may have arrived in Rome (see Minty's report, 16 May 1864, OR, ser. 1, vol. 38, pt. 2, 816).

[25] Davis was a troubled officer who had killed a superior officer, Major General William "Bull" Nelson, for slapping him after the two had exchanged insults. Davis, a native of Indiana, was part of the Federal garrison at Ft. Sumter at the beginning of the war. He had managed to avoid court martial, chiefly because the killing had happened at a time of crisis during the Confederate invasion of Kentucky as part of the Perryville Campaign, and there had been neither time nor spare officers to conduct it (*OR*, ser. 1, vol. 38, pt. 4, 202; Davis's report, 16 May 1864, *OR*, ser. 1, vol. 38, pt. 1, 627).

[26] *OR*, ser. 1, vol. 38, pt. 1, 627–28.

reported his inability to find any bridge across the Oostenaula [*sic*] above Rome, and his determination to return and cross the river with the main column near Resaca." Due to initial reports from Garrard, however, both Sherman and Davis were under the mistaken belief that Farmer's Bridge led to passage over the Oostanaula River, not Armuchee Creek. "This condition of affairs placed me in an embarrassing position as to how to act under the circumstances. Believing, however, that the main object of the expedition could best be obtained by pushing on to Rome with my command, and try to secure the bridge and capture that place," explained Davis, "I immediately sent a communication to Major-General Thomas of my determination, and early on the morning of the 17th resumed the march in that direction." By 7 a.m., Davis's men were on the move.[27]

Davis came upon Farmer's Bridge by noon on Tuesday, 17 May, as Howard's IV Corps pressed Wheeler's cavalrymen south of Calhoun and toward Adairsville. At Farmer's Bridge, Davis encountered the first Confederate pickets, which fell back before him without contesting possession of the bridge. The division commander parked his wagon train and left two regiments, the Tenth Illinois of Morgan's First Brigade and the 125th Illinois of McCook's Third Brigade, to guard the bridge and wagons, and, after a two-hour respite for lunch, the division proceeded down the road to Rome, eight miles away. Mitchell's Brigade led the way.[28]

As they came into view of the church spires of Rome, and within range of artillery fire, the Thirty-Fourth Illinois, led by Lieutenant-Colonel Oscar Van Tassell (of Mitchell's Brigade), formed in the front, astride the road as skirmishers. Morgan's Brigade deployed to the west of the road (today's US Highway 27). The Sixteenth Illinois under Colonel Robert F. Smith moved to the right, pushing a strong skirmish line forward. Smith's men forced back the Confederate troopers who had ridden forward from Dalton to meet and retard them. The balance of Morgan's Brigade formed in a second line, with the Tenth Michigan held in reserve. The Tenth Illinois continued to guard the wagon train, but after 9 p.m., brought up the wagons to within two miles of Rome.[29]

McCook's Brigade deployed to the left of the Thirty-Fourth Illinois, left (or east) of the road (today's US Highway 27). In the first line, McCook placed the Twenty-Second Indiana next to the road on the right, and the

---

[27] Ibid.

[28] Ibid., 628, 647, 709.

[29] *OR*, ser. 1, vol. 38, pt. 3, 628, 647, 657, 660, 665, 667.

Eighty-Sixth Illinois on the left, with the Fifty-Second Ohio and the Eighty-Fifth Illinois in the second line. The Fifty-Second Ohio was behind the Twenty-Second Indiana, while the Eighty-Fifth Illinois was behind the Eighty-Sixth Illinois. Throwing three companies of the Twenty-Second Indiana in front as skirmishers, McCook's Brigade moved steadily forward, as did the Thirty-Fourth Illinois astride the road and the Sixteenth Illinois west of the road.[30]

Confederate Major General Samuel Gibbs French arrived in Rome on Monday, 16 May, just ahead of the first of his three brigades from west Alabama, Brigadier General Claudius Sears's Mississippi brigade. French was ordered to bring his brigades forward to join Johnston as soon as they arrived in Rome. Sears's men marched twenty-nine miles from Blue Mountain, Alabama (near today's Anniston, Alabama), to reach Rome just after dark. They had been marching and riding the various trains from Montevallo, Alabama, since Friday, 13 May. By 10 p.m., Sears's men, without their cooking utensils or a hot meal for three days, were on the train cars headed for Kingston, then to Adairsville to join Johnston's retreating army.[31]

Upon learning of Minty's probe to the outskirts of Rome the day before, French ordered Colonel D. T. Blakey and his 1st Alabama Cavalry of Morgan's Brigade to perform reconnaissance on the east bank of the Oostanaula River to see if any Federals had crossed the river, and if Rome was in any imminent danger from the direction of Calhoun. Blakey reported that his scouts had patrolled to the mouth of Armuchee Creek, and that they had found no Federals east of the river, at least up to eight miles from Rome. Thus, on Monday, 16 May, French had only a small portion of Morgan's Alabama brigade patrolling the east bank above Rome. In the city, Davidson's 150 men prepared the defenses at Fort Attaway and the hill east of the Fort between Summerville Road (US Highway 27) and the Oostanaula River. Huggins's Battery was also on the line, probably in Fort Attaway, where they had also likely served on 15 May against Minty's demonstration. Croft's Battery also was placed on line, again probably on the hill to the right of Huggins's guns.[32]

The next morning, Tuesday, 17 May, Brigadier General Matthew D. Ector's brigade arrived at Rome with about 1,165 men, mostly Texans who used to be cavalrymen but were now horseless. One North Carolina regiment,

---

[30] *OR*, ser. 1, vol. 38, pt. 1, 628, 709, 718, 720, 726, 728.

[31] French, *Two Wars*, 193.

[32] Ibid., 193–94; French's report, *OR*, ser. 1, vol. 38, pt. 3, 899.

the 29th North Carolina Infantry under Colonel Bacchus S. Proffit, was brigaded with Ector's Texans. Soon, the 39th North Carolina, which had fought with General Daniel Reynolds's brigade at Resaca, would join them. Throughout the day, French received constant telegraph messages from Johnston and Polk to hurry and send his brigades as soon as they arrived, without waiting for them to consolidate. As Ector's men were preparing to leave by train around 1 p.m., French received word from Davidson that the Federals were approaching Rome from Farmer's Bridge on the west bank and were presently only about two and a half miles away.[33]

With Brigadier General Francis M. Cockrell's veteran Missouri brigade still thirty-two miles away, and no rail line connecting from Rome to Blue Mountain, French needed to buy time. He needed for Cockrell to arrive before Rome fell, which would cut the Missourians off from the main body of Confederates. French quickly ordered Ector's men off the train cars and sent them to the west side of the Oostanaula River to join Davidson's small contingent that had moved to cover the Federal threat from the northwest.[34]

French had also started two batteries, Captain Henry Guibor's Missouri and Captain James A. Hoskins's "Brookhaven" Mississippi battery, to Kingston, in part by dirt road and in part by train. Upon learning of the threat to Rome, he was able to stop one section of two guns in Hoskins's Battery and send them to Jackson Hill north of Rome on the east bank of the Oostanaula River (between today's Dogwood Drive and Reservoir Street). There, Hoskins's Battery section was placed at Fort Jackson (near today's Georgia Rome Visitors Center). Additionally, one section of two guns from Captain N. H. Clanton's Alabama battery was present at Rome and saw action. Its

[33] Ector's strength is derived by taking French's present for duty figure of 4,765 men less Sears's reported present strength of 2,110 and Cockrell's reported present strength of 1,490. At Cassville, French requested rations for 6,000 men as his three brigades had marched from west Alabama so quickly that their cooking utensils had been left behind and their supply wagons had not yet caught up with the men. Added to French's present for duty strength by this time must be added about 300 artillerists in three batteries, Captain John J. Ward's Alabama battery, Captain James A. Hoskins's Mississippi battery, and Captain Henry Guibor's Missouri battery. Also added to this figure are the officers and noncombatants of French's Division (French, *Two Wars*, 193–94; French's report, *OR*, ser. 1, vol. 38, pt. 3, 899; Stroud, *Ector's Texas Brigade*, 153).

[34] Stroud, *Ector's Texas Brigade*, 153.

location and level of participation are unclear although there is some evidence to suggest it was engaged on the morning of 18 May at Fort Jackson.[35]

Ector's and Davidson's men manned the Southern lines along a range of hills overlooking Little Dry Creek, anchored on the west by De Soto Hill (the present-day location of Shorter University) and centered on Fort Attaway (at the site of the former Sumo Japanese Restaurant on Martha Berry Boulevard, NE/US Highway 27). French also sent a dispatch rider at the gallop to Cockrell to order him to move with all possible haste. Ector's Brigade was placed "in the trenches over the Oostanaula and [was ordered] to hold the town until Cockrell arrived," explained French. "A strong line of skirmishers was advanced, which was soon engaged with the enemy."[36]

French continued, "During the afternoon, Gen. J[ohn]. T. Morgan arrived and said that his command was enroute to Rome from Adairsville, and that he and Gen. Furgerson [*sic*] were both hard pressed by the enemy." Ferguson's troopers had moved toward Woodlands and Kingston while Morgan's cavalrymen continued southwest from Hermitage and the east bank of the Oostanaula River until they reached Rome. French added, "At 4 p.m. Gen. Ross (cavalry) arrived with two regiments."[37]

---

[35] French arrived in Rome with two batteries, Guibor's and Hoskins's. A third battery, Captain John J. Ward's Alabama battery would be assigned to him by or before 10 June 1864. Ward's Battery was stationed at Camp Cummings near Mobile, Alabama, on 30 April 1864. Apparently, it was sent north to Georgia during the first week of May 1864 when Cantey's Brigade was sent to Rome and then Resaca. Bill Scaife included Ward's Battery along Polk's line in his maps of Resaca, but he provided no source for his inclusion. I agree with Scaife that Ward was likely at Resaca with Cantey, but it's possible that Ward's Battery did not join the army until at or after New Hope Church. What is certain, however, is that Ward was not with French at Rome (see *OR*, ser. 1, vol. 32, pt. 3, 861, 863; *OR Supp.*, pt. 2, vol. 1, 192; Wheeler, *Confederate Military History*, 8:334–36; and Brewer, *Alabama*, 704). Brewer was unable to find any evidence linking Ward's Battery with the Army of Tennessee, which fits because Ward's Battery was previously assigned to the Department of the Gulf and stationed near Mobile until it joined Polk's Army of Mississippi at or after Resaca. Brewer also reported that at least one section of Clanton's Alabama battery saw action at Rome (see Brewer, *Alabama*, 704; Wheeler, *Confederate Military History*, 8:335).

[36] Wheeler, *Confederate Military History*, 8:335

[37] French, *Two Wars*, 194. Located in the community of Shannon along Old Calhoun Road and near the Shannon Cemetery, Hermitage was the pioneer home of Joseph Watters, an early White settler and an admirer of President Andrew Jackson ("Hermitage").

Ross's brigade had, according to the Texas brigade commander, "been posted to guard the crossings of the Oostenaula River above Rome, and was eight miles distant when [he] received a dispatch from Brigadier General Morgan informing" him of the Federal threat on Rome. That morning, Ross's men had moved at daylight from Rome toward Calhoun, and at 2 p.m., according to Lieutenant George L. Griscom, adjutant of the 9th Texas Legion, the troopers were ordered to turn around and move back to Rome with all possible speed. John Morgan and Ross moved their troopers to the crest of hills with Ross's Texans on the right. "The men were dismounted," continued Griscom, "and placed on the hills. Davidson, with a few cavalry [a few of Ross's Texans supplemented Davidson's line], moved on the enemy's right. Then, at 6 p.m., Ross, with his men, charged their line of skirmishers and drove them back to the main line."[38]

As Davis pressed his men forward, the Southern defenders held their ground on the ring of hills protecting Rome. Newton Asbury Keen of the 6th Texas Legion remembered, "The public Road [today's US Highway 27] ran along between to [*sic*] lofty hills some 400 yards apart [Fort Attaway was located on the hill just west of US Highway 27 at the Sumo Restaurant, and an unnamed hill, located on the east side of the highway opposite Fort Attaway, contained a full battery, rifle pits, and a line of infantry earthworks]. The val[l]ey was in farms on either side of the road. The Yankee force could form some 500 yards in our front in timber and low flat land where we would never see them." Describing McCook's advance, Keen continued, "Their battle line came sweeping up from this place through the val[l]ey. Our right and left rest[ed] against each side of the hills and formed a solid column right across the val[l]ey. The Yankees were determined to break through our line. While they were infantry," he explained, "so were we, our horses bein[g] some miles in the rear. On they came with a shout and fixed bayonets, but the boys poured such volleys into their line that it wavered, realed [*sic*] and fled back to the woods."[39]

After reforming, the bluecoats "returned with a determination to sweep the valley," remembered Keen, who added that they would not succeed. "Their line formed itself within twenty feet of ours," Keen added, "and it seemed they would mix it with a hand-to-hand fight. But at this juncture, our boys drew their six shooters and then the Yankees began to tumble into piles.

---

[38] Ross's report, *OR*, ser. 1, vol. 38, pt. 3, 962–63; Kerr, quoting Griscom, *Fighting with Ross' Texas Cavalry Brigade*, 143.

[39] Billingsley, "Such Is War," 103–104.

Their line came to a dead halt and stood still for at least ten seconds when it realed [*sic*] and fled in great confusion." Keen explained that the Federals tried a third time to no avail, leaving what he thought were three hundred to four hundred dead and wounded on the field.[40]

McCook's Brigade quickly seized a hill—he referred to as Howe's Hill—in his immediate front, with his left resting near the Howe house overlooking the Oostanaula River (located just east of Martha Berry Boulevard, NE/US Highway 27 and at the present-day site of Oak Hill Church of Christ). Ross's dismounted Texans advanced on foot and opened fire on the Federal skirmish line that consisted of three companies of the Twenty-Second Indiana (who had advanced across the plain at today's Greater Community Bank and moved south toward today's US Post Office, reaching to about today's Coligni Way). According to Ross, his Texans "drove in the enemy's line of skirmishers, and attacked vigorously his main force, which proved to be General Davis' division of infantry, and pressed back his center near a mile, charging and driving it from two positions."[41]

Lieutenant Colonel James W. Langley of the 125th Illinois witnessed the attack by the Texas Legion. The front line of the Twenty-Second Indiana and Eighty-Sixth Illinois to the left (east by the river) had just formed on the hill (at today's Oak Hill Church of Christ), Langley stated, "when the enemy made a vigorous attack upon the 22nd Indiana, throwing it in some confusion and pressing its right back about sixty yards, where it rallied behind a rail fence."[42]

The Twenty-Second Indiana and the right half of the Eighty-Sixth Illinois fell back in the wake of the sudden charge by the Texans. So irresistible was the attack that the veteran Hoosier regiment was forced from the field, losing all of their field officers in the action. The Twenty-Second Indiana was able to recoil and reform behind the Fifty-Second Ohio regiment posted behind them. The Ohioans then moved forward to fill the brief void in the line. At the same time, the right half of the Eighty-Sixth Illinois refused its line and formed behind a fence on the Howe Hill behind the Howe house.

Lieutenant George L. Griscom, adjutant of the 9th Texas Legion, remembered, "dismounting we send our horses back to town—leap the works driving the enemy's skirmishers back & charged their main line of infantry composed of Jeff [C.] Davis (Indiana) Infantry Division—drove them back

---

[40] Ibid.

[41] *OR*, ser. 1, vol. 38, pt. 1, 709; *OR*, ser. 1, vol. 38, pt. 3, 962–63.

[42] *OR*, ser. 1, vol. 38, pt. 1, 709.

from their position in confusion with heavy loss—they outnumbered us more than 10 to 1 & soon flanked our position when we withdrew bringing off our dead and wounded." (The Twenty-Second Indiana fell back from the field at today's Greater Community Bank.)[43]

As the Hoosiers of the Twenty-Second Indiana fell back before the furious attack, the Eighty-Sixth Illinois refused its right half and began pouring fire into the attacking Texans, checking their advance. This gave time for the Hoosiers to rally behind the Ohioans. The Fifty-Second Ohio also came forward from its reserve position and relieved the exhausted Indianans who had lost eleven men killed, and five officers and twenty-three men wounded in the action. The Hoosiers were particularly hard hit in field officers, with Lieutenant Colonel William M. Wiles being severely wounded in the right arm, Major Thomas Shea in the throat, and Adjutant William A. Adams slightly in the right arm. The Eighty-Sixth Illinois saw six men killed and eleven wounded. In all, Davis's Division sustained 149 casualties during the action, with one quarter of the losses coming from the Twenty-Second Indiana.[44]

Ross's Texans had charged through a gap in the hills that formed the Confederate defensive line, across a valley, and into the Federal position. While the hills that lined the road on both sides partially shielded the initial part of the Southern attack, once the Texans reached the hill occupied by the Federals, there was no cover. Collecting their dead and wounded, Ross's men withdrew to their lines amid a rousing cheer from fellow Texans and some North Carolina troops in Ector's Brigade who were manning the trenches. Ross lost fifty men killed and wounded in the assault. A newspaper account published the following week in Atlanta provided the names of the casualties in Ross's Brigade, including one man killed and nineteen wounded in the 3rd Texas Legion, one man killed and nine wounded in the 6th Texas Legion, one killed and two wounded in the 9th Texas Legion, and one killed and twelve wounded in the 1st and 27th Texas Legion consolidated.[45]

---

[43] Kerr, ed., *Fighting with Ross' Texas Cavalry Brigade*, 143.

[44] *OR*, ser. 1, vol. 38, pt. 1, 629, 709–10, 726, 728; Aten, *History of the Eighty-Fifth Regiment*, 171.

[45] P. B. Plummer, acting assistant adjutant general, casualty list, Brigadier General Lawrence Sullivan Ross's Texas Cavalry Brigade, 15 May–4 September, during the Atlanta, Georgia, Campaign, *OR Supp.*, pt. 2, vol. 83, 509–15, from the *Houston Daily Telegraph*, 10 November 1864; Brigadier General Lawrence Sullivan Ross's casualty report at Rome, 17 May, *OR*, ser. 1, vol. 38, pt. 3, 963; Hale, *Third Texas Cavalry*, 219–20; Kerr, ed., *Fighting with Ross' Texas Cavalry Brigade*, 220; Crabb, *All Afire to Fight*, 212–13. *Memphis Daily Appeal*, Atlanta, GA, 25 May 1864, 1.

During the action, Davis ordered the four three-inch ordnance rifles of Captain Charles M. Barnett's Battery I, Second Illinois Artillery, and four Napoleon twelve-pounder guns of Captain George Q. Gardner's Second Minnesota battery, to unlimber along the hill at the crossroads (today's Oak Hill and Martha Berry Museum). There, the Federal guns under the command of Captain Charles M. Barnett exchanged fire with the two guns of Hoskins's Mississippi battery section posted in Fort Jackson, and with Huggins's Battery and Croft's Battery at Fort Attaway and the hill to its east. Hoskins lost two men wounded in the action while French reported a total of about one hundred men killed and wounded, chiefly from Ross's Texans.[46]

Undeterred from the Confederate counterstrike, Davis brought up his reserves and tightened his hold on the range of hills, moving the Eighty-Fifth Illinois to the front left to adjoin the line to the river (at the site of the parking lot for Oak Hill Church of Christ). Davis also extended his line to the west by pushing Morgan's Federal infantry brigade out to the Alabama Road, west of the Southern defenses at DeSoto Hill that was manned by Confederate General John Morgan's Alabama cavalrymen, and close to the Confederate works. Federal General James Morgan placed a strong skirmish line along the Alabama Road to the west to protect his flank.[47]

During the night, French continued his evacuation. Cockrell's Brigade arrived at dusk, "with colors flying and drums beating," according to Lieutenant Colonel R. S. Bevier of the 5th Missouri who added that the brigade had "made a march that day of thirty-two miles over slippery, red-clay roads, besides the nineteen miles by rail." The latter was a reference to the nineteen-mile trip that the brigade took on the Rome Railroad that evening, departing Rome by 10 p.m. and arriving at Kingston by midnight.[48]

Ector's Brigade was withdrawn from the trenches around midnight and arrived in Kingston at 7:30 a.m. on Wednesday, 18 May. Hoskins's Battery had also been withdrawn during the night, leaving Rome in the hands of Ross's Texans, John Morgan's Alabamians, and Davidson's contingent. Ross had been instructed to evacuate Rome the following day with Morgan, after

---

Compare Hale, *Third Texas Cavalry*, 220, which shows two killed, seven wounded, and four captured in the 3rd Texas.

[46] Brown, Murphy, and Putney, *Behind the Guns*, 140; *OR*, ser. 1, vol. 38, pt. 1, 628–29, 829; *OR*, ser. 1, vol. 38, pt. 3, 899, 963.

[47] *OR*, ser. 1, vol. 38, pt. 1, 629–29; 646–47.

[48] *OR*, ser. 1, vol. 38, pt. 3, 899; Bevier, *Confederate First and Second Missouri Brigades*, 232.

Exhibit 1

Adairsville, Georgia
(Sketch by Theodore R. Davis *Harper's Weekly*, July 2, 1864)

Woodlands, Georgia
(Sketch by Theodore R. Davis *Harper's Weekly*, July 2, 1864)

Kingston, Georgia
(Sketch by Theodore R. Davis *Harper's Weekly*, July 2, 1864)

Exhibit 2

Rome, Georgia: View from Myrtle Hill (facing north) taken between May 18, 1864 and November 10, 1864, during the Federal occupation of Rome. Note the Etowah River in the foreground, the covered bridge over the Oostanaula River to the left, and the Coosa River which begins at the bottom left where the other two rivers join.

Exhibit 3

Brigadier General John T. Morgan
(Library of Congress)

Brigadier General Lawrence (Sul) Ross
(Library of Congress)

Both of the Federal attacks, Minty's cavalry on May 15, 1864, and Davis' infantry on May 17, 1864, came from the northwest in the upper left of the picture, while the City of Rome lies in the center and right. Sesquicentennial Committee of The City of Rome, *Rome & Floyd County: An Illustrated History 1834–1984*, revised edition, Charlotte, NC: The Delmar Company, 1986, 40-41.

Brigadier General Jefferson C. Davis
(Library of Congress)

Colonel Robert H.G. Minty
(Library of Congress)

Exhibit 4

Jonathan McDow House
This house, located just south of Adairsville on the Adairsville-Cassville Road, served as Major General Joseph Hooker's headquarters on the evening of May 18, 1864, and it was used briefly by Major General John Schofield on the morning of May 19, 1864. (Drawing by Wilbur G. Kurtz, Sept. 1947, Kurtz Papers, Keenan Research Center, Atlanta History Center)

Brigadier General George Gibbs Dibrell
(Public Domain)

Major General John M. Schofield
(Library of Congress)

Colonel Hawkins Price House
Colonel Hawkins Price served as a Georgia State Senator from 1857-1865 and was a member of the Georgia Secession Convention. The title "Colonel" appears to have been honorary due to his public service. (Photo by Wilbur G. Kurtz, Kurtz Papers, Keenan Research Center, Atlanta History Center)

Major General Jospeh Hooker
(Library of Congress)

Major General Daniel Butterfield
(Library of Congress)

Exhibit 6

Federal Cavalry Charge at Cassville, Afternoon of May 19, 1864: Cavalry of McCook's division in their charge at Cassville on the afternoon of May 19, 1864. While the artist is unknown, the sketch appeared in Dr. Homer Mead, *The Eighth Iowa Cavalry in the Civil War: Autobiography and Personal Recollections of Homer Mead*, M.D., Augusta, Illinois, Carthage, IL: S.C. Davidson,1925. Dr. Mead participated in the attack with the Iowa regiment and lost his horse in the charge.

Brigadier General Edward McCook
(Library of Congress)

Colonel Jospeh Bartlett Dorr, Jr.
(Library of Congress)

Colonel Richard G. Earle, 2nd Alabama Cavalry, Killed at Woodlands, May 18, 1864. (Sketch by Antonela Boyles)

Lt. James A. Park, Co. F, 39th GA, Wounded at Cassville, May 19, 1864. (Sketch by Antonela Boyles)

Captain Andrew H. Buchanan, Assistant Engineer, attended the meeting with Johnston and the lieutenant generals at Adairsville, evening of May 17, 1864.
(*Confederate Veteran*, Vol. XIV, 370)

Major Wilbur E. Foster, Engineer, supervised the map project along each side of the Western & Atlantic Railroad from November 1863 to May 1864.
(*Confederate Veteran*, Vol. XX, 369)

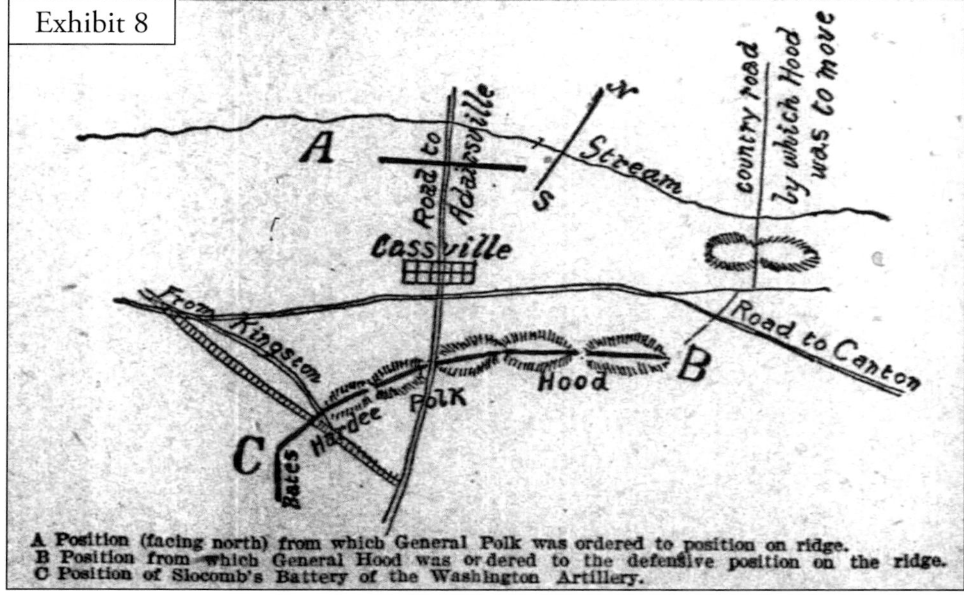

Johnston Map: Joseph E. Johnston drew this map and sent it along with a letter to Charles G. Johnsen, on June 19, 1874, from Savannah, GA. The letter was published in the *Southern Historical Society Papers*, R.A. Brock, Editor, Southern Historical Society, Richmond, VA: 1893, Vol. 21, 319. The letter and map were published in the *Times Picayune*, Sunday, October 22, 1893, New Orleans, LA. Johnston's sketch fails to include either the Copper Mine/Ironton Road or the Spring Place Road, but it does include a "country road" at the location of today's Brown Loop Road.

General Joseph Eggleston Johnston
(Library of Congress)

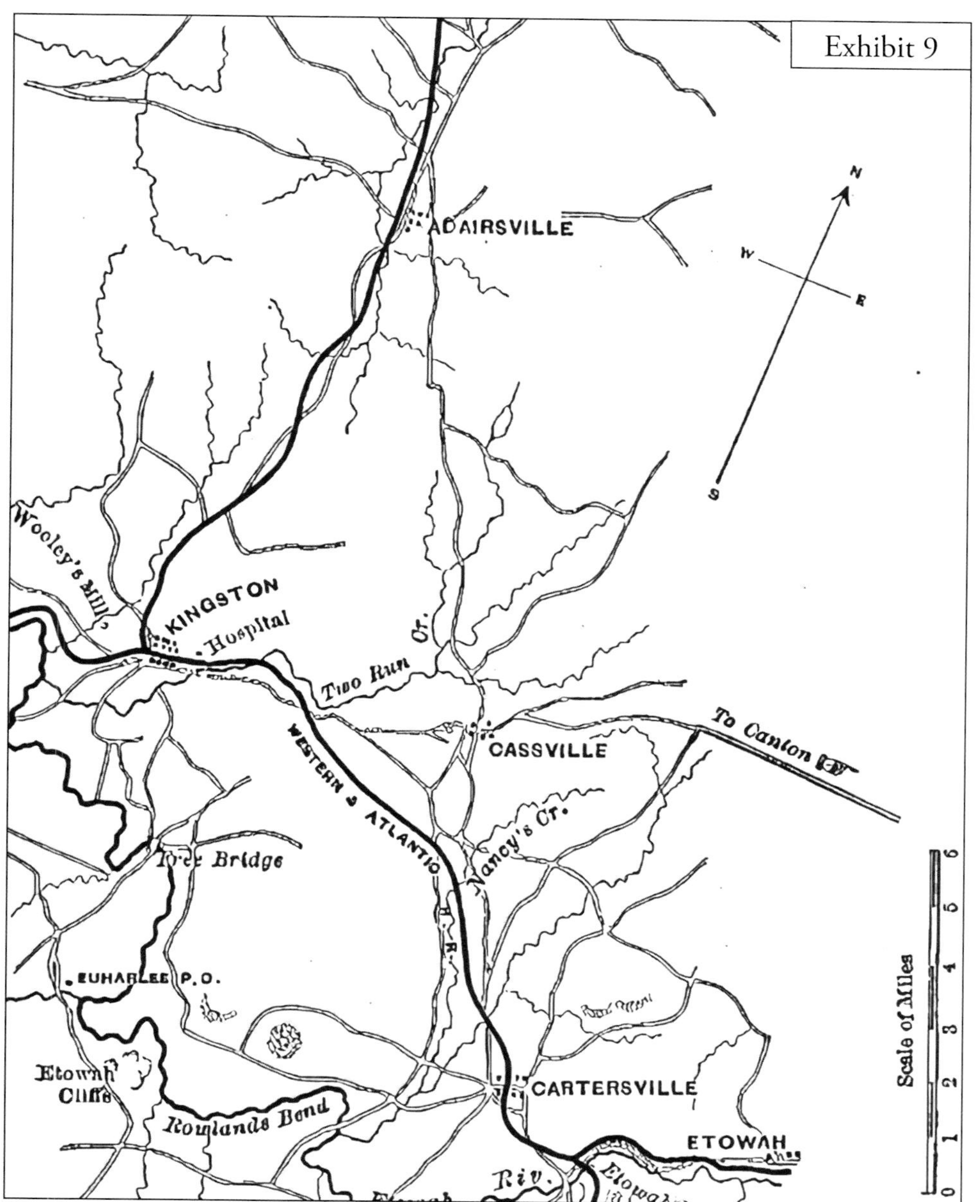

Johnston Narrative Map

This map, appearing in his post-war memoir, illuminates General Joseph E. Johnston's lack of awareness of the incompleteness and inaccuracy of the Confederate maps used at Cassville. Even a decade following the war, Johnston was still using a version of the incomplete Foster map in defending his position. His failure to understand the correct location of the (new) Spring Place Road is understandable. His alteration of the Copper Mine/Ironton Road, to the (old) "Spring Place Road" in T.B. Mackall's "O" sample "Journal," is inexcusable. Johnston's mistaken understanding of the Spring Place Road, coupled with his insistence on creating his version of the facts to preserve his reputation, and his deceitful use of the T.B. Mackall "Journal," have served to cloud and confuse the events at Cassville for a Century and a half, and have shamefully disparaged the reputation of the performance of General John Bell Hood and the soldiers of his corps at Cassville (See Joseph E. Johnston, *Narrative of Military Operations*, New York, NY: D. Appleton and Company, 1874, 320b.)

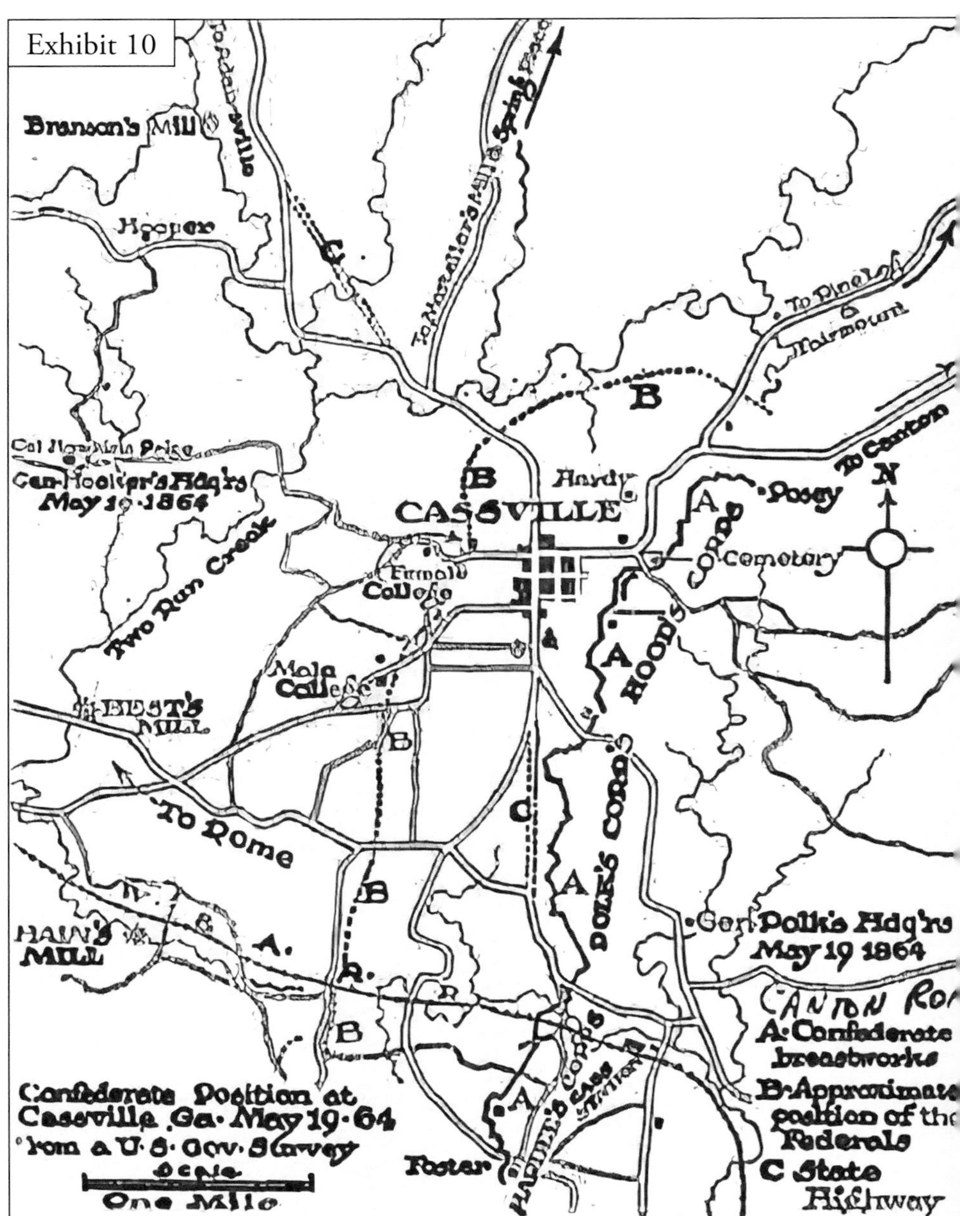

Kurtz Map 1: This map, drawn by Wilbur G. Kurtz, was published in the *History of Bartow County* in 1933 and wa relied upon by William R. Scaife in his map of the Morning Cassville Affair. Kurtz apparently relied on one of the Confederate Maps (Foster, Martin, or Wheeler) in drawing this map for he only included four roads north of Cassville instead of five. He also apparently relied on the altered T.B. Mackall "O" sample "Journal," in including in the notatio "To Mosteller's Mill & Spring Place" at the location of the Copper Mine/Ironton Road. After further study, Kurtz created a more detailed map of Cassville in 1949 (the Kurtz Map 2) in which he included five roads with the Spring Place Road in its correct location, and connected to the Pine Log Road at Five Forks. In his 1949 map, Kurtz also removed the notation "Spring Place," (leaving only "To Mostellar's Mill"), he apparently having discovered that the references to "Spring Place Road" in T.B. Mackall's published version, or "O" sample, "Journal" was inaccurate. (See Lucy Josephine Cunyus, *History of Bartow County, Georgia (Formerly Cass County)*, Atlanta, GA: Southern Historical Press, Inc., 1933, 233.)

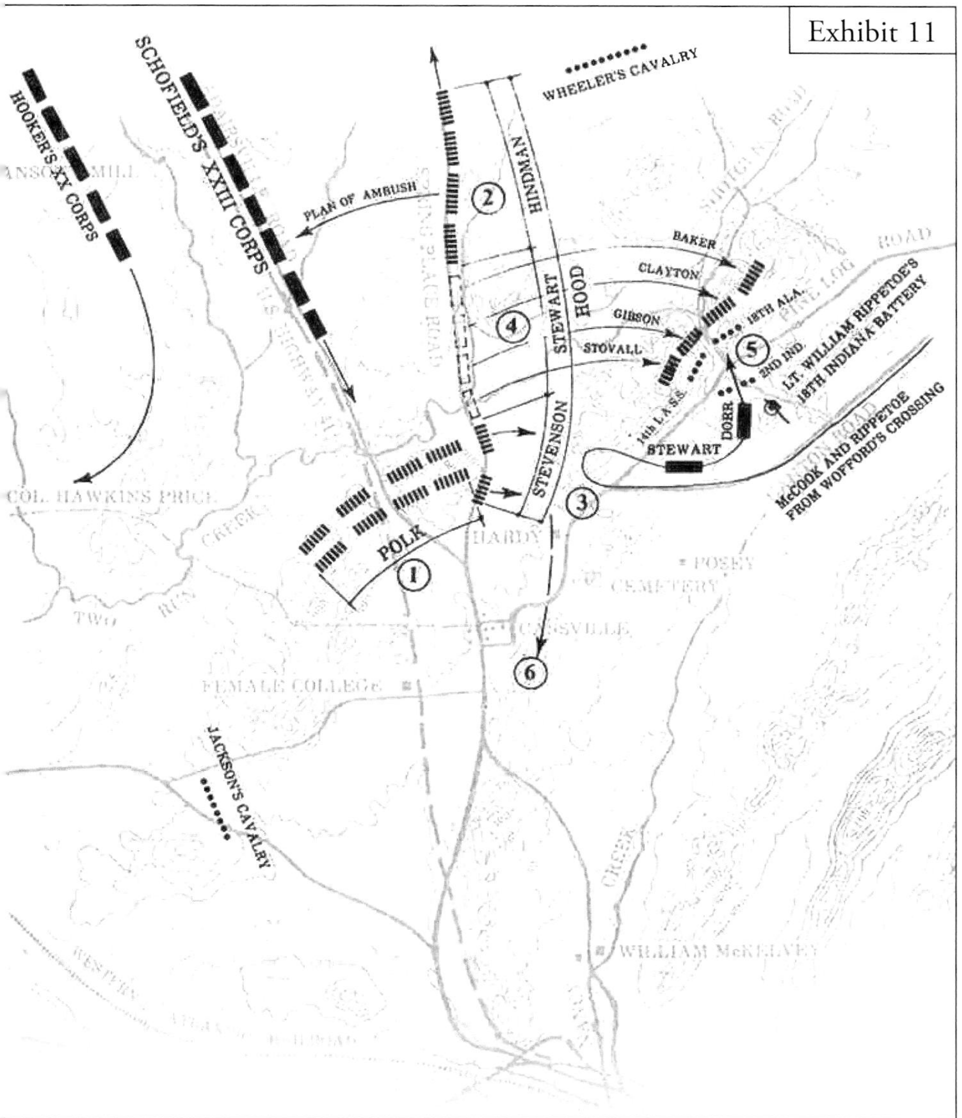

Scaife Map 1 "The Morning Cassville Affair"

This map, created by William R. Scaife in 1993, ironically also suffers from an incompleteness of the area northeast of Cassville and fails to include either the Five Forks intersection or the correct (new) Spring Place Road. Relying on the 1933 Kurtz map, Scaife also incorrectly referred to the Copper Mine/Ironton Road as the "Spring Place Road." He also incorrectly placed Schofield's XXIII Corps on the Adairsville-Cassville Road, instead of the Copper Mine/Ironton Road. Scaife's map correctly depicted a portion of the action of 10:30 a.m. at the Canton Road at its intersection with the Pine Log Road with the 2nd Indiana Cavalry, but he then blurred it with the fighting after 3:30 p.m. with Stewart's Confederate division in the Two Run Creek valley. McCook's Federal cavalry left the area for several hours and then returned with Stoneman after 3:00 p.m. Scaife also incorrectly placed Stewart's division facing south at the gap at today's Brown Loop Road. Stewart's division actually faced north and northeast, defending the gap from the afternoon Federal cavalry assault that came from the Five Forks area. (See William R. Scaife, *The Campaign for Atlanta*, Atlanta, GA: Scaife, 1993, 48c; Scaife, "Waltz Between the Rivers, and Overview of the Atlanta Campaign from the Oostanaula to the Etowah," Theodore P. Savas & David A. Woodbury, editors, *The Campaign for Atlanta & Sherman's March to the Sea*, 2 vols., Campbell, CA: Savas Woodbury Publishers, 1994, insert 278a.)

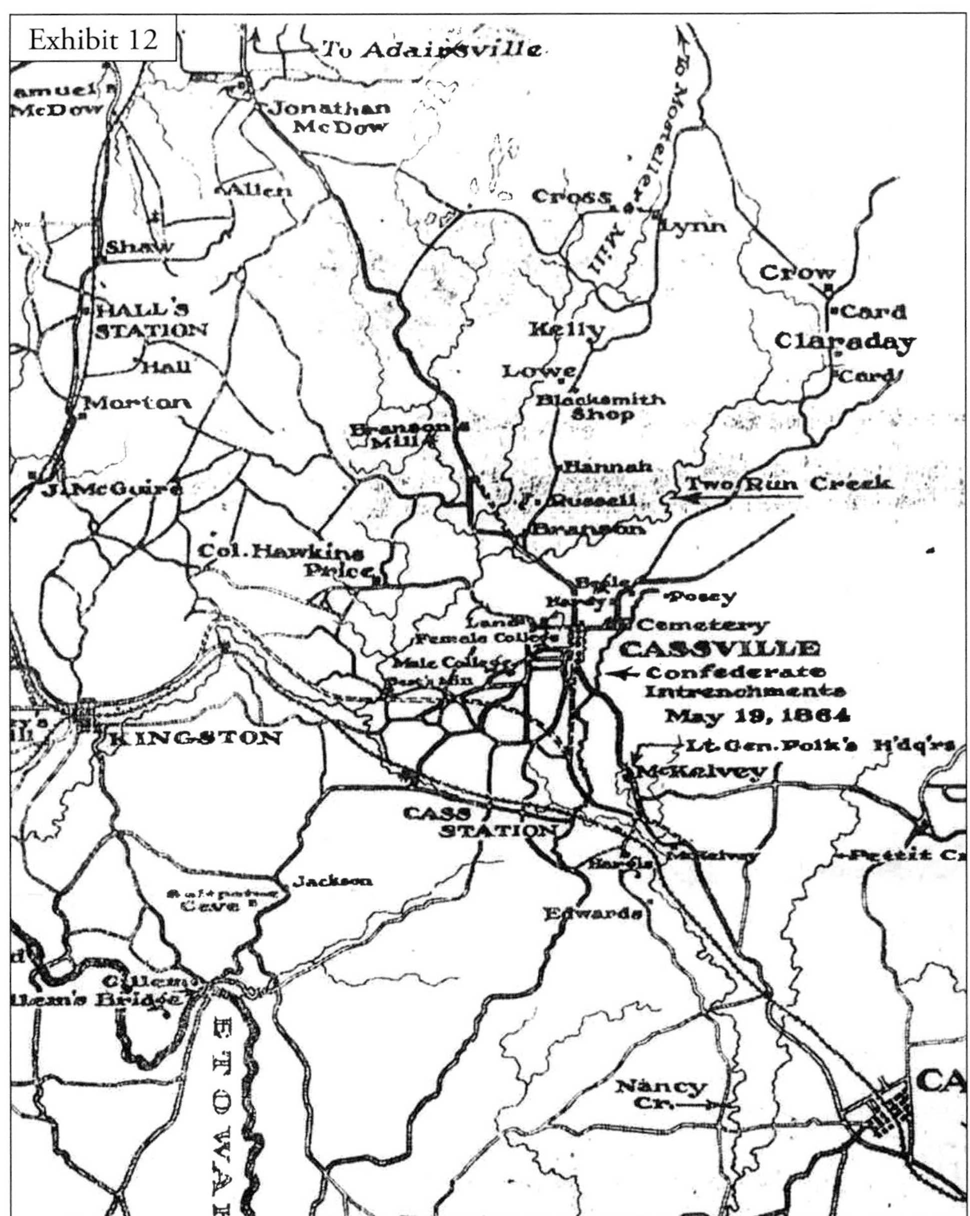

Kurtz Map 2: Wilbur Kurtz spent 50 hours creating this map for Colonel Thomas Spencer. In this map, Kurtz added a fifth road, the Spring Place Road, in its correct location connected with Pine Log Road at Five Forks. On the Copper Mine/Ironton Road, Kurtz removed the notation "Spring Place," (leaving only "To Mostellar's Mill"), having discovered that the references to "Spring Place Road" in T.B. Mackall's "O" sample, "Journal" was inaccurate. Kurtz also added a number of homesteads to this map. (*The Daily Tribune News*, Cartersville, GA, November 8, 1949. Courtesy Bartow History Museum)

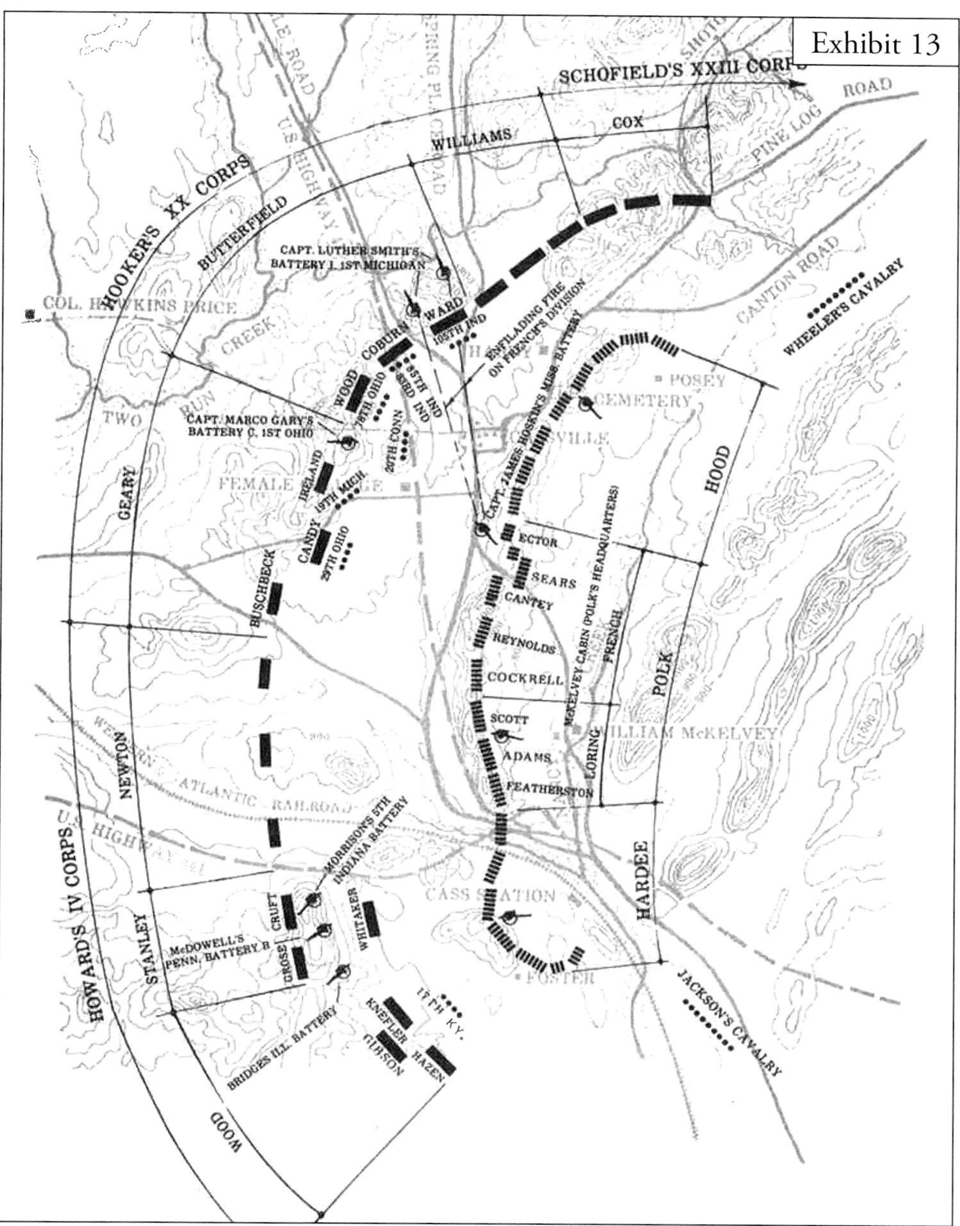

Scaife Map 2 "The Evening Cassville Affair:" In this map, Scaife has incorrectly placed Hoskins' battery at the gap where today's Mac Johnson Road (the old Cartersville Road) splits the ridge southeast of Cassville. Hoskins was actually in the gap formed by today's Shinall-Gaines Road with half of Ector's brigade north of the gap connecting with Hood's corps at the cemetery. Also, Rippetoe's Federal battery was on the hill north of Hardy's place. (See William R. Scaife, *The Campaign for Atlanta, Atlanta*, GA: Scaife, 1993, 48e; Scaife, "Waltz Between the Rivers, and Overview of the Atlanta Campaign from the Oostanaula to the Etowah," Theodore P. Savas & David A. Woodbury, editors, *The Campaign for Atlanta & Sherman's March to the Sea*, 2 vols., Campbell, CA: Savas Woodbury Publishers, 1994, insert 284a.)

Exhibit 14

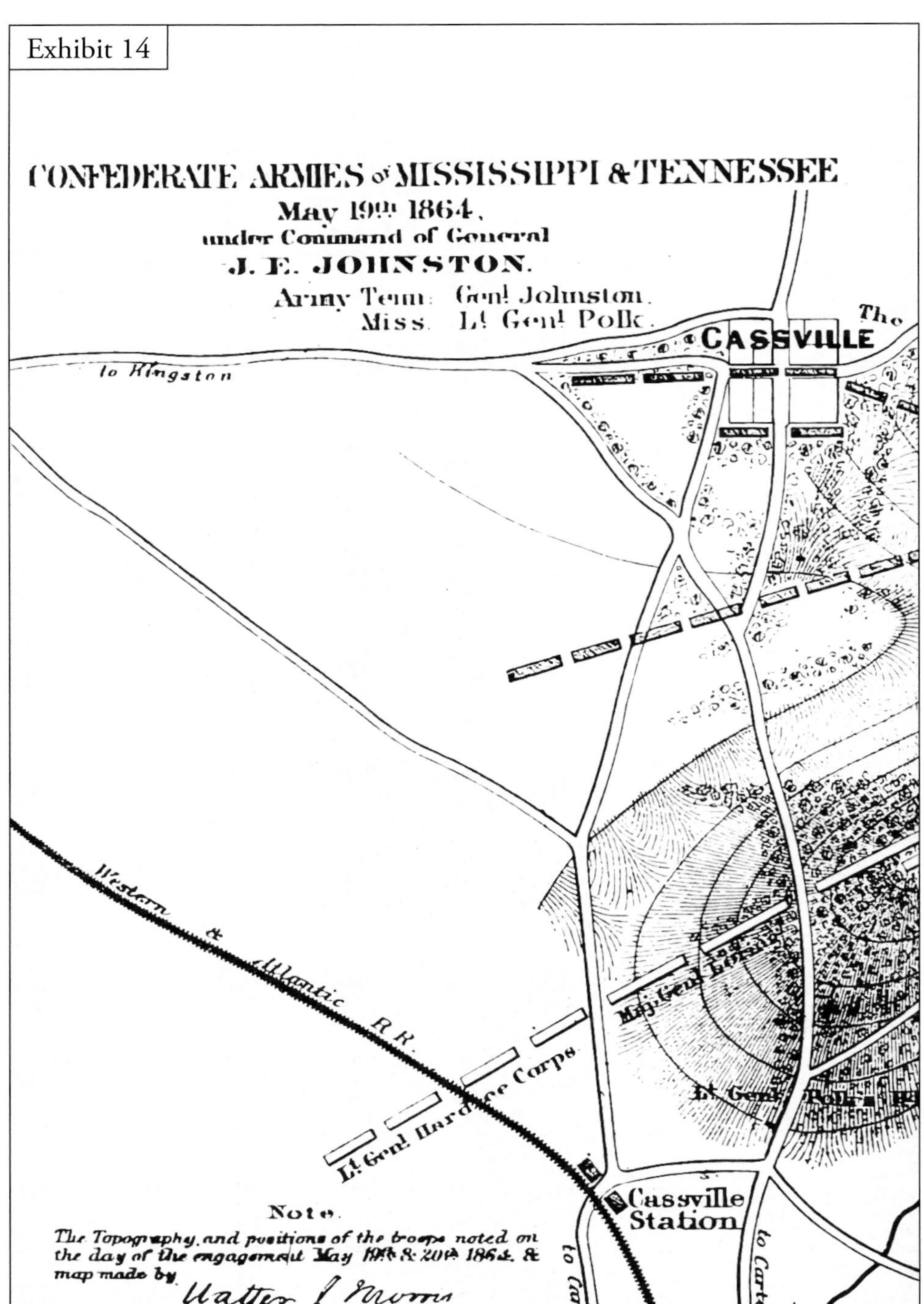

Morris Map: On the afternoon of May 19, 1864, Captain Walter J. Morris, Chief Engineer for Polk's Army of Mississippi, was tasked with examining the position of Polk's right and Hood's left in Johnston's newly-selected line of defense. Morris' opinion, like that of Polk, Hood, and Johnston's Chief of Artillery, Francis Shoup, was that the Confederate position was untenable for defense. Note the location of Hoskins' battery to the left of the gap (at

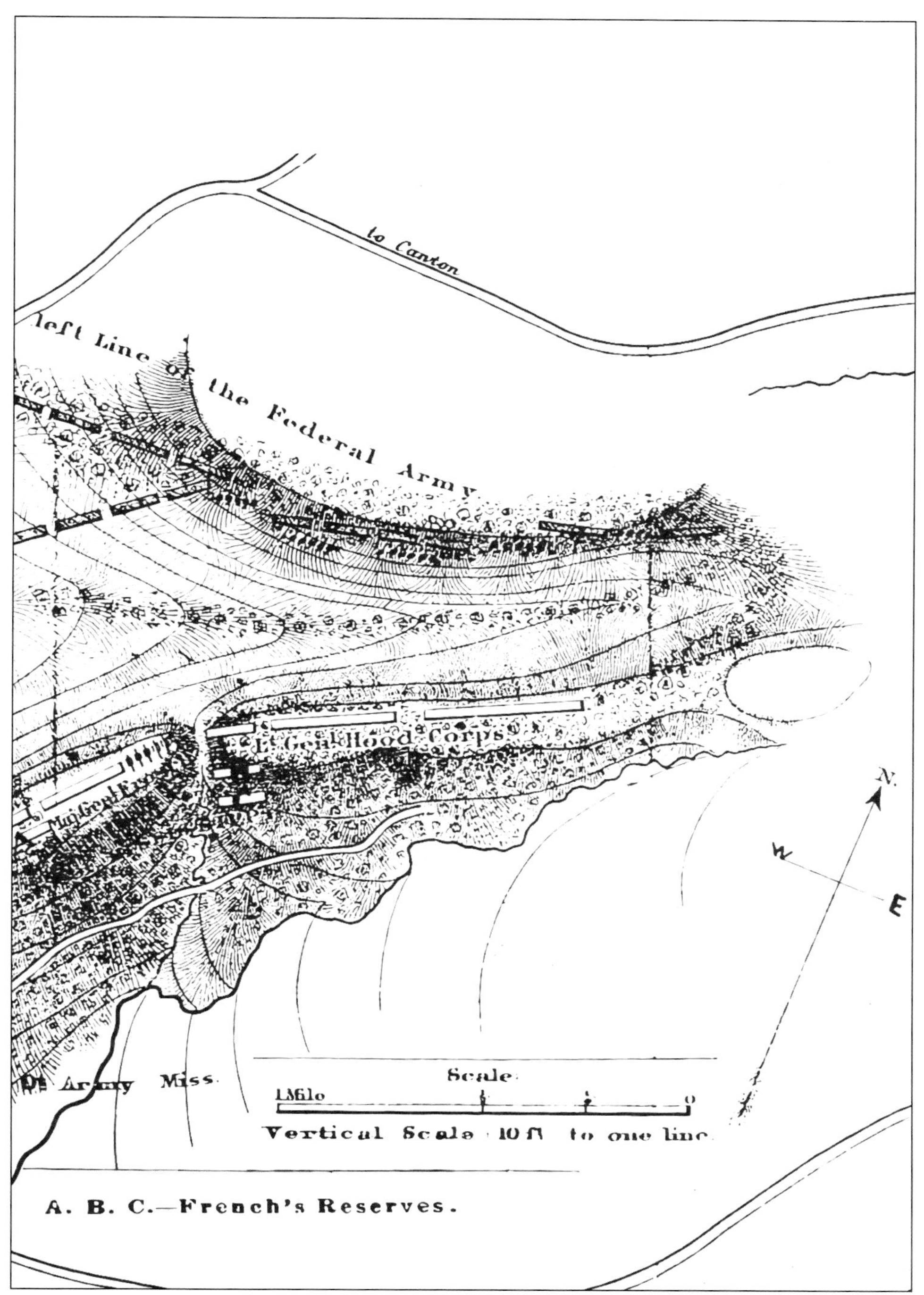

today's Shinall Gaines Road). Hood's line begins at its connection with French from above the Cassville Cemetery and continues to the east. French's reserves are both in the gap at Shinall Gaines Road, and behind the hill to his left (today's Latimer Lane). Loring's division is located between Cassville Road (old U.S. 41) and the Carterville Road (today's Mac Johnston Road), while Hardee's corps is covering Cass Station.

Exhibit 15

Thomas Van Buren Hargis House
This house was the site of General Sherman's headquarters from May 19-23, 1864, at Kingston, Georgia. From here, Sherman planned the next phase of the Atlanta Campaign to move south toward Dallas, Georgia, and around Johnston's defenses along the Etowah River and the Allatoona Mountains. (Photo by Wilbur G. Kurtz, February 22, 1947, Kurtz Papers, AHC)

Major General William Tecumseh Sherman
(Library of Congress)

Major General James McPherson
(Library of Congress)

William Neal McKelvey House
This house was the site of Lieutenant General Polk's headquarters at Cassville, and where General Johnston and Lieutenant General Hood had dinner on the evening of May 19, 1864, before retiring across the road to a cabin to discuss and debate the next day's plans for battle. (Photo by Wilbur G. Kurtz, September 14, 1937, Kurtz Papers, AHC)

Lieutenant General John Bell Hood
(Library of Congress)

Lieutenant General Leonidas Polk
(Library of Congress)

Exhibit 17

Barnard Photo #1

This photograph, taken by George Barnard in the Fall of 1864, shows the Federal earthworks on the north bank of the Etowah River. The Hightower Bridge and Allatoona Mountains are seen in the distance. (See George N. Barnard, *Photographic Views of Sherman's Campaign*, New York, NY: Dover Publications, Inc., 1977, Image 23.)

Barnard Photo #2

This photograph, also taken by George Barnard in the Fall of 1864, shows a close-up angle of the Federal earthworks on the north bank of the Etowah River. The Hightower Bridge appears to the right and below the ridge. The Allatoona Mountains are again seen in the distance. (See George N. Barnard, *Photographic Views of Sherman's Campaign*, New York, NY: Dover Publications, Inc., 1977, Image 24.)

General George H. Thomas' headquarters, Cassville, Georgia
This image by an unknown photographer shows the headquarters and camp of General George H. Thomas, commander, Army of the Cumberland, while the army was encamped west of Cassville near the Colonel Price House from May 19 to May 23, 1864. (Public Domain)

Major General George Henry Thomas
(Library of Congress)

Major General George Stoneman, Jr.
(Library of Congress)

Exhibit 19

Major General Samuel G. French
(Library of Congress)

Major General Alexander P. Stewart
(Library of Congress)

Major General Thomas C. Hindman
(Library of Congress)

Major General Carter L. Stevenson
(Library of Congress)

Major General Joseph Wheeler
(Library of Congress)

Lieutenant General William J. Hardee
(Library of Congress)

Cass Station Depot
(Bartow History Museum)

Exhibit 21

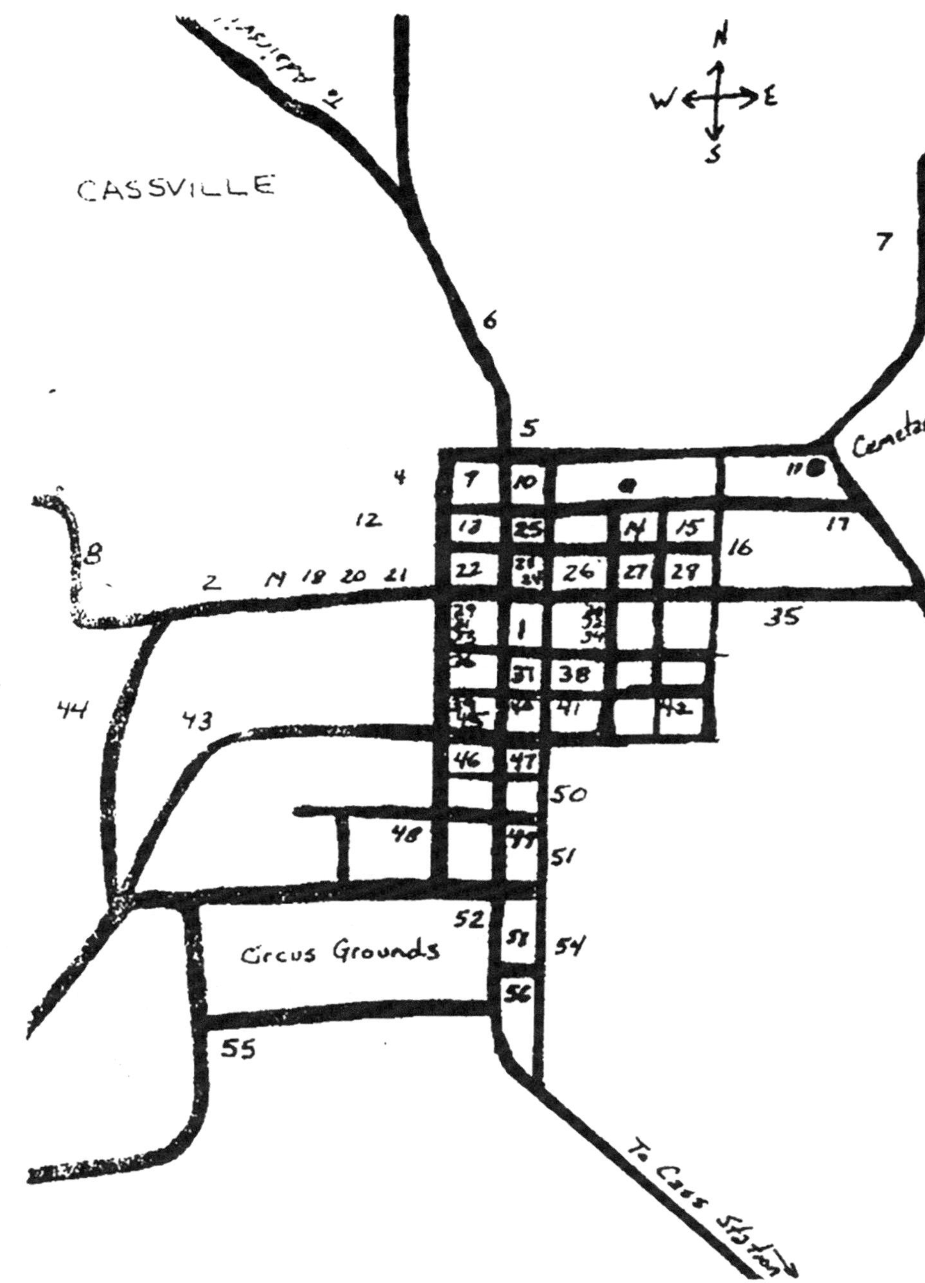

Kurtz Map 3
Map copied from a drawing by Joe Mahan which appeared in the *Tribune News*, Cartersville, Thursday, November 2, 1939.

Key to Kurtz Map 3

1. Cass County Court House
2. Cassville Female College
3. Cherokee Baptist College
4. Chunn home
5. John Laudermilk
6. Original site of Baptist Church
7. Dr. Weston Hardy
8. Judge Nathan Land
9. H. H. Holmes
10. H. H. Holmes carriage and wagon shop
11. John F. Milhollin
12. Chester Hawkes
13. Levi Branson
14. Nelson home
15. Jesse R. Wykle
16. Dr. Griffin
17. Mrs. Kenny
18. Tom Word
19. Original site of Methodist Church
20. Silah home
21. Silah furniture shop
22. Unidentified
23. Latimer Hotel
24. Post Office
25. Madison McMurrey
26. Col. Abda Johnson
27. Livery stable
28. Collins home
29. Levy store
30. J. D. Carpenter store
31. George L. Upshaw store
32. Store
33. Chunn & Patton Dry Goods store
34. Store
35. Jail
36. M. Murray store
37. Printing Shop, home of the Cassville Standard
38. Hotel
39. William Headden Carriage Shop
40. Headden home
41. Hotel
42. Methodist Church
43. Miss Lizzie Gaines
44. Col. Warren Akin
45. Brick kiln
46. Hotel
47. Rev. A. G. Johnson
48. Goldsmith home
49. Presbyterian Church
50. J. D. Carpenter
51. A. C. Day, tailor
52. Baptist Church
53. Saxon home
54. Rev. B. Arborgast
55. Rev. Ranbaut
56. Mercer home

Brigadier General Kenner Garrard
(Library of Congress)

Lieutenant Solomon Stanbrough,
Co. C, 5th Indiana Cavalry
(Library of Congress)

Exhibit 22

Saxon House, Adairsville, Georgia
Painting by Wilbur G. Kurtz of the Robert Saxon House, an octagon-shaped farmhouse made of gravel. The 1st and 27th Tennessee Infantry Regiments used the house and outbuildings for defense during the May 18, 1864 action at Adairsville. (Annie Pye Kurtz, ed., *Atlanta and the Old South, Paintings & Drawings by Wilbur G. Kurtz: Artist and Historian*, Atlanta, GA: American Lithograph CO., 1969, 34)

Major General Benjamin Franklin Cheatham
(Library of Congress)

Major General Oliver Otis Howard
(Library of Congress)

Exhibit 23

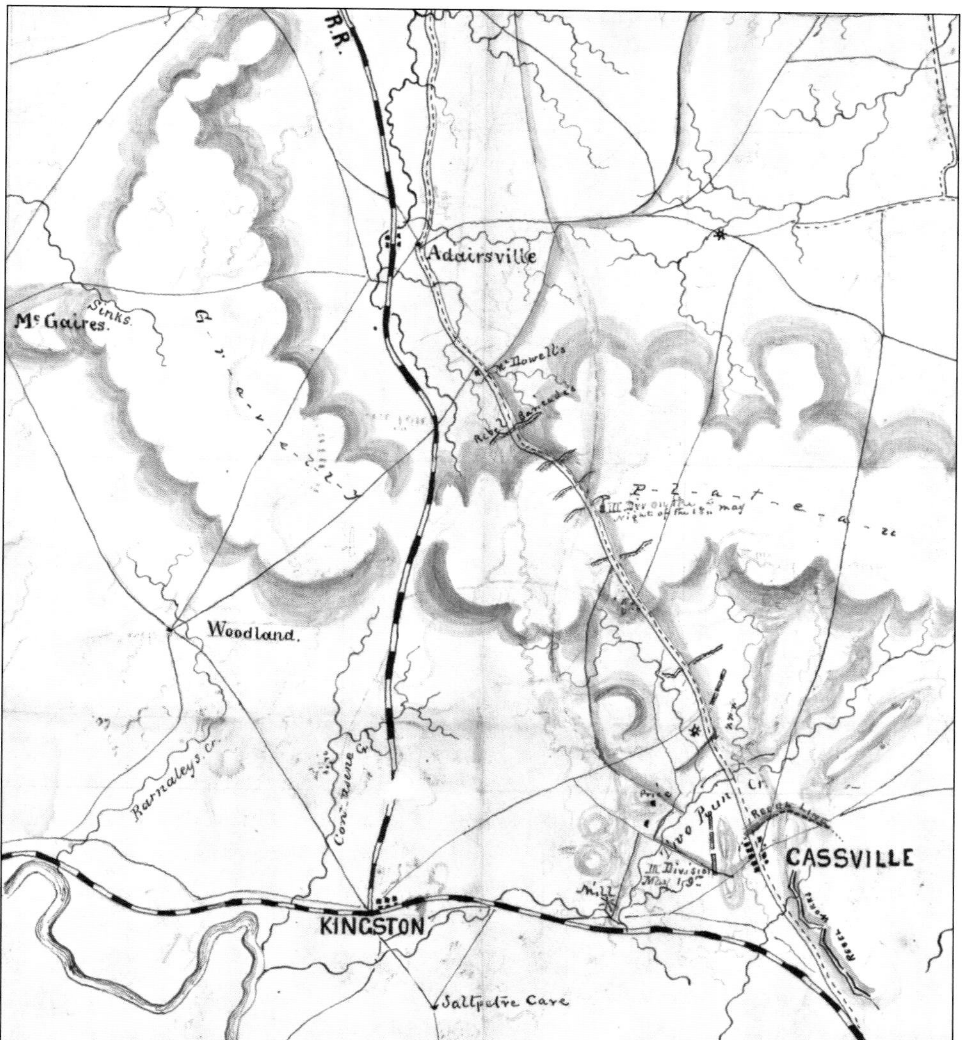

Butterfield Map

Map accompanying Major General Daniel Butterfield's Report, 3rd Division, XX Corps, Army of the Cumberland, "Advance of 3rd Div. 20th C. from Snake Creek Gap to Cassville, Engineer's office, 3rd Division, 20th A.C." Note the Confederate barricades along the Adairsville-Cassville Road used by the Southern cavalry to slow Butterfield's progress. (Wisconsin Historical Society, Image ID 90851, Map Collection, Georgia, Original Format Number: GX8678 G66 1864 US [see https://www.wisconsinhistory.org/Records/Image/IM90851, accessed May 17, 2023].)

Merrill Map: The "Merrill Map," sometimes referred to as the "Poe Map," is a compilation from a survey by J. T. Dodge, Civil Engineer, Map of the Atlanta Campaign by Captain O. M. Poe and Lieutenant H. C. Wharton, U.S. Engineers, Map of Northern Georgia compiled under the direction of Captain W.E. Merrill, U.S. Engineer, and captured Rebel Maps and Official Reports, compiled by Captain Edward Ruger, received at the Office of Engineers, United States Army on May 31, 1871. It is the origin for the "Map Illustrating The Second Epoch of the Atlanta Campaign." The Author has termed it the "Merrill Map" because the details in the terrain and road structure found

with this map were due to Merrill's work. Subsequent versions of this map have removed certain details in order to be readable in mass-produced, and smaller scale, publications. Note the five roads leading to Cassville from the north and east: (1) Adairsville-Cassville, (2) Copper Mine/Ironton, (3) Spring Place, (4) Pine Log, & (5) Canton. (NARA [See https://nara.getarchive.net/media/the-second-epoch-of-the-atlanta-campaign-embracing-the-region-from-resaca-to-c2587b, accessed May 17, 2023].) All roads identified by number are listed in the Road Number Key to Maps.

Exhibit 25

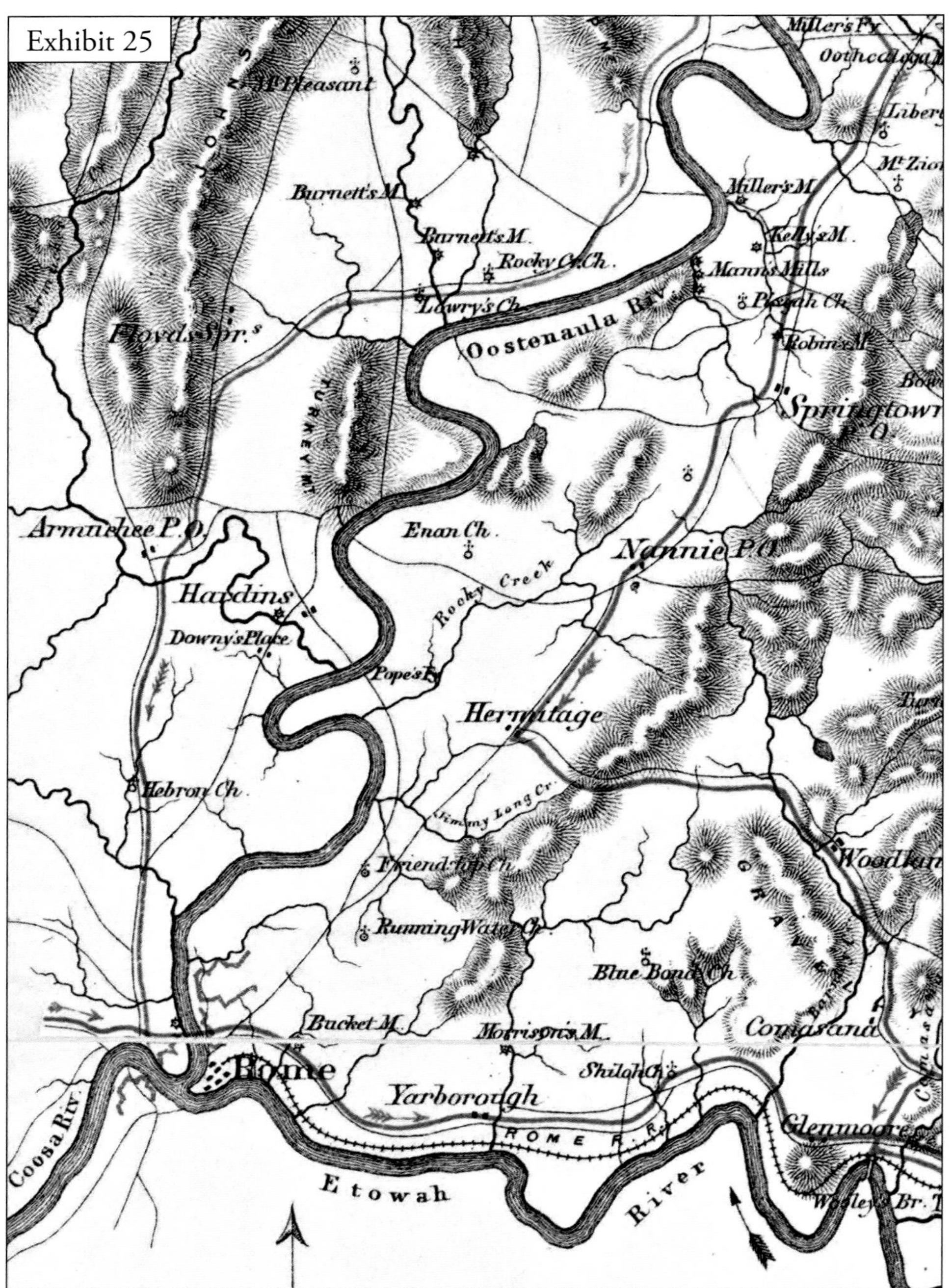

Ruger Map: Topographical Engineer Office, Army of the Cumberland, was published in 1875 by T.B. Van Horne, as part of a series of maps depicting the action of this army during the war. This map, although less detailed than the "Merrill Map" of 1871, from which this one is derived, highlights in color the movements of each of the Federal Corps during the Second Epoch (or phase) of the Atlanta Campaign between the Oostanaula and the Etowah Rivers. This map also highlights in blue and red the Federal and Confederate earthworks respectively. Subsequent variations of this map do not provide the length, or detail of these earthworks. Note the five roads leading to Cassville from the north and east: (1) Adairsville-Cassville, (2) Copper Mine/Ironton, (3) Spring Place, (4) Pine Log,

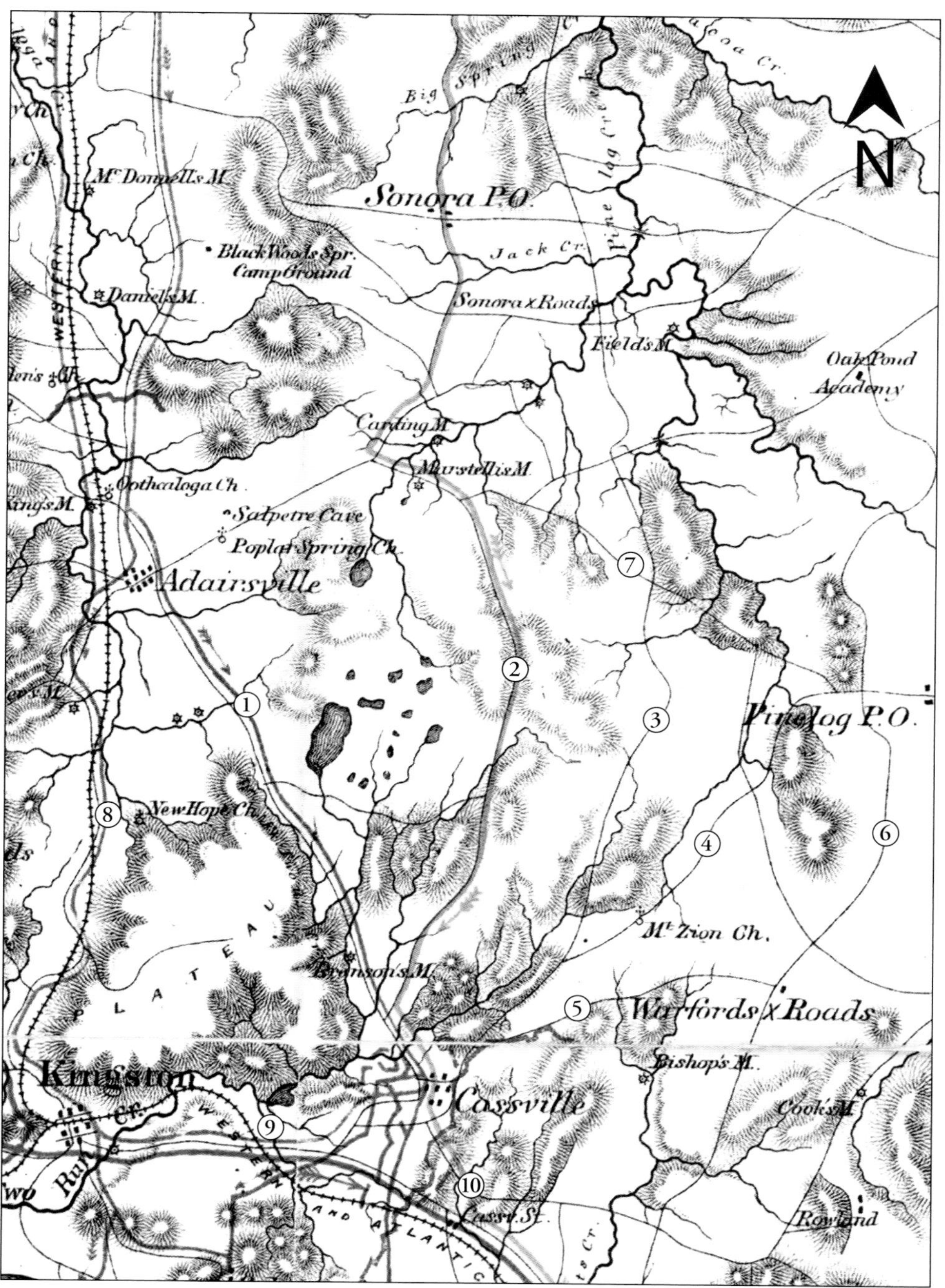

& (5) Canton. (See T.B. Van Horne, *History of the Army of the Cumberland, Its Organization, Campaigns, and Battles, Written at the Request of Major General George H. Thomas, Chiefly from his Private Military Journal and Official and Other Documents from Him*, two volumes and Atlas, Cincinnati, OH: Robert Clarke & Co., 1875, page 14, image 12 [copy found at Library of Congress, Washington, D.C.: 1875, image no. 136058; also https://www.loc.gov/resource/g3866sm.gcw0102000/?sp=1&r=-0.188,0.851,1.422,0.641,0., accessed May 17, 2023].) All roads identified by number are listed in the Road Number Key to Maps.

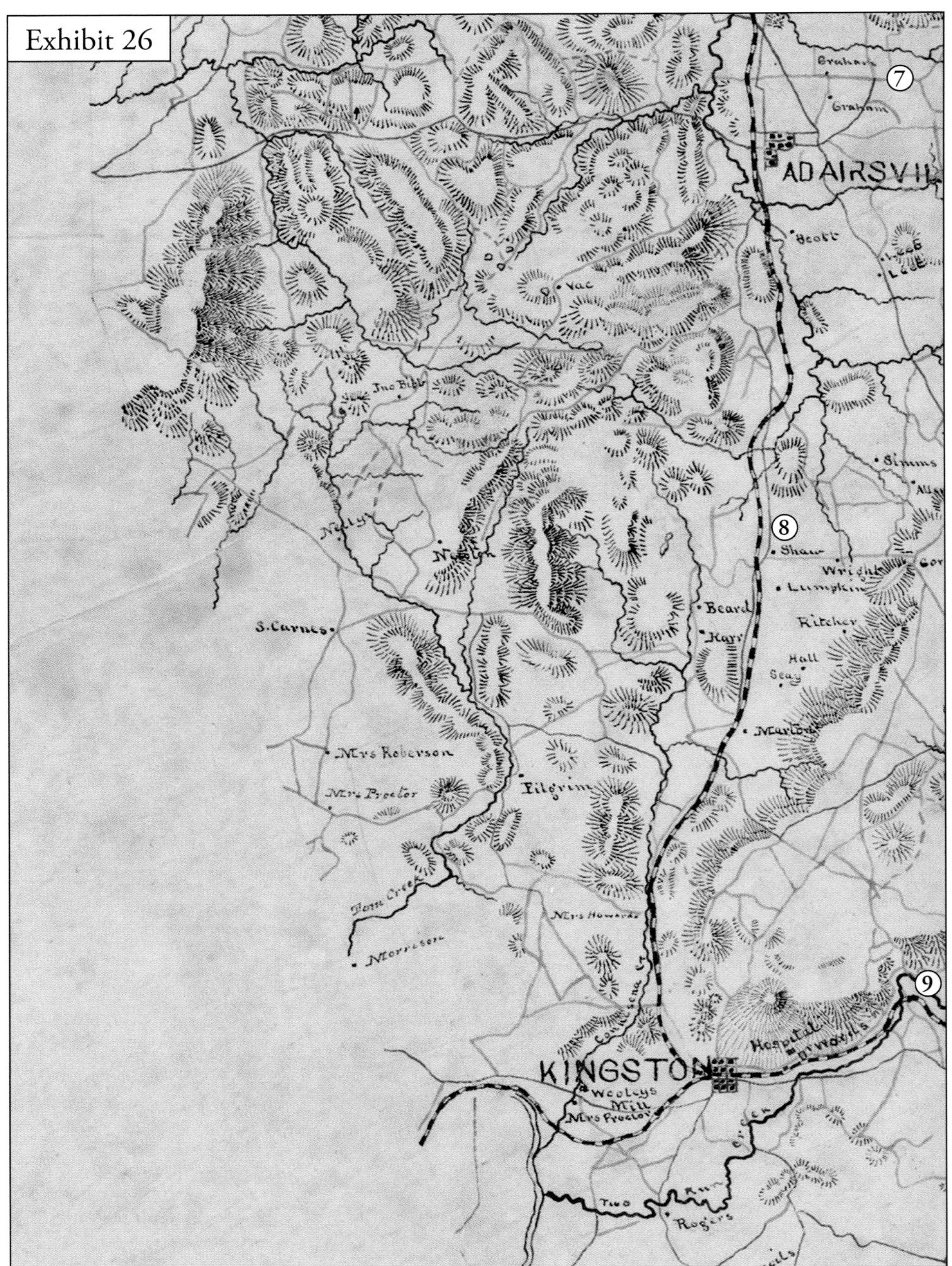

Foster Map: Commissioned November 1, 1863, by General Braxton Bragg, this map, as part of a series of three maps, was designed to provide the Confederate Army with a detailed description of the terrain and roads within ten miles on either side of the Western & Atlantic Railroad from Missionary Ridge to Atlanta, to include Rome and the Rome Railroad. Captain (promoted to Major on March 17, 1864) Wilbur T. Foster, Engineers Office, led the team of surveyors, engineers, and draftsmen who completed their work in the Spring of 1864. Although quite detailed for the area portrayed, this map failed to include the critical area northeast of Cassville, including the Five Forks intersection of the (3) Spring Place, (4) Pine Log, and nearby (5) Canton Roads (today found northeast of the TA Truckstop at I-75, Exit 296). Five Forks is located approximately nine miles east of the Western & Atlantic Railroad, at its closest

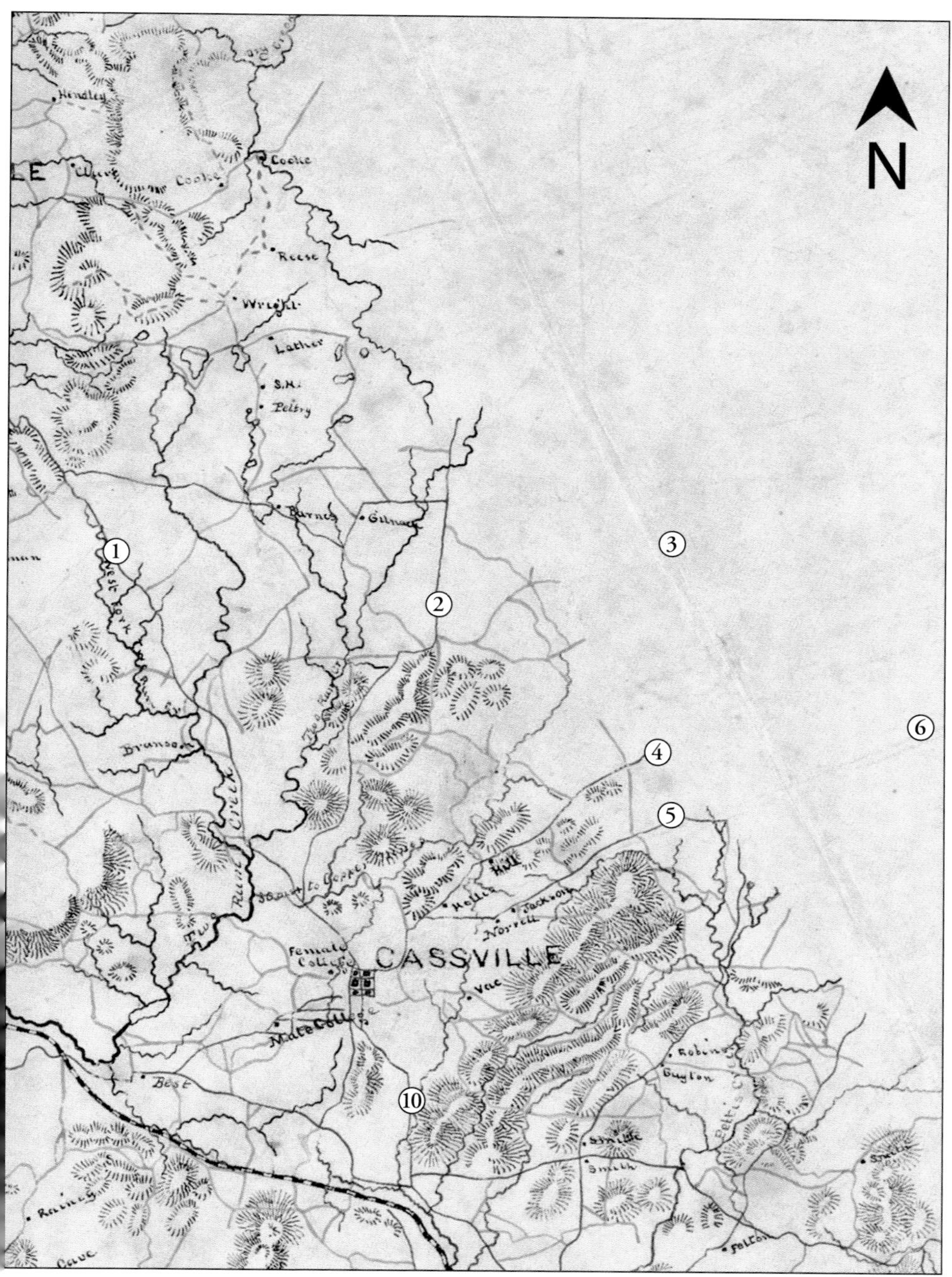

point near Hall Station. Major Generals Will T. Martin and Joseph Wheeler and their teams of engineers relied on this map in preparing their maps during the Spring of 1864, and none of the Confederate maps included the connection of the Spring Place Road with Five Forks. General Joseph E. Johnston was still missing the Spring Place Road in the map that he included in his *Narrative of Military Operations* in 1874, at page 320b. Note the empty space in the northeast corner of this map and the one in Johnston's *Narrative.* (See National Archives, Record Group 109, Georgia Maps, Map of Roads between Marietta and Dalton, Ga., ID number: 70652905, Captured Confederate maps, Macon, Ga., November 10, 1864, https://catalog.archives.gov/id/70652905?objectPage=4, accessed May 17, 2023.) All roads identified by number are listed in the Road Number Key to Maps.

Martin Map: This map, part of a series of twenty maps contributed to the Alabama Department of Archives and History by Major General Henry D. Clayton, is often called the "Clayton Map." It is one of six maps covering northwest Georgia prepared for Major General Will T. Martin in the Spring of 1864 by John M. Stewart, Engineer, and J.S. Tyner, Assistant Engineer, Cavalry Corps, Army of Tennessee. Although this map covered the missing space northeast of Cassville from the "Foster Map," it failed to connect (3) Spring Place Road with the Five Forks

intersection and (4) Pine Log Road. Although this copy was dated July 2, 1864, another map in this series that covers the area between Dalton and Resaca immediately to the north was dated May 11, 1864. (See Clayton Papers, CB 075, Alabama Department of Archives and History, Montgomery, AL, https://digital.archives.alabama.gov/digital/collection/maps/id/20/, accessed May 17, 2023.) All roads identified by number are listed in the Road Number Key to Maps.

Exhibit 28

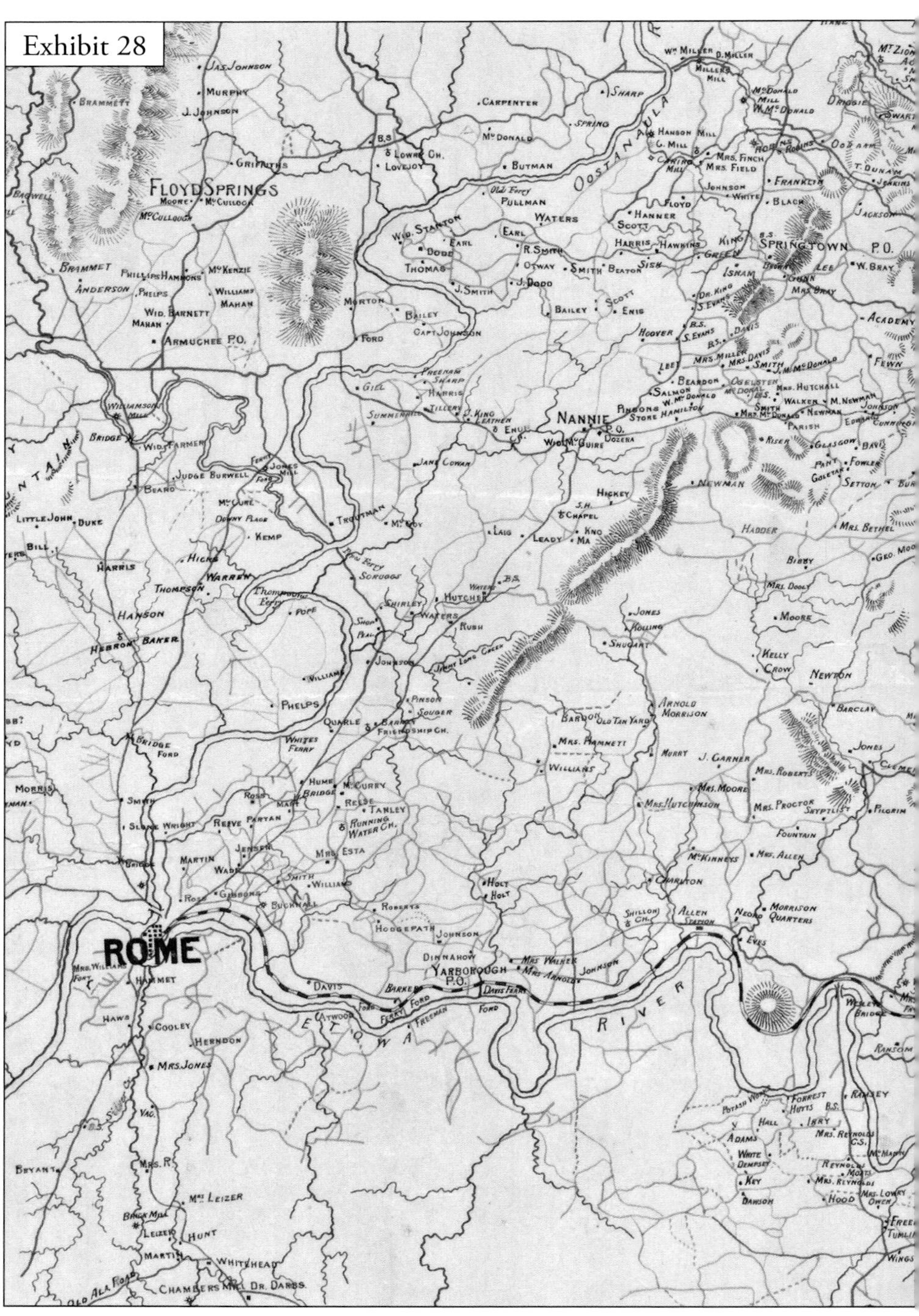

Wheeler Map: This map, part of a series of five maps used by Major General Joseph Wheeler during the Atlanta Campaign, was turned over to the National Archives by the War Department in 1879. It was also prepared by John M. Stewart, Engineer, Cavalry Corps, Army of Tennessee, and it also failed to connect (3) Spring Place Road with the Five Forks intersection and (4) Pine Log Road (see map insert). Wheeler likely used this map to prepare his cavalry screen north of Cassville as described in his Report (OR, Serial 74, 946), when he covered four of the five

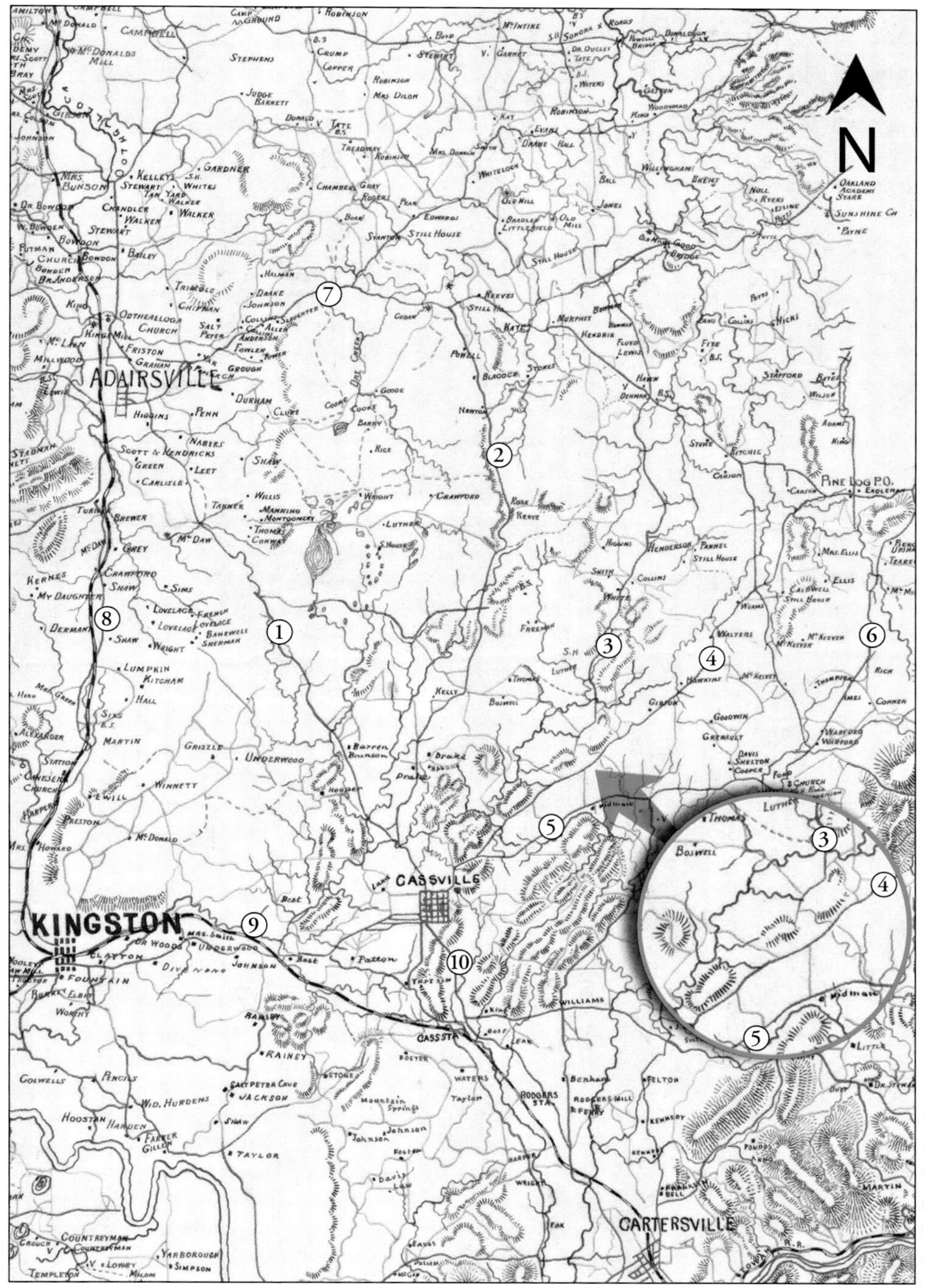

roads, leaving Spring Place Road unguarded. (See National Archives, Record Group 77, Records of the Office of the Chief of Engineers, United States, ID Number 122206872, Copy of a Rebel Map received from War Department showing Georgia, https://catalog.archives.gov/id/122206872?objectPage=5, accessed May 18, 2023.) All roads identified by number are listed in the Road Number Key to Maps.

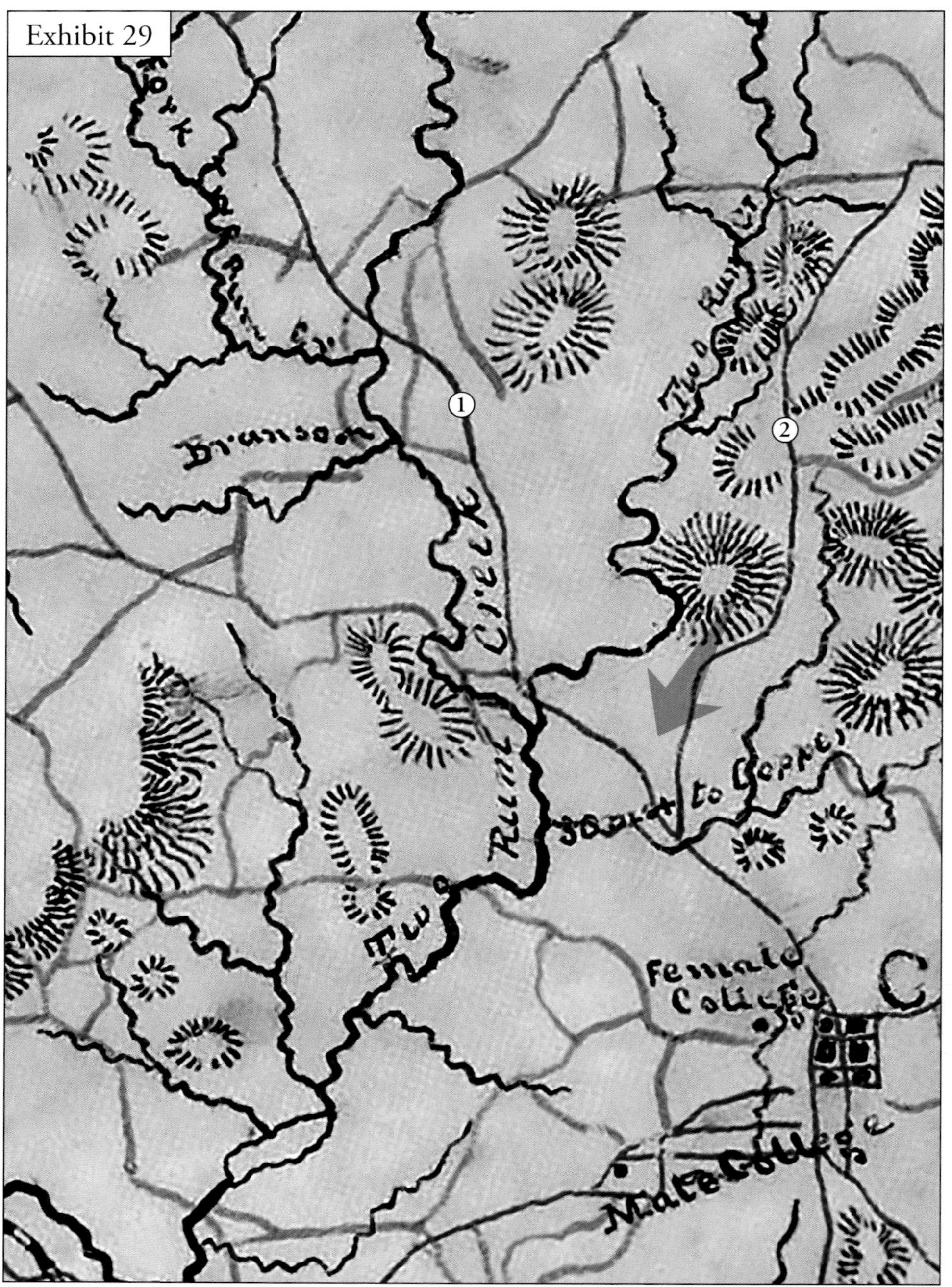

Foster Map (enlarged): This enlargement of the "Foster Map" shows the location of the (2) Copper Mine Road, and its connection with the (1) Adairsville-Cassville Road just north of Cassville. Marked with and "X" which signifies the beginning of the Copper Mine Road, the description "30 OLD X to Copper Mines" is included (see map insert). Since the Mark A. Cooper mine, an iron mine is only about 10 miles north of this location, the description, the only one of its kind on the map, does not seem to refer to distance. Mark Cooper's mine originally included some speculating for copper although very little copper was found, but significant iron ore was discovered. It is still being mined today by Vulcan Mines just east of I-75 at Exit 306. The Copper Mine Road is shown in red as are all of the

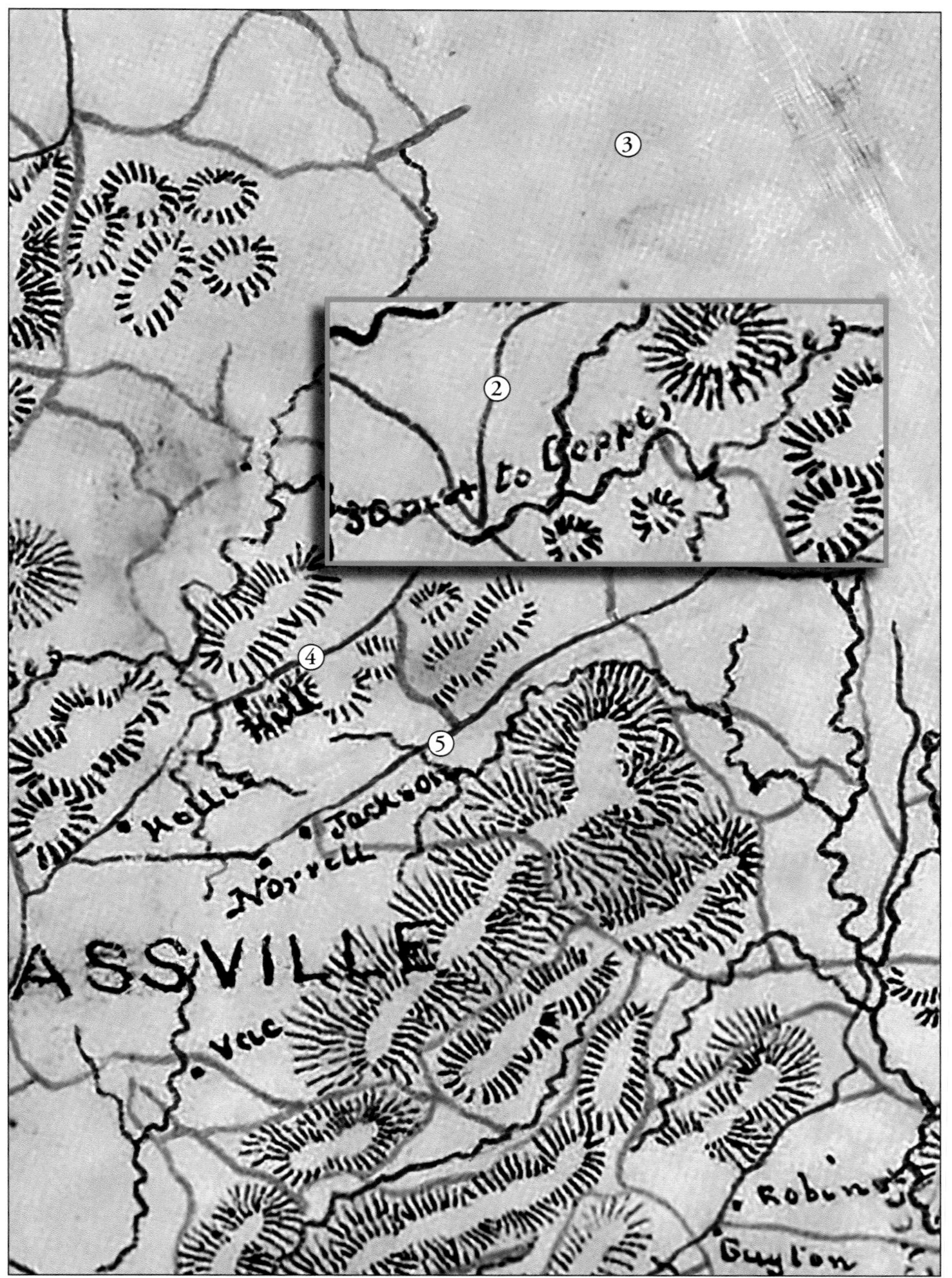

other improved roads on the map that were at least 30 feet wide and improved, meaning that they were suitable for two-wagon width military use. The author suspects that this description added by Foster and his assistants was to point out that this road was suitable for military use and that the reference was to the width and condition of the road, and not the distance to the original Copper (or "Cooper") Mine. (See National Archives, Record Group 109, Georgia Maps, Map of Roads between Marietta and Dalton, Ga., ID number: 70652905, Captured Confederate maps, Macon, Ga., November 10, 1864, https://catalog.archives.gov/id/70652905?objectPage=4, accessed May 17, 2023.) All roads identified by number are listed in the Road Number Key to Maps.

Cassville Aerial Photo, circa 1940s (enlarged): This enlargement of the photo taken by Carl Forrester shows the area north and northeast of Cassville where Hood's planned strike was to take place. The (1) Adairsville-Cassville Road is shown in blue. The (2) Copper Mine/Ironton Road has been highlighted in green. The (3) Spring Place Road is off-frame to the east. The (4) Pine Log Road is today called the Cass-White Road. The (5) Canton Road is indicated in yellow and is today called the Old Cass-White Road. The large, open field, runs from the center to the

top right of the photo. Hood's route of march is shown in red. Hood moved east on the Pine Log Road, then turned left on today's Brown Loop Road, crossed Two Run Creek, and then continued across the large, open field toward the Ironton Road above the far side of the field. The photo, like the Confederate maps, suffers from failing to include the land to the northeast of the image where McCook's Federal cavalry first appeared. Kurtz, "Kurtz Papers," Keenan Research Center, Atlanta History Center, Atlanta, GA, MSS-130.

Cassville Aerial Photo, circa 1940s

This aerial photograph was taken for Wilbur G. Kurtz in the late 1940's by Carl Forrester. Note that the Confederate afternoon-evening position was along the wooded ridge southeast of Cassville. Today, the ridge is filled with neighborhood streets and houses. Note the gap between French and Hood at Shinall Gaines Road located at the 90-degree bend of Cass-White Road. It appears to be quite large, and much wider than the 150-200 yards estimated by Johnston. (See Wilbur G. Kurtz, "Kurtz Papers," Keenan Research Center, Atlanta History Center, Atlanta, GA, MSS-130.)

Confederate Earthworks at Cassville
These three photographs, taken by Matthew Beard, show the Confederate infantry earthworks that were located between the Pine Log Road (Cassville-White Road) and the Canton Road (Old Cassville-White Road) facing east, at the former KOA campground site. The works have since been destroyed, and the land altered with the construction of the Chick-Fil-A Distribution Center. The works were discovered by Dale Black. The author believes that these works were the extreme right flank of Hood's line, and erected by portions of his corps between 11:00 a.m. and 3:30 p.m. before being abandoned in favor of the afternoon line selected by Johnston. (Photos courtesy Matthew Beard)

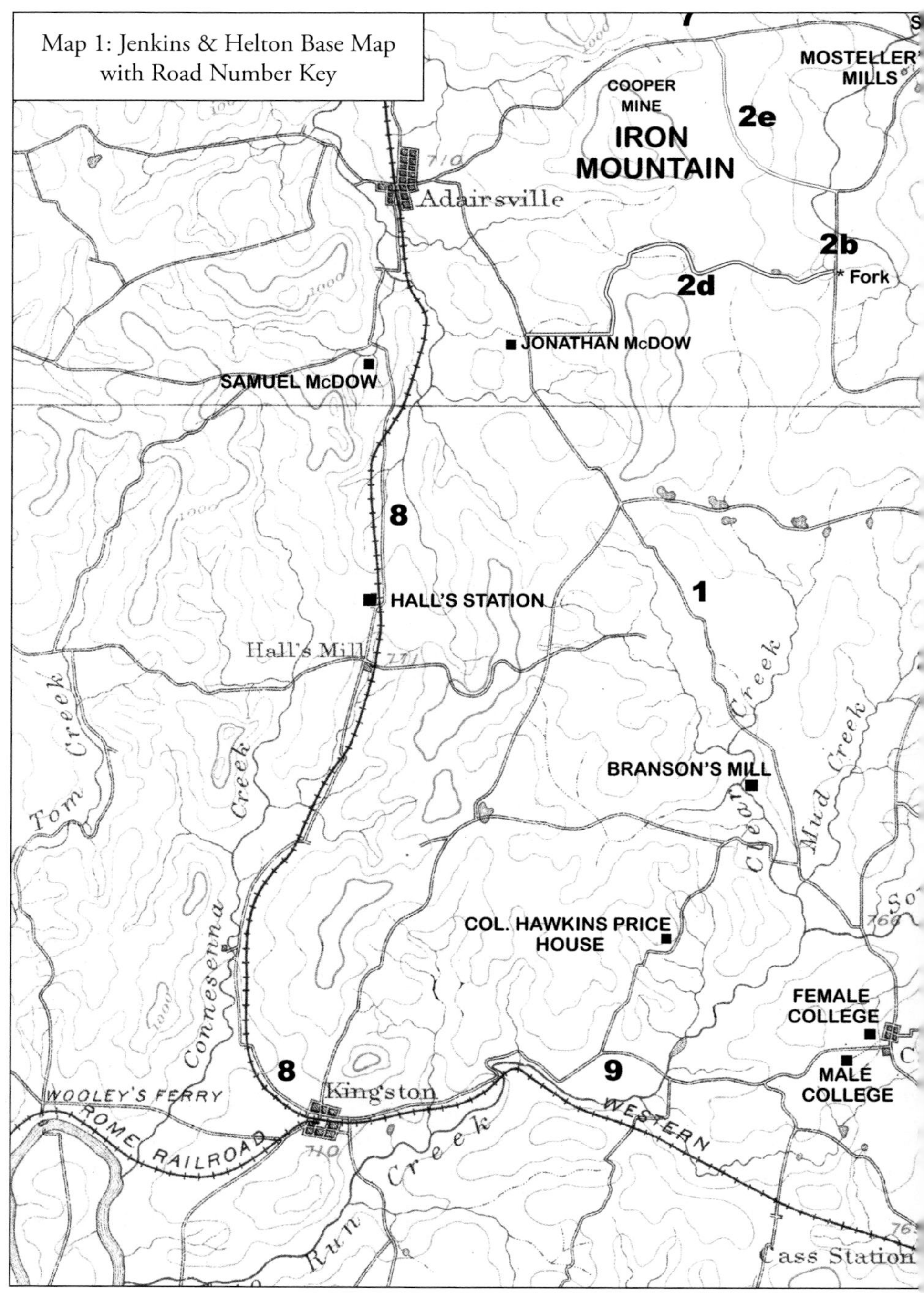

The roads identified in this map and provided throughout the text are: 1-Adairsville-Cassville Road (today U.S. 41, Ga. 3, Joe Frank Harris Hwy.); 2-Copper Mine Road, Ironton Road, "old" Spring Place Road (1820s-1840s) (today, south to north, Kimsey Circle, Janice Lane, Cedar Creek Road); 2a-Mosteller's Mill Road; 2b-Section of Ironton (Iron Mountain) Road (no longer in existence); 2c-By-Road (Wheeler) (no longer in existence); 2d-Unnamed cut off road from "the forks in the road" (Hooker's term) (today Manning Mill Road); 2e-Section of Ironton (Iron Mountain) Road (no longer in existence); 3-Spring Place Road (since about 1851); 3a-"Country

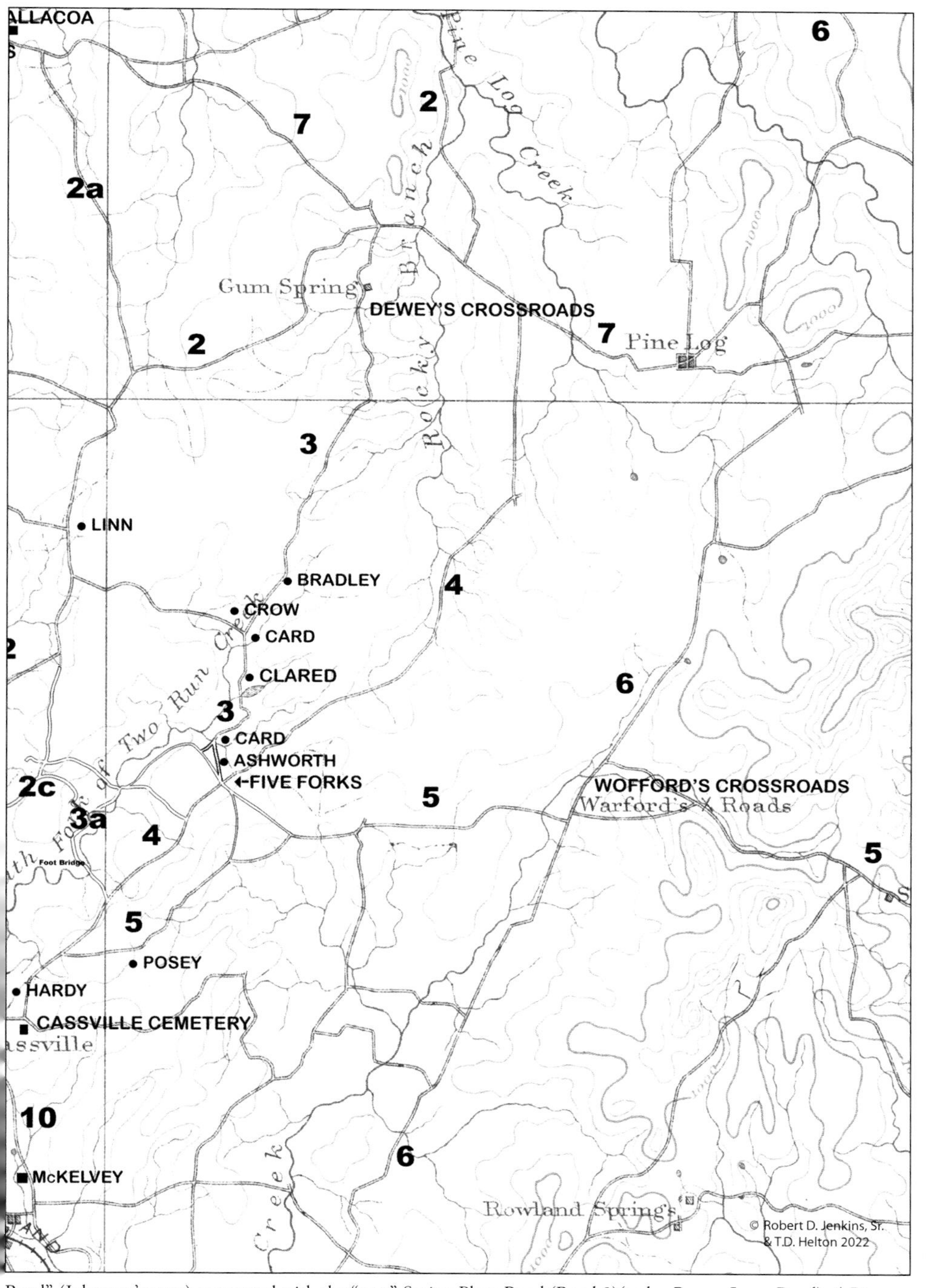

Road" (Johnston's term) connected with the "new" Spring Place Road (Road 3)(today Brown Loop Road); 4-Pine Log Road, also Fairmount Road (today Cass-White Road); 5-Canton Road (today Old Cass-White Road); 6-Tennessee Road, also Jackson Military Road (1825), also Old Federal Road (today U.S. 411 and Ga. 61 Hwy.); 7-Adairsville-Pine Log-Canton Road (today Ga. 140); 8-Adairsville-Kingston Road (today, Hall Station Road); 9-Kingston-Cassville Road (today Kingston Hwy, Ga. 293, Fire Tower Road); 10-Cartersville Road (today, Mac Johnson Road).

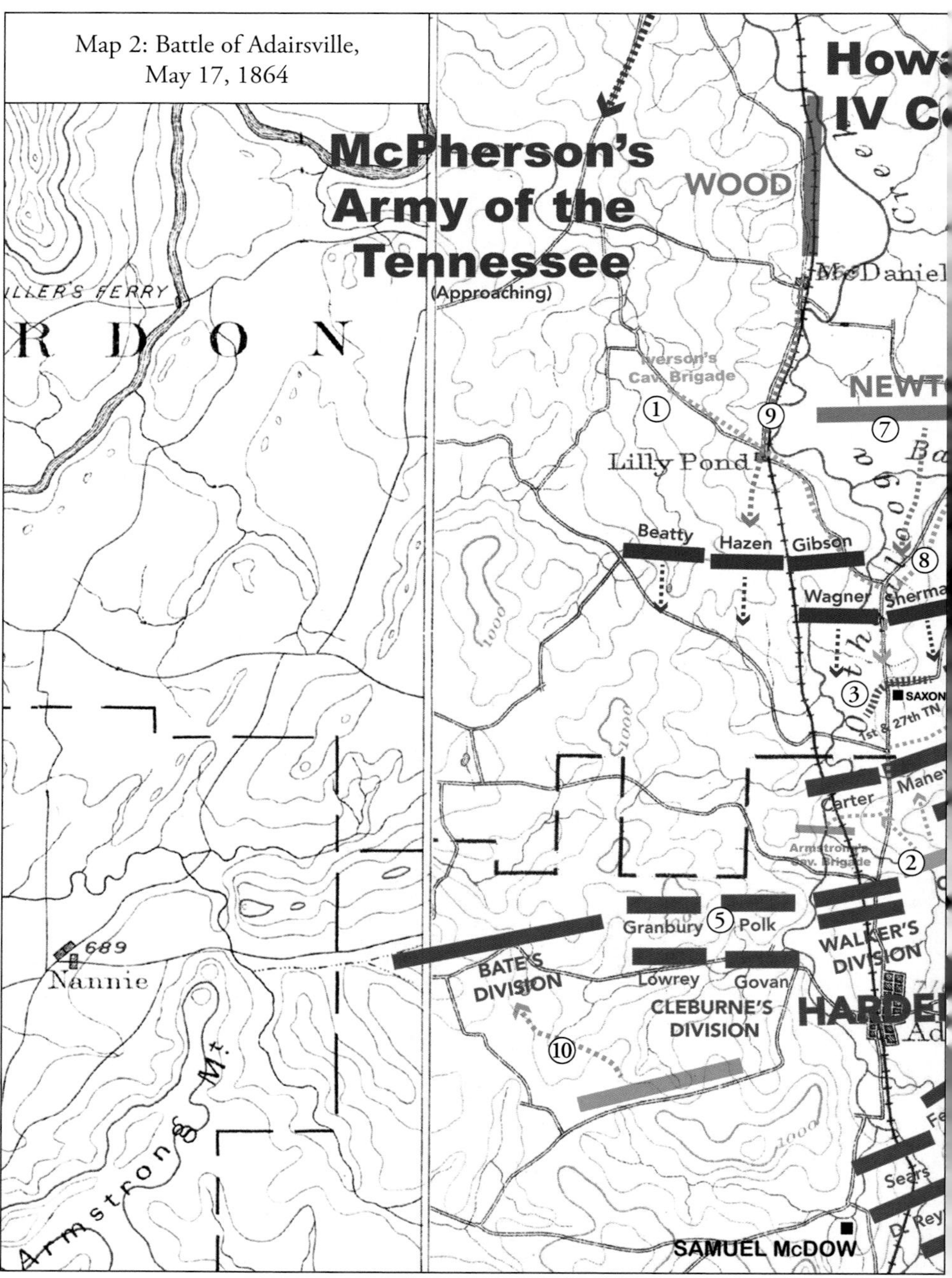

About 3:00 p.m., (1) Howard's IV Corps pressing from Calhoun, caused the Confederate cavalry screen of Ashby and Harrison (Kelly's division) to fall back along today's U.S. 41 Hwy., and Iverson to withdraw via today's Darby/ Taylor Bridge Road. (2) Cheatham's division, Johnston's rear guard, scrambled to reach high ground along a low ridge at the Gordon-Cass (now Bartow) County line before the Federals arrived. (3) Seizing a knoll located about 200 yards in advance, the 1st and 27th Tennessee Infantry regiments took up positions in and around the Saxon house, an octagon-shaped farm house made of gravel. Joining them was (4) Armstrong's Mississippi cavalry brigade who formed on the right. (5) Cleburne formed 800 yards to the left and rear in support, west of Oothkalooga Creek. (6) Hindman deployed to the east along a high ridge just north of Iron Mountain (along the east side of

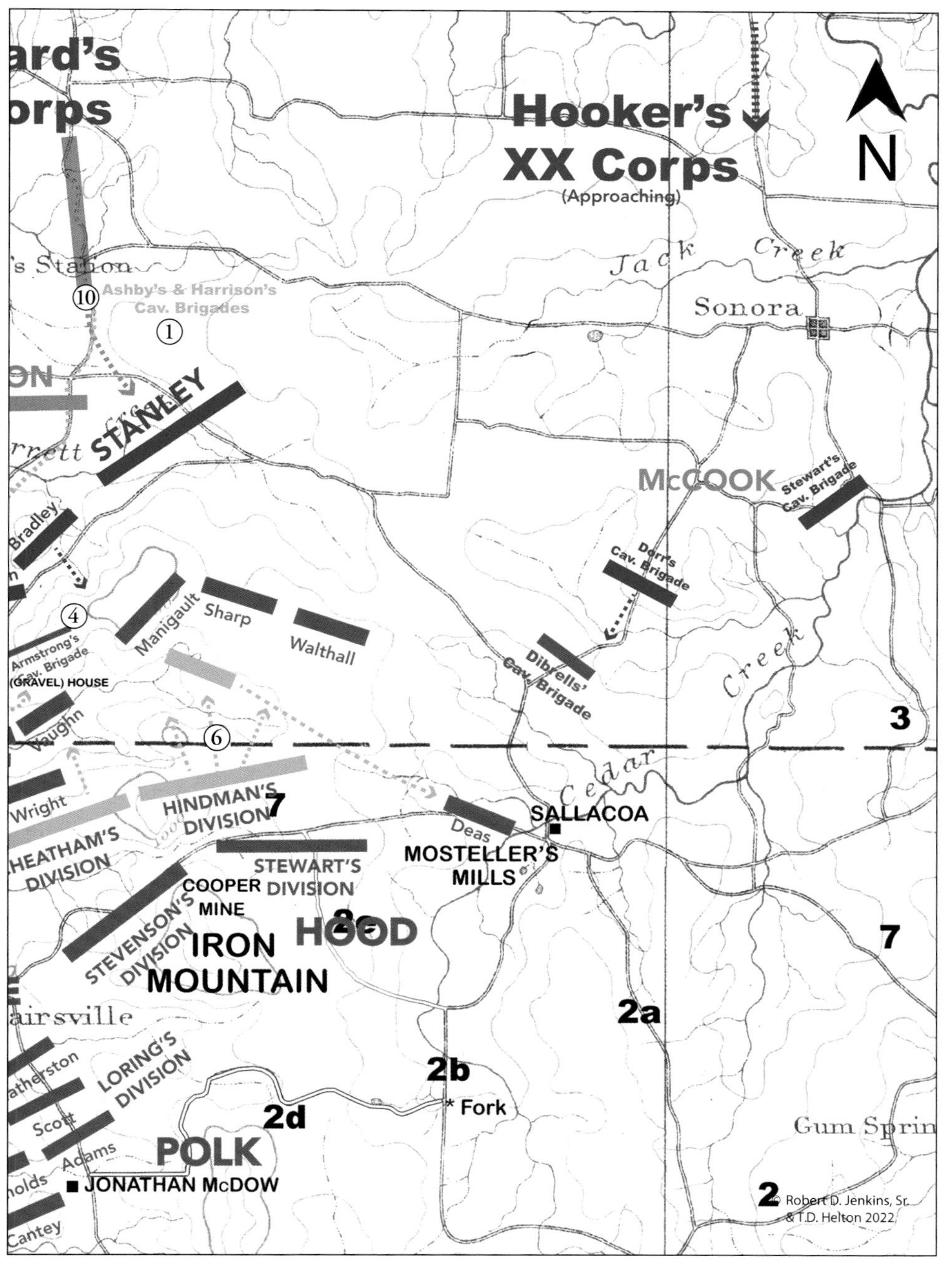

today's I-75). (7) After brushing the Southern cavalry aside, Newton entered the large valley and deployed. (8) Believing that only a small detachment awaited, the Federals advanced until sustaining heavy casualties. (9) Wood advanced along the W&A RR, and deployed to the west of Newton, threatening to flank Cheatham's line. (10) Cleburne reinforced his left, below a swampy bog and tributary, until Bate's division arrived to extend Cleburne's lines. (11) Stanley was added to the east of Newton as the Federals prepared to renew the assault. After sustaining about 200 casualties, Howard's order to attack was countermanded by Thomas as twilight approached and a light rain began to fall. Overnight, the Confederates, who sustained about 100 casualties including 31 in Armstrong's brigade, withdrew to Cassville.

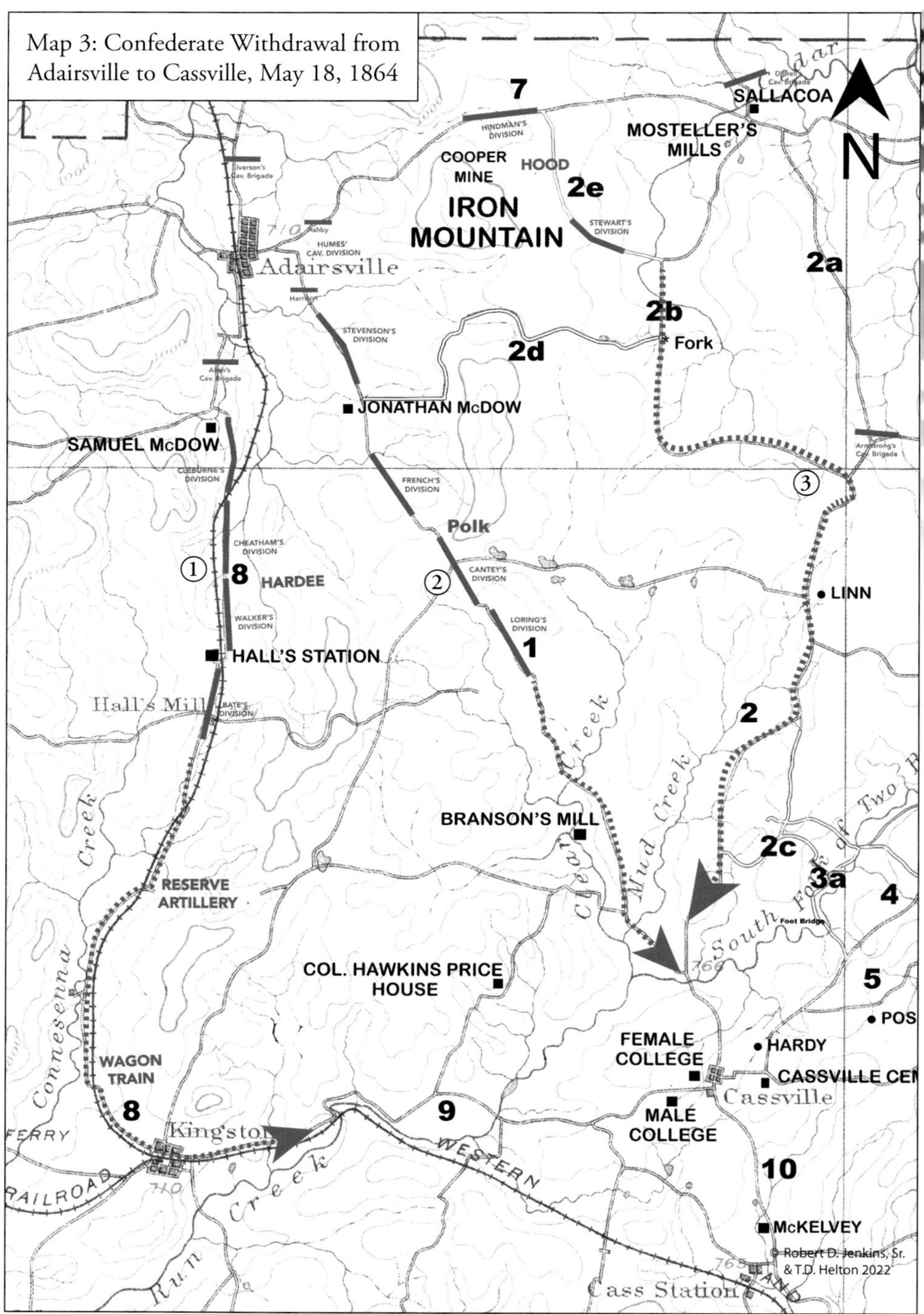

Looking to withdraw safely from Adairsville in the face of approaching Federal forces believed to be marching toward multiple directions including Rome, Adairsville, and Hightower Bridge, Johnston's army utilized three roads to make their escape. (1) Hardee's corps, the Reserve artillery, and the Wagon train took the Kingston Road, (2) Polk's corps and Stevenson's division followed the Cassville Road, while the rest of (3) Hood's corps, Stewart's and Hindman's divisions, positioned east of Iron Mountain, took the Copper Mine/Ironton Road to Cassville.

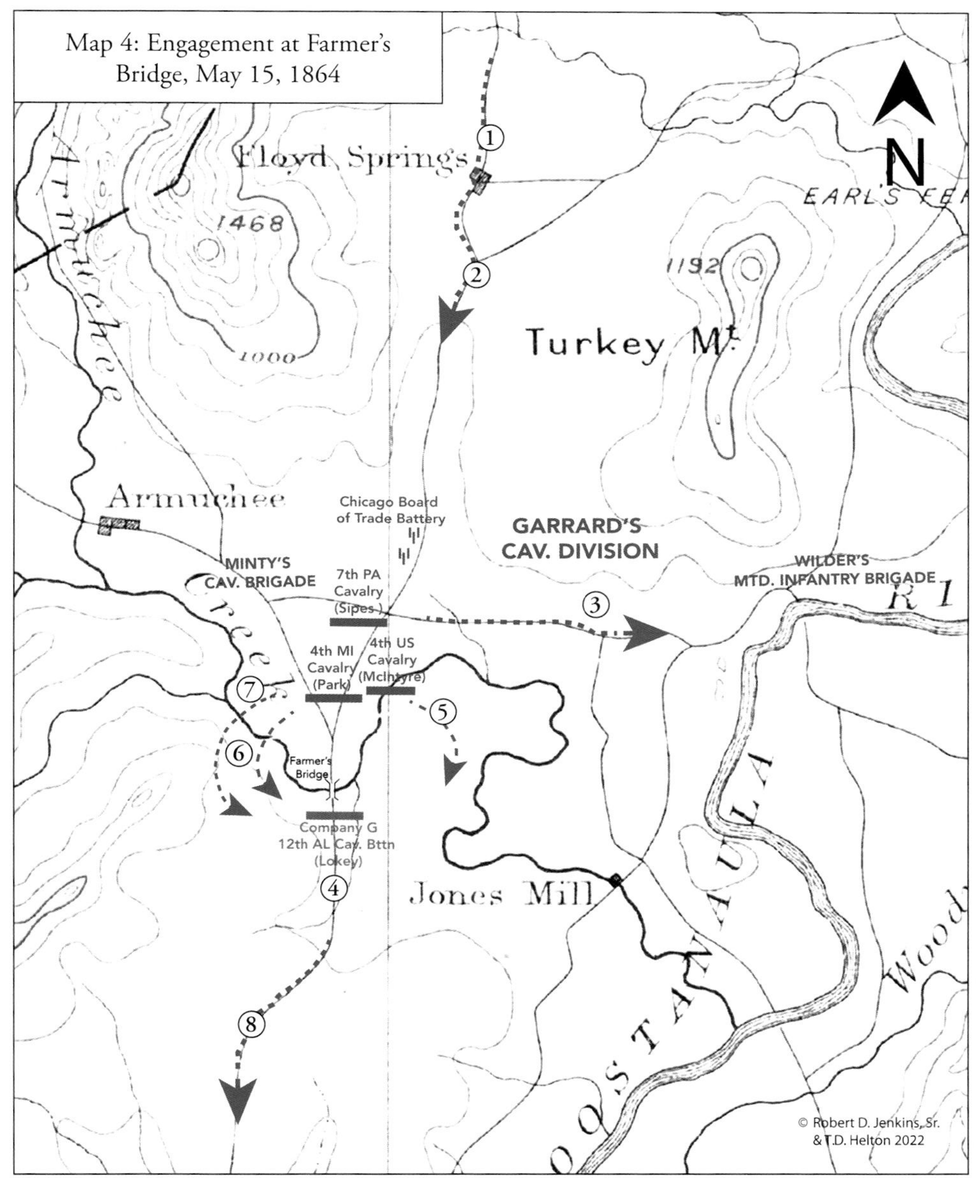

Map 4: Engagement at Farmer's Bridge, May 15, 1864

(1) Ordered by Sherman to find a crossing over the Oostanaula River and strike the Western & Atlantic RR in the Confederate rear, and/or threaten Rome, Garrard's cavalry left Villanow and proceeded south via the Pocket Road, camping at Floyd Springs. (2) Following the Old Summerville Road, Garrard reached Armuchee Creek at Farmer's Bridge on May 15 at mid-day. Garrard ordered Minty's brigade (2,200 troopers) to take the bridge and drive back the Southern pickets who had checked the Federal advance. (3) Garrard, with Wilder's brigade, searched for a crossing over the Oostanaula River. (4) Guarding the bridge was Co. G, 12th Alabama Cavalry Battalion commanded by Captain William Lokey who had held off the blue-clad troopers for two hours. (5) Sending two companies of the 4th Michigan to cross the creek below, and (6) six companies of the 4th Michigan and the 4th U.S. above, (7) Minty followed them with the remaining four companies of the 4th Michigan and the 7th Pennsylvania in a simultaneous attack. Overwhelmed by the Federal numbers, Lokey's Alabamians lost 10 men killed including Lokey, and 10 captured, while Minty lost 1 man killed and 4 horses wounded in the initial approach to the bridge. (8) Minty then moved his men southward along the Old Summerville Road toward Rome, while Confederate cavalry forces from Ross, Morgan, and Davidson prepared to receive them.

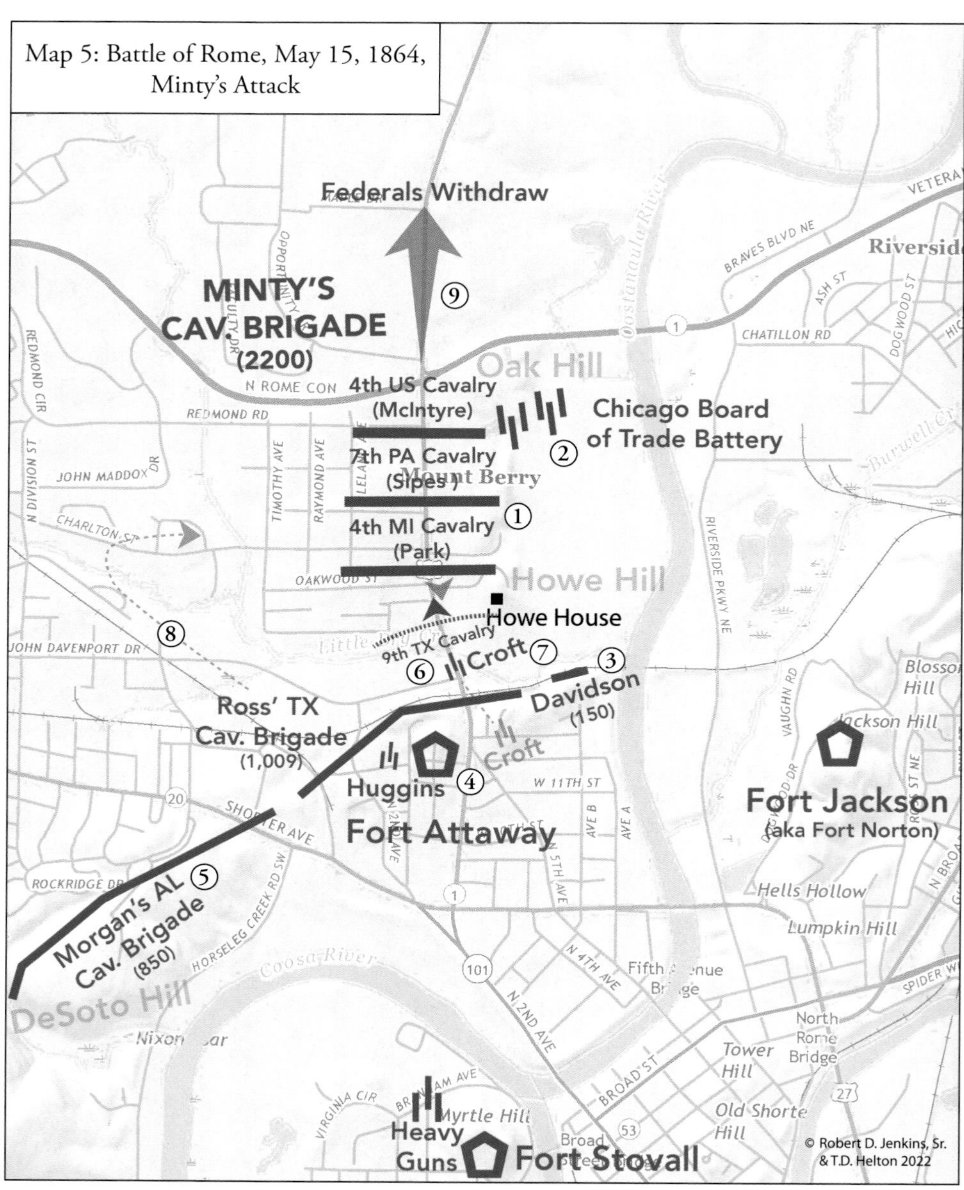

After taking Farmer's Bridge, (1) Minty advanced toward Rome using the Summerville Road (today's U.S. 27 Hwy.) with the 4th Michigan Cavalry in the lead. (2) Minty placed the Chicago Board of Trade Battery on Oak Hill to provide covering fire and to cover the crossroads. (3) On the Confederate side, Davidson's demi-brigade of some 150 dismounted troopers from Martin's division who were either too sick to ride or were without mounts, covered the river. (4) Huggins Battery was placed in Fort Attaway, while (5) a portion of Morgan's brigade extended the Confederate defenses to DeSoto Hill. The balance of Morgan's Alabama horsemen were away covering various assignments, scouting and picketing in the region. Ross, with his Texas legions having just arrived at Rome, ordered (6) the 9th Texas Cavalry to dismount and advance in a skirmish line to meet the Federals with (7) Croft's Battery to move in support. Hoping to lure the blue-coat troopers closer, (8) Ross moved with the balance of his brigade to the west of Summerville Road as he prepared to attack Minty in his right flank. Seeing Ross' Texans preparing to ambush him from the west, Minty wisely withdrew to Farmer's Bridge to rejoin Garrard and Wilder's Brigade. Minty lost four wounded and one captured, while Davidson lost two wounded and the 9th Texas Cavalry lost one killed and one scout captured in the brief action. Rome remained free from Federal occupation, at least for the moment.

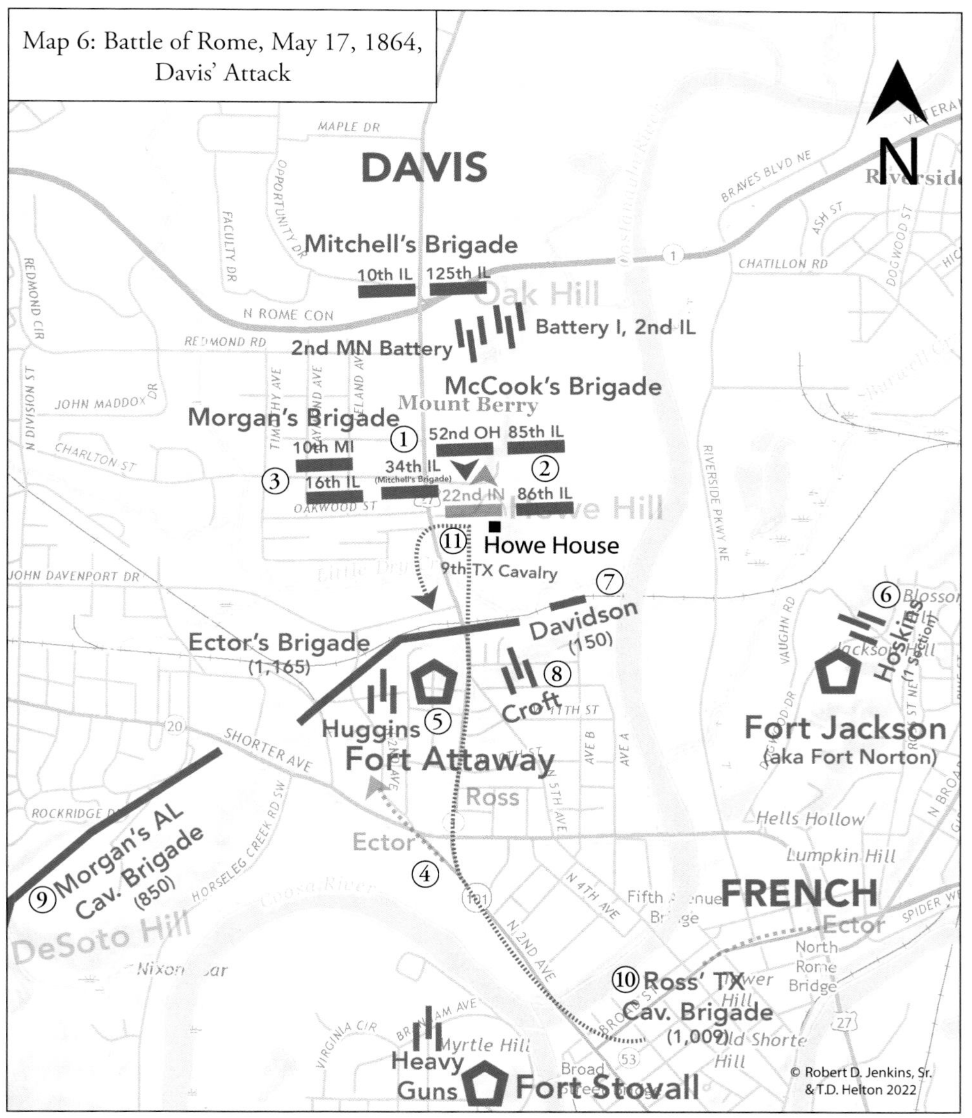

Map 6: Battle of Rome, May 17, 1864, Davis' Attack

After retaking Farmer's Bridge at Noon on May 17 after being ordered to move on Johnston's flank and rear, Federal Brigadier General Jefferson C. Davis resumed the march on Rome (8 miles distant) at 2:00 p.m. with (1) the 34th Illinois and Mitchell's brigade in front. Arriving 2 miles above Rome around 5:00 p.m., Davis deployed (2) McCook's brigade to the east of the Summerville Road. The 22nd Indiana formed to the left of the 34th Illinois while the 86th Illinois was posted to the left of the Hoosiers and atop Howe Hill. (3) Morgan's brigade was placed to the west of the 34th Illinois with the 16th Illinois in front. In Rome, Confederate Major General Samuel G. French hastily withdrew (4) Ector's brigade from the train cars before they were to leave for Kingston, and placed them along the ridge supporting Fort Attaway with (5) Huggins' battery in support and (6) one section of Hoskins' battery at Fort Jackson. (7) Davidson was posted on the hill east of the road with (8) Croft's battery, and (9) Morgan's troopers covered DeSoto Hill to the west. (10) Ross' Texas cavalry having just traveled 8 miles from up the east side of the Oostanaula River, galloped quickly through town, over the bridge, and up the Summerville Road. (11) With the 9th Texas Cavalry in front, Ross moved rapidly through the two hills that split the road, surprising and overwhelming the 22nd Indiana which fell back to its support regiment, the 52nd Ohio. The right half of the 86th Illinois refused its line to fire into the flank of the Texans while the 52nd Ohio checked their further advance, forcing Ross' men to withdraw.

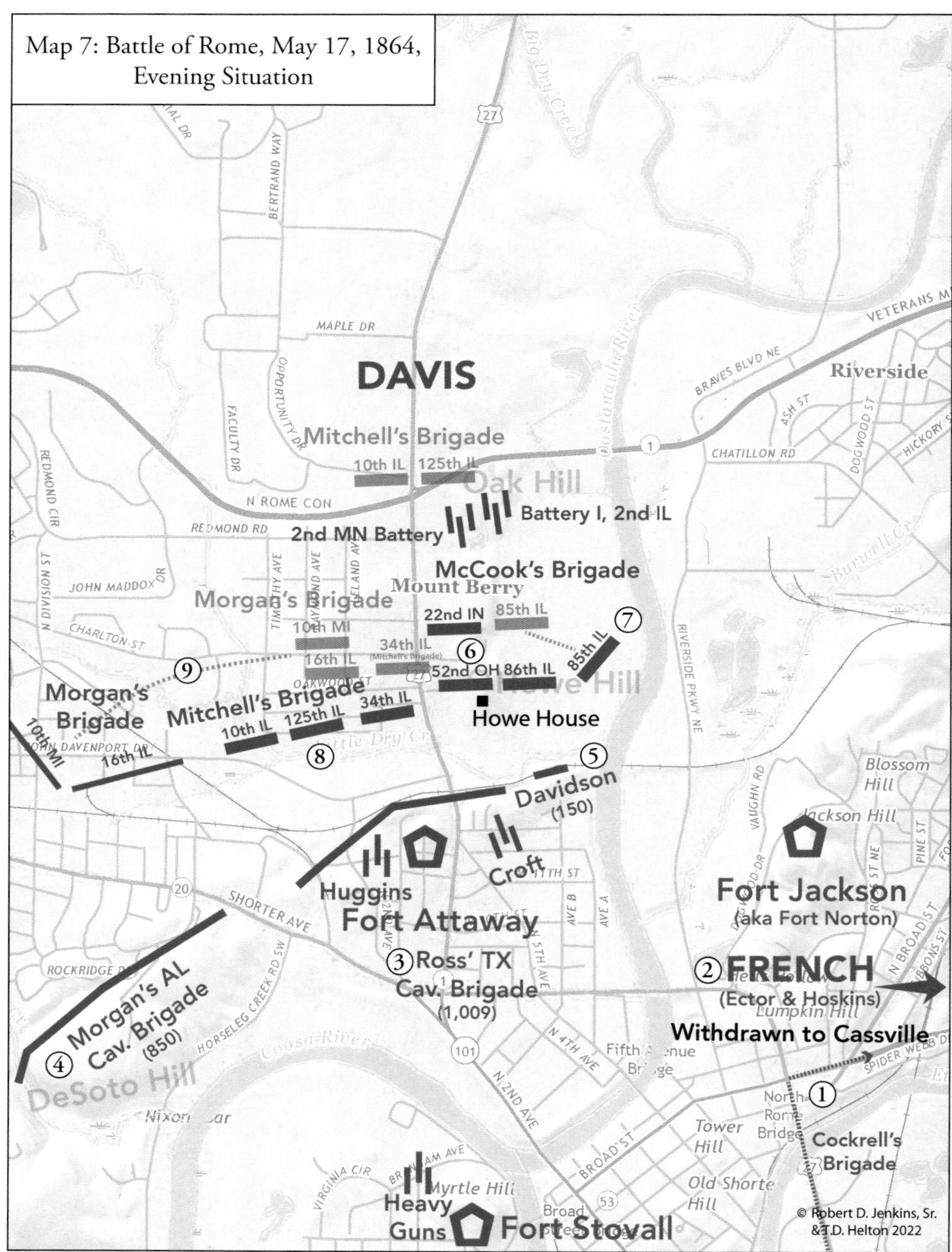

Map 7: Battle of Rome, May 17, 1864, Evening Situation

After checking Davis' advance on Rome to buy time for (1) Cockrell's Missouri brigade to arrive from Alabama and be put on trains bound for Kingston, French withdrew (2) Ector's brigade and Hoskins' artillery and headed for Cassville to join Johnston's main army as ordered. (3) Ross, (4) Morgan, and (5) Davidson remained overnight with orders to destroy everything of military value and evacuate the next day. On the Federal side, the (6) 52nd Ohio replaced the 22nd Indiana in line, the (7) 85th Illinois moved up to the bluff overlooking the river to the left of the 86th Illinois, (8) Mitchell's brigade deployed in the center and to the west of the Summerville Road, while (9) Morgan's brigade was extended to cover the Alabama Road (today's John Davenport Road). Davis prepared to renew his attack on Rome the next morning, while Ross and the Confederates prepared to evacuate and join Johnston's main body as ordered by the Southern commander.

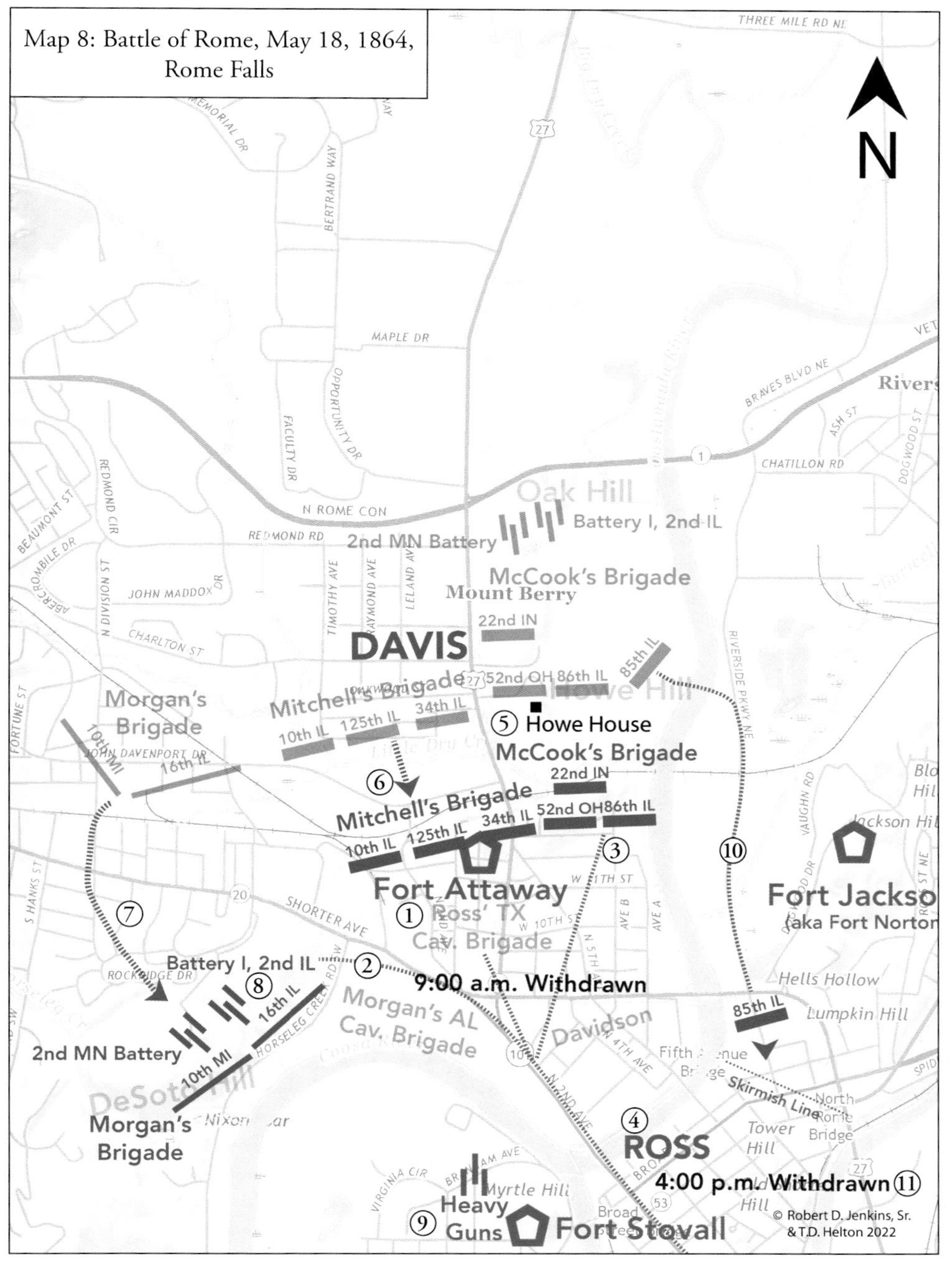

At daylight a heavy fog shielded the Confederate withdrawal from the northwest bank of the Oostanaula River as the last of (1) Ross', (2) Morgan's, and (3) Davidson's men left the works by 9:00 a.m. and burned the (4) bridge. On the Federal side, (5) McCook, (6) Mitchell, and (7) Morgan's lead regiments advanced as soon as enough of the fog lifted only to find abandoned earthworks in their front. (8) Batteries I, 2nd Illinois, and the 2nd Minnesota Battery, were moved forward to DeSoto Hill (at the site of the present-day Shorter College), to silence the fire coming from some (9) heavy guns atop Fort Stovall on Myrtle Hill which was covering the Southern retreat. (10) the 85th Illinois crossed the Oostanaula River on makeshift rafts of logs and boards, and threatened Rome from the northeast as (11) Ross and the remaining Confederates withdrew from the city by 4:00 p.m. as ordered by Johnston.

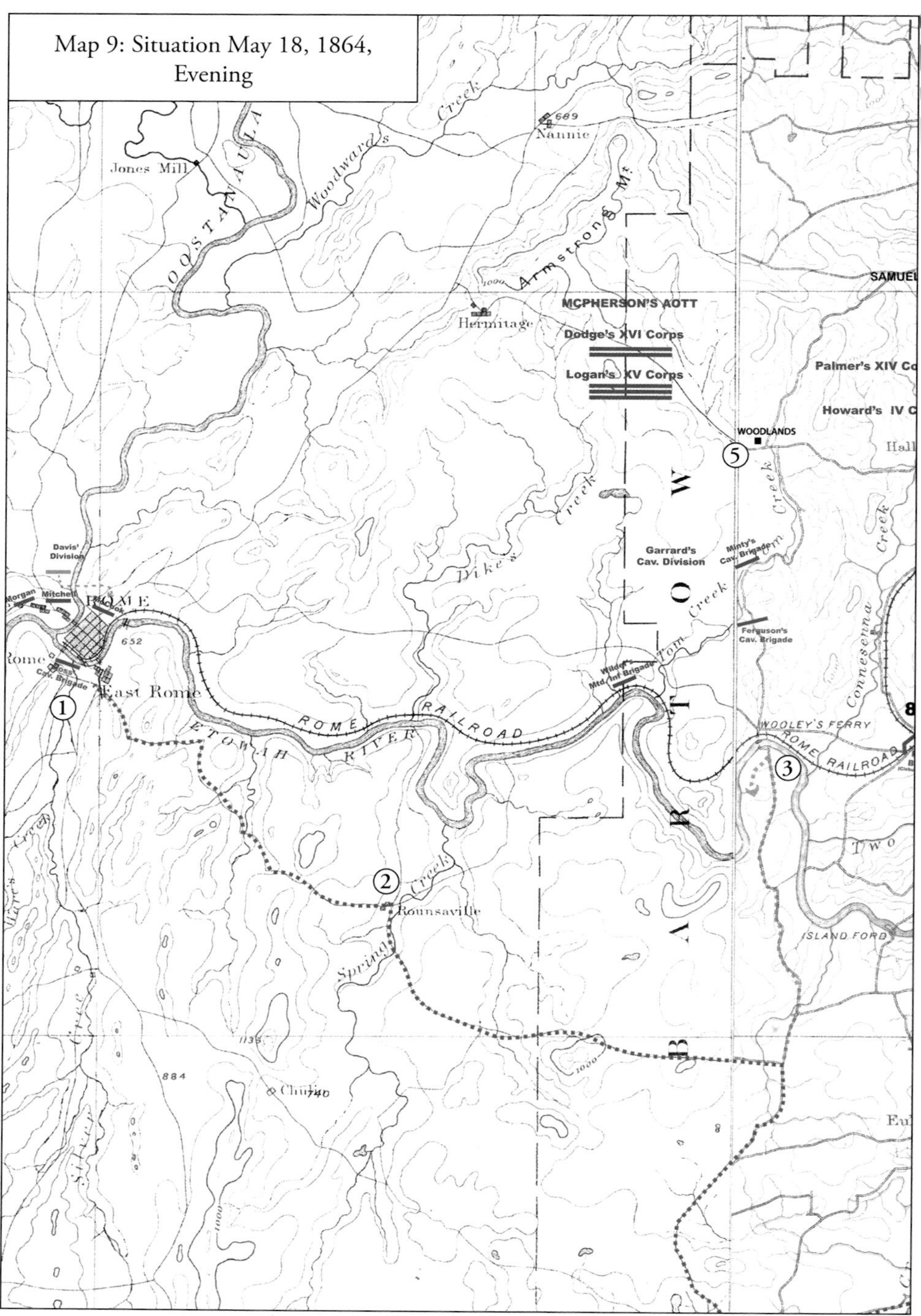

Map 9: Situation May 18, 1864, Evening

Wednesday, May 18, was a day of marching with little combat for the opposing forces except for the cavalrymen who saw plenty of action. After evacuating Rome by 4:00 p.m., (1) Ross' and Morgan's brigades moved east 8 miles where they stopped for the night along (2) Spring Creek. The next day, finding (3) Wooley's Ferry occupied by Federals, Ross and Morgan finally reached (4) Hightower Bridge by evening, traveling 35 miles in just over 24 hours. (5) Ferguson's Southern troopers clashed with Minty's horsemen near Woodlands (today's Barnsley Gardens), while

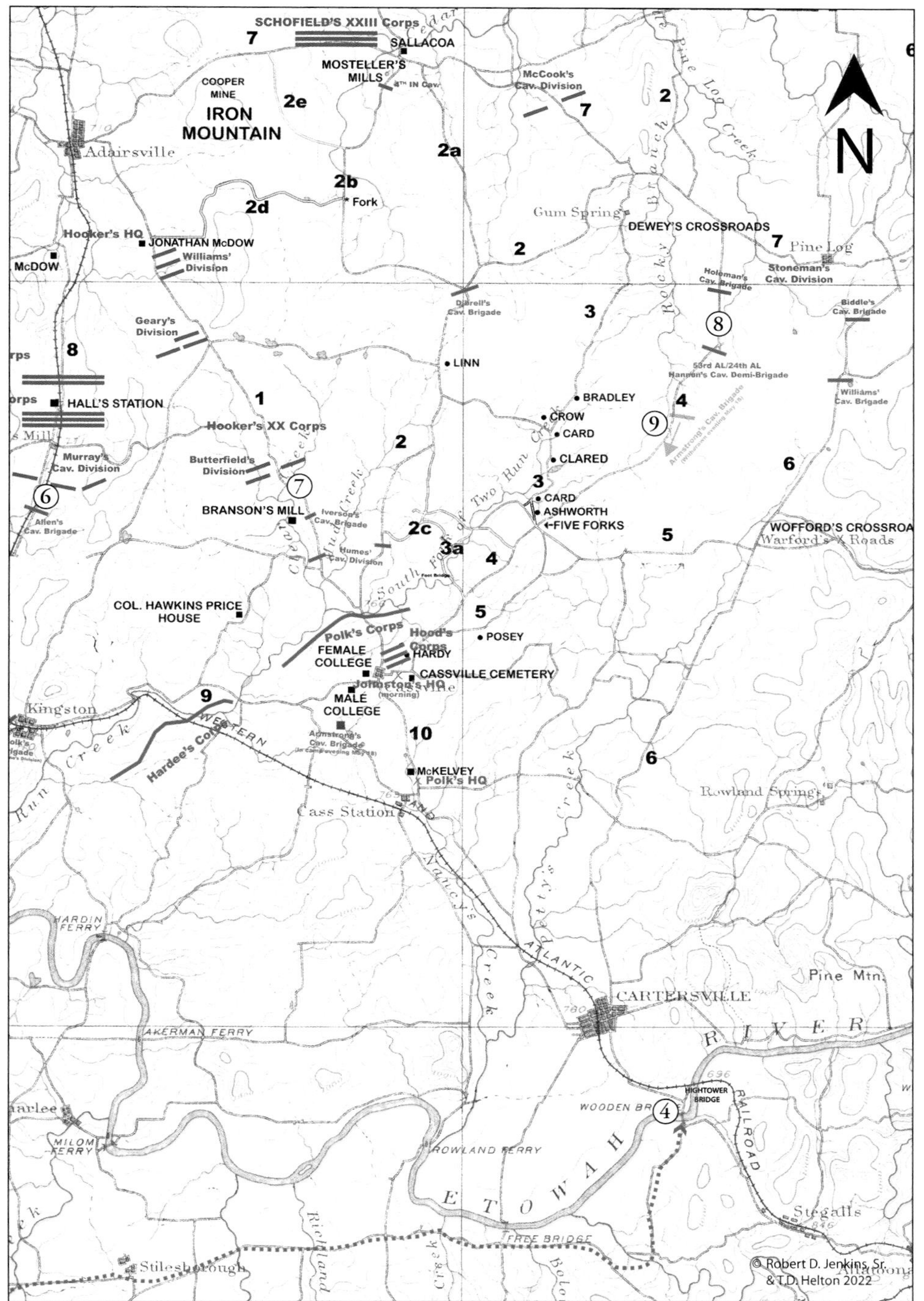

(6) Allen's cavalrymen sparred with portions of Murray's blue-clad troopers on the Adairsville-Kingston Road (Road 8). On the Adairsville-Cassville Road (Road 1), (7) Iverson's Georgians and Humes' cavalrymen slowed the progress of Butterfield's advance using barricades and ambuscades. (8) On the Pine Log (Fairmount) Road (Road 4), Hannon's Alabamians made contact with Holeman's Federal Kentucky troopers at a branch of Pine Log Creek. (9) Armstrong's Mississippi troopers were sent in support but were withdrawn that evening.

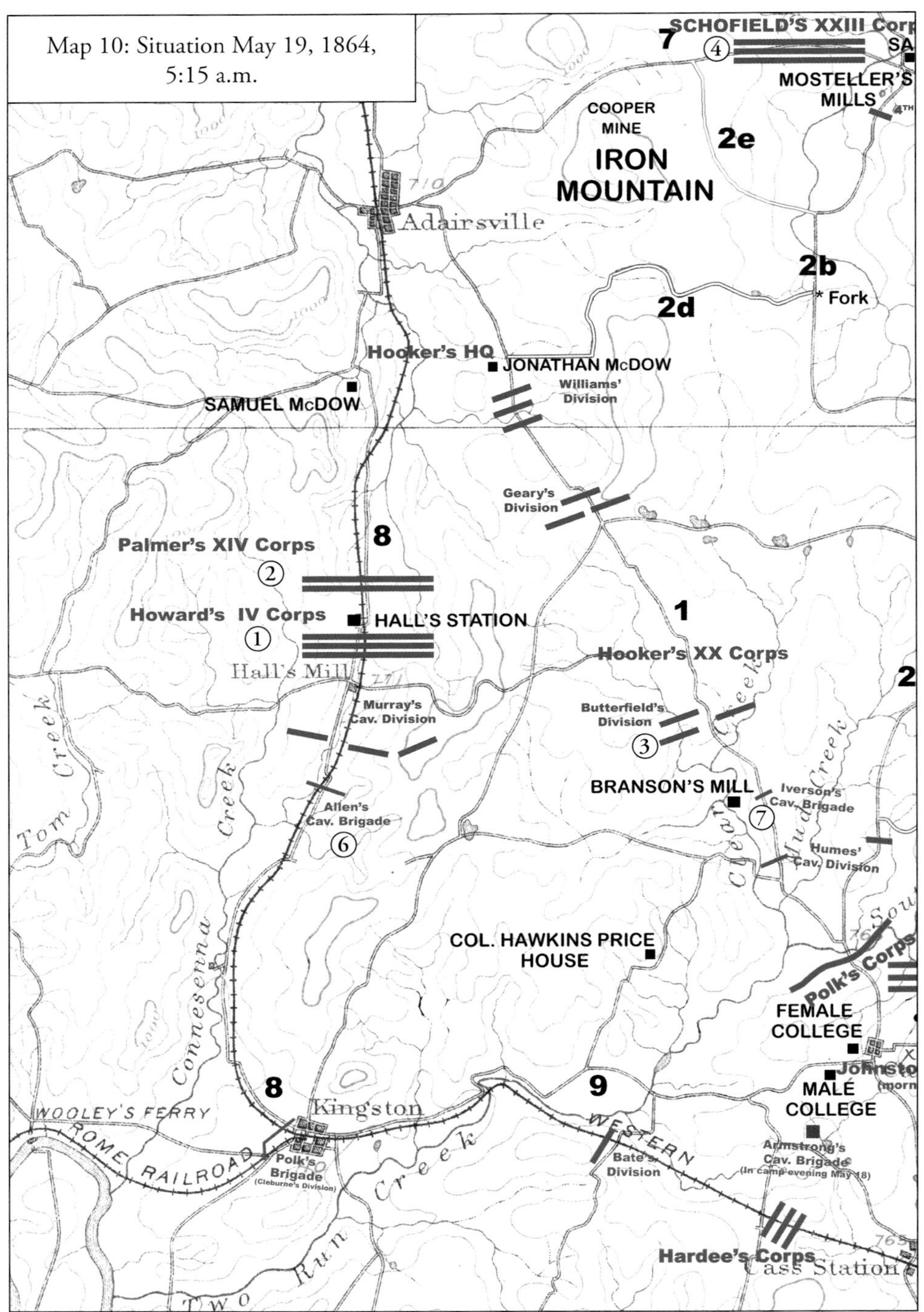

At 5:00 a.m., (1) Howard's IV Corps started south from Hall Station on the Adairsville-Kingston Road (Road 8), with Stanley's division in the van, and two divisions of (2) Palmer's XIV Corps following. At 5:15 a.m., (3) Ward's and Wood's brigades of Butterfield's division prepared to advance, as (4) Schofield's XXIII Corps began to move toward Hooker's rear at the Jonathan McDow house using the Ironton Road (Road 2b), and the unnamed road (today's Manning Mill Road, Road 2d). (5) McCook proceeded along today's Georgia Hwy. 140 (Road 7) toward

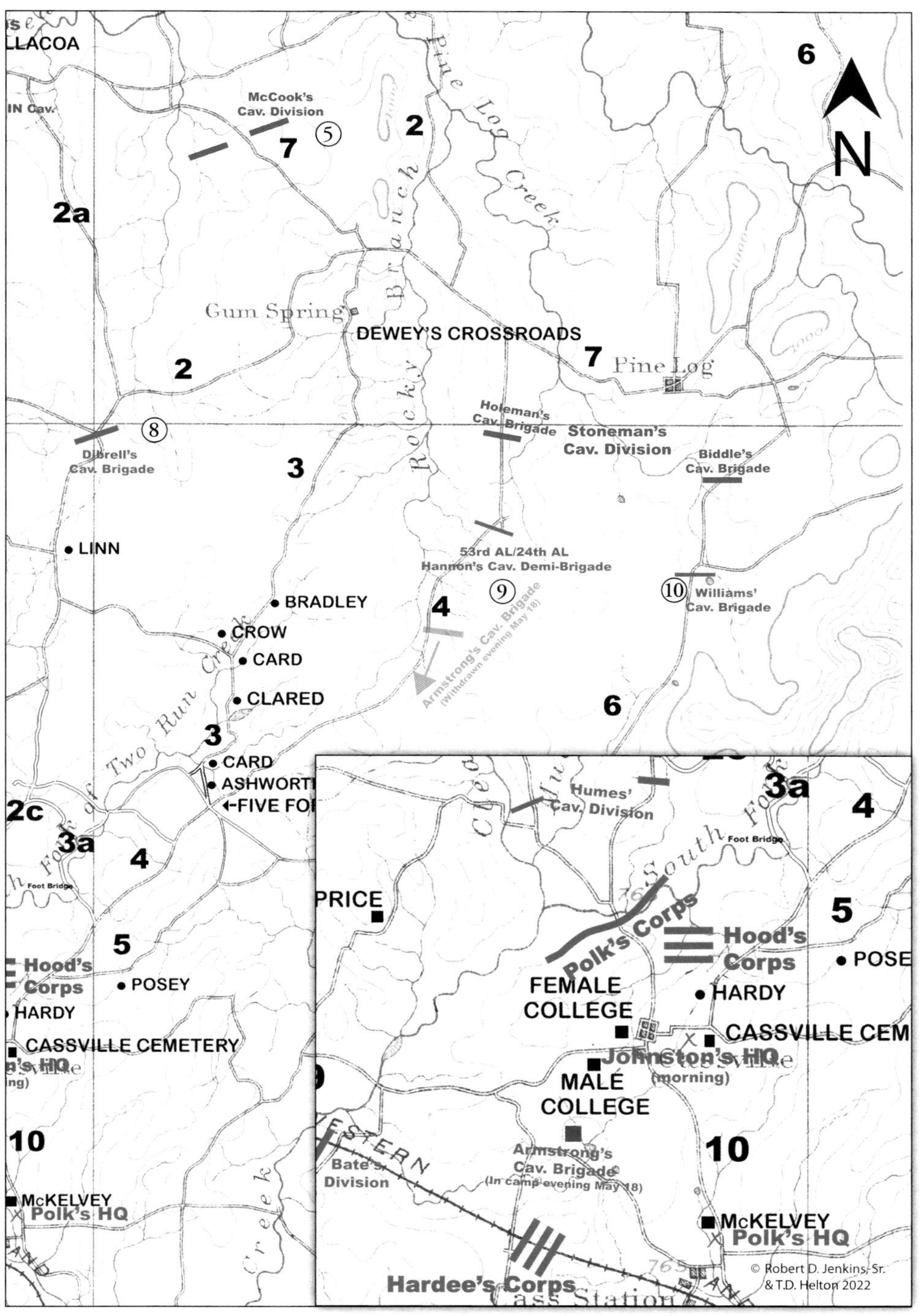

Dewey's Crossroads and Spring Place Road (Road 3). Wheeler posted his Southern cavalry screen with (6) Allen's brigade to the west with Jackson's division, (7) Iverson's brigade and Humes' division (Ashby and Harrison) on the Adairsville-Cassville Road (Road 1), (8) Dibrell's Tennessee brigade on the Copper Mine/Ironton Road (Road 2), (9) Hannon's Alabamians on the Pine Log (Fairmount) Road (Road 4), and (10) Williams' (formerly Grigsby's) Kentucky troopers on the Tennessee Road (Road 6).

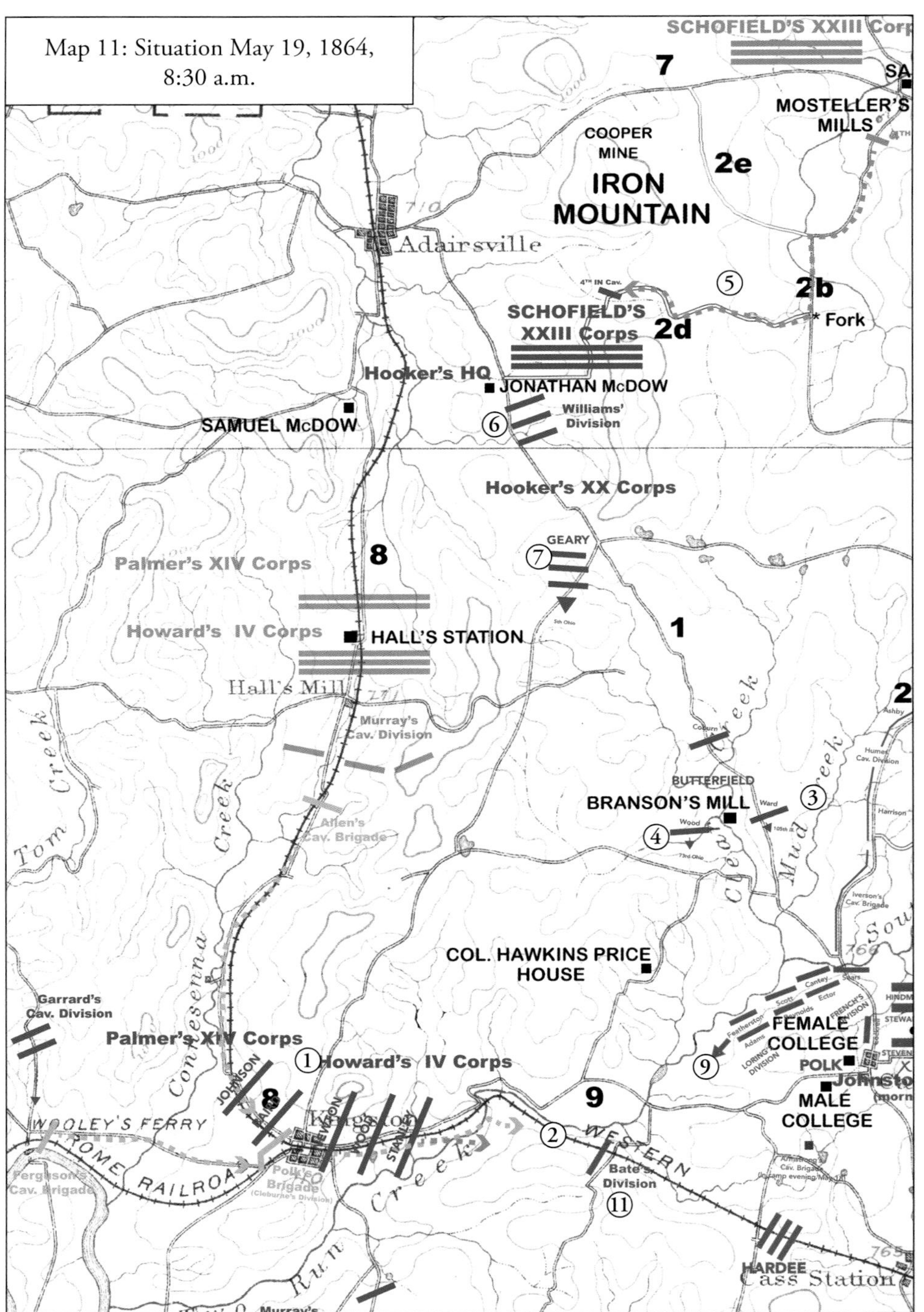

(1) Howard's IV Corps reached Kingston by 8:00 a.m. as (2) Lucius Polk's Confederate brigade and Ferguson's and Allen's troopers withdrew in the direction of Kingston. (3) Ward's brigade moved slowly down the Adairsville-Cassville Road (Road 1) while (4) Butterfield with Wood's brigade probed the valley to the west of the road. (5) The head of Schofield's XXIII Corps arrived at the Jonathan McDow House by 8:00 a.m. finding (6) Hooker and Williams' division still there. (7) Geary's division was ordered to support Butterfield and connect with Palmer's XIV Corps

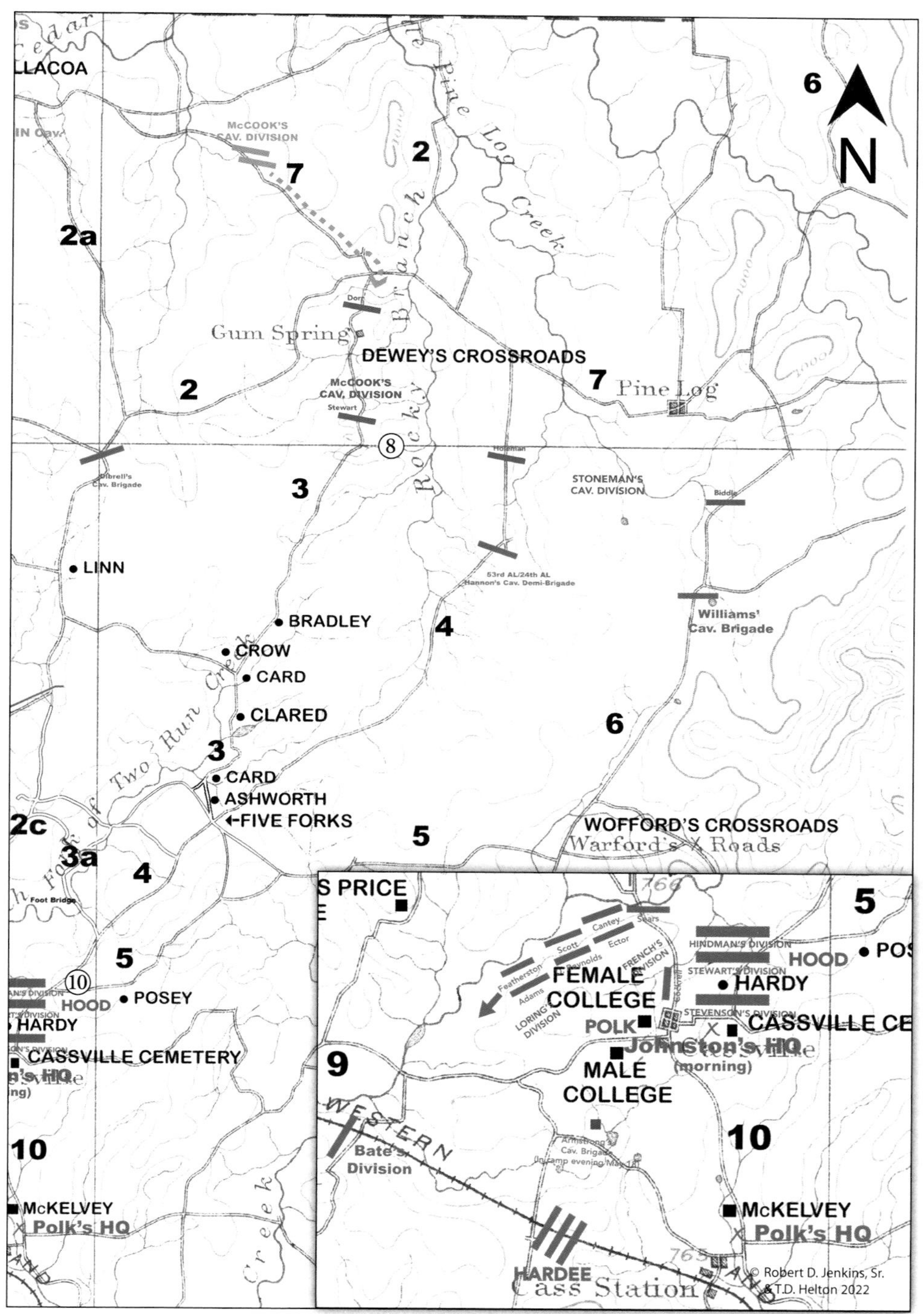

to the west, if possible. (8) McCook connected with Stoneman's pickets at Dewey's Crossroads, and then proceeded down the Spring Place Road (Road 3) undetected by Confederate pickets. On the Southern side, (9) Polk began to shift his corps to the southwest to cover Cassville below Two Run Creek, as (10) Hood began to move for his attack. Hardee held (11) Bate's division forward to retard the advance of the Federals on the Kingston-Cassville Road (Road 9).

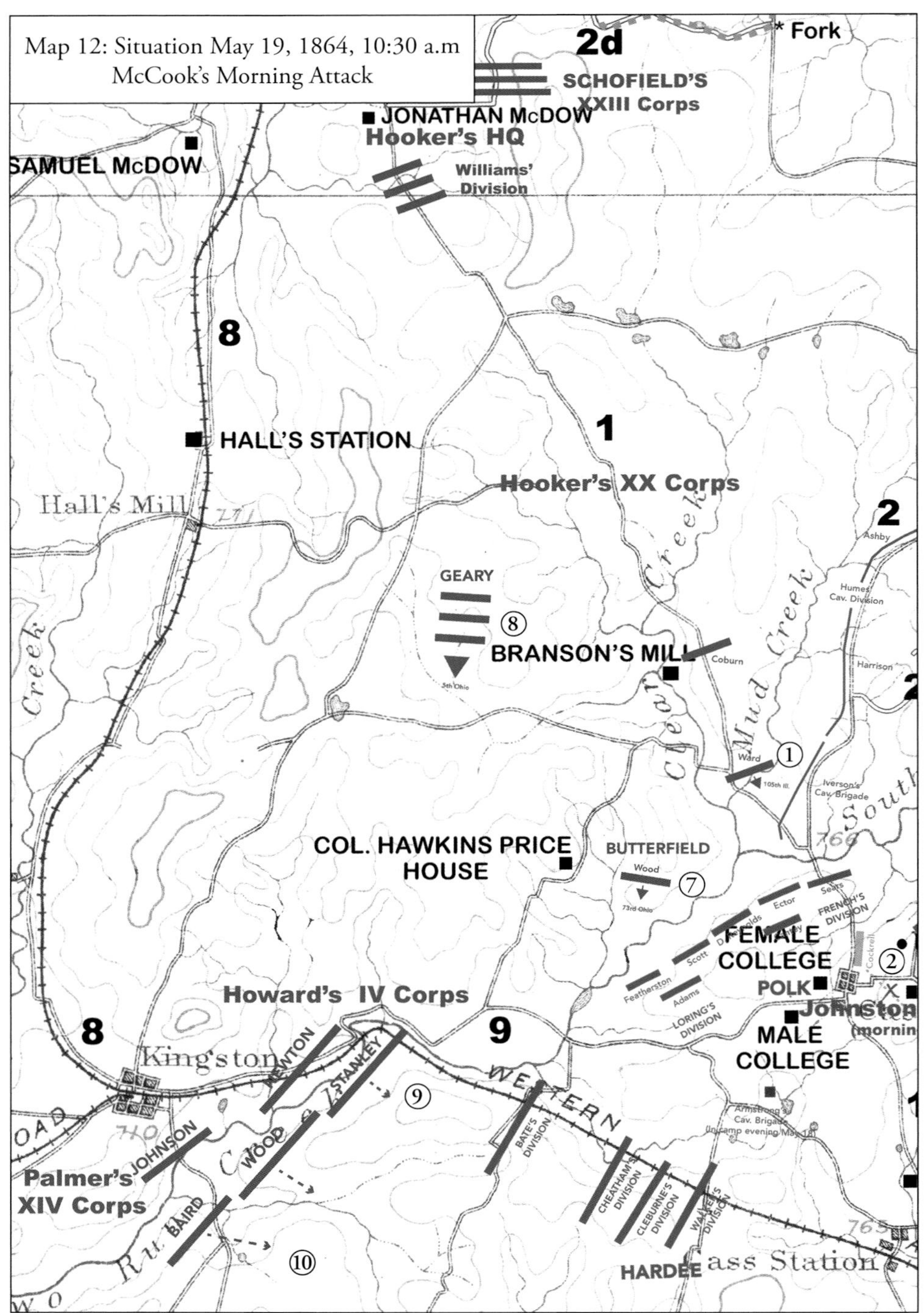

At 10:20 a.m., (1) Ward's brigade and Iverson's troopers exchanged fire which was heard at (2) Johnston's headquarters, while (3) Hood was within 200 yards of the Ironton Road. At the same time, (4) McCook's cavalry appeared to the east on the Spring Place Road at Five Forks. (5) The 9th Mississippi Battalion and the 41st Mississippi of Sharp's brigade were sent to develop the enemy. At 10:30 a.m., Rippetoe's 18th Indiana Battery opened on the Mississippians. Meanwhile, (6) the 2nd Indiana Cavalry continued down the Canton Road until

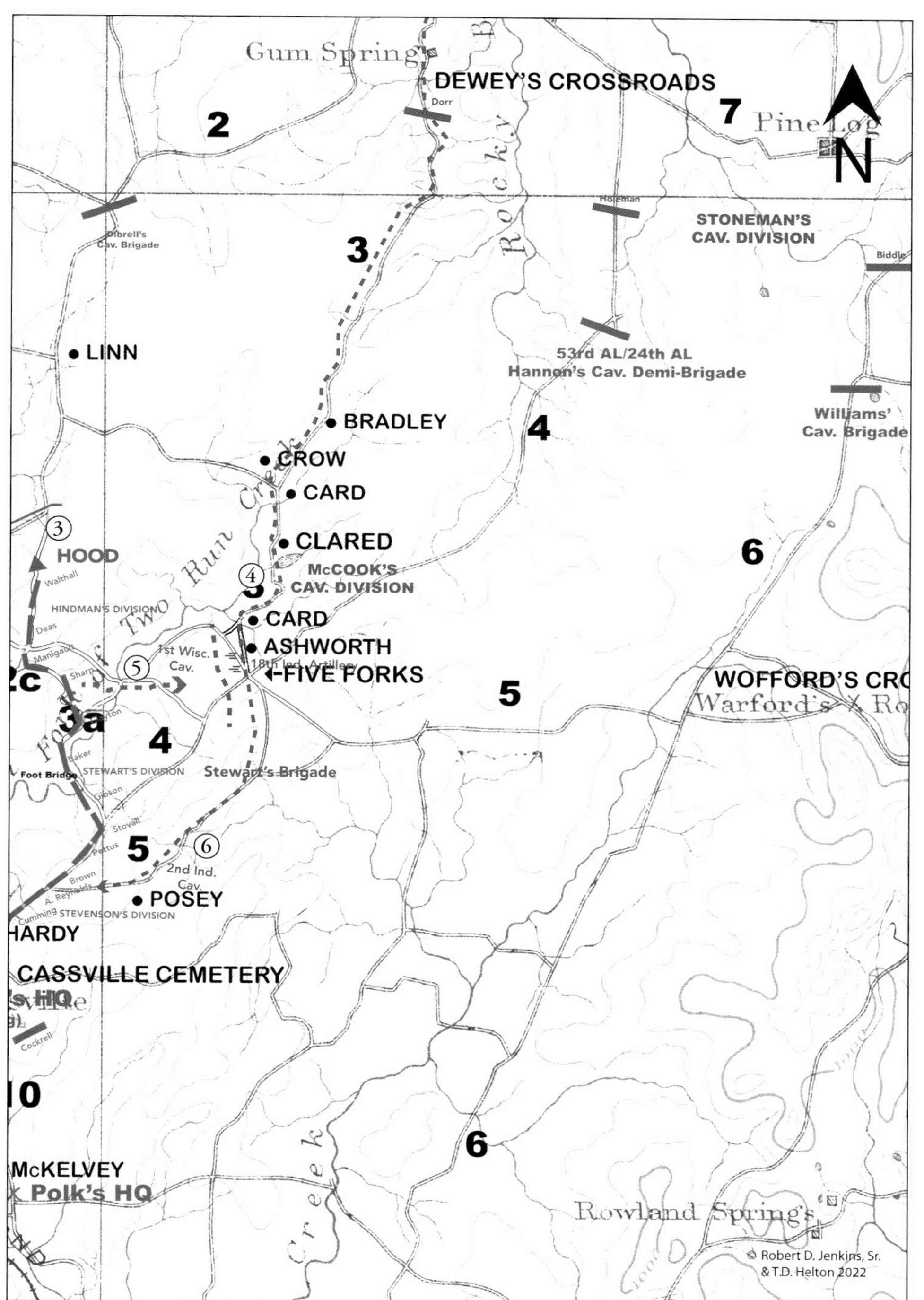

running into the 63rd Virginia of A. Reynolds' brigade and firing a few shots before turning and withdrawing at a gallop. (7) Butterfield with Wood's brigade probed along the Two Run Creek valley west of Cassville, while (8) Geary continued to progress slowly through the rough country. (9) Howard pressed Bate's men on the Kingston-Cassville Road (Road 9), while (10) Palmer was ordered to move Baird's division in support.

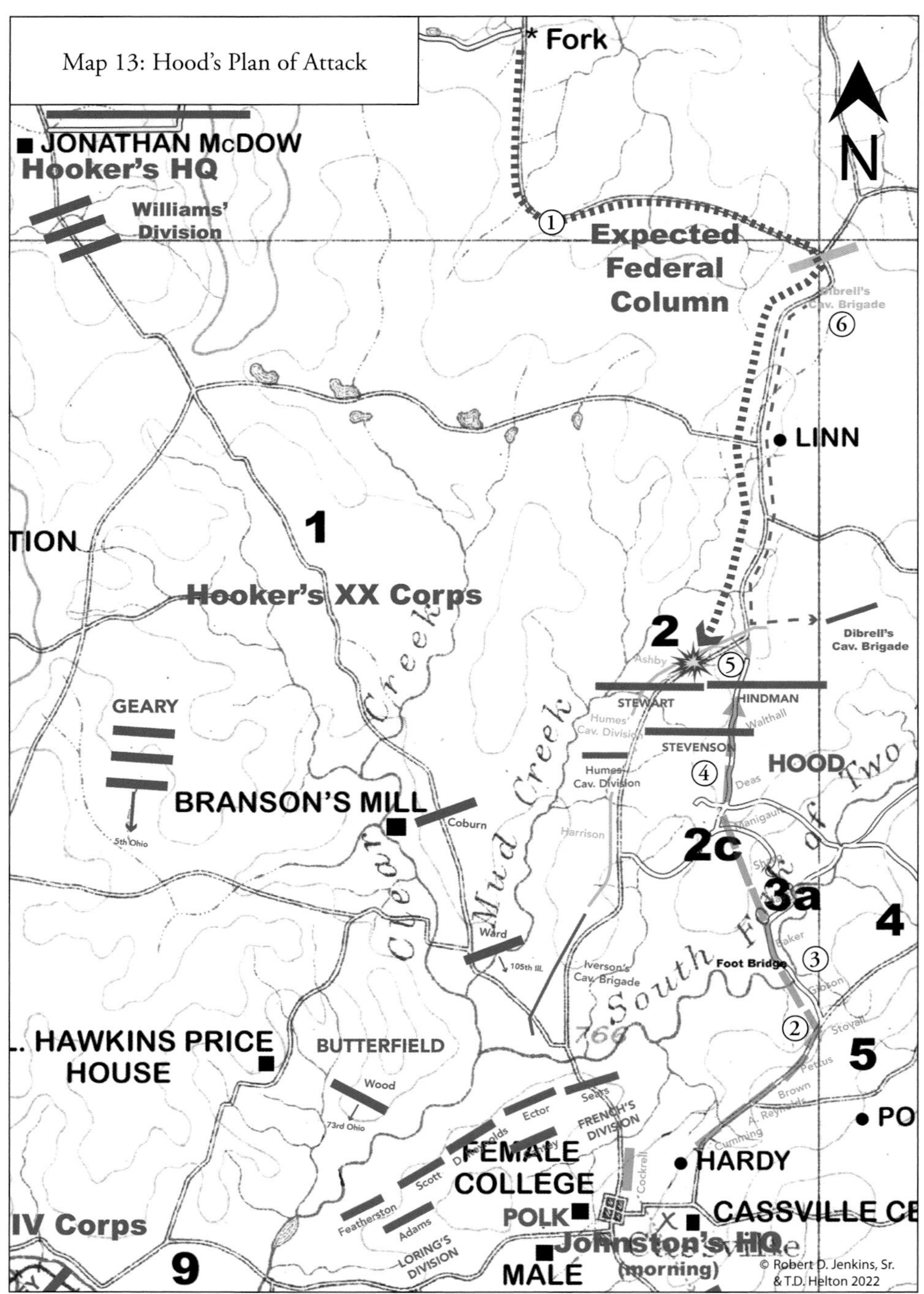

Believing that a (1) Federal column would approach Cassville from the Ironton/Copper Mine Road (Road 2) and separated from the balance of the Northern forces, Hood's plan called for moving his corps east on the (2) Pine Log/Fairmount Road (Road 4), then left through a gap at today's (3) Brown Loop Road (Road 3a), cross Two Run Creek at a foot bridge, and advance across (4) a large, open field to the (5) Ironton Road where Humes' division of cavalry was waiting to set the trap. (6) Dibrell's brigade was posted well to the north on the Ironton Road to report on the Federal progress and bait the unsuspecting foe into the trap.

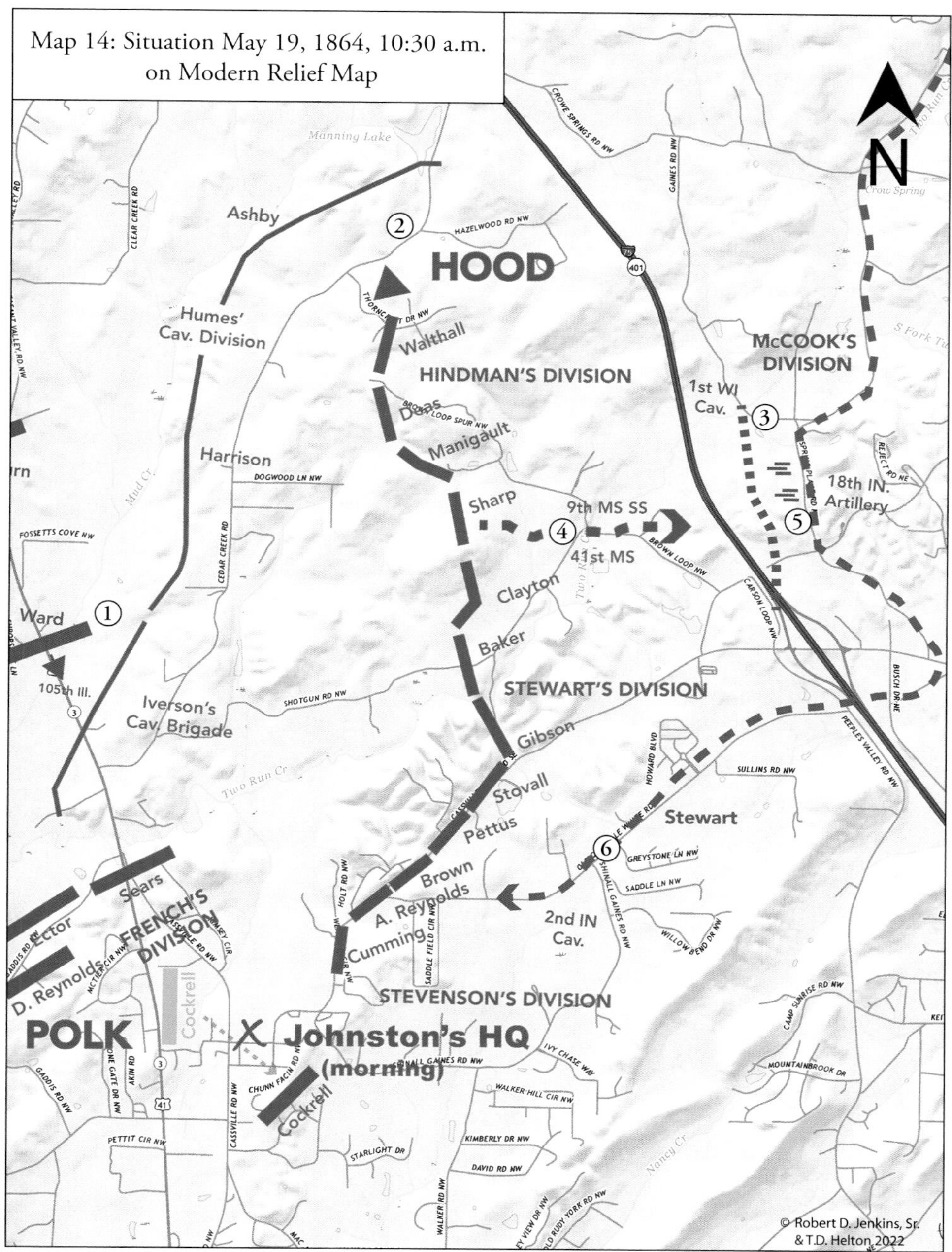

At 10:20 a.m., (1) Ward's brigade and Iverson's troopers exchanged fire, while (2) Hood and the van of his column was nearing the Ironton Road. At the same time, (3) McCook's cavalry appeared to the east on the Spring Place Road at Five Forks. There, McCook deployed Rippetoe's two 3" guns of the 18th Indiana Battery, and ordered the 1st Wisconsin Cavalry to dismount and provide support. (4) The 9th Mississippi Battalion and the 41st Mississippi of Sharp's brigade were sent to develop the enemy. At 10:30 a.m., (5) Rippetoe opened on the Mississippians, firing 6 rounds from each gun, which killed 4 men and wounded several others. Meanwhile, (6) the 2nd Indiana Cavalry continued down the Canton Road until running into the 63rd Virginia of A. Reynolds' brigade and firing a few shots which killed 3 and wounded 2 before withdrawing at a gallop losing just one man wounded in the arm, the lone Federal casualty in McCook's morning attack.

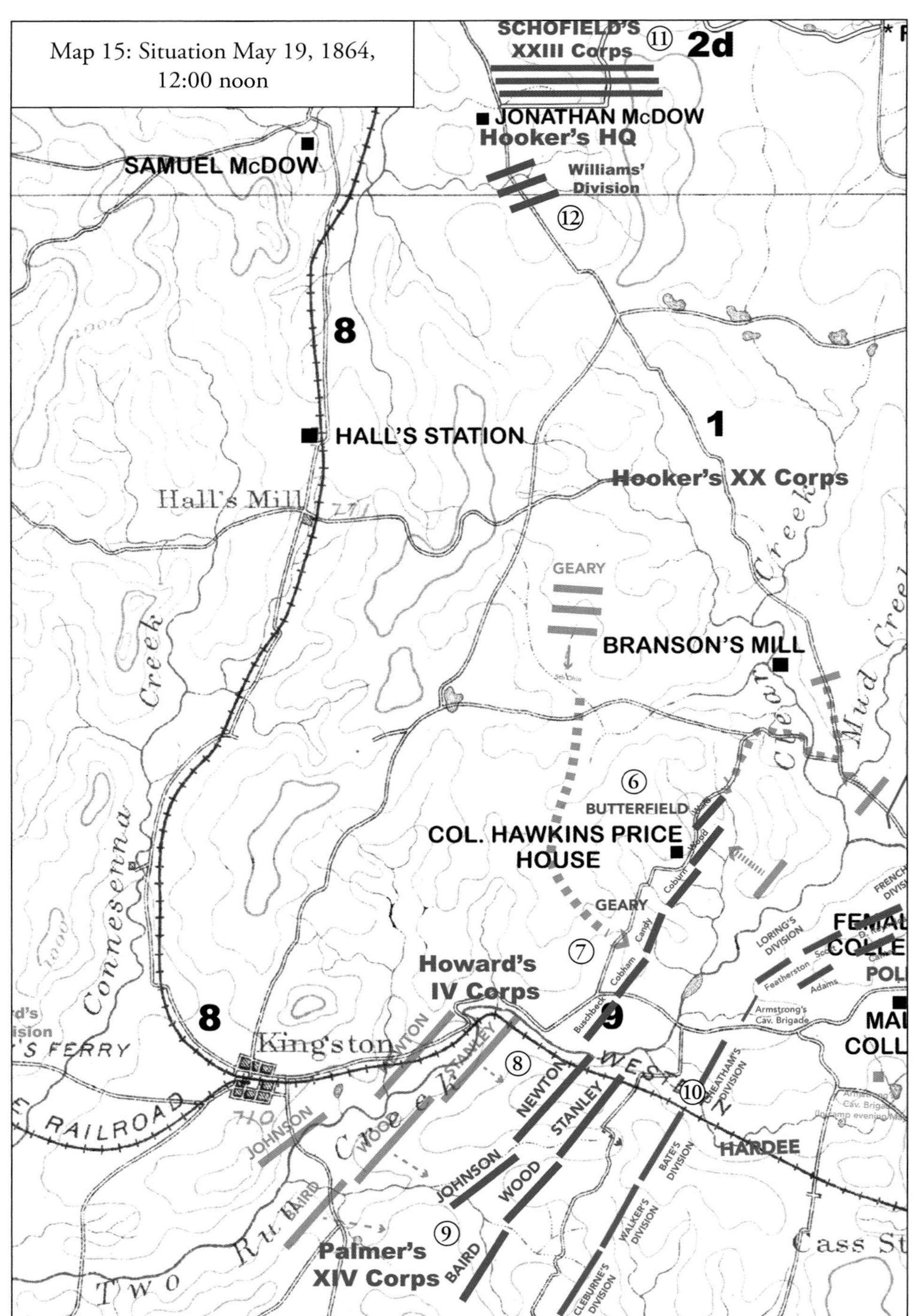

McCook's cavalry having withdrawn about a mile north to (1) Crow Springs, Hood swung his right to cover the Pine Log and Canton Roads to the east by deploying (2) Stevenson's division to the right, (3) Stewart's division in the center covering the north hill and the gap at Brown Loop Road, and (4) Hindman's division remaining on the north end of the open field in anticipation of the expected Federal column coming from the Ironton Road. Polk

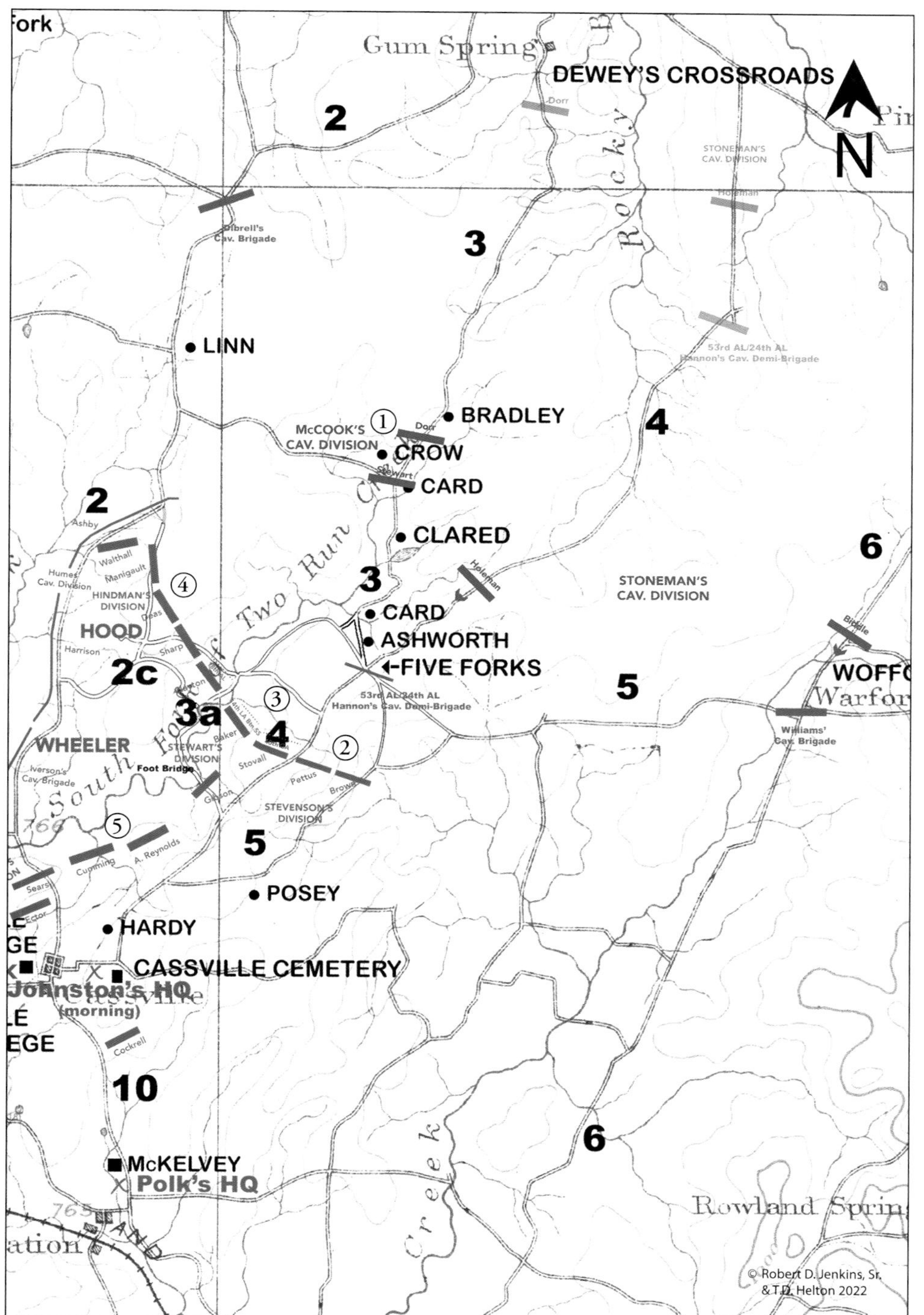

withheld two of Stevenson's brigades, (5) Cummings and probably A. Reynolds, to cover the field between his right and the south hill. (6) Butterfield consolidated his vulnerable division at the Colonel Price house, while (7) Geary arrived to connect with his right. (8) Howard and (9) Palmer continued to press from Kingston as (10) Bate withdrew to join Hardee. (11) Schofield and (12) Williams remained idle at the Johnathan McDow house.

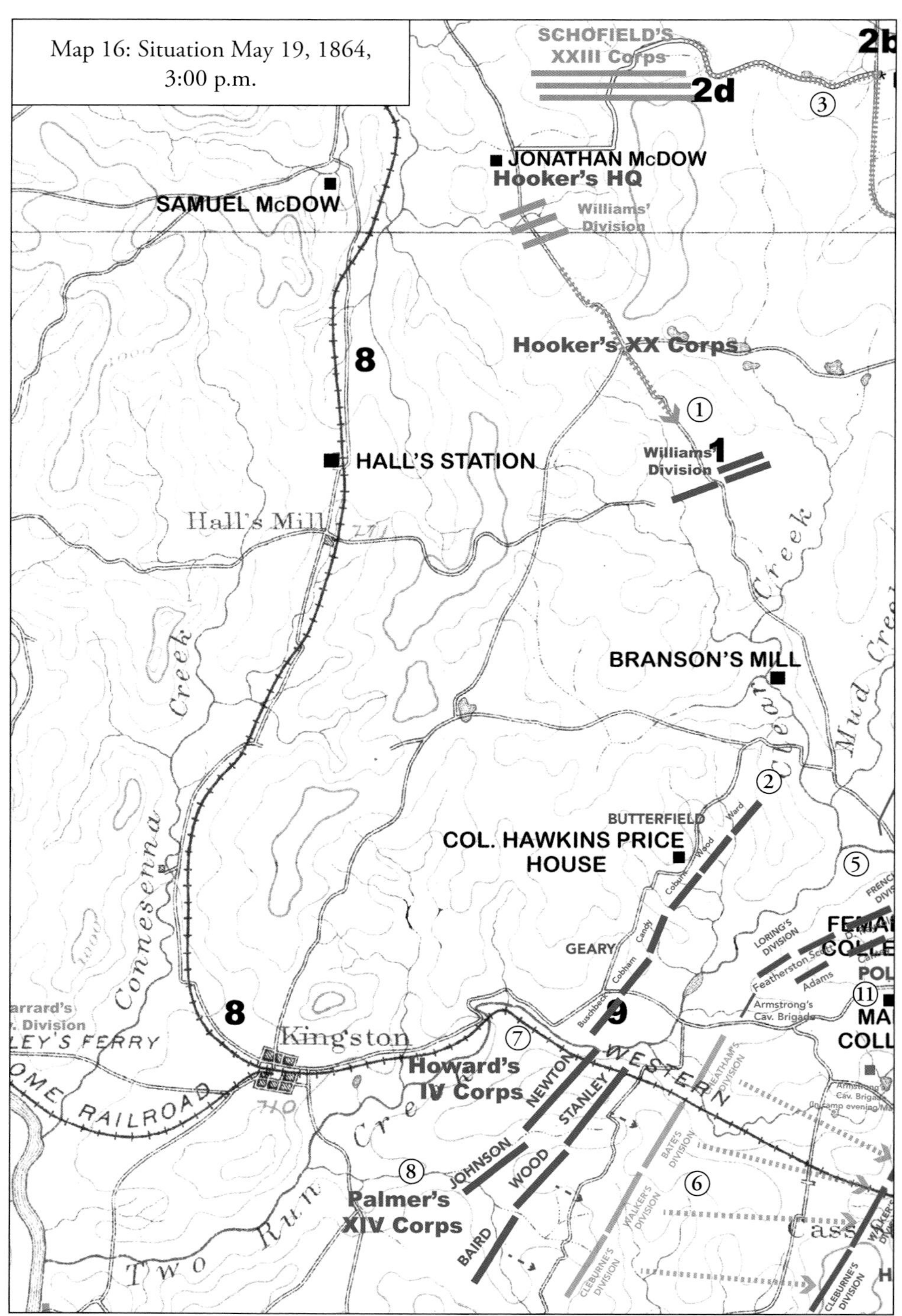

Williams' division was ordered to move down the (1) Adairsville-Cassville Road (Road 1) to connect with Butterfield's left (2), while Schofield was ordered to advance on Cassville east of Hooker. Schofield took today's (3) Manning Mill Road (Road 2d), and the (4) Ironton Road (Road 2), but would not arrive until after 4:00 p.m. just after Williams

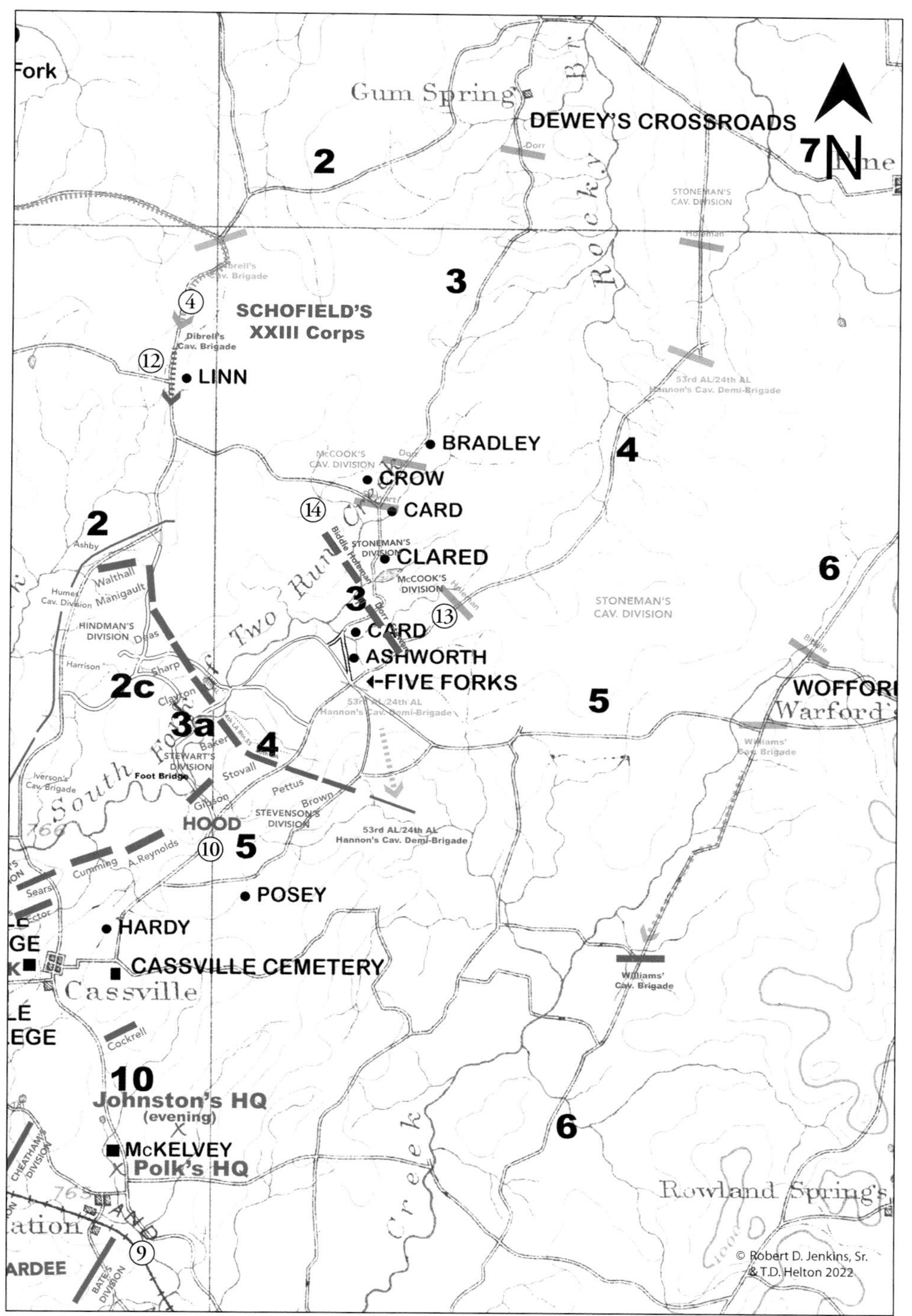

reached (5) Two Run Creek. (6) Hardee formed to slow (7) Howard and (8) Palmer, withdrawing to Johnston's new line by 4:00 p.m. with (9) Bate posted in the rear. (10) Hood and (11) Polk would begin to move at 3:00 p.m. to the new line as Wheeler recalled (12) Dibrell. (13) McCook, now with (14) Stoneman prepared to strike from Five Forks.

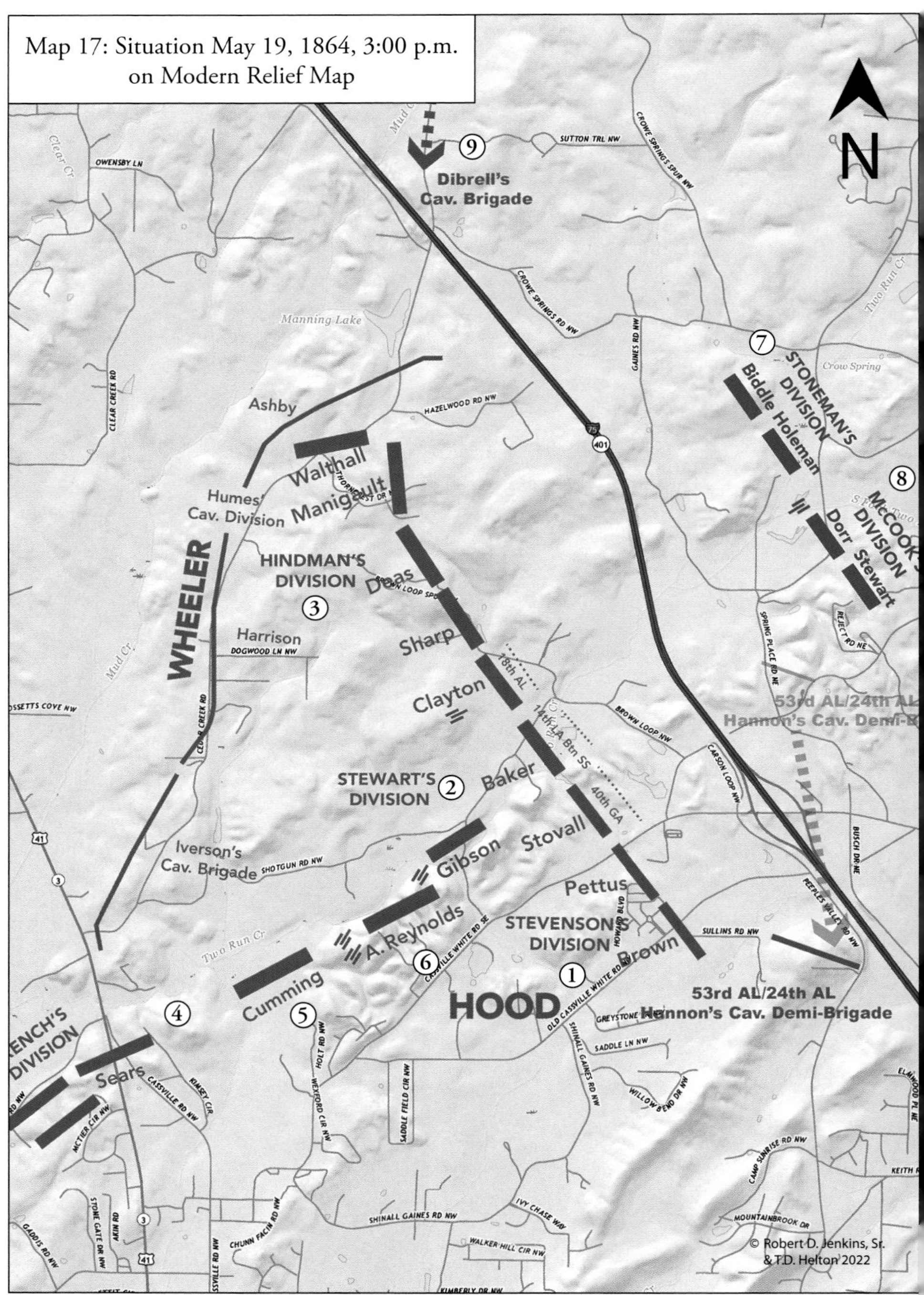

Having deployed two brigades of (1) Stevenson to cover the Canton and Pine Log Roads to the east, and (2) Stewart's division to cover the east side of Two Run Creek valley and the north hill, Hood began to pull back (3) Hindman's division to the south hill to connect with (4) Polk's right which Polk had temporarily filled with (5) Cummings and probably (6) A. Reynolds. (7) Stoneman had joined (8) McCook by now, and the two divisions prepared to advance. Discovering the danger of the advancing Federals from multiple directions, Wheeler recalled (9) Dibrell's brigade, but it would take them some time to return from their advanced post.

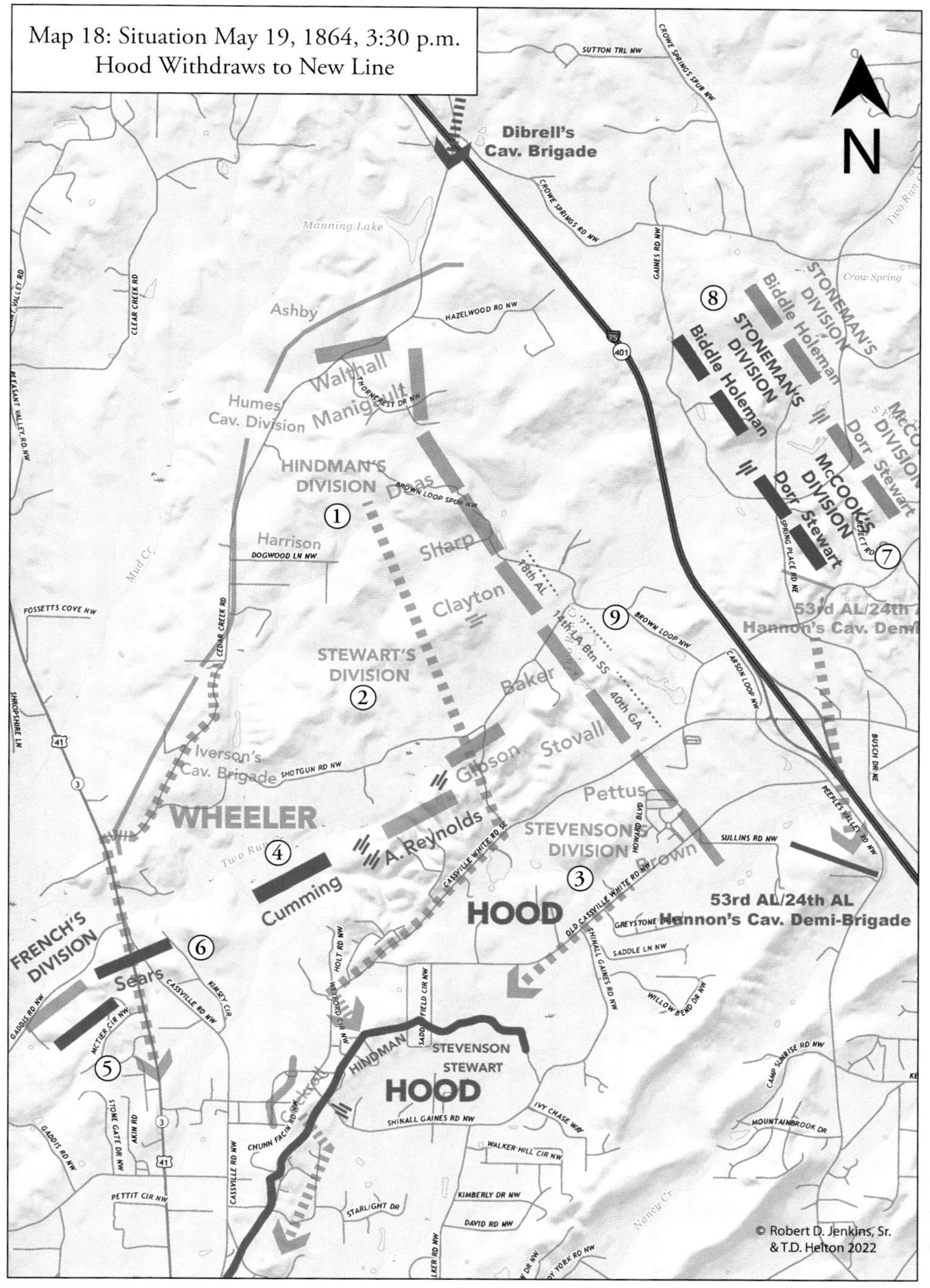

By 3:30 p.m., (1) Hindman's division, which was on its way to the south hill, was ordered to withdraw to Johnston's new line, as well as (2) Stewart's and (3) Stevenson's division except (4) Cumming's brigade which received orders to return to the field to cover (5) French's withdrawal. (6) Sears' brigade was the last to leave the morning position, Sears being struck in the boot by a shell fragment while moving through the streets of Cassville. (7) McCook and (8) Stoneman drew closer as the unsuspecting Confederate skirmish line of (9) Major Austin's 14th LA, and some companies of the 40th GA and 18th AL, covered Hood's withdrawal.

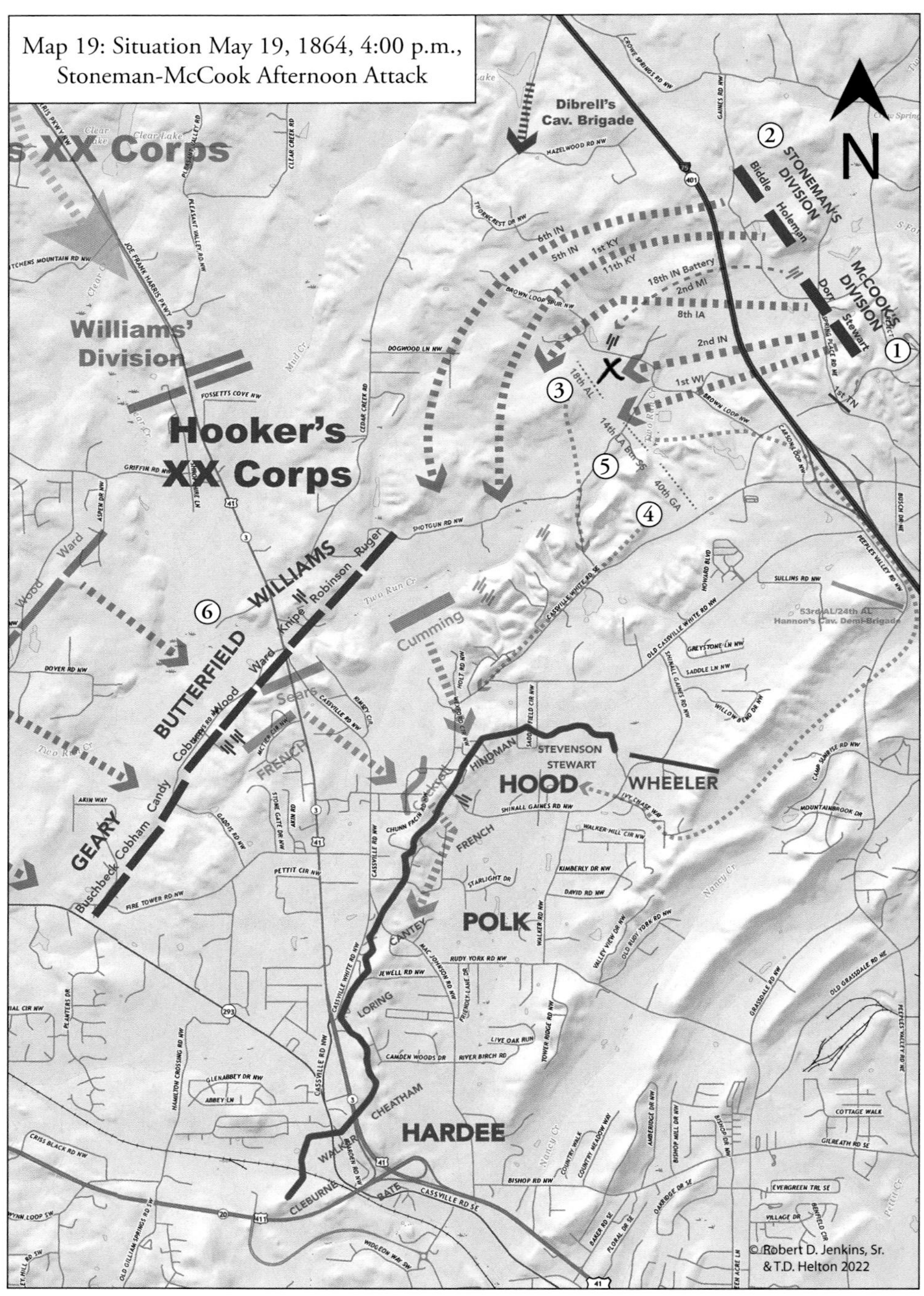

After most of Hood's corps had moved from the field, (1) McCook and (2) Stoneman charged across the field toward the Southern skirmish line, capturing one company of the (3) 18th AL and routing two others, and causing the skirmishers of the (4) 40th GA to withdraw from the field, leaving Major Austin's (5) 14th LA cut off, forcing Austin to withdraw to the east via an 8- or 9-mile circuitous route before rejoining their brigade at 2:00 a.m. the following morning, just in time to join in the retreat. (6) Hooker's corps advanced toward the abandoned village as Williams' division arrived.

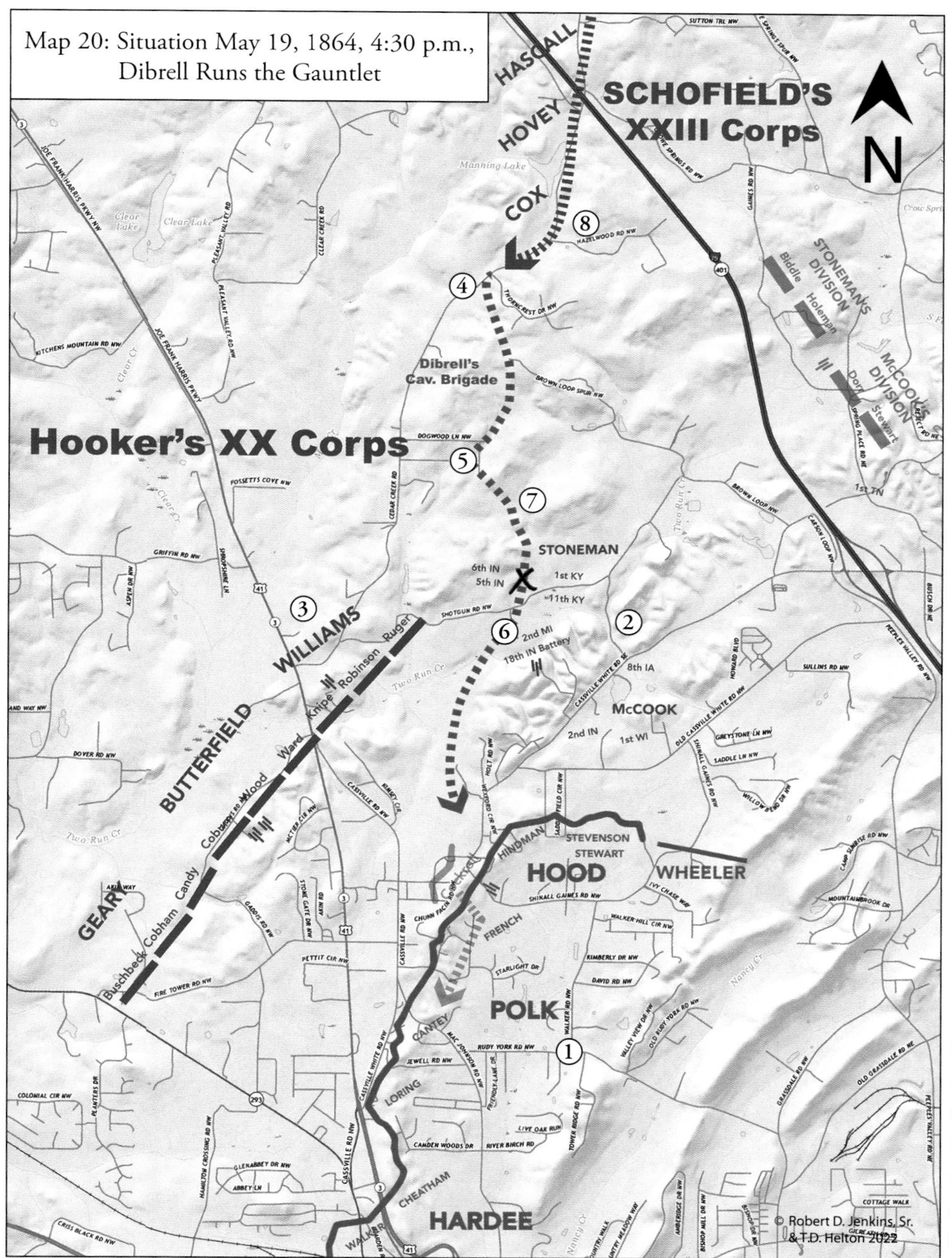

With the withdrawal of the Confederate army to (1) Johnston's new line, and the advance of (2) Stoneman's and McCook's Federal cavalry across the Two Run Creek valley and (3) Williams' division down the Adairsville-Cassville Road (Road 1), Dibrell's brigade was forced to take a (4) by road from the Ironton Road (Road 2) before reaching the (5) large, open field. There, Dibrell's first column surprised a portion of the Federal cavalry and may have captured a guidon of the 5th Indiana Cavalry before being chased by additional (6) Federal troopers toward the new Confederate line. Then, the rest of Dibrell's retreating column and his escort reached the field and (7) chased the Federal cavalrymen back, thus opening their line of escape, losing 11 killed and wounded in the dash. Meanwhile, (8) Schofield's column continued down the Ironton Road.

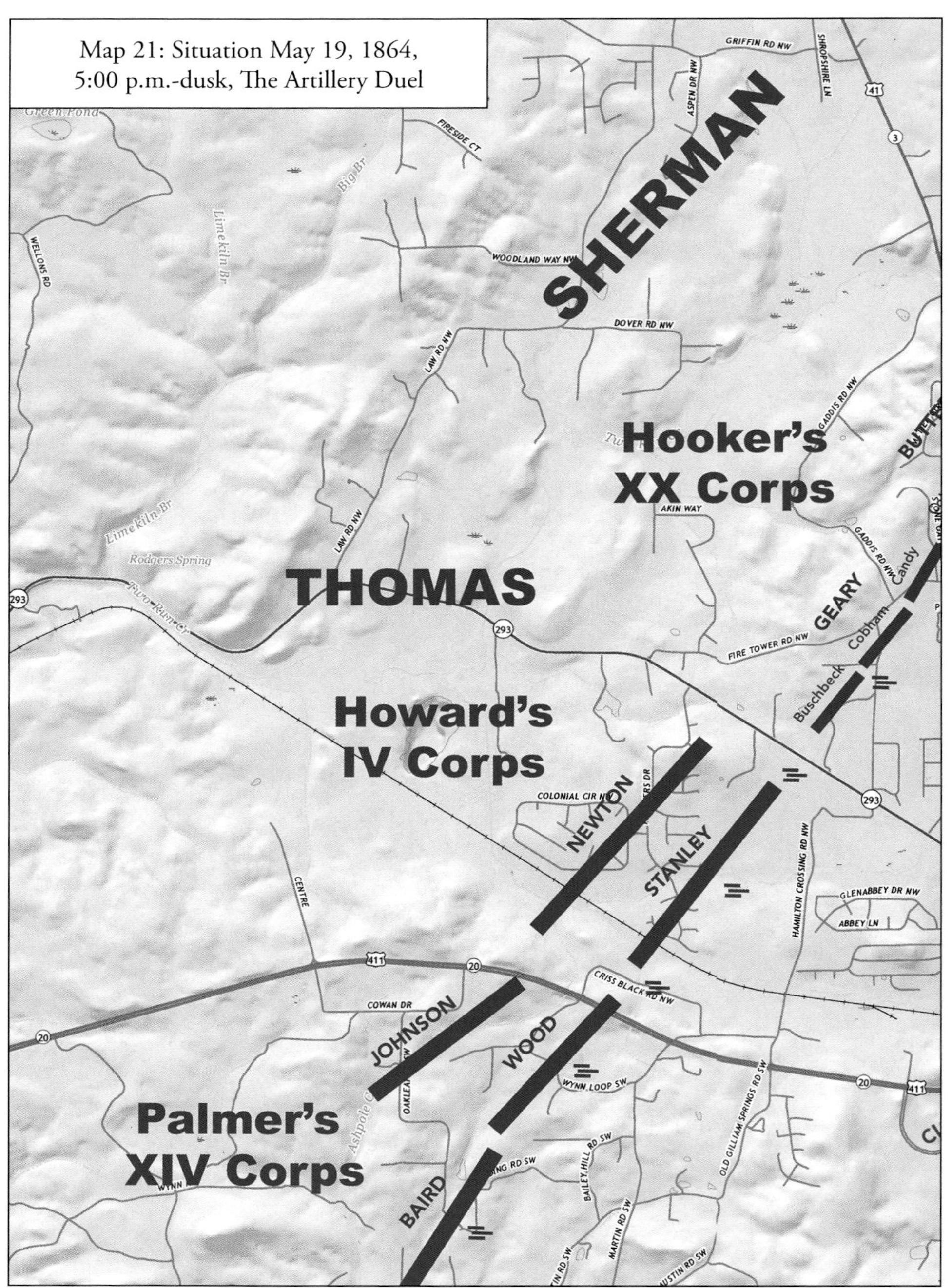

Johnston's new line (1) as shown from the Ruger (Second Epoch) Map, was exposed to enfilade fire on (2) French's right and Hindman's left. French ordered (3) Hoskins' battery to fire on the Federal cavalry that had swept Two Run Creek valley, forcing their withdrawal. In response, Federal artillery from (4) Rippetoe's 18th Indiana battery, and (5) Stephens' Battery C, 1st Ohio, supported by Smith's Battery I, 1st Michigan, silencing Hoskins' battery. (6) Sears' brigade sustained 8 wounded, while (7) in Hindman's division Walthall's brigade had 1 killed and 4 wounded, and Deas' brigade lost 1 killed and 2 wounded during the artillery duel. Before dark, (8) Winegar's Battery I, 1st New York, also fired 6 rounds as Federal artillery struck the angle in the Confederate line from three

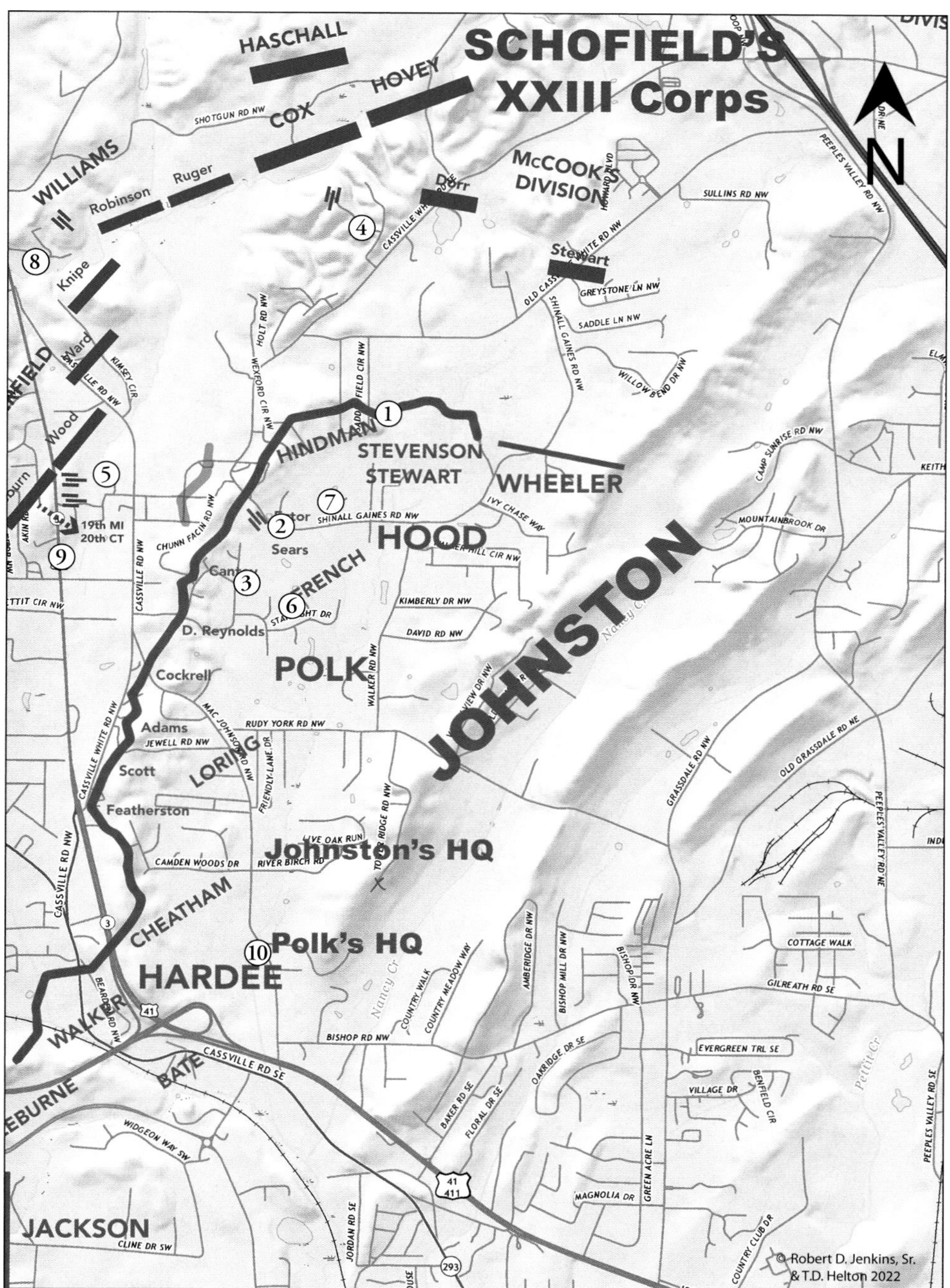

directions. (9) At dusk, the 19th Michigan and the 20th Connecticut of Coburn's brigade moved into and occupied the village of Cassville amid fleeing citizens. After dark, Johnston met Polk and Hood for dinner at the (10) McKelvey House before retiring to a cabin to discuss the battle plan for the next morning where Hood and Polk argued for either an offensive or withdrawal from the exposed line. Hardee arrived in time to learn that Johnston had ordered a withdrawal after receiving news from Ross at Cartersville that Federals had crossed the Etowah River at Wooley's Bridge west of Kingston and Johnston's Army was apparently again flanked by Sherman.

Exhibit 33

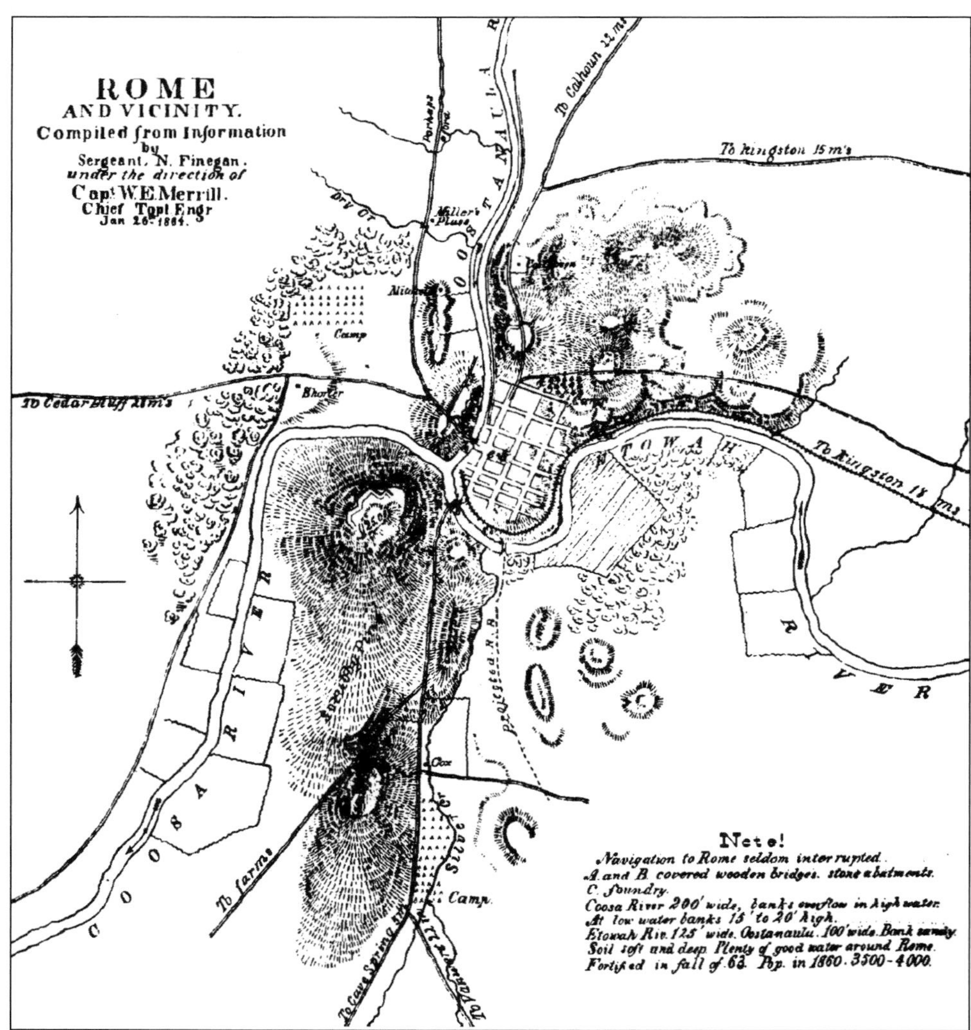

Map of Rome, Georgia, by William E. Merrill

This map was compiled by Sergeant N. Finegan under the direction of Captain W.E. Merrill, Chief Topographical Engineer, Army of the Cumberland, January 26, 1864, lithographed and printed at Topographical Engineer's Headquarters, Chattanooga, Tennessee, June 30, 1864. It appears to be based upon a copy of a captured Georgia Militia Map that was created in late 1863, but the fortifications were not completed until February 1864 (See Report of Retired Lieutenant Colonel David Chuber, https://web.archive.org/web/20120307175544/http:/www.fortattaway.com/Chuber_Report/Chuber_Report.htm, accessed May 17, 2023.)

destroying anything of military value. He was also told to have Davidson and his demi-brigade leave Rome as well and rejoin the rest of Johnston's army via the High Tower Bridge south of the Etowah River.[49]

In the morning, Ross's men busied themselves with the general destruction of any equipment, weapons, mechanical devices, and machinery—anything that they could not carry with them, and the rest, including tobacco, clothing, and commissary goods, were stuffed by the men in their haversacks and saddlebags. Lieutenant Griscom of the 9th Texas remembered that they were up at daylight and skirmished with the enemy "all day till 2 p.m. when the enemy came into town via [the] Calhoun road." At that point, they burned "the North & RR bridge and retire[d] to [the] west bridge," and skirmished until 4 p.m., then plundered the depot and stores before retiring across the bridge to the south at 8 p.m. Griscom noted one man, a scout named E. A. Shults of Company A, 9th Texas, was left behind after being wounded slightly in the knee. The Texas adjutant added that there were no other soldiers left in Rome other than some "boomerangs," soldiers who were sent to the front only to return quickly to escape the hazards of combat. They were left to the peril of the approaching Federals.[50]

That morning, Ross's Texans set fire to the wagon bridge over the Oostanaula River and, after withdrawing to the south bank of the Etowah along with John Morgan's cavalry brigade and Davidson's contingent, destroyed the bridges over that river, as well. Ross led his men eight miles to the southeast, where they stopped for the night, probably along Spring Creek.[51]

Davis's men awoke on the morning of Wednesday, 18 May, to a dense fog that prevented visibility for more than a few yards. By 9 a.m., the fog began to rise, allowing the men to see sufficiently for operations. The Federal division commander ordered each brigade to attack the enemy works vigorously, with a strong line of skirmishers before each attacking column. As the bluecoats charged across the field between the two lines and reached the Confederate works, they found that the Southerners had abandoned them in the night, leaving only a skirmish line. The gray-clad skirmishers were only then

---

[49] French, *Two Wars*, 194; *OR*, ser. 1, vol. 38, pt. 4, 725.

[50] Kerr, ed., *Fighting with Ross' Texas Cavalry Brigade*, 143–44.

[51] This creek was likely incorrectly misidentified as Raccoon Creek by 9th Texas biographer Martha Crabb, perhaps because the 9th Texas saw action the following week at Racoon Creek near Dallas, Georgia (Crabb, *All Afire to Fight*, 214–15; Scaife, *Campaign for Atlanta*, 42; Hale, *Third Texas Cavalry*, 220).

withdrawing and were pursued by the Federals, according to Davis, who claimed that the enemy was only partially successful in burning the bridge.[52]

Some of Davis's men reached the abandoned Confederate positions on the northwest side of the river at De Soto Hill, where they received artillery fire from a Confederate two-gun battery in the fort on the hill (known locally as Jackson Hill), located above the city and on the east bank of the Oostanaula River. They also began to receive artillery fire from the hill on the south side of the Coosa River, at Fort Stovall on Myrtle Hill. Davis ordered Barnett's and Gardner's batteries to be placed on De Soto Hill in response.[53]

Captain Charles M. Barnett's battery, the Second Illinois Light Artillery battery with its four three-inch ordnance rifled guns, went to work on the enemy defenses, and Captain George Q. Gardner's Second Minnesota battery joined the effort with its four Napoleons. Texas trooper Keen remembered that Northern artillery fired a number of shells into their position, and into a graveyard (Myrtle Hill Cemetery), which was in front of them atop Myrtle Hill. He said some of the "shots knocked some nice monuments into thousands of pieces."[54]

Davis's guns silenced the Confederate batteries as the Southerners began their withdrawal from the beleaguered city, but Davis believed that his guns had caused the Seccessionists to cease firing. "To complete the capture of the city it was necessary to throw troops across the Oostenaula [*sic*]," he explained. He then ordered Colonel Caleb J. Dilworth with his Eighty-Fifth Illinois to cross "on rafts built of rails and logs hastily collected on the bank. The regiment was [*sic*] crossed in an astonishingly short space of time, and soon began to drive in the enemy's pickets in the direction of the city." One veteran of the Eighty-Fifth Illinois explained that the men "placed their arms, ammunition

---

[52] Davis's report, *OR*, ser. 1, vol. 38, pt. 1, 629. By this time, Hoskins's Battery had left Fort Jackson and Rome and was at Cassville with the balance of French's Division. It is likely that this two-gun section that remained to fight in Fort Jackson on the morning of 18 May was Clanton's Alabama battery (see Brewer, *Alabama*, 704; Wheeler, *Confederate Military History*, 8:335). The guns that were located at Fort Stovall on Myrtle Hill were described by the Federals as "heavy guns." According to Davis, "Three field pieces, five 32-pounder garrison guns, and two 8-inch howitzers were abandoned, and fell into our hands" (629).

[53] Davis's report, *OR*, ser. 1, vol. 38, pt. 1, 629.

[54] Brown, Murphy, and Putney, *Behind the Guns*, 140; Billingsley, "Such Is War," 103–104.

and clothing [on the log and rail rafts]," and "then swimming the Oostanaula they pushed these rafts before them to the opposite shore."[55]

"The enemy," according to Davis, "finding himself unexpectedly attacked from a direction which soon must result in his capture, retreated in the most precipitate manner over the Etowah River." Ross's brigade was forced to withdraw from Rome to the south bank of the Etowah River. This opened the door for Davis's Division to capture the "City of Seven Hills" on the afternoon of 18 May, with the Eighty-Fifth Illinois of Colonel Daniel McCook's Third Brigade leading the way. By 2 p.m., McCook's Brigade crossed the river.[56]

Ross's Texans held off the Federals until they were able to burn the bridges and evacuate Rome by 4 p.m. Davis's Division "captured three pieces of field artillery, five 32-pounder garrison guns, and two 8-inch Howitzers, together with large stores of quartermaster, commissary and medical supplies, great quantities of cotton and tobacco, and train loaded with salt, and the extensive ironworks, foundries and machine shops," all located at Rome. The Federals would use the captured guns and forts built to repel them to outfit their own defenses of Rome against Confederate threats for the balance of the war. In addition, Ross and his weary troopers would have to make a twenty-five-plus mile detour south of the Etowah River to reunite with Johnston's army via High Tower Bridge.[57]

Rome Crossroads

Sergeant Magee of the Seventy-Second Indiana Mounted Infantry remembered Wilder's Brigade did not cross over the Oostanaula River at Lay's Ferry until near midnight on 16 May. Division commander Garrard had doubled back from above Rome to join the main body of the Federal army. After receiving Sherman's scolding for his failure either to effect a river crossing or to attack Rome, Garrard now prepared to provide screening duty for

---

[55] *OR*, ser. 1, vol. 38, pt. 1, 629; Aten, *History of the Eighty-Fifth Regiment*, 170–72.

[56] Davis's report, *OR*, ser. 1, vol. 38, pt. 1, 630; Captain James R. Griffith's report for the Eighty-Fifth Illinois, *OR*, ser. 1, vol. 38, pt. 1, 718; Aten, *History of the Eighty-Fifth Regiment*, 170–72; Stewart, *Dan McCook's Regiment*, 103.

[57] Aten, *History of the Eighty-Fifth Regiment*, 170–72; Brown, Murphy, and Putney, *Behind the Guns*, 140; Ross's report, *OR*, ser. 1, vol. 38, pt. 3, 962–63; Kerr, ed., *Fighting with Ross' Texas Cavalry Brigade*, 142–44; Crabb, *All Afire to Fight*, 214–15; Hale, *Third Texas Cavalry*, 219–20.

McPherson's two corps, the XV and XVI, as they moved south of Lay's Ferry. Saddling up early on the morning of Tuesday, 17 May, and prepared to move, Magee said that for some reason his brigade did not leave the area around Lay's Ferry until 4 p.m. During that time, Magee and his fellow troopers examined the battlefield below Lay's Ferry, at a place called Rome Crossroads, where many of McPherson's men had been killed the day before. Some of Hardee's Confederates had fought a delaying action while the two divisions of Major General Grenville Dodge sought unsuccessfully to cut off the Confederate retreat from Resaca and Calhoun. By the end of the bloody Monday, 16 May, at Rome Crossroads, Dodge had lost more than seventy men killed and wounded. The Confederates lost a similar number.[58]

Woodlands

Magee recalled the day's march: "At 4 p.m. our division moved down the river on the east side, toward Rome. We took a direct course through the woods and fields regardless of roads, going through many swamps and sloughs. Bivouacked at 9 p.m., 12 miles from Rome." Wilder's Brigade stopped on the evening of 17 May at "Hermitage."[59]

The next morning, Garrard's two brigades, Wilder's and Minty's, turned to the southeast and headed toward Kingston. After proceeding about eight miles, they came into a "beautiful valley," remembered Magee, "surrounded on three sides by high hills. In this valley lived an English gentleman by the name of Blanchford [*sic*]." Sir Godfrey Barnsley of Liverpool, England, had built an estate modeled after the Italian farm estates of the Tuscany region in the 1840s. Magee continued, "His house was a mansion, and his plantation embraced the whole valley. This delightful situation was six miles from Kingston. When we approached this place Minty's Brigade, in the advance, encountered the rebels, a skirmish ensued, and the pickets were driven in."[60]

Minty's troopers had run into the Alabama and Mississippi cavalry of Brigadier General Samuel Ferguson. While most of the Seventy-Second Indiana was patrolling various roads as pickets, the balance of the regiment dismounted, retrieved their Spencer rifles from their saddles, and prepared to meet the oncoming Confederates. Magee continued, "Immediately our

---

[58] Magee, *History of the 72nd Indiana Volunteer Infantry*, 298; Dodge's report, *OR*, ser. 1, vol. 38, pt. 3, 378–79. For a detail of Confederate losses on 16 May 1864, see the Table of Confederate Casualties at appendix D.

[59] Magee, *History of the 72nd Indiana Volunteer Infantry*, 298.

[60] Ibid.

cavalry [the Fourth Michigan] came hurrying back in confusion, a regiment of Southern cavalry at their heels, yelling like demons; the [Federal] cavalry passed through our brigade and the Johnnies came on like a whirlwind, and when within range of our Spencers we opened on them." He explained that the Southerners came suddenly to a halt when "the colonel leading the charge fell dead from his horse within 10 feet of our lines."[61]

Ferguson's men, some two thousand troopers, came to Georgia as part of Polk's Army of Mississippi. Skirmishing with Brigadier General Kenner Garrard's Second Cavalry Division at Woodlands (today's Barnsley Gardens) on 18 May, Ferguson slowed McPherson's advance toward Kingston from the northwest. Colonel Richard Gordon Earle of the 2nd Alabama Cavalry led a counterstrike against the Federal cavalry, surprising Lt. Colonel Josiah B. Park and his Fourth Michigan Cavalry between Kingston and Woodlands before the blue-clad troopers restored order. As the Confederate horsemen withdrew, Colonel Earle could not be found and was believed to have been captured. Instead, his men later learned from captured Federals that Earle had been killed.[62]

Captain Knox Miller of the 8th Confederate Cavalry remembered a Federal column had "pressed back a brigade [Ferguson's] guarding a road to our left and attempted to get in our rear." Miller noted that General Allen quickly ascertained the situation and "took our [the 8th Confederate cavalry] Regt. & a small detachment of the 3rd Confed. [cavalry] & suddenly fell upon the Yankees left flank. Our Regt. was leading and coming thro' thick woods and] unfortunately received a volley from our own men which threw us into confusion for a moment. We soon rallied," added Knox, "and pressing down on

---

61 Ibid.

62 Garrard's report, *OR*, ser. 1, vol. 38, pt. 2, 803–804; Minty's report, *OR*, ser. 1, vol. 38, pt. 2, 811. Park's report, *OR*, ser. 1, vol. 38, pt. 2, 828. Park reported that he lost three officers wounded and one officer captured, with three men killed, nine wounded, and nine captured, for a total of twenty-five casualties, plus thirty-four horses killed, wounded, or missing. See also Rowland, *Mississippi*, 422, 424, 429; Hatley, *First Texas Legion*, 120; Brewer, *Alabama*, 678, 668, in which the wounding of Captain Thomas D. Hall of the 56th Alabama Mounted Infantry near Kingston is chronicled. See also letters of Hoole, "Letters of Harden Perkins Cochrane," 285–87. On 6 June, Cochrane explained that Col. Earle was missing, and that prisoners reported that "a gray-haired Colonel rode up on four Yankees and ordered them to surrender and they shot him." On 14 June, Cochrane reported that seven horses were wounded and that three men were wounded, two severely, in action by the 2nd Alabama Cavalry near Kingston.

the enemy at a full charge drove him from his ground when they began a hasty retreat." Knox "collected about 20 scattered men and taking a short cut poured a volley into the scoundrels unexpectedly," the Southern captain proudly recalled. "This turned retreat into flight and for six miles we pursued them and scattered their forces in every direction. The first prisoner captured told me that he belonged to the 4th Michigan, & this only gave me new vigor. We drove them until our horses were so fatigued that they could not go faster than a walk."[63]

Writing to his wife, Celestine Miller, two days later, the Confederate cavalry captain saw, "Along the road where the Yankees stampeded there were piled up horses, saddles, & their villainous riders. Some killed by running against trees. Others shot down by our pistols. We killed quite a number." Knox Miller proudly added, "I captured Maj. Grant, a relative of the General, one Capt., one Lt., & some 20 or more privates." Miller's company also captured "five Spenser [*sic*] rifles," some "pistols, saddles," and "several horses."[64]

During the action, Federal trooper John G. Lemmon of the 4th Michigan Cavalry, vividly remembered a horrifying scene. "After discharging all of our magazine," Lemmon recorded in his diary, "we fell back to another hill on the opposite side of the road to [re]load and to repel [the next] attack as before. The sights and sounds of war were becoming painful," he added. "Poor Jones Stark, next man in line [to me], was struck just under the collar bone at the left. His blood poured out in a full stream to a distance of six feet as he turned a ghastly look upon his companions. J. J. Babcock caught him and succeeded in bringing him nearly off of the field." Lemmon remembered that "Sergeant Halfrin Co. H and one of [Co.] K were also killed at this point."[65]

The Fourth Michigan Cavalry had run into an ambush set by some of Ferguson's troopers. In their hasty retreat, the Michigan troopers had led

---

[63] McMurry, *An Uncompromising Secessionist*, 203.

[64] Ibid., 203–204. In footnote 3, McMurry notes that Major Horace D. Grant of the 4th Michigan Cavalry was captured on 18 May, and that his relationship to general, later president, U. S. Grant, if any, is unknown (see *OR* Supp., Serial 41, 818 which claimed "One officer, Major Grant, was cut off from his command and captured," but compare Robertson, *Michigan in the War*, 661, which reported "Captain [not Major] Grant, having been cut off from his command, was taken prisoner." Also, "Among the wounded were Major [Richard R.] Robbins and Lieutenants [Julius M.] Carter and Randolph—the latter mortally, and on the 30th [of May] he died of his wounds.").

[65] Lemmon, "Memoirs," 1866, entry for 19 May 1864, Special Collections, Huntington Library, San Marino, CA, courtesy David A. Powell.

Colonel Earle and his Alabamians into an unanticipated Federal trap. The 2nd Alabama Cavalry lost one killed (Colonel Earle) and five wounded, while Ferguson's Brigade saw five men killed, nineteen wounded, and four missing during the action. Lieutenant Colonel J. B. Park, commander of the Fourth Michigan, remembered losing three men killed and twelve wounded with ten captured along with thirty-four horses killed, wounded, and missing. "The enemy's loss must have been severe," he noted, "5 were seen to fall at a single volley, and 7 others were seen to fall within a few yards of our lines."[66]

In the meantime, portions of Colonel John T. Wilder's Third Mounted Infantry "Lightning Brigade" struck the Confederate telegraph and rail lines. Six companies of the Seventeenth Indiana Cavalry led by Lieutenant Colonel Henry Jordan were, according to Garrard, "detached to cut the railroad and telegraph wire from Rome to Kingston, which was accomplished [albeit too late to prevent the movement by the rest of French's Division from Rome the evening before]. They also captured a wagon and 3 rebel soldiers," he proudly added. "The railroad was cut near the mouth of Bradley Creek" (also known as Barnsley Creek, today called Tom's Creek) on the Etowah River. Also, "from Woodlands [Barnsley Gardens] Major [Jacob G.]Vail, with four companies of the 17th Indiana, was sent to cut the telegraph between Adairsville and Kingston, two miles north of Kingston. They skirmished up to the railroad," explained Garrard, "and under the fire of a rebel battery cut the telegraph wire."[67]

Kingston

On 18 May, Brigadier General William Wirt Allen's brigade, which included the 3rd, 5th, 10th, 11th, and 12th Confederate cavalry regiments, defended Kingston. Allen's men were made up of men mostly from Alabama and were a part of Major General John H. Kelly's division of Wheeler's Corps. During the skirmishing of 18 May, Captain Georg Knox Miller of Company A, 8th Confederate cavalry, remembered engaging the enemy near Kingston,

[66] The biographer for the Fourth Michigan recorded three men killed, three officers and sixteen men wounded, and ten more men missing (Robertson, *Michigan in the War*, 661; Brewer, *Alabama*, 678–79; Cochrane, letter to his wife, in Hoole, "Letters of Harden Perkins Cochrane," 287; Rowland, *Mississippi*, 421–22, 426, 433, 457–58; Park's report, *OR*, ser. 1, vol. 38, pt. 2, 828; *OR Supp.*, pt. 2, vol. 29, 818).

[67] Garrard's report, *OR*, ser. 1, vol. 38, pt. 2, 806. The identity of this battery has not been determined.

"routing and pursuing, saber in hand, six miles." In the action, Private Lee of Company I, 8th Confederate Cavalry was wounded.[68]

Meanwhile, in Kingston, after two weeks of marching and fighting, and spending the past three days of defending the rear of the army from Resaca, Calhoun, and Adairsville, Cleburne's Division was exhausted and needed a good and unmolested night's sleep. "Had whiskey issued to us last night," remembered Captain Samuel T. Foster of Granbury's Brigade, "and for once we did not move. Had a good night's rest, and this morning heard some good news from the Army in Va. and also in La." John Jackman of the Kentucky "Orphan Brigade" of Bate's Division remembered that they also were issued "'spiroots,' which the boys appreciate, after being exposed to inclement weather—at 10 p.m." Soldier Robert Davis Smith recorded, "I slept 7 hours last night and feel like another man today." Perhaps the shot of whiskey had something to do with it; then again, perhaps the chance to sleep outside the zone of enemy shell and skirmish fire for the first time in ten days was the cause. Regardless, the men of Cleburne's Division, the watchdog of the army and regarded as the best of them, were happy to have the sorely needed night of rest.[69]

At 5 a.m. on 19 May, Major General David S. Stanley's First Division of Howard's IV Corps was up and by sunrise was on the move toward Kingston. Brigadier General Walter C. Whitaker's Second Brigade "was in advance of the army," according to Whitaker, who explained that he placed the Ninety-Ninth Ohio on the right of the Twenty-First Kentucky Federal, which was in the center. The Ninety-Sixth Illinois occupied the left of the front line with its right along the railroad. In the second line, the Eighty-Fourth Indiana was placed on the right and the Thirty-Fifth Indiana formed on the left with both Hoosier regiments serving as flankers.[70]

Captain Evangelist Gilmore of the Ninety-Sixth Illinois remembered, "the 96th [Illinois] was in the lead of a column which marched along the line of the railroad. A half hour after the start the Confederates were encountered. One Company after another was sent into the skirmish line until most of the command was deployed." Gilmore's regiment was a part of Whitaker's Brigade. "At Kingston, which was the junction of the Rome branch of the main line of the Railroad from Chattanooga, the Confederates opened up on the

---

[68] *OR Supp.*, pt. 2, vol. 73, 292, 302.

[69] N. D. Brown, ed., *One of Cleburne's Command*, 78; Jackman, *Diary of a Confederate Soldier*, 126–27; R. D. Smith, *Confederate Diary of Robert D. Smith*, 129.

[70] Whitaker's report, *OR*, ser. 1, vol. 38, pt. 1, 242.

advancing troops with artillery. The skirmishers however kept up the advance and soon were threatening to flank them. At this point," explained the Illinois veteran, "the artillery moved back. Skirmishing was very severe and even approached what would be called a battle. They were ordered to stay near the railroad, so the line swung to the left and moved rapidly forward. The rebels stopped at every road and ridge and compelled the Ninety-Sixth Illinois to keep up a heavy fire constantly."[71]

Allen's Southern horsemen continued to harass the advance of Howard's men on the Kingston Road, contesting his progress, before retiring to the main Confederate line at Cassville by midday. With the withdrawal of Allen's and Ferguson's troopers and Polk's Brigade from Cleburne's Division, Kingston was open for the arrival of Howard's IV Corps by 8:30 on the morning of Thursday, 19 May.

---

[71] Gilmore, Ninety-Sixth Illinois Infantry, 120. Gilmore would be mortally wounded on 20 June and die on 24 June 1864 in action before Kennesaw Mountain at a place called Bald Hill by one Federal account (see report of Lieutenant Colonel William T. Chapman, *OR*, ser. 1, vol. 38, pt. 1, 238).

Chapter 4

Correcting the Errors in the *Official Records*

General John Bell Hood submitted his report of operations to adjutant and inspector general Samuel Cooper on 15 February 1865, at Richmond, Virginia. Following his description of events while he was in command of the Confederate Army of Tennessee from 18 July 1864 to 23 January 1865, Hood added an explanation of his conduct at several controversial places when he had been in command of a corps during the first half of the Atlanta Campaign under the leadership of General Joseph E. Johnston. Hood had by then seen Johnston's report, written 20 October 1864, from Vineville, Georgia, near Macon. Included in Hood's comments was a detailed explanation of his conduct at Cassville, which had become one of the greatest sources of contention between the two generals. In the version as published in the *Official Records*, Hood quoted Johnston: "You can, if you desire, move your corps to the *Canton Road* and if *Howard's corps* is there you can attack it."[1]

Two important statements made in this quote have discredited Hood over the past century and a half. First, the evidence is clear that Howard's IV Corps was west of Cassville, not east of it, as his corps traveled from Adairsville south to Kingston and then east toward Cassville. Hood's confusion about the identity of the Federal troops that he was supposed to attack, as well as the Northerners who appeared on his flank and rear, will be addressed herein. The second, and more curious statement, has to do with the reference to the Canton Road. Clearly, Canton Road is east of Cassville, and certainly not north or northwest of the village, in the direction of the expected advance by the Union troops from Adairsville.

In contrast, in Hood's postwar account, *Advance and Retreat*, he referred to a road he called the Ironton Road, a name that appears to have been ignored or not understood in all previous studies of Cassville. In *Advance and Retreat*, Hood explained that "Howard's Corps having been reported on the *Ironton Road* (the *country road* referred to [by Johnston]), I asked his authorization to march my command across an open field, and attack this

[1] General John B. Hood's report, *OR*, ser. 1, vol. 38, pt. 3, 635. Emphasis added.

detachment of the enemy, in case the report was correct. He consented."[2] Hood's statement presents another question, that of whether Hood requested permission to make the attack or whether Johnston ordered Hood to attack. It also sheds light on the difference between the two generals' understandings of the plan of the attack. This, too, will be addressed herein.

Hood assumed that Johnston's use of the term "country road" in his *Narrative* was in reference to the Ironton Road. Johnston was instead referring to the road that Hood's Corps took on their way to cross Two Run Creek and the large, open field, as demonstrated by Johnston's sketch map. Johnston drew a map that accompanied a letter dated 18 June 1874 to Charles Johnsen. In it, Johnston showed the "country road" at a different location from the Ironton Road. Johnston's "country road" was east of Cassville, at the location of today's Brown Loop Road (Road 3a). This is the road on which Hood marched his column out of town, and after passing through the gap on today's Brown Loop Road, crossed Two Run Creek on a log bridge. The front of his column then proceeded north across a large, open field *toward* the Ironton Road. Hood would never see the map drawn by Johnston in 1874, as it was not published until it appeared in the *Times Picayune* on Sunday, 22 October 1893, fourteen years after Hood's death. If Hood had seen the map, he would have been able to clarify that Johnston's "country road" was the road *on* which his men had marched to conceal themselves behind the two ridges before crossing Two Run Creek and proceeding across the large, open field on their way *to* the Ironton Road.[3]

If Hood intended to refer to the Canton Road for his planned attack, as the published version of his report in the *Official Records* indicates, there is no plausible explanation. Either Hood was mistaken in the identity of the road, or he was misleading the reader by using it. These are the explanations that all prior studies have apparently concluded, perhaps because no one has looked beyond the *Official Records* to consult original manuscripts, nor has anyone determined the identity or location of the Ironton Road to which Hood referred to in his postwar account, *Advance and Retreat*. In his response to Johnston's *Narrative of Military Operations*, written in 1874, Hood referred

---

[2] Hood, *Advance and Retreat*, 99. In *Advance and Retreat*, Hood responded to the statements Johnston had published in 1874 (Johnston, *Narrative of Military Operations*, 320–22).

[3] Johnston to Johnsen, 19 June 1874, 319; also, *New Orleans Times Picayune*, 22 October 1893. This map is reproduced herein with the express thanks to the *Times Picayune* for this valuable map, heretofore lost to history.

to the Ironton Road three times while also linking it to the "country road" that Johnston described in his *Narrative*. Johnston explained that "Hood was directed to move with his corps to a *country road* about a mile to the east of that from Adairsville, and parallel to it, right in front."[4]

Hood distinguished his reference to the Ironton Road as the road *toward* which his corps was to march and prepare for an attack, a road that Hood said was the same road that Johnston called the "country road." Also, the "country road" described by Johnston was one that ran parallel with the Adairsville-Cassville Road, and about a mile to the east of it. Hood explained that unknown Federal forces appeared on his right *and* rear. He specifically referred, in his wartime report and in his postwar writing, to the unexpected Northern force, or forces, as being on his right on the Spring Place Road, and on his rear on the Canton Road.[5] Clearly, the Ironton Road was *not* the same as the Canton Road. And, clearly, the Ironton Road was one that ran in a northerly direction from Cassville and paralleled the Adairsville-Cassville Road, about a mile to the east of it while the Canton Road ran to the east from Cassville. Further, the Ironton Road was also not the Spring Place Road Hood referred to, as will be seen herein.

In searching for the original manuscript, or an earlier version of Hood's report dated 15 February 1865, I discovered a copy of a *New York Times* article dated 29 March 1865, in which Hood's report had been copied from a *Richmond Enquirer* edition dated 25 March 1865 and republished in its entirety. Apparently, Hood's report to the Confederate War Department dated 15 February 1865 had found its way to the Richmond, Virginia, press, and had been published there on 25 March 1865. Then, a captured copy of the Southern newspaper had made its way to the *New York Times*, where it was republished on 29 March 1865. Remarkably, this was just forty-two days after its submission by Hood to the Confederate government. In the *New York Times* version, Hood's quote of Johnston reads, "You can, if you desire, move with your corps to the *Ironton Road*, and if Howard's corps is there you can attack it." Just a few lines later, the Ironton Road is referenced a second time in lieu of the Canton Road.[6]

---

[4] Johnston, *Narrative of Military Operations*, 321. Emphasis added.

[5] See Hood's report, *OR*, ser. 1, vol. 38, pt. 3, 635; Hood, *Advance and Retreat*, 100.

[6] "Gen. Hood's Report of the Operations of the Army of the Tennessee," *New York Times*, 29 March 1859, https://www.nytimes.com/1865/03/29/archives/news-from-the-south-gen-hoods-report-of-the-operations-of-the-army.html, accessed 31

In Hood's *Advance and Retreat*, published in 1880 following his death the previous year, a copy of his report was included in the appendix. Presumably, this version is derived from his personal copy of his report. This version also includes the mention of Ironton Road in the same two places.[7] There can be no mistake that Hood referred to the Ironton Road as the intended point of his attack, and that it was clearly different from the Canton Road. The reason Hood failed to correct the *Official Records* error is obvious; the five volumes on the Atlanta Campaign were not published until 1891, more than a decade after his death. He never saw it and could never have anticipated the confusion it would cause for future historians. He did provide an ironic admonition to Johnston in his *Advance and Retreat*, however, about the importance of leaving a full and accurate "contribution for the use of the future historian."[8] Whether his former chieftain, Old Joe (as some of his men referred to him), would follow this warning is about to be tested in the next point.

The second and most troubling revelation concerning errors related to the Confederate controversies at Cassville is found in T. B. Mackall's journal as published in the *Official Records*.[9] Lieutenant Thomas Bennett Mackall was a cousin to Brigadier General William Whann Mackall, Johnston's chief of staff during the Atlanta Campaign. Young Lt. Mackall kept a series of unofficial notes in a journal that served as the apparent basis for document Number 728 in the *Official Records*. It was purported to be a "Journal of Operations of the Army of Tennessee May 14—June 4 [1864]." This report notably was "kept at headquarters Army of Tennessee by Lieut. T. B. Mackall, aide-de-camp to Brig. Gen. W.W. Mackall, chief of staff, and *furnished by General J. E. Johnston*." It is important to note that the secretary of war and the Board of Publications Staff of the War Department, which oversaw the publication of the 128-volume *Official Records*, added the clarification that this document, or journal, was furnished by General J. E. Johnston. This statement in itself should raise suspicions of future historians.[10]

July 2023. In the caption of the article, "the" was erroneously included before "Tennessee." Federal armies were named thus, "Sherman's Army of the Tennessee," named after the river. But in the Confederacy, armies were named after states, thus "Hood's Army of Tennessee." Emphasis added.

[7] Hood, *Advance and Retreat*, 334.

[8] Ibid., 104.

[9] *OR* ser. 1, vol. 38, pt. 3, 978–91.

[10] Ibid., 978. Emphasis added.

In his research of the Joseph E. Johnston papers held in the repository of the Special Collections Library at William & Mary College, Williamsburg, Virginia, Richard M. McMurry discovered two previously unidentified diaries, or portions of diaries, that appear to be from the same handwriting source. After determining that these are the original diaries of Lieutenant Mackall, McMurry conducted a thorough study of the journal and published his findings in 1974.

One diary, referred to as the "A" sample by McMurry in his published findings, appears to be the original, while the second account, the "B" sample, appears to have been written by the same person as a revision (or more complete version) of "A." In other words, in the "A" sample, there are more abbreviations while more complete sentences appeared in the "B" source, but with many of the same terms from "A." In comparisons with other known sources, it was determined that T. B. Mackall wrote both the "A" and "B" documents.

McMurry also discovered at least two other T. B. Mackall–related writings. The first one was from the J. P. Nicholson Collection of Joseph E. Johnston Papers at the Henry E. Huntington Library in San Marino, California, in which a detailed set of entries for 14 May and 15 May concerning the Confederate activities during the Battle of Resaca appeared to have been written by T. B. Mackall. The second, a manuscript found in the National Archives in Washington, D.C., was not dated, but appeared to have been written by at least two other people and did *not* appear to be the same handwriting of T. B. Mackall.

McMurry labeled the Huntington document as "H" for comparison, and the one found in the National Archives written by two persons (who were not T. B. Mackall) as "N" for National Archives. This "N," or manuscript version, was different from the other three sources labeled "A," "B," and "H," all of which were clearly written by T. B. Mackall. Importantly, this "N" version was the one that was presented by Johnston to the War Department and published in the *Official Records*. McMurry refers to the published *Official Records* version as "O" in his conclusions.[11]

In the original, or "A" version, of the Mackall Journal, the following entry was recorded for 19 May:

> "Heard first skirmishing on Adairsv[ille]. & Cassv[ille] rd. 10:20 AM. In ten minut[es], artillery on Sp[rin]g. Place road & on Ad[airsville] rd. After a few guns Genl. M[ackall] sent [word] more en[em]y close to H[ood] on

[11] McMurry, "The Mackall Journal and Its Antecedents," 311–28.

> Canton rd. Lt. Genls sent for. Wagons moved [to] rear. Line changed 2:25 PM. Change going on. Artillery on Hardee's front. Change of line effected under fire. Report of column on Canton Road not afterwards confirmed. Battle expected next day. General Ross reports from Cartersville enemy across at Wooley's Bridge.[12]

In the rewritten, or "B" version, of the Mackall Journal, the following entry was recorded for 19 May: "Line of battle formed to attack enemy. First skirmishing on Adairsville & Cassville road 10:20 AM. Ten minutes later artillery heard in direction of Spring Place road. After a few discharges report recd. from Genl. Hood that enemy was advancing on Canton road. Line of battle changed. At night army withdrawn."[13]

In contrast, the published *Official Records* version, or "O" version as McMurry describes it, is much longer than the "A" version. A substantial amount of additional information was added to the "O" sample, which was more than seven times longer than the original "A" sample. The "O" sample contains seventy-four lines of typed manuscript, whereas the "A" sample consists of only ten lines, and the corresponding entry for 19 May in the "B" sample is only five lines of typed manuscript. The "O" sample also contains several assertions negative to Hood that are not found in either the "A" or "B" samples.

For purposes of this study, however, the focus is on the subtle, but important, differences between the samples as to time, place, and manner in which events are described—that is, what T. B. Mackall said that he saw and heard, and when and where events occurred from his perspective, as written in his own handwriting. Critically, the published *Official Records*, "O" version, changed the first report of sounds of battle at 10:20 a.m. from "heard first skirmishing on the Adairsville & Cassville Road," as it appeared in the "A" version,[14] to "a few discharges of artillery on Adairsville and Cassville Road, and in ten minutes *report* of artillery in *easterly* direction."[15]

---

[12] Mackall Journal, "A" sample, 5 May–31 July 1864.

[13] Mackall Journal, "B" sample, 1 May–9 July 1864.

[14] Mackall Journal, "A" sample, 5 May–31 July 1864.

[15] The "O" sample, *OR*, ser. 1, vol. 38, pt. 3, 983. In his article, "The Mackall Journal and Its Antecedents," McMurry cautioned historians against relying upon the "O" sample of the Mackall Journal due to its inherent corruption (327–28). However, in applying the evidentiary standard, its inclusion, or admission, by Johnston permits its use when a statement contained therein provides an inference which would tend to impeach Johnston's position, or to repudiate his contradictory statements. In courts, it is called an admission by a party opponent. While I did not begin this study

While it may seem like an innocent series of changes from T. B. Mackall's original diary accounts, these changes substantially altered the meaning and understanding of the circumstances at Cassville during the morning of 19 May. First, the *Official Records* version dropped the all-important word "heard" from the original versions. In other words, T. B. Mackall, from his position at Johnston's morning headquarters east of Cassville, recorded that he first *heard* skirmish fire from the Adairsville & Cassville Road at 10:20 a.m. This agreed with other reports of contact along that route at that time between Brigadier General William Ward's Federal brigade of Hooker's XX Corps and troopers of Brigadier General Alfred Iverson's Georgia brigade and Brigadier General William Y.C. Humes's division of Confederate cavalry.[16]

Second, T. B. Mackall reported that he *heard* artillery ten minutes later from the Spring Place Road. This supported the account of Brigadier General Edward M. McCook, who was commanding a division of Federal cavalry that approached Cassville that morning from the Spring Place Road, and the account of Lieutenant William B. Rippetoe, who led a two-gun section of the Eighteenth Indiana Battery of three-inch ordnance rifles, which accompanied McCook along the Spring Place Road that morning. It also agreed with Hood's account of events east of Cassville, as well as the accounts of multiple officers under Hood.[17]

These changes and others found in the published "O" sample were not accidental slights or oversights, but deliberate attempts to mask from history the true nature of the events that occurred. Removing the term "heard" from

---

in a manner adverse to Johnston's position, in the process of following the evidence and in cross-examining each piece of primary source material, I concluded that the use of both T. B. Mackall's journal, all samples, as well as the use of William Mackall's "Memoranda," provided multiple opportunities for the impeachment of Johnston's claims at Cassville. Emphasis added. See Appendix F for a comparison of the "A," "B," and "O" samples.

[16] Ward's report, *OR*, ser. 1, vol. 38, pt. 2, 342; Colonel F. S. Smith's report (102nd Illinois), *OR*, ser. 1, vol. 38, pt. 2, 353; Colonel Daniel Dustin's report (105th Illinois), *OR*, ser. 1, vol. 38, pt. 2, 361; Colonel Benjamin Harrison's report (Seventieth Indiana), *OR*, ser. 1, vol. 38, pt. 2, 372; Captain Samuel A. West (Seventy-Ninth Ohio) *OR*, ser. 1, vol. 38, pt. 2, 376; Wheeler, *OR*, ser. 1, vol. 38, pt. 3, 946; Mackall Journal, "A" sample.

[17] McCook, *OR*, ser. 1, vol. 38, pt. 2, 752. Compare to Rippetoe's report in which he claimed artillery began shelling the enemy at about 10 a.m. (See *OR*, ser. 1, vol. 38, pt. 2, 801; Hood, *Advance and Retreat*, 98–103. See also Manigault and Tower, *A Carolinian Goes to War*, 185–86.)

the published account raised a level of doubt that T. B. Mackall ever heard anything but instead simply recorded what Hood reported.

The subtle changes to the account also led to other unfortunate consequences in the subsequent understanding of events. Ward's Brigade did not initially have artillery in support. The Southern troopers, however, did have artillery covering Ward's approach, which accounts for the artillery sounds that Mackall heard from the northwest, or Adairsville and Cassville Road, around 10:30 a.m., ten minutes after the first skirmish fire was heard from the northwest. Lt. Rippetoe reported that he opened with two guns from his position on the road, which was the Spring Place Road to the northeast, on the Confederate infantry of Major General Thomas C. Hindman's division, which was in a large field. This accounts for the sounds of artillery heard by T. B. Mackall at 10:30 a.m. from *both* directions and is supported by multiple reports.[18]

Equally important were the changes in the "O" sample relative to the events to the east, or on the Spring Place and Canton Roads. In the "A" and "B" samples, Mackall reported that he *heard* artillery about 10:30 a.m. on the Spring Place Road. In the *Official Records* account, not only were no artillery *heard* (only a *report* of artillery), but the reference to Spring Place Road was dropped, leaving merely a "report of artillery in *easterly* direction."[19] In changing "Spring Place Road" to "easterly," the writer of this entry in the "O" sample as published in the *Official Records*, understood and verified that the artillery heard at 10:30 a.m. was *east* of Cassville. Since Johnston submitted the "N" sample to the Board of Publication of the *Official Records,* which then formed the basis for the "O" sample, Johnston affirmed by its inclusion that the artillery heard at 10:30 a.m. referred to by T. B. Mackall was east of Cassville. Additionally, by its alteration, T. B. Mackall understood that the Spring

---

[18] Ward's report, *OR*, ser. 1, vol. 38, pt. 2, 342; Colonel F. S. Smith's report (102nd Illinois), *OR*, ser. 1, vol. 38, pt. 2, 353; Colonel Daniel Dustin's report (105th Illinois), *OR*, ser. 1, vol. 38, pt. 2, 361; Colonel Benjamin Harrison's report (Seventieth Indiana), *OR*, ser. 1, vol. 38, pt. 2, 372; Captain Samuel A. West's report (Seventy-Ninth Ohio), *OR*, ser. 1, vol. 38, pt. 2, 376; Wheeler's report, *OR*, ser. 1, vol. 38, pt. 3, 946; Mackall Journal, "A" sample, "O" sample, *OR*, ser. 1, vol. 38, pt. 3, 983. See also Hood's report, *OR*, ser. 1, vol. 38, pt. 3, 635; Manigault and Tower, *A Carolinian Goes to War*, 185–86.

[19] Merriam Webster gives one definition of "report" as "an explosive noise," but I do not believe this was the intended meaning by the alteration.

Place Road was *east* of Cassville (in its correct location), and that Johnston believed that the Spring Place Road was located somewhere else.[20]

Vital to the analysis of the failed Cassville Offensive is the correct location of the Spring Place Road. Most previous studies have shied away from determining a specific location due to the conflicting information in accounts. A previous study by William Scaife notably claimed that it was at today's Cedar Creek Road, but this location does not match any of the other contemporaneous accounts except for the altered T. B. Mackall, "O" sample account supplied by Johnston. It does not conform with Hood's detailed description of the Spring Place Road as being to his right flank along with the Canton Road to his rear. It is not consistent with McCook's description, nor of those of his subordinates. And it does not fit the current location of the route of the Spring Place Road, which can still be found today in Bartow County, Georgia. With several antebellum houses still surviving today along this road, the route has remained largely unchanged since its early settlement dating back to the Dewey Crossroads Community with the Dewey Baptist Church in the 1850s.[21]

However, the "report of artillery in [an] easterly direction" in the *Official Records* account, which supplanted the "artillery heard in direction of Spring Place road" of both the "A" and "B" original diaries, when compared to all other contemporaneous accounts except the altered, "O" sample journal necessarily placed the location of the Spring Place Road *east* of Cassville, or northeast of it, and east of Hood's march that morning, not north or northwest of the town, which was the intended destination of Hood's attack. In other words, both the "A" and the "B" samples agree with all the other contemporaneous sources as well as with the geography of the area. Johnston's inclusion of the "O" sample, with its alteration of the Spring Place Road reference, was additional affirmation that 1. T. B. Mackall heard artillery at 10:30 a.m. east of Cassville and in a direction that was unexpected and threatened the Confederate rear; and 2. Johnston's understanding of the location of Spring Place Road was different from T. B. Mackall's (and Hood's, and McCook's, and all of the other contemporaneous accounts).[22]

---

[20] *OR*, ser. 1, vol. 38, pt. 3, 983.

[21] Thomas McCreary was buried at Dewey Baptist Church Cemetery on Spring Place Road in 1858, as was Henry McCreary in 1861 (author's field study, 28 August 2022); "Dewey Baptist Church Cemetery."

[22] This conclusion may be reached by a comparison of the three samples of T. B. Mackall's journal, "A," "B," and "O" samples.

After accounting for the discrepancies in the *Official Records* version of the Mackall Journal, and after correctly substituting the Ironton Road from the original manuscript account, instead of the Canton Road from the published *Official Records* version, the pieces began to fit together and provide a clearer, more accurate, picture of the events at Cassville.

Chapter 5

Cartography and the Confusing Roads across the Gravelly Plateau

The Gravelly Plateau is a formidable and rugged, high dome-like ridge that spans for eight miles north to south between Adairsville and Cassville and is about fifteen miles wide from east to west between Pine Log and Hall Station (located between Adairsville and Kingston, on Road 8). Prior to the advent of bulldozers following the turn of the twentieth century, a rail line typically ran along the lowest and most level terrain possible. This caused engineer Stephen H. Long, commissioned in 1836 by Georgia governor Wilson Lumpkin, to lay out the Western & Atlantic Railroad from Adairsville to Kington instead of directly to Cassville across the Gravelly Plateau.[1] In addition, the early residents of the village of Cassville did not want for their town to become "demoralized—nor their horses frightened—by having a railroad through the town," so the rail line was built two miles south of the village, and the Cass Station Depot was established there.[2]

According to the traditional interpretation of Johnston's battle plan, two roads led south from Adairsville. The first followed the Western & Atlantic Railroad directly south for eleven miles to Kingston. This was the Adairsville-Kingston Road, today called Hall Station Road (Road 8). At Kingston, the Western & Atlantic Railroad joined a spur rail line from Rome to the west and turned abruptly east to Cass Station, before continuing southeast to the Etowah River at Hightower Bridge, and then south through the Allatoona Mountains. Kingston and Cassville formed the bottom of the triangle, separated by seven miles, and the Kingston-Cassville Road (Road 9) is known today as the Kingston Highway (Ga. Hwy 293) and Fire Tower Road.

The second road led southeast from Adairsville to Cassville, ten miles away. This was the Adairsville-Cassville Road, today known as US 41, or Joe Frank Harris Parkway (Road 1). However, the assumption that this was the only road that led to Cassville from Adairsville is erroneous, and it has caused students of the Cassville Affair to ignore the additional roads that led to Cassville from the northeast and east, across which access may be gained from Adairsville. Hood understood the geography. However, Johnston apparently

---

[1] J. H. Johnston, *Western and Atlantic Railroad.*

[2] Cunyus, *History of Bartow County*, 19–21, 29.

did not, and many students of history have not either—or have been duped over the years by Johnston's alleged battle plan.

Several additional roads led to Cassville from east of Adairsville, one at Iron Mountain (east of today's I-75 at the Adairsville Exit 306), and one at Mosteller's (or Marstellar's) Mill. These two roads merged on the Gravely Plateau at Pleasant Valley and continued south to Cassville on what was called the Copper Mine Road by Wheeler, the Ironton Road by Hood, and by the Old Spring Place Road by some historians (Scaife and Kurtz). These roads (Road 2, 2a, and 2b) are the source of much of the confusion and controversy surrounding the failed Confederate offensive at Cassville. They have been called various names by Confederate and Federal officers, as well as by historians in the intervening years. Identified as road numbers 2, 2a, and 2b in the accompanying maps, the Copper Mine Road, Mosteller's Mill Road, and Ironton Road will be addressed in detail.[3]

To the east, Adairsville is linked to Pine Log by a road (known today as US Highway 140 but known as the Adairsville-Pine Log-Canton Road at the time of the Civil War) that passes Iron Mountain and continues to Mosteller's Mill. This road, identified as road number 7, continues east-southeast to Gum Springs, where it crosses the Spring Place Road and continues southeast to Pine Log and joins the Tennessee Road (today's US Hwy 411, Road 6) just east of Pine Log. The Tennessee Road, identified as road number 6, was the original Jackson Military Road constructed in 1825. It is also known as the Old Federal Road in several locations in north Georgia.

I discovered that the Confederate cavalry maps show only four roads leading into Cassville on an arc between Adairsville and Canton, as may be envisioned between 11 o'clock to 3 o'clock on the face of the clock and omit the Spring Place Road (Road 3), while the Federal maps of Merrill, Ruger, Van Horne and Dodge, as shown in the *Official Atlas to the OR,* each show five roads including the Spring Place Road (Road 3). Also, in his report of his deployment of troopers from Adairsville to the Canton Road, Wheeler only covered four roads with his cavalry screen, not five. [4]

---

[3] Hood explained that he and Polk had urged a counterattack at or near Adairsville on 18 May, the day before, because "our three corps could move back, each upon a separate road, while the enemy had but one main road upon which he could approach that place" (Hood's report, *OR*, ser. 1, vol. 38, pt. 3, 634). See also Hood, *Advance and Retreat*, 99; Wynne and Taylor, *This War So Horrible*, 73–74.

[4] Wheeler's report, *OR*, ser. 1, vol. 38, pt. 3, 946. Compare the Martin Map with the Merrill Map. Additional sources consulted for the base map include Wilbur

In 1933, artist and cartographer, Wilbur G. Kurtz, who was also the Atlanta City Manager, a Civil War historian and Atlanta Campaign expert, drew a map of Cassville that appeared in Lucy Cunyus's *History of Bartow County*. Called "Kurtz Map 1" in this text, Kurtz drew only four roads on the Adairsville-Canton Road arc, and he included a reference to a Spring Place Road in the location of Road 2 to Mosteller's Mill (shown as Road 2 and 2a). Kurtz failed to include the Spring Place Road (Road 3) on this map. Apparently, Kurtz was relying on the incomplete "Foster Map," and the inaccurate "Martin Map" and "Wheeler Map," and perhaps the "Johnston Map," none of which had included the Spring Place Road.[5]

In 1949, after studying Cassville for thirteen additional years, and after spending fifty hours drawing it, Kurtz completed a new map. In his new map, Kurtz refrained from including a reference to Spring Place at Road 2 and added a fifth road in the correct location for the Spring Place Road (Road 3) northeast of Cassville. He correctly connected this road with the Pine Log Road (Road 4) at the Five Forks intersection. It is called the "Kurtz Map 2" in this study.[6]

Unfortunately, historian and cartographer Bill Scaife found the Kurtz Map 1 and relied on it while producing his map of the morning of 19 May 1864, which was first published in 1992. In what this text refers to as the "Scaife Map 1," Scaife incorrectly labeled the Copper Mine/Ironton Road (Road 2) as the Spring Place Road, apparently because of the reference to Spring Place in Kurtz Map 1. Scaife also incorrectly placed the modern Shotgun Road in the location of today's Brown Loop Road (Road 3a) and with Spring Place Road (Road 3). Shotgun Road connects Brown Loop Road and Cedar Creek Road.[7]

Prior to the beginning of the Atlanta Campaign, Confederate engineers worked on a series of maps of northwest Georgia. Commissioned on 1 November 1863 by General Braxton Bragg when he was in command of the

---

G. Kurtz's 1949 hand-drawn map prepared for Colonel Thomas Spencer (hereafter "Kurtz Map 2"). Also consulted was a map prepared by Captain Walter J. Morris, *Atlas to the OR*, Plate 62, Map 7 (hereafter "Morris Map"). This map features prominently in the Evening Cassville Controversy concerning the Confederate defensive operations at Cassville during the evening of 19 May 1864. Also consulted were the maps prepared by William R. Scaife, one each for the Morning and Evening Affairs (hereafter "Scaife Map 1" [Morning Affair] and "Scaife Map 2" [Evening Affair]).

[5] Cunyus, *History of Bartow County*, 233; Kurtz Map 1.

[6] Kurtz Map 2.

[7] Scaife Map 1; Scaife Map 2.

Southern Army of Tennessee, the engineering department was tasked with creating a set of maps from the Tennessee-Georgia border at Missionary Ridge to Rome and Atlanta, Georgia, along the Western & Atlantic Railroad, and for ten miles on either side. Captain Wilbur F. Foster led the task force which completed their assignment and delivered a set of maps to Johnston and his army in Dalton just before the campaign began. It included five maps. A portion of Captain Foster's map covering the area between Adairsville, Cassville and Kingston, is included in this study as the "Foster Map." An enlargement of a section of the Foster Map, which includes a reference to the Copper Mine Road, is also provided.[8]

Unfortunately, because the purpose of these maps was to cover a ten-mile span on either side of the Western & Atlantic Railroad, and because the railroad extended from Adairsville to Kingston and not Cassville, Major Foster's maps did not cover the area northeast of Cassville, area that included the new Spring Place Road (Road 3), the Five Forks intersection (the confluence of Roads 3 and 4), or the upper Two Run Creek valley. Also, subsequent Confederate maps failed to include the connection of the Spring Place Road with the Pine Log Road at Five Forks. The map prepared for Major General Will Martin, called the "Martin Map," and the map prepared for Wheeler, called the "Wheeler Map," both failed to include the connection of the Spring Place Road with the Pine Log Road. Even the map used by Johnston in his *Narrative*, published ten years after the events at Cassville, failed to include the area northeast of Cassville, and failed to include the Spring Place Road.[9]

Johnston apparently relied on the incomplete Foster map and/or its succeeding maps, the Martin and Wheeler maps, during the events at Cassville. Ten years after the war, Johnston was still relying on these maps as he wrote

---

[8] Foster, "Battlefield Maps in Georgia," 369–70. Captain Foster received his instructions to make a series of maps from Brigadier General Danville Leadbetter who had been made chief engineer on 23 October 1863 (see *OR*, ser. 1, vol. 31, pt. 3, 561). Bragg apparently ordered Leadbetter between 23 October and 1 November 1863, to get a detail of engineers started on the "10 mile" road maps on either side of the railroad from Missionary Ridge to Atlanta and Rome. Foster was subsequently promoted to major on 17 March 1864 (see Porter, *Tennessee*, 480).

[9] Foster Map, Martin Map, and Wheeler Map. "Johnston *Narrative* Map" is not to be confused with his sketch map as published in the *Times Picayune*. Both maps are provided in the exhibits. The Johnston *Narrative* Map fails to include the area northeast of Cassville, which would become a vital oversight as the events of the morning of 19 May 1864, unfolded from that direction.

his *Narrative*, a factor that provides further evidence of his lack of knowledge and understanding of the road network around Cassville.

In discussing historical roads, an important point should be addressed. Today, formal directions refer to the specific (or US Post Office–approved) name of a road while local citizens may refer to it by a more traditional name. For example, the main street in downtown Dalton, Georgia, is called "Hamilton Street," named for the civil engineer who oversaw the construction of the Western & Atlantic Railroad in north Georgia, but local residents often refer to it as "Main Street."

In the mid-1800s, residents often referred to a road based on where it would lead from their location, or perhaps based on the name of a mill, house, or other feature on the road. Thus, one road could have many names. For example, Daltonians once called the road to Cleveland, Tennessee, the "Cleveland Road" and today call it the "Cleveland Highway," while Tennesseans from Cleveland, both then and now, refer to the same road as the "Dalton Pike." There was simply no uniformity in the naming of roads at the time of the Civil War.

One road with confusing names is the one called by historian Albert Castel the "Sallacoa Road."[10] (It is shown as roads 2 and 2a in the accompanying map.) In the 1840s, the lower part of this road was part of the old Spring Place Road, which passed by the A. M. Linn House. This road is indicated as Road 2 (not 2a) on the map, and it veered to the east just north of the A. M. Linn House toward Dewey's Crossroads. Here, portions of the Old Spring Place Road still crisscross with Spring Place Road, which, by the 1850s, supplanted it as the main road from Cassville to Spring Place. The Mosteller's Mill Road, indicated as Road 2a, is a spur road to the old Spring Place Road. The A. M. Linn House[11] is located between the intersection of the old Spring Place Road (Road 2) and Mosteller's (Marsteller's in Federal accounts) Mill Road (Road 2a) and the road to Crow Springs. A portion of the old Spring Place Road can be traced today from US 41 north from Cassville, continuing north on Kimsey Circle, NW, and then to Janice Lane, NW. The old road can be seen again across today's Cedar Creek Road, in the tree line between the Gateway Church and Cedar Creek Road. [12]

---

[10] Castel, *Decision in the West*, 199, 203.

[11] Called the "Lynn house" on the "Ruger map" in the *Atlas to the OR*, Plate 58, Map 1.

[12] Cunyus, *History of Bartow County*, 39.

By the 1850s, a newer road to Spring Place was more widely used. This "new" Spring Place Road is indicated as Road 3 in the attached map and is still in use today. It is referred to as the "Spring Place Road via Ashworth's North" in Lucy Cunyus's 1933 *History of Bartow County*, which included the 1871 survey/list of roads.[13] But, this road, and any details to the north and east, was not included in Kurtz's map, which also appeared in the same *History of Bartow County*.[14] The "new" Spring Place Road is also shown in the Ruger and Van Horne Atlanta Campaign maps of 1875 and 1877. Critically, this road is found in the map prepared by Captain W. E. Merrill, chief topographical engineer for the Army of the Cumberland, which was used by the Federal forces in the Atlanta Campaign.

The 1871 survey/list of roads in *History of Bartow County* is the source Wilbur Kurtz relied upon for the location of the old Spring Place Road that passed the A. M. Linn house. In Cunyus's 1933 *History of Bartow County*, Kurtz referred to the road to the Linn house as the Spring Place Road because of its original name, but he stopped at that point and did not further include the other road names to the northeast, nor did he discover the connection between the roads to Pine Log, Fairmount, and Spring Place to the northeast. Unfortunately, prior studies of Cassville, in particular Bill Scaife's work, relied on this reference. Additionally, the map used by the Confederate Army for the region between Adairsville and Cassville, prepared by engineer John M. Stewart and assistant engineer J. S. Tyner for Major General Will T. Martin and Major General Joseph F. Wheeler (hereafter called the "Martin Map"), failed to delineate the "new" Spring Place Road. Instead, it only showed

[13] Ibid. I located Jasper Ashworth's property on the Spring Place Road in the 5th District for Bartow County, Georgia. Ashworth obtained a warranty deed to the property from Robert Horrisburger, dated 24 February 1869, recorded 20 April 1869 (Bartow County, Georgia, Land Records). Ashworth married Miss Mary Annis Bradley on 26 June 1874, marriage license recorded on 24 July 1874, Probate Court, Bartow County, Georgia. Miss Bradley was the daughter of Calvin and Cary Bradley (spelled Bradly in the 1860 US Census for Cass County, Georgia) who lived immediately to the north of the Ashworth property on the Spring Place Road near its intersection with today's Gaines Road. Miss M. A. Bradley was eight years old at the time of the 1860 US Census and was twenty-two when she married Jasper Ashworth (1860 US Census Records, Cass [now Bartow] County, Georgia, District 936, 892–98). The Bradley house is indicated along the Spring Place Road and appears on the Ruger Map.

[14] Cunyus, *History of Bartow County*, 233.

broken portions of it and, most importantly, did not show its connection to Five Forks where it joins the Pine Log and Canton roads.[15]

In his 1992 work, Castel realized that identifying the correct Spring Place Road was problematic. Instead, he refrained from referring to it, and he used a safer approach by referring to the road to Mosteller's Mill as the road to Sallacoa (Road 2 and Road 2a). Historian Keith Hebert also avoided this confusion by referring to the road as the Marstellar's Mill Road (Road 2 and Road 2a), using the Federal misspelling of the Southern Appalachian vernacular of the name.[16]

Road 2 also leads to Iron Mountain, which is the high ground just east of Adairsville. Hood called it the Ironton Road (Road 2 and 2b). Hood referred to *two roads* leading from Adairsville to Cassville (Road 1), *in addition* to the road from Adairsville to Kingston (Road 8). He clearly distinguished this road from the Spring Place Road (Road 3), which is the one he said was to his right flank, or east, and across the large, open field across which his men were moving when they were interrupted by an unexpected Federal column.[17]

Following this logic, Hood's response to William Mackall's question during the morning while they were in the large, open field can be understood. Mackall asked him, "What road are the enemy moving on?" Hood responded that the Federal cavalry was "on both the Spring Place and the Canton Road"; he then added, "Did you not see them?" He was referring to the Federal columns he had observed to the east and south of his position on the northern part of the large field.[18]

Historians have criticized Hood for saying that he believed that Howard's IV Corps was moving down the Ironton Road, and that Howard's IV Corps was the column that he was planning to ambush. However, on 18 May, Confederate cavalry captured a Federal prisoner from the XX Corps who had

---

[15] Unfortunately, Scaife apparently relied on the 1933 map by Kurtz (Kurtz Map 1) and therefore reached the incorrect conclusion that the current Cedar Creek Road was located at the Spring Place Road. It should be noted, however, that Kurtz Map 2, published in 1949, corrects his earlier assumption (see Martin Map for the broken pieces of Spring Place Road).

[16] Castel, *Decision in the West*, 203, 199 (map); Hebert, *Long Civil War*, 133, 135 (Castel's map).

[17] Hood, *Advance and Retreat*, 99–100, Hood's report, 15 February 1865, appears in appendix to *Advance and Retreat*, 317–37.

[18] Mackall, "Memorandum of the Operations at Cassville on May 19, 1864," 22 September 1864, *OR*, ser. 1, vol. 38, pt. 3, 622.

become lost while walking from Adairsville to his camp southeast of town and passed through the IV Corps columns. T. B. Mackall included in his journal that he had personally questioned the prisoner at headquarters when the lieutenant generals and Johnston were present. Given this information, as well as knowledge that Howard's IV Corps was the lead and attacking column just north of Adairsville the day before (17 May), it is understandable that the Confederate high command assumed that Howard's IV Corps was still close to Adairsville and southeast of the village, where the prisoner had been captured.[19]

The Confederates were aware of the identity of the Federal corps located on the Adairsville-Cassville Road as being the XX Corps because Iverson's Georgia brigade remained in close contact with the pickets of Butterfield's Division, Hooker's leading column of the XX Corps. Iverson's advance scouts remained in contact with and skirmished with Butterfield's men throughout the afternoon and evening of 18 May along the Adairsville-Cassville Road, as well as at first light on 19 May. Therefore, if the XX Corps was identified as the column moving south along the Adairsville-Cassville Road, then the IV Corps appeared to the Southern leaders as the most likely unit that would move toward Cassville from east of Iron Mountain, along the Ironton Road (Road 2 and 2b).[20]

The Confederate leadership was also under the incorrect assumption that all of Palmer's XIV Corps was headed toward Rome. Two divisions, Brigadier General Absalom Baird's Third Division, followed by Brigadier General Richard Johnson's First Division of Palmer's Corps, marched behind Howard's IV Corps along the Adairsville-Kingston Road (Road 8) toward Kingston on the evening of 18 May.[21]

---

[19] Interview of Federal XX Corps prisoner captured in the Ironton Road area (*OR*, ser. 1, vol. 38, pt. 3, 982). The same Federal soldier also said that there was a third corps behind the IV and XX Corps at Adairsville, although the Northerner did not know which one. This may be compared with the interview of a Confederate prisoner captured by Hooker's XX Corps on the Ironton Road, in which the captured Southerner stated that Dibrell's Tennessee Brigade had passed by on that road (Hooker to Whipple, *OR*, ser. 1, vol. 38, pt. 4, 238).

[20] Butterfield to Hooker, *OR*, ser. 1, vol. 38, pt. 4, 240; Hooker to Whipple, *OR*, ser. 1, vol. 38, pt. 4, 239; Wheeler, *OR*, ser. 1, vol. 38, pt. 3, 946.

[21] Provost General B. F. Hill obtained a statement from a scout that Palmer's XIV Corps was in advance of move on Rome on Calhoun and Rome Road (Mackall Journal, "O" sample, *OR*, ser. 1, vol. 38, pt. 3, 982; Johnson's report, *OR*, ser. 1, vol. 38, pt. 1, 522; Baird's report, *OR*, ser. 1, vol. 38, pt. 1, 736).

McPherson's Army of the Tennessee (XV and XVI Corps) was at Woodlands (today's Barnsley Gardens), with Garrard's Division between him and Davis's Division near Rome. Kilpatrick's Division, under the temporary command of Colonel Eli H. Murray (Brigadier General Judson Kilpatrick being wounded on 13 May near Resaca), guarded McPherson's front and left flank. The Southerners had lost connection with Schofield's XXIII Corps and were apparently unaware of the identity of the Federal troops who were traveling down the Adairsville-Kingston Road (Road 8). Hardee obtained information on 17 May above Adairsville that McPherson's "corps" (as he called it) was "in the neighborhood of Rome and another had been sent to Virginia" to reinforce General Ulysses Grant and the Federal Army of the Potomac, which was facing General Robert E. Lee's force.[22]

Hood claimed in his postwar *Advance and Retreat* that the Ironton Road (Road 2 and 2b) was the one referred to by Johnston in his postwar *Narrative of Military Operations* as the "country road." However, Hood never saw the sketch that Johnston drew for Johnsen in 1874, which was not published until 1893. Johnston's sketch map showed the "country road" in the location of Hood's movement to the east of Cassville on the morning of 19 May as he marched through a gap in two hills toward the large, open field (today's Brown Loop Road, Road 3a). Clearly, this is not the Ironton Road that Hood said that he was marching *toward* to make his surprise attack. The "country road" in Johnston's sketch is merely a connecting road to the large, open field to the north, though it *led to* the Ironton Road (Road 2) at the northern end of the field.[23]

In his 15 February 1865 report, Hood explained that there were three roads by which the three separate Confederate corps could attack the Federals at Adairsville on 18 May, the day before the Cassville events. Hood explained that he and Polk had argued for an attack to be made on 18 May because the three Southern corps could each advance on Adairsville from separate and converging directions, presumably Hardee on the Adairsville-Kingston Road, Polk on the Adairsville-Cassville Road in the center, and Hood on the Ironton Road parallel to Polk and to the east.[24] Moreover, he argued that the

[22] McPherson's Special Field Order #12, *OR*, ser. 1, vol. 38, pt. 4, 231–32; Major Henry Hampton, "Itinerary of Hardee's Army Corps May 15–June 14," *OR*, ser. 1, vol. 38, pt. 3, 704.

[23] Johnston to Johnsen, 19 June 1874, 319; also, *New Orleans Times Picayune*, 22 October 1893.

[24] Hood, *OR*, ser. 1, vol. 38, pt. 3, 634.

disadvantage of having only one route of retreat north of Adairsville was one of the reasons for the Confederate withdrawal on the evening of 17 May. This disadvantage could now be turned on the advancing Federals, should they be compelled to fall back from Adairsville toward Calhoun or, in the event of a defeat, be bottled up in the forks of the Oostanaula and Etowah Rivers near Rome.[25]

Finally, I discovered a key map that had been prepared by Johnston in 1874 but not published until 22 October 1893 in the *New Orleans Times Picayune*. This map is important because it provides Johnston's understanding of the location of the "country road" that he referred to in his writings, as he gave specific geographic references which can be identified today. The "country road" drawn by Johnston is east of the intersection of the Canton Road (Road 5) and the Pine Log Road (Road 4), and splits two hills north of the Pine Log Road at today's Brown Loop Road (Road 3a). It is the road on which Hood's Corps traveled to get to the large, open field, across which Hood's Corps was traveling when surprised by Federal cavalry.[26]

To make matters more confusing, the Ironton Road (Hood), or old Spring Place Road (Kurtz Map 1/Scaife Map 1), is also referred to as the "Copper Mine Road" or "Cooper Mine Road" by Major General Joseph Wheeler. In his report of his operations on 18 and 19 May between Adairsville and Cassville, Wheeler referred to the next road to the east of the Adairsville-Cassville Road as the Copper Mine Road. The Copper Mine Road is the same road as the Ironton Road (Road 2 and 2b on the map).[27]

A soldier using the pen name of "Osceola," in Dibrell's Tennessee cavalry brigade, also referenced the Copper Mine Road (or Coppermine Road) in a dispatch to the *Memphis Daily Appeal*. According to Osceola, Dibrell's Brigade was posted on the Coppermine Road about two and a half miles north of Cassville on 19 May before being recalled. Osceola described the Coppermine Road as being "united" with the Adairsville-Cassville Road one-half

---

[25] Ibid.; Hood, *Advance and Retreat*, 99.

[26] Johnston to Johnsen, 19 June 1874, 319; also, *New Orleans Times Picayune*, 22 October 1893.

[27] Wheeler's report, *OR*, ser. 1, vol. 38, pt. 3, 946. This may be compared with the online transcription at Ohio State University that shows "Cooper Mine Road" (https://ehistory.osu.edu/books/official-records/074/0946) and with the online transcription at Cornell University, which provides "Copper Mine Road," (https://babel.hathitrust.org/cgi/pt?id=coo.31924077722993&view=1up&seq=948&skin=2021). Ohio State University's use of an optic scanner to read the *Official Records* in creating its digital file sometimes led to slight imaging errors.

mile north of Cassville. This location corresponds to today's intersection of Kimsey Circle NW and US Highway 41 (the Adairsville-Cassville Road), which is located approximately one-half mile north of the four-way stop in downtown Cassville.[28]

In the 1850s, Mark A. Cooper developed several mines in Bartow County, purchased a mine at Iron Mountain, and, in 1859, wrote about the rich minerals and ores in the area.[29] Iron Mountain is located east of Adairsville and today lies just east of Interstate I-75 at Exit 306, where the current Vulcan Mine operates. It is named after Iron Mountain, Missouri, a site Cooper had visited and for which he likely named the Adairsville site "Iron Mountain." During the 1850s, speculation for copper occurred on and around Iron Mountain. Very little copper was found, but iron ore deposits were discovered that are still being mined today by the Vulcan Mine.[30]

Because most of the mines in Bartow County, including copper mines, were in the southeast part of the county in the Allatoona mountains, it may have been assumed that Wheeler was referring in his report to a road in that direction, southeast of Cassville near the Etowah River. Thus, historians may have ignored Wheeler's reference because it did not seem to fit. However, close examination reveals that in the 1850s and 1860s, Mark Cooper owned a mine just east of Adairsville at Iron Mountain, and it logically follows that a road down the middle of the Gravelly Plateau to Cassville from Iron Mountain would be called the Iron Mountain, or Ironton Road, Copper Mine, or Cooper Mine Road.

As previously explained, the Copper Mine Road appears on the Foster Map in the location described by Wheeler and Osceola. In addition, James "Bo" Blalock, an attorney with a law practice in neighboring Cartersville, identified the road as the Copper Mine Road. Blaylock was reared along the road in the section known today as Janice Lane. He explained that longtime local historians Reba Allen and Herman Bearden referred to this road as the "Copper Mine Road." Using multiple identifiers, including Wheeler's report, Osceola's account, the existence of Mark A. Cooper's mine, the Foster Map,

---

[28] Osceola, "Camp Dibbrell's [*sic*] Brigade Cavalry, Etowah River, May 23, 1864," *Memphis Daily Appeal*, 24 May 1864.

[29] Cunyus, *History of Bartow County*, 187–205.

[30] Ibid., 190–94; Kesler, *Geology and Mineral Deposits*, 61, 62, 92.

and current accounts, the location of the Copper Mine Road can be confirmed as today's Kimsey Circle-Janice Lane-Cedar Creek Road (Road 2).[31]

Today there is a spur road called the Iron Mountain Road located just east of Adairsville and I-75, Exit 306, and east of Iron Mountain. It is located just north of the Adairsville-Pine Log-Canton Road (Road 7) and branches off about a half mile from the interstate exit. Hood's Ironton Road is Wheeler's and Osceola's Copper (or Cooper) Mine Road (identified herein as Road number 2 and 2b), perhaps originally named for the man and not the mineral.

Historically, the Morning Cassville Affair has focused on the triangle created between the towns of Adairsville, Kingston, and Cassville, as scholars have relied on Johnston's postwar account in his *Narrative*. However, since it was published ten years after the actual events at Cassville, and when comparing it to the T. B. Mackall Journal "A" and "B" samples, Johnston's *Narrative* is suspect. Unfortunately, the veracity of Johnston's account could not be fully tested with other contemporaneous accounts by previous studies because the road system was confused and mistaken.

I have focused on the geographic area between Adairsville, Pine Log, and Cassville, that also forms a triangle, where the mysterious events about the Morning Cassville Affair occurred. Here, in this triangle, the true "Cassville Triangle," Hood's Corps moved out of town to strike an imaginary enemy on the Ironton Road. Here, Federal cavalry moved, undiscovered and unmolested, into the right flank and rear of Hood's unsuspecting column. Here, Howard's IV Corps was believed to be traveling toward Cassville via the Ironton Road. And here, Wheeler's cavalry covered four roads that led to Cassville from this direction. However, in this "Cassville Triangle," there were five roads that provided access to Cassville, and one road, the Spring Place

[31] Telephone interview with James "Bo" Blalock, 25 January 2023. Blaylock, age seventy-one, explained that a longtime moonshiner, Darby Fowler, now deceased, owned a still in the woods off Copper Mine Road and referred to the road as the "Copper Mine Road." The local usage of "Copper Mine Road" is corroborated by attorney Blake Scoggins, age thirty-seven, who grew up in nearby Rydal/Pine Log community. Scoggins was also aware of the "Copper Mine Road" and confirmed that it was in the area described by Blalock and other, older residents of the county (telephone interview with Blake Scoggins, 9 March 2023). Also, attorney Brad Stephens grew up on Janice Lane and corroborates the use of the term "Copper Mine Road" for the road. For decades, Stephens's father owned the store that was located at the northeast intersection of the four-way stop in Cassville (interview with Brad Stevens, 26 April 2023).

Road, remained unguarded. It was down this Spring Place Road that McCook's cavalrymen successfully maneuvered and struck Hood's marching column in two places.

To help illustrate the road structure across the Gravelly Plateau, or "Cassville Triangle," it may be helpful to envision the roads north of Cassville as five fingers on the left hand with the palm facing away from the viewer. Following this illustration, Cassville would be at the bottom of the left hand at the wrist, Adairsville would be up the smallest (little) finger, Iron Mountain would be up the ring finger, and Spring Place would be up the middle finger, and beyond by a considerable distance (two counties away in Murray County). Pine Log would be up and beyond the index finger (and Fairmont is beyond Pine Log on the same road), and the route to Canton would be located well to the east along the thumb. Now, by reviewing Wheeler's Report, and following along with Wheeler from west to east in the placement of his cavalry screen on 18 May, his deployment may be traced as follows:[32]

1. Wheeler placed Iverson's Brigade and Humes's Division on the Cassville and Adairsville Road, which would be the little finger (Road 1). They were in front of Butterfield's Division of the XX Corps, which camped where they had found water on the evening of 18 May just south of the downward slope of the Gravelly Plateau, approximately four miles north of Cassville.[33]

2. Wheeler deployed Colonel George G. Dibrell's brigade on the Copper Mine Road, which is the same road that Hood referred to as the Ironton Road, or Iron Mountain Road (Road 2 and 2b). Mosteller's Mill Road (Road 2a) connects with this road from the north, and some of Schofield's XXIII Corps referred to it as the road from Marsteller's Mill.[34] This Road 2 would be the ring finger.

3. The middle finger represents Road 3, which is the Spring Place Road that Wheeler missed, and which has eluded previous studies of Cassville for

---

[32] *OR*, ser. 1, vol. 38, pt. 3, 946.

[33] Major General Joseph Hooker, dispatch to Brigadier General William D. Whipple, chief of staff to General George H. Thomas, Army of the Cumberland, 18 May 1864, 10:30 p.m., *OR*, ser. 1, vol. 38, pt. 4, 239.

[34] See Wheeler, *OR*, vol. 38, pt. 3, 946; compare with the OSU transcription at https://ehistory.osu.edu/books/official-records/074/0946. Note that on the afternoon of 19 May, Dibrell's Confederate cavalry brigade had to find a byroad (probably Road 2c) to avoid the pincer trap formed by Federal units advancing on both of their flanks (see Wheeler's report, *OR*, ser. 1, vol. 38, pt. 3, 946; Osceola, "Camp Dibbrell's [*sic*] Brigade Cavalry, Etowah River, May 23, 1864," *Memphis Daily Appeal*, 24 May 1864).

over a century and a half—despite common knowledge of its location and usage by local citizens in the area.[35]

4. According to Wheeler's report, the 53rd Alabama and 24th Alabama Battalion of Colonel Moses W. Hannon's demi-brigade were on the next road, the name of which he omitted, but left two blanks, as the ___ ___ Road. The two most obvious possibilities to fill these blanks are the Spring Place Road or the Pine Log Road. Perhaps Wheeler had forgotten the name when he made out his report on 1 June 1864. Or, perhaps he purposely omitted the name because by then he should have been aware of his failure to cover *both* the Spring Place (Road 3) and the Pine Log (Road 4) Roads. These two roads meet at the Five Forks intersection, just east of today's TA Truck Stop at Interstate I-75 east of Exit 296.[36]

Ironically, the omission of the name of the third road in Wheeler's Report was a key factor in the Confederate cavalry's mistake at Cassville. Wheeler screened four roads, but there were five roads that needed to be covered. The Spring Place Road was the one that McCook slipped through undetected until he had proceeded as far as what is known today as Five Forks (Intersection of Roads 3 and 4). Because we know that, on the evening of 18 May, Hannon's Alabamians clashed with Colonel Alexander W. Holeman's Kentucky (Union) cavalry brigade in Major General George Stoneman's division along the Big Pine Log Creek on the Pine Log (Fairmont) Road (Road

---

[35] Just as the adage that all politics is local, so, too, is geography. Local residents are usually the best source for locations and geographic features in their communities. Residents of the Gravelly Plateau know where the Spring Place Road is located and have known it for more than 170 years. Since the 1850s, Spring Place Road has provided passage across the eastern portion of the Gravelly Plateau for local travelers from Highway 140 south to Cassville via the Five Forks intersection, where it joins the Cassville-Pine Log Road proceeding southwest into Cassville. However, some historians have been misled by Johnston's alterations of the Mackall Journal and by Kurtz's unintended original (prewar) designation of a portion of the Copper Mine/Ironton Road, that passed by the Linn (or Lynn as shown on the Ruger Map) house because the lower part of it (Road 2) was also the "old" Spring Place Road. This road had been supplanted by the time of the Civil War with the newer (and now more than 170 years "new") Spring Place Road. Kurtz amended his findings from his map in the 1933 *History of Bartow County* to his 1949 map that was published in the *Daily Tribune News*. However, Scaife did not note the correction when he relied on the earlier map and on the falsified Mackall Journal in creating his maps in the 1990s. See Cunyus, *History of Bartow County*, 233; *OR*, ser. 1, vol. 38, pt. 3, 978–91, at 982.

[36] Wheeler, *OR*, ser. 1, vol. 38, pt. 3, 946.

4), we know that Spring Place Road (Road 3) was left unguarded by Wheeler, according to his deployment.[37] From Five Forks, these two roads converge and form one road today. Together, they proceed to the southwest (today's Cassville-White Road, Road 4), which leads into Cassville from the east. This road (Road 4), joins the old Canton Road (today called the Old Cassville-White Road, Road 5) on the outskirts of town near today's Holt Road and the old Hardy house (today called Watkins Farms).[38]

Thus, in 1864, the road leading east out of town by the cemetery could correctly be referred to as the Canton Road, the Pine Log Road, the Fairmont Road or the Spring Place Road, because the Canton and Spring Place roads split from the Pine Log/Fairmount Road (the Canton Road just out of town at the Hardy house, and the Spring Place Road later at Five Forks).

On 18 May, Hannon's Demi-brigade of the 53rd Alabama and 24th Alabama Battalion encountered Federal cavalry on the "Fairmount Road" four miles from Cassville.[39] The Fairmount Road is also the Pine Log Road.[40] (The road to Pine Log eventually goes to Fairmount.) Brigadier General Frank C. Armstrong's brigade from Jackson's Division of cavalry was ordered to support Hannon. That clash, or skirmish, on 18 May between Hannon and Armstrong on the Confederate side, and Stoneman's cavalry on the Federal side, occurred south of Pine Log, likely near the Big Pine Log Creek because Stoneman's Kentucky troopers reached the Big Pine Log Creek that

[37] Tarrant, *Wild Riders of the First Kentucky Cavalry*, 330; Mackall Journal, "O" sample, *OR*, ser. 1, vol. 38, pt. 3, 982; Wheeler, *OR*, ser. 1, vol. 38, pt. 3, 946.

[38] Johnston never referred to the "Spring Place Road" when describing his ambush plan, and he merely described a "country road" to the north of Cassville. (See Johnston's Map, *New Orleans Times Picayune*, 22 October 1893). However, Mackall Journal, "O" sample, states that, during the confusion in the middle of the day of 19 May, Johnston rode out to Hood's lines on the Spring Place Road and that he crossed a creek to look at Hood's redeployment. Two Run Creek crosses the old roadbed of old Spring Place Road between Janice Lane and Cedar Creek Road.

[39] See Mackall Journal, "O" sample, *OR*, ser. 1, vol. 38, pt. 3, 982. Private Moseby of Company D, 53rd Alabama Cavalry was wounded in the arm during this encounter. One Alabama trooper noted, "We were skirmishing on the right of our army near Cassville," with "no results of importance" (J. F. Gaines, letter to the *Montgomery (AL) Weekly Advertiser*, 8 June 1864). Also, Private C. Murray in Company K, 53rd Alabama Cavalry, was wounded by a "gunshot in the left leg," while privates J. Davidson, J. J. Haynie, and J. P. Jones in Company C were captured on 18 May 1864 (McLendon Jr., *History of the 53rd Regiment*, 367–77).

[40] See Kurtz Map 1 in Cunyus, *History of Bartow County*, 233.

afternoon.[41] Thus, taking all of this into consideration, it is clear that Hannon's Demi-brigade, followed by Armstrong's Brigade, was on the Pine Log Road, which is also the road to Fairmount, during the afternoon and into the evening of 18 May. This road is Road 4, the index finger. Hannon's troopers were thus *not* on Spring Place Road.

5. According to Wheeler's report, his final disposition, or deployment of his cavalry screen on 18 May, was Brigadier General John S. Williams's (formally Grigsby's) Kentucky brigade on the Tennessee Road. The Tennessee Road was the old Jackson Military Road, which was built in 1825 and generally follows the course of today's US 411 in northern Bartow County. This road is well to the east. It is a north-south road on the extreme eastern part of Bartow County and links Pine Log south toward Cartersville. This road number is identified as Road 6. Williams's Kentucky cavalrymen were responsible for keeping the Federals from reaching the all-important Hightower Brigade, Johnston's escape route over the Etowah River.[42]

This fourth road, or Tennessee Road, described in Wheeler's report, connects with the Canton Road, or the road from Cassville to Canton (today's Old Cassville-White Road, Road 5) which splits off the Pine Log Road (today's Cassville-White Road, Road 4) just northeast of the Cassville Cemetery and near the Hardy House (today's Watkins Farm) and today's Holt Road. The Canton Road is represented by the thumb. This is Road 5.

The Canton Road connects with the Tennessee Road, which runs north to south from the Pine Log Community through today's White down to Cartersville. Several changes since the war make matters visualizing the geography difficult. The town of White did not exist at the time of the war; it is a postwar railroad town.[43] Also, two of the roads, the Pine Log Road (Road 4) and the Canton Road (Road 5), have been supplanted by the Cassville-

[41] See Tarrant, *Wild Riders of the First Kentucky Cavalry*, 330. This account suggests that on 18 May 1864, Holeman's Independent Brigade, consisting of the First Kentucky Cavalry and Eleventh Kentucky Cavalry, was on the Pine Log (Fairmount Road) while Stoneman's other brigade, Colonel James Biddle's Second Brigade, which included the Fifth Indiana Cavalry, the Sixth Indiana Cavalry, and the Twelfth Kentucky Cavalry, was on the Tennessee Road facing Williams's Kentucky (Confederate) Cavalry. See also Goodall, *Glory Gone Forgotten*, 95.

[42] This road is known as the Old Federal Road in Murray County where, at the northern part of Murray County, it bends to the west and passes by Prater's Mill and continues into Red Clay, Georgia (see Cunyus, *History of Bartow County*, 40–41).

[43] White, Georgia, was incorporated in August 1919 following the construction of the Louisville & Nashville Railroad. See Cunyus, *History of Bartow County*, 28.

White Road and the Old Cassville-White Road, respectively. Also, Interstate 75, Exit 296, along with its entrance and exit ramps and multiple commercial developments, have significantly altered the landscape and road network east of Cassville.

Another way to visualize the confusing roads across the Gravely Plateau, or Cassville Triangle, is to return to the face of clock example with Cassville at the center of the clock, Adairsville to the northwest at eleven o'clock, and Canton to the east at three o'clock. Road 1, the Adairsville-Cassville Road, is at eleven o'clock; Road 2, the Ironton, Copper Mine, old Spring Place, or Mosteller's Mill Road is roughly twelve o'clock; Road 3, the Spring Place Road, is at one o'clock; Road 4, the Pine Log/Fairmount Road is at two o'clock; and Road 5, the Canton Road is at three o'clock.

Using the "hand" illustration, visualize a scene in which Wheeler's cavalry screen, by securing the Tennessee Road (Road 6) above its connection with the Canton Road (Road 5), covered the thumb. Wheeler's cavalry also covered the little finger (Road 1), the ring finger (Road 2), and the index finger (Road 4). This left only the middle finger (Road 3), the Spring Place Road, or one o'clock on the face of the clock, uncovered.

Now, envision that McCook's cavalry proceeded undetected from the northeast via the Spring Place Road to Crow Springs and Five Forks, where it joined the Pine Log Road and turned to the west/southwest toward Cassville.[44] McCook's cavalry was spotted by some of Hood's men as McCook neared the Five Forks juncture with the Pine Log Road. Hannon's demi-brigade was northeast of that intersection on the Pine Log Road and in contact with Colonel Alexander W. Holeman's brigade of Stoneman's Division and was thus not in position to spot McCook's blue-coated horsemen. Between Crow Springs and Five Forks, McCook's force became visible to Hood and his men across the large open field in the valley of Two Run Creek.[45] The appearance by McCook's force at Five Forks from the Spring Place Road corresponds with Hood's description, with the detailed explanation by Colonel Taylor Beattie, who had accompanied Hood's Corps for the attack and who

---

[44] McCook's report, *OR*, ser. 1, vol. 38, pt. 2, 751–2; McCook, dispatch to Brigadier General Elliott, 19 May 1864, 5:40 p.m., *OR*, ser. 1, vol. 38, pt. 4, 255; Rowell, *Yankee Artillerymen*, 198–99.

[45] Hood's report as republished in the *New York Times*, 29 March 1865, 8; Hood, *OR*, ser. 1, vol. 38, pt. 3, 635; Hood, *Advance and Retreat*, 99–100, 101–103; Major J. E. Austin, 14th Louisiana Battalion Sharpshooters, *OR*, ser. 1, vol. 38, pt. 3, 862. For an excellent analysis of these sources, see S. Davis, *John Bell Hood*, 144–52.

was present in the large, open field when the Federal column appeared from the east, and with the Federal descriptions by McCook and several of his officers.[46]

When Johnston was subsequently told that Hood was changing course, and it was reported that Federals were on both the Spring Place and the Canton roads, Johnston remarked "It can't be! Armstrong on that road reported none." Johnston thought Armstrong's Brigade was covering the Canton Road (the thumb of the hand), which also contributed to his disbelief about Hood's claims. Apparently, Johnston believed that Armstrong's troopers were still east of Cassville patrolling the Canton Road.[47]

Armstrong's tired Mississippians had come from Alabama with Jackson's cavalry division when Polk's Army of Mississippi was called to Georgia. After traveling from Alabama as rapidly as they could, Armstrong's troopers had been in action at Adairsville on 17 May, where they had been deployed and extended the Confederate line to the right or east, sustaining thirty-one casualties. They had then proceeded on 18 May to the Pine Log Road, also called the Fairmount Road by T. B. Mackall (Road 4), in support of Hannon's Alabamians. The exhausted Mississippians had been recalled to the rear of Cassville on the evening of 18 May to rest overnight. By the midday Thursday, 19 May they would be ordered to line up on the left flank of Polk's Corps to cover the gap between Polk's and Hardee's men.[48]

The officer who ordered Armstrong's cavalry to retire from duty on the evening of 18 May, and then to fill the gap between Polk's left and Hardee's right around noon on 19 May, remains unconfirmed. There are two reasons it may have been General Polk. First, according to Mackall's journal, "O" sample,[49] Polk detained two of Hood's brigades, Cumming's and probably Reynolds's, to shore up the space on his right flank, and he likely ordered Armstrong's Brigade of his cavalry division, who were resting near his headquarters to move to the left flank to do the same. Second, on 22 May, following the events at Cassville, which included the detour of Ross's Texas brigade

---

[46] Hood, *Advance and Retreat*, 99–102; Taylor Beattie to Hood, 29 March 1874, in Hood, *Advance and Retreat*, 102–103; McCook's report, *OR*, ser. 1, vol. 38, pt. 2, 751–52; McCook, dispatch to Brigadier General Elliott, 19 May 1864, 5:40 p.m., *OR*, ser. 1, vol. 38, pt. 4, 255; Dorr Journal, 19–20.

[47] Mackall Journal, "O" sample, *OR*, ser. 1, vol. 38, pt. 3, 983.

[48] Champion diary, 22 May 1864, 28–29; Montgomery, *Reminiscences of a Mississippian*, 164, 168; Roland, "First Mississippi Cavalry," 94–95; *Jackson [MS] Clarion-Ledger*, 9 June 1864.

[49] *OR*, ser. 1, vol. 38, pt. 3, 984.

from Rome south across the Etowah River where it rejoined the army at the Hightower Bridge, Polk wrote to W. W. Mackall, Johnston's chief of staff, "I have concluded that some embarrassment might arise from my continuing to direct the movements of the cavalry force under my command during the present military operations, and I therefore turn over to you the brigades of Armstrong, Ferguson, and Ross...[and] ask to be relieved from any responsibility."[50]

One other point about the geography at Cassville should be addressed. Two Run Creek features prominently in the story. This large creek with its tributaries begins north and northeast of Cassville and runs in a westerly direction north of the range of hills and ridges that protect Cassville from the north. After running in a westerly direction past Cassville and the Adairsville-Cassville Road (today's US Highway 41 and Joe Frank Harris Parkway, Road 1), Two Run Creek turns sharply to the south, then continues past the west side of the village and the range of hills that protects Cassville on the west. Thus, various commands of both North and South record crossing the creek on numerous occasions, but the locations could be miles apart from one another and the military actions completely unrelated.

---

[50] Polk to Mackall, *OR*, ser. 1, vol. 38, pt. 4, 735.

Chapter 6

Johnston's Battle Plan

The best evidence of a battle plan is a written order with specific directions to the subordinate commanders concerning each party's role. Sometimes circumstances do not permit the time for written instructions, and an oral order must be given. Johnston had ample opportunity to prepare a written battle order to his corps commanders, particularly if his story that he first planned it two days earlier at Adairsville is to be believed. Instead, he wrote what may be described as a "pep rally speech."

An order or battle plan is one that is given to the subordinate commander or commanders to conduct a desired action. It is not typically something that is given to all the troops. Johnston's "General Order" was not a battle plan. It was merely a speech to inspire his men. Johnston delivered his "order" after he consented to Hood's request to move into position for a surprise attack. Hood, Johnston and the other leaders mistakenly believed that a Federal column, perhaps Howard's IV Corps, would soon be approaching Cassville via the Copper Mine/Ironton Road (Road 2). One officer would later sarcastically refer to Johnston's order as the "celebrated battle order!"[1]

Following the Civil War, the US Army under the leadership of General Sherman, created a "School of Application" at Leavenworth, Kansas. There, young lieutenants were sent for a two-year course of instruction. At first, the school struggled to find its purpose. After the arrival of Colonel Alexander McDowell McCook in 1886, and the addition of Captain Arthur L. Wagner, however, the school became an important institution for the preparation of brigade and division officers. One development at the school was the creation of a standard for issuing battle plans or orders. Known as the "Leavenworth Order," the standard order was given in five separate paragraphs with the acronym, SMEAC, that stood for situation (friendly and enemy), mission (the intent of the operation), execution (how is it to be accomplished), attachment (the support that will be given the operation, including artillery and additional forces), and command (how will communication during the operation occur, including who is in charge, who is second in command, etc., and what code words, radio, signal flags, rally-points, etc. will be used). In more modern times, the US Army began using a new acronym, METT-T, which stands for

---

[1] Sykes, *Walthall's Brigade*, 568.

mission, enemy, terrain, troops and, if necessary, time. Johnston's order provided none of these details; it merely informed the men that he was ready to lead them to battle.[2]

Two-thirds of Johnston's army, Polk's and Hood's corps, arrived at Cassville by noon on Wednesday, 18 May, via the Adairsville-Cassville Road (Road 1), called the direct road by Johnston, and the Copper Mine/Ironton Road (Road 2). Polk's Corps traveled the Adairsville-Cassville Road with Loring's Division, together with Cantey's two brigades and Sears's Brigade of French's Division, which had just arrived from Rome. Following Polk's six brigades was Stevenson's Division of Hood's Corps down the "direct road" (Adairsville-Cassville Road, Road 1).[3]

Butterfield's Division was in the vanguard of Hooker's XX Corps from Mosteller's Mill on 18 May. They traveled down the upper portion of the Copper Mine/Ironton Road (Road 2b) until they reached the "forks in the road," and turned west onto today's Manning Mill Road (Road 2d) and continued until they reached the Adairsville-Cassville Road near the Jonathan McDow House, where Hooker made his headquarters on the evening of 18 May. Butterfield's Division pressed south along the Adairsville-Cassville Road and began to run into resistance from the Confederate cavalry of Colonel Henry M. Ashby's Tennessee brigade, and Colonel Thomas H. Harrison's brigade of Brigadier General William Y. C. Humes's division, and Iverson's Georgia brigade of Major General William T. Martin's division. The Southern cavalry erected barricades about every half of a mile to impede the Federal advance (see Butterfield Map).[4]

Georgia cavalryman O. P. Hargis, who had grown up in the vicinity, remembered that when "Johnston fell back in the direction of Cassville" on the morning of 18 May, "our cavalry covered his retreat and we were skirmishing with them all day, and when we fell back to the McDow farm, we built a temporary breastwork across the field with fence rails." As the Southern infantry columns withdrew down the road toward Cassville, Hargis saw

---

[2] Powell, "Following Orders"; Nenninger, *Leavenworth Schools and the Old Army*, 20.

[3] French's report, *OR*, ser. 1, vol. 38, pt. 3, 899; Butterfield to Hooker, 18 May 1864, 10:30 p.m., *OR*, ser. 1, vol. 38, pt. 4, 240.

[4] Butterfield to Hooker, 18 May 1864, 6:30 p.m. and 10:30 p.m., *OR*, ser. 1, vol. 38, pt. 4, 240; Wheeler, *OR*, ser. 1, vol. 38, pt. 3, 946; Sloan Diary (Company D, 5th Tennessee Cavalry, Ashby's Brigade), 18 May 1864; Hargis Journal, 18 May 1864, 38.

Mrs. McDow at the smokehouse where she was cutting slices of ham to give to passing soldiers. When Hargis approached her, she was glad to see him, and inquired about her two sons who were in his company. She cut him about four pounds of ham to take to take with him.[5]

The reason that barricades were used by the Confederate cavalry along the Adairsville-Cassville Road (Road 1) and that three brigades of cavalry were deployed here whereas on every other route covered only one brigade was used was likely in keeping with Johnston's plan to withdraw from Adairsville to Cassville safely. By slowing the Federal advance down the "direct route" as Johnston called it, Hardee's Corps and the wagon train could safely escape Adairsville and reach Cassville via the Kingston Road (Roads 8 and 9) before the Federals could threaten Johnston. Once his force had reunited, Johnston began to feel both relieved and more confident.

Butterfield's men continued south along the Gravely Plateau until they began to reach the downhill slope. They proceeded until they were about a half-mile south of the plateau, where they could access water, and stopped to camp about 6:30 p.m. There, Butterfield wrote Hooker to report his progress and on the enemy cavalry resistance. Later that evening, he pushed his advance pickets forward to the next line of barricades, which were found unoccupied. The Confederate cavalry had evacuated after dark and moved to about a mile north of Cassville. Butterfield's men captured about fifteen prisoners from Stevenson's Division, which had been the last Southern infantry to retire along the Adairsville-Cassville Road. These men were apparently "stragglers" from Brigadier General Alexander W. Reynolds's North Carolina and Virginia brigade.[6]

---

[5] Hargis Journal, 18 May 1864, 38–39.

[6] Butterfield to Hooker, 18 May 1864, 10:30 p.m., *OR*, ser. 1, vol. 38, pt. 4, 240. The 58th North Carolina suffered or lost fourteen men captured or deserted between Adairsville and Cassville, 18–19 May (Hardy, *Fifty-Eighth North Carolina Troops*, 19). The 60th North Carolina saw three men captured or deserted following Adairsville (Jordan, *North Carolina Troops*, 502). The 54th Virginia lost sixteen men captured or deserted between Adairsville and Cassville. Stevenson claimed that the 54th Virginia, who did not get the order to stop the attack, lost one hundred men in just fifteen minutes during assault on 15 May at Resaca (*OR*, ser. 1, vol. 38, pt. 3, 813). But see Sherwood and Weaver, *54th Virginia Infantry*, 157, which shows losses for Dalton and Resaca as twenty-one killed, twenty wounded, and twenty-eight captured for a total of sixty-nine men. The 63rd Virginia lost nine men captured or deserted at or above Cassville (Weaver, *63rd Virginia Infantry*, 98).

In the predawn hours of 18 May, from their position east of Adairsville along the ridge just north of and adjoining Iron Mountain, Stewart's Division, followed by Hindman's Division, took the Copper Mine/Ironton Road (Road 2). Manigault's Brigade was posted along a high ridge east of Adairsville, just north of Iron Mountain (at today's Exit 306 on I-75), where he and his men had a panoramic view of the countryside, and of the Federal attack on Cheatham's Division and Armstrong's troopers in the valley the previous evening. Several miles to the east of Manigault's South Carolinians and Alabamians, Deas's Alabama Brigade was sent to contest the Federal advance on Mosteller's Mill from the north.[7]

---

[7] Hood, *OR*, ser. 1, vol. 38, pt. 4, 726. Hood, through his assistant adjutant general J. W. Ratchford, told his three division commanders that "in order that you may be prepared for any move, that the enemy are advancing on both roads *we* marched on this morning," meaning his corps (emphasis added). Also see Hood, *OR*, ser. 1, vol. 38, pt. 3, 634, in which Hood explained that each of the three Confederate corps had a separate road from which to approach Adairsville. And see Hood, *Advance and Retreat*, 99 and 107, in which Hood corroborated his previous claims in his report.

Also, see Manigault (Tower, *A Carolinian Goes to War*, 185), who explained that he had a difficult time in the fog searching for the road that his brigade was to take toward Cassville, and that his division (Hindman's) was the rear of the column on that route. Presumably, if Hindman was in rear of the column on the Copper Mine/Ironton Road (Road 2), then they followed Stewart's Division, which was also east of Adairsville, while Stevenson's Division, which saw fifteen men captured by Butterfield's Division was on the Adairsville-Cassville Road (Road 1). This matches Hood's statement about his three divisions using two roads on 18 May to travel to Cassville.

See also, Henderson Diary, in which Henderson recorded on 17 May, "Taken up line of march and marched until late in the evening, got in the neighborhood of Adairsville and remained all night" (ibid., 18 May 18). Williams (*This War So Horrible*, 73–74), a pioneer in the 40th Alabama of Baker's Brigade in Stewart's Division, was tasked with the duty of improving the Copper Mine/Ironton Road for use during the night by his division. Williams described the road as a "rough stumpy road" (73–74).

See also Captain G. W. Welch's report, 38th Alabama, Clayton's Brigade, Stewart's Division (*OR*, ser. 1, vol. 38, pt. 3, 840) in which Welch explained that his brigade was placed in line east of Adairsville and withdrew south in the direction of Cassville at 1 a.m. See also Colonel Richard W. Turner's report, 19th Louisiana, Gibson's Brigade, Stewart's Division (*OR*, ser. 1, vol. 38, pt. 3, 867), in which he reported that his regiment moved from his bivouac to the right (east) of Adairsville, "right in front" to Cassville. In other words, his regiment traveled east and then south

On the morning of 19 May, while Johnston and his three corps commanders were assembled at Johnston's headquarters, which was located just east of Cassville along the Pine Log Road (today's Cass-White Road) between Chunn Facin Road and Shinall Gaines Road, overlooking the south end of the large, open field.[8]

Butterfield's men were reported one mile from Cassville on the Adairsville-Cassville Road by the Confederate cavalry posted on that road. With the knowledge that the Federal infantry from Hooker's XX Corps—the same Federals that had clashed with Ashby's Tennesseans and Iverson's Georgians farther north on the Adairsville-Cassville Road the previous evening—was driving in the cavalry on that road, Johnston and his lieutenant generals quickly mounted and rode to the right of Polk's line, northward on the Copper Mine/Ironton Road. This road was incorrectly altered by Johnston and identified as the Spring Place Road in the Mackall Journal "O" sample.[9]

There, Hood again renewed his request to make an attack on the "other" Federal column that he believed would be traveling from east of Adairsville and down the Copper Mine-Ironton Road, following the trail blazed by Stewart's and Hindman's divisions of his corps the day before. Since the Confederate leaders had learned that the XX Corps was south of Adairsville on the Adairsville-Cassville Road, and since they had learned from a Federal soldier of the XX Corps captured the evening before on the Copper Mine/Ironton Road, that the IV Corps wagon train was apparently east of Adairsville, and since Butterfield's men were pressing them on the Adairsville-Cassville Road, it was logical for Hood, Johnston, and the others to assume that Federal

on a road east of Adairsville (the Copper Mine/Ironton Road, Road 2) toward Cassville.

[8] Johnston's headquarters on 18 May and the morning of 19 May was located east of Cassville (see Mackall Journal, "O" sample, *OR*, ser. 1, vol. 38, pt. 3, 983). However, around noon, Johnston ordered the headquarters wagons sent beyond Cassville. By 2:25 p.m., Johnston had laid out a new line and ordered the headquarters' wagons to return and set up camp again. It was completed about 6:00 p.m. at a new location east of the Cartersville Road (today's Mac Johnson Road) near a muddy brook and just north of Polk's headquarters (see Mackall Journal "A" and "O" samples, *OR*, ser. 1, vol. 38, pt. 3, 983.

[9] Compare Mackall Journal "A" sample to the "O" sample, *OR*, ser. 1, vol. 38, pt. 3, 983.

troops would also be advancing down the Copper Mine Road/Ironton Road simultaneously, or nearly so, and that it would likely be Howard's IV Corps.[10]

A decade following the war, Johnston claimed that "When Brig. General Jackson's reports showed that the head of the Federal column following the railroad was near Kingston, Lieutenant-General Hood was directed to move with his corps to a country road about a mile to the east of that from Adairsville, and parallel to it, and to march northward on that road, right in front." This statement, written in his *Narrative*, does not comport with the facts, or with Johnston's two purportedly supportive sources, the two Mackalls. First, according to Howard, Stanley's Division of Howard's IV Corps did not reach Kingston until 8:00 a.m.[11]

Second, the Southern commander could not have received Jackson's news (which would have required Jackson to have sent a dispatch rider seven miles from Kingston to Johnston's headquarters) until after he and the three lieutenant generals, Hood, Polk, and Hardee, had already gone to Polk's right. While assembled before daylight at his headquarters, Johnston and his three lieutenant generals received a report early that morning that *Wheeler's cavalry* was being driven down the Adairsville-Cassville Road (Road 1) in front of Polk's line. Johnston and his lieutenant generals, apparently *without his chief of staff, William Mackall*, then rode from his headquarters east of Cassville, through the village, then turned north at the four-way stop and passed Cockrell's Brigade resting in reserve along the road side (following an exhausting march from Alabama the two days prior) as they reached the Y-split with the Adairsville-Cassville Road (Road 1) and the Coppermine/Ironton Road (Road 2, which Johnston mistakenly believed was the Spring Place Road). Johnston and his generals then continued up the Copper Mine/Ironton Road, passing Sears's Brigade posted astride the road just south of the creek, then crossed Two Run Creek, and proceeded to Wheeler's skirmish line along the heights just north of the creek (near the mouth of today's Cedar Creek Road and the County Transfer Station), where they learned that some of Wheeler's troopers were engaged with elements of Ward's Brigade a mile or two up the Adairsville-Cassville Road. Hood repeated his request from the day before to move his corps into position to ambush and attack the anticipated Federal column coming from the Copper Mine/Ironton Road, and here

---

[10] Hood's report, *New York Times*, 29 March 1865, quoting the *Richmond Enquirer*, 25 March 1865; correct copy of report also found in appendix, Hood, *Advance and Retreat*, 334.

[11] Johnston, *Narrative*, 321; Howard's report, *OR*, ser. 1, vol. 38, pt. 1, 191.

Johnston *first* consented to *any* offensive operation at Cassville. Johnston then returned to his headquarters to write his general orders between 7:00 a.m. and 8:00 a.m., while the three corps commanders returned to their corps to prepare for their roles in Hood's plan, Hardee to cover the Kingston Road and slow the Federals from that direction, and Polk to cover the Adairsville-Cassville Road and slide to the west to connect with Hardee.[12]

It is likely that Hood had already renewed his request to attack at Johnston's headquarters that morning, given his passion and his statements in both his report and in *Advance and Retreat*, and that the reconnaissance to Polk's right may have been at Hood's urging. Johnston, who had reached Cassville the day previous via the Kingston Road with Hardee's Corps, was clearly not as familiar with the roads and terrain north and northwest of Cassville, and this inspection after daylight probably afforded him his first opportunity to see the land and how Hood's plan of attack was to unfold.

Third, Mackall's Journal, "O" sample, the published version that is most favorable to Johnston, recorded "The signal corps and General Hardee reported in *forenoon* that enemy in front of Cassville were moving toward Kingston, all advantageous to the designed attack on his left flank." This statement is not found in Mackall's "A" or "B" samples, and it appears that this statement in the "O" sample was inserted for the purpose of bolstering Johnston's story because it is out of sequence from the next statement in the "O" sample, which reads, "An order was written about 7 or 8 a.m. thanking troops for patience, and telling them they would be led against enemy." The next line also does not match, either. It reads, "General J(ohnston) rode over to General Hood's and then passing by general headquarters rode out Spring Place road, north of creek, with Hood and Polk and Hardee to show former where he was to form his line for attack." By the time that Johnston was writing his order, Hood was already busy with preparing his troops for the movement.[13]

Fourth, in contrast to this statement, Hood, in his official report written on 15 February 1865, claimed that "The next morning, while we were assembled at Johnston's headquarters, it was reported that the enemy was driving in the cavalry on the *Adairsville road* [Road 1], in front of Polk's position. Polk's corps was in line of battle and my corps was in bivouac on his right. We all rode to the right of Polk's line in front of my bivouac. Hardee soon left and

---

[12] Cockrell's Missouri Brigade had traveled from northwest Alabama during the past week, making the final thirty-two miles to Rome in about fifteen hours (French, *Two Wars*, 194; Mackall Journal "A," "B," and "O" samples, Appendix F).

[13] Mackall Journal, "O" sample, Appendix F.

went to his position, which was on the left, *there being some report of the enemy being in that direction.*" Hood's statement is more reliable here. First, it was written only nine months from the events at Cassville and during the war while the events were fresh and the various reports and correspondence of the armies was available, whereas Johnston's *Narrative* was written nine years after the war and ten years after the events at Cassville. Moreover, little in Johnston's statements can be corroborated with other events while each of Hood's statements such as why the four generals rode to Polk's right and why Hardee left to tend to his line are interlocked with contemporaneous facts. The claim that Johnston rode to Hood's headquarters, presumably to issue an attack order if his version is to be believed, does not match the reality that Polk and Hardee were also present on Polk's right when the order to attack was either given, if Johnston is to be believed, or consent to his request to make an attack was given, if Hood is to be believed.[14]

Fifth, William Mackall, who was apparently not present when Johnston agreed to permit Hood to make his requested attack, subsequently learned of Hood's attack when Johnston returned to write his general orders. William Mackall made two writings of his experience at Cassville. The most known account was his "Memoranda of the Operations at Cassville on May 19, 1864," written by him on 22 September 1864 at Vineville, Georgia, while William was with Johnston following their departures from the Army of Tennessee. Tellingly, he picked up the story of the morning's events from his first apparent participation with it. It began, "On the morning of the 19th, *after General Johnston returned* from the right of the line, and while Lieutenant-General Hood's corps was moving to attack the enemy, I was by General Johnston ordered to return to General Hood and inform him that General Hardee reported a heavy force advancing on him…." The indication in William's "Memoranda" is that he did not accompany Johnston, Hood, Polk, and Hardee to go to Polk's right. Also, a second indication in William's "Memoranda" is that Hood was moving to attack the enemy, there being no mention about Polk moving to make any attack, a claim that Johnston would also make. Third, if Johnston had indeed planned an attack that morning, surely his chief of staff would have accompanied him and his three lieutenant generals on their reconnaissance. Finally, if Johnston had planned his master stroke of divide and conquer two days earlier at Adairsville, surely William

[14] Hood, *OR*, Serial 74, 634; T Mackall Journal, "O" sample, Appendix F.

would have included some mention of it in his "Memoranda." But he did not.[15]

Sixth, William Mackall also wrote to his wife, Aminta Elizabeth Douglass Sorrel Mackall, the half-sister of Confederate Brigadier General Gilbert Moxley Sorrel, during the Atlanta Campaign. In his letter dated 18 May from Cassville, William made no mention of any plan for attack or of any discussion of a master plan from a meeting at Adairsville the night before. Instead, he repeated much of the same information found in Mackall's journal samples "A," "B," and "O," including "we could hear the cannon at Rome where they were attacking my old staff [chief of staff officer] General Davison," and "Last night the Bishop, General Polk, baptized General Joe." In another letter, dated 21 May, William lamented, "This retreat will damage the General in public estimation till we beat the foe," and then added, "I was so sure the other day that I could not restrain my tears when I found we could not strike." While one could argue that this statement supports Johnston's claim that he had a plan, looking critically that both William's "Memoranda" and his two contemporaneous letters to his wife, to whom he was not shy in disclosing military command decisions and details, there is no mention of any plan for an attack by Johnston, made either while at Adairsville, or the morning of 19 May at Cassville. There is only found his frustration in failing to force a battle north of the Etowah River.[16]

In T. B. Mackall's original "A" sample, Spring Place Road to the east of Cassville was correctly described as located. From that direction, Mackall heard the sounds of artillery firing at 10:30 a.m. ("A" sample). Mackall's "A" sample correlates with Hood's, Beattie's, McCook's, and Rippetoe's accounts. In the "O" sample, which was altered some time prior to 1891 while under the control of Johnston and submitted by him to be published as part of the 128-volume *Official Records*, Mackall's entry was changed to "in ten minutes [after 10:20 a.m.] *report* of artillery in *easterly* direction" ("O" sample).[17]

In the added lines found in the "O" sample, and at the location of the Copper Mine/Ironton Road, the "O" sample included, "General J[ohnston] rode over to General Hood's and then passing by general headquarters rode out *Spring Place Road*, *north* of creek, with Hood and Polk and Hardee to show

[15] W. W. Mackall, "Memoranda of the Operations at Cassville on May 19, 1864," *OR*, ser. 1, vol. 38, pt. 3, 622.

[16] W. W. Mackall Jr., *A Son's Recollections*, 210–11.

[17] Compare Mackall Journal "A" and "B" samples to the "O" sample in Appendix F, *OR*, ser. 1, vol. 38, pt. 3, 983. Emphasis added.

former where he was to form his line for attack." A few lines later in the "O" sample: "After a few moments in town [General Johnston] rode rapidly back out Spring Place Road; general saw Hood and returned to camp-ground and dismounted; Hood's Corps passing, Polk's troops shifting."[18]

The road that Johnston traveled on with Hood, Polk, and Hardee on the right of Polk's line was the Copper Mine/Ironton Road. Hood pointed out the large open field, the range of hills behind which he would move his corps, and the distant ridge behind where he planned to place his men in an ambush position. It was located just below the Copper Mine/Ironton Road, to the north of the large field. Hood asked for Johnston's permission to put his corps in position to make the surprise attack on the Federal column that was believed to be approaching from the Copper Mine/Ironton Road, "in case the report was correct."[19]

Hood later explained the events of the morning of 19 May: "Howard's Corps having been reported on the Ironton road (the country road referred to [by Johnston]), I asked his authorization to march my command across an open field, and attack this detachment of the enemy, *in case the report was correct*. He consented." Hood assumed that the "country road" referred to by Johnston in his *Narrative* was the Ironton Road (Road 2), and not the road on which he took his corps out to the large field (today's Brown Loop Road, Road 3a). Hood, as previously pointed out, never saw Johnston's sketch map as it was not published until 1893.[20]

After resting the previous afternoon and overnight, Hood's men began to move into position by 8:30 on the morning of Thursday, 19 May. Polk adjusted his line westward to a line of hills northwest of Cassville as Hood began to move to the northeast in preparation for his surprise assault. There was ample time for Johnston to write orders for his planned attack. However, he did not plan an attack.

Instead, between 7 and 8 a.m. on 19 May, Johnston wrote and issued a "General Order" to all the troops. (See complete copy in appendix C.) The order complimented the soldiers for their bravery in the recent battles (at Dalton, Resaca, Calhoun, and Adairsville), and assured them that their communications were secure, meaning that their lines of supply and communications (and retreat) were protected. Most importantly, the order explained that the

---

[18] Mackall Journal, "O" sample, *OR*, ser. 1, vol. 38, pt. 3, 983. Emphasis added.

[19] Hood, *Advance and Retreat*, 99.

[20] Ibid.; Johnston, *Narrative of Military Operations*, 321; Johnston's Sketch Map. "Johnston's Map. Emphasis added.

army "will now turn and march to meet his [the enemy's] advancing columns," and that he [Johnston] would "lead you to battle."[21]

For about twenty-four hours, from noon on 18 May when he and his army arrived at Cassville, until midday on 19 May, when the situation began to deteriorate, Johnston was confident. He had extracted himself from the four positions he believed were untenable: Dalton, Resaca, Calhoun, and Adairsville. For months, he had felt constant pressure from President Jefferson Davis and the Richmond authorities to act aggressively and force a battle. With the addition of the last of the reinforcements from Polk's Army of Mississippi, Old Joe had finally consolidated his army at Cassville. If he had to retreat, he could now easily fall back with one night's march to the safety of the Allatoona Mountain range and the Etowah River. And, if Sherman's forces were spread out for miles between Adairsville and Rome, then perhaps Hood's plan of attack might work.

On the afternoon of 18 May, after learning from a newspaper account that General Robert E. Lee's Army of Northern Virginia had badly damaged General U. S. Grant's forces in action at the Wilderness and Spotsylvania, Virginia, including inflicting forty-five thousand casualties on the Federal troops and the loss of thirty-one generals, Johnston bragged to his staff that the "Confederacy was as fixed an institution as England or France!"[22]

The day before, Johnston's staff had received a telegram from Lieutenant General Stephen D. Lee. Originally sent 16 May, but not decipherable until it had been re-sent on 17 May, the message informed the Southern commander that his repeated wish would finally be coming true: General Nathan Bedford Forrest and his feared cavalrymen would be striking middle Tennessee and Sherman's line of supply beginning 20 May![23]

Johnston's confidence was tempered on the afternoon of 18 May when he received another cipher from S. D. Lee that Forrest's move into Tennessee had been suspended due to increased Federal activity from Memphis. Regardless, the time had come for Johnston and his army to fight and win the battle that would help win the war. He preferred to continue to try to delay Sherman's parry into Georgia until the terms of enlistment, for many of the Federal veteran regiments expired in late June. General Hood and the other lieutenant generals had been pressing him to make an attack and engage the

---

[21] Johnston's General Orders, *OR*, ser. 1, vol. 38, pt. 4, 728.

[22] Mackall Journal, "O" sample, *OR*, ser. 1, vol. 38, pt. 3, 982–83.

[23] Ibid.; Symonds, *Joseph E. Johnston*, 288–92; Castel, *Decision in the West*, 198–201; S.D. Lee to Johnston and Polk, *OR*, ser. 1, vol. 38, pt. 4, 719, 726.

enemy. Maybe he should offer battle at Cassville? He had been baptized the night before, after all; surely Divine Providence would bestow favor upon the newly-converted disciple and his cause![24]

Johnston's order, read to the various regiments and units as copies reached them throughout the morning and into the afternoon, was met with wild enthusiasm and cheers. However, there was nothing in the "order" directing any specific action. It was intended that each regiment heard the "order" by noon. By the time many of the soldiers heard the order, they were shifting to a new line of hills south and east of town. This led most of the men to believe that the order had been given because they were preparing to dig in and defend against an expected Federal attack, not due to any offensive operation. Some believed, however, that the right wing (Hood) was going to make an attack the following morning.[25]

During the years following his failure to launch an attack on 19 May, and his subsequent withdrawal from Cassville that night, Johnston took advantage of at least four opportunities to leave a record of his battle plan. First, in his report prepared on 20 October 1864, at Vineville, near Macon, and published in the *Official Records*, Johnston reported that at Adairsville he divided his forces by sending Hardee and the wagon train to Kingston and Polk and Hood to Cassville via the direct road. He stated that "about half of the Federal army took each road" in pursuit. Johnston explained that "the two corps at Cassville [Polk and Hood] were ordered to advance against the troops that had followed them from Adairsville, Hood's leading on the right."[26]

---

[24] S.D. Lee to Johnston and Polk, *OR*, ser. 1, vol. 38, pt. 4, 719, 726.

[25] Hardee to Cleburne, 19 May 1864, note accompanying Johnston's Order with instruction that Johnston wanted it read to all troops by 12 noon (NARA, RG109, Naid: 24468091, vol. 265, p. 135); Colonel Columbus Sykes to his wife, 21 May 1864; Wynne and Taylor, *This War So Horrible*, 74–75; Manigault in Tower, *A Carolinian Goes to War*, 186. These may be compared with Sykes, *Walthall's Brigade*, 568–89, in which it was assumed that Johnston's order meant an attack, not a defensive action. See the account of Major Henry Hampton, who recorded on the evening of 19 May at Cassville following the proclamation of Johnston's general order, "Here, then, all agreed the stand would be made or an advance projected, but before midnight again went our order 'fall back'" (Hampton, itinerary of Hardee's Army Corps, *OR*, ser. 1, vol. 38, pt. 3, 704). See also the accounts of Dr. George Little and James R. Maxwell, veterans of Lumsden's Battery, who recollected that Johnston's "order" meant that they were preparing for an "attack of our right wing on the enemy the next morning" (Little and Maxwell, *History of Lumsden's Battery*, 38).

[26] Johnston's report, *OR*, ser. 1, vol. 38, pt. 3, 615.

In his postwar *Narrative of Military Operations*, published in 1874, Johnston related that Polk's Corps was "deployed in two lines, crossing the road [Adairsville-Cassville Road, Road 1], and facing Adairsville," with Hood's Corps "halted on its [Polk's] right."[27] Johnston added that Jackson's cavalry was to monitor the Federal column approaching Kingston (Road 8) while Wheeler's cavalry was to observe the other Federal units moving toward Cassville and that "those two officers were instructed to keep me accurately informed of the enemy's progress."[28]

The Confederate leader explained that when Jackson reported that the Federal column was near Kingston, "Lieutenant-General Hood was directed to move with his corps to a *country road* about a mile to the east of that from Adairsville, and parallel to it, and to march northward on that road, right in front."[29]

Johnston described a road running parallel to the Adairsville-Cassville Road (Road 1), and about a mile to the east of it, and called it a "country road." Johnston explained that Polk was ordered "to advance to meet and engage the enemy approaching from Adairsville; and [that] it was expected that Hood's [corps] would be in position to fall upon the left flank of those troops as soon as Polk attacked them in front."[30] In his 1874 *Narrative*, for the first time in published sources, Johnston used the term "country road" and stated that Polk was to advance and attack the enemy *first*, a claim not seen before.[31]

In 1878, Johnston wrote an article titled "The Dalton-Atlanta Operations" in response to Sherman's *Memoirs*, which had just been released. In "The Dalton-Atlanta Operations," Johnston disparaged Hood by titling one

---

[27] A double line is typically an indication of placing a field army into a defensive position, with a front line and a supporting line behind it. (See Cameron, *U.S. Infantry Tactics*, 348–50, and Hess, *Civil War Infantry Tactics*, 103–22. Originally compiled by General Winfield Scott and adopted by the US Army in 1935, *U.S. Infantry Tactics* has been commonly referred to as "Scott's Tactics.")

[28] This statement comes closer to explaining to the truth behind the Confederate failure during the morning of 19 May at Cassville, as the greatest mistake may have been Wheeler's failure to patrol and screen the Spring Place Road.

[29] Johnston, *Narrative of Military Operations*, 320–21. Emphasis added.

[30] Ibid.

[31] Ibid., 321. In response, Hood, in *Advance and Retreat*, tried to clarify this issue and explained that the "country road" referred to by Johnston was the Ironton Road that he had previously referred to in his original report, as published in the *Richmond Enquirer* on 25 March 1865, in the *New York Times* on 29 March 1865, and in Hood, *Advance and Retreat*, 317–37, 334.

of his sections "Hood's Erratic Movement." He had previously described Hood's redeployment at Cassville as "erratic" in his report and *Narrative*, but by this time he had coined the new phrase, and, unfortunately, it was one that both his contemporary disciples and subsequent historians continued to use.[32]

In his article, Johnston did not mention the country road, but instead merely stated that Hood was to march on a road to Polk's right. Referring to himself in the third person, he wrote that "Johnston determined to attack the column on the direct road [Adairsville-Cassville Road, Road 1], with Polk's and Hood's corps when the other [column] was at Kingston, three hours' march to the west." Johnston continued, "Polk was to meet and attack the head of the column; Hood, marching a little in advance of him on a road on his right, was to join in the action as the enemy deployed."[33] Interestingly, in his initial report in 1864, Johnston had indicated that Hood "advanced some two miles" northeast of town. In his *Narrative* in 1874, he said Hood "moved two or three miles." In this account in *Annals* in 1878, Johnston maintained that Hood "marched some miles in the proper direction."[34]

In 1889, Johnston had a fourth opportunity to tell his version of the events at Cassville. Published in January 1889, *Battles and Leaders* was a massive undertaking to obtain contributions from various officers about events during the war. Johnston contributed his views in an article titled "Opposing Sherman's Advance to Atlanta," which was included in volume four. In it, he explained that "Hood was instructed to move and follow northwardly a *country road* a mile east of that from Adairsville, to be in position to fall upon the flank of the Federal column when it should be engaged with Polk." Johnston added that "after going some three miles, General Hood marched back about two, and formed his corps facing to our right and rear."[35]

In this fourth account, Johnston used the term "country road" a second time and extended Hood's march out of Cassville to three miles. He also retreated from his claim that Polk was to attack first, but merely stated that Polk was to engage the enemy—just as he had originally claimed in his wartime report.

---

[32] Johnston, "The Dalton-Atlanta Operations," 4–5.

[33] Ibid.

[34] *OR*, ser. 1, vol. 38, pt. 3, 616; Johnston, *Narrative of Military Operations*, 321; Johnston, "The Dalton-Atlanta Operations," 5.

[35] Johnston, "Opposing Sherman's Advance to Atlanta," 287–88. Emphasis added.

This version follows Johnston's original report more closely and perhaps provides the best version of Johnston's understanding of Hood's battle plan: namely, that Hood would take his corps out of town via the "country road" (today's Brown Loop Road, Road 3a) and form his troops along the Copper Mine/Ironton Road (Road 2), the road that Johnston thought was about a mile east of and parallel to the Adairsville-Cassville Road (Road 1). Then, when Polk engaged the Federal column coming down the Adairsville-Cassville Road, the blue-clad troops in the lead would be forced to assume a battleline formation, thereby exposing their left, or eastern flank. Hood's Corps, which was formed on the other road, would then sweep from east to west across the flank of the Federals in front of Polk.

Johnston's understanding of the plan did not conform to Hood's plan to attack a different column of Federals that Hood believed was coming via the Copper Mine/Ironton Road (Road 2). Additionally, Johnston seemed unaware of the names Ironton or Copper Mine (Road 2 and 2b), instead believing that Road 2 was the Spring Place Road. He was unaware of the correct location of the Spring Place Road (Road 3), probably because Road 3 was "off the map" and outside the scope of what he understood concerning Hood's battle plan. A decade later, when Johnston wrote his *Narrative*, he was still apparently unaware of the existence and location of Road 3 (the correct Spring Place Road) as evidenced by the map he used in his book. Johnston also confused Hood with the "country road" (Road 3a) reference, mostly likely because Johnston was himself confused. This confusion may explain why the four published variations of his alleged "battle plan" do not comport with either the road structure or the contemporaneous accounts. Also, his four accounts remain vague and varied. Even still, it helps to understand what Johnston may have been thinking and how he remembered, or perceived, Hood's request.

On 19 June 1874, Johnston wrote to Charles G. Johnsen, a former lieutenant with the Washington Artillery (Slocum's Battery) that served in Hardee's Corps during the Atlanta Campaign. In the letter, written while Johnston was in Savannah, the former commander included a hand-drawn map, on which he drew, to the best of his recollection, the location of the places at Cassville.[36] In fairness to Johnston, the letter offers his best explanation for his understanding of the battle plan at Cassville and provides some continuity for his four published accounts.

---

[36] Johnston to Johnsen, 19 June 1874, 319; also, *New Orleans Times Picayune*, 22 October 1893.

Hood never saw Johnston's hand-drawn map since it was not made public until it was published in 1893 in the *Times Picayune*, fourteen years after his death. Hood would have been surprised to see the location of the "country road" (at today's Brown Loop Road, Road 3a) that Johnston attributed in his hand-drawn map because Johnston's previous reference to the "country road" that Hood had read in Johnston's 1874 *Narrative* fit the location Hood was heading *toward* in preparation for his surprise attack. *That* road was the Ironton Road as he explained in *Advance and Retreat* and was not the same road as the one on which his columns marched *from* town.

In the letter, Johnston stated, "Hood was to march by his right flank on the country road, east of and parallel to that [the "direct" road] to Adairsville. When his rear was opposite A [as shown in Johnston's accompanying sketch], Polk was to move towards Adairsville, in order of battle, until he met the enemy." He continued, "when he [Polk] became engaged, Hood was to face to the left and take the Federals in flank. Before the time came to order General Polk forward, General Hood, moving towards Adairsville on the country road, upon a wild report, turned back, and formed his corps on the line marked B [on the sketch]." The old chieftain complained, "This frustrated the design of attacking, and put us on the defensive."[37]

Two important factors that Johnston failed to take into account should be considered in evaluating his statements. The first is that there are absolutely no accounts from anyone in Polk's Corps, either contemporary, or postwar, to corroborate a claim that any order was given to Polk and his men to make any kind of advance, engagement, or attack. If there had been, then Ward's and Wood's brigades would have been met, engaged, or attacked. That did not happen, and Butterfield was permitted to extract his two exposed brigades from harm's way unmolested and to move them to the Colonel Price house and grounds where he consolidated his division. The second important fact that does not comport with Johnston's version of events concerns his claim that Hood reversed course based upon "a wild report," a claim Johnston also made in his official report when he stated that a staff officer who had told Hood that Federals had appeared on the Canton Road in Hood's rear was "mistaken." In his *Narrative*, Johnston called it Hood's "erratic" movement.

In all of his accounts, Johnston failed to address the reality that Hood sustained casualties during the 10:30 a.m. action in both Sharp's Mississippi brigade (the 9th Mississippi Battalion Sharpshooters and the 41st Mississippi) from the Federal artillery fire (Rippetoe's Eighteenth Indiana artillery)

---

[37] Ibid.

which came from the Spring Place Road at Five Forks, and in the 63rd Virginia in Alexander Reynolds's brigade on the Canton Road.[38]

Hood was correct to turn back and redeploy in a defensive position to cover the roads to his right and rear until he could better develop and determine the enemy force that had surprised him. Johnston ratified Hood's course of conduct when he first learned of it, exclaiming, as he called for a map, "If that's so, General Hood will have to fall back at once." Johnston subsequently looked for and found a defensive position, a range of hills south and east of Cassville which covered the Canton Road.[39]

While the hand-drawn Johnston map is clearly not to scale and was drawn a decade after the events occurred, it had several key components that may be informative to a study of the events at Cassville today. First, Johnston identified and placed Polk's Corps on the map indicating them at point "A," which was a range of hills northwest of Cassville, in a defensive position. Second, he included the location of the "country road" and added "country road by which Hood was to move."[40] Third, the location of the "country road" as sketched by Johnston was east of the junction of two roads northeast of Cassville. These two roads were the Canton Road (Road 5) and the Pine Log Road (today's Cassville White Road, Road 4). Fourth, the mouth of the "country road" is on the Pine Log Road and in a gap between two hills. This specific description can only be found in one place along the Pine Log Road (today's Cassville-White Road, Road 4). It is known today as the Brown Loop Road and is indicated as Road 3a. This road may also be found on the Ruger Map in the *Official Atlas*, which shows its connection to the Spring Place Road to the northeast.[41]

The intersection of today's Brown Loop Road (Road 3a) with today's Cassville-White Road is the place Johnston understood to be the origin of the "country road" near Cassville. Johnston also referred to this road as being about a mile east of, and parallel to, the Adairsville-Cassville Road. By straight line, the distance between the Adairsville-Cassville Road, at its crossing of Two Run Creek, and Brown Loop Road, at its crossing of Two Run Creek, is 1.6 miles.

Hood described the Ironton Road as the road that he was headed *toward*, and not the road that his men traveled when leaving Cassville. Johnston did

---

[38] Ibid.; Johnston, *Narrative of Military Operations*, 322.

[39] Mackall Journal, "O" sample, *OR*, ser. 1, vol. 38, pt. 3, 983–84.

[40] Johnston Map.

[41] Ibid.; Ruger Map.

not understand Hood's battle plan, and he did not know the name of the road that Hood was headed toward. If Hood had been able to see Johnston's sketched map, he could have corrected the confusion caused by Johnston's lack of understanding.

A final factor to contemplate is Johnston's failure to consider the threat of Federal approaches east of the "direct route," as he referred to the Adairsville-Cassville Road (Road 1). Johnston never mentioned the possibility of multiple Federal columns advancing on Cassville from the north by way of different roads. This possibility apparently did not fit Johnston's narrative.

Johnston maintained that Polk was to advance and attack the Federals approaching from the direct road to force them to deploy, presumably to aid in Hood's flank attack. While this may have been a potentially sound offensive strategy, the record is silent as to Polk's alleged participation in the morning offensive, other than to serve as a blocking unit across the ridge north and west of Cassville and just below Two Run Creek at the Adairsville-Cassville Road. Johnston, in his official report written on 20 October 1864, merely stated that the two corps, Polk's and Hood's, were to advance on the enemy approaching from Adairsville, as he indicated, "Hood's leading on the right." Johnston's own redeployment of his army to the second line south and east of Cassville was made for the purpose of covering any Federal approach to his right and rear from the Canton Road.[42]

There is no mention of a plan for Polk's men to attack first in any literature from Polk's Corps (or Army of Mississippi, as it was called at the time). Polk was killed on 14 June at Pine Mountain and left no report, but major generals William Wing Loring and Samuel G. French in Polk's Corps both published reports of the operations of their divisions during the campaign, and neither report mentioned advancing to attack the enemy. Loring merely explained that "on arriving at Cassville the division was placed in position, skirmished with the enemy, and retired at night with the main body of the army."[43]

In addition to his report, French kept a diary from which he quoted in his postwar autobiography, *Two Wars*. His diary entry for 19 May reads, "This morning the army was formed in line of battle. At first I was on the extreme right, but soon after, by change of dispositions, I occupied the line from the hills, on Loring's right, across the valley to the top of the first hill on my right."

---

[42] Johnston's report, *OR*, ser. 1, vol. 38, pt. 3, 615.

[43] Loring's report, *OR*, ser. 1, vol. 38, pt. 3, 875. See also French's report, *OR*, ser. 1, vol. 38, pt. 3, 899.

Importantly, French adds, "Hood's Corps was on my right, maneuvering to attack the enemy, but from some cause no fight was made."[44] French pointed out that Hood was preparing to attack, but he made no mention of Polk's Corps, or any other unit making similar advances.[45]

Of note concerning Johnston's claim that Polk was also ordered to attack is the absence of any such recorded statement by either of the two Mackalls, who each left memorandums and journals of the events. In T. B. Mackall's "O" sample version of his journal, the one most favorable to Johnston and the one that Johnston caused to be published in the *Official Records*, Mackall (or someone writing for him) wrote that Johnston "rode out Spring Place road, north of creek, with Hood and Polk and Hardee to show former where he was to form his line for attack."[46] There was no mention of Polk making any attack. Nor did any of the other T. B. Mackall journal samples report that Polk was to initiate an attack.

Finally, the most serious piece of evidence to refute Johnston's claim that Polk was to attack first comes from Brigadier General William W. Mackall, Johnston's own chief of staff, who wrote a memo that, ironically, was intended to support his commander. Mackall wrote on 22 September 1864, while he was with Johnston at Vineville, Georgia, that "while Lieutenant-General Hood's Corps was moving to attack the enemy, I was by General Johnston ordered to return to General Hood and inform him that General Hardee

[44] French, *Two Wars*, 196. While French's diary and postwar autobiography tended to support Hood's version of the Morning Cassville Affair, he was inclined to support more of Johnston's version of the events concerning the Evening Cassville Affair.

[45] During extensive research on Polk's Army of Mississippi in the Atlanta Campaign, I have not found any source that supported Johnston's claim that Polk was ordered to attack first. All, in fact, gave evidence to the contrary. As an example, Colonel M. D. L. Stephens, commander of the 31st Mississippi Infantry in Featherston's Brigade of Loring's Division, recorded in his *Recollections* that Loring's Division "marched to Cassville where we formed line of battle in [on] the crest of a hill southeast of Rome and waited the advance of the enemy. The enemy advanced and opened fire on our line with artillery which was promptly answered from our side" (Stephens, *Recollections*, 30).

[46] The Pine Log Road (Road 4) merged with the Spring Place Road (Road 3) at Five Forks. Thus, the stretch of road from Five Forks into town could have accurately been called by any of three names, the Pine Log Road, the Fairmount Road, or the Spring Place Road. T. B. Mackall referred to the road east of town as the Spring Place Road (Mackall Journal, "A" and "B" samples).

reported a heavy force advancing on him...[and] if the enemy advanced upon him to strike him promptly and hard."[47] If Polk was supposed to meet and attack the enemy first, why then was Mackall ordered to tell Hood that "if the enemy advanced upon him to strike him promptly and hard"?[48] William Mackall was never sent to hurry Polk. He was sent to hurry Hood. William Mackall's memo supports Hood's version of the battle plan.

[47] W. W. Mackall, "Memoranda of the Operations at Cassville on May 19, 1864," *OR*, ser. 1, vol. 38, pt. 3, 621–22. Additionally, William Mackall wrote a letter to his wife, 21 May 1864, in which he expressed his disappointment when they were unable to strike a blow to the enemy and added that he believed General Johnston's reputation would be damaged (W. W. Mackall, Jr., *A Son's Recollections of His Father*, 211).

[48] W. W. Mackall, "Memoranda," *OR*, ser. 1, vol. 38, pt. 3, 983.

Chapter 7

Hood's Battle Plan

In contrast to Johnston's multiple opportunities to explain his plan of battle at Cassville and leave a record for future historians, Hood had only two chances to leave his story. First, his report, dated 15 February 1865 and submitted to Adjutant and Inspector General Samuel Cooper and the Confederate War Department, provided his explanation of his intended plan of attack. In the correct version of his report, as found in the *New York Times*, 29 March 1865 (reprinted from the *Richmond Enquirer* 25 March 1865 and also included in the appendix to *Advance and Retreat*), Hood explained,

> After the army had arrived at Cassville [midday Wednesday, 18 May], I proposed to Gen. Johnston, in the presence of Gens. Hardee and Polk, to move back upon the enemy, and attack him at or near Adairsville, urging as a reason, that our three corps could move back, each upon a separate road, while the enemy had but one main road upon which he could approach that place.[1]

After relating that no decision had been reached, Hood said that he, Hardee, and Polk left Johnston's headquarters together and, while riding, continued their discussion. According to Hood, Polk enthusiastically agreed to Hood's proposal, and Hardee also was in favor of it. The three corps commanders decided to wait until the following morning to renew the discussion with Johnston.

While the Confederate army reached Cassville by noon on 18 May, this meeting at Johnston's headquarters likely occurred in the evening. T. B. Mackall recorded in his journal, "O" sample, that "Hood and Hardee and Polk [were] at headquarters discussing over map plans for morning."[2] Hood pointed out that Johnston failed to mention Hood's proposal to attack the day before, on 18 May, while Sherman was still at Adairsville, a point that Hood said offered the best chance for success because the Confederates had *three routes* south of Adairsville while Sherman had only one route north of the town. Hood reasoned that the single lane north of Adairsville to Calhoun, which had been a liability for the Confederate army the day before, could now

---

[1] Hood's report, *New York Times*, 29 March 1865; Hood, *Advance and Retreat*, 317–37, 334.

[2] Mackall Journal, "O" sample, *OR*, ser. 1, vol. 38, pt. 3, 983.

be used against Sherman and his columns. The Federals would not be able to be reinforced easily from the scattered units between Mosteller's Mill to the east and Rome to the west. Sherman's only route of escape from Adairsville, in the event of a defeat, was the single lane leading to Calhoun, and the Oostanaula River would be at his back.[3]

In addition, on 18 May Hood had issued a circular order to all his division commanders to be prepared for any move, including an advance or a further retreat. The order, sent on behalf of Hood by J. W. Ratchford, assistant adjutant general, explained "in order that you may be prepared for any move, that the enemy are advancing on *both roads* we marched on this morning." In other words, Hood had anticipated that in his 18 May meeting with Johnston and the other corps commanders, either Johnston would approve his suggestion to turn back and attack the pursuing Federals, or the Confederate leader might order the army to continue to retreat to the south side of the Etowah River.[4]

The most important point here, however, is that Hood's order referred to two roads on which his corps had marched on, a point which previous historians could have assumed meant the Adairsville-Cassville (Road 1) and the Adairsville-Kingston Roads (Road 8). However, Ratchford's dispatch referred to the Adairsville-Cassville Road and the Ironton Road (Road 2) because portions of Hood's Corps used both routes to reach Cassville. General Schofield would eventually use the Ironton Road (Road 2b and Road 2) to reach Cassville following a frustrating day of marching and countermarching. Schofield also described the road from Mosteller's Mill to Cassville (Road 2a to Road 2) as the route in which he intended to use before Sherman's dispatch redirected him to move to "get up to General Hooker" on the Adairsville-Cassville Road (Road 1).[5]

Hood's three divisions were east of Hardee's Corps and northeast of Adairsville on the evening of 17 May. Manigault's Brigade of Hindman's Division was posted along a ridge east of Adairsville (just east of today's I-75 at Exit 306, between the Rest Area to the north and Iron Mountain, the site of Vulcan Mine, to the south). The ridge overlooked the plain to the north and

---

[3] Hood, *Advance and Retreat*, 99.

[4] Ratchford to division commanders, 18 May 1864, *OR*, ser. 1, vol. 38, pt. 4, 726. Emphasis added.

[5] *OR*, ser. 1, vol. 38, pt. 4, 726; Schofield to Sherman, note 19, May 1864, 12:40 p.m., *OR*, ser. 1, vol. 38, pt. 4, 255; Sherman to Schofield, note 18 May 1864, *OR*, ser. 1, vol. 38, pt. 4, 242–43.

northwest where the Federal army deployed and attacked Cheatham's Division. Deas's Brigade was posted another mile or two to the east near Mosteller's Mill to support Confederate cavalry operating in that area.[6]

Johnston and his three corps commanders were concerned about withdrawing from Adairsville using multiple roads to move more quickly and efficiently. Thus, it made no sense for Hood's Corps to march west and into the village of Adairsville, where they would be behind both Polk's Corps as it began its withdrawal via the Adairsville-Cassville Road (Road 1), and Hardee's Corps, as it covered the retreat and the wagon train south via the Adairsville-Kingston Road (Road 8).

General Manigault described having difficulty finding the road. "Whilst laying on the top of our ridge, we could hear the movements of our troops, as they marched off during the night, and when the time came for us to start, everything from that part of the field had departed. A thick fog had risen during the night," Manigault explained, "and it was with much difficulty that I could find my way out to the road to join the division, which was that day to be the rear guard."[7]

Confederate pioneer Hiram Williams, a native of New Jersey, had migrated to Alabama just two years prior to the war, but when hostilities began, he cast his lot with the Yellowhammer State and joined the 40th Alabama Infantry. Charged with cutting timbers, clearing brush, erecting log breastworks, erecting crude log bridges over streams, and clearing paths to make wagon roads, Williams and his team of pioneers were frequently called upon. After fixing bridges just south of Adairsville on 17 May, they were ordered at 2 a.m. on 18 May to improve another road to Cassville. "Two miles to the east of this," Williams recorded in his diary, "there is another road running to the town of Cassville, county seat of Cass County. Nobody knew the road, but several pretended to know it. Up a long narrow lane half-a-mile, then—where then. Ah, 'that's the question,'" he wrote, clearly exasperated.[8] "The Captain rides off to inquire. Soon returns with all the needful information, so he says. Off again. Over a rough stumpy road! Across nearby creeks, where one gets his feet wet in getting over despite his utmost care. Up to the corner of a field. No road to be traced any farther. What then?" Williams continued to describe his frustration at his officer's efforts to find the road (Ironton Road, Road 2) he and his pioneers were supposed to repair during the night.

---

[6] Manigault and Tower, *A Carolinian Goes to War*, 185.

[7] Ibid.

[8] Wynne and Taylor, *This War So Horrible*, 73.

Finally, the captain ordered his pioneers corpsmen to lie down for the balance of the night. At daylight the pioneers were off again, "through deep forests, over fields of young corn, along rough hilly lanes, we marched until we reached the road we were in search of, when we found that we had just struck the head of our [Stewart's] division—just in time."[9]

Hindman's Division withdrew from east of Adairsville via the Ironton Road (Road 2e and Road 2) and went around the east side of Iron Mountain and through Pleasant Valley, following Stewart's Division, while Stevenson's Division marched down the Adairsville-Cassville Road (Road 1) along with the smaller-sized corps of Polk. Only the three brigades of Loring, two brigades of Cantey, and Sears's Brigade of French's Division withdrew south from Adairsville. Cockrell's and Ector's brigades joined the army at Kingston and Cassville. For a better understanding of the routes of withdrawal by Polk's and Hood's corps south from Adairsville, see Map 3, "Confederate Withdrawal from Adairsville to Cassville, May 18, 1864."[10]

By process of elimination, the remaining division, Stevenson's, took the Adairsville-Cassville Road along with Polk's Corps. The route of Stevenson's Division on the Adairsville-Cassville Road is corroborated by the capture of fifteen prisoners from Stevenson's Division by Butterfield's men on the Adairsville-Cassville Road (Road 1), as explained in detail in the previous chapter. Also, Stevenson's Division was in the rear of Hood's attacking column on 19 May, with Stewart's Division in the center and Hindman's Division in the lead. Hindman's Division, following Stewart's men on the Copper Mine/Ironton Road on 18 May, arrived at Cassville last.

"The next morning [Thursday, 19 May]," Hood recorded, "while we were all assembled at Gen. Johnston's headquarters, it was reported that the enemy was driving in the cavalry on the Adairsville road, in front of Polk's position. Polk's Corps was in line of battle and my corps was in bivouac on his right," he continued. "We all rode to the right of Polk's line in front of my bivouac. Hardee soon left and went to his position, which was on the left, there being some report of the enemy being in that direction. Gen. Johnston

---

[9] Ibid., 73–74.

[10] Mackall Journal, "A," "B," samples show Sears's Brigade arrived at Adairsville, but the presence of Sears's Brigade at Adairsville is not mentioned in the "O" sample despite it being more than five time longer than either the "A" or "B" samples (Mackall Journal, "O" sample, *OR*, ser. 1, vol. 38, pt. 3, 982); French, *OR*, ser. 1, vol. 38, pt. 3, 899; Manigault and Tower, *A Carolinian Goes to War*, 185; Wynne and Taylor, *This War So Horrible*, 73–74.

said to me, 'You can, if you desire, move with your corps to the Ironton road, and if Howard's corps is there you can attack it.'"[11]

The evening before, during the meeting between Johnston and his three corps commanders, a prisoner from Hooker's XX Corps had been brought in for questioning. In their presence, T. B. Mackall questioned the captured Federal soldier, who explained that "his command was behind Howard's [IV Corps which had]...skirmished with Cheatham [on the] afternoon of [May] 17th, and all [the Federal] army was assembled close by. Next morning (on [the] 18th) [the prisoner reported that the] whole command [was] in motion. Howard moved into Adairsville, halted, and cooked dinner." T. B. Mackall continued, "Prisoner got lost among Howard's men and was told Hooker had moved toward our right, and endeavoring to join his regiment was captured by our cavalry; was told that an additional corps was following behind Hooker; knew nothing of other commands."[12]

Based upon this intelligence, the Confederate leaders believed that Howard's IV Corps and Hooker's XX Corps, and perhaps one other corps behind these two, were at or east of Adairsville and would likely be headed toward Cassville, while the other half of Sherman's army would be marching toward Kingston, or perhaps further to the west. Thus, on the morning of 19 May, when Wheeler's cavalry began to report skirmishing with his outposts on the Adairsville-Cassville Road, the Southern leaders expected that Howard and Hooker were on their way to Cassville following the same two roads that they had taken the morning before, the Adairsville-Cassville Road (Road 1) and the Ironton Road. (Road 2). Wheeler explained in his report for 19 May, "at daylight, my line was formed about a mile in front of the infantry line. The enemy advanced a heavy line of skirmishers from a woods toward the field in our front."[13]

Wheeler's outpost on the Adairsville-Cassville Road consisted of the Georgia troopers of Brigadier General Alfred Iverson's brigade, supported by the two brigades of Brigadier General William Y. C. Humes's division,

---

[11] Hood's report, *New York Times*, March 29, 1865; Hood, *Advance and Retreat*, 317–37, 334.

[12] Mackall Journal, "O" sample, *OR*, ser. 1, vol. 38, pt. 3, 983. The additional corps behind the XX Corps was Schofield's XXIII Corps, which spent the night of 18 May at Mosteller's Mill (Schofield, *OR*, ser. 1, vol. 38, pt. 4, 41–42).

[13] Wheeler's report, *OR*, ser. 1, vol. 38, pt. 3, 946.

Ashby's Tennesseans and Harrison's Arkansans, Texans, and Tennesseans. Wheeler also had his artillery present, covering the road (Road 1).[14]

Opposing Wheeler along this road was Butterfield's Division. These men had bivouacked the night before on the Adairsville-Cassville Road about four miles away, at the foot of the Gravelly Plateau, where they had found water.[15] Early on the morning of 19 May, Butterfield reported, "The enemy's cavalry are about a mile and a quarter beyond my advance pickets…partly mounted, partly dismounted."[16]

Howard's IV Corps was on the Adairsville-Kingston Road (Road 8) and headed for the Kingston-Cassville Road (Road 9) by mid-morning on 19 May, but the Confederate high command did not know that. It was reasonable for Hood and the other Southern leaders to believe that if Butterfield's Division (XX Corps) was on the Adairsville-Cassville Road (Road 1) at dawn on 19 May, then the other Federal corps that had been reported at Adairsville by the Federal prisoner, Howard's IV Corps, would be on the easterly road from Adairsville, the Ironton Road (Road 2). When Hood was surprised by Federal cavalry on the Spring Place Road and Canton Road later that morning, it was reasonable for him to conclude that the mysterious column could have been the front of the remaining Federal corps that had been trailing the IV and XX Corps at Adairsville. However, Hood correctly deduced that the Federals who struck his right and rear while he was on the march were likely cavalry.[17]

After Johnston gave him permission to attack, Hood explained that "my troops were put in motion. At the head of the column, I moved over to this road [the Ironton road] and found it in possession of our own dismounted cavalry, and [found] no enemy there." Hood had no doubt hoped that he would reach Wheeler's cavalrymen, probably Ashby's and Harrison's brigades, before any Federals had yet approached, in the hopes that he could move his men into position to set the trap.[18]

---

[14] Ibid.

[15] Hooker to Whipple, 18 May 1864, 10:30 p.m., *OR*, ser. 1, vol. 38, pt. 4, 239.

[16] Butterfield to Hooker, 19 May 1864, 5:15 a.m., *OR*, ser. 1, vol. 38, pt. 4, 253.

[17] Hood's report, *New York Times*, 29 March 1865, quoting *Richmond Enquirer*, 25 March 1865; Hood, *Advance and Retreat*, 334.

[18] Hood's report, *New York Times*, 29 March 1865, quoting *Richmond Enquirer*, 25 March 1865.

Meanwhile, Johnston returned to his headquarters and composed his "eloquent, blood-stirring order"[19] from 7 a.m. to 8 a.m. while waiting for the planned attack to begin. Hearing only small arms fire on the Adairsville-Cassville Road at 10:20 a.m., and some artillery from there, as well as from the Spring Place Road to the east around 10:30 a.m., but hearing no general engagement, Johnston was no doubt puzzled. Then, upon receiving a report from Hardee that Federals were pressing him from the direction of Kingston, Johnston dispatched William Mackall to Hood to hasten his attack. Johnston did not send a message to Polk, however, then or at any other time, to "hurry up" or engage the enemy.[20]

Hood explained that, as his men neared the Ironton Road, "a body of the enemy, which I supposed to be cavalry, made its appearance on the Canton road in rear of the right of my original position. Major Gen. Hindman was then [sent] in that direction with his division, to ascertain what force it was, keeping the other two divisions in the vicinity of the Ironton road."[21]

In his *Advance and Retreat*, Hood's second and final chance to record his view of the events at Cassville, the subordinate commander paraphrased his previous report concerning his battle plan by stating, "On the following day, Howard's Corps having been reported on the Ironton road (the county road referred to [in Johnston's *Narrative*]), I asked his authorization to march my command across an open field, and attack this detachment of the enemy, in case the report was correct. He consented."[22]

While the events are confusing, the key point is that Hood's battle plan was to strike a federal column that was thought to be headed down the Ironton Road (Road 2), purportedly Howard's IV Corps. Hood's plan called for marching to the east along the Pine Log/Spring Place Road (Road 3–4), through a gap in a ridge, crossing Two Run Creek, then turning left and marching across a large, open field to lie in wait on the back side of a ridge that commanded the Ironton Road. There, Hood's divisions would be hidden from view from the unsuspecting Federals, who were assumed to be headed

---

[19] S. Hood, *John Bell Hood*, 47. Richard McMurry described Johnston's general order as "bombastic" (*Atlanta 1864*, 83). One of Johnston's officers, Colonel E. T. Sykes, adjutant general of Walthall's Mississippi brigade of Hindman's Division in Hood's Corps, which was in the vanguard of Hood's attacking column, sarcastically termed it the "celebrated battle order" (Sykes, *Walthall's Brigade*, 568).

[20] Mackall Journal, "O" sample, *OR*, ser. 1, vol. 38, pt. 3, 983.

[21] Hood's report, *New York Times*, 29 March 1865; Hood, *Advance and Retreat*, 334.

[22] Hood, *Advance and Retreat*, 99.

down the old, wooded country road, Ironton Road (Road 2) on the other side of the slope.

Hood described both the Spring Place Road and the Canton Road as being to his right and rear, respectively, after his lead division (Hindman's) had reached the open field and was proceeding to cross it.

The only other contemporaneous usage of the term "Spring Place Road" was by T. B. Mackall in his "A" and "O" samples. In the "A" sample, T. B. Mackall described hearing artillery from the Spring Place Road at 10:30 a.m. In his "O" sample, he (or the unidentified author[s] under Johnston's supervision) explained that General Johnston "rode out Spring Place Road, north of creek, with Hood and Polk and Hardee." As discussed in the previous chapter, the road Johnston and his lieutenant generals took out of town in order to reach Polk's right, across the creek north of town, to determine which Federal columns were approaching from the Adairsville-Cassville Road, was the Copper Mine/Ironton Road (Road 2).[23] Hood's Corps moved out of Cassville to the east, turned to the north, traveled through a range of hills, then crossed the creek and moved across the large field toward the Copper Mine/Ironton Road. Johnston's own hand-drawn map supported Hood's position concerning the route of his march.[24]

Finally, Johnston's chief of staff, William Mackall, by his own admissions in his *Memoranda*, supported Hood's version of the battle plan. Mackall did not record any plan for Polk to make an attack. Instead, Mackall remembered that he was sent to Hood by Johnston with an admonition to hurry his attack because the Federals were advancing with "a heavy force" on Hardee from the Kingston Road. In keeping with his instructions from Johnston, Mackall told Hood "*if the enemy advanced upon him* to strike him [the enemy] promptly and hard." However, according to Mackall, there was no such record of any admonition to Polk. Additionally, Mackall's statement to Hood to attack "if the enemy advanced upon him" is consistent with Hood's claims that that he had been given permission by Johnston to move his corps to the Ironton (Copper Mine) Road, and "*if Howard's corps is there* you can attack it."[25]

---

[23] Mackall Journal, "O" sample, *OR*, ser. 1, vol. 38, pt. 3, 983.

[24] Johnston Map.

[25] W. Mackall, *Memoranda, OR*, ser. 1, vol. 38, pt. 3, 622; Hood's report, *New York Times*, 29 March 1865; Hood, *Advance and Retreat*, 334. Emphasis added.

Chapter 8

Sherman's Analysis and Plan

As Johnston evacuated Adairsville and moved southward down the Adairsville-Kingston Road (Road 8), his heavy wagons left behind a deeply rutted trail on the roads that had become wet from rain the evening before. Sherman became convinced, or perhaps hoped, that Johnston was retreating to Kingston to gain time to evacuate his vast machinery and supplies at Rome. To the east, Sherman knew that the Hightower Bridge, by which the Western & Atlantic Railroad cars crossed over the Etowah River, was a key link in the critical route of supply and communication to Atlanta for Johnston's army. If Sherman could overtake him before he crossed the bridge, he might be able to force a battle between the Etowah and Oostanaula Rivers. If Johnston was planning on Kingston as his place of defense, then Sherman could cut off the Confederate supply and retreat line to Atlanta by destroying the railroad to the east. Then, he could do the same to the west by capturing Rome and destroying the rail line there. Johnston would have the Etowah River at his back and would be compelled to cross it with Sherman at his front, and no rail line nearby. Thus, Sherman hoped, the Southern army would be forced either to fight north of the river or to cross it and retreat twenty-five miles southeast on back roads to Acworth south of the Allatoona Mountains.

Sherman issued orders to his cavalry divisions accordingly. At 6:15 p.m. on 17 May, from his headquarters just north of Adairsville, Sherman sent an order to McPherson directing him to have "Garrard and Murray to make a dash at the railroad between Rome and Kingston (if not already done) to-night.... If not done to-night there will be no use in doing it at all."[1] Sherman sent a similar order the same evening to Stoneman that would produce significant results.[2]

Sherman told Stoneman that he wanted him to advance along the Pine Log corridor toward the Etowah River Bridge (the Hightower Bridge), and to break the railroad between Cassville and Cartersville. Sherman strengthened Stoneman's probing force with McCook's cavalry division from Schofield's Army of the Ohio. To both Stoneman and McCook, Sherman

---

[1] Sherman, dispatch to McPherson, 17 May, 6:15 p.m., *OR*, ser. 1, vol. 38, pt. 4, 227.

[2] Castel, *Decision in the West*, 202.

added, "It is also important that you should measure your fighting qualities with the enemy's cavalry about Cassville. I am sure you can beat them, but it should be done suddenly so as to produce a salutary effect and be of moral force to you in after operations." Sherman's admonition for aggression by the Federal troopers would soon yield much fruit.[3]

Believing that Johnston would not offer battle north of the Etowah River, Sherman issued orders to all his commands to advance on Kingston as their point of direction. Thus, like spokes of a wagon wheel, McPherson's Army of the Tennessee proceeded from the northwest, Thomas with the IV Corps and two divisions of the XIV Corps came from the north, and Hooker and Schofield approached from the northeast. At 11:40 a.m. on 18 May, Thomas delivered Sherman's orders to Hooker and his corps who were located at Mosteller's Mill. Thomas added, "We are informed that there are neighborhood roads which will lead you along the back [east] of the hills past here [Adairsville]. With the aid of the guide Cooper, who has been sent you, and a neighborhood guide, you will be able to march abreast of Howard's corps and connect with him." Ironically, the guide who helped the Federals find their way around Iron Mountain and across the Gravelly Plateau was named Cooper, the same surname of the family who owned the iron mine located at Iron Mountain between Adairsville and Mosteller's Mill.[4]

As they neared Adairsville from the northeast, first Hooker, and then Schofield, realized that they could march on Cassville via the Ironton Road (Road 2 and 2b) or Mosteller's Mill Road (Road 2a) and accomplish their mission by cutting off Johnston at Cassville and Cass Station. Each commander wrote dispatches to this effect, but Sherman remained focused on Kingston. On 18 May at 6:20 p.m., Hooker wrote Thomas that his men had proceeded down *to the forks of the road* that afternoon, and that they had captured a Confederate prisoner who said that Kingston is "no place," but that he believed Johnston would fight at Hightower Bridge. The Southern prisoner also reported that Dibrell's Tennessee (Confederate) cavalry brigade was patrolling the Ironton Road (Road 2 and 2b). Although Hooker had been ordered to proceed the next day toward Kingston, "if I can hear that the enemy

---

[3] Sherman, dispatch to Stoneman, 17 May, Evening, *OR*, ser. 1, vol. 38, pt. 4, 224.

[4] Whipple, dispatch to Hooker, 18 May, 11:40 a.m., *OR*, ser. 1, vol. 38, pt. 4, 237. Although possible, it is not likely that the guide "Cooper" was Mark A. Cooper, for he was a staunch supporter of the South (Cunyus, *Cass County*, 282).

are falling back from Kingston," he asked, "would it not be advisable to push for Cassville?"[5]

Schofield reached the same conclusion as he wrote Sherman from Mosteller's Mill on 18 May at 6 p.m., about the same time that Hooker was writing Thomas from his headquarters at the Jonathan McDow House. Schofield's XXIII Corps arrived at Mosteller's Mill at 1:30 p.m. before Hooker left. Hooker showed Schofield his orders from Thomas directing the XX Corps to march to within four miles of Kingston. Hooker's divisions, which were guided by Mr. Cooper, proceeded down the Ironton Road (Road 2b) two miles west of Mosteller's Mill, then turned west at a fork in the road on top of the Gravelly Plateau, and moved west along an unnamed road (today's Manning Mill, Road 2d)[6] until they reached the Adairsville-Cassville Road (Road 1), where they turned left and traveled south.

Anticipating Sherman's blessing for his proposed move directly on Cassville via either the Mosteller's Mill Road (Road 2a) or the Ironton Road (Road 2b), Schofield wrote "I will take the nearest road I can find to the one taken by General Hooker, and endeavor to come up within supporting distance of his left. I have my scouts out looking for roads."[7] Thus, Schofield planned to march south via the Mosteller's Mill Road (2a) until it merged with the Ironton Road (2b) then continue south (Road 2) to Cassville so that his corps could remain on the left flank of Hooker instead of in the rear of it.

After seeing Schofield's message, Sherman wrote him again at 10:30 p.m. the same night, redirecting him to move toward Kingston, not Cassville. This order, coupled with the directive to Stoneman and McCook, likely saved Schofield's Corps from disaster the following day, 19 May. If Schofield had proceeded at daylight south toward Cassville via the Mosteller's Mill (Road 2a) and Ironton Road (Road 2, south of 2b) as he had planned, his men would have been heading directly toward the trap being set by Hood that morning. If Stoneman and McCook had remained east along the Dewey's Crossroads and Pine Log corridor, then Hood's legions would have been in position to strike Schofield. With only the Fourth Indiana Cavalry escorting Schofield, Dibrell's Tennesseans likely could have kept them from discovering Hood's ambuscade before it was too late. As it turned out, by the time Schofield's

---

[5] Hooker, letter to Whipple, 18 May, 6:20 p.m., *OR*, ser. 1, vol. 38, pt. 4, 238. Emphasis added.

[6] Road 2d appears to be a portion of today's Manning Mill Road at the location where it intersects with US Highway 41/Joe Frank Harris Parkway (Road 1).

[7] Schofield to Sherman, *OR*, ser. 1, vol. 38, pt. 4, 241–42.

column reached Cassville using the Ironton Road, it was late afternoon. By then, Hood's Corps had left the ambush position and retired south to a defensive position.[8]

Lamenting that Schofield's divisions had not proceeded farther south on 18 May, Sherman admitted in his dispatch to Schofield that "the roads are not suited to one concentric movement on Kingston," but, he tellingly added, "we must approach the game as near as the case admits of." The Federal commander continued, "All the signs continue [to point to] Johnston's having retreated on Kingston, and why he should lead to Kingston, if he designs to cover his trains to Cartersville, I do not see." Reasoning that Johnston already had sent his trains and cars south of the Etowah River to Allatoona Pass, and that the Confederates were planning to take their wagons and army south of Kingston via backroads, Sherman concluded, "In any hypothesis our plan is right. All of General Thomas' command will follow his trail straight, let it lead to the fords or toward Allatoona. You must shape your course to support General Hooker and strike the line of railway to his left." Then, Sherman gave the pivotal instruction to Schofield: "As soon as you can march in the morning get up to General Hooker and act according to the developments."[9]

Thus, by 5 a.m., Schofield's columns were on the move, headed for the McDow House on the Adairsville-Cassville Road (Road 1) via the Ironton Road (Road 2b) and the fork to the west (Road 2d), *not* to Cassville via the Mosteller's Mill Road (Road 2a) and its junction with the Ironton Road (Road 2b) and then to the south down the Copper Mine/Ironton Road (Road 2).[10]

Upon discovering that Johnston's main body had apparently retreated toward Kingston, Sherman was unsure of the Southern commander's intentions. Sherman was faced with three possibilities: (1) Johnston was headed toward Cass Station and the Hightower Bridge over the Etowah River following the route of the Western & Atlantic Railroad; (2) Johnston was heading toward Rome and Alabama; or (3) Johnston, after sending his wagons and equipment south of the Etowah River via the Hightower Bridge, would make

---

[8] According to General Jacob Cox, who was commanding the lead division in Schofield's march, they drove back cavalry (Dibrell's Brigade) as they approached Cassville, and they did not deploy and form a line of battle on the outskirts of town until 4 p.m. (Cox's report, *OR*, ser. 1, vol. 38, pt. 2, 679–80).

[9] Sherman, dispatch to Schofield, 18 May, 10:30 p.m., *OR*, ser. 1, vol. 38, pt. 4, 242–43.

[10] Cox's report, *OR*, ser. 1, vol. 38, pt. 2, 679–80.

a brief stand at Kingston to allow time to cross his infantry over the river directly to the south of Kington. Historian Dave Powell has concluded that whichever direction Johnston chose, Sherman correctly followed the military maxim to drive toward the center at Kingston and then move to strike the enemy in detail as the situation developed before him.[11]

Ironically, after Sherman discovered that Johnston had evacuated Cassville overnight on 19–20 May and escaped safely over the Etowah River at the Hightower Bridge, Sherman wrote Schofield, scolding him for not striking directly for Cassville instead of "get[ting] up to General Hooker" as Sherman had ordered him to do.[12] "My instruction for you to move toward Cassville Depot was based on my theory or supposition that after reaching the 'divide' on Gravelly Plateau, roads would divide naturally, one set leading to Kinston and one to Cassville Depot." Sherman was disappointed that Schofield's Corps had failed to trap a portion of what he perceived as the fleeing Confederates from Kinston to the Hightower Bridge via Cass Station.[13]

"Yesterday I was very anxious that Stoneman or yourself should reach the road from Kingston to Etowah, for I saw by the singular maneuvering of the enemy and the confusion of his wagon trains, how uneasy he was to prevent our capturing a part of his forces.... Knowing that Hooker would take one toward Kingston," Sherman continued, "I wanted you to take one toward Cassville, with some rapidity of movement, to increase the chances of interposing between Etowah [Hightower] bridge and the enemy's falling back before Thomas' head of column."[14]

Sherman incorrectly believed that the chaos created by the Confederate change of position midday of 19 May from the line of hills north and west of Cassville to the hills south and east of the village—a move that had been caused by McCook's surprise attack on Hood's right flank and rear at 10:30 a.m.—was due to Johnston's single route of escape and the resulting delay. "Had 10,000 men reached the railroad any time after 10 a.m. of yesterday, we should have had a signal success," wrote Sherman, "whereas now Johnston will encourage his men by his skillfully saving his army and baggage in the face of such odds." Sherman was wrong about this conclusion. Had Schofield with his corps of thirteen thousand men reached the vicinity of Cassville around 10 a.m., as the Federal commander had hoped, Schofield's Corps

---

[11] Powell, *Atlanta Campain,* Vol. 1, forthcoming.

[12] Sherman to Schofield, 18 May, 10:30 p.m., *OR*, ser. 1, vol. 38, pt. 4, 242–43.

[13] Sherman to Schofield, 20 May, 1:15 a.m., *OR*, ser. 1, vol. 38, pt. 4, 266.

[14] Ibid.

might have been destroyed in detail along the Cooper Mine/Ironton Road (Road 2), along the northern reaches of the large, open field—provided Wheeler's Cavalry had been able to screen the Spring Place Road at or above Five Forks, thereby preventing McCook from getting close to Hood's column and causing havoc.[15]

To soften his chastisement to Schofield, Sherman added, "I know the difficulties of the roads and country, and merely mean to explain what I aimed to accomplish. I did expect to catch a part of the army retreating before us, but I take it for granted that it is now impossible." Upon receiving Sherman's last letter late in the night, Schofield replied in defense, "The theory upon which your orders were based yesterday morning was correct, except the supposition that Hooker would take the road toward Kingston; he sent only one division on that road, while the other two took the Cassville road."[16]

There was an undertone in Schofield's reply to Sherman, that Hooker was purposefully seeking to detach from the main body and operate independently. Hooker's Corps had taken a route following the Battle of Resaca that blocked Schofield's Corps and forced him to find other roads. Schofield reminded Sherman that, in his opinion, Hooker was repeating this conduct before Cassville. After the war, Schofield wrote, "General Hooker's habit of swinging off from the rest of General Thomas's army, and getting possession of roads designated for McPherson or for me, was a common subject of remark between Sherman, Thomas, McPherson and myself; and his motive was understood to be," continued Schofield, "as General Sherman states, to get command of one of the armies, in the event of battle, by virtue of his senior commission." Sherman and Grant also recorded their frustrations with Hooker's apparent design.[17]

---

[15] Ibid.

[16] Ibid.; Schofield, reply to Sherman, 20 May, 5:15 a.m., *OR*, ser. 1, vol. 38, pt. 4, 266.

[17] Schofield, *Forty-Six Years in the Army*, 136. Grant recorded in his memoirs that he "regarded him [Hooker] as a dangerous man. He was not subordinate to his superiors. He was ambitious to the extent of caring nothing for the rights of others. His disposition was, when engaged in battle, to get detached from the main body of the army and exercise a separate command, gathering to his standard all he could of his juniors" (see Grant, *Personal Memoirs*, 2:539; Jenkins, *Battle of Peach Tree Creek*, 391–92). Hooker bypassed Thomas in writing Sherman directly, and, in doing so, created the false impression that his corps was not supported by Schofield's at the Battle of Kolb Farm, or Zion Church, on 22 June 1864. (See McDonough, *Schofield*, 81–82.) Sherman was pleased that Hooker, who had seniority, resigned following

As will be shown, Sherman's intended show of force by Stoneman and McCook, coupled with his unintended delay of Schofield's approach on Cassville due to his fixation on Kingston, would serve to frustrate the Confederate battle plan on the morning of 19 May.

Sherman's decision to promote Howard to command of the Army of the Tennessee following McPherson's death. Sherman told Major General Henry Halleck, chief of staff, that Hooker was "not qualified or suited to [command of the Army of the Tennessee]" (Sherman to Halleck, 27 July 1864, 8:30 p.m., *OR*, ser. 1, vol. 38, pt. 5, 272).

Chapter 9

The Morning Events at Cassville: The McCook Morning Attack

Butterfield

At 5:15 on the morning of Thursday, 19 May, Butterfield's Third Division of Hooker's XX Corps began advancing cautiously down the Adairsville-Cassville Road (Road 1). Ward's First Brigade led the division's advance with Wood's Third Brigade following. As the road slanted to the southeast, Wood's Brigade moved due south, off the road and into the low-lying wooded basin, headed for Two Run Creek west of the town. Butterfield was in personal command of this reconnaissance brigade while Ward's Brigade continued down the road to the southeast. Captain Paul A. Oliver of Butterfield's staff accompanied Ward and his men. They had gone about two miles by 7:30 a.m.[1]

On the afternoon before, the leading skirmish line of Butterfield's Division, in the form of the 136th New York of Colonel James Wood's Third Brigade, probed slowly but steadily down the Adairsville-Cassville Road (Road 1) searching for water as they descended the Gravelly Plateau. Together with other portions of Butterfield's Division, the New Yorkers encountered barricades that blocked their progress about every half a mile.[2] Confederate horsemen of Ashby's and Harrison's brigades of Humes's Division, together with Iverson's Brigade, impeded the progress of the bluecoats. Trooper Thomas H. Williams of the 1st Tennessee Cavalry in Ashby's Brigade remembered, "skirmishing very little in our front. Formed line of fight twice during the day. Make breastwork but enemy did not come up to us." According to diarist John T. McMahon, the 136th New York lost one man wounded during the 18 May action.[3]

---

[1] Butterfield to Hooker, 5:15 a.m., *OR*, ser. 1, vol. 38, pt. 4, 253; Butterfield to Hooker 7:30 a.m., *OR*, ser. 1, vol. 38, pt. 4, 251; Paul A. Oliver to Daniel Butterfield, 5 March 1877, in S. Hood, *Lost Papers of Confederate General John Bell Hood*, 96–98.

[2] See map accompanying Major General Daniel Butterfield's report, for a depiction of the barricades faced by Butterfield's Division, included as Exhibit 23 as the "Butterfield Map."

[3] *OR*, ser. 1, vol. 38, pt. 2, 436–37; Cater, "Civil War Papers of John Bell Hamilton," 119; Priest, ed., *John T. McMahon's Diary*, 95; *OR*, ser. 1, vol. 38, pt. 3, 946.

Schofield

At 5:30 a.m. on Thursday, 19 May, Schofield's XXIII Corps, escorted by the Fourth Indiana Cavalry of some 175 horsemen under Captain Albert J. Morley, left Mosteller's Mill and proceeded south from the mill to the Ironton Road (Road 2b) to support Hooker's force. Schofield may have disagreed with Sherman's orders of the evening before to join Hooker rather than take the eastern road so that he could be positioned on Hooker's flank instead of his rear, but he followed orders. Taking the right-hand turn at the "forks in the road" described by Hooker the day previous, Schofield's army followed the same path traced by Hooker's Corps.[4]

In a day filled with frustration and countermarching, the Army of the Ohio commander arrived at the Jonathan McDow House by 8 a.m. where he found Hooker and Williams's First Division of the XX Corps blocking any further advance down the Adairsville-Cassville Road (Road 1). There, Schofield sent a note to Sherman at 8:30 a.m. "The head of my column arrived at this place at 8 o'clock. General Hooker is here with one division [Williams]; his other two are scouting toward Kingston and Cassville. I am massing my troops, and will await further developments or further instructions from you."[5]

Turning south onto the Ironton Road (Road 2b), and then right on the spur road to the west (Road 2d), the head of Schofield's column reached the McDow House where Hooker had spent the night and still remained. Because of Sherman's order to Schofield to "get up to General Hooker," no troops were headed down Wheeler's "Copper Mine Road" (Road 2) as Dibrell's Brigade awaited, and none were headed down the "Ironton Road" (the same Road 2) as Hood had anticipated. Schofield would soon receive a different order from Sherman, which would change his direction of march and put him on the Ironton Road, the road with multiple names and references (Road 2d to Road 2), but his men would arrive on the outskirts of Cassville too late to receive Hood's malevolent surprise reception.[6]

---

[4] Schofield to Sherman, 19 May 1864, 8:30 a.m., *OR*, ser. 1, vol. 38, pt. 4, 255.

[5] Ibid.

[6] Sherman dispatch to Schofield, *OR*, ser. 1, vol. 38, pt. 4, 242–43; Sherman to Halleck, *OR*, ser. 1, vol. 38, pt. 4, 232, Sherman dispatch to Thomas, *OR*, ser. 1, vol. 38, pt. 4, 233. The estimated size of Fourth Indiana Cavalry is based on 217 men present for duty at the start of the Campaign on 3 May, minus four officers and seventeen men captured and several wounded at Varnell Station (Albert J. Morley's report, Fourth Indiana Cavalry, *OR*, ser. 1, vol. 38, pt. 2, 788).

Those instructions came in the form of a directive from Sherman that Schofield received just after noon. Following Howard's IV Corps that morning as they reached Kingston virtually unopposed by 8:30 a.m., and in apparent pursuit of one division of Confederate infantry east toward Cassville, Sherman sent a new order directing Schofield to move rapidly toward Cassville and Cass Station in the hopes of cutting off the lone division. "I want you to put the head of your column at Cassville Depot, your line facing east…" Sherman directed, prompting Schofield to respond quickly at 12:40 p.m.[7]

Following Sherman's previous order to get up on Hooker at daylight, the Army of the Ohio commander was now out of position from Sherman's new order. "Your dispatch directing me to put the lead of my column at Cassville Depot reached me a few minutes ago," replied Schofield. "General Hooker is ahead of me, but is about to move. I will move as soon as the road is clear." The fellow Ohio leader added, "I presume you are aware that I am on the Adairsville and Cassville road [Road 1]. My cavalry reports the enemy in force on the road from Cassville to my camp of last night (at Marsteller's [*sic*] Mill), and about two miles from Cassville." Schofield was describing the presence of Dibrell's Confederate cavalrymen on the Ironton Road (Road 2) just south of the junction of the Ironton Road (Road 2b) and Mosteller's Mill Road (Road 2a) near the A. M. Linn House (on Road 2, see Ruger Map), as reported to him by elements of Morley's Fourth Indiana Cavalry.[8]

Schofield explained that because Hooker still had most of his corps on the Adairsville-Cassville Road (Road 1), blocking his progress, he would move back over to the Ironton Road to march on Cassville. "General Hooker has two divisions on this road. I will get onto the road to the east as soon as I can, and keep my communication with General Hooker." Unaware that McCook with a part of his cavalry force had already run into Hood's infantrymen, Schofield added, "Stoneman, with his own and a part of McCook's force, started before daylight this morning to strike the railroad between Cassville and Allatoona." Schofield's lead division under Brigadier General Jacob Cox, would reach the outskirts of Cassville via today's Manning Mill Road (Road 2d) and the Ironton/Copper Mine Road (Road 2b & 2).[9]

Ironically, Schofield would later receive a letter from Sherman, written at 1:15 a.m., 20 May, admonishing him for not going directly to Cassville at daylight on 19 May: "Knowing that Hooker would take one [a road] toward

[7] Sherman to Schofield, 19 May 1864, *OR*, ser. 1, vol. 38, pt. 4, 255.

[8] Schofield to Sherman, 19 May 1864, 12:40 p.m., *OR*, ser. 1, vol. 38, pt. 4, 255.

[9] Ibid., 255–56; Cox's report, *OR*, ser. 1, vol. 38, pt. 2, 679–80.

Kingston, I wanted you to take one toward Cassville, with some rapidity of movement, to increase the chances of interposing between Etowah bridge and the enemy's falling back before Thomas' lead of column." If Schofield had done so, then it is possible that Hood's planned attack could have succeeded, that is, if McCook's cavalry had not been permitted to probe his flank and rear unmolested.[10]

Geary

At 6 a.m., Brigadier General John W. Geary, commanding the Second Division of Hooker's XX Corps, received an order from Hooker dated 4:45 a.m. that morning. In it, he was ordered to send one of his "most active regiments," supported by the balance of his division, to move toward the railroad west of Butterfield's position and east of the XIV and IV Corps on the Adairsville-Kingston Road (Road 8). Ordered to leave his wagon train behind, Geary sent the Fifth Ohio followed by the balance of his division into the tangled woods and byways. By early afternoon, Geary's men made connection with Butterfield on his left and Howard's IV Corps on his right west of the Two Run Creek valley and just south of the Colonel Price House.[11]

Johnston

On the morning of 19 May 1864, Johnston and his lieutenant generals met to discuss options for the day. There, they learned of the approach of a Federal infantry column that was pressing Wheeler's cavalry on the Adairsville-Cassville Road (Road 1). Ward's Brigade of Butterfield's Division was approaching Cassville via the "direct road" as Johnston termed it. Riding to the north of Cassville and up the Copper Mine Road (also known as the Ironton Road, Road 2) to look at the land in front of Polk's right, and to see how Hood's proposed plan of attack would take shape, Johnston and his corps commanders surveyed the land. Johnston knew that he should strike a blow on Sherman while his forces were divided and while he was still north of the Etowah River, and Hood's plan provided the details of how to do it. Johnston clearly felt the pressure from President Davis and the Richmond government to try and force

---

[10] Sherman to Schofield, 20 May 1864, 1:15 a.m., *OR*, ser. 1, vol. 38, pt. 4, 266.

[11] Major W.H. Lawrence dispatch to Geary, 4:45 a.m., *OR*, ser. 1, vol. 38, pt. 4, 252–53; Geary's report, *OR*, ser. 1, vol. 38, pt. 2, 121–22; Lieutenant Colonel R. L. Kilpatrick's report, *OR*, ser. 1, vol. 38, pt. 2, 163–64.

the issue with a general engagement as soon as possible and somewhere in northwest Georgia.

Hood renewed his request from the day before to launch a counterstrike on the Federal column that he supposed was coming south, down the Ironton Road, from the east side of Adairsville. Johnston and his corps commanders had learned the previous evening from a captured Federal soldier in the XX Corps that Howard's IV Corps was apparently east of Adairsville. While the information proved to be incorrect as to the identity of the Federal column east of Adairsville during the evening of 18 May (Howard's IV Corps was on the Adairsville-Kingston Road [Road 8]), Schofield's XXIII Corps [Army of the Ohio] had camped the night before at Mostellar's Mill, five miles east of Adairsville. Thus, Schofield's XXIII Corps might head for Cassville via the Ironton/Copper Mine Road and into the trap set by Hood.

Believing that the Northern force that would take this route would be isolated, Hood wanted to strike it in an ambush-style attack while the Federal column was on the march and not prepared. Polk and Hardee also liked the idea, and they would each hold their corps in readiness to block any Federals approaching from their fronts, Polk along the Adairsville-Cassville Road (Road 1), and Hardee along the Kingston-Cassville Road (Road 9). Johnston consented.

At this point, Johnston and his lieutenant generals believed that Palmer's XIV Corps was pressing Rome, Hooker's XX Corps was proceeding down the Adairsville-Cassville Road (Road 1), and Howard's IV Corps was east of Adairsville and coming from the Ironton Road. The Southern leaders had mixed intelligence on McPherson's "corps" (as some of the Confederate accounts called his two corps, Logan's XV, and Dodge's XVI). Hardee thought that some of McPherson's men had disengaged and were headed toward Virginia to reinforce Grant.

While Brigadier General Jefferson C. Davis's Second Division of Palmer's XIV Corps was indeed pressing Rome, the balance of Palmer's Corps, the two divisions of brigadier generals Robert Johnson and Absalom Baird, were proceeding down the Adairsville-Kingston Road (Road 8) behind Howard's IV Corps. Also, McPherson's two corps had gone from west of Adairsville first to Hermitage and then to Woodlands (today's Barnsley Gardens).

Around 7 a.m., Johnston returned to his headquarters to write his general order, or "pep speech," while the three lieutenant generals returned to their corps to prepare to execute the plan. The general order was completed by 8 a.m. and multiple copies began to be circulated. The general order did not provide any details about how the Confederates would meet the enemy. It contained no battle plan. It did not even reveal whether the plan was to attack or to defend. Colonel Edward T. Sykes, adjutant in Walthall's Brigade, later called it the "celebrated battle order."[12]

The generals understood that Hardee was to hold off the approaching Federals from the Kingston-Cassville Road (Road 9), Polk was to block the Federals advancing from the direct Adairsville-Cassville Road (Road 1), and Hood was to move his divisions under the cover of a ridge line to the east and then across a large field to lie in wait along the Ironton Road (Road 2) for the anticipated foe, and then strike them as they neared Cassville, isolated along the Ironton Road.[13]

Howard

After marching at 5 a.m., Howard's IV Corps reached Kingston by 8 a.m. with Thomas and Sherman accompanying his force.[14] Two divisions of Palmer's XIV Corps, Baird's and Johnson's, followed Howard's column. At 9:20 a.m., believing that the Confederates were in full retreat, Thomas sent a note to Hooker to "Push your column down upon the railroad, between Kingston and Cassville. The rebels are pulling back from here." With Major General David S. Stanley's division in the van, Howard's men pressed forward along the Kingston-Cassville Road (Road 9).[15]

Hood

By 8 a.m., while Johnston was finishing his "pep speech," Hood's men were beginning their march out of town and along the Pine Log (or Spring Place, or Fairmount, or Canton) Road to the east (Road 4, today called the Cassville-White Road, NW). Hindman's Division led Hood's advance, with Major General Alexander P. Stewart's division following, and Major General Carter L. Stevenson's four brigades were in the rear of the column. Hood's Corps of three divisions, containing a total of twelve brigades, consisted of about twenty thousand men. Passing the Canton Road (Road 5), Hindman's

---

[12] Sykes, *Walthall's Brigade*, 568.

[13] Johnston, *Narrative of Military Operations*, 321; Hood, *OR*, ser. 1, vol. 38, pt. 3, 625; Hood, *Advance and Retreat*, 99; Mackall Journal, "O" sample, *OR*, ser. 1, vol. 38, pt. 3, 983.

[14] Thomas's report, *OR*, ser. 1, vol. 38, pt. 1, 142.

[15] Thomas, dispatch to Hooker, *OR*, ser. 1, vol. 38, pt. 4, 252.

Division continued along the Pine Log Road (Road 4) until they reached today's Brown Loop Road (Road 3a), a connecting route to Spring Place Road (Road 3).

Hindman's men turned left onto today's Brown Loop Road, called the "country road" by Johnston (Road 3a), and proceeded through a gap between two hills, as indicated on Johnston's sketch map. Hood's lead division crossed the south branch of Two Run Creek on a log bridge and proceeded to march across a large, open, field to the north with the ground rising steadily as they continued. Brigadier General Arthur M. Manigault, in command of one of Hindman's four brigades, remembered "we were under arms by eight o'clock, and were marched several miles east of the town, for the purpose of finding out something about the enemy in that direction." As they marched through the field by the right flank, Hood, who was as the head of his column, rode forward to the top of the field, where he found, as he expected, some of Wheeler's troopers guarding the Ironton Road. Wheeler had deployed a cavalry screen along the Copper Mine/Ironton Road (Road 2) with Dibrell's Brigade posted well to the north, two miles up the road and near the Linn House to provide early warning of the approaching Federals, and to serve as the bait to lure the bluecoats into the trap. By this time, it was after 10 a.m.[16]

Ward

At 10:20 a.m., Ward's Federal brigade came into a large field along the Adairsville-Cassville Road (Road 1) and in sight of the Confederate line northwest of Cassville. They had been marching through a forest of cedars as they descended the Gravelly Plateau and cleared a tree-lined ridge.[17] On the far side of the field, and less than a mile away, Ward's men could see the butternut and gray lines of Polk's Corps on high ground lining the south side of Two Run Creek. Polk's infantry line trailed off to the south to their right. On their left front, and much closer to them, Ward's Midwesterners saw a range of hills topped with Confederate cavalry, some mounted and some dismounted. Iverson's Georgia cavalry brigade and troopers from Humes's

[16] The cavalry force that Hood met was probably a part of Humes's Division that was covering the range of hills separating the Adairsville-Cassville Road from the Copper Mine/Ironton Road. Dibrell's Brigade was considerably farther north on the Ironton Road as no Federals had begun to advance down the Ironton Road in their sector by this hour (see Manigault and Tower, *A Carolinian Goes to War*, 185–86; Sykes, *Walthall's Brigade*, 568).

[17] Castle Diary, 19 May 1864.

cavalry division continued the Southern defense around the east side of the hills that ringed the bowl-shaped field. The Southern horsemen were posted atop a series of ridges that overlooked the Adairsville-Cassville Road from the east on Polk's right.

As they came down the Adairsville-Cassville Road, Ward's men were funneled into the bowl-shaped field and into the view of the Confederate cavalry and Polk's infantry. A wooded valley lay to their west, where Butterfield with Wood's Brigade had disappeared that morning. Entering the bowl-shaped field, Ward deployed his brigade with the 105th Illinois, armed with Henry repeating rifles, on point as skirmishers. Captain J. S. Forsyth, with Companies H and I, was assigned to proceed forward with a thin line of skirmishers. Other men from this regiment deployed as flankers to the right. Forsyth's two companies began to exchange fire with Wheeler's cavalrymen across the field. These were the first sounds of gunfire heard at Johnston's headquarters that morning and were recorded by T. B. Mackall at 10:20 a.m.[18]

Ward deployed the balance of his brigade behind the 105th Illinois with the Seventieth Indiana and the 102nd Illinois in the front line, and the 129th Illinois and the Seventy-Ninth Ohio in the second line, as they began to ease forward. The 102nd Illinois sent skirmishers out in an arc on the left front and left flank of the brigade. By 10:30 a.m., the Confederate horse artillery opened up on Ward's Brigade with two guns from Lieutenant Colonel Felix H. Robertson's horse artillery battalion, as Ward's men found themselves advancing into a trap. Moving farther into the field would likely prove fatal.[19]

Captain Paul Oliver of Butterfield's staff accompanied Ward's Brigade that morning. Ward's Brigade had been ordered by Butterfield to create a diversion down the Adairsville-Cassville Road (Road 1), while Butterfield with Wood's Brigade would strike for the Western & Atlantic Railroad between Kingston and Cassville. As Ward's men advanced into the field in front of the enemy lines, Oliver recognized the danger. "The Col. [Colonel Daniel Dustin of the 105th Illinois] intended to attract the enemy's attention toward him as far as he dared without bringing on an engagement. The enemy's

[18] Ward's report, *OR*, ser. 1, vol. 38, pt. 2, 342; Daniel Dustin's report, 105th Illinois, *OR*, ser. 1, vol. 38, pt. 2, 361; Strong, *A Yankee Private's Civil War*, 26; Wheeler's report, *OR*, ser. 1, vol. 38, pt. 3, 946; Mackall Journal, "A" and "B" samples.

[19] Ward's report, *OR*, ser. 1, vol. 38, pt. 2, 342.

cavalry scouts watched us very closely but were kept far enough off to prevent their learning our actual force," remembered the staff officer.[20]

Recalling the harrowing adventure, Oliver wrote Butterfield following the war. "On our left was an open country, bounded by mounds slightly undulating and gradually sloping down from our position. Some cavalry made their appearance in this quarter, and ours was certainly a position inviting an attack from this arm," he explained. "Fearing that a dash might be made upon us in this quarter, I placed Smith's Battery on our left in a very formidable position concealing it partly only by brush. The artillery men were placed on the flanks like infantry in order to give as much a show of force as possible." Smith's battery did not have any ordinance to fire as the artillery train was at that time three miles up the Adairsville-Cassville Road on the Gravely Plateau.[21]

Oliver, who was born on an American ship while it was in the English Channel and migrated to New York when he was nineteen, reflected, "I must confess that it seemed important to give any demonstration of cavalry on our left a very effectual check. Our skirmishers met but little resistance, but finally [the] enemy formed line of battle and commenced to shell us." The New York captain added, "Matters began to look serious and as though we were in turn to be attacked at any moment[;] just at this time a dispatch was received from you to join you immediately."[22]

Extracting the brigade and Smith's Battery from the peril was no easy task, remembered Oliver. It appeared that the Confederates "had formed line of battle with the apparent intention of attacking us," he said. "Any notice on their part of our retreating would have caused them to charge down upon us like a shot," believed the captain. "Orders were given in an undertone, and the Brigade moved as silently as possible," he said, "together with artillery under cover of woods, knolls, and hollows to join you." Colonel Dustin and the 105th Illinois were ordered to "bring up the rear, with the exception of 30 men who were to maintain a show of force by keeping up their fire as would seem judicious. Col. Dustin did remarkably well," recalled Oliver, "for the enemy was completely deceived for he threw shells into the woods for at least two hours, after our junction to your force." The 102nd Illinois sustained a loss of one man killed and one man mortally wounded from exposure to shell fire

---

[20] Oliver to Butterfield, 5 March 1877, in S. Hood, *Lost Papers of Confederate General John Bell Hood*, 96–98.

[21] Ibid.

[22] Ibid.

from the Confederate battery, while the 105th Illinois saw two men wounded during the exchange.[23]

Ward's Brigade delicately withdrew from its exposed position in the field on the Adairsville-Cassville Road. Colonel H. G. Kennett of the Seventy-Ninth Ohio Infantry remembered of the morning of 19 May, "We pushed forward in a heavy reconnaissance to within one and a half miles of Cassville." In charge of Ward's second line, which included the 129th Illinois Infantry, Colonel Kennett added, "We threw up works at [the] crossroads (near the intersection of today's Shropshire Lane and Griffin Road), the enemy appeared strong in our front. We moved by the flank under cover of [a] dense woods due south and formed [a] second line of battle." According to Samuel Merrill of the Seventieth Indiana, "By some mistake the Brigade took the wrong road, and the troops, as J. M. Wills expressed it, 'were pressed up so close to the enemy that we were almost surrounded by Wheeler's cavalry. Orders came for us to march to the rear at trail arms and for no one to speak above a whisper.'" The Hoosiers together with the rest of Ward's Brigade carefully extracted themselves from the front of the gray-clad troopers.[24]

Hood

Meanwhile, to the east, as the vanguard of his column reached within two hundred yards of the Ironton Road, Hood was suddenly alerted to what appeared to be an enemy force in the distance. As Colonel Taylor Beattie later recalled, one of the soldiers in Hindman's Division drew his attention to "a dark line off to our right, saying they were Yankees." Beattie, who initially did not believe it was a sighting of the enemy, replied that he "thought the dark line was a fence or hedge." But the officer nevertheless rode forward to notify Hood. Unalarmed, Hood replied that "it could not be so, but [it] must be our cavalry, if it was a body of men." As Beattie returned to the line, the same observant soldier then said that "they were throwing out skirmishers in our direction." Beattie immediately returned to Hood who then halted the

---

[23] Oliver to Butterfield, 5 March 1877, S. Hood, *Lost Papers of Confederate General John Bell Hood*, 96–98; F. C. Smith's report, 102nd Illinois, *OR*, ser. 1, vol. 38, pt. 2, 353.

[24] Kennett's report, *OR Supp.*, pt. 1, vol. 7, 26; S. Merrill, *Seventieth Indiana*, 113.

advance and ordered Hindman to send a brigade forward to investigate the mysterious force.[25]

McCook's Morning Attack

Across the large, open field to the east, some two miles away, the approaching horsemen of Brigadier General Edward McCook and Lieutenant Colonel James P. Stewart with his Second Brigade together with a section of artillery (two guns), were coming into view of Hood and his men. McCook's troopers had traveled that morning from their bivouac at the intersection of the Spring Place Road (Road 3) and the Adairsville-Pine Log Road (Road 7). After connecting with the pickets of Stoneman's Division above Dewey's Crossroads that morning, and mindful of Sherman's orders to be aggressive, McCook and his troopers began their approach to Cassville via the Spring Place Road (Road 3). Stoneman's forces continued to proceed slowly down the Pine Log Road (Road 4) and Tennessee Road (Road 6), encountering opposition from Hannon's Alabamians on the Pine Log Road and Williams's Confederate Kentuckians on the Tennessee Road. However, McCook found no opposition in his front as he moved down the Spring Place Road (Road 3). By around 10:20 a.m., McCook's men approached a clearing as they rounded the curve on the Spring Place Road just south of the Card House and the road to Crow Springs. McCook remembered that they were only about four miles from Cassville at this point.[26]

McCook's troopers trotted down the Spring Place Road, and were nearing the Five Forks crossroads when, to the west, they could see a large body of Confederate infantry in the distance across the Two Run Creek valley. The blue horsemen were led by Lieutenant Colonel James P. Stewart, with two of his three regiments, the Second Indiana Cavalry and the First Wisconsin Cavalry (the small Fourth Indiana Cavalry having been previously detached to escort Schofield's XXIII Corps from Mosteller's Mill). Also, with Stewart and McCook was a section of the Eighteenth Indiana Horse Artillery led by Lt. William B. Rippetoe with two of their six three-inch ordinance rifle guns. Stewart's two cavalry regiments totaled about 1,050 men, with some 350 Hoosiers in the Second Indiana Cavalry and about 700 Badgers in the First

[25] Taylor Beattie to Hood, 29 March 1874, in Hood, *Advance and Retreat*, 102–103.

[26] McCook, *OR*, ser. 1, vol. 38, pt. 2, 751–52; McCook, *OR*, ser. 1, vol. 38, pt. 4, 255.

Wisconsin Cavalry, while Rippetoe's entire artillery battery, also called the "Eli Lilly battery," contained just three officers and seventy-nine men.[27]

At this time, McCook's First Brigade under Colonel Joseph P. Dorr, and the other two sections of Rippetoe's Battery, were near the Dewey Crossroads four miles north on the Spring Place Road. Dorr's three regiments, the Eighth Iowa, the Second Michigan, and the First Tennessee (Union) Cavalry, were patrolling other roads that morning in the Dewey's Crossroads sector. They would join the Second Brigade, along with portions of two brigades of Stoneman's Division, between 3 p.m. and 5 p.m. for a second attack on Hood's lines.[28]

As he entered the large valley, McCook and his troopers could see a long line of Confederate infantrymen in the distance on the other side of the field. One of his officers estimated the Southern infantry to be about two miles away. McCook ordered the Second Indiana Cavalry to continue quickly down the road to the south to investigate what lay ahead. He then ordered a section of Rippetoe's Eighteenth Indiana Battery to unlimber on the high ground to the right of the Spring Place Road (Road 3) at the Five Forks, and the Wisconsin troopers were instructed to dismount and form a line of skirmishers on the left of the road to support the battery. On the far side of the field, as the South Carolinian General, Manigault later recalled, "A part of the division [Hindman's] came in contact with a large body of cavalry, and before we were aware of it a battery of artillery opened on us, doing some mischief."[29]

Stewart and the Second Indiana Cavalry continued south through the Five Forks, crossing the Pine Log Road (Road 4) onto the Canton Road (Road 5), which connected just below and then bent sharply to the west past a range of hills. The Second Indiana Cavalry proceeded rapidly down the Canton Road until they encountered the tail of Hood's column. Bringing up the rear of Hood's strike force was Major General Carter Stevenson's division of four brigades. Led by Major David A. Briggs, the Second Indiana fired into the 63rd Virginia Infantry Regiment of Brigadier General Alexander W. Reynolds's North Carolina and Virginia brigade, killing three men and

---

[27] McCook, *OR*, ser. 1, vol. 38, pt. 2, 751–52; McCook, *OR*, ser. 1, vol. 38, pt. 4, 255; Albert J. Morley's report (Fourth Indiana Cavalry), *OR*, ser. 1, vol. 38, pt. 2, 788–89; Harris Diary, 21; Horace P. Lamson, report of Second Brigade, *OR*, ser. 1, vol. 38, pt. 2, 780–81.

[28] Dorr Journal, 18–19.

[29] Manigault and Tower, *A Carolinian Goes to War*, 186; Rippetoe, *OR*, ser. 1, vol. 38, pt. 2, 801; Rowell, *Yankee Artillerymen*, 198.

wounding two others, all of whom were in Company C. The Hoosiers quickly turned and dashed back up the Canton Road, but one fast-acting Virginian managed to get a shot off, wounding Hoosier trooper W. H. Underwood of the Second Indiana in the arm as the blue horsemen galloped away as suddenly as they had appeared.[30]

Meanwhile, on the north side of the large field, two and a half miles away, Hood and his staff watched the events to his right unfold. Tucker's Mississippi brigade of Hindman's Division drew the assignment of engaging the unknown blue force on the far side of the field to the east. Known as the "High Pressure Brigade," a moniker given them for their heroism under fire at the Hornet's Nest during the Battle of Shiloh, Tucker's Brigade was now commanded by Colonel Jacob H. Sharp (General William F. Tucker having been wounded on 14 May at Resaca). Sharp sent the 9th Mississippi Battalion Sharpshooters forward in a skirmish line, followed by the remainder of the brigade. As the Mississippians advanced at the double-quick, Rippetoe's men prepared their loads and waited for the Confederates to move closer.[31]

As they came within range, the lieutenant opened with both guns on the Mississippians, killing and wounding five men with one shot. Three men of

---

[30] Briggs's report, *OR*, ser. 1, vol. 38, pt. 2, 785; Weaver, *63rd Virginia Infantry*, 98. The five casualties were privates Morgan Phipps and Lewis W. Brewer, who were killed; First Sergeant Wiley Cornett, who was wounded and died on 11 June 1864; privates Joseph M. Phillips, who was wounded, and Macagah Phipps, who was wounded in the side (Weaver, *63rd Virginia Infantry*, 112, 117, 140–41). During the second clash with the blue horsemen around 4 or 5 p.m., another nine men from the 63rd Virginia would be captured (privates James DeFreece, Peyton Houndshell, Nelson Kilby, Edward A. Leonard, Stith Lovern, Charles F. McDaniel, Isaiah C. Patton, James A. Spradlin, and Peter S. Wix), together with sixteen men captured from the 54th Virginia, and fourteen men surrendered from the 58th North Carolina in Alexander Reynolds's brigade. See also Sherwood and Weaver, *54th Virginia Infantry*, 157; Hardy, *Fifty-Eighth North Carolina Troops*, 118. Ironically, no men were reported as captured from the 60th North Carolina in Reynolds's Brigade although three were reported as captured on 18 May between Adairsville and Cassville (Jordan, *North Carolina Troops*, 502). Dr. V. W. Cooper, a surgeon in the 60th North Carolina, remembered a different order at Cassville, one he called the "English Order." It provided that "a surgeon should go on the field of battle and take care of the wounded as they fell. I was proud of that order," explained Cooper, "and thought it right for a doctor to be present when the men were shot" (V. W. Cooper, *Some Experiences of Dr. V. W. Cooper in the Confederate Army, 1861–1865*, unpublished, vertical files, Confederate NC-3, Kennesaw Mountain NMP, 5–6).

[31] Rowell, *Yankee Artillerymen*, 198.

41st Mississippi Infantry were killed while one man from the 9th Mississippi Battalion Sharpshooters was killed during the shelling.[32] Rippetoe managed to fire twelve rounds (six by each piece) before McCook, according to Henry Campbell of the Eighteenth Indiana Horse Artillery Battery, "rode up and ordered us to get back off the field as quick as possible as a column of rebel Infantry was charging up the woods and would cut us off."[33] One witness from the First Wisconsin Cavalry recalled,

> some artillery officer placed two parrott rifles, where shells could be thrown into a marching column of confed.[erates] it was done, and at once a detachment swung out to secure [capture] the guns, but an aide-de-camp from a division commander sent the guns to the rear. [Company G of the

---

[32] Privates William Jernigan of Company F; J. H. Priest and W. Y. Robertson of Company L, from the 41st Mississippi Infantry; and Corporal W. S. Sartin of Company C, 9th Mississippi Battalion Sharpshooters, were all killed during the shelling on the morning of 19 May. All four are buried in the Cassville Confederate Cemetery (see Cassville Cemetery list, transcr. Raymond W. Watkins). Also wounded from the 41st Mississippi was John Mitchell, the nephew of General Nathan Bedford Forrest (see Ora, letter, Army of Tennessee, Allatoona, Georgia, six miles south of the Etowah, Friday, 20 May 1864, *Weekly Advertiser*, Montgomery, AL, 23 May 1864, 2).

The casualties in Walthall's Mississippi brigade of Hindman's Division occurred during the evening action. Manigault's diary, published as part of his book, *A Carolinian Goes to War*, does not indicate that his brigade sustained any casualties or participated in any combat, either in the morning or the evening although they witnessed both events.

As for Brigadier General Zachariah C. Deas's Alabama brigade, the final brigade in Hindman's Division, the record of their participation at Cassville is minimal. A review of the vertical regimental files from Alabama Department of Archives and History, which include monthly reports and casualty lists for the Atlanta Campaign, reveals only three casualties in Deas's Brigade at Cassville. David A. McCollough and Alden E. Hyatt of Company G, 19th Alabama, were reported as wounded at Cassville (Civil War Muster Rolls 1861–1865, 19th Alabama Infantry, Company G, box 11, folder 8, images 3 and 6, ADAH). There are conflicting reports concerning the death of Captain Nathan J. Venable of Company K, 19th Alabama of Deas's Brigade. According to *OR Supp.*, pt. 2, vol. 1, 519, Venable, from Blount County, was killed 19 May 1864, at Cassville. See Civil War Muster Rolls, 1861–1865, 19th Alabama Infantry, Company A, image 45. However, in Brewer's treatise on Alabama, Venable was reported as being killed at Marietta (Brewer, *Alabama*, 621).

[33] Rippetoe's report, *OR*, ser. 1, vol. 38, pt. 2, 801; Rowell, *Yankee Artillerymen*, 198.

> First Wisconsin Cavalry] was ordered to turn the rebs back, but never a shot was fired by either side

because the Federal troopers mounted and withdrew before the Southerners could come any closer. Lt. John D. Cooper of the 7th Mississippi of Tucker's (Sharp's) Brigade remembered, we "got in position at about 8 o'clock near Cassville, brisk engagement—sharpshooters and artillery—suffered very little—our regiment now entrenched again,"[34] as Hood ordered his divisions to move to the right to cover the range of hills along the Pine Log (Road 4) and Canton Roads (Road 5).[35]

Thus ended the brief morning encounter by Hood and his divisions with two of McCook's cavalry regiments and two of his three-inch ordinance rifles. As the quick-striking Second Indiana Cavalry raced back up the Canton Road through Five Forks and onto Spring Place Road to their comrades, McCook became concerned that the gray-clad units who were now moving rapidly up the Canton and Pine Log Roads in pursuit, would overtake the unsuspecting artillerymen. McCook's troopers withdrew up the Spring Place Road about a mile to the Crow Springs Road intersection and waited for Stoneman's, Dorr's, and Schofield's men to arrive. According to Henry Campbell of the Eighteenth Indiana Horse Artillery, "We have advanced to[o] rapidly for them which leaves our right flank exposed." Referring to Schofield's Corps, "We are nearly 10 miles ahead of them."[36]

Hood

Amid the confusion caused by McCook's appearance on Hood's flank and rear, Hood sent Major James Hamilton of his staff "to report to General Johnston the fact that the enemy had appeared on the Canton road." At the same time, and "during Major Hamilton's absence Brigadier General Mackall, chief of staff, rode up in great haste and said that General Johnston directed

[34] Skellie, *Lest We Forget*, 664.

[35] Rowell, *Yankee Artillerymen*, 198. The Wisconsin trooper was mistaken about the type of guns used by the Eighteenth Indiana at Cassville. They were three-inch ordnance rifles, not Parrott rifles (Clark, *History of "G" Company*, 18). For a discussion of the guns issued to the Eighteenth Indiana Light Artillery Battery, also known as "Eli Lilly's Battery," see Rowell, *Yankee Artillerymen*, 25–26, in which he explains that the artillerymen received three-inch ordnance rifles, sometimes referred to as "Rodman guns."

[36] Rowell, *Yankee Artillerymen*, 198.

that I [Hood] should not separate myself so far from General Polk," he explained.[37]

T. B. Mackall reported that "General M[ackall], who had ridden out to Hood with directions 'to make quick work,' sent word back by courier, who reported to me that 'enemy in heavy force close to Hood on Canton road.'" Johnston and T. B. Mackall initially believed that Major Hamilton had been sent by William Mackall and not Hood based on T. B. Mackall's original, "A" sample entry in his journal. However, when T. B. Mackall penned his revision in his "B" sample, he corrected himself. Mackall's "B" sample recorded, "report recd. from Genl. Hood that enemy was advancing on Canton road. Line of battle changed. At night army withdrawn." But Johnston would later deny that Hood reported the enemy column.[38]

Butterfield-Wood

Meanwhile, to the west of Cassville, Wood's Brigade, accompanied by General Butterfield, neared Two Run Creek and found themselves confronted with a long line of Confederate infantry on a ridge to their left. According to Colonel James Wood, his brigade had been "ordered to make a reconnaissance toward Two Run Creek. My instructions were to march due south until I struck the Creek."[39]

Deploying the Seventy-Third Ohio Infantry with skirmishers ahead, Wood formed his other four regiments in "two columns on the right and left of the [Seventy-Third Ohio] regiment." As Wood's men continued to probe in search of Two Run Creek, they realized they were precariously close to the Southern lines. "When within about a half a mile from the creek," explained Wood, "it was discovered that the enemy in force was in dangerous proximity on our left flank." Explaining that his brigade had become isolated from the other brigades and divisions of its corps, the New York colonel continued, "it became necessary to withdraw the reconnaissance and take up a defensive position, I withdrew hence about 1,000 yards from my most advanced position and threw up a slight protection of boards and rails, the enemy having shown no disposition to attack."[40]

---

[37] Hood, *OR*, ser. 1, vol. 38, pt. 3, 635.

[38] Mackall Journal, compare "A," "B," and "O" samples, *OR*, ser. 1, vol. 38, pt. 3, 983. Comparison available at appendix F.

[39] Wood's report, *OR*, ser. 1, vol. 38, pt. 2, 437.

[40] Ibid.

After falling back from their exposed position, Wood's Brigade reached the home of Colonel Hawkins F. Price where Butterfield established his headquarters.[41] From the Price House, Butterfield busily sent dispatches, one to recall Ward's Brigade to fall back to his location, one to Coburn to send reinforcements, and three to Hooker between about noon and 1:30 p.m. to advise of his status and of his continuing desire to strike for the railroad.[42]

In this series of correspondence, Butterfield admitted that he might have been mistaken in his direction of march. Believing that he had struck Two Run Creek shortly after his men had begun the march at daylight, Butterfield explained in the first note to his commander about noon that he had then proceeded "due south as directed" by Hooker, for two miles. Butterfield's two brigades had crossed the branches of Cedar Creek and Mud Creek early in their march, and after continuing south for two miles, Wood's Brigade came into sight of Two Run Creek west of Cassville. At 1 p.m., Butterfield sent a second letter to Hooker, this time confessing, "The enemy came near catching me in a bad position on my reconnaissance and compelled me to take a defensive position and draw in Wood's Brigade, pushing for the railroad, until I could get Ward's up." Observing Polk's lines to the east and portions of Hardee's Corps to the south, the zealous division commander continued, "They [the enemy] are now in my front with two batteries, cavalry, and about twenty regiments of infantry, as counted by those who saw them pass to our right." Confidently, if not naively, Butterfield added, "If Geary and Williams were up I think we could attack them."[43]

---

[41] Price was a Georgia state senator from 1857 to 1865 and had been a member of the Georgia Secession Convention. The title "Colonel" appears to have been one given out of respect or due to his political career, not from any military position. When I first began practicing as a young lawyer in the South, I was occasionally called "Colonel" by old-timers, a reference to my title as a lawyer. I think that usage has now been all but forgotten in local society.

[42] Wood's report, *OR*, ser. 1, vol. 38, pt. 2, 437; Pula, *Sigel Regiment*, 241. Pula, the regiment's biographer, outlined the diary of 2nd Lt. Karl M. Karsten of Company F, Twenty-Sixth Wisconsin, in which he recorded that the "Sigel Regiment deployed near a farmhouse, constructing a makeshift breastwork out of material from nearby slave shacks to receive the anticipated Confederate attack, but the rebels declined the invitation." A copy of Karsten's diary is in the State Historical Society of Wisconsin, Madison (microfilm 251).

[43] Butterfield, notes to Hooker, circa noon and 1 p.m., 19 May 1864, *OR*, ser. 1, vol. 38, pt. 4, 254.

Butterfield also wrote to Colonel John Coburn, commander of his Second Brigade, who was guarding the division wagons on the Adairsville-Cassville Road near their previous night's bivouac. Butterfield asked Coburn to send two regiments quickly to proceed straight south and report to him and Wood's isolated brigade. Coburn chose the Nineteenth Michigan and the Twentieth Connecticut to move out, while the Thirty-Third Indiana and Eighty-Fifth Indiana remained with the wagons. The Hoosiers were ordered to hold the road and fortify it. Additionally, Gary's Battery C, First Ohio Light Artillery, and Captain Luther R. Smith's Battery I, First Michigan Light Artillery, supported Butterfield's advance.[44]

Butterfield sent a third note to Hooker from the Price House, this one at 1:30 p.m., in which he explained, "The enemy are moving their trains from Kingston to Cassville. I withdrew Wood's brigade, as I wrote you [at 1 p.m.], when it was within about half a mile of the railroad in consequence of a large force, larger than my division." Butterfield continued, stating that this force was "threatening him [Wood's Brigade] on his left and moving at a double-quick to cut him off or attack in flank." Lt. Colonel Samuel Hurst, who led the Seventy-Third Ohio Infantry in Wood's reconnaissance, recalled, "Coming to an open country, Gen. Ward's brigade bore to the left, while Col. Wood's went to the right and in the direction of Kingston, which was only a few miles away." The Ohioan continued, "When we had gone a couple of miles, we discovered quite a body of troops a short mile in our left front."[45]

Initially unaware of the danger, Hurst remembered, "They were moving in the same direction as ourselves, and it was at first supposed to be Gen. Ward's brigade." However, the other body of troops was Polk's Corps of gray-clad infantry who were shifting to the southwest to cover Cassville. The Ohio colonel explained, "But, just as they rose upon a small hill beyond Nancy's [Two Run] Creek, another column coming from the direction of Kingston, met the one we had first seen; and directly we knew there was some misapprehension." As Loring's Division of Polk's Corps turned south along the heights west of Cassville, Major General William B. Bate's and Cheatham's divisions from Hardee's Corps were falling back from Kingston to line up

[44] Coburn's report, *OR*, ser. 1, vol. 38, pt. 2, 380; Lt. Colonel Philo B. Buckingham's report (Twentieth Connecticut Infantry), *OR*, ser. 1, vol. 38, pt. 2, 452; Welcher and Liggett, *Coburn's Brigade*, 179; 1st Lt. Thomas King's report for the First Ohio Light Artillery, *OR*, ser. 1, vol. 38, pt. 2, 485; Smith's report, *OR*, ser. 1, vol. 38, pt. 2, 473.

[45] Hurst, *Journal-History of the Seventy-Third Ohio*, 122.

with Polk's men west of town. Also, Armstrong's Mississippi cavalry brigade was ordered to fill the space between the two corps.[46]

Hurst and his Seventy-Third Ohio Infantry continued in front of the brigade, "marching," according to the Ohio leader, "in a line across a large wheatfield, scarcely half a mile from the hill on which these mysterious demonstrations were being made." Hurst and his fellow Ohioans could see the bayonets glistening in the sunlight as the distant soldiers moved at the double-quick up the hill and batteries of artillery began to be positioned. "Our skirmishers were two hundred yards in advance of the regiment when a line of skirmishers was discovered advancing to meet us, and we knew certainly [for the first time] they were foes." Alarmed at their predicament, Hurst explained, "Our brigade was completely isolated, and the rebels might have almost crushed it at a blow; but they seemed perfectly willing to 'let us alone,' if we would be equally generous." There was no attack or engagement by Polk's lines. His men were busy with preparing a line of defense. Hurst and his Seventy-Third Ohio Infantry joined the remainder of Wood's Brigade in falling back to the west to Colonel Price's house, where they, together with the balance of the brigade, erected a line of works.[47]

During Wood's (with Butterfield) excursion, there were some lighter moments. Colonel Adin Underwood was a veteran of the Thirty-Third Massachusetts, which was trailing the Seventy-Third Ohio, and the biographer of its unit history. He explained, "The enemy's skirmishers were so near that they amused themselves by repeating the orders of Colonel Faulkner, commanding Wood's skirmish line, 'Move up a little Captain Wood, on the right, move up,'" recorded Underwood, "while our men shouted in derision at their old field piece which was harmlessly firing blank cartridges for want of something better."[48]

---

[46] Ibid., 123; compare Mackall Journal, "A" sample, and "O" sample, *OR*, ser. 1, vol. 38, pt. 3, 983–84; Montgomery, *Reminiscences of a Mississippian*, 166; Roland, "First Mississippi Cavalry," 95. Walker's Division was in the center of Hardee's line west of Cassville and southwest of the railroad while Cleburne's Division was on the far left. Like Polk's Corps, Hardee's men formed in two lines (Major General Patrick Cleburne's report, *OR*, ser. 1, vol. 38, pt. 3, 723; Major General William Brimage Bate's report, *OR Supp.*, pt. 1, vol. 7, 93).

[47] Hurst, *Journal-History of the Seventy-Third Ohio*, 123–24.

[48] Underwood was grievously wounded in the leg at the Battle of Lookout Mountain in November 1863, but he remained close to the unit and recorded its actions and events (Underwood, *Three Years' Service of the Thirty-Third Mass. Infantry Regiment 1862–1865*, 212).

As veterans of the Eastern battles from Bull Run to Gettysburg before transferring to the Western Theater, the Ohioans had seen plenty of action. It was a miracle that they sustained no casualties at Cassville. After the drama of the morning, Butterfield's Third Division suffered fewer than twenty killed or wounded on 19 May, including four men wounded in the 136th New York and two men wounded in the Thirty-Third Massachusetts of Wood's Brigade.[49]

Howard

By midday on 19 May, Major General O. O. Howard's IV Corps was within three miles of Cass Station. His men began their march at 5 a.m., reaching Kingston by 8 a.m., and finding only some cavalry and Brigadier General Lucius Polk's Tennessee brigade of Major General Patrick R. Cleburne's division there. The Confederates quickly withdrew to the east along the Western & Atlantic Railroad and across Two Run Creek. Hardee's Corps was posted along the east bank of Two Run Creek about three miles west of Cassville. "As soon as our troops came in view he [the enemy] opened fire upon us from a 6-gun battery," remembered Howard as his corps neared the creek. "General [David] Stanley promptly brought up his artillery, supported by a brigade of infantry, and replied to the enemy's guns. He silenced them and drove them off," exclaimed Howard.[50]

Brigadier General Walter C. Whitaker's Second Brigade of Stanley's First Division of Howard's IV Corps led the advance on Kingston from the IV Corps camps around Hall Station. Deploying the Twenty-First Kentucky to the right of the Adairsville-Kingston Road (Road 8), and the Ninety-Ninth

[49] William Grinsted, surgeon's report for Third Division, *OR*, ser. 1, vol. 38, pt. 2, 335; Priest, ed., *John T. McMahon's Diary*, 95; Lt. Colonel Godfrey Rider's report of Thirty-Third Massachusetts, *OR*, ser. 1, vol. 38, pt. 2, 458; Hurst, *Journal-History of the Seventy-Third Ohio*, 123–24. About 6 p.m., the Twentieth Connecticut and Nineteenth Michigan of Coburn's Second Brigade were ordered to take the village of Cassville after the Confederates withdrew to the east side of town. The Nineteenth Michigan reported one killed and four wounded (Robertson, *Michigan in the War*, 394); the Twentieth Connecticut claimed four men wounded during the evening action (Storrs, *Twentieth Connecticut*, 253). In Ward's First Brigade, the 102nd Illinois reported one man killed and one mortally wounded, while the 105th Illinois had two men wounded. Total reported loss for Butterfield's Division at Cassville: two killed, sixteen wounded, one mortally, for a total of eighteen men (*OR*, ser. 1, vol. 38, pt. 2, 335–464).

[50] Howard's report, *OR*, ser. 1, vol. 38, pt. 1, 192.

Ohio to the left of the road, Whitaker advanced using the Eighty-Fourth Indiana on the right and the Thirty-Fifth Indiana on the left as flankers. Whitaker's men experienced "heavy skirmishing all the way to Kingston," remembered the commander. "Beyond the town, the enemy formed in line of battle and opened upon us with a battery."[51]

Earlier that morning, Brigadier General William Wirt Allen's brigade, consisting of the 3rd, 5th, 10th, 11th, and 12th Confederate Cavalry (made up of men mostly from Alabama), loaned to Jackson by Wheeler to help impede the Federal advance from the west, had fallen back before the advance of Howard's men on the Kingston Road. At Kington, Allen joined Brigadier General Samuel W. Ferguson's Alabama and Mississippi brigade who had been patrolling the roads to Rome and Woodlands. Brigadier General Lawrence (Sul) Ross's Texas brigade, and the brigade of Brigadier General John T. Morgan, were cut off and on the south side of the Etowah River after having evacuated Rome.[52]

At Cassville, Johnston's general orders, which one colonel remembered as a "flaming address," continued to be announced to regiments, and cheers were heard across the hills and valleys around the village. But chaos and confusion lasted through the afternoon as the cavalry charges ceased and artillery barrages commenced. A second Cassville Controversy was about to begin.[53]

---

[51] Whitaker's report, *OR*, ser. 1, vol. 38, pt. 1, 241–42.

[52] *OR*, ser. 1, vol. 38, pt. 3, 642. In May and June 1864, Allen commanded a Confederate brigade of cavalry until they reached Marietta, Georgia, when Allen was transferred to command Morgan's Brigade of Alabama troopers, and the Confederate brigade was assigned to Colonel Robert H. Anderson. Anderson would subsequently be wounded at the Battle of Brown's Mill, 30 July 1864, during McCook's Raid (*OR*, ser. 1, vol. 38, pt. 3, 650; Wheeler's report, *OR*, ser. 1, vol. 38, pt. 3, 956).

[53] Sykes to his wife, 21 May 1864.

Chapter 10

Conclusions to Part 1

Johnston stated that his battle plan called for Hood to march out to the east via a "country road" (Road 3a), then double back and connect with the right flank of Polk's Corps. Polk would then move out first to strike, or "engage," the approaching Federals from the Adairsville-Cassville Road (Road 1) with Hood joining as soon as Polk engaged. Poppycock.

The evidence does not demonstrate Johnston's claims to be accurate. Johnston did not have a battle plan. He had a hope, an expectation, but he had no real plan or understanding of what Hood was intending to do. He was relying on Hood, just as he had relied on him on 12 May in Crow Valley, north of Dalton, and again on 14–15 May at Resaca, to provide the details and execute an attack. He would do so again at the end of May following the Battle of Pickett's Mill, and again on 22 June at Kolb Farm. Johnston relied on Hood to provide the details and the execution of an attack on each of those fields of battle.

Johnston had no specific plan, other than a general desire to strike Sherman's divided legions when they were separated. Johnston's varying explanations over the course of some half-dozen accounts, and his hand-drawn map that shows where Hood's columns departed from Cassville to make their surprise attack, indicate that he did not understand Hood's plan at all, and he did not understand the geography north of the village.

Johnston's inclusion of the doctored T. B. Mackall "O" sample journal and William Mackall's *Memoranda* in the *Official Records,* coupled with his varying explanations in a half-dozen postwar accounts and the rediscovery of his hand-drawn map, expose his lack of understanding of the nature of the ground, the disposition of his forces, and the approach directions of the Federals. His distortions to the T. B. Mackall "O" sample journal have served to cloud the issue, to confuse students of the Cassville Affairs, and unfairly to discredit Hood and disparage the men of Hood's Corps who faced Federal horsemen east of Cassville.

One of the most alarming alterations to the T. B. Mackall journal is seen in the change of the location of the Spring Place Road from the young Mackall's original "A" sample to the published "O" sample. In the "A" sample, T. B. Mackall recorded,

> Heard first skirmishing on Adairsv[ille]. & Cassv[ille] rd. 10:20 AM. In ten minut[es], artillery on Sp[rin]g. Place road & on Ad[airsville] rd. After a few guns Genl. M[ackall] sent [word] more en[em]y close to H[ood] on Canton rd. Lt. Genls sent for. Wagons moved [to] rear. Line changed 2:25 PM. Change going on. Artillery on Hardee's front. Change of line effected under fire. Report of column on Canton Road not afterwards confirmed. Battle expected next day. General Ross reports from Cartersville enemy across at Wooley's Bridge.[1]

T. B. Mackall rewrote his "B" version with complete sentences, dropping a couple factual statements, but not adding anything to the original "A" version: "Line of battle formed to attack enemy. First skirmishing on Adairsville & Cassville road 10:20 AM. Ten minutes later artillery heard in direction of Spring Place road. After a few discharges report recd. from Genl. Hood that enemy was advancing on Canton road. Line of battle changed. At night army withdrawn."[2]

Importantly, in both the "A" and "B" samples, T. B. Mackall clearly recorded that he heard artillery in the direction of the Spring Place Road (Road 4), ten minutes after he heard the first sounds of skirmishing of the day on the Adairsville-Cassville Road (Road 1), to the northwest of town. T. B. Mackall's description matches every other contemporaneous account as has been detailed previously.

In contrast, the "O" sample changes the 10:20 a.m. action from "heard first skirmishing on the Adairsville & Cassville Road" in the "A" version or sample,[3] to "a few discharges of artillery on Adairsville and Cassville Road, and in ten minutes *report* of artillery in *easterly* direction."[4]

Additionally, in the "O" sample, which was lengthened at the hands of Johnston to over seven times longer than either the "A" or "B" samples, Spring Place Road is in a different location from the original location where T. B. Mackall had placed it. In the "O" sample, Johnston included,

> "General J[ohnston] rode over to General Hood's and then passing by general headquarters rode out Spring Place road, north of creek, with Hood and Polk and Hardee to show former where he was to form his line for

---

[1] Mackall Journal, "A" sample; transcription interpretation by author on a few missing words related to wagons being moved to the rear and change of line going on and effected under fire.

[2] Mackall Journal, "B" sample.

[3] The "A" and "B" samples.

[4] The "O" sample, *OR*, ser. 1, vol. 38, pt. 3, 983. Emphasis added.

> attack. General M[ackall] rode from headquarters east of town to join him; found Generals J[ohnston], P[olk], and Hardee returning (Sears's Mississippi brigade formed across road). Riding back, all passed Cockrell's Missouri brigade resting on road, and in town met Hindman's columns, advance of Hood's corps, moving to take position on Polk's right. After a few moments in town, rode rapidly back out Spring Place Road; general saw Hood and returned to camp-ground and dismounted....[5]

Twice, the Johnston-altered "O" sample referred to the Spring Place Road. Thankfully, there are several specific references that are included that assist in determining where the author of the altered "O" sample believed the Spring Place Road was located. First, a reference to crossing a creek is given. The Old Spring Place Road, Hood's Ironton Road, and Wheeler's Copper Mine Road (Road 2) crossed Two Run Creek just north of Cassville. Today, this route, as previously described, can be traced from the four-way intersection at Cassville by proceeding north on the Adairsville-Cassville Road until it reaches Kimsey Circle NW. There, the Old Spring Place Road/Ironton Road/Copper Mine Road (Road 2) continued straight north on Kimsey Circle NW until it reaches Janice Lane NW. The road continued along Janice Lane NW, then crossed the creek, and then connected to today's Cedar Creek Road north of the creek and just before reaching today's Shotgun Road.

Additionally, Sears's Brigade was in this area prior to being shifted to the west, and Cockrell's Brigade was in reserve along this road between the creek and village. Also, the author of the "O" sample referred to William Mackall as coming from the east ("from headquarters east of town") in search of Johnston and his lieutenant generals. Several critical revelations may be found concerning Johnston's understanding of the road locations and the battle plan.

First, Johnston believed that the Copper Mine, or Ironton Road (Road 2), was the Spring Place Road, and he was not aware of the existence or the location of the correct Spring Place Road (Road 4). His confusion, and his alteration of the Mackall Journal, "O" sample, has unfortunately confused and misled historians for decades.

Second, Johnston seemed unaware of the existence of five roads north of Cassville instead of four. Even when Johnston penned his *Narrative of Military Operations* a decade after the war, he continued to be unaware that there were five connecting roads north of Cassville instead of just four roads. In his *Narrative*, Johnston used a map from the Foster Map origins that failed to cover the space northeast of Cassville because it was outside the scope of its

[5] Ibid.

project to provide the road network adjacent to the Western & Atlantic Railroad. The blank space on the northeast portion of the map selected by Johnston for his book is as revealing as it is bare.[6]

Third, Johnston's use of the term "country road" provides additional proof of his lack of understanding of the roads or of Hood's battle plan. Johnston claimed that he ordered Hood "to move with his corps to a *country road* about a mile to the east of that from Adairsville, and parallel to it, and to march northward on that road, right in front."[7] When Hood read Johnston's *Narrative*, this sentence confused him, and rightly so, because Johnston's reference to moving to a country road that was parallel with the Adairsville-Cassville Road (Road 1), meant to Hood that Johnston was talking about the Ironton Road (Road 2).

The subsequent finding of Johnston's hand-drawn map, prepared in 1874 and contemporaneous with his *Narrative* that was published the same year, provides another indication of Johnston's confusion about the roads north of Cassville. In his hand-drawn map, Johnston indicated the location of the "country road" is at today's Brown Loop Road (Road 3a). While this is the correct route of Hood's march out of town, it is not the road that is parallel to the Adairsville-Cassville Road (Road 1), and it is not the road that Hood was marching *to*, i.e., the Ironton Road (Road 2), as Johnston had said in his *Narrative*.

Fourth, if Johnston's purported "battle plan" was true, then Hood's Corps would have to march about three miles east and north out of town and then countermarch to the southwest another two or three miles to return to the right flank of Polk's Corps. Ironically, this is course that Hindman's Division had to take when it fell back to get into a defensive position following the 10:30 a.m. surprise by McCook's troopers.

Fifth, if Johnston was committed to make an offensive movement between the Oostanaula and Etowah Rivers instead of merely looking for an opportunity to defend, why did he not order French to remain at Rome with portions of Jackson's cavalry to defend it? Johnston was not convinced that northwest Georgia was the place to engage in a decisive battle. During the Atlanta Campaign, Johnston acted, in the words of Sherman to Major General Henry Halleck, chief of staff of US forces, "totally on the defensive," a predictive statement made in just the first week of the campaign.[8]

---

[6] See Johnston, *Narrative of Military Operations*, 320a, see Exhibit 9.

[7] Ibid., 321. Emphasis added.

[8] Sherman to Halleck, 10 May 1864, *OR*, ser. 1, vol. 38, pt. 4, 111.

"We passed Gen. Johnston a day or two after [crossing the Oostanaula River following the withdrawal from Resaca], sitting on his horse with his staff and escort near him. The troops would cheer him as they passed and with his hat in his hand (he) would salute the boys. Our battery was stopped," remembered William Talley, of Havis's Georgia battery. "[A]nd the troops would pass by. Some of the infantry would holler out 'Hey Joe, we thought we were not to retreat anymore.' The General's face would turn red, but he never said a word but continued to salute with his hat." Talley captured the sentiment in his observations; the men seemed to love Johnston, but many would, in time, grow weary of the constant fallbacks.[9]

By the evening of 19 May, Sherman confessed to Halleck that he "apprehend[ed] more trouble from our long trains of wagons than from the fighting," but then added, "though, of course, Johnston must fight hard for Atlanta."[10] Major General Daniel E. Sickles, who had been attached to Sherman's army group by President Lincoln, astutely observed following the Battle of Resaca that "if Georgia cannot be defended on its northern frontier it cannot be defended anywhere."[11]

While researching this project, I was surprised by the lack of depth of prior comparative studies between Hood's and Johnston's battle plans at Cassville. Other than a discussion as to which general may have been more truthful, prior analyses have neither examined the details of either plan nor evaluated either plan for accuracy in light of other available primary source materials. Confusion created by irregular names of roads and inconsistent interpretations of their locations may have significantly contributed to this omission.

Additionally, I reached disappointing conclusions about General Johnston's postwar writings concerning the conflict at Cassville. In previous research for my book *Battle of Peach Tree Creek*,[12] I found multiple sources to corroborate the fact that Johnston had a well-conceived battle plan at Peach Tree Creek. Based on this experience, when I began this project, I expected to find substantial evidence for a battle plan by Johnston at Cassville. I did not. Worse, he was at the controls of evidence-tampering and of attempting, through his writings after the war, to influence the narrative to reflect more

---

[9] Talley autobiography, Kennesaw Mountain NBP.

[10] Sherman to Halleck, 19 May, received in Washington, D.C., 11:30 p.m., *OR*, ser. 1, vol. 38, pt. 4, 248.

[11] Sickles to Lincoln, 16 May 1864, *OR*, ser. 1, vol. 38, pt. 4, 215–16.

[12] Mercer University Press, 2014.

positively on his own role at Cassville. While many post-event writings are understandably written to be self-serving, Johnston went much further. His contribution of the altered Mackall Journal, "O" sample, was intentional, misleading, and dishonest. Richard McMurry, through his careful research, reached this conclusion in 1974.

Other historians have reached the conclusion that Hood was more likely truthful than Johnston, at least as far as the Morning Cassville Affair is concerned. In 1960, in an unpublished paper, Wilbur G. Kurtz criticized Johnston's review of General Sherman's *Memoirs*. In it, Kurtz, who had reviewed the *Official Records*, found that the likely Federal units on Hood's flank came from McCook's horsemen on the Spring Place Road, and he concluded, according to Albert Castel, that "Johnston had lied about what happened on May 19 in order to preserve his reputation."[13]

In 1992, Castel agreed with Kurtz's conclusions and emphasized the importance of McMurry's findings concerning the Mackall Journal and its five samples. Castel also pointed out that Thomas Connelly was without benefit of McMurry's discoveries concerning the Mackall Journal when he surmised that Hood's version was false in his 1971 book, *Autumn of Glory: The Army of Tennessee, 1862–1865*. Castel added that when Connelly wrote, "he did not realize that the Mackall 'Journal' as published was spurious, and evidentially he did not have access to Beattie's diary." Professor Richard McMurry believes that the alterations may have been made in fall 1864 from William Mackall's residence at Vineville, Georgia, just north of Macon, where Johnston, William, and T. B. Mackall spent time together with all the records they had taken with them, or that Johnston acquired possession of T. B. Mackall's "A" and "B" journal samples at that time.[14]

---

[13] Kurtz Sr., "General Joseph E. Johnston's Review of Sherman's *Memoirs*," 15, 18; Castel, *Decision in the West*, 590n102.

[14] Castel, *Decision in the West*, 589n101; Connelly, *Autumn of Glory*, 347–48; author's conversation with Richard McMurry, 16 April 2023. I believe that Johnston's alterations of the Mackall Journal happened much later and in anticipation of its use in the *OR*; otherwise, Johnston would likely have referred to it in his postwar writings. I believe that Johnston may have obtained (or remembered that he had) the "A" and "B" Journals from T. B. Mackall in preparation for his article "Opposing Sherman's Advance to Atlanta" in *Battles and Leaders* published in 1889, and that when Johnston learned of the *OR* project, sometime shortly after the publication of *Battles and Leaders*, he determined to rewrite the T. B. Mackall Journal and submit it. Johnston died unexpectedly on 21 March 1891 after catching pneumonia while attending Sherman's funeral service and famously not wearing a hat in a cold rain out of respect for his old

Castel pointed out that the T. B. Mackall's "A" sample journal follows "Hood's version [of the Cassville Affair], as presented in his [Hood's] official report and memoirs, and it rejects for the most part Johnston's version as given in his report and postwar writings. Hood is not necessarily more reliable than Johnston." Castel was unaware of the veracity of Hood's claim about the Ironton Road, "but when it comes to what happened at Cassville, Hood's testimony is explicitly and implicitly supported by others, whereas the only backing for Johnston's assertions comes from the 'Journal' of Lieutenant [T.B.] Mackall as published in the Official Records." Additionally, Castel pointed out, "General [William] Mackall, in a May 21, 1864, letter to his wife merely states that 'we could not strike' the Federals on May 19, and makes no allegations against Hood." T. B. Mackall's "O" sample journal and William Mackall's *Memoranda* are the only two documents that Johnston used to bolster his story of the events at Cassville.[15]

Those who have criticized Hood's explanation of the events at Cassville have pointed to Kurtz's statement that Hood's reply to Johnston's charge of "blatant mendacity" in Hood's report dated 15 February 1865 was met with "a tissue of denials and accusations which ignore his singular opportunity for contributing to the annals of the Atlanta Campaign," in his *Advance and Retreat*. On this, the Hood naysayers hang their belief that Hood was lying and that Kurtz agreed.[16]

However, these naysayers failed to include the rest of Kurtz's comments concerning Hood's account. Kurtz first pointed out that it is regrettable that Hood failed to include the accounts of McCook and Rippetoe (Eighteenth Indiana Light Artillery battery), in either his 15 February 1865 report or in his *Advance and Retreat*. However, it is doubtful that Hood had access or knowledge of these accounts, which were not published until 1891 with the *Official Records*, eleven years after Hood's death.[17]

If, according to Kurtz, "Hood's Richmond report included a detailed account of the battle with McCook's cavalry and artillery, Johnston would have found it impossible to maintain his adopted thesis that Hood—to put it

---

adversary a month before. The two hands that wrote the "N" sample that was submitted to the Board of Publications I believe were likely Johnston and someone close to him who helped to complete it prior to its submission (Johnston, "Opposing Sherman's Advance to Atlanta," 267–69).

[15] Castel, *Decision in the West*, 589n100.

[16] Kurtz Sr., "General Joseph E. Johnston's Review of Sherman's *Memoirs*," 16.

[17] Ibid.

mildly—was mistaken; neither would the historians have assumed that Johnston knew whereof he spoke."[18]

Kurtz found at Cassville, "there was a pitched battle which, according to Rippetoe, lasted six hours." Corroborating accounts from both sides provided specific details about the capture of an entire company of the 18th Alabama Infantry Regiment by McCook's troopers, explained Kurtz, who added, "Didn't Johnston wonder what all the shooting was about? Didn't the noise of musketry and cannon rise 'to the dignity of a battle,' (one of Sherman's phrases, facetiously quoted by Johnston)? Far from that, in Johnston's book," quipped Kurtz, "it didn't rise to the dignity of a simple fact."[19]

In perhaps the most revealing statement of his findings, Kurtz summarized, "It is doubtful if any battle of its size, in world history, has been so effectually erased from its pages by the simple process of declaring the commanding officer a deluded prevaricator, and an embattled enemy mere phantoms. Hood may have had a woeful countenance, but he never tilted with windmills."[20]

Upon critical analysis of the Mackall accounts, considering all the other available sources, it is clear that Johnston's story of Cassville was fabricated. Even without sorting out the complicated road structure, or the identity and location of the approaching Federals toward the town, both Kurtz and Castel were able to sniff out Johnston's misrepresentations. The additional sources discovered through research for this book have both supported and strengthened these opinions.

Confederate maps of the Gravelly Plateau, or Cassville Triangle, are suspect. The map of the region prepared by engineer John M. Stewart, and assistant engineer J. S. Tyner for cavalry leaders Will Martin and Joseph Wheeler failed to include an accurate, fully connecting Spring Place Road. Instead, it showed only broken portions of the road on the northern half of it on the Plateau and indicated no connection by Spring Place Road to the all-important Five Forks intersection.

In contrast, the map used by the Federal units of the Army of the Cumberland had a much clearer picture of the Gravelly Plateau. Sherman's forces used the map prepared for the campaign by Captain W. E. Merrill, chief topographical engineer for the Army of the Cumberland. Though not as

---

[18] Ibid.

[19] Ibid., 17.

[20] Ibid. Historian Steve Davis also found Kurtz's remarks compelling, for he included them in his book *John Bell Hood*, 150.

detailed as the Confederate map, the Merrill Map clearly shows five roads leading to Cassville across the Gravelly Plateau, not just four, as the Southern maps indicate.[21]

A large part of the untold story of Cassville is that Wheeler and his cavalrymen failed to cover the Spring Place Road. Wheeler provided protection for four of the approach routes to Cassville, but he missed one, the Spring Place Road. This failure proved to be Hood's undoing on the morning of 19 May when McCook's cavalry advanced on Hood's flank and rear undetected.

McCook's aggression that morning, coupled with his resourcefulness in dismounting part of his force in support of his two guns, deceived Hood and many of Hindman's men. Perhaps some of them thought they were facing a line of infantry supported by artillery on the Spring Place Road to the east while a part of Stevenson's marching column faced Federal cavalry on the Canton Road to the south. However, Hood always maintained that he faced only cavalry.

Generals Butterfield and Hooker were aggressive, as well. They correctly determined that Johnston was headed for Cassville, and that Cassville, not Kingston, was the key position. By moving quickly that morning in isolated brigade spearheads, however, Butterfield's two probing brigades (those of Ward and Wood) could have been seriously damaged had the Confederate attack been as Johnston described it in his plan, that is, an assault on the Federals coming down the Adairsville-Cassville Road. If Polk had attacked or engaged the enemy first, then Butterfield's two lone brigades would have faced the onslaught of eight brigades in three divisions, Loring's, Cantey's, and French's, northwest of Cassville. Instead, they were left to probe and move around for several hours in the face of overwhelming numbers until they withdrew westward to Colonel Price's House where they could consolidate that afternoon with other Federals arriving on the scene.

Though Sherman was wrong about Johnston's route of retreat between the Oostanaula and Etowah Rivers, he was right that aggression was the best policy, and this stance helped his forces win the day. Sherman ordered his cavalry units to show aggression. He wanted his men to erase the embarrassment of their earlier performances around Dalton and Varnell, thereby increasing their confidence for future action. While two of his cavalry divisions struck an infantry line on two separate occasions (normally a recipe for disaster

[21] Martin Map (Exhibit 27); Merrill Map (Exhibit24); Foster Map (Exhibit 26), Wheeler Map (Exhibit 28).

to cavalry), a combination of good fortune and quick, bold action helped them rule the day.

Richard McMurry surmised that, even if Hood had attacked, he would not have made a large impact on the Federals approaching Cassville. Even if Hood had tried to continue his ambush plan, Schofield was late to arrive, so there was no enemy for Hood to attack. Moreover, if Hood had moved farther to the west to strike at Ward's and Wood's isolated units, by the time he arrived, he would have risked a counterstrike on his right flank by Williams's Division, and by Schofield's late-arriving XXIII Corps.

If Johnston's understanding of the battle plan had occurred, if Polk had struck the isolated brigades of Butterfield that were probing along his front that morning, and if Hood had been in a supporting position, then it could have been a disastrous day for Butterfield and his men. With Geary's and Williams's divisions within two or three miles of Butterfield on the Adairsville-Cassville Road, and with Schofield's Corps approaching from the Ironton Road, presumably the Federals could have struck Hood or Polk in flank at some point. But this is all merely speculation.

Followed by the two divisions of Palmer's XIV Corps, brigadier generals Richard W. Johnson's and Absalom Baird's divisions, Howard's IV Corps reached the vicinity of Cassville more quickly than anticipated and before either Williams's or Schofield's legions arrived. For the Confederate attack plan to have been successful, the Northern forces along the Copper Mine/Ironton Road and Adairsville-Cassville Road needed to have arrived in the vicinity of Cassville long before Howard's legions reached the outskirts of town from the west. Furthermore, though Johnston did not learn it until the evening of 19 May during his meeting with Polk and Hood, the Federals had secured a bridge (Wooley's Bridge) over the Etowah River, and thus would have been able to flank him and make his withdrawal from Cassville inevitable unless he had been able to pull off a successful attack.[22]

A failure of Confederate reconnaissance coupled with a reliance on limited information in the form of a couple of dispatches from Rome about the Federal force that was threatening it, and on the captured Federal soldier, contributed to the flawed Southern battle plan. Also, reliance on a set of maps that failed to show the Spring Place Road (Road 3) to the northeast of Cassville and its connection with the Pine Log/Fairmount Road (Road 4) at Five Forks, led to a mistake by Wheeler and the Confederate cavalry to fail to cover this Spring Place Road in its cavalry screen. These mistakes in intelligence

[22] Mackall Journal, "A" sample, and "O" sample, *OR*, ser. 1, vol. 38, pt. 3, 983.

gathering, a lack of reconnaissance, a failure to screen all of the routes and approaches to Cassville, together with a couple of strokes of good luck for the Federals (McCook's undetected and timely arrival along the unguarded Spring Place Road, and Schofield's march to the McDow House instead of on Cassville via the Mostellar's Mill [Road 2a] and Ironton [Road 2] roads on the morning of 19 May), would serve to disrupt the Confederate battle plan and confuse the participants and future historians for decades to come.

Hood pointed out, in both his 15 February 1865 report and in *Advance and Retreat*, that the better opportunity for a Confederate attack was on 18 May because the three Southern corps could attack Sherman from three separate points (and roads) south of Adairsville while Sherman had only one route of escape to the north, and Sherman had already divided his forces, thus creating a serious threat to his exposed columns. In his report, Hood explained that he had made this proposal on 18 May when the army had reached Cassville and that he repeated it that evening. Hood stated that Polk and Hardee both agreed with him while Johnston remained noncommittal. Hood again raised the topic in his reply to Johnston's *Narrative of Military Operations* when he complained, "in no part of his [Johnston's] *Narrative*, can be found the slightest allusion to this matter."[23]

Unfortunately, no other sources have been found to support Hood's claim although it was important enough for him to mention it in both his report and again in *Advance and Retreat* and to admonish Johnston for failing to include it. Ironically, T. B. Mackall's entry for 18 May in both his "A" and "B" versions of his journal are silent on the issue. The only entry for 18 May in the "A" version is "Reached Cassville 10 m[iles] from Adairsville. Get in camp about 7 a.m. Beautiful country. Army has good rest near fine stream." There is no entry in his "B" version for that date, a point that seems suspect. More study on Hood's claim about a missed opportunity to attack at or near Adairsville on 18 May is needed.[24]

Finally, as to the central question: was Hood right at Cassville? As for the Morning Controversy, although he was surprised by McCook's aggression, he was prudent in halting his advance. Hood was also correct in sending part of Hindman's Division, Sharp's Brigade, to investigate and develop the enemy, that is, to force them to reveal themselves. Hood could not be certain that the cavalry that appeared on his rear from the Canton Road was not screening a main Federal column. While Hood believed that it was only

[23] Hood, *OR*, ser. 1, vol. 38, pt. 3, 634; Hood, *Advance and Retreat*, 99.

[24] Mackall Journal, "A" and "B" samples.

Federal cavalry, he had to protect his flank and rear. When Rippetoe's two guns began inflicting damage on Sharp's Brigade, Hood and the five thousand witnesses of Hindman's Division would certainly attest to the presence of a blue-clad body that included artillery. Once McCook had withdrawn about a mile on the Spring Place Road to the Crow Springs area, Hood was left to ponder his next steps.

When the Second Indiana Cavalry encountered the Virginians of Stevenson's Division (who were at or near the rear of Hood's marching columns at the intersection of the Canton and Pine Log/Spring Place Roads) at the same time as Rippetoe deployed his two guns and some seven hundred Badgers dismounted two miles away (at Five Forks) against the vanguard of Hood's would-be attackers, the perfect storm had been created. McCook's aggressive action, coupled with an absence of Confederate cavalry protection, forced Hood to abandon his attack. With his right flank and rear exposed, Hood had no way of knowing the character or strength of the enemy force that had surprised him. Without it, Hood was right to cancel the offensive and begin preparations to protect both his corps and the entire Confederate army at Cassville.

General Manigault agreed with Hood's assessment of the morning's events: "A part of the division," he explained, "came in contact with a large body of cavalry, and before we were aware of it a battery of artillery opened on us, doing some mischief. This cavalry covered the movement of some portion of the Federal army, who were soon afterwards discovered in force."[25]

One of the discoveries in this project was that Hood's planned flank attack was toward the Ironton Road/Copper Mine Road (or today's Cedar Creek Road), and *not* the Adairsville—Cassville Road that we have all believed for 150 years because of Johnston's *Narrative*. If the battle plan as Johnston stated were true, then Ward's Brigade and Wood's Brigade would have been struck and likely destroyed, and we would have had accounts from Polk's Corps about their supposed offensive movement instead of sliding to the west in a defensive posture. Johnston would have sent William Mackall also to Polk to "hurry up" instead of just to Hood.

Because Dibrell's Brigade had captured a Federal prisoner from the XX Corps the evening before up the Ironton/Copper Mine Road (Road 2), who stated that he stumbled across and got lost in the wagon train of the IV Corps on his way to the east while looking for his command, the Confederate leaders

---

[25] Manigault in Tower, *A Carolinian Goes to War*, 186.

believed that a Federal corps, apparently the IV Corps, would be coming down the Ironton Road the following day.

The IV Corps approached Cassville from the west, not north, and the Confederates based this proposed attack by Hood on inaccurate and flimsy information. As a result, Hood moved first east and then north out of town to get into a position to strike "air" because there were no Federals marching down the Ironton/Copper Mine Road (today's Cedar Creek Road, Road 2) during the morning of 19 May.

Because Sherman had ordered Schofield and the XXIII Corps, who had spent the night at Mosteller's Mill, to get up at daylight on Hooker's rear at the Jonathan McDow House on the Adairsville-Cassville Road, Schofield marched to the west and not to the south toward Cassville as he had originally requested of Sherman the evening before. If Schofield had gone in the direction he originally wanted, then he would have been heading into the trap that Hood and Wheeler were setting.

Ironically, Sherman later ordered Schofield to march on Cassville around 12:30 p.m. on 19 May, causing Schofield first to write to Sherman to explain why he had gone west instead of south that morning in reliance of Sherman's 10:30 p.m. order to him the evening before, and then Schofield moved east via today's Manning Mill (Road 2d) and south down the Copper Mine/Ironton road (today's Cedar Creek Road) and arrived in the vicinity north of Cassville at or after 4 p.m., according to his leading division commander on the march, Brigadier General Jacob D. Cox.[26]

Historian Bill Scaife got the movement of Schofield partially right when he labeled Schofield's Corps as going down into the planned trap in his 1990s series of maps on the Atlanta Campaign, but he placed Schofield incorrectly on the Adairsville-Cassville Road, and he incorrectly interpreted the location of the Spring Place Road, probably based on Lucy Cunyus's 1933 *History of Bartow County*, in which Wilbur Kurtz drew a map that incorrectly labeled a road. Wilbur Kurtz later corrected that mistake in 1949 with a new map that was published in the Cartersville newspaper, but apparently Bill Scaife did not know about the correction.

The Morning Cassville Affair was a complete Confederate failure in intelligence, reconnaissance, cavalry screening, inadequate and incomplete mapping of the contested area, misinterpretation of the roads, and misunderstanding and misuse of the road names, all followed by a massive postwar cover-up in Johnson's *Narrative* and in Johnston's manipulation of the Mackall Journal

[26] Cox's report, *OR*, ser. 1, vol. 38, pt. 2, 680.

as published in the *Official Records*. Hood's tarnished postwar record, due largely to the failed Fall 1864 Tennessee Campaign, discredited him and his version of the facts. Postwar, Hood's reputation was damaged, but Johnston's soldiers admired and loved him for not sending them into futile frontal assaults during his command of the Confederate army in Georgia; the perception that Hood did just that in the Atlanta-area battles and the reality that Hood also did just that at Franklin, Tennessee, led to an imbalance of scrutiny and criticism for more than a century after the war.

Despite not having the correct and full road structure or the ability to do the comparative analysis that this project has been able to accomplish, numerous historians, including Wilbur Kurtz, Albert Castel, Steve Davis, Richard McMurry, Stephen (Sam) Hood, Keith Hebert, and others have concluded that Hood was most likely telling the truth about his version of the battle plan and Johnston was not. For one reason or another, each of these historians had to make an educated guess based on the limited data available, but they all sniffed out Johnston's fibbing. In an upcoming article on the defense at Adairsville, Larry Daniel has also recently uncovered and exposed another factual misstatement in Johnston's *Narrative*.[27]

One of my "a-ha" moments in researching this project over the past several years, was concluding that Johnston's story about coming up with his game plan on the evening of 17 May at Adairsville was a complete fabrication. What the Confederate leaders were "poring" over the map about at that time was trying to figure out how to move seventy-four thousand men out of harm's way from the single road north of Adairsville via multiple routes south of the town before Johnston might be cut off either via Rome from the west, or High Tower bridge to the east. They were *not* planning a master counterstroke of divide and conquer against Sherman on the evening of 17 May but simply were seeking a safe evacuation by splitting their forces and reuniting at Cassville. The loss of the name and use of the road to Cassville five miles east of Adairsville, the Ironton/Copper Mine Road, and the loss of understanding that two of Hood's divisions used this route to withdraw from east of

---

[27] Daniel, "Adairsville," in vol. 3 of *A Series of Essays on the Atlanta Campaign*, forthcoming 2024. Johnston wrote William Mackall after the war on multiple occasions in an effort to get Mackall to support him, and on one occasion tried to get the elder Mackall to agree that Johnston planned the Cassville attack while at Adairsville, but Mackall would not do it. (Johnston to Mackall, 20 July 1874 from Savannah, GA; William W. Mackall papers, special collections UNC Chapel Hill, 48, File 1299, Folder 5).

Adairsville, and the advantage in maneuvering three army corps away from Adairsville and toward Cassville via three routes (as well as its potential use for a counterstrike on Sherman via the same three routes as argued by Hood) has been lost to history.

If there exists any contemporaneous account that supports Johnston's statement that he devised his strategy to divide and conquer Sherman on the evening of 17 May, I have not found it. All I have found is that the first time this master plan to divide and conquer Sherman ever saw print was in 1874 in Johnston's *Narrative*, but it has been repeated over the years, first by soldiers, and then by postwar writers and historians, even up to and through today.

In 1974, Richard McMurry exposed Johnston's alterations to T. B. Mackall's journal. This discovery should have set off a flood of new research, interpretation, and historiography on the Atlanta Campaign given this new and blockbuster prism by which Johnston's *Narrative* and the operations (and reports) of the campaign could be examined. Unfortunately, instead of a surge of new research, the new discoveries of the campaign have merely trickled over the past fifty years.

In 1974, McMurry cautioned historians about the altered Mackall Journal, "O" sample, following his discoveries. I echo McMurry's admonition. Unfortunately, my research has led me to conclude that Johnston lied to preserve his reputation for failing to fight or to have a plan to defend north of the Etowah River line in any significant manner. Johnston's real plan was to try and hold off Sherman and bleed him, both in men and in days off the calendar until June when he believed that Sherman would lose so many veterans due to the expiration of their terms of enlistment that he would be able to easily counterstrike at that time. Whether that occurred on the Etowah River line, the Chattahoochee River line, or the Peach Tree Creek line was apparently inconsequential to Johnston.

Hood read Johnston's official report while he was in Richmond, Virginia, in January 1865, following his failed Tennessee Campaign. In response, Hood added to his report, "After the army had arrived at Cassville, I proposed to Gen. Johnston, in the presence of Gens. Hardee and Polk, to move back upon the enemy, and attack him at or near Adairsville, urging as a reason," Hood explained, "that our three corps could move back, each upon a separate road, while the enemy had but one main road upon which he could approach that place [Adairsville]. No conclusion was obtained." After the meeting, Hood, Polk, and Hardee rode together from Johnston's headquarters for some distance while continuing their discussion about wanting to urge a counterattack to Johnston. All three agreed to make the attack on Sherman. "It was then suggested that we should return and still further urge the matter upon Gen. Johnston. We, however, concluded to delay until the morning."[28]

Hood, upon reading Johnston's *Narrative*, and in direct reply to Johnston's assertions about the events at Adairsville and Cassville, exclaimed, "the corps commanders, especially Polk and myself, urged Johnston only the day previous to march back and attack Sherman at Adairsville."[29] Hood explained,

> The three corps commanders, especially General Polk and myself, urged General Johnston, soon after our arrival at Cassville, to turn back and attack Sherman at Adairsville, as we had information of a part of his Army having been sent to cross the Etowah, in order to threaten our communications south of that river. The opportunity was the more favorable because of an open country and good roads, which would have enabled the Army to move rapidly and force the Federals, whilst divided in their forces, to accept a pitched battle, with rivers in their rear. This he [Johnston] declined to do, as stated in my official report.

Hood then delivered an indictment of Johnston's postwar apology: "in no part of his *Narrative*, however, can be found the slightest allusion to this matter."[30]

Hood never wavered from his statements about his recommendation for an attack of Sherman's columns between Adairsville and Cassville while Johnston's version has vacillated over his multiple opportunities to leave a record for the historian. Three times in the two places that Hood left a record, his statements were clear, concise, and consistent. There is an adage that the truth never changes.

There is another principle in the law, which provides that if the testimony of a party or witness is impeached by contradictory evidence, meaning that the witness or party's statement has been proven to be false, then all of that witness's testimony may be ignored or discounted. Thus, in a courtroom setting, if Johnston was found to have been untruthful about any one of his claims at Snake Creek Gap, or Calhoun, or Adairsville's defense, or about the size and strength of his army, or about the number of casualties sustained by his men during his tenure, then it can be assumed that he was also untruthful concerning his statements on the events at Cassville, as well.

---

[28] Hood's report, *New York Times*, 29 March 1865; *OR*, ser. 1, vol. 38, pt. 3, 634.

[29] Johnston, *Narrative of Military Operations*, 323 and 324; Hood, *Advance and Retreat*, 107.

[30] Hood, *Advance and Retreat*, 99.

In 1960, Wilbur Kurtz, a native Northerner but six-decade Atlantan, saw through Johnston's *Narrative* but did not have the resources (online and virtual libraries, the internet, email, and the collaboration of multiple historians and researchers) that this project has been able to bring to bear on the subject. Kurtz did not believe that Johnston was truthful on a number of points in his *Narrative*, including his excuses for Snake Creek Gap, his defense of Calhoun, or Adairsville, or his supposed battle plan for Cassville.[31]

"In the fall of 1865," Kurtz wrote, "Sherman chanced to meet General Johnston aboard a Mississippi steamboat enroute from Memphis to Cairo. Maj[or] Gen[eral] Frank P. Blair who had commanded the 17th Corps in Sherman's army, was also aboard." Kurtz continued, "Something had kept bothering Sherman for over a year and he seized this opportunity to ask Johnston about it—some such question as 'General, I heard all about your proclamation to make a stand at Cassville and fight the battle of the campaign there, but you didn't do it...why was that?'"[32]

Kurtz explained that Johnston then went on to discuss his intention to remain during the evening of 19 May and offer battle the following morning by defending the line that he had selected, but that Hood and Polk had argued against it due to being enfiladed by Federal artillery fire. Johnston made no mention to Sherman about devising a plan for attack at Cassville during his meeting at Adairsville on 17 May. Johnston made no mention to Sherman about ordering Hood or Polk to make any attack. The postwar meeting with Sherman afforded Johnston with an excellent opportunity to explain his grand "divide and conquer" strategy, or that he had ordered an attack on the morning of 19 May. However, Johnston merely talked about how he had wanted to stay and defend the new line that he had selected. Sherman subsequently had a meeting with Hood, who explained his plan for a surprise attack on Schofield's column—Hood had since discovered the identity of the Federal corps that marched down the Copper Mine/Ironton Road—that he believed was separated by five miles from Thomas's army. More information about Sherman's recollections of both visits are provided in part 2.[33]

Kurtz concluded, "Ironically, Johnston's version of the story, recited to set Sherman, and everybody else, straight about Hood's mendacity fell somewhat short of the mark. Obviously, [it was] a face-saving measure to

---

[31] Kurtz Sr., "General Joseph E. Johnston's Review of Sherman's *Memoirs*," 1–18.

[32] Ibid., 8.

[33] Ibid.; Sherman, *Memoirs*, 2:40–41.

rationalize his failure to fight at Cassville after his flaming proclamation. *It could pass for history only as long as the complete story awaited access to certain records.*"[34]

Perhaps now, what really happened during the Morning Cassville Affair has finally been discovered.

[34] Kurtz Sr., "General Joseph E. Johnston's Review of Sherman's *Memoirs*," 17–18. Emphasis added. As previously discussed in chapter 2, as early as 1927, historian Alfred P. James questioned the veracity of *Johnston's Narrative of Military Operations*, but he pointed out that Johnston's postwar popularity coupled with James's lack of knowledge of the Atlanta Campaign, prevented him from forming specific conclusions on the campaign. James did, however, refute many of Johnston's claims related to the Peninsular Campaign, a subject which he was much more familiar with, and he cited historian Francis W. Palfrey and Confederate generals G. W. Smith and E. P. Alexander who also refuted Johnston's claims about the Peninsular Campaign (see J. E. Johnston, "Storm Center of the Confederate Army," 342; also Palfrey, *Military Historical Society of Massachusetts*, 1:197; G. W. Smith, *Confederate War Papers*, part 1, *passim*, and *Battle of Seven Pines*; E. P. Alexander, *Military Memoirs of a Confederate*).

PART 2

THE EVENING AFFAIR:

THE FAILED CONFEDERATE DEFENSIVE

Chapter 11

The Issue

While the Morning Cassville Affair has been wrought with confusion, the Evening Cassville Affair involves the question: Should the Confederate army have remained and fought the next day, or, should the army have withdrawn during the night across the Etowah River and to the safety of the Allatoona Mountains? If Johnston and the Confederates chose to remain at Cassville and fight the next day, a second question arises: should the army have attacked Sherman on Friday morning, 20 May? Or, should the army have remained in its works along the ridge where it entrenched Thursday evening? Finally, in light of his decision to retreat, why did Johnston ultimately withdraw?

According to Johnston in his initial recorded version of events, when it was reported to him that an enemy column "was approaching on the Canton Road (Road 5), in rear of the right" of the Confederate position, it became necessary to fall back to cover that road. Johnston also claimed that he believed that the Federals were massing in his front preparatory to an assault, and, therefore, he needed to find a suitable defensive position: "Expecting to be attacked I drew up the troops in what seemed to me an excellent position—a bold ridge immediately in rear of Cassville, with an open valley before it."[1]

T. B. Mackall's "A" sample journal corroborates Johnston's initial explanation of his decision to change the line of his army following discovery of enemy on the Canton Road. He recorded, "After a few guns, Genl. M[ackall] sent [word] more en[em]y close to H(oo)d on Canton rd. Lt. Genls sent for. Wagons moved [to] rear. Line changed 2:25 PM. Change going on. Artillery on Hardee's front. Change of line effected under fire."[2]

In his "B" sample, T. B. Mackall simply wrote, "After a few discharges report rec[eive]d from Genl Hood that enemy was advancing on Canton Road. Line of battle changed. At night army withdrawn." One subtle, but important change can be seen in the identity of who sent word to Johnston that there were Federals on the Canton Road. In the "A" sample, T. B. Mackall and Johnston assumed that the news came from William Mackall, who had been sent to Hood to "hurry up" his attack. William Mackall had left to see Hood a few minutes before word was received at headquarters that there

[1] Johnston's report, *OR*, ser. 1, vol. 38, pt. 3, 616.
[2] Mackall Journal, "A" sample.

were Federals on the Canton Road. The news came from Hood, who sent Major James Hamilton of his staff to report the new development to Johnston as soon as Hood discovered the presence of the enemy in his rear. Apparently, T. B. Mackall discovered this information before he wrote his "B" sample.[3]

T. B. Mackall's "O" sample records, "Moved out to attack enemy, but columns reported advancing on *Cartersville* road; line changed; brisk skirmishing. General Ross reports enemy throwing pontoons across Etowah at Wooley's Bridge, and crossed a force—main force." In this published version, the enemy is reportedly on the Cartersville Road, the road that the Confederate army will use to evacuate during the night, and not the Canton Road as provided in both the "A" and "B" samples. Also, the identity of who sent word of a report that the enemy was advancing on the Canton (or Cartersville Road as indicated in the "O" sample), is not given.[4]

The next line in the "O" sample, however, suggests the real reason for Johnston's withdrawal. During the evening meeting, Johnston received a dispatch from Ross stating that the Federal army had crossed the Etowah River and that the "main body" of Northern troops was crossing and flanking the Confederate position. In the "O" sample, these brief lines provide a summary of the events at Cassville and are the only lines purportedly to have been written by T. B. Mackall on Thursday, 19 May. Two more pages containing four more paragraphs about the events of 19 May are purportedly written by T. B. Mackall two days later on Saturday, 21 May, near Allatoona.[5]

Johnston claimed, however, in his *Narrative*, that the reason he changed his line was because he heard firing on the Kingston-Cassville Road (Road 9) before Hardee, and also on the Adairsville-Cassville Road (Road 1) in front of some of Wheeler's men. "The sound of the artillery of the Federal column following Hardee's corps," explained the Southern leader, "and that of the skirmishing of Wheeler's troops with the other, made it evident in an hour that the Federal forces would soon be united before us, and indicated that an attack by them was imminent. To be prepared for it," he added, "the Confederate Army was drawn up in a position that I remember as the best that I saw occupied during the war—the ridge immediately south of Cassville, with a broad, open, elevated valley in front of it completely commanded by the fire of troops occupying its crest."[6]

---

[3] Mackall Journal, "B" sample; Hood's report, *OR*, ser. 1, vol. 38, pt. 3, 635.

[4] Mackall Journal, "O" sample, *OR*, ser. 1, vol. 38, pt. 3, 983. Emphasis added.

[5] Ibid.

[6] Johnston, *Narrative of Military Operations*, 322.

In his *Narrative*, Johnston also denied that he received a report from Hood or that he was notified Hood had changed positions. "When General Hood's column had moved two or three miles," Johnston claimed,

> that officer [Hood] received a report from a member of his staff, to the effect that the enemy was approaching on the Canton road, in rear of the right of the position from which he had just marched. Instead of transmitting this report to me and moving on in obedience to his orders, he fell back to that road and formed his corps across it, facing to our right and rear, toward Canton, without informing me of this strange departure from the instructions he had received. I heard of this erratic movement after it had caused such loss of time as to make the attack intended impracticable; for its success depended on accuracy in timing it. The intention was therefore abandoned.

As previously discussed in chapter 6, Johnston repeated the phrase "erratic movement" as a section heading in his article made in response to General Sherman's *Memoirs* and published in the *Annals of the Army of Tennessee*.[7]

In his fourth published explanation of the events at Cassville, published in 1889 in "Opposing Sherman's Advance to Atlanta," Johnston claimed that Hood was insubordinate in changing his direction and in failing to report. "Being asked for an explanation [as to why Hood had changed his line of march]," Johnston claimed, "he [Hood] replied that an aide-de-camp had told him that the Federal army was approaching on that road." Johnston said that the report of the Federals on the Canton Road was untrue. "Our whole army knew that to be impossible. It had been viewing the enemy," he explained, "in the opposite direction every day for two weeks. General Hood did not report his extraordinary disobedience—as he must have done had he believed the story upon which he professed to have acted. The time lost frustrated the design, for success depended on timing the attack properly."[8]

It must be remembered that Hood was deceased by the time Johnston's third and fourth versions about the Cassville events were published, so Hood had no opportunity to defend against Johnston's claims. For that matter, Hood never saw the *Official Records*, either. The Atlanta Campaign volumes were not published until 1891. However, there are contemporaneous accounts to compare against Johnston's claims.

First, Hood never claimed that the "Federal *army* was approaching on that [Canton] road." In his 15 February 1865 report, Hood twice claimed that

---

[7] Ibid., 321–22; Johnston, "The Dalton-Atlanta Operations," 4–5.

[8] Johnston, "Opposing Sherman's Advance to Atlanta," 268.

he suspected that the enemy was a body of cavalry. Hood explained, "While in motion a body of the enemy, *which I supposed to be cavalry*, made its appearance on the Canton road, in rear of the right of my original position."[9] Following his explanation of events that included his dispatch of Major James Hamilton of his staff to report the surprise to Johnston, Hood concluded with his explanation of the circumstances that he related to William Mackall, who had arrived on the scene. In response to Mackall's admonition to not become too separated from Polk's right, Hood said, "I called his [William Mackall's] attention to where General Polk's right was resting, and informed him that I could easily form upon it, and orders were given to that effect, throwing back my right to look after this body, *which turned out to be the enemy's cavalry*."[10]

Second, Johnston's claim that there were no Federals east of Hood's morning position has been proven to be incorrect. As Hood indicated in his *Advance and Retreat*, "Five thousand witnesses, moreover, could be produced to testify to the truth of my assertion [that Federals appeared on the Spring Place and Canton Roads]." Hood's claim is corroborated by multiple sources, both Federal and Confederate. Hindman's Division sustained casualties in both the 9th Mississippi Battalion Sharpshooters and the 41st Mississippi. Colonel Taylor Beattie and Major John E. Austin each provided letters in support. General Manigault recorded it in his diary. On the Federal side, multiple accounts can be found from McCook, Briggs, Rippetoe, and others concerning the morning clash with Hood. There is no basis for Johnston's assertion in each of his four accounts that there were no Federals on the Spring Place (Road 3) or Canton (Road 5) roads. There certainly were Federals present, and they were in the form of McCook, with the First Wisconsin Cavalry and Rippetoe's section of artillery on the Spring Place Road, and Stewart and Briggs and the Second Indiana Cavalry on the Canton road that morning as provided in part 1.[11]

Third, Johnston claimed that Hood never reported either the presence of Federals on the Canton Road, or his change of direction and deployment of his men. In his third published version of the Cassville events, Johnston wrote, "Neither this information [the presence of Federals on the Canton Road] nor his action upon it [Hood's change of direction] was reported." Both claims by Johnston are false. As the T. B. Mackall "O" sample (the sample most favorable to Johnston) records, word was sent "back by courier, who

---

[9] Hood's report, *OR*, ser. 1, vol. 38, pt. 3, 635.

[10] Ibid. Emphasis added.

[11] Hood, *Advance and Retreat*, 103.

reported to me that 'enemy in heavy force close to Hood on Canton road.' I tell general [Johnston], who says 'it can't be. (Armstrong on that road reported none.)' [Johnston] called for a map; said 'if that's so General Hood will have to fall back at once.'" At that point, General William Mackall rode up to Johnston in great haste, no doubt repeating the news that Johnston had just learned from T. B. Mackall and Major Hamilton and no doubt explaining Hood's change of line to meet the unexpected threat.[12]

Johnston would then make a critical tactical decision to change his line while in the face of the approaching enemy. His forces were at that time, around 12:30 to 1 p.m., posted along a series of high hills and ridges north and west of Cassville and in a strong defensive position. However, both the Pine Log/Fairmount Road (Road 4), and the Canton Road (Road 5), were behind the two hills that Hood was returning to (at today's Brown Loop Road [Road 3a]). In anticipation of the threat from the two roads that ran behind him, Hood moved his men into a position to cover the roads as well as to use the two large hills along his front. Also, Hood moved Hindman's Division to the west across the field to connect with the right of Polk as William Mackall desired. Hood wanted to remain in this position. He explained that it was the strongest and best position for defense. As will be seen, Johnston's decision to withdraw from it and to move to the lower set of hills immediately south and east of Cassville would have important consequences.

---

[12] Johnston, "The Dalton-Atlanta Operations," 4–5; Mackall Journal, "O" sample, *OR*, ser. 1, vol. 38, pt. 3, 983.

Chapter 12

Afternoon Confusion (12–3 p.m.)

Following Johnston's receipt of news that Federals had appeared on the Canton Road, first from Major Hamilton of Hood's staff and then from William Mackall, Johnston looked over a map and determined to change positions of the army from north and west of Cassville to south and east of town. While the exact timeline is unclear, there are enough sources to piece together a reasonable estimate of the time the events took place.

According to T. B. Mackall's "A" sample journal, Johnston's decision to change lines was made at 2:25 p.m. Also, according to all three samples ("A," "B," and "O"), the first sounds of enemy skirmish fire occurred at 10:20 a.m. on the Adairsville-Cassville Road (Road 1). Additionally, in all three samples of Mackall's journal, at 10:30 a.m. sounds of enemy artillery fire were heard from the Spring Place Road, or from an easterly direction. Major General George Thomas reported that Howard's IV Corps moved from Kingston to Cassville beginning at 11 a.m. and soon ran into two Confederate divisions under Hardee. At that point, Howard deployed artillery who began shelling the Southerners. Howard's IV Corps then advanced toward the Confederates, pushing them to within two miles of Cassville. Finally, French recorded that he received orders to withdraw from his position north and west of town to the new line at 4 p.m., and that his division was the last to leave the old line.[1]

Taking each of these accounts, we can piece together a reasonable sequence of events and calculate a fair timeline of events from the time of first contact by Hood with the Federals, and the time that the last of the Confederates under French moved to the new line. While there was no standard for time-keeping during the American Civil War—multiple time-keeping sources were used, including by banks, cities, and railroad companies—what is critical is the *sequence* in which events occurred. In this manner, we can study and understand the cause and effect of events, and in the sequence of events, we can see what event led to the next event.

At 10:20 a.m., between a mile to a mile and a half northwest of Cassville along the Adairsville-Cassville Road (Road 1), Ward's Brigade of Federals

---

[1] Mackall Journal, "A," "B," and "O" samples; W. Mackall, "Memorandum," *OR*, ser. 1, vol. 38, pt. 3, 621–22; Thomas's report, *OR*, ser. 1, vol. 38, pt. 1, 142; French, *Two Wars*, 196.

engaged Iverson's and portions of Ashby's and Harrison's cavalry brigades. At 10:30 a.m., Hood's Corps became engaged in two places with portions of Stewart's Brigade of McCook's cavalry division. By 11 a.m., Stanley's First Division of Howard's IV Corps was on the march east from Kingston and headed toward Cassville, just six miles away. Between 11 a.m. and noon, artillery guns from Howard's IV Corps were deployed, and its cannoneers began firing on Hardee's lines. At the same time, Stanley's Division, supported by the balance of Howard's Corps, pressed Hardee's lines to within two miles of Cassville.

Due to the pressure being placed on Hardee, Johnston ordered William Mackall to go to Hood to inform him that "General Hardee reported a heavy force advancing on him, he (Hardee) being on the left, and to direct General Hood not to make too wide a movement; not to separate himself too far from the left of the army, but *if the enemy advanced upon him* to strike him promptly and hard." William Mackall's *Memoranda* supports both Hood's version of events and Hood's version of the battle plan as previously discussed.[2]

As William Mackall explained, "On reaching General Hood, who was in a field in rear of one of his divisions, I informed him that the enemy was advancing in force on Hardee. He instantly said, 'And they are on me, too. The cavalry gave me no warning. I only learned the fact through officers of my own staff, and I am now falling back to form a line farther to the rear.'"[3]

Hood corroborated William Mackall's statement in both his report in the *Official Records* and his *Advance and Retreat*. In his report, Hood said that after he had sent Major James Hamilton to report the news to Johnston that the enemy was on the Canton Road,

> Brig. Gen. Mackall, Chief of Staff, rode up in great haste, and said that Gen. Johnston directed that I should not separate myself too far from Gen. Polk. I called his attention to where Gen. Polk's right was resting, and

---

[2] W. W. Mackall, "Memoranda of the Operations at Cassville on May 19, 1864," *OR*, ser. 1, vol. 38, pt. 3, 622. Emphasis added. As it was clear that Federals (Ward's Brigade of the XX Corps) were already approaching on the Adairsville-Cassville Road toward Polk's line and opposed by Iverson, Ashby, and Harrison, and it was clear that Hood was moving across the large, open field toward another road (the Ironton/Copper Mine Road), William Mackall's statement to Hood "if the enemy advanced upon him" supports Hood's position that the Confederate leaders expected a Federal column to come down the Ironton/Copper Mine Road. Also, William Mackall's statement implies that his words and directive to "strike promptly and hard" and "if the enemy advanced upon him" came from Johnston.

[3] Ibid.

> informed him that I could easily form upon it, and orders were given to that effect, throwing back my right to look after this body, which turned out the be the enemy's cavalry.[4]

In his report, Hood added "Finding that I had done all which Gen. Johnston had given me liberty to do, I then rode to his headquarters, where Gen. Johnston decided to take up his line on the ridge in rear of the one then occupied by Gen. Polk," he continued, "a line which was enfiladed by heights of which the enemy would at once possess himself, as was pointed out to Gen. Johnston by Brig. Gen. [Francis A.] Shoupe [*sic*], commanding the artillery."[5]

Following the war, and after the release of Johnston's *Narrative*, Hood wrote in his *Advance and Retreat*, "About this juncture [after the enemy had appeared on his right and rear, and after Hood had ordered Hindman to deploy and develop the enemy], General Mackall, Chief of General Johnston's staff, rode up in great haste, and said in a most excited manner that General Johnston desired I should not separate myself too far from General Polk."[6]

Hood continued, "I called his attention to the enemy, in sight, advancing in the open field, and told him I had been in person to the Ironton road; had found it in possession of our cavalry, and could, therefore, at any moment, easily form on the right of Polk [meaning that there was no present threat to Polk's flank from any Federals on the Ironton Road]. His reply was 'Very well,' or words to that effect." Hood's account in *Advance and Retreat* is substantially the same as his account in his 15 February 1865 report, and it matches with William Mackall's 22 September 1864's *Memoranda*, with one exception.[7]

In *Advance and Retreat*, Hood claimed that William Mackall arrived in the field behind Hindman's Division while the enemy was "in sight," and that Hood called Mackall's attention to the enemy. This discrepancy between Hood and William Mackall might suggest that one or the other had misrepresented the events, or been deficient in memory. However, it appears that William Mackall missed the contact with Rippetoe's Eighteenth Indiana battery section and the First Wisconsin troopers who had been west of Five Forks

---

[4] Hood's report, *OR*, ser. 1, vol. 38, pt. 3, 635.

[5] Ibid. Francis A. Shoup spelled his name without an "e" but Hood and others misspelled it by adding an "e" in their reports. (Correspondence with Stephen Hood, descendant of John Bell Hood, who has an original letter signed by Shoup John Bell Hood.)

[6] Hood, *Advance and Retreat*, 100.

[7] Ibid.

at the Spring Place Road (Road 3). McCook's cavalrymen withdrew quickly after Hindman's Division advanced. William Mackall supports Hood's claim that he tried to point out the presence of the enemy, when Hood exclaimed, "On both the Canton and Spring Place Road; and did you not see them?" William Mackall answered that he "had seen no enemy."[8]

In addition, it is possible, and indeed likely, that William Mackall never saw the brief contact between James Stewart's Second Indiana Cavalry and the 63rd Virginia on the Canton Road either, therefore providing William Mackall with the ability to claim that the report of Federal cavalry on the Canton Road was "not confirmed," a statement recorded by T. B. Mackall in his "A" sample.[9]

It is likely that William Mackall's meeting with Hood in the field behind Hindman's Division occurred around noon, or within thirty minutes either way, at most. Given the action between Rippetoe's two guns and the 9th Mississippi Battalion and 41st Mississippi of Sharp's Brigade in Hindman's Division occurring at or just after 10:30 a.m. and Howard's advance on Hardee's Corps beginning at 11 a.m., William Mackall could not have ridden to Hood before 11:30 a.m. Assuming that Hardee, who was three miles west of Cassville, sent a dispatch to Johnston at 11 a.m., when Howard's IV Corps first began to advance, by the time that the rider reached Johnston, delivered the news, and Johnston dispatched William Mackall to Hood, who was two or three miles northeast of Cassville, it would have likely taken up to thirty minutes for Hardee's note to reach Johnston, Johnston to dispatch William Mackall, and William Mackall to meet Hood in the field.

Major Henry Hampton of Hardee's staff kept a journal of events in Hardee's Corps. In it, Hampton recorded at noon that "it was determined to change the line to a stronger one in the rear." Assuming that Hardee sent his note to Johnston at that time, when his forces fell back east about two miles to the vicinity of Cassville (which also fits the statements from Butterfield and James Wood, who witnessed the arrival of a portion of Hardee's men to their right front), and assuming the same thirty minutes for Hardee's dispatch rider to reach Johnston and for William Mackall to reach Hood, then the latest time Mackall reached Hood was around 12:30 p.m. Thus, noon to 12:30 is a fair approximation of the time for the meeting between William Mackall and Hood. By then, William Mackall would not have seen any Federals on either

---

[8] Ibid.; W. W. Mackall, "Memoranda of the Operations at Cassville on May 19, 1864," *OR*, ser. 1, vol. 38, pt. 3, 622.

[9] Mackall Journal, "A" sample.

road, but Hood was still reeling from the unexpected presence of the Federals.[10]

Between 12:30 p.m. and 2:30 p.m., in response to the new threat on the Canton Road, according to T. B. Mackall's "O" sample journal, Johnston reviewed a map, called for his corps commanders, and then began looking for a new defensive position south and east of town. Joining Johnston was Polk and Brigadier Francis A. Shoup, chief of artillery, as they surveyed and rode along the new position together. During that time, Hood rode up and joined Johnston. Hood was apparently present when Shoup warned Johnston that the new line would be subject to enfilade fire. By 2:25 p.m., according to T. B. Mackall's "A" sample journal, Johnston had selected the new line. Hood was not happy with the new line and believed that the adjustment he had just made would both cover the Canton Road to the east and keep his men on the higher hills northeast of town and connected to the same range of hills that Polk's men were already on, and in line with the most-recent position of Hardee's men.[11]

According to Johnston, Brigadier General Francis Shoup "had pointed out to me what he thought a weak point near General Polk's right, a space of a hundred and fifty or two hundred yards, which, in his opinion, might be enfiladed by artillery placed on a hill more than a mile off, beyond the front of our right—so far, it seemed to me, as to make the danger trifling." The Southern commander explained that he responded by telling Shoup "to instruct the officer commanding there to guard against such a chance by the construction of traverses, and to impress upon him that no attack of infantry could be combined with a fire of distant artillery, and that his infantry might safely occupy some ravines immediately in rear of this position during any such fire of artillery."[12]

T. B. Mackall's "O" sample captured details surrounding the chaotic midday at Johnston's headquarters. The doctored "O" sample recorded,

> [Johnston] Called for map; said if that's so [Federals on the Canton Road] General Hood will have to fall back at once. Presently General M(ackall) rode up at a rapid rate, spoke with general [Johnston], who sent him back in haste, riding one of his horses. [Major Richard M.] Mason went off on

---

[10] Hampton Journal, *OR*, ser. 1, vol. 38, pt. 3, 704–705; Butterfield, *OR*, ser. 1, vol. 38, pt. 4, 254; Wood's report, *OR*, ser. 1, vol. 38, pt. 2, 437.

[11] Mackall Journal, "A" sample.

[12] Johnston, *Narrative of Military Operations*, 323.

another; still firing had ceased; confusion in passing backward and forward of Hood's and Polk's troops.[13]

Meanwhile, Johnston's "battle order" continued to reach the various Confederate units. Mackall's "O" sample entries continued, "At this time could be heard officers all around reading orders to regiments and cheers of troops. Some regiments in field where headquarters were. Polk detains two of Hood's brigades, as Hardee on his left had not closed up a gap. Headquarters wagons sent beyond Cassville. Corps commanders and Wheeler arrive."[14]

Following the meeting between Johnston and his corps commanders and Wheeler, Johnston determined to fall back. This meeting occurred after 12:30 p.m. and before 2:25 p.m. because Johnston had not yet laid out the new line. T. B. Mackall's "O" sample continued, "Instructions to change line. Generals J[ohnston] and M[ackall] and Polk ride on high hill overlooking town and back from original line. New line marked out, and troops rapidly formed on it and along a ridge."[15]

Between 2:30 p.m. and 4 p.m., Johnston's three infantry corps withdrew from their lines north and west of Cassville and to the new position. Hardee's withdrawal would come while in the face of Howard's IV Corps, the two sides having been engaged in skirmish and artillery fire since just after 11 a.m. Hood's withdrawal would occur just as McCook's cavalry would return, and together with Stoneman's troopers, the Federal calvary would make a second strike at Hood. Polk's Corps would be the last to leave their position in the center with Loring's Division withdrawing, followed by Cantey's two brigades, and finally French's two brigades, Ector's and Sears's, which were on the line (Cockrell's Brigade having been in reserve and already posted on the new defense line). Soon, the balance of Hooker's XX Corps would arrive northwest of Cassville (Williams's Division on the Adairsville-Cassville Road [Road 1]) and Geary's Division linking with Butterfield's right and Howard's left. Schofield's XXIII Corps would also arrive via the Ironton/Copper Mine Road (Road 2) as the Federal forces consolidated during the afternoon.

Johnston's withdrawal to the new position would have several consequences. First, the skirmish lines of Hood would find themselves isolated and without support from the main infantry line that was withdrawing to the new position just before they would be struck by a Federal cavalry attack. Second, Dibrell's Tennessee cavalry brigade would find their route of retreat cut off,

---

[13] Mackall Journal, "O" sample, *OR*, ser. 1, vol. 38, pt. 3, 983, 986, 993.

[14] Ibid.

[15] Ibid.

and they would have to fight their way across the lower (west) end of the large, open field to return to the Confederate line. Third, Northern units would seize the high ground given up by the Confederates, and the blue-coats would begin to place artillery on the hills and bombard the new Southern line, exposing the gray-clad soldiers to enfilade fire between Polk's and Hood's lines. Fourth, the village of Cassville would now be in between the lines of the combatants, exposing the citizens to the hazards of war and causing many to flee.

T. B. Mackall's altered "O" sample captured the chaos. "Late in afternoon considerable skirmishing and artillery. Enemy's skirmishers occupied town. At one time confusion; wagons, artillery; and cavalry hasten back; noise, dust, and heat. Disorder checked; wagons made to halt. Consternation of citizens; many flee, leaving all; some take away few effects, some remain between hostile fires."[16]

Hood

As Howard's IV Corps drew closer to Cassville and engaged with Hardee's Corps to the west, and while isolated brigades of Butterfield's Division probed in front of Polk's line northwest of the town, Hood flung his corps out to the east to cover the roads and to protect the flank of the army from the unknown force that had struck him so quickly. By noon, Hood had placed Stewart's Division in an arc along the ridge north of the Pine Log Road (Road 4), from the gap at today's Brown Loop Road (Road 3a) and to the northeast around the northern face of the ridge (reaching today's Carson Loop Road and its connection with Cassville White Road, Pine Log Road, Road 4). Hood posted Hindman's Division along the southwestern ridge left of the gap at today's Brown Loop Road connecting with Stewart's left. Hood also ordered Stevenson's Division to move east along the Pine Log (today's Cassville White Road, Road 4) and Canton Roads (today's Old Cassville White Road, Road 5) and cover the ridge spur between them as they connected with Stewart's right.

While Stevenson's four brigades began to move to the east, Polk detained two of them, Brigadier General Alfred Cumming's Georgia brigade and one other, apparently Alexander Reynolds's brigade, to cover the open field which lay between his right and Hood's left after Polk had shifted his troops to the southwest that morning. As Hindman's and Stewart's men began piling up rails and dirt along the base of the ridges, Stevenson's two brigades, which

[16] Ibid.

had moved to the east, began to dig a line of works to cover the two roads to the east.[17]

Hood's Pioneer Corps began to prepare a line of works on the ridges being occupied by Hood's men northeast of town. Pioneer Hiram Smith Williams of the 40th Alabama in Brigadier General Alpheus Baker's brigade of Stewart's Division recalled, "We were marched here and there for three or four hours up hills and down in ravines, cutting underbrush away from before our line of battle, and every thing else just to keep us busy…About five o'clock," remembered Williams, "our line of battle was changed to another range of hills and a half-mile farther back, where it is said the decisive battle is to be fought."[18]

Williams

Brigadier General Alpheus S. Williams's First Division moved at 1 p.m. from near the McDow House on the Adairsville-Cassville Road to the support of Butterfield's threatened brigades. By 1:20 p.m., the tail of Williams's Division, in the form of Brigadier General Thomas H. Ruger's Second Brigade, was on the road, remembered Colonel Ezra A. Carman of the Thirteenth New Jersey. Williams's men had camped the night before at Spring Mills just south of the McDow House. According to Williams, "The division was put in line on his [Butterfield's] left, and advancing in this order over a very rough country and through the thickest underbrush, reached the vicinity of Cassville, after some skirmishing with the enemy."[19]

Williams's blue-clad soldiers formed in line of battle as they encountered "the enemy's cavalry and flankers" at 4 p.m., remembered Colonel James S. Robinson, commanding the Third Brigade. Williams's Division arrived in the area from the northwest along the Adairsville-Cassville Road and connected

---

[17] Hood's report, *OR*, ser. 1, vol. 38, pt. 3, 635; Hood, *Advance and Retreat*, 104; Mackall Journal, "O" sample, *OR* ser. 1, vol. 38, pt. 3, 984. Between the Cassville-White Road and the Old Cassville-White Road, on the high ground just west of I-75, was located a KOA campground where a line of infantry earthworks was found. The works have since been destroyed, and this land was altered with the construction of the Chick-Fil-A Distribution Center. Photographs of these original works are included in this book, with special thanks to Mr. Dale Black, who helped locate the works, and to Mr. Matthew Beard, who made the images.

[18] Wynne and Taylor, *This War So Horrible*, 74–75.

[19] Williams's report, *OR*, ser. 1, vol. 38, pt. 2, 29; Carman's report, *OR*, ser. 1, vol. 38, pt. 2, 69.

with Butterfield's Division to its right. Between 4 and 5 p.m., as Stoneman's and McCook's cavalry brigades charged across the Two Run Creek valley two miles to the east, Williams's Brigades formed into position. Robinson's Brigade deployed in two lines, "one in support of the other," according to its leader. With Williams and Lieutenant Colonel Charles W. Asmussen of General Hooker's staff observing, Robinson's Brigade began their advance at 5 p.m. "The troops moved steadily forward over steep hills and through tangled forests and marshes, compelling the enemy to remove his light artillery and cavalry and fall back upon his infantry supports," recorded Robinson. His veterans pressed Iverson's and Humes's Southern cavalrymen along with Robertson's artillerists, who had fired on Ward's men that morning around 10:30 a.m. The Confederates withdrew from their position northwest of town to the new infantry line south and east of Cassville.[20]

As Robinson's Third Brigade led the advance of the division from the center, Ruger's Second Brigade formed to its left with the 107th New York, the 150th New York, and the Thirteenth New Jersey, from right to left, on the first line of Ruger's Brigade. Williams's First Brigade, under Brigadier General Joseph F. Knipe, formed to the right of Robinson's Brigade and on the right of the division, with the Fifth Connecticut deploying as skirmishers and the 123rd New York serving as support for a section of artillery. Lieutenant Colonel James C. Rogers, commanding the 123rd New Yorkers, remembered, "on the 19th rebel pickets were met a mile and a half from Cassville and quickly driven into the town." There, Rogers explained, the regiment "formed line of battle and advanced to the edge of the village, when the regiment was sent by General Knipe to support a section of artillery in advance. In the performance of this duty one man was wounded by a shell."[21]

Private Van R. Willard of the Third Wisconsin in Ruger's Second Brigade, witnessed the advance of Williams's Division. "We came upon their line late in the afternoon and found them strongly posted on the hills and ridges north of the town," remembered Willard. "Our line advanced, and a brisk fire was commenced by the skirmishers. Late in the afternoon, and just before

---

[20] Robinson's report, *OR*, ser. 1, vol. 38, pt. 2, 87. One man was killed in the Eighty-Second Illinois, and another man was wounded in the 123rd New York during the action (*OR*, ser. 1, vol. 38, pt. 2, 48, 97).

[21] Colonel John H. Ketchum's report, 150th New York, *OR*, ser. 1, vol. 38, pt. 2, 77; Knipe's report, *OR*, ser. 1, vol. 38, pt. 2, 41; Colonel Warren W. Packer's report, Fifth Connecticut, *OR*, ser. 1, vol. 38, pt. 2, 45; Rogers's report, 123rd New York, *OR*, ser. 1, vol. 38, pt. 2, 48.

sunset, the 1st Brigade of the 1st Division, 20th Corps, swept around to the left and fell upon the flank of the enemy while the 3rd and 2nd Brigades charged the enemy's line in front." Williams's Division approached the right of French's Division and the two brigades of Stevenson's Division to French's right (Cummings and probably A. Reynolds).[22]

"But the rebels abandoned their position," continued Willard, "without hardly firing a shot and retreated to a high ridge beyond the town. It was now sunset, and as the dusk of evening stole over the scene, the firing died away, and only the occasional flash of a skirmisher's rifle," he explained, "as it gleamed through the deepening twilight, gave proof of a hostile foe. The next morning [we] found their works beyond the town deserted. They had retreated during the night and were hurrying on toward the Allatoonas [mountains]."[23]

Geary

After connecting with Palmer's XIV Corps around 10:30 a.m., Geary's Division continued south through the unbroken forests and deep ravines in the region until reaching within sight of the railroad between Kingston and Cassville. Geary then turned east and, around 3 p.m., formed a connection with Butterfield's Division on his left near the home of Colonel Price. Geary found Butterfield's Division in line of battle and shelling the enemy in the woods on the ridge to the east with artillery fire.[24]

"By a reconnaissance sent out toward the railroad," Geary explained, "I connected with Newton's Division of the Fourth Corps, and then moved forward (crossing Two Run Creek) south of the main road to Cassville, pressing the rear guard of the retreating enemy and capturing a number of prisoners." Geary's Division, now formed with Howard's IV Corps on the right and Butterfield's Division on the left, with Williams's Division to the left of Butterfield. They now moved forward in one solid line toward the newly abandoned Confederate position.[25]

Butterfield

The veterans of the IV and XX Corps remembered it as a grand sight although perhaps a foolish move. Private Robert Hale Strong of the 105th Illinois in

---

[22] Raab, *With the 3rd Wisconsin Badgers*, 257.

[23] Ibid.

[24] Geary's report, *OR*, ser. 1, vol. 38, pt. 2, 121–22.

[25] Ibid.

Ward's Brigade, described the scene: "while we lay supporting a battery of ours on a hillside, the enemy lay on the opposite hill, waiting to charge. In between us was an open field with a creek through it. While we lay there, the enemy formed in line to charge. Our battery opened on them with cannister and they scattered." Butterfield's Division was opposite portions of Loring's Division and Cantey's two brigades between noon and 3 p.m. Private J. P. Cannon of the 27th Alabama in Scott's Brigade remembered that his company, Company C, was placed on a skirmish line in front of the main Confederate works after moving about a half mile to the left around 9 a.m. "Our command was detailed as skirmishers, and we had a lively time the balance of the day, but being in the timber we all took shelter behind the trees and a six hour battle resulted in very little loss to either side," he recalled.[26]

Private Strong of the 105th Illinois remembered one time while on the march,

> We came to a splendid line of works but found it empty. Just before we reached the works, we saw a large tree with a hole made through it by a solid shot. Low down on the other side, sitting against the tree was a headless man. He had been sitting there during the fighting, and undoubtedly thought himself safe, when a Yankee solid shot went through the tree and took his head off. His body remained against the tree. There was no trace of his head.

Judging from the circumstances that his regiment found while at Cassville, it is likely that this event occurred on the afternoon of 19 May, northwest of the village.[27]

Around 4 p.m., the entire Federal line of the IV and XX Corps advanced toward Polk's and Hardee's positions. The 129th Illinois was deployed as skirmishers as Ward's Brigade led the advance from the center of the XX Corps. Private Strong of the 105th Illinois thought that it was the craziest idea to attack the Southerners who were, no doubt, entrenched on the ridge ahead. "Then we were ordered to do a thing that I thought then, and think now, was a foolish, fool-hardy thing. Our music struck up, and with arms at 'shoulder' we infantry marched in a solid square out into that open field with our bands playing 'Behold, the Conquering Hero Comes.'" Strong added, "We stood at rest in the field for half an hour, supposing every minute of the time that the Rebs would open fire on us as we were in plain view of their position. As they

---

[26] Strong, *Yankee Private's Civil War*, 28–29; Cannon, *Bloody Banners and Barefoot Boys*, 67.

[27] Strong, *Yankee Private's Civil War*, 20.

did not accept our challenge, we then marched up to where they had been an hour or less before, and found they had left." The Illinoisan veteran moved to Nebraska after the war. There, he met a fellow Northern veteran who witnessed the demonstration before Cassville. The comrade confessed that the pageantry of the bands playing, the colors flying, and all the troops moving forward in unison, more than forty thousand strong, "was the grandest thing he ever saw."[28]

Schofield

After arriving at the McDow House and conferring with General Hooker, Schofield and his columns waited for Williams's Division to move south along the Adairsville-Cassville Road. About 12:30 p.m., Schofield received a message from Sherman ordering him to "put the head of your column at Cassville Depot, your line facing east." Until now, Schofield had proceeded toward Kingston following his previous order from Sherman although the Federal commander had hinted that he might want Schofield to move east of Kingston. This change of direction meant that Schofield's men would have to double back to the east to the "fork" in the road on the Gravelly Plateau and then turn south on the Ironton Road and to proceed toward Cassville parallel to Hooker's columns.[29]

At 12:40 p.m., Schofield sent his commander a note confirming his receipt of Sherman's change of orders, telling him of his troops' movements, and advising him that his divisions were "on the Adairsville and Cassville road." Schofield explained that he could have simply proceeded south from Mosteller's Mill that morning, but that, as he understood Sherman's orders, he was heading toward Kingston, which forced him to move to the southwest and behind Hooker's units. Schofield informed Sherman that his "cavalry [the Fourth Indiana Calvary] reports the enemy in force on the road from Cassville to my camp of last night (at Marsteller's Mill [*sic*, Mosteller]), and about two miles from Cassville." The Confederate cavalrymen that the Fourth Indiana troopers found were Dibrell's Tennesseans. Schofield pledged to Sherman that he would "get onto the road to the east [the Ironton Road] as soon as I can, and keep my communication with General Hooker." With Cox's Division leading the way and pressing Dibrell's horsemen back, Schofield's

[28] Colonel Henry Case's report, *OR*, ser. 1, vol. 38, pt. 2, 366; Strong, *Yankee Private's Civil War*, 29.

[29] Sherman, dispatch to Schofield, 19 May 1864, 12:40 p.m., *OR*, ser. 1, vol. 38, pt. 4, 255.

columns would not arrive above Cassville until 4 p.m., where they would deploy and connect with the left of Williams's Division of the XX Corps on their right.[30]

[30] Ibid., 255–56; Cox's report, *OR*, ser. 1, vol. 38, pt. 2, 679–80. However, see Schofield's report, *OR*, ser. 1, vol. 38, pt. 2, 511, in which Schofield claimed that his men proceeded from Marsteller's [*sic*] Mill to Cassville, "where we passed the Army of the Cumberland on the morning of the 19th…." This bragging, though inaccurate, statement may have caused historians who reviewed the report of Schofield and others, but not the correspondence of each of the unit commanders, to get the order of march incorrect. Schofield's men did chase the Confederate army to the Etowah River during the following days, but they did not "pass" the Army of the Cumberland until 20 May.

Chapter 13

The Afternoon Stoneman-McCook Attack (3–5 p.m.)

Between 2:30 and 4 p.m., just before the Federal cavalry was preparing to advance, Johnston's orders to withdraw to the new line were being received by the division and brigade commanders along Hood's, Polk's, and Hardee's lines. According to the Mackall Journal, sample "A," the young lieutenant noted, "Line changed 2:25 PM. Change going on. Artillery on Hardee's front. Change of line effected under fire." The next time noted by Mackall in his "O" sample journal is 5 p.m., in which he stated that after "considerable skirmishing and artillery," and "enemy's skirmishers occupied town," that disorder was "checked."

Samuel French noted in his diary that he received orders to fall back to the new line at 4 p.m. Manigault remembered that by "four o'clock, our dispositions were complete. The infantry formed in two lines each, as well as the artillery, protected by light field works, hurriedly thrown up." Importantly, Manigault added, "Between that hour [4 p.m.] and five o'clock, there was much heavy skirmishing, and a sharp cavalry engagement, in which the latter did not show to any advantage, and all our light troops [cavalry] were driven in by the steady advance of the enemy." According to T. B. Mackall, at about 5 p.m., after having lunch with Governor Harris of Tennessee, Johnston and the governor rode down to Hardee's line south of Cassville. French remembered the events at that time differently: "About 5 p.m. our pickets from the extreme front were driven in toward the second line by the enemy's cavalry."[1]

About 3:30 p.m., Hood's Divisions began to withdraw from the Two Run Creek defensive line and to the new line of defense laid out by Johnston. Covering the Confederate withdrawal was the skirmish line together with a couple of artillery batteries. It is unclear whether or which batteries from Hood's Corps participated in the action, but Captain J. A. Hoskins's Brookhaven (Mississippi) Light Artillery battery, Selden's Alabama battery, and Tarrant's Alabama battery, all from Polk's Corps, appear to have been engaged during the action in the afternoon. French ordered Hoskins's Battery to cover the space between his right and Hood's left in Johnston's new line of defense. French remembered that his division was the last to leave the

---

[1] Manigault and Tower, *A Carolinian Goes to War*, 186; Mackall Journal, "A" sample and "O" sample, *OR*, ser. 1, vol. 38, pt. 3, 984; French, *Two Wars*, 196.

morning line. During the movement to the new line, Private Joseph Pool from the 10th Texas Mounted Infantry (Dismounted) of Ector's Brigade was captured.[2]

Between 3:30 p.m. and 4 p.m., McCook returned from Crow Springs on the Spring Place Road, this time with portions of both of his brigades and with Stoneman's Division, which had arrived via the Pine Log Road. As Stoneman was his senior, he led the four Federal cavalry brigades for the afternoon's contest. Ordering an attack across the Two Run Creek valley, the available portions of Stoneman's two brigades formed on the right, or north, while the regiments of McCook's brigades, who were not scouting or screening crossroads, lined up on the left, or south side of the line.

Colonel Joseph B. Dorr, commanding McCook's First Brigade (the Eighth Iowa with about eight hundred horsemen, the Second Michigan, and the First Tennessee [Union, Brownlow's Regiment]), wrote that, "the First Brigade was directed to take the right of the division, having the Second [Stewart's] Brigade on our left and Stoneman's cavalry on the right. The 1st Tennessee," he continued, "having been sent off on a reconnaissance, [and] the 2nd Michigan ordered to support the battery [Rippetoe's Eighteenth Indiana Battery], I had only six companies of the 8th Iowa left, the [rest of the Eighth Iowa] being posted to cover certain roads and some having been sent after forage." During the action, Trooper John Craig of Company B, Second Michigan cavalry, was killed while Trooper William H. Dicker of Company C, Second Michigan cavalry, was mortally wounded and died the following day.[3]

"With these six companies" [of the 8th Iowa], Dorr continued, "I was assigned the duty of attacking the enemy in the open valley across which they had thrown a line of rushed works of rails and earth. This line of works was on the opposite side of a deep and miry creek [Two Run Creek northeast of Brown Loop Road], the existence of which was unknown to us." Trooper Homer Mead of the Eighth Iowa remembered the Federal cavalry charge at Cassville as "the most spectacular and brilliant movement in action of the 8th Iowa Cavalry as the sun was going down." Mead described the attack. "McCook's division of cavalry with drawn sabres charged the rebel line of

---

[2] Brewer, *Alabama*, 699, 704; Daniel, *Cannoneers in Gray*, 155; French, *Two Wars*, 196; Carlock, *History of the Tenth Texas Cavalry*, 132–33. Pool had been wounded in the foot at Murfreesboro two years earlier; perhaps the injury prevented him from making the rapid redeployment.

[3] Dorr Journal, 19–20; Thatcher, *A Hundred Battles in the West*, appendix.

works. We marveled at the time why our cavalry was hurled so compactly and persistently against them." Mead added, "I lost my horse in this charge."[4]

Colonel James W. Stewart's Federal cavalry brigade, which included the 350 troopers of the Second Indiana (who had surprised Stevenson's marching column that morning), was formed to the left of Dorr's men. In front of the Hawkeyes and Hoosiers was Major General Alexander P. Stewart's Confederate infantry division. To the right of Stewart's Southern foot soldiers were the two remaining brigades of Stevenson's Division (between today's Cassville White Road and Old Cassville White Road where the KOA Campground was previously located and where the eastern part of the Chick-fil-a Distribution Center is located today).

A. P. Stewart formed his division to cover the gap between the two ridges at today's Brown Loop Road, with Brigadier General Marcellus A. Stovall's Georgia brigade on the right, Baker's Alabama brigade in the center, Brigadier General Henry D. Clayton's Alabama brigade on the left, and Brigadier General Randall L. Gibson's Louisiana brigade in reserve behind Baker's men and at the mouth of the gap. In front of his line, the veteran 14th Louisiana Battalion Sharpshooters under Major John E. Austin held the center of the skirmish line, with three companies of the 18th Alabama of Clayton's Brigade on the skirmish line on the left, and some Georgians from Stovall's Brigade under Captain Singleton A. Maxwell, Company C, 42nd Georgia, joining on the skirmish line to the right of Austin's Louisianans.[5]

As Dorr's Hawkeyes and James W. Stewart's Hoosiers began their assault on A. P. Stewart's line of gray-clad skirmishers and the temporary works of brush and rails, Dorr explained, "The approach to the works was still further protected by open ground which allowed no shelter for 300 yards from their batteries or small arms." The Iowa colonel added, "A full battery was posted on the hill just to the right of the town on the left of the valley and a

---

[4] Dorr Journal, 19–20; Mead, *The Eighth Iowa Cavalry in the Civil War*, 35.

[5] Dorr Journal, 19–20; Colonel Horace P. Lamson's report, *OR*, ser. 1, vol. 38, pt. 2, 781; Stewart's report, *OR*, ser. 1, vol. 38, pt. 3, 818; Gibson's report, *OR*, ser. 1, vol. 38, pt. 3, 854–56; Austin's report, *OR*, ser. 1, vol. 38, pt. 3, 62; Austin to Hood, 26 May 1874, in Hood, *Advance and Retreat*, 101–102; Colonel Abda Johnson, report of Stovall's Brigade, *OR*, ser. 1, vol. 38, pt. 3, 825; Brigadier General Henry D. Clayton's report, *OR*, ser. 1, vol. 38, pt. 3, 831; Lt. Colonel Peter F. Hunley's report of 18th Alabama Infantry, *OR*, ser. 1, vol. 38, pt. 3, 836; Hewitt and Lawrence, *Georgia Confederate Soldiers*, 2:534.

section on the hillside northwest of the valley both in easy range of the ground over which we must pass to gain the works."[6]

Dorr described the action as his troopers engaged the Southern lines: "As the 8th Iowa moved up to the attack, the rebel batteries opened upon them from both the hillside and breastworks." Led by Lieutenant W. Carron of Company G and Captain Hoxie of Company H, the Hawkeyes "gallantly charged in line upon the works but coming upon the creek were obliged to halt and cross in column," then "deploy[ed] again when they charged over the works and the hillside to the right—sweeping everything before them and driving the enemy entirely from the valley to a line of works near the base of the hill by the town."[7]

One Iowan wrote the editor of the *Dubuque Times* describing the attack: "It is a brave thing for cavalry to charge upon the bayonets of infantry in the open field, and when that infantry is strongly entrenched behind log breastworks, covered on the outside with rails, placed one end on the logs and the other on the ground pointing towards the assaulting force." The proud Hawkeye continued, "it is only the bravest that will undertake to charge up to and over them. This our boys did at Cassville," he affirmed, "charging with pistol and saber in hand, shooting right and left as they came thundering up, then with a regular Comanche yell clearing the works, and" the trooper added, "with their sabers driving the terror-stricken rebels like sheep through the town and into the woods beyond."[8]

Those "terror-stricken rebels" were portions of Clayton's Alabama brigade, including thirty-three men of the 18th Alabama who had been placed on a skirmish line just prior to the Federal saber charge. To the left of Dorr's attackers, Stewart's Second Indiana Cavalry swept across the Two Run Creek valley, onto and through the skirmishers of the 18th Alabama, many of whom quickly threw down their guns and surrendered for fear of being struck down by the blades of the blue horsemen. Calling it unnecessary and disgraceful, Major General Alexander P. Stewart complained of the performance by the Alabamians in his report. Major John E. Austin, in command of the 14th Louisiana Battalion's veterans, who were connected to their right on the skirmish line, urged Captain Darby, who was leading the 18th Alabama

[6] Dorr Journal, 19–20.

[7] Ibid.

[8] Corbin, *Star for Patriotism*, 478.

skirmishers, to move his line forward and remain connected with his Louisianans.[9]

Instead, the Alabamians broke, and thirty-three men were captured in an instant. Austin remembered, "About an hour and a half before nightfall the enemy broke through the skirmish line of an Alabama brigade posted to my left, and moved rapidly in rear of my main line, which was threatened in front." To Austin's right, the skirmishers of Stovall's Georgians, led by Captain Maxwell, being unable to see the developments around the curve of the hill to their left, also broke, and hastily withdrew from the field to join the rest of Stovall's Georgia brigade as it retreated to the new line south of town. Captain Maxwell led a company of the 42nd Georgia. The losses in the 40th Georgia, also of Stovall's Brigade, were twenty-one missing with four captured and seventeen deserted.[10]

Ground evidence in the form of an unexploded three-inch Hotchkiss shell has been found along the southwest bank of Two Run Creek just inside the west part of the gap (on the west side of the bridge over the creek on Brown Loop Road), indicating the location of receiving fire from Rippetoe's Eighteenth Indiana Artillery Battery as it supported the afternoon attack while the Confederates withdrew through the gap. Additional ground evidence in the form of fired firing pins and multiple three-inch Hotchkiss shell fragments has also been discovered on the hill southwest of the gap indicating the position of Confederate artillery supporting the Southern infantry's withdrawal during the afternoon action.

This left Austin's veteran Louisianans isolated and cut off from their line of retreat. After the war, Austin left a vivid account of the struggle by his men in returning to their lines. "To extricate my command, I had to move to the right, fighting all the while in front and rear, until darkness put an end to hostilities. By making a detour of eight or nine miles in the night, over a country devoid of road," he continued, "I was enabled to rejoin your [Hood's] corps, massed in column about two o'clock in the night, and just in time for

---

[9] Captain James B. Darby, Company H, 18th Alabama, is incorrectly referred to as "Derby" in Major John Austin's report (*OR*, ser. 1, vol. 38, pt. 3, 862).

[10] Stewart's report, *OR* ser. 1, vol. 38, pt. 3, 818; Austin's report, *OR*, ser. 1, vol. 38, pt. 3, 862; Major J. E. Austin to Hood, in Hood, *Advance and Retreat*, 101; Brig. General Marcellus Stovall's report, *OR*, ser. 1, vol. 38, pt. 3, 825. Henderson, *Roster*, 4:341–425.

my wearied men to participate in the retreat across the Etowah, which was shortly after begun."[11]

According to Lt. Colonel Horace P. Lamson of McCook's Second Brigade, the Second Indiana Cavalry captured thirty-eight prisoners, including an entire company from the 18th Alabama, while losing just five men wounded. McCook recorded that his entire division lost thirty-four or thirty-five men killed and wounded in the day's action. Hood lamented in his post-war account, "Whilst Major Austin was still engaged with this same enemy on the Canton Road, and my corps was nearing the line occupied by General Polk on the ridge in front of Cassville, orders were issued for the Army to fall back to the ridge in rear of the town."[12]

In the confusion of the shifting of lines by the Confederates as Hood's Divisions redeployed, the two brigades from Stevenson's Division that had been detained by Polk found themselves in a "no man's land." One of the brigades was Cumming's Georgia brigade, which was posted in a field between the right of French's Division and the left of Hood's lines.

One Georgia soldier in Cumming's Brigade vividly recalled the exposure that his men faced in the field. Private Robert Magill of the 39th Georgia Infantry recorded in his diary, "3 p.m., just our brigade here. Out in an old field. Yanks advancing in sight on our front and both flanks. Lieutenant Park's left hand shot off, and James White's leg nearly so. I began to think we were about gone," continued the frightened Georgian, "just as they were coming within rifle range, we were ordered to fall back, and I was 'mighty' glad to hear it. We did not wait for a second order. Fell back in rear of Cassville, where our troops are fortifying." Magill added, "5 p.m., Federals advanced to the other side of town, when an artillery duel was kept up until dark. We afterward learned somebody blundered and gave the wrong order, that sent us back to the old line, and came very near getting us all captured."[13]

While the identity of the second brigade that was detained by Polk is unknown, the evidence points to Alexander Reynolds's North Carolina and Virginia brigade for two reasons. First, since there were three killed and two wounded in the 63rd Virginia from the 10:30 a.m. action on the Canton Road as a result of the encounter with the Second Indiana Cavalry, these units must

[11] Austin to Hood, in Hood, *Advance and Retreat*, 101.

[12] Lamson's report, *OR*, ser. 1, vol. 38, pt. 2, 781; McCook's report, *OR*, ser. 1, vol. 38, pt. 2, 752; Hood, *Advance and Retreat*, 104.

[13] Magill, *Magill Family Record*, 225. L. Henderson, *Roster of the Confederate Soldiers of Georgia 1861–1865*, 4:300, 308..

have been at or near the rear of Hood's column that morning. Second, there were thirty-nine men captured (or deserted) from Reynolds's North Carolina and Virginia brigade and twenty-eight captured (or deserted) from Cumming's Georgia brigade. The other two brigades of Stevenson's Division, Brigadier General Edmund W. Pettus's Alabamians and Brigadier General John C. Brown's Tennesseans appear to have sustained few casualties at Cassville.[14]

These facts indicate that Cumming's and Alexander Reynolds's brigades were the two that were positioned in the field north of the Cassville Cemetery, between it and Two Run Creek, and in the "no man's land" from noon to 4–5 p.m. They were thus in close contact with the advancing Federals who encircled Cassville between 3 p.m. and 5 p.m. One Confederate veteran remembered, "The Tennessee (Brown's) and Alabama (Pettus's) brigades were as good as any in the army, but the Georgians (Cumming's) and North Carolinians (A. Reynolds's) were badly commanded and when an attack was made by the division, Cummings and [Alexander] Reynolds, who were always on the left, usually gave way and left the other wing in a bad place."[15]

It seems possible that Hood was still hopeful of engaging the Federals north of Cassville until he received orders to move his men. Hindman's location in the northern part of the large, open field, is corroborated by several facts. First, Polk's right flank, the brigades of Ector and Sears of French's Division, were not connected with Hood which caused Polk to "detain" two of Stevenson's brigades that were at the rear of Hood's marching column.[16] Polk placed the two borrowed brigades of Stevenson (Cumming's and probably Alexander Reynolds's brigades) to extend his right flank across the southern end of the large, open field (just north of the Cassville Cemetery at the Hardy farm) and to tie into the left of the two ridges that are split by today's Brown Loop Road (Road 3a). Polk's right was therefore not connected with Hindman's Division between 10:30 and 3 p.m., but instead was connected by filling the space with the two "borrowed" brigades of Stevenson.

---

[14] The 31st Alabama of Pettus's Brigade lost three men captured. Private Steven Newton Hand, a blue-eyed, light-haired twenty-seven-year-old of Company C from Shelby County, lost a leg after being wounded in the left thigh. The war was over for the 5'10", 135-pound Hand, who, now with only one leg, would have to survive on a trade other than farming (R. Miller, *Hundley's Ragged Volunteers*, 52; Steven Newton Hand, 31st Alabama Infantry, CMSR, RG 109, roll 339, NARA).

[15] Wilson, *Reminiscences*, 30.

[16] Mackall Journal, "O" sample, *OR*, ser. 1, vol. 38, pt. 3, 984.

Second, around 3 p.m., when Wheeler discovered that Allen's Brigade was no longer on Kingston Road, and that a large Federal infantry force was closing in on Cassville from the west, or Kingston Road, he notified Hindman, who was near him, of the approaching Federal threat. Thus, at 3 p.m., or just after, Hindman and his division were near Wheeler somewhere in the upper part of the large, open field and close to the Ironton road, where Hood intended to spring his trap. Hood was not present at this time. After adjusting his columns to face the unexpected threat from the east side of Two Run Creek valley, Hood rode to Johnston's headquarters sometime during the early afternoon, and he was present when Johnston decided on the new line around 2:25 p.m.[17]

A third corroborating piece of evidence is found in Hood's *Advance and Retreat* when, in response to Johnston's assertion that Polk was to attack first, Hood explained that "Polk had not moved from the position in which I had left him, as I had his right in full view." Hood added that if Polk was to have attacked first, that his (Hood's) men would have already been on the Ironton Road, closer to Polk and to town (Copper Mine/Ironton Road near Janice Lane, Road 2), instead of moving east out of town, away from Polk's right flank, and then north across the large, open field. Hood planned to shield his corps behind the crest of the ridge as they prepared to ambush the expected Federal column marching south on the Ironton Road (Road 2b to Road 2). Hood subsequently said, "In accordance with General Mackall's instructions, I marched back to join Polk's right, which had remained in the same position I had left it." Hood next explained, "Whilst Major Austin was still engaged with this same enemy on the Canton road, and my corps was nearing the line occupied by General Polk on the ridge in front of Cassville, orders were issued for the Army to fall back to the ridge in rear of the town." This statement places the movement of Hindman's Division by Hood much later and during the same time that Austin's Louisianans were engaged with McCook's troopers (after 3:30 p.m.).[18]

While Hood began to redeploy his troops northeast of town to cover the roads that radiated from that direction, the Spring Place, Pine Log, and Canton roads, Johnston, upon receiving word of Hood's unexpected encounter, initially ratified the change of direction by Hood. Calling for a map, Johnston

---

[17] Hood, *OR*, ser. 1, vol. 38, pt. 3, 635; Hood, *Advance and Retreat*, 104; Mackall Journal, "A" sample.

[18] Wheeler, *OR*, ser. 1, vol. 38, pt. 3, 946; Hood, *Advance and Retreat*, 100, 104.

exclaimed, "If that's so, Hood will have to fall back at once."[19] Hood selected a line northeast of town and overlooking Two Run Creek.

Meanwhile, Johnston called for the wagons to be sent to the rear, and he called for his lieutenant generals and Wheeler to find a location for a new line of defense south of town. By 2:25 p.m., a new line south and east of Cassville had been marked off, even as cheers from the troops just hearing the general order continued. By 5 p.m., the wagons had been recalled, the Confederate infantry had withdrawn from north and west of town to the new line, and the artillery and cavalry units had hastened back to Cassville. Recording "disorder checked," Mackall's "O" sample journal added, "the "Enemy skirmishers occupied the town."[20]

Hood had earlier selected a different defensive line northeast of Cassville, one that he believed was better suited to his needs. By 3:30 p.m., as Hindman's Division was moving from the large, open field to connect with Polk's right, *north* of town and along the hill immediately west of the gap at Brown Loop Road, Hood received orders to withdraw his corps *south* of town to the new line that Johnston had just selected. Hood warned that, should his line (along Brown Loop Road and the two ridges that it bisected) be evacuated, the Federals would be able to crown those heights with artillery and enfilade Johnston's new defense line.

During this time, the Federals continued to approach and consolidate around Cassville from the west, northwest, and northeast. Between 4 and 5 p.m., McCook renewed his attack across Two Run Creek, joined by Dorr's Brigade and Stoneman's Division. In doing so, they would surprise the Confederates again with their aggressiveness, as the gray-clad soldiers had begun withdrawing from the field to proceed to Johnston's new line south of Cassville. In the confusion, a number of Southerners surrendered (or deserted) to the approaching Federals during the afternoon and evening.[21]

---

[19] Mackall Journal, "O" sample, *OR*, ser. 1, vol. 38, pt. 3, 983.

[20] Ibid., 984.

[21] Hood, *Advance and Retreat*, 101–102; Stewart's report, *OR*, ser. 1, vol. 38, pt. 3, 818; Austin's report, 14th Louisiana Battalion, *OR*, ser. 1, vol. 38, pt. 3, 861; Clayton's report, *OR*, ser. 1, vol. 38, pt. 3, 833–34; Hunley's report, 18th Alabama Infantry, *OR*, ser. 1, vol. 38, pt. 3, 836; Johnson's report, 40th Georgia Infantry, *OR*, ser. 1, vol. 38, pt. 3, 825.

Chapter 14

Hardee's Defense

By midday, Sherman had arrived at Howard's front. He ordered Howard and Major General David S. Stanley to continue to press another four miles to an old mill (Best Mill) located near the railroad. "As soon as General Stanley had dislodged the enemy from the high ground east of the creek he moved forward," Howard added. "On reaching a point about a half mile from this mill, severe resistance was made to our advance by the enemy's infantry skirmishers, and from a prominent height the enemy's infantry was discovered drawn up in two lines and advancing."[1]

After pushing the enemy cavalry pickets and taking Kingston, Stanley's Division turned east and proceeded toward Cass Station. They soon found a considerable force of Confederate infantry posted on the hills east of Kingston and beyond a creek. This was Two Run Creek, the same creek that Hood's men crossed northeast of Cassville seven miles upstream. Two Run Creek flows to the southwest around Cassville, splitting the plain between Cassville and Kingston before depositing into the Etowah River below the latter town.

Whitaker's Second Brigade led the advance into Kingston, then turned and deployed to the east and advanced southeast toward the Southern left flank. As Whitaker's men proceeded, Stanley pushed forward Brigadier General Charles Cruft's First Brigade into the space opened up on Whitaker's left and between it and the railroad. Stanley then sent Colonel William Grose's Third Brigade to the left of the railroad and on Cruft's left rear to press the right flank of the advance Confederate position.[2]

As Stanley's Division advanced, Captain Gilmore of the Ninety-Sixth Illinois in Whitaker's Brigade remembered, "bullets cut through the line but the men of the 96th responded with valor. Sometimes running and firing very rapidly toward the enemy, and sometimes flanking them out of position. The enemy was behind every tree, fence and rock and had to be driven out. It was a hot day and some of the command suffered greatly from the heat."[3]

---

[1] Howard's report, *OR*, ser. 1, vol. 38, pt. 1, 192; Cleburne's report, *OR*, ser. 1, vol. 38, pt. 3, 723.

[2] *OR*, ser. 1, vol. 38, pt. 1, 222; 242, 258.

[3] Gilmore, Ninety-Sixth Illinois Infantry database, 120.

Stanley's men pressed one Confederate division and a battery of artillery that was deployed on a rise of hills just east of Two Run Creek. "All of a sudden, the rebel firing almost stopped," remembered Gilmore. "At first the command was greatly relieved, but then, off in the distance they could see a great sea of gray uniforms heading their way. There was at least a full Corps in sight, all marching toward the Federal lines. The great battle was about to begin." At least it appeared that way.

Meanwhile, to the west and southwest of Cassville, Hardee's divisions, after making a show of force, fell back to a line south of Cassville to cover Cass Station. Major General William H. T. Walker's division, mostly Georgians and some South Carolinians, were placed in the center covering the Western & Atlantic Railroad, with Brigadier General States Rights Gist's brigade on the left of the division and Brigadier General Clement H. Stevens's brigade second to the left. Positioned just to the southwest of the railroad, Gist placed the 24th South Carolina and the 46th Georgia on the front line and 16th South Carolina and the 8th Georgia Battalion in the rear line.[4]

Captain John Henry Steinmeyer of Company A, 24th South Carolina of Brigadier General States Rights Gist's brigade, remembered of his company, "As [a] portion of the skirmish line, [we] were posted across the territory in advance of but at right angles with the line as prepared for battle." As the South Carolina captain was busy deploying his men in what they supposed would be an ambush position in the curtilage of a fine farm house, "Gen. Gist and staff rode up, suggested my placing sharpshooters in the upper story of the residence, which was done at once. The Genl. asked for water," recalled Steinmeyer, "for which [I] dispatched a man to the splendid spring (dairy) house nearby, and that party rode off."[5]

Steinmeyer explained, "The fight opened very shortly by sharpshooting from across the road on our right. Soon, the fire of the skirmishers was added to on the part of the enemy by their field artillery run down, for the purpose of driving us from the house. I ordered the men upstairs to lay flat on the floor and wait developments. In the midst of this and under pressing circumstances."

> Maj.[or] Ben Smith (of the Genl. staff) came up to me on foot through the garden from the rear. His first exclamation was 'Captain, this is a

---

[4] Ellison Capers's report, *OR*, ser. 1, vol. 38, pt. 3, 715; E. W. Jones, Jr., *Enlisted for the War*, 164–65; Steinmeyer Diary, 26; Samuel McKittrick to his wife, 22 May 1864.

[5] Steinmeyer Diary, 26.

> d____d [damned] hot place.' He had come, he added, to instruct me, as to our retiring. Gist was on the first line, supported by Stevens, in rear of us. 'The first would fall back, [explained the Major] then the next, when Stevens was beyond the ridge, or out of sight, we should retire.' [Major Smith then] ordered us to advance as though to meet the enemy, on their own ground. Our movement caused their halt, he remembered, when after a brief stand, we were quietly withdrawn.[6]

The two right brigades of Walker's Division were those of Brigadier General Hugh W. Mercer and Brigadier General John R. Jackson. Their order of alignment has not been definitively determined, but there is evidence that Mercer's Brigade was sent forward to support the skirmish line. The 63rd Georgia of that brigade sustained casualties, including one man who was shot and, while he was being carried from the field on a litter, shot again, this time fatally in the head. Another Georgian was shot in the buttocks as he made his way rearward.[7]

William O. Norwell of the 63rd Georgia in Mercer's Brigade, remembered that the brigade suffered about twenty casualties during the action. Norwell recalled that his brigade was ordered forward into a wood to support the skirmish line when "Not many minutes elapsed before our pickets became pretty warmly engaged and the balls began to fly around too thick to be pleasant." He added, "All were ordered to lie down and a more flattened set of men were never seen." Norwell explained that the enemy "balls were stray balls, fired at others [on the skirmish line ahead] as we could not have been seen." The brush and woods were so thick "that it was impossible for us to see 20 feet," added the Georgia soldier, who was relieved when the order to retire was given and quickly obeyed. Orderly Sergeant Walter A. Clark of the 63rd Georgia, recalled "H. L.[Legare] Hill [was] killed and T. F. Burbanks [was] wounded," and that there were "12 to 15 casualties in [the] regiment."[8]

Veteran Joseph T. Derry of the 63rd Georgia, witnessed the action. "Mercer's brigade was thrown out in Walker's front and the Sixty-Third Georgia was put in advance of the brigade to support the skirmish line. The skirmishers of the brigade were commanded by Maj. J. V. H. Allen, of the Sixty-Third," remembered Derry. "In the spirited skirmish which occurred, his scabbard was dented and his clothing pierced by minie [*sic*] balls, but he was unhurt. When orders came to retire the brigade to the line of battle, the

---

[6] Ibid.

[7] Norwell Diary, 8.

[8] W. Clark, *Under the Stars and Bars*, 99.

Sixty-third was nearly surrounded by the enemy." Derry was among the Georgians in peril. "The regiment was skillfully extricated from its perilous position by Lieutenant-Colonel [George Robison] Black and the acting adjutant, Lieut. George W. McLaughlin, of Company A (the Oglethorpes of Augusta), and marched in order to the position assigned it in line of battle." As Derry explained,

> Among the killed was Legare Hill, son of Hon. Joshua Hill, of Madison, Ga. Two of his comrades took up the lifeless body, conveyed it to a little abandoned cottage, pinned his name upon his jacket and left him there. Although this was done in full view of the Federal skirmishers. Not a shot was fired at the two men until they had rejoined their comrades. The Federals coming up, took the body of young Hill, buried it, and marked the grave by a headboard on which they cut the name which they found pinned to his jacket.[9]

Colonel William Grose's Third Brigade deployed to the left of Stanley's Division and north of the Kingston-Cassville Road (Road 9), with a heavy skirmish line. The Seventy-Seventh Pennsylvania lost one man killed and three wounded during the afternoon. Also deployed as skirmishers were the Seventy-Fifth Illinois, who had a sergeant severely wounded.[10]

Brigadier General Thomas J. Wood's Third Division of Howard's IV Corps had been ordered to deploy to the right or south of Stanley's Division as they neared the Confederate lines. The Seventeenth Kentucky of Brigadier General Samuel Beatty's Third Brigade were deployed as "skirmishers to cover the advance of its brigade," sustaining twenty casualties during the fighting, "bearing unmistakable evidence of the sharp fire to which it had been exposed." Colonel Alexander M. Stout of the Seventeenth Kentucky remembered, "We could not see the enemy's position, as the woods were very thick and it was dark. Our losses were heavy. Captain William J. Lendrum was killed and Lieutenant Curtis A. Brasher received a severe wound in the face; 2 privates were killed and 16 others wounded." Supporting the Unionist

---

[9] Milledgeville native Joseph T. Derry was a veteran with vast experience, serving in Virginia and Western (West) Virginia in the 1st Georgia, then with the 12th Georgia battalion of artillery with Brigadier General John Hunt Morgan in Kentucky and subsequently in the 63rd Georgia in Georgia, Alabama, Tennessee, and the Carolinas. Derry would subsequently write the Georgia volume of *Confederate Military History* (C. A. Evans, ed., *Confederate Military History*, 3:307–308, 601–603).

[10] Colonel Thomas E. Rose's report, 14 September 1864, *OR*, ser. 1, vol. 38, pt. 1, 266; Colonel John E. Bennett's report, 13 September 1864, ibid.

Kentuckians to their right or south, were the veterans of the Thirteenth Ohio under Colonel Dwight Jarvis. The Ohioans lost one man mortally wounded and two men severely wounded in the late afternoon action. The Ninth Kentucky formed behind the Seventeenth Kentucky on the left of the second line, while the Seventy-Ninth Indiana formed to the right in the second line and behind the Thirteenth Ohio. "Capt. John L. Hanna [of the 79th Indiana] was badly wounded through the hand while advancing in line of battle" although the Hoosiers did not become engaged.[11]

To the right of Walker's Division, Cheatham's all-Tennessee division was posted covering the Kingston-Cassville Road. The 13th and 154th Tennessee regiments of Brigadier General Alfred J. Vaughan's brigade were placed in front as skirmishers to engage the oncoming Federals.[12]

To the left of Walker's Division, Cleburne's Division was posted to cover the left flank of the army and the open land to the south of Cass Station. The 3rd Confederate Regiment of Brigadier General Daniel C. Govan's brigade served on the skirmish line and suffered the loss of one man killed.[13] Bate's Division had been skirmishing with Stanley's Federals three miles west of Cass Station from noon until 2 p.m. Kentuckian Johnny Green of the "Orphan Brigade" (as the Kentuckians had come to be known) remembered, "We moved forward, threw out skirmishers, found the enemy, & received from them a few shells, when we almost immediately were ordered back & marched tow[ar]ds Cassville." Around 4 p.m., they fell back and were placed in reserve on the Confederate left flank behind Cleburne's men.[14]

In Brigadier General Thomas B. Smith's brigade of Georgians and Tennesseans, Private William Caldwell was apparently unable to keep up with his command as they fell back. Caldwell, a veteran of Company I in the 37th Georgia, was captured. Having volunteered for frontier service while in the prisoner of war camp, Caldwell was released from Rock Island Prison on 25 October 1864 because he was "rejected," apparently due to poor health.

---

[11] Thomas J. Wood's report, 10 September 1864, *OR*, ser. 1, vol. 38, pt. 1, 376; Alexander M. Stout's report, 14 September 1864, *OR*, ser. 1, vol. 38, pt. 1, 467; Major Joseph T. Snider's report, 11 September 1864, *OR*, ser. 1, vol. 38, pt. 1, 473; Capt. Eli F. Ritter's report, 15 September 1864, *OR*, ser. 1, vol. 38, pt. 1, 454.

[12] Vaughan, *Personal Record of the Thirteenth Regiment*, 33; Head, *Campaigns and Battles of the Sixteenth Regiment*, 129; Cunningham, *Reminiscences of the 41st Tennessee*, 76.

[13] Dixon Diary, 1.

[14] Waters, "The Partial Atlanta Reports," 209; Kirwan, ed., *Johnny Green of the Orphan Brigade*, 180; Thompson, *History of the Orphan Brigade*, 249.

Orderly Sergeant Alexander R. Winn of Company D in the 20th Tennessee was not so lucky. He was killed during the action west of Cass Station as Smith's Brigade withdrew to the depot town. Apparently, General Bate was relieved from command for the rest of the day during the afternoon at Cassville for imbibing, or for doing so in excess. A soldier in the 37th Georgia in Smith's (Tyler's) Brigade of Bate's Division complained, "I regret to say that some of our commanding officers indulge too frequently in 'pop skull.' They go into battle drunk, and are totally incompetent to lead a body of men successfully into action. Gen. Hardee suspended our Major General [Bate] for this offence [*sic*] at Cassville, and I hope all others who so indulge will share the same fate."[15]

The Kentucky "Orphan Brigade" fell back to a reserve position at Cass Station about 4 p.m. There, they joined the balance of Bate's Division in reserve behind Cleburne's Division on the extreme left of the Confederate line.[16] Meanwhile, in Cleburne's Division, Captain Foster, commanding a company in the 24th Texas Cavalry (dismounted) in Granbury's Texas brigade, remembered, "My company was put out in the woods, which were very thick. The army soon fell back to Cass Station, and left us. When we were ordered back. We had to run about 2 miles to save ourselves from capture."[17]

After Johnston decided upon his new defensive line, Tennessee governor Isham G. Harris brought lunch to him and the two Mackalls. They ate while siting along the roadside of the Cartersville Road (today's Mac Johnson Road), as various gray-clad regiments filed by on their way to the new line. Several general officers began to gather. It seemed that the confusion of the day's uncertainties had given way to relief, as a calmness settled in around Johnston and his staff.[18]

About 5:00 p.m., Johnston rode over to Hardee's position on the left of the line apparently accompanied by Governor Harris. By about 6:00 p.m., General William Mackall "set out to find our camp [Johnston's Headquarters]," according to the younger Mackall. By then, Johnston and Harris had returned; they and the two Mackalls moved to a field near the Cartersville

---

[15] Henderson, *Roster of the Confederate Soldiers of Georgia*, 4:105; W. J. McMurray, *History of the Twentieth Tennessee, C.S.A.*, 105; F. M. G., Company K, 37th Georgia, letter, "In camp near Atlanta, May 22, 1864," *Columbus (Georgia) Daily Sun*, 28 May 1864, 2.

[16] Bate's report, *OR Supp.*, ser. 7, 93.

[17] Foster, *One of Cleburne's Command*, 79.

[18] Mackall Journal, "O" sample, *OR*, ser. 1, vol. 38, pt. 3, 984.

Road in rear of Polk's lines while brisk skirmishing could be heard along the lines in the fading daylight. According to T. B. Mackall, during this time Johnston boasted to the governor that "he will be ready for and happy to receive [the] enemy [the] next day" as darkness fell on the armies. Johnston's headquarters tents had been pitched along a muddy brook just east of the Cartersville Road. About this time, Wheeler and his staff arrived as some of his cavalry rode in and began to fall in behind the infantry lines. Next, as Johnston headed to his headquarters tent, he received an invitation to join Hood and Polk for dinner at the home of William McKelvey, just to the south on the Cartersville Road. About 8:00 p.m., Johnston walked to Polk's headquarters at the McKelvey house and cabin, unaware of Polk's and Hood's intentions.[19]

After his dispositions were made, Hardee took a few minutes to stop and eat with his staff. "After finishing his supper, he sat upon a fence near the tree under which we were bivouacked," remembered Lieutenant William Trask, a courier for Hardee, "and said he thought we had got the Yankees where they would have to fight at last; that there would be some heavy work tomorrow, though he didn't think the whole strength of the enemy was yet up in our front. When asked if it were not likely that they would try flanking again, added to the dispatch rider, "he said that if they did, we would follow them."[20]

---

[19] Dubose, *General Joseph Wheeler*, 299–300. Note that the headquarters wagon train had already packed and was sent "beyond Cassville" around noon. When Johnston determined to defend along a new line southeast of town, the wagons were recalled and the new camp was set up by dusk (see Mackall Journal, "O" sample, *OR*, ser. 1, vol. 38, pt. 3, 984).

[20] Trask, *Civil War Journal*, 148.

Chapter 15

The Cavalry Duel

Between 2 and 3 p.m., Wheeler sent three separate dispatches to General Allen, who he "supposed" was "on the Kingston Road, by three different couriers, all of whom returned, stating that they had run into the enemy's pickets on that road about one mile from Cassville." Allen's Brigade, consisting of the 3rd, 5th, 10th, 11th, and 12th Confederate Cavalry (made up of men mostly from Alabama), had been loaned to Jackson to help impede the Federal advance from the west. The Federals that these couriers found were the advance of Stanley's Division of Howard's Corps. Alarmed at the speed of the Federal advance from the west, Wheeler quickly notified General Hindman, whose division was on the left of Hood's Corps north of Cassville. He also sent orders to General Martin, who was overseeing the Confederate cavalry of Iverson's and Humes's units on the Adairsville-Cassville Road, to fall back to town. Then he sent a staff officer familiar with the local country to Brigadier General John H. Kelly, who was with Dibrell's Tennessee brigade on the Copper Mine/Ironton Road, still well north of town, to alert him of the danger. Wheeler gave the staff officer instructions to have Dibrell's men "retire by a by-road with his command to the town."[1]

According to "Osceola," the imbedded reporter/soldier for the *Memphis Daily Appeal* in Dibrell's Brigade, the Tennessee horsemen were dismounted and waiting for the Federal soldiers to appear on the "Coppermine Road" about two and a half miles north of Cassville. Their horses had been left below Cassville, about three miles away when, according to the newspaper correspondent, "we received orders to fall back." Osceola added, "Gen[eral] Martin who was guarding the other road [the Adairsville-Cassville Road] to our left, which united with the Coppermine Road one-half mile north of Cassville, had fallen back, leaving our left and rear exposed. The enemy," explained the reporter, "had speedily taken advantage of this movement, and already had possession of the road between Col[onel] Dibbrell's [*sic*] brigade and their

[1] Wheeler's report, *OR*, ser. 1, vol. 38, pt. 3, 946. Wheeler's conversation with Hindman appears to indicate that as late as 3 or 4 p.m., Hindman's Division was still well north of Cassville and in the large, open field.

horses." Osceola was describing the advance by Williams's Division in that sector that cut off their route of escape.[2]

"Why Col[one]l' Dibbrell [*sic*] was not notified of Gen[eral] Martin's retrograde sooner, is one of the mysteries which we suppose will never be explained," Osceola wrote. He was not sure who was to be blamed for the mistake, which nearly forced the capture of Dibrell's Brigade, but he believed

> someone was grievously at fault. The whole brigade for a time was in great danger of being captured or seriously cut up, and under a less skillful leader would undoubtedly have suffered severely. As it was the whole command reached their horses in safety, after double-quicking about four miles, which was by no means agreeable to us cavalrymen, with the exception of eleven men killed and wounded.[3]

The "by-road" described by Wheeler may have been a connecting road just north of the large, open field (Road 2 connecting with Road 2c and the "country road" described by Johnston). The action was described by one veteran from the 11th Tennessee Cavalry in Dibrell's Brigade:

> About 3 o'clock in the evening the Federal advance pressed heavily the Confederate right and center. The Eleventh, with the remainder of the brigade and some other cavalry [Iverson's and/or Humes's troopers], contested the advance but were pressed back by superior and overlapping numbers till the Confederate infantry lines were reached when a sharp engagement occurred. The Federals were repulsed, but a most terrific artillery duel ensued, lasting some two or three hours. The Federal artillery appeared to have the advantage in position. At any rate, their artillery was served with marked precision and effect.[4]

One Union Tennessee veteran who was a part of the First Tennessee Cavalry (Union) of Dorr's Brigade, remembered the late afternoon Federal cavalry assault at Cassville. Earlier, they had participated in a charge against the skirmish line of Stewart's Division as the Confederates were withdrawing from the Two Run Creek valley and the range of hills north of Cassville to the new line that Johnston had selected. The afternoon saber charge was a "brisk engagement [and] they were driven back 'pell-mell into town, losing thirty-eight by capture," according to W. C. Carter of the First Tennessee

---

[2] Osceola, "Camp Dibbrell's [*sic*] Brigade Cavalry, Etowah River, May 23, 1864," *Memphis Daily Appeal*, 24 May 1864.

[3] Ibid.

[4] Lindsley, *Military Annals of Tennessee, Confederate*, 2:703.

Cavalry (Union). Now, following up on their afternoon success, McCook and Stoneman pressed. "The First Tennessee Cavalry [Union] was in the advance, and near sundown drove Wheeler's advance back upon the infantry, who were behind rifle-pits. The regiment captured several prisoners." The trooper added, "Lilly's battery was sent to the front and shelled the enemy vigorously until dark. The regiment had two men wounded and several horses shot."[5]

Wheeler witnessed Kelly's and Dibrell's narrow escape from the Federal pincer from the north, east, and west. "As the rear of General Kelly's command was near the town," he later wrote, "the enemy's cavalry charged his line of skirmishers, but were stampeded by the fire from a second line of his command, and were charged in return by his escort." He added, "I retired my command at about night-fall to the rear of the infantry lines and took position to guard the right flank of the army." Dibrell's men were "charged" by portions of Stoneman's and McCook's cavalrymen as they continued their pursuit, following the route of some of Clayton's Alabama Brigade, to the edge of town in the field just north of the Cassville Cemetery.[6]

A Southern correspondent for the *Columbia Carolinian* who witnessed the Federal cavalry attack on Dibrell's men, reported,

> Heavy skirmishing commenced at 4 p.m., along our whole line. The enemy's cavalry made a desperate charge on our right, which was firmly met by Wheeler's boys supported by the Whitworth sharpshooters, who emptied many a Federal saddle. It was a grand sight and intensely exciting, while our boys cheered exultingly at the severe repulse of the Federal cavalry.

Wheeler reported casualties on 18 May near Cassville of thirty-two men and twenty-one men lost on 19 May.[7]

By 5 p.m., as most of the Confederate army had withdrawn to the new defense line south and east of town, those in French's and Hindman's divisions had a panoramic view of the cavalry clash in the field below. Manigault described it as "a sharp cavalry engagement" in which neither cavalry side "show[ed] to any advantage." One officer of Brigadier General Edward C.

---

[5] Carter, *History of the First Regiment of Tennessee Volunteer Cavalry*, 154.

[6] Wheeler's report, *OR*, ser. 1, vol. 38, pt. 3, 946.

[7] Dodson, *Campaigns of Wheeler and His Cavalry*, 200; Dubose, *General Joseph Wheeler*, 296–302; Drake, *Annals of the Army of Tennessee*, appendix, 87; also, Wheeler, *Confederate Military History*, 8:364.

Walthall's brigade remembered some Mississippians who witnessed the action, "laughed and said it was like child's play."[8]

This evening action appears to have occurred near and west of the Hardy House, today's Watkins Farm, near Holt Road and Cassville-White Road. According to Colonel Dorr, his Eighth Iowa lost two men killed and one officer and only a few men wounded. One of these men was Corporal Alfred A. Lepper of Company L, who was wounded severely in the leg and died on 16 June. Dorr added, "In the evening…[portions of the Eighth Iowa were dismounted and] advanced on foot drawing the enemy out of an orchard and buildings which afforded good cover for their sharpshooters."[9]

One member of Dibrell's Brigade remembered that many of the Tennessee troopers were dismounted up the Ironton (Copper Mine) Road (Road 2), as they waited for the anticipated arrival of the Federal column that was supposed to be attacked. The Tennessean lamented that when his unit was ordered to fall back abruptly, they found that some Federals had seized the road below them blocking their withdrawal and the path to their mounts. These Federals were some of Williams's Division who had just arrived via the Adairsville-Cassville Road from the northwest and had cut the Ironton (Copper Mine) Road just north of Two Run Creek. Moreover, the Southern cavalrymen could see other Federals, blue-clad troopers in the large open field below them.[10]

Taking a by road, the Tennesseans reached their horses and rushed south across the western edge of the field, surprising the Hoosiers of the Fifth Indiana Cavalry of Colonel James Biddle's brigade. To the northeast of the Fifth Indiana Cavalry, the Sixth Indiana Cavalry regiment was posted in reserve in some woods overlooking the field. The Sixth Indiana Cavalry was a sister regiment to the Fifth Indiana Cavalry in Biddle's brigade. Some of the 5th Indiana cavalrymen began to chase the Tennesseans as the two groups moved at a gallop, each firing wildly at one another, and few landing any hits. Just when it seemed that the Indianans might have the advantage, a second column of Dibrell's Brigade, consisting of the balance of the Tennessee troopers including Dibrell and his escort and staff, emerged from the woods along the Ironton (Copper Mine) Road to the north, surprising the Hoosiers a second

---

[8] Manigault in Tower, *A Carolinian Goes to War*, 186; Sykes, *Walthall's Brigade*, 569.

[9] Corbin, *Star for Patriotism*, 477.

[10] Osceola, Camp Dibrell's Brigade Cavalry, *Memphis Daily Appeal*, 24 May 1864, 3.

time. After seeing their comrades emerge, some of the first contingent of Dibrell's troopers turned and began chasing their former pursuers back up the large field, emptying a few saddles and possibly capturing a flag of the Fifth Indiana Cavalry.[11]

As the small size of Dibrell's second contingent was fully revealed, the Fifth Indiana Cavalry supported by the Sixth Indiana Cavalry once again took up the pursuit. The Hoosiers finally halted when the Tennesseans made it to the Confederate lines and Hoskins's Mississippi battery opened on the pursuing Federal cavalrymen. Thus ended the cavalry duel, with McCook's and Stoneman's troopers the clear winners of the day's events, but Dibrell's heroics in running the gauntlet apparently resulted in a consolation prize in the form of a company guidon of the Fifth Indiana Cavalry.[12]

According to trooper Oliver C. Haskell, the Sixth Indiana Cavalry mounted and formed about a dozen different times throughout the day as Colonel Biddle's troopers inched closer to Cassville from south of Pine Log. Later, Haskell remembered,

> 5th Indiana cavalry had a pretty sharp battle with the enemy about 4 o'clock. We were close by in the woods ready to assist if they had not retreated…about 5 o'clock. Our regiment started to make a charge. Charged across a large open field, but a very rocky one, but found no enemy there. It is a Grand site [*sic*] to [see] 2000 men mounted making a charge in open

---

[11] Osceola, *Memphis Daily Appeal*, 24 May 1864, 3; Haskell.

[12] Osceola, *Memphis Daily Appeal*, 24 May 1864, 3; Haskell. Ironically, the 9th Tennessee Cavalry of Dibrell's Brigade captured the regimental colors of the Fifth Indiana Cavalry on 15 May at Resaca, and it appears that a company guidon was captured from the same Fifth Indiana Cavalry by one of Dibrell's Tennessee troopers on 19 May at Cassville during the confusing afternoon action. Two stands of unidentified colors were reported as captured by General Joseph Wheeler (OR, ser. 1, vol. 38, pt. 3, 945) on 15 May at Resaca. One was the regimental flag of the Fifth Indiana Cavalry (see O.G.G., Camp Near Calhoun, 16 May, *Augusta [Georgia] Daily Constitutionalist*, 20 May 1864, 2). The author believes that the other flag captured on 15 May at Resaca by Wheeler's troopers appears to have been a company guidon of the First Kentucky (Union) cavalry (likely thirty-five–star Stars and Stripes guidon pattern). The captured flags at Resaca are also reported in the appendix to Drake's *Annals of the Army of Tennessee* (Appendix, 87), which shows two stands of colors captured by Wheeler's cavalry on 15 May (Day 2 at Resaca). Drake's *Annals* also show one stand of colors captured by Wheeler's cavalry on 19 May near Cassville which the author suspects is a company guidon flag from the Fifth Indiana Cavalry (a thirty-five–star Stars and Stripes guidon pattern).

> ground with several nols [knolls] and also draws. It is quite enticing. Company A was sent in pursuit of the enemy to find them move and hustle as hard as they could go over hills, hollows, and bogs two miles when we came out into an open field in full view of their batteries, which commenced playing on us as soon as we came into view. The shells burst among us, partly, but no one was injured, we was not close enough to do any injury, and with our short range guns, we retired into the woods. General Hooker had arrived by this time with some of his artillery and infantry skirmishers made the rebels get back in a hurry here, where this last engagement was in Cassville....

The Indiana troopers had linked up with Williams's Division of Hooker's XX Corps along the west end of the large, open field as the evening action drew to a close.[13]

[13] Haskell.

Chapter 16

The Artillery Duel

During the first three months of the Atlanta Campaign, the Confederate cavalry could match up equally, if not favorably, with the Federal cavalry, each side ranging from eight to ten thousand horsemen, more or less, from Resaca until late July. In infantry, from Cassville to Peach Tree Creek, Sherman outnumbered Johnston roughly three to two, or about ninety thousand to sixty thousand, more or less, as attrition whittled down both sides in similar ratios, with Sherman's legions taking a few more battle casualties, and a considerable number of Johnston's men from northwest Georgia were taking to the woods as he continued to retreat. But the real, and most telling, discrepancy between the two sides was in the artillery arm of service. The Federal artillery corps outclassed the Confederate artillery both in numbers and in quality. The disparity became noticeable almost immediately at the Battle of Resaca, and it was on display again at Cassville during the last couple of hours before sunset ended hostilities for the day.

At the beginning of the war, the most-common field artillery gun was the Napoleon smoothbore that fired a twelve-pound round of either solid shot (a round, twelve-pound iron ball), or shell (a ball with a hollow center loaded with gun powder or gun powder and small balls), or, at close range, grape shot, or cannister (a tin can filled with small, about one-inch round iron balls). By the fourth year of the war, developments in armaments had produced many new improvements and weapons, including a new three-inch ordnance rifled gun that could fire all of the loads that the Napoleons fired, but with greater accuracy and distance. For example, the Napoleon could fire a twelve-pound solid shot five-eighths of a mile with five degrees of elevation. In contrast, the three-inch ordnance rifle could fire a round up to a mile and a quarter with accuracy, or twice as far.[1]

Sherman's combined Federal armies brought 254 guns into Georgia at the start of the Atlanta Campaign. Of that number, 127 were rifled guns. In contrast, Johnston's forces contained only 144 guns, and only 16 rifled guns were placed among units that served with his infantry. Wheeler's and Jackson's cavalry each had eight rifled guns, as well. Another key difference

---

[1] Coggins, *Arms & Equipment of the Civil War*, 61–82; McKee and Mason, Jr., *Civil War Projectiles II*, 92–132, 160–64.

between the Northern and Southern artillery was that by this point in the war, Confederate batteries had switched from the conventional model of three two-gun sections for a total of six guns per battery commanded by a Captain, with two batteries per battalion commanded by a Major, to two two-gun sections for a total of four guns per battery commanded by a Captain, with three batteries per battalion commanded by a major.[2]

Since the Confederate forces were acting primarily on the defensive, and since the topography of north Georgia did not lend itself to large, open fields or plains, when a battery was sent into action, often only three or four guns could get into line while the others remained in park in the rear. Moreover, often when a battalion of twelve guns in two six-gun batteries were assigned to a division containing three or four brigades, one or two brigades were left without artillery support while reserve guns remained idle in the rear when they could not get into the line in their assigned place. To remedy this problem, the three four-gun battery organization was created.[3]

In contrast, Federal batteries continued to use the six-gun battery organization. In addition, since the Federal army was usually acting on the offense while the Confederate batteries occupied defensive positions along fixed, prepared lines, often two or three Federal batteries maneuvered to strike the Southern battery simultaneously from two or three directions. Moreover, where there was a large, open field, such as was found across the Camp Creek valley at Resaca, and also at Cassville, Federal three-inch ordnance rifles could be positioned between a half mile and one mile away from the Confederate line, just outside of the range of most of the Southern guns, but easily with range of the Northern guns, and fire unmolested.

By 5 p.m., after reaching the new defensive line, French ordered his artillery to open on Federal cavalry that had driven in the Southern pickets toward the second line. According to French, "Hoskins' battery opened on them and checked the advance [of the Federal cavalry]." Confederate artillery fire reached the newly arrived bluecoats of Ward's Brigade as they drew into the northern edge of Cassville. Private Strong of the 105th Illinois remembered, "Having occupied the Rebel position without resistance, we lay down expecting that we were safe for the rest of the day."[4]

Strong recorded in his diary that during this time, one of his comrades, Put Scott began "declaiming some funny piece to amuse us, when suddenly

[2] Scaife, *Campaign for Atlanta*, 145–90; Daniel, *Cannoneers in Gray*, 40, 141.

[3] Daniel, *Cannoneers in Gray*, 40, 133–50, 157.

[4] French, *Two Wars*, 377; Strong, *Yankee Private's Civil War*, 29.

the Rebs began to shell us. Scott kept on declaiming and the boys kept on laughing. Then," Strong recalled, "with a big shock a heavy shell struck the ground in front of our company, within ten feet of us. It buried itself in the ground, and we just held our breath expecting it to explode. Scott threw himself on the ground. I flattened myself out on the ground until I seemed to have made a hole in it," explained the Illinoisan.

> Maybe you can imagine what the suspense was, waiting for some of us to be killed. Of course, all this happened quicker than you can read it. After perhaps a minute, Mark Naper lifted his head and, with his eyes big as saucers, said, "Why don't the d—d thing bust?" That made us laugh, and we began to get up. As far as I know, that shell never has exploded, yet.

Neither has another shell exploded that was fired that day, probably by the same Confederate battery during this time, that landed in a tree on the Copper Mine/Ironton Road (Road 2), at today's Janice Lane, just north of the four-way intersection in Cassville, according to James "Bo" Blalock who grew up there and who remembered the unexploded shell imbedded in the tree in his front yard in the 1950s and 60s.[5]

The fire of the Confederate artillery drew an immediate response. French explained, "About 5:30 p.m. the enemy got their batteries in position and opened fire on my line. One battery on my right enfiladed a part of my line." This battery was probably Rippetoe's three-inch ordnance rifles from near the Hardy farm where they had followed McCook's cavalry in their pursuit of the retreating Confederates from that direction.[6]

Historian Bill Scaife believed that French's line received enfilade fire from a battery in front of a large hill on the northwest side of the large, open field northwest of the Hardy farm, and in sight of the Cassville Cemetery. This position was occupied by Williams's Division around 4 p.m., and not by Butterfield's Division as Scaife posits. While it is possible that a few shots from this hill made their mark, it is more likely that the damage to French's line, was done by Rippetoe's guns. Cox's Division of Schofield's XXIII Corps arrived after 4 p.m., as well, and deployed to the east and rear of Williams. None of the guns of Schofield's XXIII Corps were engaged on 19 May at Cassville, and of the two batteries attached to Williams's Division of the XX Corps, only one section of two guns, two three-inch ordnance rifles from Lieutenant Charles E. Winegar's First New York Light Battery I, was slightly

---

[5] Strong, *Yankee Private's Civil War*, 29–30; author's telephone interview with James "Bo" Blalock, 25 January 2023.

[6] French, *Two Wars*, 377.

engaged. According to Winegar, two of his guns fired a total six fuse shell rounds before dusk at Cassville.[7]

Rippetoe's Eighteenth Indiana Artillery Battery supported the Federal cavalry attack across Two Run Creek. One veteran described the work of the Indiana battery as "shelling the rebels over the heads of our lines." The Confederates held a line at the creek, "until the 8th Iowa made a gallant Sabre [*sic*] charge on them when they retreated across the creek. The battery then commenced shelling the woods on the other side while the Iowans crossed the stream." After the Iowans had crossed the creek, "the rebels opened out on them from a 4-gun Battery [*sic*] located on the hills ½ mile from the creek." This caused Lilly's Battery, the Eighteenth Indiana, to cross the creek on a log bridge and take position at the edge of the woods as they faced "the Confederate battery in the fortifications and the Rebel skirmishers in the open field between."[8]

According to veteran Henry Campbell of the Hoosier artillery battery, "We opened a heavy fire on the rebel battery which soon limbered up & retired behind their 2nd line of works from which they occasionally sent us a shot at long range." The second Confederate defensive position in the Two Run Creek valley that afternoon was located at the mouth of the gap between the two ridges at today's Brown Loop Road. Here, one of the Confederate batteries was posted to provide covering fire for the Southern skirmish line. McCook, commanding the left division in the Federal cavalry attack, wrote, "My artillery knocked one of their guns and one of their caissons all to pieces, which they left on the field."[9]

Campbell would later find "three dead horses where their first shell had landed" and learn from prisoners that the first shot had also taken "off the rebel captain's leg." That unlucky "rebel" was Lt. A. J. Stewart of Captain J. A. Hoskins's Brookhaven (Mississippi) light artillery battery, which had brought three of its four guns into position in front of an elderly lady's house to support the withdrawing Confederates and retard the advancing Federal horsemen. The fourth gun was still parked in the rear of the house. One of

---

[7] Scaife, *Campaign for Atlanta & Sherman's March to the Sea*, 292–93; Scaife, *Campaign for Atlanta*, 46; Brigadier General Jacob D. Cox's report, *OR*, ser. 1, vol. 38, pt. 2, 680; Colonel J. W. Reilly's report, *OR*, ser. 1, vol. 38, pt. 2, 701; Major John A. Reynolds's report, *OR*, ser. 1, vol. 38, pt. 2, 468; Captain Charles E. Winegar's report, *OR*, ser. 1, vol. 38, pt. 2, 475.

[8] Rowell, *Yankee Artillerymen*, 199.

[9] Ibid.

Rippetoe's rounds struck a caisson, causing it to explode, killing four horses and severely wounding Lt. Stewart. Private Tim Cady, formerly a part of Captain William C. Winston's Tennessee "Belmont" battery but attached to Hoskin's Mississippi battery, was also wounded. In addition, several of Hoskins's men were captured.[10]

"I saw one battery of ours knocked to pieces," remembered Manigault, "and the gunners driven from their guns in less than fifteen minutes." The South Carolinian watched the effect of Rippetoe's guns on Hoskins's Battery. He added, "I was told of another instance of the same kind that occurred in our division front, and I think it likely there may have been others." Manigault explained,

> As soon as our artillery opened on them that of the enemy came into action in beautiful style, and selecting their positions with great skill, opened fire on ours, and soon showed an almost overwhelming superiority. It must be remembered that they had two guns to our one and a greater number of rifled pieces, which also gave a great advantage in range and accuracy.[11]

In addition to Rippetoe's action before dark, Butterfield's artillery was engaged in wreaking havoc on the Confederate defensive line. Major John Reynolds, chief of artillery for the XX Corps, described the action as Polk's men withdrew through the village of Cassville. Captains [Marco B.] Gary's [First Ohio Light Battery C] and [Luther R.] Smith's [First Michigan Light Battery I] batteries were quickly placed in position by Captain Gary, division chief of artillery [Butterfield's Third Division], and after firing a few rounds the enemy fell back out of range." As previously described, Polk's Corps was in the process of withdrawing between 3 and 4 p.m. "The other divisions of the corps coming up," continued Reynolds, "an advance was ordered, one section of Captain Gary's battery, under Lieutenant [Thomas] King, keeping with the advance. The enemy was found to be behind strong works around the town, a part of his troops moving through the town in column."[12]

The Confederate column was Sears's Mississippi Brigade who, together with Ector's Texas and North Carolina Brigade, were the last to leave the earlier line. "Lieutenant King's section was quickly placed in position on the right of the seminary," continued Reynolds, "and opened on this column with solid shot, creating great confusion among them." King's two guns deployed

---

[10] Ibid.; *OR Supp.*, pt. 2, vol. 66, 387; Daniel, *Cannoneers in Gray*, 155; French, *Two Wars*, 377.

[11] Manigault and Tower, *A Carolinian Goes to War*, 186–87.

[12] Reynolds's report, *OR*, ser. 1, vol. 38, pt. 2, 468.

at the Female College located on the hill immediately west of the four-way intersection in Cassville, and at the intersection of today's Willow Lane NW and US Highway 41.[13]

According to King, his section was placed into position by Major Reynolds "near the brick female seminary in Cassville," King explained, "I immediately opened on the enemy's battery in position on the opposite side of the town, and also on a column of infantry who were marching out of the town. The enemy replied from a full battery and also kept up a rapid skirmish fire. I held the position until my ammunition was all expended…."[14]

That Confederate battery appears to have been Guibor's Missouri battery of French's Division. Commanded by Henry Guibor, the battery of four twelve-pound brass Napoleon guns usually accompanied Cockrell's Missouri brigade of the same division. W. L. Truman of Guibor's Battery remembered the afternoon action at Cassville. "My battery was just above the town and within twenty feet of the nice home Gen. Waker's mother. Gen. Walker is in Hardee's corps. Our position over looks a beautiful rich valley which extends to a ridge with timber about two thirds of a mile in our front. We have a splendid position," explained the Missourian.

> We are all, infantry and artillerymen, anxious for the battle to come off, believing, that with God's help we will gain the victory. About sunset this evening our skirmish line on the opposite side of the valley were attacked and forced out [of] the timber, and as they were retreating in nice order in a walk, they were charged by a body of the enemy's cavalry in full view of most of our army. The skirmishers ran together and formed squares in a minute and stood the ground, and we opened on the cavalry immediately with our guns and bursted a few shells among them and they beat a hasty retreat for the timber.

The Federal cavalrymen of Stonemen and McCook quickly withdrew up the Two Run Creek valley. "The skirmishers deployed again and quietly continued their retreat to within the proper distance of our line of battle," according to the proud Southern artillerist, but he added, "We were sorry to see that we had broken nearly every pane of glass in the windows of Mrs. Walker's house by the jarring of our guns."[15]

Artillerist John Wharton, also of Guibor's Battery, recorded in his diary that the battery "remained in the [morning] position until 4 o'clock, when we

---

[13] Ibid.; French, *Two Wars*, 196.

[14] Lt. Thomas King's report, *OR*, ser. 1, vol. 38, pt. 2, 485.

[15] W. L. Truman, *Memoirs of the Civil War.*

moved across the valley and occupied the opposite heights." There, the men heard Johnston's general order. As Wharton explained,

> About ½ past 5 the enemy occupied our abandoned positions, and the cavalry charged upon our sharp-shooters. Our batteries opened upon them and drove them back. The batteries on both sides soon commenced firing and the Yankees' firing was tolerable effective. Our battalion is in reserve. Hoskins went and fired awhile and they returned, the firing being too heavy for them. They had several wounded, one which was a Lt. [A. J. Stewart].[16]

Sergeant Major William Pitt Chambers of the 46th Mississippi in Sears's Brigade, remembered hearing Johnston's general order while his regiment was in line of battle at the earlier position:

> A stirring battle order was read to the men and Lt. Gen. Polk made a brief talk to each regiment along the line. Our brigade was on the reserve line and we were not brought under fire till about 3 o'clock p.m. It was the first time we had heard the zip of hostile bullets since leaving Vicksburg," and the first time that Chambers had been under fire since becoming a Christian.[17]

Chambers described the scene as the Mississippians withdrew through Cassville: "Gen. Sears, who was under fire for the first time after his promotion, was struck on the foot by the fragment of a shell. I, in passing, was within a few feet of him at the time and asked, 'General, are you hurt?' 'I believe not,' he replied as he coolly surveyed the damage. 'I wouldn't mind it if it hadn't spoiled my new boot!'"[18]

Sears's Mississippians filed into their new position in rear of Cantey's Brigade and part of Ector's Brigade east of town. As they moved into position, they passed fellow Mississippians in the 27th Mississippi regiment of Walthall's Brigade in Hindman's Division, where Chambers recognized a friend. "As we were moving from one part of the field to another we passed the 27th Miss. Regt (also in reserve). At the head of the remnant of the 'Fencibles,' with his Bible in his hand, was the youthful captain Joel R. Baugh. He was

---

[16] John Wharton, vertical files, Confederate MO-5, 13, Kennesaw Mountain NMP.

[17] Chambers, *Blood and Sacrifice*, 142.

[18] Ibid.

reading aloud to his men. There was only time for a hurried hand clasp as we marched by and I saw them no more."[19]

Meanwhile, Confederate artillery began to fire on King's guns located at the hill by the Female College to provide cover for Sears's men. "A battery behind their works now opened on Lieutenant King, to which he replied, making excellent shots until they ceased," remembered Reynolds, who added, "The other sections of Captain Gary's battery were soon in position, and fired a few shots, but eliciting no reply ceased firing."[20]

Chambers remembered, "Our regiment had five men wounded that afternoon, though we did not fire a gun." In addition to his new boot, Sears and his brigade suffered a total of eight wounded and three missing at Cassville. Two of the wounded came from the 4th Mississippi.[21] Nearby, Walthall's Brigade saw one killed and four wounded from the evening's artillery fire.[22]

Meanwhile, in Captain Maximillien van den Corput's "Cherokee" Light Artillery battery, cannoneer Wesley Connor could only feel despair. The battery had lost all four of its Napoleon twelve-pounder guns at Resaca together with six killed, two wounded, nineteen captured, and twenty missing. "God knows what will become of us if we go [fall back] much further," recorded Connor in his journal. "Members of the Cherokee Artillery becoming demoralized," he added. "Most of them believe we will not get a battery, and the men will be put into Rowan's and Marshall's Batteries. Should that be the case, I venture the assertion that in a month there will be not thirty men of the [original] 150."[23] Samuel McKittrick, of the 16th South Carolina in Gist's Brigade, remembered the Federal artillery fire. "They came in sight and shelled us away."[24]

In Brigadier General Winfield Scott Featherston's Mississippi brigade of Loring's Division, Albert Quincy Porter of Company D, 22nd Mississippi,

---

[19] Ibid.

[20] Reynolds's report, *OR*, ser. 1, vol. 38, pt. 2, 468; King's report, *OR*, ser. 1, vol. 38, pt. 2, 485.

[21] Massey, *Foremost*, 38.

[22] Chambers, *Blood and Sacrifice*, 142; appendix D.

[23] Waters and Fisher, "*The Damnedest Set of Fellows*," 249–71. Compare Russell, "List of Casualties in Johnston's Battalion Artillery May 8 to June 4, 1864," *OR Supp.*, pt. 2, vol. 83, 554–55, which shows five wounded and seventeen missing for a total of twenty-two, all on 15 May. Daniel also reports twenty-two lost by Van Den Corput at Resaca (*Cannoneers in Gray*, 154).

[24] McKittrick to his wife, 22 May 1864, vertical files, Confederate SC-1, Kennesaw Mountain NMP.

remembered in the morning that his regiment was formed in line and "threw out skirmishers" before being ordered "to double quick back to the top of the mountain [west of Cassville along the ridge located at today's US 41], and then ordered back down into the field again, back of where we first formed, about 600 yards and formed another line." Featherston's Mississippians, along with the rest of Polk's Corps, moved to the southwest as they adjusted their lines to close up on Hardee's men in the morning. As they moved along the ridge top, Butterfield and the men of Wood's Brigade could see the Confederates moving parallel with them. After falling back to Johnston's new defensive line, Porter took a few minutes to record some additional lines in his diary: "It is now nearly too dark for me to see how to write and the shells are bursting over our heads constantly. Skirmishing commenced late in the evening."[25]

Artillerist William A. Brown of Stanford's Battery recorded that his "Battalion [was] not on the lines," meaning that Oliver's "Eufaula" Alabama battery, Fenner's Louisiana battery, and Stanford's Mississippi battery, all of Major John W. Eldridge's battalion, were not engaged at Cassville. These three batteries saw plenty of action at Resaca, and they would again a week later at the Battle of New Hope Church where the battalion would lose forty-three men killed and wounded, and forty-five horses killed and wounded. It seems likely that because Hood's Corps, including Stewart's Division, was in the act of withdrawing from their morning and midday positions in the Two Run Creek valley and along the two hills north of the Pine Log Road (Road 4) as divided by today's Brown Loop Road, that Eldridge's battalion did not see action. They were apparently on the move to the new line when McCook's and Stoneman's troopers made their afternoon charge.[26]

Captain Charles C. Briant, commanding Company "K" of the Sixth Indiana in Brigadier General William B. Hazen's Second Brigade remembered, "It was here at Cassville that we got to see the grandest military display I ever saw." Wood's Division, which included Hazen's Brigade, was posted to the right or south of Stanley's Division. "The enemy had taken position near Cassville, in the woods, with a large field just in their front," explained the captain. "In this field Howard's whole corps, as it were, passed in review, in plain sight of the enemy, and then while standing closed in mass, the artillery

[25] Albert Quincy Porter, vertical files, Confederate MS, Kennesaw Mountain NMP.

[26] William A. Brown, vertical files, Confederate MS-5, 166–67, Kennesaw Mountain NMP.

was brought up and placed in position to shell the woods, in which the rebels were stationed." Briant witnessed the unleashing of the Army of the Cumberland's artillery as thirty-one pieces of field artillery from the IV Corps and another thirty-two pieces from the XX Corps were brought to bear on the new Confederate defense line. The Hoosier recalled, "There were some fifty pieces of artillery, and at a given signal they were all to open on the woods. The boys will remember that our regiment was called on to defend a battery and that we took position just in front of it. Don't you remember, how the large guns belched the fire and smoke down over us?" exclaimed Briant.[27] The Hoosier captain continued.

> The signal gun sounded, and then she opened up, and *Great Heavens*! Talk about noises! Such a noise and such a sight, is not often witnessed by mortal man. Each gun was required to fire as rapidly as it could be loaded, and this kept up for at least ten or fifteen minutes. The woods were thick and heavy, and into this the shot and shell rained like hail, in a field of standing grain. The limbs were falling and timber being knocked in every direction. When the firing ceased the only thing to be heard was the echo of Howard's destructive artillery and when this died away, we could hear away to the front a rattling, tumbling noise, which we did not fully understand, until the next day. As we passed along by the woods and through Cassville, the ground in the woods was latterly covered with the green links of the trees.

Briant and his comrades could not believe the destruction that just fifteen minutes of artillery in his front had caused. "These woods were full of rebels when the cannon[s] opened on them, and in a few minutes they all broke in wild disorder and confusion, and an old man in Cassville told me that he never saw men so confused in his life, that both officers and men were running at full speed for the rear," added the Hoosier officer, "and that there was no signs of any organization like a company or a regiment, [and] it seemed to be every fellow for himself. This occurred about sundown."[28]

---

[27] Briant, *History of the Sixth Regiment*, 312–14.
[28] Ibid.

Chapter 17

The Abandonment of Cassville

With the withdrawal from the defenses north and west of the village in favor of the ridge to the southeast of town, Cassville now lay in between the lines of the belligerents. The beleaguered city was now suddenly in harm's way and in the crosshairs of the approaching Federals who had advanced quickly to the abandoned Southern lines that had protected Cassville.

In the "O" sample of his journal, T. B. Mackall captured the chaos of the sudden Confederate withdrawal through the village that had been renamed "Manassas" following the Confederate victory by that name in Virginia in 1861. It now resembled "Bull Run," the Federal name for this same battle.

As the Federals occupied the village, many soldiers recalled seeing homes and farms in a state unprepared for the destruction of war that had been thrust upon them by the sudden and unexpected withdrawal of the Confederate army, which had been protecting them, to a position that placed the town between the lines. "We passed a house that had just been vacated by the family. The table was spread for supper, and flour and sorghum lay scattered over the floor," remembered Private Samuel Toombs, a New Jersey soldier in Williams's Division.[1]

Arriving from the north of Cassville as McCook's and Stoneman's cavalry was sweeping the Two Run Creek valley to the east, and as the balance of Hooker's XX Corps and Howard's IV Corps began to form and move forward to the southwest, Williams's Division deployed to lengthen the long, blue, line that now extended for over three and a half miles as forty thousand Northern troops of the two corps moved forward in a battle line as if on dress parade. Halting just out of range of most of the Confederate guns, additional Federal batteries moved forward to unlimber and join in the duel.[2]

Deploying in the center of a cornfield in front of Williams's line, the Thirteenth New Jersey of Ruger's Second Brigade in Williams' Division supported the skirmish line. "The enemy's works were distinctly visible, and their officers were plainly seen riding backward and forward evidently preparing to resist our advance," remembered Private Toombs. "A battle seemed probable at any moment," he added. Presently, "a [Southern] battery opened on our

---

[1] Toombs, *Reminiscences of the Thirteenth Regiment*, 136.

[2] Ibid.

lines," continued the New Jersian, "Battery 'M' [First New York Light—4 Napoleons commanded by Captain John D. Woodbury] was brought up into position and fired a few shots at the enemy who hastened off and we at once moved forward beyond the line they occupied."[3]

One section of Battery I, First New York Light Artillery, with two of its six three-inch ordnance rifles were deployed. Soldier Edmund R. Brown, of the Twenty-Seventh Indiana, also in Ruger's Brigade, remembered,

> Our division was to the left of the road upon which we were approaching Cassville [the Adairsville-Cassville Road, Road 1]. With skirmishers out, and sometimes engaged, we moved through alternating timber and brush and plowed fields up to the edge of the town. At one point the Twenty-seventh was halted near a farmhouse, on elevated ground. A section or so of Battery M, First New York Light Artillery, was unlimbered near the house, perhaps in the yard, and was firing slowly upon the enemy. Sitting in a chair near the guns was "Pap" Williams [General Alpheus Seth Williams], cooly giving orders to the gunners, between puffs at his pipe.

The section of Battery I fired a total of six rounds at the retreating Confederates until they were safely out of range. Brown also noted in his diary, "Colonel [Silas] Colgrove [commanding the Twenty-Seventh Indiana], was put under arrest today for halting the column." The New Jersians and other portions of Williams's Division joined their fellow easterners of the Nineteenth Michigan and Twentieth Connecticut in occupying the village of Cassville, ere Manassas, ere Cassville, now again, Cassville.[4] "We kept up our advance, and believing that some of the enemy might be cut off and captured, the order to 'double quick' was given," remembered Toombs, "but they escaped us. We re-formed the line, and just as we were nearing a small piece of woods, that skirted the left of the town, a heavy volley of musketry was poured into us which checked our advance." The "volley" that Colonel Ezra Carmen's

---

[3] Ibid.; Scaife, *Campaign for Atlanta*, 154; Coburn's report, *OR*, ser. 1, vol. 38, pt. 2, 381; Buckingham's report, *OR*, ser. 1, vol. 38, pt. 2, 452; Welcher and Liggett, *Coburn's Brigade*, 180.

[4] Apparently, the colonel was released from arrest without incident for no other record exists for the infraction, and Colgrove was grievously wounded during the Battle of Peach Tree Creek on 20 July (E. R. Brown, *History of the 27th Indiana*, published by author, Monticello, Ind., 1899, 482; Captain Charles E. Winegar's report, September 7, 1864, *OR*, ser. 1, vol. 38, pt. 2, 474–77; Toombs, *Reminiscences of the Thirteenth Regiment*, 136; Scaife, *Campaign for Atlanta*, 154; Coburn's report, *OR*, ser. 1, vol. 38, pt. 2, 381; Buckingham's report, *OR*, ser. 1, vol. 38, pt. 2, 452; Welcher and Liggett, *Coburn's Brigade*, 180.

New Jersians received appears to have come from some of Wheeler's cavalrymen, either from one of Iverson's, or Ashby's or Harrison's brigades, or from a portion of Dibrell's Brigade as they made their escape through the mouth of the Two Run creek valley just above town, as, according to Sergeant Chambers of the 46th Mississippi of Sears's Brigade, the last infantry unit north of Cassville, the Mississippians did not fire a gun despite having five men wounded during the withdrawal. "Skirmishers were at one deployed," continued the New Jersey veteran, "while the remainder of the men threw up a protecting line of old logs and rails. There was heavy firing on the skirmish line until late at night and every indication pointed to a stubborn fight at Cassville the next day, but when morning dawned the enemy had disappeared." Despite the close contact with the retreating Southerners that day, Carmen's Thirteenth New Jersey did not record a single casualty.[5]

While Federals pressed from the north of Cassville, Daniel Reynolds's small Arkansas brigade covered the withdrawal of French's Division west of town. According to the Arkansas brigade commander, after falling back to the second line, "Skirmishing commenced about 5 p.m., pretty heavy and our cavalry was driven in and just after dark the enemy advanced into Cassville. The pickets on my right came in and thus the enemy occupied a part of the town and my men the other part and the pickets' line being at nearly right angles to my line of battle." Reynolds, who commanded the new line immediately to the southeast of Cassville, had deployed his skirmish line at the outskirts of town. "My skirmishers on the right being near the line so as to connect with those on my right and my left being several hundred yards advanced. During the early part of the night, we commenced moving our wagons and building field works."[6]

To the left or south of Daniel Reynolds's Arkansas brigade, Cockrell's Missourians busily worked on improving their line as they prepared for the battle that they assumed would take place the following day. That evening, after his battery had retired to Cass Station, Artillerist Philip Daingerfield Stephenson of the Washington Artillery, Captain Cuthbert H. Slocumb's Louisiana battery, 5th Company, had obtained permission to make a visit on some of his comrades in the Missouri brigade who had just arrived the previous day from Alabama. "I found them in a dense woods on level ground and the enemy so close that skirmishers could hardly operate," remembered Stephenson. The Missourians were located just north of today's Mac Johnston

[5] Toombs, *Reminiscences of the Thirteenth Regiment*, 136.

[6] Bender, ed., *Worthy of the Cause*, 126.

Road (Road 10) near its intersection with today's Cassville Road and in front of and along the low ridge at the entrance to today's Antigua Subdivision. "Bullets flew all about us and men were hit every now and then on the line," continued the young Louisiana visitor, who became a minister following the war. "I was standing near Colonel [Lieutenant Colonel Amos C.] Riley of one of the Missouri regiments [the 1st and 4th Missouri Consolidated] when he got the battle order and read it. It was almost dusk, but the news shot like electricity through every heart and received a glowing welcome."[7]

With the evacuation of Cassville by the Confederates, the Twentieth Connecticut and Nineteenth Michigan of Coburn's Brigade were assigned to take the village. They were supported by the Thirty-Third Indiana and the Eighty-Fifth Indiana of the same brigade. According to Lieutenant Colonel Philo B. Buckingham of the Twentieth Connecticut, his regiment together with the Nineteenth Michigan assaulted Cassville at 8 p.m. and were the only two regiments to enter the town.[8]

With bayonets fixed, the Wolverines and Connecticut Yankees rushed into the village only to find pitiousness. Many residents had fled the town as the Southerners had relocated to the leeward side of Cassville while the blue-coats swept in from the windward side like an irresistible north wind. One soldier from the Connecticut regiment remembered, "One sick man was found deserted by his wife and children." In the basement of another house, he found "three or four old ladies [who] had concluded to 'stand the storm.'" And in a third house, "a table was spread for dinner, upon which was a smoking boiled ham, fried chicken, young onions, strawberries and warm biscuit, all of which we partook with great satisfaction after our hard day's work."[9]

Brigade commander Colonel John Coburn remembered, "At dusk [the brigade] advanced into the town, which, after a skirmish, they held and occupied during the night. The streets were then strongly barricaded and every preparation made for a strenuous resistance of any attempt to dislodge our forces." Coburn reported one man killed and five wounded in the action. Four of the wounded were from the Twentieth Connecticut.[10]

---

[7] Hughes Jr., ed., *Civil War Memoir of Philip Daingerfield Stephenson, D.D.*, 180–81.

[8] Coburn's report, *OR*, ser. 1, vol. 38, pt. 2, 381.

[9] Fenton, *From the Rapidan to Atlanta*, 1:15.

[10] Coburn's report, *OR*, ser. 1, vol. 38, pt. 2, 381; Buckingham's report, *OR*, ser. 1, vol. 38, pt. 2, 452; Welcher and Liggett, *Coburn's Brigade*, 180.

While the artillery fire ended at dusk, sporadic skirmish fire would continue through the night. Private J. P. Cannon remembered that when his company (Company C) of the 27th Alabama was relieved from skirmish duty and returned to main line, "the pickets kept up a ceaseless firing as long as we remained awake."[11]

[11] Cannon, *Bloody Banners and Barefoot Boys*, 67.

Chapter 18

The Evening Meeting

By the late afternoon, following the chaotic turn of events from expecting a surprise attack by Hood and his corps, to the evacuation of Cassville and withdrawal to a new line of defense, Johnston was feeling good again. He had managed to withdraw from his morning line, a line he believed was subject to a flank attack via the Canton Road, while under fire, to a new line that he believed "was the best that was ever occupied during the war."[1]

His general order (appendix C), had been read to all of the soldiers, and it had been received with cheers and wild enthusiasm. While the morning surprise attack, which Hood had recommended and Johnston had consented to, did not materialize, Johnston believed that he had a great defensive position and that, as his order had suggested, his flanks were secure. The men were ready to fight, and Sherman, as the aggressor in enemy territory, would be compelled either to fight or eventually return to his former position in Chattanooga. Besides, fighting in the "active defensive" was Johnston's nature. He was now in his comfort zone once again.

T. B. Mackall's "O" sample recorded the evening's events as the busy day at Cassville began to turn to night. The evening's events would prove to be quite eventful, as well. "General M[ackall] and I remain several hours on roadside (Cassville and Cartersville road). Governor Harris brings lunch. General J[ohnston], about 5 p. m. in afternoon, rides down to Hardee's, leaving General M[ackall]; I remain." T. B. Mackall noted the presence of Governor Isham G. Harris of Tennessee in the Confederate camps.[2]

"About 6 p. m.," T. B. Mackall's "O" sample journal continued, "General M[ackall] sets out to find our camp; meets the general, [Johnston] and both go back to a field near road in rear of Polk, as skirmishing brisk. General J[ohnston] tells Governor Harris he will be ready for and happy to receive enemy next day. Wheeler comes up; cavalry falls back behind infantry." Apparently, T. B. Mackall and Johnston did not witness the gauntlet that Dibrell's Tennessee cavalrymen experienced due to Johnston's redeployment to

---

[1] Johnston, *Narrative*, 323–24.

[2] Mackall Journal, "O" sample, *OR*, ser. 1, vol. 38, pt. 3, 984.

the line southeast of town and the abandonment of the trooper's line of escape.[3]

T. B. Mackall's altered journal continued, "Dark ride to camp. By a muddy brook near General P[olk's] find supper ready and tents pitched. After supper, General J[ohnston] walks over to General P[olk]. General M[ackall] and rest turn in." By now, it was after 9 p.m. T. B. Mackall believed that everyone was turning in for the night to get some sleep in anticipation of the busy and early day the next morning. "Soon General J[ohnston] sends word by courier to send him two of inspectors-general mounted; then one of Polk's staff officers brings word that all the staff must report mounted; I was directed to remain."[4]

When Johnston returned to his headquarters (which had been relocated to a knoll overlooking a "muddy brook" just east of the Cartersville Road [today's Mac Johnson Road] and north of Polk's headquarters), he found a note.[5] Johnston recorded in his *Narrative*,

> On reaching my tent soon after dark, I found in it an invitation to meet the Lieutenant-Generals at General Polk's quarters. General Hood was with him, but not General Hardee. The two officers, General Hood taking the lead, expressed the opinion positively that neither of their corps would be able to hold its position next day; because, they said, a part of each was enfiladed by Federal artillery.

Johnston explained that "The part of [the line in] General Polk's corps referred to was that of which I had conversed with Brigadier [Francis] Shoupe. On that account they urged me to abandon the ground immediately, and cross the Etowah."[6]

Johnston continued, "A discussion of more than an hour followed, in which they very earnestly and decidedly expressed the opinion, or conviction rather, that when the Federal artillery opened upon them next day it would render their positions untenable in an hour or two." Johnston subsequently complained, "Although the position was the best we had occupied, I yielded at last, in the belief that the confidence of two of the commanders of the three corps of the army, of their inability to resist the enemy, would inevitably be communicated to their troops, and produce that inability."[7]

---

[3] Ibid.

[4] Ibid.

[5] Mackall Journal "A" and "O" samples, *OR*, ser. 1, vol. 38, pt. 3, 984.

[6] Johnston, *Narrative of Military Operations*, 323–24.

[7] Ibid.

General Hardee, who could not be located prior to the meeting, finally arrived at Polk's headquarters as the meeting was nearing its conclusion. Upon learning of Hood's and Polk's request to move, Hardee, according to Johnston, "remonstrated against it strongly, and was confident that his corps could hold its ground, although less favorably posted." But Johnston had already made his mind up to withdraw again. "The error," Johnston recorded, "was adhered to, however, and the position abandoned before daylight." In his official report, Johnston stated that the abandonment of the Cassville line was "a step which I have regretted ever since."[8]

Hood, on the other hand, had a much different recollection of the afternoon and evening. He explained in his official report that during the afternoon, when Johnston was selecting the new line, that General Francis Shoup, Johnston's chief of artillery, had pointed out that the new line would be subject to enfilade, or flanking, fire from the heights that they would be abandoning. As soon as Hood's and Polk's troops withdrew from these heights, Hood's prediction, in his mind, came true. Hood detailed the result in his report: "In a very short time thereafter the enemy placed his artillery on these heights and began to enfilade General Polk's line. Observing the effect upon the troops of this fire, I was convinced that the position was unsuited for defense." Hood then met with Polk and, after a consensus was reached between them, sent a note to ask Johnston for a meeting.[9]

Hood recorded in his report that at the meeting, "General Polk and myself said to General Johnston that our positions would prove untenable for defense, but that we were in as good [a] position to advance upon the enemy as could be desired. We told him that if he did not intend to take the offensive he had better change our position." Hood then added, "He accordingly ordered the army across the Etowah."[10]

After the war and following his review of Johnston's *Narrative*, Hood repeated his statements from his report, and included a letter from Revered Dr. [Brigadier General Francis A.] Shoup. The former general (now reverend) supported Hood's position in his letter. Explaining that he had "a very distinct recollection," Shoup wrote "I pointed out the fact to General Johnston that his line would be enfiladed before the troops were posted, and suggested a change of position to obviate the trouble."[11]

---

[8] Ibid.; *OR*, ser. 1, vol. 38, pt. 3, 616.

[9] Hood's report, *OR*, ser. 1, vol. 38, pt. 3, 635.

[10] Ibid.

[11] Shoup to Hood, 3 June 1874, in Hood, *Advance and Retreat*, 105–106.

The reverend added, "The General [Johnston] replied that the troops could not hope to be always sheltered from fire, and that they must make the best of it by traversing." Shoup continued, "As soon as the enemy got into position, my fears were fully verified. The line, at that point, fell back from the crest of the ridge, but was poorly sheltered even upon the slope. I should say that there was as much as a quarter of a mile badly exposed to the enemy's fire." Johnston had said that the distance exposed was only about 150–200 yards.[12]

Concerning the afternoon meeting, Shoup added, "General Polk was present at the time the conversation between General Johnston and myself took place, and strongly supported my objections." Not wanting to be caught in the middle of the dispute between Hood and Johnston, the reverend close his letter with, "I am indeed sorry to have my name mixed up in the difference between General Johnston and yourself, but I do not see that I can decline to reply to such questions as you please to ask." The preacher's conscious would not let him remain silent.[13]

In addition to Johnston, Polk, and Hood, General French and Captain Walter J. Morris were also present during portions of the evening. French recorded in his diary, "After dark, as I was returning from dinner, I met Gen. Hood, who asked me to ride over with him to see Gen. Johnston at Gen. Polk's headquarters, and take supper."[14]

French had previously noted concerns with the new line when his division, the last to withdraw from the previous line, arrived. He wrote, "At 4 p.m., I was ordered to fall back and form *behind* the division of Gen. Cant[e]y and Cockrell's Brigade, which I did. But as there was an interval between Hood's line and Cant[e]y without troops, I placed there in position Hoskin's [*sic*] Battery and half of Ector's Brigade." The division commander continued, "This left me Sears's Brigade and half of Ector's in reserve. Then came an order adding to my command the division of Cant[e]y, which was directly in front of me. Cockrell, on Canty's left, was put, for the occasion, under the orders of Loring."[15]

French added, "About 5 p.m. our pickets from the extreme front were driven in toward the second line by the enemy's cavalry. Hoskin's [*sic*] battery opened on the cavalry and checked them." He then witnessed the onslaught

---

[12] Ibid.

[13] Ibid.

[14] French, *Two Wars*, 196–98.

[15] Ibid.

of the Federal artillery fire. "About 5:30 p.m. the Federals, having placed some batteries in position on a ridge in front of Hood's right, opened fire on our line, and the shells from their extreme left (in front of Hood's right) enfiladed Hoskin's [*sic*] gun[s] and the line that for a little while curved out to the battery." This Federal battery was likely the Eighteenth Indiana Light artillery that had followed the blue-clad troopers to the edge of the town. "Hood's line was not a prolongation of Polk's line," French explained, "because it *fell back* at the point of junction about twenty-five degrees." In support of his claim about the break in the line between his right and Hood's left, French then referred to a map that Captain Walter J. Morris, engineer for Polk's Corps had drawn.[16]

In his postwar memoir, French wrote about his time at the meeting: "When supper was over Hood and Polk asked Johnston to a conference that they had previously arranged, and Johnston asked me to go with him." The party had dined at the residence of William McKelvey but then retired to a cabin across the road where Polk had set up his headquarters. "At this conference, at this time, Hardee *was not* present," remembered French. "Hood commenced by declaring that his line and Polk's line were so enfiladed by the Federal artillery that they could not be held. Polk was not so strenuous. Johnston insisted on fighting." Quoting from his diary, French added, "At 9 p.m., it was, I am sure, determined to fight at Cassville, and, after remaining at the conference sometime longer, I hastened to camp to entrench. Soon after it was intimated to me by an officer riding along past me that we would fall back, owing to the enemy moving so far on our left."[17]

After the war, French wrote much more about the subject as he found himself having to defend his position from some bare allegations that were published in letters to the editor in the *New Orleans Times Picayune*. Assertions were made from a few veterans who had served in the Washington Artillery (Captain Cuthbert H. Slocumb's battery) under generals Bate and Hardee. Hardee's men had heard that Johnston wanted to stay and fight and that Hood and Polk (and presumably French) wanted to withdraw. Hardee arrived at the conclusion of the meeting in time only to receive the verdict that the army would fall back, but he missed the deliberation. Surprised, he

---

[16] Ibid.
[17] Ibid.

offered to trade places with the troops of Polk or Hood with his corps and remain and fight, but Johnston had already made his decision.[18]

As to the question of whether Hood and Polk argued for the offensive during the evening meeting, some historians have pointed to French's statements that he never heard Hood or Polk mention making an attack while he was present at the meeting. However, French was not present for much of the meeting at the McKelvey cabin after dinner. According to the DuBose account, Johnston walked to the McKelvey house at 8:00 p.m. to have dinner. Thus, French, whom Hood invited to join the party for dinner, was only with the group for the time spent having dinner at the McKelvey house, perhaps up to about an hour, and then he joined them briefly at 9:00 p.m. at the McKelvey cabin across the road, which was serving as Polk's headquarters. According to French, he left the meeting at 9:00 p.m., or just after, to tend to his defenses as he anticipated that there would be a defensive battle the following morning based on Johnston's initial response to Hood's and Polk's entreaties to move from the line that Johnston had selected. However, in his memoir, French was careful to add that "whilst I was there, [Hood] made no reference to being in a good position for action on the aggressive and making an attack."[19]

However, Johnston subsequently admitted that indeed Hood and Polk had argued for making an attack the following morning. In a letter to Dr. William M. Polk, son of the late General Leonidas Polk, dated 24 May 1869 from Savannah and written in response to a letter from Dr. Polk requesting clarification on the issue, Johnston replied, "You say *truly* that General Polk advocated offensive fighting. He was anxious that we should assail the enemy, and if he, instead of General Hood," added Johnston, in an effort to change the subject to the morning episode, "had been on the right in the morning, the attack ordered would have been executed." Johnston added that there was a "discussion of about two hours," that General "Hardee joined the party near eleven o'clock," and that he recalled that "General Clayton was occasionally present during the evening," but that he had "no recollection of seeing General French during the evening."[20]

In contrast to French, Captain Walter J. Morris, Polk's chief of engineers, was present during the entirety of the evening meeting, and, in a letter

---

[18] Ibid.; Major Henry Hampton, "Itinerary of Hardee's Army Corps May 15–June 14," *OR*, ser. 1, vol. 38, pt. 3, 704.

[19] French, *Two Wars*, 198.

[20] Polk, *Leonidas Polk, Bishop and General*, 357.

to Dr. William M. Polk dated 25 June 1874, from New York City, Morris provided a detailed explanation of the issue and of the roles played by the chief participants, Hood, Polk, and Johnston. The letter, which was first published in Hood's *Advance and Retreat*, is the most thorough and most accurate account of the evening meeting.[21]

In his letter, Morris explained that in addition to being ordered by General Polk to determine if the newly selected line of defense could be held, he was also ordered by Polk "[t]o examine the ground immediately in his front in reference to advancing, and to note in reference the positions then occupied by the Federal batteries in front and to the right of Lieutenant General Hood's line." Morris added that he was also ordered to determine "If those [the enemy's] batteries to the front and right of Hood's line could be taken by a special movement." Morris wrote that he inspected the lines in front of Polk's right (French's Division) and Hood, jotting down all of his carefully calculated measurements until darkness prevented his further examination on Hood's extreme right. Morris then prepared a detailed sketch (exhibit 14) of the lines, and reached the following conclusions: 1) "The right of the line occupied by...Polk's command could not be held... by constructing rifle pits along the crest"; 2) "That traverses would be of no avail, either"; 3) "That it would be extremely hazardous for...Polk to advance his line to make an attack upon the enemy while their batteries held the positions they then occupied"; and 4) That he could not form an opinion as to whether "a special flank movement," from Hood's right to the Federal left could be successful, "as it had grown dark" before he could complete his examination, but that "judging from the stream, as located on the skeleton map, there must have been a very narrow ridge to approach the enemy upon their left," implying that it was possible to make such an attack.[22]

---

[21] Morris to William Polk, 25 June 1874, in Hood, *Advance and Retreat*, 110–16; compare Polk, *Leonidas Polk, Bishop and General*, 376–72, where the letter is dated 25 June *1878*. See appendix E.

[22] Ibid. Bill Scaife found fault with Morris's sketch, claiming that it was "misaligned by some 35 degrees," and that the "deployment of the troops and the configuration of both the Federal and Confederate lines were inconsistent with Federal and Confederate reports of the engagement." However, I found Morris's map to be quite accurate and detailed, despite his limitations of time and daylight. I was able to fairly line up Morris's map to the modern topography as well as the various unit locations, both Federal and Confederate. Also, I positively compared them to the trench lines as depicted in the Ruger Map (exhibit 25). However, I was unable to reconcile Scaife's placements of French's Division, Hoskins's Battery, or the "gap" in between the lines

Morris explained that after completing his reconnaissance (together with his calculations and drawing of his sketch map), he returned to Polk's headquarters just after dark. "I placed before him my sketches and notes, and explained to him substantially these facts. General Polk went at once to ask General Johnston to come to his headquarters. Lieutenant General Hood was already with General Polk," remembered Morris. Evidently, Morris did not sup with the generals across the road at the McKelvey house. Instead, he probably used the time to complete his map drawing and calculations. "General Johnston arrived about *9 o'clock*. I remained in the *cabin* during the conversation as to holding the position then occupied *or advancing* or retiring the Armies to the south of the Etowah River, about seven or eight miles to our rear."[23]

Morris remembered,

> these Generals [Hood and Polk were] both advocating to the Commanding General to take the offensive, and advance on the enemy from these lines. In reference to this proposed forward movement. General Johnston's attention was particularly called to the advantages of taking possession of the positions occupied by the batteries of the enemy on their extreme left, either by a special flank movement or by prompt action at the time when the Confederate lines would be advanced. Lieutenant General Polk expressed himself entirely willing and ready to co-operate with General Hood to accomplish this object.[24]

Morris then said, "After some moments of silence, General Johnston decided to withdraw the Armies to the south of the Etowah [River]. Soon after this, Lieutenant General Hardee arrived. General Johnston informed him of this decision to cross the river, stating that Generals Polk and Hood had informed him that they could not hold their lines." Repeating their positions to Hardee, including their "urging the offensive rather than await the enemy," Hood and Polk again tried to no avail to move Johnston to attack. Shortly thereafter, Johnston gave the orders to withdraw. Polk then called his assistant

---

of Polk and Hood (Scaife puts the gap at the Mac Johnston Road instead of Shinall Gaines Road), in his "Evening Cassville Affair" map (exhibit 13). Also, Scaife's omission of Rippetoe's 18th Indiana battery makes the Scaife map unreliable and unfortunately inadvertently misleading. See Scaife, "Waltz between the Rivers," 290.

[23] Ibid. Emphasis added.

[24] Ibid.

adjutant general to issue orders to effect the movement. "This was about 10:30 or 11:00 o'clock," remembered Morris."[25]

In addition to Morris's vivid portrayal of the events between Johnston, Hood, and Polk at the McKelvey cabin during the Evening Cassville Affair, others were aware of Hood's and Polk's desire to make an attack and of Johnston's timidity. General Joseph "War Baby" Wheeler and his staff were well aware of it. Wheeler's admirer and biographer John Witherspoon DuBose recorded, "About 8:00 o'clock he [Johnston] walked to Polk's [headquarters]. Both [Hood and Polk] agreed that a direct advance upon the foe might be made the next morning. General Johnston refused to accept their conclusions." However, explained DuBose, "As Johnston walked out of Polk's quarters, Hardee met him on the steps," where he learned the news that the army would fall back again.[26]

Unfortunately, Johnston left a trail of untruths for future historians to follow and be led astray. DuBose recorded an incident that occurred shortly after the evacuation from Cassville. "Johnston told Colonel J. L. M. Curry, of Wheeler's staff, two or three days later, that it was a sad blunder, the contention of Hood and Polk, but he could not order battle opposed by two of the three corps commanders." This face-saving statement by Johnston would be the first of many misleading comments.[27]

Also, because Hardee arrived at the conclusion of the meeting, he did not hear the full discussion and debate between Johnston and Hood and Polk. In addition, when another retreat was by then a foregone conclusion in Johnston's mind, in which Hardee's entreaty to offer to switch his corps with one of the other two and remain and defend was not an option, it is no wonder that Hardee and his staff returned to their corps with limited information about the Evening Meeting.

As the entries to the diaries, letters, and journals from officers and soldiers in Hardee's Corps spawned, the story that Johnston withdrew from Cassville due to Hood's and Polk's timidity, although only a part of the story of the Evening Meeting, grew into legend. For example, Captain Samuel T. Foster, of Granbury's Texas brigade, recorded on 19 May, "We hear that some of Genl. Johnston's Genls made a slip some way, and disarranged his whole plan for the fight. Consequently, he had to fall back." When the news that the army would again fall back was delivered to General Cleburne,

---

[25] Ibid.

[26] Dubose, *General Joseph Wheeler*, 296–302.

[27] Ibid.

Cleburne asked why. "Hardee replied," according to Captain Irving A. Buck, Cleburne's assistant adjutant general, "that at a conference between the commanding general and two of his corps commanders, Lieutenant-Generals Polk and Hood had stated that they could not hold their positions for an hour after the Federal artillery should open upon them." Soldier John Jackman in Lewis's Kentucky "Orphan" Brigade, recorded, "Tis said the reason we did not fight at Cassville was, Hood and Polk declared they could not hold their position." The next day, courier William L. Trask noted in his entry of 20 May, "It now appears that after our lines were formed yesterday, General Hood and Polk informed Johnston that if attacked they would be unable to hold their positions more than two hours. Hardee told them that if they would fight he would reinforce them with three of his divisions and that he would hold his part of the line always, with only Cheatham's Division. General Johnston at once ordered a retreat."[28]

But in Polk's and Hood's corps, the reason for the withdrawal was understood very differently by the men. Compare the diary of Claudius Sears, a brigade commander in French's Division of Polk's Corps, who remembered the reason for the withdrawal was because of the report that Federals had crossed the Etowah River to the west. "Enemy shelled our position *and flanked us*, and we resumed our retreat at dark and on morning of [May] 20th at sun rise, crossed the Etowah at Cartersville." Lieutenant Colonel Christopher Columbus Sykes, of the 43rd Mississippi in Adams's Brigade of Loring's Division, wrote to his wife, on Saturday, 21 May 1864, that the Southern army was across the Etowah River, "but I am satisfied that we will not have an engagement here, as the enemy are still flanking us on the left." Artillerist William A. Brown of Stanford's Battery recorded in his diary, "Enemy said to be flanking our left and crossing the river." The diary of Chaplain Thomas Deavenport, from the 3rd Tennessee in Brown's Brigade of Stevenson's Division, recorded "heavy skirmishing was kept up through the evening, but again the enemy refused to fight and *marched to the left* compelling us to evacuate." Also, in the diary of E. D. Willet of the 40th Alabama in Baker's

[28] N. D. Brown, ed., *One of Cleburne's Command*, 79; Buck, *Cleburne and His Command*, 216; Jackman, *Diary of a Confederate Soldier*, 130; Hafendorfer, *Civil War Journal of William L. Trask*, 150.

Brigade of Stewart's Division, Willet noted, "Being flanked at Rome compelled further retreat."[29]

The men in Wheeler's cavalry corps seemed to understand that the reason for the withdrawal was the report of another Federal flanking movement. Trooper William Thornton of the 3rd Georgia Cavalry of Iverson's Brigade, in a letter to his father dated Sunday, 22 May 1864, wrote, "I heard that 30,000 yankees were across the Hightower [*sic*; Etowah] or cross[ed] it about the time he [Johnston] cross[ed] it. They crossed on his (Johnston)['s] extreme left—reliable news it is said. I think that is their programme of subjugating the South as they have been successful in every undertaken [*sic*] in this army."[30]

Perhaps the most revealing evidence on the cause for Johnston's withdrawal following the Evening Cassville Affair, is found in correspondence to General Bragg from Brigadier General Marcus J. Wright commanding troops at Atlanta. In a letter dated 23 May 1864, written in an effort to assure Bragg and the Richmond authorities that Johnston intended to seek a battle, Wright explained, "General Johnston intended to fight at Cassville. A flank movement of the enemy crossing [the] Etowah [River] on the left, he [Johnston] retired to Allatoona, where the army has remained for the past two days to enable wagon trains to pass to the rear." Wright's dispatch did not contain any reference to Hood or Polk, of the evening meeting, or of Hood's failure to make an attack the morning of 19 May.[31]

In his letter to President Davis, written the day after the withdrawal from Cassville, Johnston mentioned neither the evening meeting nor the dispute with Hood and Polk. On 20 May 1864, from the Etowah River, Johnston wrote, "In the last eight days the enemy have pressed us back to this place, thirty-two miles." Explaining that he had remained in close contact so as to prevent Sherman from detaching a force and reinforcing Grant in Virginia, Johnston said that his plan for an attack at Resaca was "defeated by his

---

[29] Claudius Sears's Diary, vertical files, Confederate MS-1, 17, Kennesaw Mountain NMP; Christopher Columbus Sykes to wife, 21 May 1864, Along the banks of the Etowah, vertical files, Confederate MS-4, 13, ibid.; William A. Brown, vertical files, Confederate MS-5, 166, ibid.; Reverend Thomas Deavenport's diary, vertical files, Confederate TN-13, 24, ibid.; E. D. Willet's diary, vertical files, Confederate AL-4, 101, ibid.

[30] William Thornton to father, 22 May 1864, camp near Altonia [*sic*], Ga., vertical files, Confederate GA-26, ibid.

[31] Marcus J. Wright to Braxton Bragg, 23 May 1864, *OR*, ser. 1, vol. 52, pt. 2, 672.

[Sherman's] crossing a column at Calhoun close to my communications," and on 19 May at Cassville, "having ordered a general attack, while the officer charged with the lead [Hood] was advancing he was deceived by a false report that a heavy column of the enemy had turned our right and was close upon him, and took a defensive position. When the mistake was discovered, it was too late to resume the movement." Also, in a second letter written on 21 May 1864, to correct an error related to the date of the intended attack at Resaca, Johnston told the president, "The direction of the railroad to this point has enabled him [Sherman] to press me back by steadily moving to the left and by fortifying the moment he halted." Again, in this letter as in the first one, Johnston made no mention of the evening meeting or of any timidity by Hood and Polk, at Cassville, at Adairsville, or at any other place.[32]

As the time following the war grew, Johnston would subsequently flatly deny that Hood and Polk had ever recommended an offensive during the evening meeting. In a letter he wrote to Charles Johnsen in 1874, the same year that his *Narrative of Military Operations* was released, Johnston wrote in sharp contrast to his earlier letter to Dr. William Polk. Apparently forgetting his statements written to Dr. William Polk in 1869 (or perhaps believing that they would never be published to impeach him), Johnston wrote in his 19 June 1874 letter to Johnsen, "In the discussion at night between Generals Hood, Polk and myself, the question was *only* of holding the position sketched" (see exhibit 8). Johnston subsequently added, "To attack Sherman's concentrated army would have been inexpressibly absurd. General Hood expressed no such idea at the time. To postpone the attack from the afternoon, when the Federals were entrenching, until the next morning, when they were entrenched, would have been stupid."[33]

In his *Memoirs*, Sherman recorded perhaps the best explanation of the evening controversy. While meeting with Johnston on a Mississippi riverboat in fall 1865, Sherman asked Johnston about the events at Cassville and what

---

[32] Joseph E. Johnston to Davis, 20 May 1864, *OR*, ser. 1, vol. 38, pt. 4, 728; Joseph E. Johnston to Davis, 21 May 1864, *OR*, ser. 1, vol. 38, pt. 4, 736. Compare these letters with Johnston's 20 October 1864 official report where he claimed the reason for his withdrawal was due to Hood's and Polk's timidity (Johnston's report, 20 October 1864, Vineville, Ga., *OR*, ser. 1, vol. 38, pt. 3, 616.

[33] Johnston to Charles G. Johnsen, 19 June 1874, Savannah, Ga., *Southern Historical Society Papers*, 21:319–20; also found with hand-drawn map at the *New Orleans Times Picayune*, 22 October 1893, 20. Emphasis added.

he meant by his general order. Sherman had read a copy of the order and was puzzled as to Johnston's intentions at Cassville.[34]

In response, Johnston told him about the events of the afternoon and of his evening meeting with Hood and Polk. Sherman's recollections of that meeting are reproduced in their entirety here:

> In the autumn of 1865, when in command of the Military Division of the Missouri, I went from St. Louis to Little Rock, Arkansas, and afterward to Memphis. Taking a steamer for Cairo, I found as fellow-passengers Generals Johnston and Frank Blair [former commander of the Federal XVII Corps]. We were, of course, on the most friendly terms, and on our way up we talked over our battles again, played cards, and questioned each other as to particular parts of our mutual conduct in the game of war.
>
> I told Johnston that I had seen his order of preparation, in the nature of an address to his army, announcing his purpose to retreat no more, but to accept battle at Cassville. He answered that such was his purpose; that he had left Hardee's corps in the open fields to check Thomas, and gain time for his formation on the ridge, just behind Cassville; and it was this corps which General Thomas had seen deployed, and whose handsome movement in retreat he had reported in such complimentary terms.
>
> Johnston described how he had placed Hood's corps on the right, Polk's in the centre, and Hardee's on the left. He said that he had ridden over the ground, given to each corps commander his position, and orders to throw up parapets during the night; that he was with Hardee on his extreme left as the night closed in, and as Hardee's troops fell back to the position assigned them for the intended battle of the next day; and that, after giving Hardee some general instructions, he and his staff rode back to Cassville.
>
> As he entered the town, or village, he met Generals Hood and Polk. Hood inquired of him if he had had any thing to eat, and he said no, that he was both hungry and tired, when Hood invited him to go and share a supper which had been prepared for him at a house close by.
>
> At the supper they discussed the chances of the impending battle, when Hood spoke of the ground assigned him as being enfiladed by our (Union) artillery, which Johnston disputed, when General Polk chimed in with the remark that General Hood was right; that the cannon-shots fired by us at nightfall had enfiladed their general line of battle, and that for this reason he feared they could not hold their men.
>
> General Johnston was surprised at this, for he understood General Hood to be one of those who professed to criticize his strategy, contending

[34] Sherman, *Memoirs*, 2:39–41.

> that, instead of retreating, he should have risked a battle. General Johnston said he was provoked, accused them of having been in conference, with being beaten before battle, and added that he was unwilling to engage in a critical battle with an army so superior to his own in numbers, with two of his three corps commanders dissatisfied with the ground and positions assigned them. He then and there made up his mind to retreat still farther south, to put the Etowah River and the Allatoona range between us; and he at once gave orders to resume the retrograde movement.[35]

Following this meeting, Sherman had an occasion to give an after-dinner speech to a Society of the Army of the Cumberland around 1868 in Cleveland, Ohio. In an impromptu speech, Sherman related his steamboat meeting with Johnston to the group, and subsequently, according to the veteran Federal commander, "it got into print." In spring 1870, while Sherman was at New Orleans on his way to Texas, General Hood invited Sherman to meet him at the St. Charles Hotel. Hood told Sherman that

> he had seen my speech reprinted in the newspapers and gave me his version of the same event, describing the halt at Cassville, the general orders for battle on that ground, and the meeting at supper with Generals Johnston and Polk, when the chances of the battle to be fought the next day were freely and fully discussed; and he stated that he had argued against fighting the battle purely on the defensive, but had asked General Johnston to permit him with his own corps and part of Polk's to quit their lines, and to march rapidly to attack and overwhelm Schofield, who was known to be separated from Thomas by an interval of nearly five miles, claiming that he could have defeated Schofield, and got back to his position in time to meet General Thomas's attack in front.
>
> He also stated that he had then contended with Johnston for the "offensive-defensive" game, instead of the "pure defensive," as proposed by General Johnston; and he said that it was at this time that General Johnston had taken offense, and that it was for this reason he had ordered the retreat that night.[36]

"As subsequent events estranged these two officers, it is very natural they should now differ on this point," explained Sherman. "But it was sufficient,"

[35] Ibid.

[36] Ibid.

he continued, "for us that the rebel army did retreat that night, leaving us masters of all the country above the Etowah River."[37]

The critical questions from the Cassville Evening Affair are: 1) Should the Confederates have stayed or withdrawn? 2) If they chose to stay, should they have defended or attacked? 3) Why did Johnston withdraw? 4) Did Hood request another attack for the following morning?

Following a dispute with Hood and Polk in which Johnston became, according to his own words to Sherman, *provoked*, because Hood had challenged him to stand and risk a general engagement the following morning by striking at the enemy before they could strike him, Johnston said that he ordered a retreat. He had delivered his "stirring address" that the army would turn and fight, and that his "communications were secure." A couple of hours of exertion by Polk and Hood would not dissuade him. When he left the meeting, French was convinced that they would be defending the following day. But when Hood called Johnston's strategy of "pure defensive" into question, Johnston, according to his own words, if his comments to Sherman are to be believed, became "provoked" and ordered the withdrawal.

About this same time, Johnston received a dispatch from General Ross, whom he had not heard from for forty-eight hours since communication with Rome had been broken. After riding twenty-five miles that day from below Rome to Cartersville Ross had sent a dispatch rider with news that Federals had effected a crossing over the Etowah River at Wooley's Bridge.

In the T. B. Mackall "A" sample, the young lieutenant recorded what he thought was his last entry for the evening when William Mackall turned in for bed after 9 p.m.: "Battle expected next day." However, when T. B. Mackall was alerted that the staff was to mount their horses and report (probably around 11 p.m.), he learned the reason for the withdrawal, and he recorded, "General Ross reports from Cartersville enemy across at Wooley's Bridge."[38]

The most telling piece of evidence (in addition to T. B. Mackall's journal entry), was French's last line in his diary entry for 19 May. After French left the meeting and "hastened to camp to entrench," he was surprised to receive the news that the army would be soon withdrawing. He wrote, "Soon after it was intimated to me by an officer riding along past me that we would fall back, *owing* to the enemy moving so far on our left."[39] The staff officer who rode by French delivering the news to prepare to withdraw provided the

---

[37] Ibid.

[38] Mackall Journal, "A" sample.

[39] Emphasis added.

reason: the enemy had flanked the Confederates again. T. B. Mackall, at Johnston's headquarters, also received the news around the same time from a different staff officer, and he also heard the reason: "General Ross reports from Cartersville enemy across at Wooley's Bridge."[40]

In an article in the *Augusta Chronicle*, the reason for Johnston's evacuation was provided: "The anticipated battle of Friday morning in front of Cassville," explained the reporter, "was prevented by the unexpected movements of the enemy, and the sending a column across the Etowah above Rome by Cedar Town Valley, leading to Marietta." A second article in the same paper provided more details: "By the train from the front this morning, we learn that a column of the enemy crossed the Etowah river eight miles above the railroad bridge, yesterday, and were marching on Marietta. And McPherson with 15,000 crossed, the night before, twelve miles below Etowah Station, to flank our left. This maneuvering made a change of position necessary to our army, in order to preserve its communication."[41] Sherman, though, had not yet crossed the Etowah River west of Johnston at Kingston or Rome, as was reported to and relied upon by Johnston, but that is precisely what Sherman would do just days later on Monday, 23 May 1864.[42]

It is clear from an inspection of the ground and a review of a topographic map that the line Johnston selected was both commanded by and subject to enfilade fire by Federal artillery on the heights he had just abandoned. It is also clear that Johnston felt tremendous pressure from the Richmond authorities to make a stand north of the Etowah River. Also, he had just delivered a "turn and fight" speech. Since Hood's morning attack proposal did not work out, he could still remain and fight and no one would question his decision—besides, this strategy was more comfortable to him and less risky. But when the news arrived that Federals had crossed the river far to his left, he resigned to the decision to withdraw. The reason Johnston ordered the evacuation was his receipt of the news from Ross. The excuse he would give for his evacuation

---

[40] French, *Two Wars*, 196–98; Mackall Journal, "A" sample.

[41] "Latest for Johnston's Army, Flank Movements of the Enemy," and "From the Front, More Flank Movements, Etowah Bridge Burnt, No General Engagement Yet," *Augusta Chronicle*, 21 May 1864.

[42] "From the Front," *Augusta Chronicle*, 21 May 1864.

was Hood's and Polk's alleged timidity. In reality, he told Sherman it was their temerity that had "provoked" him.[43]

T. B. Mackall then recorded the hasty withdrawal from Cassville in the middle of the night: "General Mackall returned to camping-place, where all staff waited until about 2 a.m., when they rode to Cartersville, passing trains and artillery parked in field; all hurried off without regard to order." The officers and staff, teamsters, pioneers, troopers, infantrymen, artillerymen, and camp followers all slogged along throughout the night in a disorganized withdrawal. "Reach Cartersville before day," T. B. Mackall recalled, "troops come in after day. General Johnston comes up-all hurried over bridges; great confusion, caused by mixing trains and by trains which crossed first parking at river's edge and others winding around wrong roads; about 2,000 wagons crowded on bank."[44]

In just two weeks since the beginning of the campaign, Johnston had fallen back over two rivers. Sherman's legions now controlled northwest Georgia from the Etowah River to Chattanooga, and Dalton and Rome were squarely in Federal hands. Despite receiving reinforcements in infantry and cavalry in numbers that swelled Johnston's force to more than seventy-four thousand men—a force larger than Lee took to Gettysburg, or Bragg led at Chickamauga, or that Lee was presently using against Grant—Johnston had still not forced a general engagement.

---

[43] Two veterans of Lumsden's Alabama battery expected that the right wing (Hood) would attack the following morning. See also Little and Maxwell, *History of Lumsden's Battery*.

[44] Mackall Journal, "O" sample, *OR*, ser. 1, vol. 38, pt. 3, 984.

Chapter 19

Conclusions to Part 2

After cheering to an order earlier in the day proclaiming that they were going to stand and fight, the men were surprised by Southern army's withdrawal during the evening. As the Confederate soldiers made their way south and across Hightower Bridge, confidence in Joe Johnston began to fade. After the strange set of events that had occurred in the morning followed by the evening disagreement at the William McKelvey house and cabin—Polk's headquarters where he and Hood had quarreled with the Southern commander—Johnston's confidence in John Bell Hood had begun to erode.

Enmity had not yet taken root within the Confederate high command, but its seeds had been planted. With the passing of another two months and two more rivers, Johnston would be removed in favor of Hood. The former chieftain would always lament his failure to bring battle at Cassville. In time, Johnston's disillusionment with Hood, and the events of 19 May, would fester and grow into a passionate mission to leave his own version of the day's history. His views have dominated the literature ever since, and they have clouded our understanding of the subject for over a century and a half.

Brigadier General Edward M. McCook of the famous "fighting McCooks" family was unquestionably the star of the day, with Stoneman playing best supporting actor. The two cavalry leaders had their best day of service in the Atlanta Campaign at Cassville, and clearly, as Albert Castel aptly stated in *Decision in the West*, "it [was] the most valuable service that will be performed by Sherman's cavalry during the entire campaign."[1]

By striking Hood's marching infantry columns that morning, McCook completely deranged Hood's plan of attack. Later in the day, when McCook (with Stoneman) attacked a second time, the Federal cavalrymen caught the Confederates out of position again as the gray-clad infantry withdrew to a new defense line south of town. Thus, the Northern troopers were able to rout and capture small detachments of skirmishers. Later, the superior firepower of the Federal artillery outdueled the Confederate guns.

Cassville was supposed to be the place where the Confederate army surprised the pursuing Federals while on the move. Instead, McCook's and

---

[1] Castel, *Decision in the West*, 202.

Stoneman's horsemen surprised the Southerners twice in aggressive and successful parries, catching the gray-clad infantry on the move.

With the correction of the errors in Cassville's historiography, her story can now be examined with more accuracy than before. The events there exposed the failure of the Confederate forces to gather accurate intelligence on their enemy. It revealed the incompleteness, inadequacy, and inaccuracy of the Southern maps. The events at Adairsville and Cassville also demonstrated a level of incompetency within the high command. At Adairsville, Johnston did not anticipate the speed at which Sherman's legions spilled into the plains below the Oostanaula River. While successfully withdrawing from the potential trap at Adairsville, Johnston again was slow to accept Hood's proposal for an offensive on 18 May.

The Confederate plan of attack on the morning of 19 May was based on limited and flimsy intelligence. Hood assumed that because a portion of his corps used the Ironton (Copper Mine) Road to reach Cassville, that the Federals would follow suit. Had Hooker or Schofield been in command, based upon their requests to Sherman to march early on 19 May to Cassville, it is likely that one or the other of the two corps, the XX or XXIII, would have fallen into the trap. However, Sherman's determination to focus on Kingston at the center first and then move east or west as the situation developed likely saved Hooker and Schofield from a potential disaster.

The Confederate leaders believed that Howard's IV Corps would use the Ironton (Copper Mine) Road based on the information from a captured soldier from the XX Corps who claimed to have gotten tangled up with some the IV Corps wagons southeast of Adairsville. That soldier was captured along the Ironton (Copper Mine) Road by pickets from Dibrell's Brigade who were patrolling that road. Hood explained that he sought and obtained permission to take his "command across an open field, and attack this detachment of the enemy, *in case the report* was correct" and that Johnston "consented." Subsequently, William Mackall was ordered by Johnston to go to Hood to admonish him that "*if the enemy advanced upon him* to strike him promptly and hard." Both statements indicate that the Confederate high command assumed that a Federal column, possibly Howard's IV Corps, would approach Cassville via Ironton (Copper Mine) Road, and that they would be isolated from the balance of the Northern force.[2]

[2] Hood, *Advance and Retreat*, 99; W. W. Mackall, "Memoranda of the Operations at Cassville on May 19, 1864," *OR*, ser. 1, vol. 38, pt. 3, 622. Clearly, Hood and the Confederates had staked much on the statements from the lone captured Federal.

Had Hood and Polk been able to strike the head of the approaching Federals near Adairsville on 18 May instead of waiting twenty-four hours, it is possible that the Confederates could have achieved some success. On 18 May, Hooker's column was spread out on the northern part of the Adairsville-Cassville Road (Road 1) and a strike by Polk (who now had eight brigades with the addition of French's complete division) up the Adairsville Road and Hood (with twelve brigades) up the Ironton Road could have hit him in rear. Moreover, Schofield had not yet reached Mosteller's Mill, and Howard and Palmer were in the vicinity of Hall Station on the Adairsville-Kingston Road (Road 8). These forces were a half-day's march away from providing any relief to Hooker.

Luck always plays a part in any battle, and in the fog of war, good fortune is perhaps the most important asset. On the morning of 19 May, had Schofield continued down the path to Cassville along the Ironton Road (Road 2) as he had requested, then he could have fallen into the trap being set by Hood. Instead, Sherman's directive to "get up on Hooker" at first light changed Schofield's direction and with it, the course of the battle. A leader can often create his own luck by certain command decisions. Had Sherman not pressed his cavalry commanders for action and aggression, then McCook's troopers from Stewart's Second Brigade might not have ventured so far that morning or been so bold as to strike a column of Confederate infantry over twenty times their size.

In contrast, had Braxton Bragg, in October 1863, ordered General Danville Leadbetter to have his engineers prepare a set of maps twenty or fifteen miles (or even one mile farther) on either side of the Western & Atlantic Railroad, then Major Wilbur F. Foster and his team (that included Andrew H. Buchanan) might have correctly identified and included the Spring Place Road (Road 3) and its juncture with the Pine Log/Fairmount Road (Road 4) at Five Forks. Had Foster's men gone the extra mile, they might have had the Spring Place Road included on their map.

Had the team sent by Major General William T. Martin, who began with the Foster Map and then traveled the countryside to fill in the spaces not covered, picked up the connection of the Spring Place Road with the Pine Log/Fairmount Road at Five Forks, perhaps Johnston would have known that there were five roads that led to Cassville from the north, and not four.

Had Wheeler's mapmaker, who relied on the Martin Map, reconnoitered and surveyed the roads himself, then Wheeler's Map might have included the Spring Place Road. In that event, Wheeler could have accounted for it in his deployment of the Confederate cavalry screen above Cassville.

Then perhaps McCook would not have been able to penetrate so deeply into the flank and rear of the Southern army undetected, and Hood's battle plan might not have been interrupted.

The fortunes of war are made on calculations, risk, and preparation. Prussian military theorist General Carl Von Clausewitz coined the phrase "the fog of war," defining it as being placed in a circumstance of receiving incomplete, uncertain, and often erroneous or misunderstood information, coupled with being saddled with great fear, doubt, and excitement while under the stress of battle. Von Clausewitz believed that rapid decisions by alert commanders were best when facing the fog of war. His theory sharply contrasted that of Frenchman Antoine-Henri Jomini, who believed war could be reduced to science by appropriate calculations. Von Clausewitz argued that war could not be reduced to science or to any degree of mathematical certainty, but that it contained a level of uncertainly that could only be overcome by impulses and exertions of a skilled leader.[3]

Von Clauswitz wrote, "The great uncertainty of all data in war is a peculiar difficulty, because all action must, to a certain extent, be planned in a mere twilight, which in addition not infrequently—like the effect of a fog or moonshine—gives to things exaggerated dimensions and unnatural appearance." The Prussian leader explained that to achieve success on a battlefield when facing the fog of war, a leader must have a combination of three things, which have been translated into English as a combination of "violent emotion, chance, and rational calculation." In modern terms, and often used when describing successful athletic coaches, this is referred to as the "it" factor. For one who has the combination of passion, opportunity, and preparation.

Whether Sherman, and McCook, and Stoneman were lucky or good at Cassville thus becomes a rhetorical question, for they created their fortune by the decisions they made, and they acted with such a "violent emotion" and with such a speed so as to tilt the odds of success in their favor. In contrast, the Confederates, acting in a defensive posture throughout the campaign, struggled to find opportunities to unleash a "violent emotion," except in defense.

Following the Confederate withdrawal overnight, Sherman ordered Schofield and the XXIII Corps to pursue the retreating Confederates as far as the Etowah River and then stop and return to Cassville to join the rest of the Federal armies, who had been given a three-day respite. Schofield's pursuers bagged a considerable number of Southern soldiers who had either given

[3] Von Clausewitz, *On War*, 24.

up or played out the war from the latest retreat. By 20 May, Johnston's army was safely across the Etowah River with only some cavalry units operating on the north bank of the river. The retrograde moves by his forces had cost him at least 869 men lost to capture or desertion between Dalton and Cassville. Contrary to Johnston's subsequent claims that he had only lost 444 men killed and 2,828 wounded for a total loss of 3,272 between 7 May and 20 May,[4] I have compiled losses to date of 736 killed, 3,687 wounded, and 869 missing for a total of 5,292 in two weeks. With additional research, the number confirmed as missing (captured or deserted) will only increase.

In contrast, Sherman lost 1,209 at Dalton, 5,500 at Resaca (653 killed, 3,786 wounded, and 316 missing confirmed so far), about 70 at Rome Crossroads, 149 at Rome, about 200 at Adairsville, and about 200 at Woodlands, Kingston, and Cassville, for a total of about 7,328 between 7 May and 20 May. Ironically, historian Steven Newton estimated that Sherman's losses for this timeframe were 7,308.[5]

More importantly, however, was the effect on the morale of both armies. Johnston's retrogrades were met with Confederate soldiers' increasing disillusionment about the South's chances for winning. While many still hoped for success and continued to have faith in Johnson, others were beginning to become resigned to ultimate defeat. Johnston, in the aftermath, may have wanted desperately to justify his miliary performance in north Georgia, but it

---

[4] As reported by Johnston, using the table supplied by Dr. A. J. Foard. Note that in *OR*, ser. 1, vol. 38, pt. 3, 686–87, Foard reported 441 killed and 2,943 wounded, but in Johnston (*Narrative of Military Operations*, 576), losses were shown at 444 killed and 2,828 wounded. Johnston deducted the wounded of Jackson's cavalry division and never included Wheeler's Cavalry losses under the novel fiction that since cavalry typically operated outside the immediate zone of his control (i.e., the battlefield), cavalry losses were not his responsibility. The discrepancy in the number of killed appears to be from an updated return from Hardee's Corps where three soldiers were moved from the wounded column to the killed column. A complete table (or as near a complete table as the author has been able to compile to date) of casualties among the Confederate forces is included at appendix D.

[5] Figures are based on author's research and calculations. Newton estimated Sherman's losses 6 May–18 July 1864, the date of Johnston's removal from command at 21,925, and one-third of this figure, or 7,308, covers his estimate of Sherman's losses for the first third of this period (Newton, *Lost for the Cause*, 106). The 5,500 estimate of Sherman's losses at Resaca comes from Dave Powell, unpublished manuscript on the Atlanta Campaign and my conversations with him between December 2022 and June 2023.

seems some of his soldiers realized the gravity of the situation. Private J. B. Sanders of Company H, 37th Mississippi, captured both the hope and the despair of many of the Confederate soldiers in Georgia when he wrote to his wife on 13 July 1864, less than a week before Johnston's removal: "I beleave [*sic*] Johns[t]on is doing all in his power to save our c[o]untry," he wrote, "[but] unless the people do turn out and stand by the side of those [w]ho [would fight], we ar[e] a lost and ruin[ed] people."[6]

By the end of May, Sherman's legions would report capturing and turning over to the provost marshal at Chattanooga and Nashville 34 officers and 1,795 men as prisoners and another 610 men as deserters. No doubt, some of these were captured or turned themselves in at various places in north Georgia, north Alabama, or central Tennessee during the month, but most of them were from Johnston's army and resulted from Johnston's fallbacks.[7]

It is clear that the retreats were beginning to have an effect. In a letter to his wife dated 21 May 1864, William Mackall confessed that he feared that Johnston's reputation would be damaged as a result of their failure to strike a blow upon the enemy at Cassville. Lieutenant William Trask, a currier on Hardee's staff, was more direct, recording in his journal, "they [the soldiers] now begin to think Johnston is being outgeneraled and that Sherman is beating him at a game he was thought to be the champion of." And where it mattered most, President Davis and the Richmond authorities were beginning to grow impatient. Following news of the withdrawals from Dalton and Resaca, Davis wrote Johnston curtly, "Your dispatch of 16th received; read with disappointment. I hope the re-enforcements sent will enable you to achieve important results."[8]

Johnston received Davis's telegram at Allatoona on Friday, 20 May, as his army lay along the south bank of the Etowah River. There, they rested, out of harm's way, for the next three days. Soon, a new kind of warfare would erupt twelve miles away at a church named New Hope where five roads met in the Georgia wilderness of Paulding County. In what the soldiers would call the "Hell Hole," the two sides would engage in a constant, sometimes

---

[6] J. B. Sanders to his wife, 13 July 1864.

[7] *OR*, ser. 1, vol. 38, pt. 1, 147.

[8] W. W. Mackall to his wife, 21 May 1864, in W. W. Mackall, Jr., *A Son's Recollections of His Father*, 211 (original Mackall letters located in Special Collections, No. 01299, UNC-Chapel Hill Library); Hafendorfer, *Civil War Journal of William L. Trask*, 144–45; *OR*, ser. 1, vol. 38, pt. 4, 725.

desperate, always stressful struggle in the tangled woods and ravines for ten days with no respite.

Richard McMurry argues convincingly in his new book that Johnston was "the central military figure in the history of the Southern Confederacy, not just of the 1864 operations in North Georgia." McMurry points out that while Robert E. Lee may have been most successful, and while Lee's successes may have lengthened the war by two or three years, it is Johnston and his role in the war that were most consequential. From Virginia in 1861 and 1862, to Mississippi in 1863, and Georgia in 1864, and finally in North Carolina in 1865, Johnston was present in every theater where the action was the greatest and the results most important.[9]

In Georgia, Johnston's "active defensive" strategy would continue to be put to the test. So, too, Sherman's blend of "spirited offensive" and "flanking" strategies would be tested in various places throughout the balance of May and into June, where the pressure for him to force the issue culminated in the resounding defeat at Kennesaw Mountain. Neither side was willing to risk all their forces in a general engagement, however. Richard McMurry called the struggle between Sherman and Johnston in Georgia, "the red-clay minuet."[10] There would be no Shiloh, or Gettysburg, or Chickamauga, or Wilderness, with Johnston and Sherman. And the war in Georgia would go on.

---

[9] McMurry, *Civil Wars of General Joseph E. Johnston*, 1:xiii–xiv.

[10] McMurry, at any lecture or meeting when discussing the Atlanta Campaign.

Appendix A

Confederate Order of Battle from Dalton to Cassville

ARMY OF TENNESSEE
General Joseph E. Johnston
(removed 17 July 1864)
General John Bell Hood
(from 18 July 1864)

Chief of Staff: Brigadier General William W. Mackall
Chief of Artillery: Brigadier General Francis A. Shoup
Chief Engineer: Lt. Colonel Stephen W. Presstman (until 20 July 1864)
Chief Engineer: Major General Martin L. Smith (from 20 July 1864)
Medical Director: Surgeon-Major A. J. Foard
Chief Ordnance Officer: Captain W. D. Humphries

HARDEE'S CORPS
Lieutenant General William J. Hardee

CHEATHAM'S TENNESSEE DIVISION
Brigadier General George E. Maney

Maney's Brigade
Colonel Francis M. Walker

1st & 27th Tennessee, Lt. Col. John L. House
4th Tennessee (Confederate), Lt. Col. Oliver A. Bradshaw
6th & 9th Tennessee, Col. George C. Porter, Lt. Col. John W. Buford
19th Tennessee, Maj. James G. Deaderick
50th Tennessee, Col. Stephen H. Colms

Strahl's Brigade
Brigadier General Otho F. Strahl

4th & 5th Tennessee, Major Henry Hampton
24th Tennessee, Col. John A. Wilson
31st Tennessee, Lt. Col. Fountain E. P. Stafford
33rd Tennessee, Lt. Col. Henry C. McNeill
41st Tennessee, Lt. Col. James D. Tillman

Carter's (Wright's) Brigade
Colonel John C. Carter

8th Tennessee, Col. John H. Anderson
16th Tennessee, Capt. Benjamin Randals
28th Tennessee, Lt. Col. David C. Crook
38th Tennessee, Lt. Col. Andrew D. Gwynne
51st & 52nd Tennessee, Lt. Col. John W. Estes

Magevney's (Vaughan's) Brigade
Colonel Michael Magevney, Jr.

11th Tennessee, Col. George W. Gordon
12th & 47th Tennessee, Col. William M. Watkins
29th Tennessee, Col. Horace Rice
13th & 154th Tennessee, Maj. William J. Crook

CLEBURNE'S DIVISION
Major General Patrick R. Cleburne

Polk's Brigade
Brigadier General Lucius Polk

1st & 15th Arkansas, Lt. Col. William H. Martin
5th Confederate, Col. James C. Cole
2nd Tennessee, William D. Robison
48th Tennessee (Nixon's regiment), Capt. Henry G. Evans

Granbuy's (Smith's) Texas Brigade
Brigadier General Hiram M. Granbury
Brigadier General James A. Smith (wounded 22 July 1864)

6th Texas & 15th Texas Cavalry (dismounted), Col. Robert R. Garland
7th Texas, Capt. T. B. Camp
10th Texas, Col. Roger Q. Mills
17th & 18th Texas Cavalry (dismounted), Capt. George D. Manion
24th & 25th Texas Cavalry (dismounted) Lt. Col. William M. Neyland

Lowrey's Brigade
Brigadier General Mark P. Lowrey

16th Alabama, Lt. Col. Frederick A. Ashford
33rd Alabama, Col. Samuel Adams
45th Alabama, Col. Harris D. Lampley
32nd Mississippi, Col. William H. H. Tison
45th Mississippi, Maj. Elisha F. Nunn

Govan's Arkansas Brigade
Brigadier General Daniel C. Govan

2nd & 24th Arkansas, Col. E. Warfield

5th & 13th Arkansas, Col. John E. Murray
6th & 7th Arkansas, Col. Samuel G. Smith
8th & 19th Arkansas, Col. George F. Baucum
3rd Confederate, Capt. M. H. Dixon

WALKER'S DIVISION
Major General William H. T. Walker

Mercer's Georgia Brigade
Brigadier General Hugh W. Mercer
1st Volunteer Georgia, Col. Charles H. Olmstead
54th Georgia, Lt. Col. Morgan Rawls.
57th Georgia, Lt. Col. Cincinnatus S. Guyton
63rd Georgia, Maj. Joseph V. H. Allen

Gist's Brigade
Brigadier General States Rights Gist
2nd Georgia Battalion Sharpshooters, Maj. Richard H. Whiteley
8th Georgia Battalion, Col. Zachariah L. Watters
46th Georgia, Maj. Samuel J. C. Dunlop
65th Georgia, Capt. William G. Foster
5th Mississippi, Lt. Col. John B. Herring
8th Mississippi, Col. John C. Wilkinson
16th South Carolina, Col. James McCullough
24th South Carolina, Col. Ellison Capers

Stevens's Georgia Brigade
Brigadier General Clement H. Stevens (mortally wounded 20 July 1864)
1st Georgia Battalion Sharpshooters, Maj. Armur Shaaff
1st Georgia (Confederate), Col. George A. Smith
25th Georgia, Col. William J. Winn
29th Georgia, Capt. J. W. Turner
30th Georgia, Lt. Col. James S. Boynton
66th Georgia, Col. J. Cooper Nisbet

BATE'S DIVISION
Major General William B. Bate

Tyler's Brigade
Brigadier General R. C. Tyler
Brigadier General Thomas B. Smith
4th Georgia Battalion Sharpshooters, Maj. Theodore D. Caswell
37th Georgia, Col. Joseph T. Smith

15th & 37th Tennessee, Lt. Col. R. Dudley Frayser
20th Tennessee, Lt. Col. William M. Shy
30th Tennessee, Lt. Col. James J. Turner

Lewis's Kentucky "Orphan Brigade"
Brigadier General Joseph H. Lewis

2nd Kentucky, Col. James W. Moss
4th Kentucky, Lt. Col. Thomas W. Thompson
5th Kentucky, Lt. Col. Hiram Hawkins
6th Kentucky, Col. Martin H. Corer
9th Kentucky, Col. John W. Caldwell

Finley's Florida Brigade
Brigadier General Jesse J. Finley
Lt. Col. Robert Bullock

1st & 4th Florida, Lt. Col. Edward Badger
1st Florida Cavalry (dismounted) & 3rd Florida, Capt. Matthew H. Strain
6th Florida, Lt. Col. Daniel L. Kenan
7th Florida, Lt. Col. Robert Bullock

HOOD'S CORPS
Major General Benjamin F. Cheatham

HINDMAN'S DIVISION
Major General Thomas C. Hindman

Deas's Brigade
Brigadier General Zachariah C. Deas
Colonel John G. Coltart

17th Alabama Battalion Sharpshooters, Capt. James F. Nabers
19th Alabama, Lt. Col. George R. Kimbrough
22nd Alabama, Col. Benjamin R. Hart
25th Alabama, Col. George D. Johnston
39th Alabama, Lt. Col. William C. Clifton
50th Alabama, Capt. George W. Arnold

Tucker's Brigade
Colonel Jacob H. Sharp

9th Mississippi Battalion Sharpshooters, Maj. William C. Richards
7th Mississippi, Col. William H. Bishop
9th Mississippi, Lt. Col. Benjamin F. Johns
10th Mississippi, Lt. Col. George B. Myers
41st Mississippi, Col. J. Byrd Williams

44th Mississippi, Lt. Col. R. G. Kelsey

Manigault's Brigade
Brigadier General Arthur M. Manigault

24th Alabama, Col. Newton N. Davis
28th Alabama, Lt. Col. William L. Butler
34th Alabama, Col. Julius C. B. Mitchell
10th South Carolina, Col. James F. Pressley
19th South Carolina, Maj. James L. White

Walthall's Brigade
Brigadier General Edward C. Walthall

24th & 27th Mississippi, Colonel Samuel Benton, Col. Robert P. McKelvaine
29th & 30th Mississippi, Col. William F. Brantly
34th Mississippi, Capt. T. S. Hubbard

STEVENSON'S DIVISION
Major General Carter L. Stevenson

Brown's Brigade
Brigadier General John C. Brown
Colonel Joseph B. Palmer

3rd Tennessee, Lt. Col. Calvin J. Clack
18th Tennessee, Lt. Col. William R. Butler
26th Tennessee, Col. Richard M. Saffell
32nd Tennessee, Capt. Thomas D. Deavenport
23rd Tennessee Battalion & 45th Tennessee, Col. Anderson Searcy

Reynold's Brigade
Brigadier General Alexander W. Reynolds

58th North Carolina, Capt. Alfred T. Stewart
60th North Carolina, Col. Washington M. Hardy
54th Virginia, Lt. Col. John J. Wade
63rd Virginia, Capt. David O. Rush

Cumming's Brigade
Brigadier General Alfred Cumming

2nd Georgia State Troops, Col. James Wilson
34th Georgia, Maj. John M. Jackson
36th Georgia, Maj. Charles E. Broyles
39th Georgia, Capt. J. W. Cureton
56th Georgia, Col. E. P. Watkins

Pettus's Brigade
Brigadier General Edmund W. Pettus

20th Alabama, Col. James M. Dedman
23rd Alabama, Lt. Col. Joseph B. Bibb
30th Alabama, Col. Charles M. Shelley
31st Alabama, Capt. J. J. Nix
46th Alabama, Capt. George E. Brewer

STEWART'S DIVISION
Major General Alexander P. Stewart

Stovall's Brigade
Brigadier General Marcellus A. Stovall

1st Georgia State Troops, Col. E. M. Galt (wounded)
40th Georgia, Capt. John F, Groover
41st Georgia, Maj. Mark S. Nall
42nd Georgia, Col. Robert J. Henderson
43rd Georgia, Maj. William C. Lester
52nd Georgia, Capt. Rufus R. Asbury

Baker's Brigade
Brigadier General Alpheus Baker

37th Alabama, Lt. Col. Alexander A. Greene
40th Alabama, Col, John H. Higley
42nd Alabama, Capt. R. K. Wells
54th Alabama, Lt. Col. John A. Minter

Gibson's Brigade
Brigadier General Randall L. Gibson

Austin's Louisiana Battalion Sharpshooters, Maj. John E. Austin
1st Louisiana (Regulars), Capt. W. H. Sparks
4th Louisiana Battalion, Maj. Duncan Buie
4th Louisiana (transferred from Quarles's Brigade 17 July 1864), Col. S. E. Hunter
30th Louisiana (transferred from Quarles's Brigade 17 July 1864), Lt. Col. Thomas Shields
13th Louisiana, Lt. Col. Francis L. Campbell
16th & 25th Louisiana, Lt. Col. Robert H. Lindsay
19th Louisiana, Col. Richard W. Turner
20th Louisiana, Col. Leon Von Zinken

Clayton's Brigade
Brigadier General Henry D. Clayton

18th Alabama, Col. James T. Holtzclaw, Lt. Col. Peter F. Hunley

32nd & 58th Alabama, Col. Bushrod Jones
36th Alabama, Lt. Col. Thomas H. Herndon
38th Alabama, Maj. Shep. Ruffin

CAVALRY CORPS
Major General Joseph Wheeler

MARTIN'S DIVISION
Major General William T. Martin

Morgan's Alabama Brigade
Brigadier General John Morgan
Later called Allen's Alabama Brigade
Brigadier General William Wirt Allen
12th Alabama Battalion, Capt. Warren S. Reese
1st Alabama, Lt. Col. D. T. Blakey
3rd Alabama, Col. James Hagan
4th Alabama, Col. Alfred A. Russell
7th Alabama, Capt. George Mason
51st Alabama, Col. M. L. Kirkpatrick

Iverson's Georgia Brigade
Brigadier General Alfred Iverson
1st Georgia, Lt. Col. James H. Strickland
2nd Georgia, Maj. James W. Mayo
3rd Georgia, Col. Robert Thompson
4th Georgia, Maj. Augustus R. Stewart
6th Georgia, Col. John R. Hart

HUMES'S DIVISION
Brigadier General William Y. C. Humes

Ashby's Tennessee Brigade
Colonel Henry M. Ashby
1st (formerly the 6th) Tennessee, Col. James T. Wheeler
2nd Tennessee, Capt. William M. Smith
5th Tennessee, Col. George W. McKenzie
9th Tennessee Battalion, Maj. James H. Akin

Harrison's Brigade
Colonel Thomas H. Harrison
3rd Arkansas, Col. Amson W. Hobson
4th Tennessee, Lt. Col. Paul F. Anderson

8th Texas, Lt. Col. Gustave Cook
11th Texas, Col. George R. Reeves

KELLY'S DIVISION
Brigadier General John H. Kelly

Dibrell's Tennessee Brigade
Colonel George G. Dibrell
4th Tennessee, Col. William S. McLemore
8th Tennessee, Capt. Jefferson Leftwich
9th Tennessee, Capt. James M. Reynolds
10th Tennessee, Maj. John Minor
11th Tennessee (a portion was detached to East Tennessee 11 July 1864), Col. Daniel W. Holman

Williams's Brigade
Brigadier General John S. Williams
1st (Butler's, also called the 3rd) Kentucky, Col. John Russell Butler
2nd Kentucky Battalion, Capt. John Basket Dortch
2nd Kentucky (Woodward's regiment), Maj. Thomas Wilson Lewis
9th Kentucky, Col. William Campbell Preston Breckinridge
Allison's (Tennessee) Squadron, Capt. J. S. Reese
Hamilton's (Tennessee) Battalion, Maj. Joseph Shaw

Allen's Alabama Brigade
Brigadier General William Wirt Allen
Later called Anderson's Brigade
Brigadier General Robert H. Anderson
3rd Confederate, Lt. Col. John McCaskill
8th Confederate, Lt. Col. John S. Prather
10th Confederate, Capt. W. J. Vason
12th Confederate, Capt. Charles H. Conner
5th Georgia, Lt. Col. Edward Bird

Hannon's Alabama Brigade
Colonel Moses W. Hannon
53rd Alabama, Lt. Col. John F. Gaines
24th Alabama Battalion, Maj. Robert B. Snodgrass

ARTILLERY
HARDEE'S CORPS
Col. Melancthon Smith

Hoxton's Battalion (8 Napoleons & 4 12-pounder howitzers)
Major Llewelyn Hoxton

Perry's (Florida) battery, Capt. Thomas J. Perry
Phelan s (Alabama) battery, Lt. Nathaniel Venable
Turner's (Mississippi) battery, Capt. William B. Turner

Martin's Battalion (6 Napoleons & 6 12-pounder howitzers)
Major Robert Martin

Bledsoe's (Missouri) battery, Capt. Hiram M. Bledsoe
Ferguson's (South Carolina) battery, Lt. John A. Alston; Lt. René Beauregard
Howell's (Georgia) battery, Capt. Evan P. Howell

Hotchkiss's Battalion (8 Napoleons & 4 12-pounder howitzers)
Major Thomas R. Hotchkiss

Goldthwaite's (Alabama) battery, Capt. Richard W. Goldthwaite
Key's (Arkansas) battery, Capt Thomas J. Key
Swett's (Mississippi) battery, Lt. H. Shannon

Cobb's Battalion (8 Napoleons & 4 12-pounder howitzers)
Major Robert Cobb

Gracey's (Kentucky) battery, Lt. R. B. Matthews
Mebane's (Tennessee) battery, Lt. J. W. Phillips
Slocomb's (Louisiana) battery, Capt. Cuthbert H. Slocomb

HOOD'S CORPS
Colonel Robert F. Beckham

Courtney's Battalion (4 Napoleons, 4 12-pounder howitzers & 4 3-inch ordnance rifles)
Major Alfred R. Courtney

Dent's (Alabama) battery, Capt. Staunton H. Dent
Douglas's (Texas) battery, Capt. James P. Douglas
Garrity's (Alabama) battery, Lt. Philip Bond

Eldridge's Battalion (6 Napoleons, 2 12-pounder howitzers & 4 3-inch ordnance rifles)
Major John W. Eldridge

Eufaula (Alabama) battery, Capt. McDonald Oliver
Fenner's (Louisiana) battery, Capt. Charles E. Fenner
Stanford's (Mississippi) battery, Lt. James S. McCall

Johnston's Battalion (12 Napoleons)
Captain Maximilien van den Corput

Corput's (Cherokee Georgia) battery, Lt. William S. Hoge
Marshall's (Tennessee) battery, Capt. Lucius G. Marshall
Rowan's (Georgia) battery, Capt. John B. Rowan

WHEELER'S HORSE ARTILLERY

(8 12-pounder howitzers, & 8 3-inch ordnance rifles)
Lieutenant Colonel Felix H. Robertson

Ferrell's (Georgia) battery (one section), Lt. Nathan Davis
Huggins's (Tennessee) battery, Lt. Nat. Baxter
Ramsey's (Tennessee) battery, Lt. D. Breck. Ramsey
White's (Tennessee) battery, Lt. Arthur Pue, Jr.
Wiggins's (Arkansas) battery, Lt. J. Wylie Calloway

ARTILLERY RESERVE

Lieutenant Colonel James H. Hallonquist

Williams's Battalion (4 Napoleons, 4 12-pounder howitzers & 4 3-inch ordnance rifles)
Lieutenant Colonel Samuel C. Williams

Barbour (Alabama) battery, Capt. Reuben F. Kolb
Jefferson (Mississippi) battery, Capt. Putnam Darden
Jeffress's (Virginia) battery, Capt. William C. Jeffress

Palmer's Battalion (8 Napoleons & 4 3-inch ordnance rifles)
Major Joseph Palmer

Lumsden's (Alabama) battery, Capt. Charles L. Lumsden
Anderson's (Georgia) battery, Capt. Ruel W. Anderson
Havis's (Georgia) battery, Capt. Minor W. Havis

Waddell's Battalion (10 12-pounder howitzers, & 2 12-pounder Blakely rifles)
Major James F. Waddell

Barret's (Missouri) battery, Capt. Overton W. Barret
Bellamy's (Alabama) battery, Capt. Richard H. Bellamy
Emery's (Alabama) battery, Capt. Winslow D. Emery

FIRST DIVISION GEORGIA MILITIA[1]

Major General Gustavus W. Smith

1st Brigade
Brigadier General Reuben W. Carswell

1st Regiment, Col. Edward H. Pottle

---

[1] Not present between Dalton and Cassville.

2nd Regiment, Col. James Stapleton
3rd Regiment, Col. Q. M. Hill

2nd Brigade
Brigadier General Pleasant J. Phillips
4th Regiment, Col. James N. Mann
5th Regiment, Col. S. S. Stafford
6th Regiment, Col. J. W. Burney

3rd Brigade
Brigadier General Charles D. Anderson
7th Regiment, Col. Abner Redding
8th Regiment, Col. William B. Scott
9th Regiment, Col. J. M. Hill

4th Brigade
Brigadier General Henry Kent McCay
10th Regiment, Col. C. M. Davis
11th Regiment, Col. William t. Toole
12th Regiment, Col. Richard Sims

ARMY OF MISSISSIPPI
Lieutenant General Leonidas Polk

LORING'S DIVISION
Major General William Wing Loring

Adams's Mississippi Brigade
Brigadier General John Adams

6th Mississippi, Col. Robert Lowry
14th Mississippi, Lt. Col. Washington L. Doss
15th Mississippi, Col. Michael Farrell
20th Mississippi, Col. William N. Brown
23rd Mississippi, Col. Joseph M. Wells
43rd Mississippi, Col. Richard Harrison

Featherston's Mississippi Brigade
Brigadier General Winfield S. Featherston

1st Mississippi Battalion Sharpshooters, Maj. James M. Stigler
3rd Mississippi, Col. Thomas A. Mellon (wounded)
22nd Mississippi, Maj. Martin A. Oatis (wounded)
31st Mississippi, Col. Marcus D. L. Stephens (absent sick), Lt. Col. James Drane (wounded)
33rd Mississippi, Col. Jabez L. Drake (killed)
40th Mississippi, Lt. Col. George P. Wallace (wounded)

Scott's Brigade
Brigadier General Thomas M. Scott

27th, 35th, & 49th Alabama, Col. Samuel S. Ives
55th Alabama, Col. John Snodgrass
57th Alabama, Lt. Col. W. C. Bethune (wounded)
12th Louisiana, Col. Noel L. Nelson

FRENCH'S DIVISION
Major General Samuel G. French
Colonel William H. Young

Ector's Brigade
Brigadier General Mathew D. Ector

29th North Carolina, Lt. Col. Bacchus S. Proffitt
39th North Carolina, Col. David Coleman
9th Texas Cavalry (dismounted), Col. William H. Young
10th Texas Cavalry (dismounted), Col. C. R. Earp
14th Texas Cavalry (dismounted), Col. John L. Camp

32nd Texas Cavalry (dismounted), Col. Julius A. Andrews

Cockrell's Missouri Brigade
Brigadier General Francis M. Cockrell
Colonel Elijah Gates

1st Missouri Cavalry & 3rd Missouri Bttn. Cavalry (dismounted), Lt. Col. D. Todd Samuel
1st & 4th Missouri, Lt. Col. Hugh A. Garland
2nd & 6th Missouri, Col. Peter C. Flournoy
3rd & 5th Missouri, Col. James McCown

Sears's Mississippi Brigade
Brigadier General Claudius W. Sears
Colonel William S. Barry

7th Mississippi Battalion, Lt. A. J. Farmer
4th Mississippi, Col. Thomas N. Adaire
35th Mississippi, Lt. Col. Reuben H. Shotwell
36th Mississippi, Col. William W. Witherspoon
39th Mississippi, Maj. R. J. Durr
46th Mississippi, Col. William H. Clark

CANTEY'S DIVISION
Brigadier General James Cantey

Quarles's Brigade[2]
Brigadier General William A. Quarles

1st Alabama, Maj. Samuel L. Knox
42nd Tennessee, Col. Isaac N. Hulme
46th & 55th Tennessee, Col. Robert A. Owens
48th Tennessee, Lt. Col. Aaron S. Godwin
49th Tennessee, Col. William F. Young
53rd Tennessee, Col. John R. White

Cantey's Brigade
Colonel Virgil S. Murphey

17th Alabama, Col. Virgil S. Murphey
26th Alabama, Maj. David F. Bryan
29th Alabama, Col. John F. Conoley
37th Mississippi, Col. Orlando S. Holland

Reynolds's Arkansas Brigade

[2] Arrived after 25 May 1864 at New Hope Church.

Brigadier General Daniel H. Reynolds

1st Arkansas, Col. Lee M. Ramsaur
2nd Arkansas, Col. James A. Williamson
4th & 31st Arkansas, Col. Henry G. Bunn
9th Arkansas, Col. Isaac L. Dunlop
25th Arkansas, Col. Charles J. Turnbull

ARMY OF MISSISSIPPI (STEWART'S) CAVALRY CORPS
Brigadier General William H. (Red) Jackson

Armstrong's Mississippi Brigade
Brigadier General Frank C. Armstrong

1st Mississippi, Col. R. A. Pinson
2nd Mississippi, Maj. John J. Perry
28th Mississippi, Col. Peter B. Starke
Ballentine's Mississippi Regiment, Lt. Col. William L. Maxwell

Ross's Texas Brigade
Brigadier General Lawrence S. Ross

1st Texas Legion, Col. Edwin R. Hawkins
3rd Texas, Lt. Col. Jiles S. Boggess
6th Texas, Lt. Col. Peter F. Ross
9th Texas, Col. Dudley W. Jones

Ferguson's Brigade
Brigadier General Samuel W. Ferguson

2nd Alabama, Lt. Col. John N. Carpenter
56th Alabama, Col. William Boyles
12th Mississippi Battalion, Col. William M. Inge
Miller's (Mississippi) regiment, Col. Horace H. Miller
Perrin's (Mississippi) regiment, Col. Robert O. Perrin
Scout Company (Mississippi Cavalry), Capt. Thomas C. Flournoy

ARMY OF MISSISSIPPI (STEWART'S) ARTILLERY
Lieutenant Colonel Samuel C. Williams

Myrick's Battalion (12 Napoleons)
Major John D. Myrick

Barry's (Tennessee) battery, Capt. Robert L. Barry
Bouanchaud's (Louisiana) battery, Capt. Alcide Bouanchaud
Cowan's (Mississippi) battery, Capt. James J. Cowan

Preston's Battalion (12 Napoleons)

Major William C. Preston (killed)
Selden's (Alabama) battery, Lt. Charles W. Lovelace (wounded)
Tarrant's (Alabama) battery, Lt. Seth Shepard
Yates's (Mississippi) battery, Capt. James H. Yates

Storrs's Battalion (10 Napoleons & 2 3-inch ordnance rifles)
Major George S. Storrs
Guibor's (Missouri) battery, Lt. Aaron W. Harris
Hoskins's (Mississippi) battery, Capt. James A. Hoskins
Ward's (Alabama) battery, Capt. John J. Ward

JACKSON'S HORSE ARTILLERY
Waties's Battalion (8 3-inch ordnance rifles)
Captain John Waties
Croft's (Georgia) battery, Capt. Edward Croft
King's Missouri) battery, Capt. Houston King
Waties's (South Carolina) battery, Lt. R. B. Waddell

Appendix B

Federal Order of Battle from Dalton to Cassville

Major General William T. Sherman, Commanding
Headquarters Guard: 7th Company Ohio Sharpshooters, Lt. William McCrory
Artillery: Brigadier General William F. Barry, Chief of Artillery

ARMY OF THE CUMBERLAND
Major General George H. Thomas
Escort: Company I, 1st Ohio Cavalry, Lt. Henry C. Reppert
Artillery: Brigadier General John M. Brannan, Chief of Artillery

IV ARMY CORPS
Major General Oliver O. Howard

FIRST DIVISION
Major General David S. Stanley

First Brigade
Colonel Isaac M. Kirby

21st Illinois, Maj. James E. Calloway, Capt. William H. Jamison
38th Illinois, Lt. Col. William T. Chapman
31st Indiana, Col. John T. Smith
81st Indiana, Lt. Col. William C. Wheeler
1st Kentucky, Col. David A. Enyart
2d Kentucky, Lt. Col. John R. Hurd
90th Ohio, Lt. Col. Samuel N. Yeoman
101st Ohio, Col. Isaac M. Kirby, Lt. Col. Bedan B. Mc Danald

Second Brigade
Colonel Jacob E. Taylor

59th Illinois, Col. P. Sidney Post
96th Illinois, Col. Thomas E. Champion, Maj. George Hicks
115th Illinois, Col. Jesse H. Moore
35th Indiana, Maj. John P. Dufficy, Capt. James A. Gavisk, Lt. Col. Augustus G. Tassin
84th Indiana, Lt. Col. Andrew J. Neff, Capt. John C. Taylor
21st Kentucky, Col. Samuel W. Price, Lt. Col. James C. Evans
23d Kentucky, Lt. Col. George W. Northup

40th Ohio, Col. Jacob E. Taylor, Capt. Charles G. Matchett, Capt. Milton Kemper
45th Ohio, Col. Benjamin P. Runkle, Lt. Col. Charles H. Butterfield, Capt. John H. Humphrey
51st Ohio, Lt. Col. Charles H. Wood, Col. Richard W. McClain
99th Ohio, Lt. Col. John E. Cummins, Capt. James A. Bope

Third Brigade
Colonel P. Sidney Post

59th Illinois, Col. P. Sidney Post, Lt. Col. Clayton Hale
75th Illinois, Col. John E. Bennett, Lt. Col. William M. Kilgour
80th Illinois, Lt. Col. William M. Kilgour, Maj. James M. Stookey
84th Illinois, Col. Louis H. Waters
9th Indiana, Col. Isaac C. B. Suman
30th Indiana, Lt. Col. Orrin D. Hurd, Capt. William Dawson
36th Indiana, Lt. Col. Oliver H. P. Carey
84th Indiana, Capt. John C. Taylor, Capt. Martin B. Miller
77th Pennsylvania, Capt. Joseph J. Lawson, Col. Thomas E. Rose

Artillery
Captain Theodore S. Thomasson

Indiana Light 5th Battery, Capt. Alfred Morrison
Pennsylvania Light, Battery B, Capt. Samuel M. McDowell, Capt. Jacob Ziegler

SECOND DIVISION
Brigadier General John Newton

First Brigade
Brigadier General Nathan Kimball

36th Illinois, Col. Silas Miller, Capt. James B. Mc Neal, Lt. Col. Porter C. Olson
44th Illinois, Col. Wallace W. Barrett, Lt. Col. John Russell, Maj. Luther M. Sabin, Lt. Col. John Russell
73d Illinois, Maj. Thomas W. Motherspaw
74th Illinois, Col. Jason Marsh, Lt. Col. James B. Kerr, Capt. Thomas J. Bryan
88th Illinois, Lt. Col. George W. Smith
28th Kentucky, Lt. Col. J. Rowan Boone
2d Missouri, Lt. Col. Arnold Beck, Col. Bernard Laiboldt (stationed at Dalton, Ga.)
5th Missouri, Col. Joseph Conrad
24th Wisconsin, Maj. Arthur MacArthur, Jr.

Second Brigade
Brigadier General George D. Wagner (sick 10–25 July)
Colonel John W. Blake

100th Illinois, Maj. Charles M. Hammond
40th Indiana, Col. John W. Blake,
57th Indiana, Lt. Col. Willis Blanch
28th Kentucky, Lt. Col. J. Rowan Boone, Maj. George W. Barth
26th Ohio, Lt. Col. William H. Squires
97th Ohio, Col. John Q. Lane

Third Brigade
Brigadier General Luther P. Bradley

27th Illinois, Lt. Col. William A. Schmitt
42d Illinois, Lt. Col. Edgar D. Swain, Capt. Jared W. Richards, Maj, Frederick A. Atwater
51st Illinois, Capt. Theodore F. Brown, Capt. Albert M. Tilton
79th Illinois, Lt. Col. Henry E. Rives, Maj. Terrence Clark, Capt. Oliver O. Bagley
3d Kentucky, Col. Henry C. Dunlap, Capt. John W. Tuttle
64th Ohio, Lt. Col. Robert C. Brown, Maj. Samuel L. Coulter
65th Ohio, Lt. Col. Horatio N. Whirbeck, Capt. Charles O. Tannehill, Maj. Orlow Smith
125th Ohio, Col. Emerson Opdycke, Lt. Col. David H. Moore

Artillery
Captain Wilbur F. Goodspeed

1st Illinois Light, Battery M, Capt. George W. Spencer
1st Ohio Light, Battery A, Lt. Charles W. Scovill

THIRD DIVISION
Brigadier General Thomas J. Wood

First Brigade
Colonel William Gibson
Colonel Richard H. Nodine

25th Illinois, Col. Richard H. Nodine
35th Illinois, Lt. Col. William P. Chandler
89th Illinois, Col. Charles T. Hotchkiss, Lt. Col. William D. Williams
32d Indiana, Col. Frank Erdelmeyer
8th Kansas, Col. John A. Martin, Lt. Col. James M. Graham
15th Ohio, Col. William Wallace, Lt. Col. Frank Askew
49th Ohio, Col. William H. Gibson, Lt. Col. Samuel F. Gray
15th Wisconsin, Maj. George Wilson, Lt. Col. Ole C. Johnson

Second Brigade
Brigadier General William B. Hazen

59th Illinois, Capt. Samuel West

6th Indiana, Lt. Col. Calvin D. Campbell
5th Kentucky, Col. William W. Berry
6th Kentucky, Maj. Richard T. Whitaker, Capt. Isaac N. Johnston
23d Kentucky, Lt. Col. James C. Foy, Maj. George W. Northup
1st Ohio, Maj. Joab A. Stafford (guarded Western & Atlantic Railroad)
6th Ohio, Col. Nicholas L. Anderson (guarded Western & Atlantic Railroad)
41st Ohio, Lt. Col. Robert L. Kimberly
71st Ohio, Col. Henry K. McConnell
93d Ohio, Lt. Col. Daniel Bowman
124th Ohio, Col. Oliver H. Payne, Lt. Col. James Pickands

Third Brigade
Colonel Frederick Knefler

79th Indiana, Col. Frederick Knefler, Lt. Col. Samuel P. Oyler, Maj. George W. Parker
86th Indiana, Col. George F. Dick
9th Kentucky, Col. George H. Cram
17th Kentucky, Col. Alexander M. Stout
13th Ohio, Col. Dwight Jarvis, Jr., Maj. Joseph T. Snider
19th Ohio, Col. Charles F. Manderson, Lt. Col. Henry G. Stratton
59th Ohio, Capt. Charles A. Sheafe, Capt. John L. Watson, Capt. Robert H. Higgins

Artillery
Captain Cullen Bradley

Bridges Illinois Lt. Battery, Capt. Lyman Bridges, Lt. Morris D. Temple, Lt. Lyman A. White
Ohio Light, 6th Battery, Lt. Oliver H. P. Ayres, Lt. Lorenzo D. Immell

ARTILLERY BRIGADE
Major Thomas W. Osborn
Captain Lyman Bridges

XIV ARMY CORPS
Major General John M. Palmer

FIRST DIVISION
Brigadier General Richard W. Johnson

Provost Guard: 16th United States, Company D, 1st Battalion, Capt. Charles F. Trowbridge

First Brigade
Colonel Anson G. McCook

104th Illinois, Lt. Col. Douglas Hapeman, Capt. James H. Masters, Capt. Gideon R. Kellams
88th Indiana, Lt. Col. Cyrus E. Briant
15th Kentucky, Col. Marion C. Taylor, Lt. Col. William G. Halpin
2nd Ohio, Capt. James F. Sarratt
33d Ohio, Lt. Col. James H. M. Montgomery, Capt. Thaddeus A. Minshall
94th Ohio, Lt. Col. Rue P. Hutchins
10th Wisconsin Capt. Jacob W. Roby
21st Wisconsin, Lt. Col. Harrison C. Hobart, Maj. Michael H. Fitch

Second Brigade
Brigadier General John H. King

11th Michigan, Col. William L. Stoughton, Capt. Patrick H. Keegan
69th Ohio, Col. Marshall F. Moore, Lt. Col. Joseph H. Brigham, Capt. Lewis E. Hicks
15th US (9 Cos. 1st & 3rd battalions), Maj. Albert Tracy, Capt. Albert B. Dod
15th US (6 Cos. 2nd Battalion), Maj. John R. Edie, Capt. William S. McManus
16th US (4 Cos. 1st Battalion), Capt. Alexander H. Stanton, Capt. Ebenezer Gay
16th US (4 Cos. 2nd Battalion), Capt. Robert P. Barry
8th US (8 Cos. 1st & 3rd battalions), Capt. George W. Smith, Capt. Lyman M. Kellogg
18th US (2nd Battalion), Capt. William J. Fetterman
19th US (1st Bttn. and Co. A, 2nd Bttn.), Capt. James Mooney, Capt. Lewis Wilson

Third Brigade
Colonel Marshall F. Moore

37th Indiana, Lt. Col. William D. Ward, Maj. Thomas V. Kimble
38th Indiana, Lt. Col. Daniel F. Griffin
21st Ohio, Col. James M. Neibling, Lt. Col. Arnold McMahan
74th Ohio, Col. Josiah Given, Maj. Joseph Fisher
78th Pennsylvania, Col. William Sirwell
79th Pennsylvania, Maj. Michael H. Locher, Capt. John S. McBride
1st Wisconsin, Lt. Col. George B. Bingham

Artillery
Capt. Lucius H. Drury

1st Illinois Light, Battery C, Capt. Mark H. Prescott
1st Ohio Light, Battery I, Capt. Hubert Dilger

SECOND DIVISION
Brigadier General Jefferson C. Davis

First Brigade
Brigadier General James D. Morgan
10th Illinois, Col. John Tillson
16th Illinois, Col. Robert F. Smith, Lt. Col. James B. Cahill
60th Illinois, Col. William B. Anderson
10th Michigan, Col. Charles M. Lure, Maj. Henry S. Burnett, Capt. William H. Dunphy
14th Michigan, Col. Henry R. Mizner
17th New York, Col. William T. C. Grower, Maj. Joel O. Martin (regiment joined Aug. 21st)

Second Brigade
Colonel John G. Mitchell
34th Illinois, Lt. Col. Oscar Van Tassell
78th Illinois, Col. Carter Van Vleck, Lt. Col. Maris R. Vernon
98th Ohio, Lt. Col. John S. Pearce, Capt. John A. Norris, Capt. David E. Roatch
108th Ohio, Lt. Col. Joseph Good (guarded Western & Atlantic Railroad)
113th Ohio, Lt. Col. Darius B. Warner, Maj. Lyne S. Sullivant, Capt. Toland Jones
121st Ohio, Col. Henry B. Banning

Third Brigade
Col. Caleb J. Dilworth
85th Illinois, Maj. Robert G. Rider, Capt. James R. Griffith
86th Illinois, Lt. Col. Allen L. Fahnestock, Maj. Joseph F. Thomas
110th Illinois, Lt. Col. E. Hibbard Topping
125th Illinois, Lt. Col. James W. Langley
22d Indiana, Maj. Thomas Shea, Capt. William H. Taggart, Capt. William H. Snodgrass
52d Ohio, Lt. Col. Charles W. Clancy (captured 19 July at Moore's Mill), Maj. James T. Holmes

Artillery
Captain Charles M. Barnett
2nd Illinois Light, Battery I, Lt. Alonzo W. Coe
Wisconsin Light, 5th Battery, Capt. George Q. Gardner, Lt. Joseph Mc Knight

THIRD DIVISION
Brigadier General Absalom Baird

First Brigade
Brigadier General John B. Turchin (sick from 15 July)
Colonel Moses B. Walker

19th Illinois, Lt. Col. Alexander W. Raffen (regiment mustered out of service 9 June)
24th Illinois, Capt. August Mauff (regiment mustered out of service 28 June)
82d Indiana, Col. Morton C. Hunter
23d Missouri, Col. William P. Robinson
11th Ohio, Lt. Col. Ogden Street (regiment mustered out of service 10 June)
17th Ohio, Col. Durbin Ward
31st Ohio, Col. Moses B. Walker, Lt. Col. Frederick W. Lister
89th Ohio, Maj. John H. Jolly, Col. Caleb H. Carlton
92d Ohio, Col. Benjamin D. Fearing

Second Brigade
Colonel Newell Gleason

75th Indiana, Lt. Col. William O'Brien (wounded 20 July at Peach Tree), Maj. Cyrus J. McCole
87th Indiana, Lt. Col. Edwin P. Hammond
101st Indiana, Lt. Col. Thomas Doan
2d Minnesota, Col. James George, Lt. Col. Judson W. Bishop
9th Ohio, Col. Gustave Kammerling (regiment mustered out of service 22 May)
35th Ohio, Maj. Joseph L. Budd.
105th Ohio, Lt. Col. George T. Perkins

Third Brigade
Colonel George P. Este

10th Indiana, Lt. Col. Marsh B. Taylor
74th Indiana, Lt. Col. Myron Baker (killed 5 August at Utoy Creek), Maj. Thomas Morgan
10th Kentucky, Col. William H. Hays
18th Kentucky, Lt. Col. Hubbard K. Milward (stationed at Ringgold, Georgia)
14th Ohio, Maj. John W. Wilson (wounded 1 September at Jonesboro), Capt. George W. Kirk
38th Ohio, Col. William A. Choate, Capt. Joseph Wagstaff

Artillery
Captain George Estep

Indiana Light, 7th Battery, Capt. Otho H. Morgan
Indiana Light, 19th Battery, Lt. William P. Stackhouse

Artillery Brigade
Major Charles Houghtaling

Reserve Artillery: Indiana Light, 20th Battery, Capt. Milton A. Osborne

XX ARMY CORPS

Major General Joseph Hooker
Escort: 15th Illinois Cavalry, Company K, Capt. William Duncan

FIRST DIVISION
Brigadier General Alpheus S. Williams

First Brigade
Brigadier General Joseph F. Knipe
Colonel Warren W. Packer (commanded 3–17 July and 28 July–28 August)

5th Conn., Col. Warren W. Packer, Lt. Col. Henry W. Daboll, Maj. William S. Cogswell
3d Maryland (detachment), Lt. David Gove (Gore?), Lt. Donald Reid
123d New York, Lt. Col. James C. Rogers
141st New York, Col. William K. Logie (killed 20 July at Peach Tree), Lt. Col. Andrew J. McNett
46th Pennsylvania, Col. James L. Selfridge

Second Brigade
Brigadier General Thomas H. Ruger

27th Indiana, Col. Silas Colgrove (wounded 20 July at Peach Tree), Lt. Col. John R. Fesler
2d Massachusetts, Col. William Cogswell, Lt. Col. Charles F. Morse
13th New Jersey, Col. Ezra A. Carman
107th New York, Col. Nirom M. Crane
150th New York, Col. John H. Ketcham
3d Wisconsin, Col. William Hawley

Third Brigade
Colonel James S. Robinson (sick from 24 July)
Colonel Horace Boughton

82d Illinois, Lt. Col. Edward S. Salomon
101st Illinois, Lt. Col. John B. LeSage
45th New York, Col. Adolphus Dobke (sent to Nashville 6 July)
143d New York, Col. Horace Boughton, Lt. Col. Hezekiah Watkins, Maj. John Higgins
61st Ohio, Col. Stephen J. McGroarty (wounded 20 July at Peach Tree), Capt. John Garrett
82d Ohio, Lt. Col. David Thomson
31st Wisconsin, Col. Francis H. West (regiment joined brigade 21 July)

Artillery
Captain John D. Woodbury

1st New York Light, Battery I, Lt. Charles E. Winegar

1st New York Light, Battery M, Capt. John D. Woodbury

SECOND DIVISION
Brigadier General John W. Geary

First Brigade
Colonel Charles Candy

5th Ohio, Lt. Col. Robert L. Kilpatrick, Maj. Henry E. Symmes, Capt. Robert Kirkup
7th Ohio, Lt. Col. Samuel McClelland (mustered out 11 June)
29th Ohio, Col. William T. Fitch, Capt. Myron T. Wright, Capt. Wilbur F. Stevens
66th Ohio, Lt. Col. Eugene Powell, Capt. Thomas McConnell
28th Pennsylvania, Lt. Col. John Flynn
147th Pennsylvania, Col. Ario Pardee, Jr., Lt. Col. John Craig

Second Brigade
Colonel Patrick H. Jones

33d New Jersey, Col. George W. Mindil, Lt. Col. Enos Fourat, Capt. Thomas O'Connor
119th New York, Col. John T. Lockman, Capt. Charles H. Odell, Capt. Chester H. Southworth
134th New York, Lt. Col. Allan H. Jackson (wounded 20 July Peachtree), Capt. Clinton C. Brown
154th New York, Lt. Col. Daniel B. Allen, Maj. Lewis D. Warner
27th Pennsylvania, Lt. Col. August Riedt (mustered out 23 May)
73d Pennsylvania, Maj. Charles C. Cresson (wounded 15 June at Pine Mountain)
109th Pennsylvania, Capt. Frederick L. Gimber (wounded), Capt. Walter G. Dunn, Capt. Hugh Alexander

Third Brigade
Colonel David Ireland
(wounded 15 May at Resaca, returned to command 2 June)

60th New York, Col. Abel Godard, Capt. Thomas Elliott
78th New York, Lt. Col. Harvey S. Chatfield, Col. Herbert von Hammerstein
102d New York, Col. James C. Lane, Maj. Lewis R. Stegman, Capt. Barent Van Buren
137th New York, Lt. Col. Koert S. Van Voorhis
149th New York, Col. Henry A Barnum
29th Pennsylvania, Lt. Col. Thomas M. Walker, Maj. Jesse R. Millison
111th Pennsylvania, Col. George A. Cobham, Jr. (killed 20 July), Lt. Col. Thomas M. Walker

Artillery
Captain Charles C. Aleshire
13th New York Light Battery, Lt. Henry Bundy
Pennsylvania Light, Battery E, Capt. James D. McGill (resigned 8 July), Lt. Thomas S. Sloan

THIRD DIVISION
Brigadier General William T. Ward

First Brigade
Colonel Benjamin Harrison
102d Illinois, Col. Franklin C. Smith (wounded 16 June Gilgal Church), Lt. Col. James M. Mannon
105th Illinois, Col. Daniel Dustin, Lt. Col. Everell F. Dutton
129th Illinois, Col. Henry Case
70th Indiana, Lt. Col. Samuel Merrill
79th Ohio, Col. Henry G. Kennett, Lt. Col. Azariah W. Doan, Capt. Samuel A. West

Second Brigade
Colonel John Coburn
33rd Indiana, Maj. Levin T. Miller (wounded 2 June at Mars Hill) Capt. Edward T. McCrea
85th Indiana, Col. John P. Baird (replaced 17 July), Lt. Col. Alexander B. Crane
19th Michigan, Maj. Eli A. Griffin, Capt. John J. Baker, Capt. David Anderson
22d Wisconsin, Col. William L. Utley, Lt. Col. Edward Bloodgood

Third Brigade
Colonel James Wood, Jr.
20th Connecticut, Col. Samuel Ross (replaced 16 July), Lt. Col. Philo B. Buckingham
33d Massachusetts, Lt. Col. Godfrey Rider, Jr.
136th New York, Lt. Col. Lester B. Faulkner, Maj. Henry L. Arnold
55th Ohio, Lt. Col. Edwin H. Powers, Capt. Charles P. Wickham
73d Ohio, Maj. Samuel H. Hurst (wounded 15 May at Resaca)
26th Wisconsin, Lt. Col. Frederick C. Winkler

Artillery
Captain Marco B. Gary
1st Michigan Light, Battery I, Capt. Luther R. Smith
1st Ohio Light, Battery C, Lt. Jerome B. Stephens

Reserve Artillery Brigade

Major John A. Reynolds
5th United States, Battery K, Capt. Edmund C. Bainbridge

Reserve Brigade
Colonel Heber Le Favour

10th Ohio, Col. Joseph W. Burke (mustered out 27 May)
9th Michigan, Lt. Col. William Wilkinson
22d Michigan Lt. Col. Henry S. Dean (joined 31 May)

Pontoniers
Colonel George P. Buell

58th Indiana, Lt. Col. Joseph Moore
Pontoon Battalion, Capt. Patrick O'Connell (battalion sent to Chattanooga 17 June)

Siege Artillery

11th Indiana Battery, Capt. Arnold Sutermeister

Ammunition Train Guard

1st Battalion Ohio Sharpshooters, Capt. Gershom M. Barber

ARMY OF THE TENNESSEE
Major General James B. McPherson (killed 22 July at Atlanta)
Escort: 4th Company Ohio Cavalry, Capt. John S. Foster, Capt. John L. King
1st Ohio Cavalry, Company B, Capt. George F. Conn

XV ARMY CORPS
Major General John A. Logan

FIRST DIVISION
Brig. Gen. Peter J. Osterhaus (sick 15 July–15 August)
Brigadier General Charles R. Woods

First Brigade
Brigadier General Charles R. Woods
Colonel Milo Smith

26th Iowa, Col. Milo Smith, Lt. Col. Thomas G. Ferreby
30th Iowa, Lt. Col. Aurelius Roberts
27th Missouri, Col. Thomas Curly, Maj. Dennis O'Connor
76th Ohio, Col. William B. Woods

Second Brigade
Colonel James A. Williamson

4th Iowa, Lt. Col. Samuel D. Nichols, Capt. Randolph Sry
9th Iowa, Col. David Carskaddon, Maj. George Granger
25th Iowa, Col. George A. Stone
31st Iowa, Col. William Smyth

Third Brigade
Colonel Hugo Wangelin

3d Missouri, Col. Theodore Meumann
12th Missouri, Lt. Col. Jacob Kaercher, Maj. Frederick T. Ledergerber
17th Missouri, Maj. Francis Romer
29th Missouri, Lt. Col. Joseph S. Gage, Maj. Philip H. Murphy
31st Missouri, Lt. Col. Samuel P. Simpson, Maj. Frederick Jaensch
32d Missouri, Capt. Charles C. Bland, Maj. Abraham J. Seay

Artillery
Major Clemens Landgraeber

2d Missouri Light, Battery F, Capt. Louis Voelkner, Lt. Lewis A. Winn
Ohio Light, 4th Battery, Capt. George Froehlich, Lt. Louis Zimmerer

SECOND DIVISION
Brigadier General Morgan L. Smith

First Brigade
Brigadier General Giles A. Smith (transferred to XVII Corps 20 July)
Colonel James S. Martin

55th Illinois, Lt. Col. Theodore C. Chandler, Capt. Jacob M. Augustin, Capt. Francis H. Shaw
111th Illinois, Col. James S. Martin, Maj. William M. Mabry
116th Illinois, Capt. John S. Windsor
127th Illinois, Lt. Col Frank S. Curtiss, Capt. Alexander C. Little, Capt. Charles Schryver
6th Missouri, Lt. Col. Delos Van Deusen
8th Missouri, Lt. Col. David C. Coleman (mustered out 16 and 25 June)
30th Ohio, Lt. Col. George H. Hildt
57th Ohio, Lt. Col. Samuel R. Mott

Second Brigade
Brigadier General Joseph A. J. Lightburn

111th Illinois, Col. James S. Martin
83d Indiana, Col. Benjamin J. Spooner (wounded 27 June at Kennesaw), Capt. George H. Scott
30th Ohio, Col. Theodore Jones
37th Ohio, Lt. Col. Louis von Blessingh (sick from 23 May), Maj. Charles Hipp

47th Ohio, Col. Augustus C. Parry (wounded 27 June at Kennesaw), Lt. Col. John Wallace
53d Ohio, Col. Wells S. Jones, Lt. Col. Robert A. Fulton
54th Ohio, Lt. Col. Robert Williams, Jr., Maj. Israel T. Moore

Artillery
Captain Francis De Gress (commanded from 12 July)
1st Illinois Light, Battery A, Capt. Peter P. Wood, Lt. George McCagg Jr., Lt. Samuel S. Smyth
1st Illinois Light, Battery B, Capt. Israel P. Rumsey (consolidated with Battery A, 12 July)
1st Illinois Light, Battery H, Capt. Francis De Gress

THIRD DIVISION[3]
Brigadier General John E. Smith
Escort: 4th Missouri Cavalry, Company F, Lt. Alexander Mueller

First Brigade
Colonel Jesse I. Alexander
Colonel Joseph B. Mc Cown
63d Illinois, Col. Joseph B. Mc Cown, Lt. Col. James Isaminger
48th Indiana, Lt. Col. Edward J. Wood
59th Indiana, Lt. Col. Jefferson K. Scott
4th Minnesota, Lt. Col. John E. Tourtellotte, Maj. James C. Edson
18th Wisconsin, Lt. Col. Charles H. Jackson

Second Brigade
Colonel Green B. Raum
13th Illinois (detachment), Lt. Mark M. Evans
56th Illinois, Lt. Col. John P. Hall
17th Iowa, Col. Clark R. Wever
10th Missouri, Col. Francis C. Deimling, Capt. Joel W. Strong
24th Missouri, Company E, Lt. Daniel Driscoll
80th Ohio, Lt. Col. Pren Metham

Third Brigade
Brigadier General Charles L. Mattheis
Colonel Benjamin D. Dean
Colonel Jabez Banbury
93d Illinois, Lt. Col. Nicholas C. Buswell, Maj. James M. Fisher
5th Iowa, Col. Jabez Banbury, Lt. Col. Ezekiel S. Sampson

---

[3] Guarded railroad at Cartersville.

10th Iowa, Lt. Col. Paris P. Henderson, Lt. David H. Emry
26th Missouri, Lt. Col. John McFall, Col. Benjamin D. Dean

Artillery
Captain Henry Dillon
Wisconsin Light, 6th Battery, Lt. Samuel F. Clark, Lt. James G. Simpson
Wisconsin Light, 12th Battery, Capt. William Zickerick

Cavalry
5th Ohio, Col. Thomas T. Heath

FOURTH DIVISION
Brigadier General William Harrow

First Brigade
Colonel Reuben Williams
26th Illinois, Lt. Col. Robert A. Gillmore
90th Illinois, Lt. Col. Owen Stuart, Capt. Daniel O'Connor
12th Indiana, Lt. Col. James Goodnow, Col. Reuben Williams
100th Indiana, Lt. Col. Albert Heath

Second Brigade
Brigadier General Charles C. Walcutt
40th Illinois, Maj. Hiram W. Hall (regiment joined 3 June)
103d Illinois, Lt. Col. George W. Wright (wounded 27 June at Kennesaw), Capt. Franklin C. Post
97th Indiana, Col. Robert F. Catterson (sick from 25 June), Lt. Col. Aden G. Cavins
6th Iowa, Lt. Col. Alexander J. Miller (wounded 28 May at Dallas), Maj. Thomas J. Ennis
46th Ohio, Capt. Joshua W. Heath (killed 22 July at Atlanta), Lt. Col. Isaac N. Alexander

Third Brigade
Colonel John M. Oliver
48th Illinois, Col. Lucien Greathouse (killed 22 July at Atlanta), Maj. Edward Adams
99th Indiana, Col. Alexander Fowler (on leave from 26 July), Lt. Col. John M. Berkey
15th Michigan, Lt. Col. Austin E. Jaquith (disabled 5 June), Lt. Col. Frederick S. Hutchinson
70th Ohio, Maj. William B. Brown (killed 3 August), Capt. Louis Love, Capt. Henry L. Philips

Artillery
Major John T. Cheney
Captain Henry H. Griffiths
Captain Josiah H. Burton

1st Illinois Lt., Battery F, Capt. Josiah H. Burton, Lt. Jefferson F. Whaley, Lt. George P. Cunningham
Iowa Lt., 1st Battery, Lt. William H. Gay, Capt. Henry H. Griffiths

XVI ARMY CORPS (LEFT WING)
Major General Grenville M. Dodge
Brigadier General Thomas E.G. Ransom

Escort: 1st Alabama Cavalry, Lt. Col. George L. Godfrey., Col. George E. Spencer
52d Illinois, Company A, Capt. George E. Young

SECOND DIVISION
Brigadier General Thomas W. Sweeny (relieved 25 July)
Brigadier General John M. Corse

First Brigade
Brigadier General Elliott W. Rice

52d Illinois, Lt. Col. Edwin A. Bowen
66th Indiana, Lt. Col. Roger Martin (sick July 23), Maj. Thomas G. Morrison, Capt. Alfred Morris
2d Iowa, Lt. Col. Noel B. Howard (wounded 22 July), Maj. Mathew G. Hamill
7th Iowa, Lt. Col. James C. Parrott, Maj. James W. McMullin, Capt. Samuel Mahon

Second Brigade
Colonel Patrick E. Burke (wounded 16 May Rome)
Lieutenant Colonel Robert N. Adams (commanded 16–23 May)
Colonel August Mersy (commanded 23 May–24 July)
Colonel Robert N. Adams (commanded from 24 July)

9th Illinois Mounted, Lt. Col. Jesse J. Phillips (wounded 9 May at Snake Creek Gap), Maj. John H. Kuhn
12th Illinois, Maj. James R. Hugunin, Lt. Col. Henry Van Sellar
66th Illinois, Maj. Andrew K. Campbell, Capt. William S. Boyd
81st Ohio, Lt. Col. Robert N. Adams, Maj. Frank Evans, Capt. Noah Stoker

Third Brigade (stationed at Rome from 22 May)
Colonel Moses M. Bane

7th Illinois, Col. Richard Rowett, Lt. Col. Hector Perrin
50th Illinois, Maj. William Hanna

57th Illinois, Lt. Col. Frederick J. Hurlbut
89th Iowa, Col. Henry J. B. Cummings, Lt. Col. James Redfield, Maj. Joseph M. Griffiths

Artillery
Captain Frederick Welker
1st Michigan Light, Battery B, Capt. Albert F. R. Arndt
1st Missouri Light, Battery H, Lt. Andrew T. Blodgett
1st Missouri Light, Battery I, Lt. John F. Brunner

FOURTH DIVISION
Brigadier General James C. Veatch (sick from 17 July)
Brigadier General John W. Fuller (commanded 17 July–4 August and after 20 August)
Brigadier General Thomas E.G. Ransom

First Brigade
Brigadier General John W. Fuller (commanded 17 July–4 August and after 20 August)
Colonel John Morrill (wounded 22 July at Atlanta)
Lieutenant Colonel Henry T. Mc Dowell
64th Illinois, Col. John Morrill, Lt. Col. Michael W. Manning
18th Missouri, Lt. Col. Charles S. Sheldon, Maj. William H. Minter
27th Ohio, Lt. Col. Mendal Churchill
39th Ohio, Col. Edward F. Noves, Lt. Col. Henry T. McDowell, Maj. John S. Jenkins

Second Brigade
Brigadier General John W. Sprague
35th New Jersey, Col. John J. Cladek, Lt. Col. William A. Henry, Capt. Charles A. Angel
43d Ohio, Col. Wager Swayne
63d Ohio, Lt. Col. Charles E. Brown (wounded 22 July at Atlanta), Maj. John W. Fouts
25th Wisconsin, Col. Milton Montgomery (wounded 22 July at Atlanta), Lt. Col. Jeremiah M. Rusk

Third Brigade (joined 7 August from Decatur, Alabama)
Colonel James H. Howe
Colonel William T. C. Grower
Colonel John Tillson
10th Illinois, Capt. George C. Lusk (regiment joined 20 August)
25th Indiana, Lt. Col. John Rheinlander, Capt. James S. Wright

17th New York, Maj. Joel O. Martin
32d Wisconsin, Col. Charles H. De Groat

Artillery
Captain Jerome B. Burrows
Captain George Robinson

1st Michigan Light, Battery C, Capt. George Robinson, Lt. Henry Shier
14th Ohio Light Battery, Capt. Jerome B. Burrows, Lt. Seth M. Laird, Lt. George Hurlbut
2d US, Batt. F, Lt. Albert M. Murray, Lt. Joseph C. Breckinridge, Lt. Lemuel Smith

XVII ARMY CORPS (joined 8 June)
Major General Frank P. Blair, Jr.
Escort: 1st Ohio Cavalry, Company M, Lt. Charles H. Shultz,
9th Illinois (mounted infantry), Company G, Capt. Isaac Clements,
11th Illinois Cavalry, Company G, Capt. Stephen S. Tripp

THIRD DIVISION
Brigadier General Mortimer D. Leggett
Escort: 1st Ohio Cavalry, Company D, Lt. James W. Kirkendall

First Brigade
Brigadier General Manning F. Force (wounded 22 July at Atlanta)
Colonel George E. Bryant

20th Illinois, Lt. Col. Daniel Bradley, Maj. George W. Kennard, Capt. John H. Austin
30th Illinois, Col. Warren Shedd (captured 22 July at Atlanta), Lt. Col. William C. Rhoads
31st Illinois, Col. Edwin S. Mc Cook (sick from 27 June), Lt. Col. Robert N. Pearson
45th Illinois, Lt. Col. Robert P. Sealy (guarded Western Atlantic Railroad at Etowah)
12th Wisconsin, Col. George E. Bryant, Lt. Col. James K. Proudfit
16th Wisconsin, Col. Cassius Fairchild, Maj. William F. Dawes

Second Brigade
Colonel Robert K. Scott (captured 22 July at Atlanta)
Lieutenant Colonel Greenberry F. Wiles

20th Ohio, Lt. Col. John C. Fry (wounded 22 July at Atlanta), Maj. Francis M. Shaklee
32d Ohio, Col. Benjamin F. Potts
68th Ohio, Lt. Col. George E. Welles (wounded 22 July at Atlanta)

78th Ohio, Lt. Col. Greenberry F. Wiles, Maj. John T. Rainey

Third Brigade
Colonel Adam G. Malloy

17th Wisconsin, Lt. Col. Thomas McMahon, Maj Donald D. Scott
Worden's Battalion, Maj. Asa Worden

Artillery
Capt. William S. Williams

1st Illinois Light, Battery D, Capt. Edgar H. Cooper
1st Michigan Light, Battery H, Capt. Marcus D. Elliott, Lt. William Justin
3rd Ohio Light Battery, Lt. John Sullivan

FOURTH DIVISION
Brigadier General Walter Q. Gresham (wounded 20 July at Bald Hill)
Brigadier General Giles A. Smith
Escort: 11th Illinois Cavalry, Company G, Capt. Stephen S. Tripp

First Brigade
Colonel William L. Sanderson (commanded until 18 July)
Colonel Benjamin F. Potts

53d Illinois, Lt. Col. John W. McClanahan (transferred from 2nd Brigade 18 July)
23d Indiana, Lt. Col. William P. Davis, Lt. Col. George S. Babbitt
53d Indiana, Lt. Col. William Jones (killed 22 July at Atlanta), Maj. Warner L. Vestal
3d Iowa (3 cos.), Capt. Daniel McLennan, Capt. Pleasant T. Mathes, Lt. Lewis T. Linnell
32d Ohio, Capt. William M. Morris, Lt. Col. Jeff. J. Hibbets (transferred from 3rd Div. 18 July)

Second Brigade
(guarded Western & Atlantic Railroad)
Colonel George C. Rogers
Colonel Isaac C. Pugh (commanded 5–19 July)

14th Illinois, Capt. Carlos C. Cox
15th Illinois, Maj. Rufus C. McEathron
32d Illinois, Col. John Logan (transferred from 1st Brigade 18 July), Lt. Col. George H. English
41st Illinois, Maj. Robert H. McFadden
53d Illinois, Lt. Col. John W. McClanahan

Third Brigade
Colonel William Hall

Brigadier General William W. Belknap

11th Iowa, Lt. Col. John C. Abercrombie
13th Iowa, Col. John Shane, Maj. William A. Walker
15th Iowa, Col. William W. Belknap, Maj. George Pomutz
16th Iowa, Lt. Col. Addison H. Sanders (captured 22 July at Atlanta with most of regiment)

Artillery
Captain Edward Spear, Jr.
Captain William Z. Clayton

2nd Illinois Light, Battery F, Lt. Walter H. Powell (Battery and Powell captured 22 July at Atlanta)
Minnesota Light, 1st Battery, Capt. William Z. Clayton, Lt. Henry Hurter
1st Missouri Light Battery C, Capt. John L. Matthaei (posted at Allatoona & Big Shanty)
10th Ohio Light Battery, Capt. Francis Seaman (posted at Big Shanty from 11 July)
15th Ohio Light Battery, Lt. James Burdick

ARMY OF THE OHIO
(XXIII ARMY CORPS)
Major General John M. Schofield
Escort: 7th Ohio Cavalry, Company G, Capt. John A. Ashbury

Engineer Battalion
Captain Charles E. Mc Alester
Captain Oliver S. Mc Clure (commanded from 23 June)

FIRST DIVISION
(disbanded and dispersed among 2nd & 3rd Divisions 9 June)
Brigadier General Alvin P. Hovey (on leave from 9 June)

First Brigade
Colonel Richard F. Barter

120th Indiana, Lt. Col. Allen W. Prather
124th Indiana, Col. James Burgess (sick from 10 June), Col. John M. Orr
128th Indiana, Col. Richard P. De Hart (wounded 7 June at Lost Mountain), Lt. Col. Jasper Packard

Second Brigade
Colonel John C. Mc Quiston
Colonel Peter T. Swaine (commanded from 23 June)

123d Indiana, Lt. Col. William A. Cullen, Col. John C. Mc Quiston
129th Indiana, Col. Charles Case (resigned 15 June), Col. Charles A. Zollinger

130th Indiana, Col. Charles S. Parrish
99th Ohio, Lt. Col. John E. Cummins

Artillery

Indiana Light, 23d Battery, Lt. Luther S. Houghton, Lt. Aaron A. Wilber
Indiana Light, 24th Battery (transferred to Stoneman's Cavalry Division 6 July and captured 31 July)

SECOND DIVISION

Brigadier General Henry M. Judah (dismissed 18 May for incompetency at Resaca)
Brigadier General Milo S. Hascall

First Brigade

Brigadier General Nathaniel C. McLean
Brigadier General Joseph A. Cooper (commanded from 4 June)

91st Indiana, Lt. Col. Charles H. Butterfield, Col. John Mehringer
25th Minnesota, Lt. Col. Benjamin F. Orcutt (sick from 10 July), Capt. Samuel L. Demarest
3d Tennessee, Col. William Cross, Maj. R. H. Dunn
6th Tennessee, Col. Joseph A. Cooper, Lt. Col. Edward Maynard, Capt. Marcus D. Bearden

Second Brigade

Colonel William E. Hobson

107th Illinois, Maj. Uriah M. Laurance, Lt. Col. Francis H. Lowry
80th Indiana, Lt. Col. Alfred D. Owen, Maj. John W. Tucker, Capt. Jacob Ragle
13th Kentucky, Col. William E. Hobson, Lt. Col. Benjamin P. Estes
23d Michigan, Lt. Col. Oliver L. Spaulding, Maj. William W. Wheeler
111th Ohio, Col. John R. Bond, Lt. Col. Isaac R. Sherwood
118th Ohio, Lt. Col. Thomas L. Young (sick from 18 June), Capt. Edgar Sowers

Third Brigade

Colonel Silas A. Strickland

14th Kentucky, Col. George W. Gallup
20th Kentucky, Lt. Col. Thomas B. Waller
27th Kentucky, Lt. Col. John H. Ward, Capt. Andrew J. Bailey
50th Ohio, Lt. Col. George R. Elstner (killed 8 August at East Point), Maj. Hamilton S. Gillespie

Artillery

Captain Joseph C. Shields

Indiana Light, 29d Battery, Capt. Benjamin F. Denning (mortally wounded July near Kennesaw)

1st Michigan Light. Battery F, Capt. Byron D. Paddock, Lt. Marshall M. Miller
Ohio Light, 19th Battery, Capt. Joseph C. Shields

THIRD DIVISION
Brigadier General Jacob D. Cox

First Brigade
Colonel James W. Reilly

112th Illinois, Col. Thomas J. Henderson (wounded 14 May at Resaca), Lt. Col. Emery S. Bond, Maj. Tristram T. Dow
16th Kentucky, Col. James W. Gault (sick from 29 May), Maj. John S. White, Capt. Jacob Miller
100th Ohio, Col. Patrick S. Slevin (wounded 6 August at Utoy Creek), Capt. Frank Rundell
104th Ohio, Col. Oscar W. Sterl
8th Tennessee, Col. Felix A. Reeve, Maj. William J. Jordan, Capt. Robert A. Ragan

Second Brigade
Brigadier General Mahlon D. Manson (wounded 14 May at Resaca)
Colonel John S. Casement (commanded 14 May–4 June)
Colonel Daniel Cameron

65th Illinois, Lt. Col. William S. Stewart
63d Indiana, Col. Israel N. Stiles, Lt. Col Daniel Morris
65th Indiana, Lt. Col. Thomas Johnson, Capt. Walter G. Hodge, Capt. William F. Stillwell
24th Kentucky, Col. John S. Hurt, Lt. Col. Lafayette North
103d Ohio, Col. John S. Casement
5th Tennessee, Col. James T. Shelley, Maj. David G. Bowers

Third Brigade (organized 5 June)
Brigadier General Nathaniel C. McLean (sent to Kentucky 17 June)
Colonel Robert K. Byrd (commanded 17 June–14 July)
Colonel Israel N. Stiles

11th Kentucky, Col. S. Palace Love, Lt. Col. Erasmus L. Mottley
12th Kentucky, Lt. Col. Laurence H. Rousseau
1st Tennessee, Col. Robert K. Byrd, Lt. Col. John Ellis
5th Tennessee, Col. James T. Shelley (resigned 22 July), Maj. David G. Bowers

Dismounted Cavalry Brigade
Colonel Eugene W. Crittenden

16th Illinois, Capt. Hiram S. Hanchett
12th Kentucky, Lt. Col. James T. Bramlette, Maj. James B. Harrison

Artillery
Major Henry W. Wells
Indiana Light, 15th Battery, Capt. Alonzo D. Harvey
1st Ohio Light, Battery D, Capt. Giles J. Cockerill

CAVALRY CORPS
Brigadier General Washington L. Elliott
Escort: 4th Ohio, Company D, Capt. Philip H. Warner

FIRST DIVISION
Brigadier General Edward M. McCook

First Brigade
Colonel Joseph B. Dorr (captured 30 July at Brown's Mill)
Lieutenant Colonel James P. Brownlow (commanded 20 July–12 August)
Brigadier General John T. Croxton (commanded from 12 August)
8th Iowa, Lt. Col. Horatio G. Barrier, Col. Joseph B. Dorr, Maj. Richard Root, Maj. John H. Isett
4th Kentucky (mounted infantry), Col. John T. Croxton, Lt. Col. Robert M. Kelly, Capt. James H. West, Lt. Granville C. West, Capt. James I. Hudnall
2d Michigan, Maj. Leonidas S. Scranton, Lt. Col. Benjamin Smith (regt. sent Franklin, TN, 29 June)
1st Tennessee, Col. James P. Brownlow

Second Brigade
Colonel Oscar H. La Grange (captured 9 May at Varnell Station)
Lieutenant Colonel James W. Stewart (captured 26 May at Acworth)
Lieutenant Colonel Horace P. Lamson (commanded from 26 May)
Lieutenant Colonel William H. Torrey (captured 30 July at Brown's Mill)
2d Indiana, Lt. Col. James W. Stewart, Maj. David A. Briggs
4th Indiana, Lt. Col. Horace P. Lamson, Maj. George H. Purdy, Capt. Albert J. Morley
1st Wisconsin, Maj. Nathan Paine (killed 28 July at Palmetto), Lt. Col. William H. Torrey

Third Brigade (stationed at Wauhatchie, Tennessee)
Colonel Louis D. Watkins
Colonel John K. Faulkner (commanded 5 July–10 August)
4th Kentucky, Col. Wickliffe Cooper
6th Kentucky, Maj. William H. Fidler
7th Kentucky, Col. John K. Faulkner, Maj. Robert Collier

Artillery

18th Indiana Battery, Lt. William B. Rippetoe, Capt. Moses M. Beck

SECOND DIVISION

Brigadier General Kenner Garrard

First Brigade

Colonel Robert H. G. Minty

4th Michigan, Lt. Col. Josiah B. Park, Maj. Frank W. Mix, Capt. L. Briggs Eldridge
7th Pennsylvania, Col. William B. Sipes, Maj. James F. Andreas, Maj. William H. Jennings
4th United States, Capt. James B. McIntyre

Second Brigade (in North Alabama until 6 June)

Colonel Eli Long (wounded 20 August at Lovejoy Station)

Colonel Beroth B. Eggleston

1st Ohio, Col. Beroth B. Eggleston, Lt. Col. Thomas J. Patten
3d Ohio, Col. Charles B. Seidel
4th Ohio, Lt. Col. Oliver P. Robie

Third Brigade (mounted infantry) "Lightning Brigade"

Colonel John T. Wilder (sick from 14 June)

Colonel Abram O. Miller

98th Illinois, Lt. Col. Edward Kitchell
123d Illinois, Lt. Col. Jonathan Biggs
17th Indiana, Lt. Col. Henry Jordan, Maj. Jacob G. Vail
72d Indiana, Col. Abram O. Miller, Maj. Henry M. Carr, Lt. Col. Samuel C. Kirkpatrick

Artillery

Chicago (Illinois) Board of Trade Battery, Lt. George I. Robinson

THIRD DIVISION

Brigadier General Judson Kilpatrick (wounded 13 May at Resaca, resumed July 28)

Colonel Eli H. Murray (commanded 12–21 May)

Colonel William W. Lowe (commanded 21 May–23 July)

First Brigade

Lieutenant Colonel Robert Klien

Lieutenant Colonel Matthewson T. Patrick

Major J. Morris Young

3d Indiana (four companies), Maj. Alfred Gaddis
5th Iowa, Maj. Harlon Baird, Maj. J. Morris Young, Capt. Martin Choumee

Second Brigade
Colonel Charles C. Smith
Major Thomas W. Sanderson (commanded 2 July–6 August)
Lieutenant Colonel Fielder A. Jones

8th Indiana, Lt. Col. Fielder A. Jones, Maj. Thomas Herring, Maj. Thomas Graham
2d Kentucky, Maj. William H. Effort (killed 4 August at Triune, TN), Maj. Owen Star
10th Ohio, Maj. Thomas W. Sanderson, Maj. William Thayer

Third Brigade
Colonel Eli H. Murray
Colonel Smith D. Atkins

92d Illinois Mounted Infantry, Col. Smith D. Atkins, Capt. Matthew Van Buskirk, Maj. Albert Woodcock
3d Kentucky, Maj. Lewis Wolfiey, Lt. Col. Robert H. King
5th Kentucky, Col. Oliver L. Baldwin, Maj. Christopher T. Cheek

Artillery
10th Wisconsin Battery, Capt. Yates V. Beebe

STONEMAN'S CAVALRY DIVISION (destroyed 31 July at Sunshine Church)
Major General George Stoneman (captured 31 July at Sunshine Church)
Colonel Horace Capron
Escort: 7th Ohio, Company D, Lt. Samuel Murphy, Lt. Washington W. Manning

First Brigade[4]
Colonel Israel Garrard

9th Michigan, Col. George S. Acker
7th Ohio, Lt. Col. George G. Miner

Second Brigade
Colonel James Biddle (captured 31 July at Sunshine Church)
Colonel Thomas H. Butler

5th Indiana, Col. Thomas H. Butler (captured 31 July at Sunshine Church), Maj. Moses D. Leeson
6th Indiana, Lt. Col. Courtland C. Matson, Maj. William W. Carter (captured 3 August at King's Tanyard)

Third Brigade

[4] Not present at Dalton to Cassville.

Colonel Horace Capron

14th Illinois, Lt. Col. David P. Jenkins
8th Michigan, Lt. Col. Elisha Mix (captured 31 July), Maj. William L. Buck (captured 3 August)
McLaughlin's Ohio Squadron, Maj. Richard Rice

Independent Brigade
Colonel Alexander W. Holeman
Lieutenant Colonel Silas Adams (commanded from 27 July)

1st Kentucky, Lt. Col. Silas Adams
11th Kentucky, Lt. Col. Archibald J, Alexander

Artillery

24th Indiana Battery, Capt. Alexander Hardy (captured with battery 31 July at Sunshine Church)

Appendix C

GENERAL ORDERS, HEADQUARTERS ARMY OF TENNESSEE, No. --.

Cassville, Ga., May 19, 1864.
Soldiers of the Army of Tennessee, you have displayed the highest quality of the soldier-firmness in combat, patience under toil. By your courage and skill you have repulsed every assault of the enemy. By marches by day and by marches by night you have defeated every attempt upon your communications. Your communications are secured. You will now turn and march to meet his advancing columns. Fully confiding in the conduct of the officers, the courage of the soldiers, I lead you to battle. We may confidently trust that the Almighty Farther will still reward the patriots' toils and bless the patriots' banners. Cheered by the success of our brothers in Virginia and beyond the Mississippi, our efforts will equal theirs. Strengthened by His support, those efforts will be crowned with the like glories.
J. E. JOHNSTON,
General.

Appendix D

Table of Confederate Casualties at Dalton, Resaca, Calhoun, Adairsville and Cassville May 6-20

	Dalton (5/6-12)	Resaca (5/9-15)	Calhoun (5/16)	Rome/Adairsville (5/17)	Cassville (5/19)	Total[1]	Adjusted Total[2]
Hardee's Corps:							
—Bate's Division: (4,054)[3]	5k/25w	25k/239w/55m				21k/121w	[28k/249w/58m][4]
Finley's Brigade:[5] (1,200)	1w	9k/29w				7k/54w	[9k/90w/7m][6]
1st FL Cav.:	0						[4k/23w/0m][7]
1st FL:	1w						[0k/5w/4m][8]
3rd FL:	2c						[1k/25w/5m][9]
4th FL:[10]	0						
6th FL:	0						[0k/12w/2m][11]
7th FL:	0	3k/16w[12]					[2k/25w/0m][13]

---

[1] As reported by General Joseph E. Johnston from A. J. Foard, medical director, Army of Tennessee (*OR*, ser. 1, vol. 38, pt. 3, 686–87). In this column, if there is no other fn, then the tally is from Johnston's report herein.

[2] Adjusted totals in brackets as found by author by compiling data from all available sources.

[3] Numbers in parentheses indicate effective number present at engagement for that unit; figure typically based upon *Official Records of the War of the Rebellion* (hereinafter *OR* or *OR Supp.*); otherwise, it will be specifically cited. Major General William Brimage Bate's report, *OR Supp.*, Serial 7, 92–93.

[4] [ ] indicates working figure by RDJ (a running tally). Figure includes 2 wounded on Bates's staff. *Memphis Daily Appeal*, Atlanta, GA, 25 May 1864.

[5] Board of State Institutions, *Soldiers of Florida*, Live Oak, FL: 14 May 1903.

[6] *Memphis Daily Appeal*, Atlanta, GA, 25 May 1864, 1, shows 7 killed, 91 wounded, and 11 missing between Dalton and Cassville, 6–20 May 1864.

[7] *Memphis Daily Appeal*, Atlanta, GA, 25 May 1864, 1, shows 4 killed, 23 wounded (5 mortally), and 0 missing between Dalton and Cassville, 6–20 May 1864.

[8] *Memphis Daily Appeal*, Atlanta, GA, 25 May 1864, 1, shows 0 killed, 5 wounded, and 4 missing between Dalton and Cassville, 6–20 May 1864. (Figures include 4th FL).

[9] *Memphis Daily Appeal*, Atlanta, GA, 25 May 1864, 1, shows 1 killed, 25 wounded, and 5 missing between Dalton and Cassville, 6–20 May 1864.

[10] Figures included with 1st FL.

[11] *Memphis Daily Appeal*, Atlanta, GA, 25 May 1864, 1, shows 0 killed, 12 wounded, and 2 missing between Dalton and Cassville, 6–20 May 1864.

[12] *Memphis Daily Appeal*, Atlanta, GA, 18 May 1864, 1, shows 1 killed, 18 wounded (2 mortally), on 14 May 1864 at Resaca.

[13] *Memphis Daily Appeal*, Atlanta, GA, 25 May 1864, 1, shows 2 killed, 25 wounded (2 mortally), and 0 missing between Dalton and Cassville, 6–20 May 1864.

Lewis's Brigade:[14]	6w[15]	15k/70w[16]	23m[17]	14k/67w	[15k/76w/23m][18]
2nd KY:	1w[19]	6k/17w[20]	8m[21]		[6k/18w/8m][22]
4th KY:	2w[23]	1k/30w[24]	10m[25]		[1k/32w/10m][26]
5th KY:	1w[27]	1k/5w[28]	2m[29]		[1k/6w/2m][30]

[14] Figures includes Dalton and Resaca. Author's research of CMSR., record No. 1158, 3847, 1887 (Ga. 36)/War Dept. Carded Apr. 9, 1927, and Thompson, *History of the Orphan Brigade*, 548–691, 806–57.
[15] *Memphis Daily Appeal*, Atlanta, GA, 25 May 1864, 1, shows 6 wounded at either Dalton, Adairsville, or Cassville (Resaca is separately given), 6–20 May 1864.
[16] *Memphis Daily Appeal*, Atlanta, GA, 25 May 1864, 1, shows 15 killed, 70 wounded at Resaca, 14–15 May 1864.
[17] *Memphis Daily Appeal*, Atlanta, GA, 25 May 1864, 1, shows 23 missing between Dalton and Cassville, 6–20 May 1864. See also William L. Trask's journal; he recorded on 17 May 1864 following the evacuation of Adairsville, "Several of the Kentuckians, no doubt disgusted with the prospect [of another retreat], threw their guns into the bushes as they marched along and no doubt sought the first opportunity to fall out and hide themselves for the purpose of falling into the enemy's hands and getting a chance to go home" (Hafendorfer, ed., *Civil War Journal of William L. Trask*, 144–45).
[18] *Memphis Daily Appeal*, Atlanta, GA, 25 May 1864, 1, shows 15 killed, 76 wounded, and 23 missing between Dalton and Cassville, 6–20 May 1864.
[19] *Memphis Daily Appeal*, Atlanta, GA, 25 May 1864, 1, shows 1 wounded at either Dalton, Adairsville, or Cassville (Resaca is separately given), 6–20 May 1864.
[20] *Memphis Daily Appeal*, Atlanta, GA, 25 May 1864, 1, shows 6 killed, 17 wounded at Resaca, 14–15 May 1864.
[21] *Memphis Daily Appeal*, Atlanta, GA, 25 May 1864, 1, shows 8 missing between Dalton and Cassville, 6–20 May 1864. See also Thompson, *History of the Orphan Brigade*, 548–97, which records 3 captured at or after Resaca.
[22] *Memphis Daily Appeal*, Atlanta, GA, 25 May 1864, 1, shows 6 killed, 18 wounded, and 8 missing between Dalton and Cassville, 6–20 May 1864.
[23] *Memphis Daily Appeal*, Atlanta, GA, 25 May 1864, 1, shows 2 wounded at either Dalton, Adairsville, or Cassville (Resaca is separately given), 6–20 May 1864.
[24] *Memphis Daily Appeal*, Atlanta, GA, 25 May 1864, 1, shows 1 killed, 30 wounded at Resaca, 14–15 May 1864. Compare Thompson, *History of the Orphan Brigade*, 548–97, which records 2 killed and 31 wounded at either Dalton or Resaca. Thus, the 2 wounded provided in footnote 22 can be attributed to Dalton, and 1 of the wounded at Resaca apparently died shortly after his wounding.
[25] *Memphis Daily Appeal*, Atlanta, GA, 25 May 1864, 1, shows 10 missing between Dalton and Cassville, 6–20 May 1864. Also, see Lewis's Brigade footnote for Adairsville.
[26] *Memphis Daily Appeal*, Atlanta, GA, 25 May 1864, 1, shows 1 killed, 32 wounded, and 10 missing between Dalton and Cassville, 6–20 May 1864.
[27] *Memphis Daily Appeal*, Atlanta, GA, 25 May 1864, 1, shows 1 wounded at either Dalton, Adairsville, or Cassville (Resaca is separately given), 6–20 May 1864.
[28] *Memphis Daily Appeal*, Atlanta, GA, 25 May 1864, 1, shows 1 killed, 5 wounded at Resaca, 14–15 May 1864.
[29] *Memphis Daily Appeal*, Atlanta, GA, 25 May 1864, 1, shows 2 missing between Dalton and Cassville, 6–20 May 1864. Also, see Lewis's Brigade footnote for Adairsville.
[30] *Memphis Daily Appeal*, Atlanta, GA, 25 May 1864, 1, shows 1 killed, 6 wounded, and 2 missing between Dalton and Cassville, 6–20 May 1864.

6th KY:	2w[31]	2k/3w[32]		3m[33]		[2k/5w/3m][34]
9th KY:	-	5k/15w[35]		-		[5k/15w][36]
Tyler's Brigade:						[4k/81w/28m][37]
4th GA SS:[38]	0	0k/1w				[1k/10w/5m][39]
37th GA:[40]	1c	0k/7w/0c[41]	1k/10w/2c	10c	1c	[0k/26w/18m][42]
10th TN:[43]		1w				
15th TN:		-				
20th TN:	1k	2k/5w			1k	[1k/23w/1m][44]
30th TN:[45]	10k&w					[2k/19w/4m][46]
37th TN:		-				[0k/3w/0m][47]

31 *Memphis Daily Appeal*, Atlanta, GA, 25 May 1864, 1, shows 2 wounded at either Dalton, Adairsville, or Cassville (Resaca is separately given), 6–20 May 1864.

32 *Memphis Daily Appeal*, Atlanta, GA, 25 May 1864, 1, shows 2 killed, 3 wounded at Resaca, 14–15 May 1864.

33 *Memphis Daily Appeal*, Atlanta, GA, 25 May 1864, 1, shows 2 missing between Dalton and Cassville, 6–20 May 1864. Also, see Lewis's Brigade footnote for Adairsville.

34 *Memphis Daily Appeal*, Atlanta, GA, 25 May 1864, 1, shows 2 killed, 5 wounded, and 3 missing between Dalton and Cassville, 6–20 May 1864.

35 *Memphis Daily Appeal*, Atlanta, GA, 25 May 1864, 1, shows 5 killed, 15 wounded at Resaca, 14–15 May 1864.

36 *Memphis Daily Appeal*, Atlanta, GA, 25 May 1864, 1, shows 5 killed, 15 wounded between Dalton and Cassville, 6–20 May 1864. Author's research of CMSR, record no. 1158, 3847, 1887 (Ga. 36)/War Dept. Carded 9 April 1927, and Thompson, *History of the Orphan Brigade*, 806–57, reveal that all these casualties appear to have occurred at Resaca.

37 *Memphis Daily Appeal*, Atlanta, GA, 25 May 1864, 1, shows 4 killed, 81 wounded, and 28 missing between Dalton and Cassville, 6–20 May 1864.

38 Author's research of CMSR and L. Henderson, *Roster of the Confederate Soldiers of Georgia*, 4:1–116.

39 *Memphis Daily Appeal*, Atlanta, GA, 25 May 1864, 1, shows 1 killed, 10 wounded, and 5 missing between Dalton and Cassville, 6–20 May 1864.

40 Author's research of CMSR and L. Henderson, *Roster of the Confederate Soldiers of Georgia*, 4:1–116.

41 *Columbus (Georgia) Daily Sun*, 24 May 1864, 2.

42 *Memphis Daily Appeal*, Atlanta, GA, 25 May 1864, 1, shows 1 killed, 26 wounded, and 18 missing between Dalton and Cassville, 6–20 May 1864.

43 Lindsley, *Military Annals of Tennessee, Confederate*, 1:288–90. Lt. Col. O'Neill severely wounded at Resaca.

44 *Memphis Daily Appeal*, Atlanta, GA, 25 May 1864, 1, shows 1 killed, 23 wounded, and 1 missing between Dalton and Cassville, 6–20 May 1864.

45 Lindsley, *Military Annals of Tennessee, Confederate*, 1:454–55; see "Sketch of 30th Tennessee" that says a shell from enemy at Rocky Face Ridge killed and wounded 10 men from the 10th and 30th TN on page 454.

46 *Memphis Daily Appeal*, Atlanta, GA, 25 May 1864, 1, shows 2 killed, 19 wounded, and 4 missing between Dalton and Cassville, 6–20 May 1864.

47 *Memphis Daily Appeal*, Atlanta, GA, 25 May 1864, 1, shows 0 killed, 3 wounded, and 0 missing between Dalton and Cassville, 6–20 May 1864. (Figures include 13th TN).

Cleburne's Division:	3w			21k/144w	[23k/144w/8c][48]
Lowrey's Brigade:				10k/45w	
16th AL:					
33rd AL:					
45th AL:					
32nd MS:		5k/7w[49]			
45th MS:[50]		1k/1w/6c	2c	1k/1w/8c	
Polk's Brigade:		25k&w[51]			[6k/46w]
1st & 15th AR:		-			
5th Conf.:		-			
2nd TN:		-			
35th & 48th TN:		-			
Govan's Brigade:				3k/31w	
2nd & 24th AR:					
5th & 13th AR:					
6th & 7th AR:					
8th & 19th AR:					
3rd Conf.[52]	0	7w	1k		
Granbury's Brigade: 3w		4k/17w		2k/21w	[4k/20w]
6th TX Cav.:	3w[53]	1k[54]			[1k/3w]
7th TX:		1k/1w[55]			[1k/1w

[48] Apparently, 2 staff officers wounded in Cleburne's Division between 7 May and 20 May.
[49] Rowland, *Military History of Mississippi*, 299.
[50] D. Williamson, *Third Battalion Mississippi Infantry*, 325–72.
[51] Drake, *Annals*, Appendix, 51
[52] Captain Mumford H. Dixon's report, *OR Supp*., Serial 7, 68. Note: he says had 6 to 8 men wounded while at Resaca, so the author listed 7. In the engagement at Calhoun on 16 May, called Battle of Lay's Ferry or Rome Crossroads, he does not report any casualties but reports capturing 1 Federal.
[53] Lundberg, *Granbury's Texas Brigade*, 141. Lundberg cites his source as Danny M. Sessums, "A Force to Be Reckoned With: Granbury's Texas Brigade *1861–1865*," Sessums Collection, Houston, Texas.
[54] Lundberg, *Granbury's Texas Brigade*, 141, show 1 killed at Resaca. Compare *Memphis Daily Appeal*, Atlanta, GA, 24 May 1864, 2, which shows 1 wounded severely at Resaca.
[55] *Memphis Daily Appeal*, Atlanta, GA, 24 May 1864, 2.

10th TX:		5w[56]						[5w]
15th TX Cav.:		3w[57]						[3w]
17th TX Cav.:		1k/1w[58]						[1k/1w]
18th TX Cav.:		3w(1mw)[59]						[3w(1mw)]
24th TX Cav.:		1k/2w(1mw)[60]						[1k/2w(1mw)]
25th TX Cav.:		2w[61]						[2w]
Walker's Division:						28k/269w		[32k/269w/38c][62]
Mercer's Brigade:						4k/41w		
1st Vol. GA:[63]	(arrived from Savannah May 29, 1864 at Elsberry Mountain, Dallas-New Hope Line)							
54th GA:[64]	2w	1k/8w	3w/2c	1w/2c	6c			
57th GA:[65]	(arrived from Andersonville May 20, 1864 and joined at Allatoona Station)							
63rd GA:[66]	1k		1w		15c			
Jackson's Brigade:							13k/113w	
2nd GA Bttn. SS:								
47th GA:[67]		2k/23w/6c/5m						
65th GA:								

---

[56] *Memphis Daily Appeal*, Atlanta, GA, 24 May 1864, 2, shows 2 wounded at Resaca. Compare Lundberg, *Granbury's Texas Brigade*, 141, which shows 3 wounded at Resaca.

[57] *Memphis Daily Appeal*, Atlanta, GA, 24 May 1864, 2.

[58] *Memphis Daily Appeal*, Atlanta, GA, 24 May 1864, 2.

[59] *Memphis Daily Appeal*, Atlanta, GA, 24 May 1864, 2.

[60] *Memphis Daily Appeal*, Atlanta, GA, 24 May 1864, 2, shows 1 killed, 2 wounded, at Resaca, 14–15 May 1864.

[61] *Memphis Daily Appeal*, Atlanta, GA, 24 May 1864, 2.

[62] Discrepancy of 5 killed due to losses in 2nd GA Bttn., 65th GA, 46th GA, and 16th SC unaccounted for but included in Resaca Cemetery. Once added, the number of wounded and missing will also increase.

[63] S. Walker, *Hell's Broke Loose in Georgia*, 125.

[64] Bowers, *54th Georgia Volunteer Infantry Regiment*, 43, 45–50. Bowers notes 1 killed on 10 May, 3 wounded on 13 May at Lay's Ferry and 5 wounded on 15 May at Lay's Ferry.

[65] S. Walker, *Hell's Broke Loose in Georgia*, 122.

[66] W. A. Clark, *Under the Stars and Bars*, 97–99.

[67] Bowers, 47th *Georgia Volunteer Infantry Regiment*, 302–303. Bowers reports 1 killed, 1 wounded, and 1 captured on 14 May at the Oostanaula River, and the remaining casualties all on 15 May at Lay's Ferry.

5th MS:[68]		4k/19w(5/15)					
8th MS:[69]		3k/60w					
Gist's Brigade:		7w (5/15)[70]				7k/62w	
8th GA Bttn.(465): [71]	3w/19m	2k/10m	7m	9m	7m		[2k/3w/52m]
46th GA:							
16th SC:							
24th SC: [72]	2k/9w	9k/30w/2m		1w[73]			
Stevens's Brigade:						4k/53w	
1st GA SS:							
1st GA Confederate:							
25th GA:							
26th GA Bttn (w/66th):							
29th GA:							
30th GA:							
66th GA:[74]		3k/2w					
Cheatham's Division:						46k/316w	[49k/335w/1m][75]
Maney's Brigade:						11k/86w	

---

[68] Rowland, *Military History of Mississippi*, 168, shows 4 killed, 19 wounded at Turner's Ferry 15 May. *Neshoba Democrat Supplement*, 27 April 1911, shows 2 killed and 1 missing in Company K at Resaca on 15 May at Tanner's Ferry.

[69] Rowland, *Military History of Mississippi*, 194.

[70] Colonel Ellison Capers's report (*OR*, ser. 1, vol. 38, pt. 3, 714) lists 7 men were wounded in Gist's Brigade while crossing the pontoon bridge over the Oostanaula River from Gideon's Ford (Calhoun Ferry) to Resaca on the afternoon of 15 May while under fire from Federal artillery on Bald Hill.

[71] 8th GA Battalion, vertical files, File No. 1, 295, Georgia Department of Archives and History, Virtual Vault. About half of this 7-company battalion came from Calhoun while the other half hailed from Savannah. During the Atlanta Campaign, the following numbers of total present and total deserted (P/D) were recorded between 8 May at Dalton and 31 August at Jonesboro: Co. A-61/32, Co. B-85/42, Co. C-81/46, Co. D-66/33, Co. E-67/22, Co. F-67/24, Co. G-38/21. Total present at beginning of campaign: 465; total deserted: 220; total present 1 September 1864: 245.

[72] Ellison Capers's report, *OR*, ser. 1, vol. 38, pt. 3, 713, 715, 718.

[73] Bowers, *47th Georgia Volunteer Infantry Regiment*, 52.

[74] Cone, *Last to Join the*, 120.

[75] Increase of 3 killed due to Resaca Cemetery. Division casualties will increase after missing and captured are added.

1st & 27th TN:					30k&w[76]			
4th Conf.:								
6th & 9th TN:[77]		3k/1w						[3k/1w]
41st TN:								
50th TN:								
Wright's Brigade:							18k/97w	
8th TN:								
16th TN:								
28th TN:		1k/24w[78]						
38th TN:		2k[79]						
51st & 52nd TN:								
Strahl's Brigade:							9k/76w	
4th & 5th TN:								
19th TN:[80]		-2k/1w	--		3k/5w	--		[5k/6w]
24th TN:								
31st TN:								
33rd TN:								
Vaughan's Brigade:							8k/57w	[10k/76w/1m][81]
11th TN:[82]	1k	1k/11w[83]		1k				[3k/11w][84]
12th &47th TN:		3k/22w/1m[85]						[3k/22w/1m][86]

[76] S.R. Watkins, *"Co. Aytch,"* 151, shows the 1st TN had about 30 killed and wounded at Adairsville at the Octagon House, 17 May. There is 1 killed in 27th TN; name listed in Lindsley, *Military Annals of Tennessee, Confederate*, 1:429.
[77] Fleming, *Confederate Ninth Tennessee Infantry*, 188–287, 311. These figures are for the 9th TN only.
[78] Lindsley, *Military Annals of Tennessee, Confederate*, 1:431–32.
[79] Ibid., 1:507–508.
[80] W. J. Worsham, *Old Nineteenth Tennessee Regiment C.S.A.*, 114–16, 204.
[81] *Memphis Daily Appeal*, Atlanta, GA, 25 May 1864, 1.
[82] Lindsley, *Military Annals of Tennessee, Confederate*, 1:303–305.
[83] *Memphis Daily Appeal*, Atlanta, GA, 25 May 1864, 1, shows 1 killed, 11 wounded, at Resaca and Adairsville, 13–17 May 1864.
[84] *Memphis Daily Appeal*, Atlanta, GA, 25 May 1864, 1. See also Lindsley, *Military Annals of Tennessee, Confederate*, 1:303–305, which gives names of 1 killed at Dalton, 1 killed at Resaca, and 1 killed at Calhoun.
[85] *Memphis Daily Appeal*, Atlanta, GA, 25 May 1864, 1, shows 3 killed, 22 wounded, and 1 missing, at Resaca and Adairsville, 13–17 May 1864.
[86] *Memphis Daily Appeal*, Atlanta, GA, 25 May 1864, 1, shows 3 killed, 22 wounded, and 1 missing, at Resaca and Adairsville, 13–17 May 1864.

29th TN:	4k/12w[87]	[4k/12w][88]
13th	16w(1mw)[89]	[16w/1mw][90]
154th TN:	15w(1mw)[91]	[15w(1mw)][92]
Smith's Regiment (Hardee's Corps) Artillery:		[46k&w (3k)][93]
Hoxton's Battalion:		
Phelan's AL Battery:		
Perry's Marion FL Battery:	2w[94]	[2w]
Turner's MS Battery:		
Martin's Battalion:		
Bledsoe's MO Battery:		
Ferguson's SC Battery:		
Howell's GA Battery:		
Hotchkiss's Battalion:		
Key's AR Battery:		
Semple's/Goldwaithe's AL Battery:	12[95]	[12k&w]
Warren (MS) Lt. Art. (Swett/Shannon):	16[96]	[16k&w]
Cobb's Battalion:		

[87] *Memphis Daily Appeal*, Atlanta, GA, 25 May 1864, 1, shows 4 killed, 12 wounded, at Resaca and Adairsville, 13–17 May 1864.
[88] *Memphis Daily Appeal*, Atlanta, GA, 25 May 1864, 1, shows 4 killed, 12 wounded, at Resaca and Adairsville, 13–17 May 1864.
[89] *Memphis Daily Appeal*, Atlanta, GA, 25 May 1864, 1, shows 16 wounded, 1 mortally, at Resaca and Adairsville, 13–17 May 1864.
[90] *Memphis Daily Appeal*, Atlanta, GA, 25 May 1864, 1, shows 16 wounded, 1 mortally, at Resaca and Adairsville, 13–17 May 1864.
[91] *Memphis Daily Appeal*, Atlanta, GA, 25 May 1864, 1, shows 15 wounded, 1 mortally, at Resaca and Adairsville, 13–17 May 1864.
[92] *Memphis Daily Appeal*, Atlanta, GA, 25 May 1864, 1, shows 15 wounded, 1 mortally, at Resaca and Adairsville, 13–17 May 1864.
[93] Of the 46 killed and wounded, 3 are confirmed as killed. Author estimates another 7 of the remaining 43 were killed, resulting in an estimated 10 killed and 36 wounded.
[94] Board of State Institutions, *Soldiers of Florida*, 14 May 1903.
[95] Daniel, *Cannoneers in Gray*, 154.
[96] Ibid.

Cobb's KY Battery:		3w[97]			[3w][98]
Mebane's TN Battery:		3w[99]			[3w][100]
Slocumb's LA Washington Art. (5th Co.)		3k/7w[101]			[3k/7w][102]
Total Smith's Regiment (Hardee's Corps) Artillery:					[46k&w]
Total Hardee's Corps: (25,782)[103]				116k/850w	[144k/1,031w/139m]
Hood's Corps:					
Stevenson's Division:	(6,589) 138[104]	(6,429)	575k&w	84k/442w	[101k/492w/235m][105]
Brown's Brigade:		15k		24k/143w	
3rd TN:[106]		7k/35[107]			

[97] *Memphis Daily Appeal*, Atlanta, GA, 25 May 1864.
[98] *Memphis Daily Appeal*, Atlanta, GA, 25 May 1864, 1, shows 3 wounded, between Dalton and Cassville, 6–20 May 1864. Author believes casualties occurred at Resaca.
[99] *Memphis Daily Appeal*, Atlanta, GA, 25 May 1864.
[100] *Memphis Daily Appeal*, Atlanta, GA, 25 May 1864, 1, shows 3 wounded, between Dalton and Cassville, 6–20 May 1864. Author believes casualties occurred at Resaca.
[101] *Memphis Daily Appeal*, Atlanta, GA, 25 May 1864, 1, shows 3 killed, 7 wounded, between Dalton and Cassville, 6–20 May 1864. Compare Daniel, *Cannoneers in Gray*, 154, which confirms 10 casualties at Resaca.
[102] *Memphis Daily Appeal*, Atlanta, GA, 25 May 1864, 1, shows 3 killed, 7 wounded, between Dalton and Cassville, 6–20 May 1864.
[103] The total present figures come from the 30 April 1864 report. (See *OR*, ser. 1, vol. 38, pt. 3, 676.)
[104] *OR*, ser. 1, vol. 38, pt. 3, 815.
[105] Brown's Brigade's wounded at Resaca is completely missing, as are several other brigade reports for Resaca. However, Stevenson's figure of 575 in killed and wounded is higher than his entire return for 6 May to 20 May (84k + 442w= 526. Therefore, his 575 figure in casualties at Resaca, less the 526 figure given as a total for 6–20 May, leaves about 50 men as casualties at Resaca who are *not* on the total report. Plus, the missing and captured are wholly missing, as well, of course.
[106] Lindsley, *Military Annals of Tennessee, Confederate*, 1:179.
[107] *Memphis Daily Appeal*, Atlanta, GA, 27 May 1864, 1, shows 7 killed and 35 wounded at Resaca.

18th TN:[108]		4k/22w/1m[109]						
26th TN:[110]		2k/9w[111]						
32nd TN:	3k/1mw (5/13)[112]	1k/3w (5/15)[113]						
45th TN:[114]		5k/44w[115]						
23rd TN Bttn.:[116]		8k						
Reynolds's Brigade:(1,116)[117]							36k/100w	
58th NC: (327)[118]	1w/4c	5k/30w/11c/2m			14c			[5k/31w/29c/2m]
60th NC: (141)[119]		2k/6w/7c	3c		3c			
54th VA: (390)[120]		21k/20w/28c[121]		16c				[21k/20w/44c]
63rd VA: (303)[122]	1w/3c	5k/11w/20c				3k/2w/9c		[8k/14w/32c]
Pettus's Brigade:							9k/129w	

---

[108] Lindsley, *Military Annals of Tennessee, Confederate*, 1:370–72.

[109] John M. Douglass, Adj., *Memphis Daily Appeal*, Atlanta, GA: 24 May 1864, 2. Compare *Memphis Daily Appeal*, Atlanta, GA, 27 May 1864, 1, which shows 2 killed and 18 wounded at Resaca.

[110] Lindsley, *Military Annals of Tennessee, Confederate*, 1:413–15.

[111] *Memphis Daily Appeal*, Atlanta, GA, 27 May 1864, 1, shows 2 killed and 9 wounded at Resaca.

[112] Lindsley, *Military Annals of Tennessee, Confederate*, 1:478.

[113] *OR Supp*., Serial 79, 158.

[114] Lindsley, *Military Annals of Tennessee, Confederate*, 1:541–42.

[115] *Memphis Daily Appeal*, Atlanta, GA, 27 May 1864, 1, shows 5 killed and 44 wounded at Resaca. This figure includes 45th TN and 23rd TN Battalion casualties at Resaca.

[116] Lindsley, *Military Annals of Tennessee, Confederate*, 2:603.

[117] Sherwood and Weaver, *54th Virginia Infantry*, 101. See Claiborne's journal, which shows 1,774 total present and 1,376 effective total present on 25 March 1864 (Willis H. Claiborne Journal, *OR Supp*., Serial 6, 207).

[118] Hardy, *Fifty-Eighth North Carolina Troops*, 111–19; Sherwood and Weaver, *54th Virginia Infantry*, 101.

[119] Sherwood and Weaver, *54th Virginia Infantry*, 101. But see W. T. Jordan, Jr., *North Carolina Troops 1861–1865: A Roster*, 14:468, 501–92, which shows 27 officers and 189 men present in May 1864 for a total present of 216.

[120] Sherwood and Weaver, *54th Virginia Infantry*, 101.

[121] Stevenson's report shows 54th VA lost 100 men in just 15 minutes during assault on 15 May (*OR*, ser. 1, vol. 38, pt. 3, 813); but see Sherwood and Weaver, *54th Virginia Infantry*, 157, which shows losses for Dalton and Resaca at 21 killed, 20 wounded, and 28 captured for a total of 69 men.

[122] Weaver, *63rd Virginia Infantry*, 98; Sherwood and Weaver, *54th Virginia Infantry*, 101.

20th AL:[123]	1k/2w(5/8), 2k/6w(5/9), 1k(5/10), 1k(5/11), 4w(5/14), 3w(5/15)			1m(5/20)			[5k/15w/1m]
23rd AL:[124]	5w	3k/37w	-		-		3k/42
30th AL:[125]	3k/7w	9k/9w/12c					
31st AL:							
46th AL:							
Cumming's Brigade:							
2nd GA State Line (joined June 15)[126]							15k/70w
34th GA:[127]	1w/7c	1k/1w/6c		2c	3c		[1k/2w/18c]
36th GA:[128]	28c	4k/5w/15c	2c	11c	9c		[4k/5w/65c]
39th GA:[129]			1c		2c	1w/7c	
56th GA:[130]				10c			
Stewart's Division:	16k/57w/21m					110k/689w	[148k/741w/142m][131]

[123] Colonel James M. Deadman, "Report of Casualties of 20th Alabama Infantry Regiment May 8–25 1864," *OR Supp.*, Serial 95, 544–46, from S*elma (Alabama) Morning Reporter*, 4 June 1864. Additionally, losses from the Hell Hole battles are included that showed 1 killed and 3 wounded on 26 May, and 1 killed and 2 wounded on 27 May.

[124] Report of Dr. J. M. Hunt, Surgeon, 23rd Alabama Volunteers. Of the wounded at Resaca, 4 died and 1 was left on the field.

[125] L. D. Stephens, *Bound for Glory*, 226, 232.

[126] From 15 June to 17 September 1864, of 436 men present at start of campaign, 36 killed, 17 died of disease, 195 wounded, 158 deserted or AWOL, and 29 supposed to be captured. A comparison of the author's hand count of microfilm rolls shows 37 killed, 19 died of wounds or disease, 157 wounded, 148 AWOL or deserted, and 21 captured or missing (2nd Regiment, Georgia State Line, Storey's Co. K list of casualties 17 September 1864 (includes regimental total at end of columns), Confederate Muster Rolls, Georgia's Virtual Vault, Georgia Archives).

[127] Author's research and compilation shows 1 wounded at Dalton, 1 killed and 1 wounded at Resaca, and 18 captured between Dalton and the Etowah River 12–19 May (CMSR and L. Henderson, *Roster of the Confederate Soldiers of Georgia*, 3:763–843). Note: this figure does *not* include number of desertions from this time and further review of records is needed.

[128] Ibid., 3:929–1013.

[129] Ibid., 4:249–340.

[130] Ibid., 5:836–917. Roster shows 1 captured on 19 May and 9 others captured, not stated but fit between Oostanaula and Etowah Rivers.

[131] There are 4 more confirmed killed that should be added to this figure.

Clayton's Brigade:	5k/24w/12m								47k/278w [64k/242w/132m][132]
18th AL:[133]		2k/4w/7m	6k/41w/27m				33c[134]		8k/45w/67m
32nd AL:		--included in 58th AL--							
36th AL:[135]		1k/5w/2m	14k/70w/8m						15k/75w/10m
38th AL:[136]		2k/15w/3m		7k/53w/30m					9k/68w/33m
58th AL:[137]		(345) 0		15k/54w/32m(5/15)					15k/54w/32m
Gibson's Brigade:[138] (85off/889men)	5k/17w/7m								17k/75w [38k/163w/19m][139]
1st LA:									2k/6w/5m[140]
4th Bttn. LA:									?[141]
13th LA:[142] (14 off/76men)		0	2k/1w		0	0		0	2k/1w
14th LA Bttn. SS:[143] (60men)		1m	(60) 2k/5w					0	2k/6w/1m
16th LA:		--included in the 25th LA—							
19th LA: (278)[144]	1k/2w/2m	2k/16w							

[132] Author's research and compilation. Note: the number of wounded is lower than the initial after-action report. This is likely due to the increase in those who since died and were added to the killed list. The first calculation is from the day of the battle or shortly afterward whereas the second report comes from the end of May or first of June, approximately 2 to 3 weeks later. The other explanation for the lower figure is that those who were only slightly wounded or injured may have been since removed. Finally, the number of missing may account for some of the discrepancy for a myriad of unknowable reasons without matching each missing soldier with a Federal capture report for that soldier.

[133] *OR*, ser. 1, vol. 38, pt. 3, 834.

[134] Ibid. See Major Austin's report from 14th LA SS, which shows 33 men surrendered to cavalry without attempting to fight, ibid at 862.

[135] Ibid.; also see Clement A. Evans, *Confederate Military History*, 8:171.

[136] *OR*, ser. 1, vol. 38, pt. 3, 834.

[137] Ibid., 834, 844; Evans, *Confederate Military History*, 8:160.

[138] As reported by General Joseph E. Johnston from A. J. Foard, medical director, Army of Tennessee (*OR*, ser. 1, vol. 38, pt. 3, 686–87). Figures also repeated in Salling, *Louisianans in the Western Confederacy*, 169.

[139] Brigadier General Randall Gibson's report includes casualties at New Hope Church (*OR*, ser. 1, vol. 38, pt. 3, 855).

[140] Major S. S. Batchelor's report includes casualties at New Hope Church (*OR*, ser. 1, vol. 38, pt. 3, 859).

[141] Major Duncan Buie's report shows casualties at New Hope Church of 3 killed and 8 wounded, but 8–15 May not reported (*OR*, ser. 1, vol. 38, pt. 3, 859).

[142] Lieutenant Colonel Francis L. Campbell's report, *OR*, ser. 1, vol. 38, pt. 3, 860–61. Campbell's report also shows 2 wounded slightly on 25 May at New Hope Church and no casualties at Dalton, Calhoun, Adairsville, or Cassville.

[143] Major John E. Austin's report, *OR*, ser. 1, vol. 38, pt. 3, 862.

[144] Salling, *Louisianans in the Western Confederacy*, 161; Lieutenant Colonel H. A. Kennedy's report, *OR*, ser. 1, vol. 38, pt. 3, 865.

20th LA: (58)[145]							
25th LA: (233)[146]	2k/9w	2k/13w					[6k/22w/1m][147]
Stovall's Brigade:[148]	0k/5w/2m 270k&w					24k/195w	[440k&w]
1st GA State Line (joined May 28)							
40th GA:[149]	1w/1m (1w 5/13)	4k/12w/60m	4m	16m	21m	7k/36w/43m[150]	[4k/14w/102m][151]
41st GA:[152]	2w/1m	4k/29w/8m					4k/31w/9m
42nd GA:[153]	1k/3w/3c	12k/60w/17c (117)	0	0	1c		13k/63w/21c
43rd GA:[154]		4k/27w/7m					
52nd GA:[155]	1w	2k/23w/3m					
Baker's Brigade:[156]	6k/11w/0m	1k/@5w(5/14), 178(5/15)				22k/141w	[44k/231w/25m][157]

---

[145] Salling, *Louisianans in the Western Confederacy*, 161, which shows 13th & 20th LA combined at 148, but 13th LA is shown in *OR* at 14 officers and 76 men.

[146] Ibid.; figure includes 16th & 25th LA combined; Colonel J. C. Lewis's report, *OR*, ser. 1, vol. 38, pt. 3, 863.

[147] *Memphis Daily Appeal*, Atlanta, GA, 25 May 1864, 1, which shows 6 killed and 22 wounded and 1 missing from Dalton, 8 May, to Resaca, 15 May.

[148] Brigadier General Marcellus A. Stovall's report of casualties from 7 May to date of report, 2 June, includes New Hope Church (*OR*, ser. 1, vol. 38, pt. 3, 823).

[149] L. Henderson, *Roster of the Confederate Soldiers of Georgia*, 4:341–425. One man wounded at Swamp Creek, 13 May; 25 of missing were captured, 35 of missing deserted at Resaca; 4 men captured at Calhoun, 16 May; 10 men captured and 6 men deserted at Adairsville, 17 May; 4 men captured and 17 men deserted at Cassville on 19 May.

[150] Captain J. N. Dobbs's report of casualties from 7 May to 29 May includes New Hope Church (*OR*, ser. 1, vol. 38, pt. 3, 826).

[151] Author's research and compilation shows 4 killed, 14 wounded and 25 captured at Resaca with 35 deserted following the retreat from Resaca, with a total of 43 men captured and 58 men deserted between Resaca and Cassville, i.e., between the Oostanaula and Etowah rivers, and 1 man deserted after Dalton.

[152] Major Mark S. Nall's report of casualties on 25 May at New Hope Church were 5k/55w, date of report, 29 May (*OR*, ser. 1, vol. 38, pt. 3, 827). Report includes casualties at Dalton, Resaca and New Hope Church but nothing at Cassville.

[153] Roberts and Clark, *Atlanta's Fighting Forty-Second*, roster 347–496. *Atlanta Constitution*, 2 February 1890, reports a loss of 117 in killed, wounded, and missing at Resaca. Captain Lovick P. Thomas's report of casualties from 14–29 May reported more than 100 killed and wounded, with 2k/20w/3m at New Hope Church on 25 May (*OR*, ser. 1, vol. 38, pt. 3, 828).

[154] Major William C. Lester's report of casualties shows 1k/4w on 14 May, and 3k/23w/7m on 15 May at Resaca (*OR*, ser. 1, vol. 38, pt. 3, 829). Report dated 30 May also includes 1k/22w on 25 May and 7 wounded 26–28 May at New Hope Church.

[155] *OR*, ser. 1, vol. 38, pt. 3, 830. Asbury's report of casualties dated 29 May also includes 17 wounded on 25 May at New Hope Church.

[156] Brigadier General Alpheus Baker's report shows 1 killed, a few wounded on 14 May, and 178 total killed, wounded, and missing on 15 May at Resaca (*OR*, ser. 1, vol. 38, pt. 3, 844–45).

[157] James M. Loughbrough, casualty list, Brigadier General Alpheus Baker's Brigade, 7–31 May 1864, *OR Supp.*, Serial 95, 495–501, from *Memphis Appeal*, newspaper, Atlanta, Georgia, 7 June 1864, includes casualties from the Battle of New Hope Church and the Hell Hole battles. Baker's report, 2 June 1864, includes casualties from 7 May through 2 June 1864, of 47 killed, 230 wounded, and 34 missing, and indicates on 1 and 2 June, Baker's Brigade saw 3 men killed

37th AL:[158]		1k	4k/33w/6m[159]	2m[160]	0	0	5k/33w/8m	[15k/90w/11m]
40th AL:[161] (416)	4k/5w	(398)5k/37w/3m	0	0	0		9k/42w/3m	[17k/60w/3m]
42nd AL:[162] (300)	0	2k/39w/17m	0	0	0		2k/39w/17m	[2k/47w/8m]
54th AL:[163]		3w	4k/21w/2m	0	0	0	4k/24w/2m	[10k/34w/3m]
Hindman's Division:							85k/391w	[103k/436w/57c][164]
Deas's Brigade:						1k/2w[165]		17k/91w
17th AL SS:								0
19th AL:								1k/2w[166]
22nd AL:								0
25th AL:								0
39th AL:			8k/25w/4m[167]					0
50th AL:								0

(or 2 men killed and 1 man who since died) from the 231 reported as wounded on 31 May 1864, and an additional 7 men missing (*OR*, ser. 1, vol. 38, pt. 3, 847).

158 Lieutenant Colonel John A. Minter's report of 54th AL includes 1 man killed in detached Company of 37th AL on 9 May at Mill Creek Gap (*OR*, ser. 1, vol. 38, pt. 3, 852). Author suspects 2 more killed and 3 more wounded not reported in 37th AL at Dalton due to brigade reconciliation being short these figures and the other three regiments being specific with their reports at Dalton and Resaca, but 37th AL did not report Dalton.

159 *OR*, ser. 1, vol. 38, pt. 3, 849–52; Evans, *Confederate Military History*, 8:173, shows captains C. Pennington and C. E. Evans among the wounded at Resaca, 15 May.

160 Lieutenant Colonel Alexander A. Greene's report includes 2 men lost between Resaca and the Etowah River because they were unable to march (*OR*, ser. 1, vol. 38, pt. 3, 849).

161 Colonel John H. Higley's report, shows 3 wounded and 3 missing with one killed on 14 May, and 5 killed and 34 wounded on 15 May at Resaca (*OR*, ser. 1, vol. 38, pt. 3, 850).

162 Captain William D. McNeill's report shows 2 slightly wounded and 3 missing on 14 May, and 2 killed (including Reverend J. P. McMullen), 32 wounded and 14 missing on 15 May at Resaca (*OR*, ser. 1, vol. 38, pt. 3, 851). Compare Willet's diary, ADAH, which shows 7 killed, 44 wounded on 15 May.

163 Lieutenant Colonel John A. Minter's report shows 1 wounded, 1 missing on 14 May, and 4 killed, 20 wounded, and 1 missing on 15 May at Resaca (*OR*, ser. 1, vol. 38, pt. 3, 852–53).

164 Figure includes 8 additional killed from Resaca Cemetery.

165 Vertical files, Regimental folders, ADAH.

166 Vertical files, 19th AL, ADAH.

167 Five men were killed and 12 wounded with one shell (*Columbus [Georgia] Daily Sun*, 29 May 1864, 1, but see the *Columbus [Georgia] Daily Sun*, 24 May 1864, 2, which reports 15 killed and wounded in 1 shell).

Walthall's Brigade: (1,158men)[168]		49k/119w/1m[169]					40k/123w	[50k/123w/2m]
24th MS: (46/559)[170]			24k/28w					
27th MS: (see 24th MS) 0[171]		6k/27w/1m (add 3 mw)			1c		0	
29th MS: (30/421)[172]			5k/23w					1w[173]
30th MS: (see 29th MS)[174]		10k/29w				1k/3w		
34th MS: (20/178)[175]			4k/11w					
Manigault's Brigade: (1,963)		119[176]						12k/59w
24th AL:			2k/18w[177]					
28th AL:			17w					[17w][178]
34th AL:			2k/24w					[2k/24w][179]
10th SC: [180]	2w		1k/11w	1c				[1k/16w/3c][181]
19th SC: [182]	1c		1k/1w/1c			1c	1k/1w/3c	

[168] Evans, *Confederate Military History*, 9: 213.

[169] Brigadier General Edward C. Walthall's report of brigade casualties at Resaca includes one staff officer wounded (*OR*, ser. 1, vol. 38, pt. 3, 798).

[170] *OR*, ser. 1, vol. 38, pt. 3, 798, shows 49 officers and 559 men present in the 24th & 27th MS combined.

[171] R. C. Wells, *27th Mississippi Infantry*, 101, provides a list of 5 killed, 4 mortally wounded, 27 wounded, and 1 missing at Resaca; see also Rowland, *Military History of Mississippi*, 270; *OR*, ser. 1, vol. 38, pt. 3, 798.

[172] Rowland, *Military History of Mississippi*, 279, and *OR*, ser. 1, vol. 38, pt. 3, 798, which shows 30 officers & 421 men present in 29th & 30th MS combined.

[173] Rowland, *Military History of Mississippi*, 279, reports 1 man wounded at Cassville by artillery fire.

[174] *OR*, ser. 1, vol. 38, pt. 3, 798; see also Ashley and Ashley, *Oh for Dixie!*, 38, figure includes the 27th and 30th MS at Cassville; compare Rowland, *Military History of Mississippi*, 287, which shows 1 killed and 1 wounded from artillery fire at Cassville.

[175] *OR*, ser. 1, vol. 38, pt. 3, 798, shows 20 officers and 178 men present.

[176] Manigault, *A Carolinian Goes to War*, 181.

[177] Newton Davis, 24th AL, to wife Bettie, 17 May 1864, ADAH, typed copy incorrectly says 13 wounded. Copy in author's possession. Compare *Memphis Daily Appeal*, Atlanta, GA, 26 May 1864, 1, which shows 10 wounded between 7 May and 20 May.

[178] *Memphis Daily Appeal*, Atlanta, GA, 26 May 1864, 1, which shows 17 wounded between 7 May 7 and 20 May.

[179] *Memphis Daily Appeal*, Atlanta, GA, 26 May 1864, 1, which shows 2 killed and 24 wounded between 7 May 7 and 20 May.

[180] Baxley, *Walk in the Light*, 185–374, shows 2 were wounded at Dalton, 1 of the wounded at Resaca was also captured, and 1 was captured on 18 May at Calhoun.

[181] *Memphis Daily Appeal*, Atlanta, GA, 26 May 1864, 1, which shows 16 wounded between 7 May 7 and 20 May.

[182] Baxley, *Walk in the Light*, 375–511.

Tucker's Brigade:			4k/3c[183]		16k/118w	
F&S:		1w[184]				
9th MS SS:			1k			
7th MS:	9k/38w[185]		3c			[9k/38w/3c]
9th MS:						
10th MS:						
41st MS:			3k			
Hood's Corps Artillery: (Beckham's Regiment):				4k/42w		
Courtney's Battalion (F&S):	1w[186]					[1k/15w]
Garrity's AL Battery:	1k/6w[187]					[1k/6w]
Dent's AL Battery:	7w[188]					[7w]
Douglas's TX Battery:	1w[189]					[1w]
Eldridge's Battalion:						
Oliver's Eufaula AL Battery:						
Fenner's LA Battery:						
Stanford's MS Battery:						
Johnston's Battalion:[190]	1w(5/14)					[2k/31w/30m]

[183] RG 109 CMSR, National Archives, Washington, DC, Cemetery list transcribed by Raymond W. Watkins, Falls Church, VA; list donated to Bartow County Museum by Bob Crowe.

[184] *OR*, ser. 1, vol. 38, pt. 3, 761; Hood's Corps report includes Brigadier General William F. Tucker's severe wounding (arm shattered).

[185] Skellie, *Lest We Forget*, 2:661–62. Note: Diarist Lt. John D. Cooper, Co. G, 7th MS, reports "no protection from artillery," and 9 killed and 30 to 40 wounded, presumably mostly on 14 May during the heavy artillery shelling, but Skellie reports only 9 killed or mortally wounded and 13 seriously wounded. Compare *Memphis Daily Appeal*, Atlanta, GA, 24 May 1864, 2, which lists 7 killed and 38 wounded. Skellie notes that all 3 captured at Cassville were apparently wounded at Resaca and left behind in a field hospital as too sick to move any farther.

[186] *Memphis Daily Appeal*, Atlanta, GA, 24 May 1864, 2.

[187] Ibid.

[188] Ibid.

[189] Ibid.

[190] Acting Adj. William A. Russell, "List of Casualties in Johnston's Battalion Artillery in the series of engagements, commencing May 8 to June 4, 1864" lists Major John William Johnston as wounded on 14 May (*OR Supp.*, Serial 95, 554–55).

Van Den Corput's Cherokee GA Battery: 1c (Dalton) 6k/2w/10c (Resaca-but @20 unaccounted for) 8c Cassville (b/t rivers) 6k/2w/19c (+20 missing)[191]					
Rowan's-Stevens'/3rd MD/GA: 2w[192]	3k/15w	-	-	3k/17w	
Marshall's TN Battery: [193]	0k/6w/4m				
Beckham's Regiment (Hood's Corps) Artillery:					[3k/46w/30m] Total
Hood's Corps: (24,379)[194]				283k/1,564w	[363k/1,717w/484m]
Army of Tennessee Artillery Reserve: Hallonquist's Regiment:					2k/2w
Palmer's Battalion:					
Lumsden's AL Battery:					
Anderson's GA Battery:					
Havis's GA Battery:					
Waddell's Battalion:					
Emery's AL Battery:	2w[195]				
Bellamy's AL Battery:					
Barret's MO Battery:					
Williams's Battalion: [196]					
Kolb's Barbour AL Battery: (115, 2 6-pdr, 2 12 pdr Howitzers)					
Darden's Jefferson MS Battery: (68, 4 Napoleons)					

[191] Also, 4 Napoleon 12-pounder guns lost on 15 May (Waters and Fisher, "*The Damnedest Set of Fellows,*" 249–71). Compare Russell, "List of Casualties in Johnston's Battalion Artillery May 8 to June 4, 1864," *OR Supp.*, Serial 95, 554–55, which shows 5 wounded and 17 missing for a total of 22 all on 15 May. Daniel (*Cannoneers in Gray,* 154) also reports 22 lost by Van den Corput at Resaca.

[192] W. W. Goldsborough, *Maryland Line Confederate Army*, 308, shows 2 wounded on 8 May. Compare Russell, "List of Casualties in Johnston's Battalion Artillery May 8 to June 4, 1864," *OR Supp.*, Serial 95, 555, which shows 1 killed, 13 wounded, and 4 missing at Resaca 14–15 May, and 2 killed, 19 wounded, and 9 missing, including 1 killed and 4 wounded in the Hell Hole battles. See also Daniel, *Cannoneers in Gray,* 154, which shows 18 lost at Resaca.

[193] Russell, "List of Casualties in Johnston's Battalion," *OR Supp.*, Serial 95, 554–55; Daniel, *Cannoneers in Gray,* 154. Shows 12 lost at Resaca.

[194] The total present figures come from the 30 April 1864 report. (See *OR*, ser. 1, vol. 38, pt. 3, 676.)

[195] *Columbus (Georgia) Daily Sun*, 21 May 1864, 2.

[196] Weaver, *Nottoway Artillery*, 67.

Jeffress's Nottoway VA Battery: 0 (80, 4 10 pd Parrots)	1k		0		1k	
Polk's Corps:						
Loring's Division: (5,405)[197]	184kwm[198]				16k/106w	[27k/156/1c][199]
Featherston's Brigade: (arrived May 12)					3k/33w	[41k/135w/1m][200]
1st MS Bttn. SS:[201]	--1k/6w					[1k/6w/0m]
3rd MS:[202]	--8k/17w/1c	0	0	0		[10k/34w/0m]
22nd MS:						[9k/22w/0m]

197 *OR*, ser. 1, vol. 32, pt. 3, 862, shows Loring's Division with 393 officers, 4,322 men present for duty, 4,259 effective total present, and 5,405 aggregate present on 30 April 1864, at Demopolis, AL. But note *OR*, ser. 1, vol. 38, pt. 3, 677, which shows Loring's Division at 6,390 aggregate present on 10 June. This increase of 985 men is from the net of the addition of the 27th, 35th, and 49th AL, plus perhaps a few men who rejoined their regiments from furlough or from being rounded up in early May who were AWOL in MS or AL, less the subtraction of the 9th AR (which was transferred to Daniel Reynolds's AR Brigade) and battlefield casualties and illnesses from 1 May to 10 June in Loring's Division. Thus, assuming 150 men from the 9th AR and 200 in losses due to the campaign, there is an increase of 1,335 men from the 27th, 35th, and 49th AL, plus a few other soldiers who rejoined their regiments after 30 April—say, 400 men each from the three arriving AL regiments and 135 men returning to their units between 1 May and 10 June. Note: the 43rd MS was transferred from Featherston to Adams after the 30 April and before the 10 June returns, but the 43rd MS is still counted in Loring's Division in both returns.

198 Loring's report, *OR*, ser. 1, vol. 38, pt. 3, 875.

199 Loring's report shows 184 killed, wounded, and missing but is not broken down. A conservative estimate, 27 killed, is less than 1/6 the total number of killed and wounded provided by Loring. Also, there are probably about this number of buried at Resaca Cemetery from Loring's Division. Loring lost 184 at Resaca, 26 between 16 May and 30 May, and 131 overnight on 30–31 May in a hot fight for possession of each other's forward line as part of the Hell Hole battles, near the Widow Brown's Mill, or Brooks house (*OR*, ser. 1, vol. 38, pt. 3, 875).

200 Casualty list, Brigadier General Winfield Scott Featherston's Brigade, 12 May, 4 June 1864, *OR Supp.*, Serial 95, 504–507, from *Memphis Appeal*, Atlanta, Georgia, 8 June 1864. While the sum of the regiment figures in killed equals only 38, and the total of wounded adds up to only 129, it appears that 3 of the wounded men since died, and 9 men may have been slightly wounded and not reported in the newspaper published account. Of these figures, Featherston lost 24 killed and 98 wounded during an overnight battle on 30–31 May 1864 during the Hell Hole battles. Thus, Featherston's losses from Resaca to Cassville total only 17 killed, 37 wounded, and 1 missing. (See Loring's report, 31 May 1864, *OR*, ser. 1, vol. 38, pt. 3, 874).

201 J. L. Power Scrapbook 1864, Special Collections (Z 742), MDAH, 9, newspaper clipping; Rowland, *Military History of Mississippi*, 145, shows 1 killed, Lt. W.C. Dodson of Company C but compare *OR Supp.*, Serial 44, at 649, which shows 2nd Lt. William T. Dodson was killed 31 May 1864. This is possible as Featherston's Brigade was heavily engaged at Brown's Mill, near New Hope Church, on 31 May, or it could be transposed as a casualty on 13 May at Resaca where the 1st MS Battalion Sharpshooters were also engaged.

202 Howell Jr., *To Live and Die in Dixie*, 293–94.

31st MS:[203]		--2k/9w	0	0	0	2k/9w[204]	[1k/19w/1m]
33rd MS:							[15k/41w/0m]
40th MS:		--				8k/47w/9m[205]	[2k/7w/0m]
Adams's Brigade: (arrived May 11)						6k/22w	
6th MS:	--	considerable loss at Resaca[206]					
14th MS:							
15th MS:[207]		--	2k/9w	0	0	2k/9w	
20th MS: (520)[208]							
23rd MS:							
43rd MS:		--	1k/2w[209]				
Scott's Brigade:	(arrived May 10)					7k/51w	
27th AL:							
35th AL:	-joined May 25 at New Hope-[210]						
49th AL:	-wintered at Dalton, assigned to Loring's Division-[211]						
55th AL:							
57th AL:			5w[212]				
9th AR:			1k/8w[213]				

(9th AR arrived Resaca 5/10 with Scott's Brigade) transferred to Reynolds's Brigade May ___ (after Resaca)

---

[203] Author's research of CSR, National Archives, microfilm records, RG 9 Mississippi, rolls 341–46, one of the wounded men later died in the Fair Ground Hospital in Atlanta on 24 May, and another wounded man was captured and sent to the US hospital in Chattanooga.

[204] Author's research of CSR, National Archives, microfilm records, RG 9 Mississippi, rolls 341–46.

[205] Rowland, *Military History of Mississippi*, 342–43, which shows all casualties from arriving at Resaca 12 May–6 July, which includes New Hope, Pine Mtn., and Kennesaw.

[206] Ibid., 176, shows 6th MS had considerable loss from skirmishing and artillery at Resaca 13–15 May.

[207] J. L. Power Scrapbook 1864, 9, newspaper clipping. This figure includes accounting through Cassville.

[208] *OR Supp.*, Serial 45, 565, reports 520 men aggregate present for duty on 20 May at Allatoona Hills, and lost 120 men in 20th MS from Resaca through Ezra Church, 28 July.

[209] W. S. Bell, *Camel Regiment*, 153.

[210] Banning, *Regimental History of the Thirty-Fifth Alabama*, 45.

[211] W. Brewer, *Alabama*, 662–63.

[212] Joel Dyer Murphree to wife, Ursula, 16 May 1864, *Alabama Historical Quarterly* 19/1 (Spring 1957).

[213] Willis, *Arkansas Confederates in the Western Theater*, 479–83; Willis's review of the Compiled Service Records reveals 1 wounded on 11 May who died three days later, 2 wounded on 13 May defending Bald Hill with Scott's Brigade, 1 wounded on 14 May, and 1 killed and 4 wounded on 15 May.

12th LA:									
French's Division: (4,765)[214]					5w		18w		[5k/18w/11m][215]
Cockrell's Brigade (1,490)[216]	--joined at Cassville 5/18--				0				
1st MO: (240)[217]									
2nd MO: (560)[218]									
3rd MO: (340)[219]									
4th MO:									
5th MO:									
6th MO:									
1st MO Cav.: (350)[220]									
3rd MO Cav.:									
Ector's Brigade:[221]	--joined at Cassville 5/18, except 39th NC already present at Resaca--				2w/2m				[5k/12w/5m]
Staff:					0				
29th NC:					0				
39th NC:	0		5k/8w/3m[222]		0				
9th TX:					1w				
10th TX Cav:[223]	--	--	-	--	1m			1m	
14th TX Cav.:						1m			

---

[214] *OR*, ser. 1, vol. 32, pt. 3, 862, includes French's Division of Ector and Cockrell, and adds Sears's Brigade, which has been added to French, shows 5 wounded and 3 horses killed during skirmishing and shelling afternoon of 19 May at Cassville (*OR*, ser. 1, vol. 38, pt. 3, 899).

[215] French's casualties are small because only the 39th NC was engaged at Resaca that listed 5k, 8w, and 3m. French had several wounded and missing at Cassville.

[216] McGhee, *Guide to Missouri Confederate Units*, 55. Figure is the sum of the four combined regiment returns herein.

[217] Figure includes the 1st & 4th MO Infantry combined.

[218] Figure includes the 2nd & 6th MO Infantry combined.

[219] Figure includes the 3rd & 5th MO Infantry combined.

[220] Figure includes 1st & 3rd MO Cavalry (dismounted) combined.

[221] French's report (*OR*, ser. 1, vol. 38, pt. 3, 908) provides each of the regimental casualties for Cassville.

[222] Jordan Jr., *North Carolina Troops 1861–1865*, 10:107, but see French's report (*OR*, ser. 1, vol. 38, pt. 3, 908) of 2 missing. Jordan's review of the roster is more complete. Also, see Carlock, *History of the Tenth Teas Cavalry*, 132, which finds that the 39th NC arrived at Resaca on 11 May.

[223] French's report, *OR*, ser. 1, vol. 38, pt. 3, 908. Also, Carlock, *History of the Tenth Teas Cavalry*, 132–33, identifies the missing soldier as Private Joseph Pool, Co. K, who was captured at Cassville. He had previously been wounded in the foot at Murfreesboro.

32nd TX Cav.:						1w	
Sears's Brigade:	(2,110)[224]	--joined at Adairsville 5/17--			8w/3m		[8w/3m]
7th MS Bttn.:					1m		
4th MS:					2w[225]		
35th MS:		--	--	--	2w/2m		
36th MS:					0		
39th MS:					0		
46th MS:					4w		
Cantey's Division:	(3,254)					26k/405w	[104/315w/86c][226]
Reynolds's Brigade:	(1,024)[227]	20k/95w/17m[228]				34k/198w[229]	[35k/135w/19c][230]
1st AR Mtd.:	(250)	10k/28w[231]					[17k/42w/4c][232]
2nd AR Mtd.:	-inc. w/1st AR-	6w/3c[233]					[7k/33w/7c][234]
4th AR:		1k/1w[235]					[3k/15w/0c][236]

---

224 *OR*, ser. 1, vol. 32, pt. 3, 862; French's report, *OR*, ser. 1, vol. 38, pt. 3, 908; Rowland, *Military History of Mississippi*, 188, 162.

225 Massey, *Foremost.*

226 Cantey's wounded count includes both Reynolds's and his own brigade figures, but his killed is underreported. It appears that he neglected to include Reynolds's killed completely. Also, the missing and captured, like all the divisions, is missing.

227 *OR*, ser. 1, vol. 32, pt. 3, 860, shows Reynolds's Brigade near Mobile/Pollard, AL, and 812 effective total (infantry) present. Also, this number does not include the 9th AR in the tally as it joined Reynolds's Brigade from Scott's Brigade on 25 May.

228 Willis, *Arkansas Confederates in the Western Theater*, 482; Daniel Reynolds recorded that he lost 130 men killed & wounded on 14 May (Bender, ed., *Worthy of the Cause*, 125).

229 Ibid., 490.

230 Ibid., appendix E, 713–17.

231 Ibid., 475–76. Willis's totals are for both the 1st and 2nd Arkansas Mounted Rifles (dismounted) during the Battle of Dug Gap Mountain, 8 May 1864, and he notes that he could not find any casualties for the 3rd AR Cavalry, which detached from Grigsby's KY Cavalry Brigade to fight with the other Arkansas troops south of the road at Dug Gap.

232 Ibid., appendix E, 713–14.

233 Leeper, *Rebels Valiant*, 230.

234 Willis, *Arkansas Confederates in the Western Theater*, 714–15; Leeper, *Rebels Valiant*, 230.

235 *OR Supp.*, Serial 13, 333; Willis, *Arkansas Confederates in the Western Theater*, 480.

236 Willis, *Arkansas Confederates in the Western Theater*, 715.

4th AR Battn.:			[0k/5w/0c][237]
9th AR:	3k/12w/0m[238]		[3k/12w/0c][239]
(arrived Resaca 5/10 with Scott's Brigade) transferred to Reynolds's Brigade May 25 (but casualties included here)			
25th AR:			[1k/17w/5c][240]
31st AR:	1k/1w/3c[241]		[4k/11w/3c][242]
Cantey's Brigade: (2,230)			[69k/180w/67m][243]
17th AL: (720)[244] 1c	6k/50w/7c	6c	
26th AL: (joined by June 10; stationed at Andersonville Prison April 26, 1864)[245]			
29th AL: (1,110)[246]	58k/85w/32c		
37th MS: (400)[247]	5k/45w/21m (5/9)[248]		
Quarles's Brigade: (1,141)[249] (joined May 24)			
1st AL: (610)[250]			

---

237 Ibid., 716.
238 Ibid., 717.
239 Ibid., 715.
240 Ibid., 716–17.
241 Bass, *History of the Thirty-first Arkansas Confederate Infantry*, 71, 87.
242 Willis, *Arkansas Confederates in the Western Theater*, 715–16.
243 Compare Robert W. Banks to Father and Mother, 23 May 1864, which shows 250 total casualties from 9–23 May (Osborn, ed., "Civil War Letters of Robert W. Banks," 211).
244 Derived by deducting the 29th Alabama total present from Cantey's report on 30 April 1864 (*OR*, ser. 1, vol. 38, pt. 3, 686). Thompson and Thompson, *Seventeenth Alabama Infantry*, 434–43. The Thompsons's casualty lists (in the appendix) notes 6 captured at Cassville, plus 1 captured at Hightower Bridge and 1 captured at Cartersville.
245 *OR*, ser. 1, vol. 38, pt. 3, 646; *OR Supp*., Serial 17, 577–78.
246 Zorn, *Hold at All Hazzards*, 62.
247 *OR*, ser. 1, vol. 38, pt. 3, 67fn.
248 *Mobile Register and Advertiser*, 14 May 1864, ADAH; Willis, *Arkansas Confederates in the Western Theater*, 478; Rowland, *Military History of Mississippi*, 328. Compare J. B. Sanders letter to wife, 10 May 1864, Co. H, 37th MS, where he claims that his regiment lost 81 on 9 May (vertical files, MDAH).
249 *OR*, ser. 1, vol. 32, pt. 3, 860, shows Quarles aggregate present on 30 April at and near Mobile, AL. This tally does not include the 1st AL or the 30th LA, which were added to Quarles's Brigade after 30 April. Thus, the 1st AL and the 30th LA must be added to this figure to derive a full strength of this brigade from approximately 1 June forward, but the 30th LA will be transferred to Gibson's LA Brigade in mid-July.
250 Brewer, *Alabama*, 589–90, records that 610 were with Johnston in fall 1863 in Mississippi, then sent to Mobile, AL, then Pollard, AL, and then to Georgia by 24 May. There were no engagements by that unit from fall 1864 to the action at New Hope Church beginning 25 May. The 1st AL lost half its number at

4th LA:				
30th LA:				
42nd TN:				
46th TN:				
55th TN:				
48th TN:				
49th TN:				
53rd TN:				
Polk's Corps Artillery:	1k/1w	2	5c	[1k/3w/5c]
Myrick's Battalion (Attached to Loring's Division):				
Cowan's MS Battery: --	1k/1w[251]			
Barry's Lookout TN Battery:				
Bouanchaud's Pointe Coupee LA Battery				
Storrs's Battalion (Attached to French's Division):				
Ward's AL Battery:				
Hoskins's Brookhaven MS Battery:		2[252]	@5c	
Guibor's MO Battery:				
Preston's Battalion (Attached to Cantey's/Walthall's Division):				
Tarrant's AL Battery:				
Selden's AL Battery:				
Yates's MS Battery:				

Ezra Church, heavily at Franklin and Nashville, TN, and 100 men surrendered at Goldsboro, NC. Also, more than 3,000 men were among the rolls of the 1st AL at some point during the war. See McMorries, *History of the First Regiment Alabama Volunteer Infantry, C.S.A.*, 119–29. The point is that this was a large regiment for most of the war.

[251] J. L. Power Scrapbook 1864, 9, Special Collections (Z 742), MDAH, shows 1 killed 14 May, and 1 wounded 15 May.

[252] French's report shows Hoskins lost 2 men at Rome, 17 May (*OR*, ser. 1, vol. 38, pt. 3, 899); see Daniel, *Cannoneers in Gray*, 154, which shows several captured at Cassville.

Total Polk's Corps: (14,804)[253]							42k/529w	[139k/490w/98m]
Wheeler's Cavalry Corps:[254]	296k/w/m	152k/w/m	22k/w/m		120k/w/m	53k/w/m	643k/w/m	[73k/341w/53c/81m][255]
Staff:							1w	
Escort:							5w/2c	
Martin's Division:							14k/68w/25c/43m[256]	
Morgan's Brigade:								
1st AL:								
3rd AL:								
4th AL:								
7th AL:								
51st AL:								
Iverson's Brigade:								
1st GA:[257]								
2nd GA:								
3rd GA:	1k/1c[258]							
4th GA:		1w/1m[259]						
6th GA:								

[253] The total present figure for Polk's Corps comes from several sources, including *OR*, ser. 1, vol. 32, pt. 3, 862; *OR*, ser. 1, vol. 38, pt. 3, 676–77, and various diaries, letters, treatises, and regimental accounts. French's Division is conservatively placed at 4,765, but at Cassville, he requested rations for 6,000 men (see *OR*, ser. 1, vol. 38, pt. 4, 725).

[254] Drake, *Annals of the Army of Tennessee*, Chronological Summary Supplement, 85–87, shows a total of 296 casualties of all kinds in Wheeler's Cavalry from 1 May through 13 May in Catoosa and Whitfield counties (from Stone Church at Ringgold and Red Clay through Tunnel Hill, Varnell, Dalton, Swamp Creek, and Tilton).

[255] Wheeler's report includes casualties of Martin's, Kelly's, and Humes's Divisions; Williams's (Grigsby's) Brigade; and Robertson's Artillery Battalion, 6 May to 31 May, Dalton to New Hope Church, Hell Hole Line. *OR*, ser. 1, vol. 38, pt. 3, 949, includes 6 May to 31 May, Dalton to New Hope Church, Hell Hole Line.

[256] Wheeler's report, *OR*, ser. 1, vol. 38, pt. 3, 949, includes 6 May to 31 May, Dalton to New Hope Church, Hell Hole Line.

[257] Between 1 June and 15 August 1864, 39 men deserted. This regiment was from Milledgeville. 1st GA Cavalry (Galt's), Tallent's Cavalry Scouts. Georgia's Virtual Vault, Georgia Archives.

[258] At Tanner's Ferry, *OR Supp*., Serial 17, 464.

[259] Ibid., 588.

Kelly's Division:	1c[260]				39k/154w/16c/23m[261]
Allen's Brigade:					
3rd Conf.:					
8th Conf.:					
10th Conf.:					
12th Conf.: [12th AL] at Farmer's Bridge (5/15)			10k/10c[262]		
Dibrell's Brigade:				11 k&w[263]	60 k/w/m[264]
4th TN:		7w[265]			28 k/w/m
8th TN:		1k/2w[266]			1k/2w
9th TN:		1k, 2w, 2c[267]			5k/5w/3c
10th TN:	5k/5w/3c[268]				3k/2w/1c
11th TN:	1k, 4w[269]			2w/2c	1k/7w/2c
Humes's Division:					13k/88w/1c/10m[270]
Humes's Brigade:					
1st [6th] TN:					
2nd TN:					
4th TN:					
5th TN:					
9th TN:					

260 Osceola, "From the Front," *Memphis Daily Appeal*, 24 May 1864, reported capture of Captain Steiger of Gen. Kelly's staff on 13 May during withdrawal from Dalton.
261 Wheeler's report, *OR*, ser. 1, vol. 38, pt. 3, 949, includes 6 May to 31 May, Dalton to New Hope Church, Hell Hole Line.
262 Brewer, *Alabama*, 688.
263 Osceola, "Camp Dibrell's Brigade Cavalry," *Memphis Daily Appeal*, 24 May 1864, 3.
264 Ibid. Total includes losses from Dalton through Cassville, 6–20 May.
265 Unknown (Dibrell?), "The Cavalry Fight on the Cleveland Road," *Chronicle & Sentinel*, 14 May 1864.
266 Osceola, "Camp Dibrell's Brigade Cavalry," *Memphis Daily Appeal*, 24 May 1864, 3.
267 Unknown (Dibrell?), "The Cavalry Fight on the Cleveland Road," *Chronicle & Sentinel*, 14 May 1864.
268 Osceola, "Camp Dibrell's Brigade Cavalry," *Memphis Daily Appeal*, 24 May 1864, 3, reported capture of Lt. Colonel A. L. Demoss on 13 May during withdrawal from Dalton.
269 Unknown (Dibrell?), "The Cavalry Fight on the Cleveland Road," *Chronicle & Sentinel*, 14 May 1864.
270 Wheeler's report, *OR*, ser. 1, vol. 38, pt. 3, 949, includes 6 May to 31 May, Dalton to New Hope Church, Hell Hole Line.

Harrison's Brigade:					
3rd AR:					
8th TX:					
11th TX:					
Hannon's Brigade:					
24th AL Bttn.:					
53rd AL:[271]	3w(5/8) 2w(5/13)	3w(5/15)		1w	
Grigsby's Brigade:	30k&w[272]				7k/24w/9c/5m[273]
3rd AR : (detached from Grigsby on 5/7 and sent to Dug Gap with 1st & 2nd AR)					
1st [3rd] KY:					
2nd KY:					
9th KY:					
Allison's TN Squadron:					
Dortch's KY Bttn.:					
Hamilton's TN Bttn.:					
Wheeler's Artillery Battalion (Robertson):					1w[274]
Ferrell's GA Battery (1 section):					
Huwald's TN Battery:					
White's TN Battery:					
Wiggins's AK Battery:					
Army of Mississippi (Jackson's Division):					[17k/104w/9m]
Armstrong's Brigade:			31k&w	1k/7w	[5k/34w][275]

---

[271] J. F. Gaines, letter to the editor, 20 May 1864, *Montgomery (Alabama) Weekly Advertiser*, 8 June 1864.

[272] Drake, *Annals of the Army of Tennessee*, 85.

[273] Wheeler's report, *OR*, ser. 1, vol. 38, pt. 3, 949, includes 6 May to 31 May, Dalton to New Hope Church, Hell Hole Line.

[274] Ibid.

[275] This figure is derived from the report of 31 killed and wounded on 17 May at Adairsville, and an estimate of 1 killed and 7 wounded on 18 May on the Pine Log (Fairmount) Road near Cassville. Total casualties in brigade 39, with 5 conservatively estimated as killed. (See Montgomery, *Reminiscences of a Mississippian*, 164, 168; *Jackson (Mississippi) Clarion-Ledger*, 9 June 1864.

6th AL:		[lost considerably][276]
1st MS:		[1k/3w][277]
2nd MS:	4w[278]	[4w][279]
28th MS:		[lost heavily May 17]
Ballentine's MS:		
Ross's Brigade: (1,009 effective)[280]	50k&w[281]	[7k/51w/5m][282]
3rd TX:	1k/19w[283]	[2k/26w/4m]
6th TX:	1k/9w[284]	[1k/11w]
9th TX:	1k/2w[285]	[3k/2w/1m]
27th TX:		[1k/12w]
Ferguson's Brigade:		[5k/19w/4m]
2nd AL:		[1k/5w][286]
12th MS:		
56th AL:		[1w][287]
Miller's MS:		[3k/4w]

---

276 Brewer, *Alabama*, 683–84.

277 Rowland, *Mississippi*, 376.

278 *Jackson (Mississippi) Clarion-Ledger*, 9 June 1864, shows 4 wounded at Adairsville, 17 May.

279 Rowland, *Mississippi*, 406.

280 P. B. Plummer, Acting Asst. Adj. Genl., "Casualty List, Brigadier General Lawrence Sullivan Ross's Texas Cavalry Brigade, May 15–September 4, during the Atlanta, Georgia Campaign," *OR Supp.*, Serial 95, 509–15, from the *Houston (Texas) Daily Telegraph*, 10 November 1864.

281 Brigadier General Lawrence Sullivan Ross's report of casualties at Rome, 17 May (*OR*, ser. 1, vol. 38, pt. 3, 963).

282 Totals derived by adding the known casualties of Ross at Rome (5 killed and 50 wounded), plus all known casualties on other dates. This may be compared with Ross's report of casualties at Rome on 17 May, where he claimed 50 killed and wounded. (See *OR*, ser. 1, vol. 38, pt. 3, 963; Hale, *Third Texas Cavalry*, 142–44; Kerr, ed., *Fighting with Ross's Texas Cavalry Brigade, C.S.A.*, 220.)

283 *Memphis Daily Appeal*, Atlanta, GA, 25 May 1864, 1, which shows 1 killed and 19 wounded at Rome on 17 May.

284 *Memphis Daily Appeal*, Atlanta, GA, 25 May 1864, 1, which shows 1 killed and 9 wounded at Rome on 17 May.

285 *Memphis Daily Appeal*, Atlanta, GA, 25 May 1864, 1, which shows 1 killed and 2 wounded at Rome on 17 May.

286 Brewer, *Alabama*, 678–79; Harden Perkins Cochrane to wife, *Alabama Historical Quarterly* 8/4 (October 1955): 287; Rowland, *Mississippi*, 421–22, 426, 433, 457–58.

287 Brewer, *Alabama*, 668.

Perrin's (11th) MS: [1k/9w/4m]

Jackson's Artillery Battalion:
Croft's GA Battery:
King's MO Battery:
Waties's SC Battery:

Summary of Confederate Casualties at Dalton, Resaca, Calhoun, Adairsville and Cassville May 6-20

Army of Tennessee:			
Hardee's Corps:			
Bate's Division: (4,054) 5k/25w 25k/239w/55m		21k/121w	[28k/249w/58m]
Cleburne's Division:		21k/144w	[23k/144w/8c]
Walker's Division:		28k/269w	[32k/269w/38c]
Cheatham's Division:		46k/316w	[49k/335w/1m]
Smith's Regiment (Hardee's Corps) Artillery:			[12k/34w][288]
Total Hardee's Corps: (25,782)		116k/850w	[144k/1,031w/139m]
Hood's Corps:			
Stevenson's Division: (6,589) 138	(6,429) 575k&w	84k/442w	[101k/492w/235m]
Stewart's Division: 16k/57w/21m		110k/689w	[148k/741w/142m]
Hindman's Division:		85k/391w	[103k/436w/57c]
Beckham's Regiment (Hood's Corps) Artillery:			[3k/46w/30m]
Total Hood's Corps: (24,379)		283k/1,564w	[363k/1,717w/484m]
Army of Tennessee Artillery Reserve: Hallonquist's Regiment: (1,043)			2k/2w
Wheeler's Cavalry Corps: (10,058) 96k/w/m 152k/w/m 22k/w/m	120k/w/m 53k/w/m	643k/w/m	[73k/341w/53c/81m]
Total Army of Tennessee: (62,189)[289]			[582k/3,091w/757m]

[288] Of the 46 killed and wounded, 3 are confirmed as killed. Author estimates another 9 of the remaining 43 were killed, resulting in an estimated 12 killed and 34 wounded.

[289] Figure reflects aggregate present 30 April 1864, Abstract of Return for Army of Tennessee, less Cantey's Brigade, which is included in Army of Mississippi below (*OR*, ser. 1, vol. 38, pt. 3, 676). Figure also adds 927 present from 63rd Georgia (Mercer's Brigade) that joined after 30 April and before 6 May, but does not add 400 present from 37th Mississippi that is included in Cantey's Brigade, Army of Mississippi below.

Army of Mississippi:					
Loring's Division: (5,405)[290]	184kwm[291]			16k/106w	[27k/156/1c][292]
French's Division: (4,765)[293]			5w	18w	[5k/18w/11m][294]
Cantey's Division: (3,254)[295]				26k/405w	[104k/315w/86c][296]
Polk's Corps Artillery: (981)[297]	1k/1w	2	5c		[1k/3w/5c]
Total Polk's Corps: (14,405)				42k/405w	[137k/492/103m]

[290] *OR*, ser. 1, vol. 32, pt. 3, 862, shows Loring's Division with 393 officers, 4,322 men present for duty, 4,259 effective total present, and 5,405 aggregate present on 30 April 1864, at Demopolis, AL. But note *OR*, ser. 1, vol. 38, pt. 3, 677, which shows Loring's Division at 6,390 aggregate present on 10 June. This increase of 985 men is from the net of the addition of the 27th, 35th, and 49th AL, plus a few men who rejoined their regiments from furlough or from being rounded up in early May who were AWOL in MS or AL, less the subtraction of the 9th AR (which was transferred to Daniel Reynolds's AR Brigade) and battlefield casualties and illnesses from 1 May to 10 June in Loring's Division. Thus, assuming 150 men from the 9th AR and 200 in losses due to the campaign, there is an increase of 1,335 men from the 27th, 35th, and 49th AL, plus a few other soldiers who rejoined their regiments after 30 April—say, 400 men each from the three arriving AL regiments and 135 men returning to their units between 1 May and 10 June. Note: the 43rd MS was transferred from Featherston to Adams after the 30 April and before the 10 June returns, but the 43rd MS is still counted in Loring's Division in both returns.

[291] Loring's report, *OR*, ser. 1, vol. 38, pt. 3, 875.

[292] Loring lost 184 at Resaca, 26 between 16 May and 30 May, and 131 overnight on 30–31 May in a hot fight for possession of each other's forward line as part of the Hell Hole battles, near the Widow Brown's Mill, or Brooks house (*OR*, ser. 1, vol. 38, pt. 3, 875).

[293] *OR*, ser. 1, vol. 32, pt. 3, 862, includes French's Division of Ector and Cockrell and adds Sears's Brigade, which has been added to French; French's report (*OR*, ser. 1, vol. 38, pt. 3, 908) shows 5 wounded and 3 horses killed during skirmishing and shelling afternoon of 19 May at Cassville (*OR*, ser. 1, vol. 38, pt. 3, 899). This number includes French's Division of Cockrell's Missouri, Ector's North Carolina and Texas, and Sears's Mississippi brigades (see *OR*, ser. 1, vol. 32, pt. 3, 862). When these troops arrived at Cassville, however, a request was made for 6,000 rations to feed French's Division (see *OR*, ser. 1, vol. 38, pt. 4, 725). Additionally, the balance of Polk's artillery arrived with French with another 300 artillerists and 12 guns. With the addition of these men, together with the noncombatants or slightly sick men, French's Division on 10 June numbered 5,666 present, a figure tallied after the loss of casualties from Cassville through the New Hope Church battles (see *OR*, ser. 1, vol. 38, pt. 3, 677).

[294] French's casualties are small because only the 39th NC was engaged at Resaca that listed 5k, 8w, and 3m. French had several wounded and missing at Cassville.

[295] Figure does not include Quarles's Brigade of 1,141 men, who arrived 24 May.

[296] Cantey's wounded count includes both Reynolds's and his own brigade figures, but his killed is underreported. It appears that he neglected to include Reynolds's killed completely. Also, the missing and captured, like in all the divisions, is missing.

[297] *OR*, ser. 1, vol. 38, pt. 3, 677.

Jackson's Cavalry Division: (5,254)[298] [17k/104w/9m]

Total Army of Mississippi: (19,659) [154k/596w/112]

Total Confederate Forces: (81,848)[299] 444k/2,828w[300]
[736k/3,687w/869m]

Total Losses: 3,272k&w 5,292k,w&m

Total losses under General Joseph E. Johnston's command 6–20 May 21864: **5,292**. [Figures calculated as of 23 April 2023 by author].
[Note: this table and summary continues to be a working tally as additional primary sources are discovered and tabulated.]

[298] Ibid. This figure includes 19 officers and 305 men in Waties's Battalion of artillery that accompanied Jackson's cavalry. Jackson's Division, which includes Armstrong's Mississippi, Ferguson's Alabama/Mississippi, and Ross's Texas cavalry brigades, on 10 June had an effective total of 4,747, and an aggregate present of 6,056 (see *OR*, ser. 1, vol. 38, pt. 3, 677). However, Johnston claimed that Jackson came with only 3,700 troopers (See J. E. Johnston, "Opposing Sherman's Advance to Atlanta," 4:267).

[299] Figure shows the total number of Confederate soldiers present at Cassville based on total present from their units after accounting for additions and subtractions to reinforcements received after the army withdrew south of the Etowah River and to losses sustained before Cassville. Note that this figure must be reduced by the casualties from Dalton through Resaca and Adairsville, say, less 5,000, or a total present at Cassville of around 76,800.

[300] As reported by Johnston. See fn 1. Note that in *OR*, ser. 1, vol. 38, pt. 3, 686–87, Foard reports 441 killed and 2,943 wounded, but in Johnston's *Narrative*, 576, losses are shown at 444 killed and 2,828 wounded.

Appendix E

Letter from Walter J. Morris, Chief Engineer, Polk's Corps (Army of Mississippi) to Dr. W. M. Polk, June 25, 1874

New York, June 25th, 1874
Dr. W. M. Polk, 288 Fifth Avenue, New York,

Dear Sir: In response to your note of the 20th inst., asking me to give you my recollection of the circumstances in regard to the retreat of the Confederate Armies from Cassville, Georgia, to the south side of the Etowah river, I will state the facts as connected with myself, as follows:

At the time when the Confederate Armies of Tennessee and Mississippi, under the command of General J. E. Johnston, and the Federal Army under General Sherman, were manoeuvring [*sic*] in the neighborhood of Cassville, I had nearly completed my journey from Demopolis, Alabama, to that town to join Lieutenant General Polk, commanding the Army of Mississippi, who was with General Johnston in that vicinity. I had crossed the country in company with a part of that command. I arrived at Cassville railway station about half-past three or four o'clock in the afternoon of the 19th of May, 1864, and met Colonel Gale, of our staff, who informed me that the Lieutenant General desired to see me as soon as I arrived. I passed on without delay to his headquarters, about half a mile east of the railway station, and met General Polk at the door of the cabin used for headquarter purposes. I entered immediately, and he placed a skeleton map before me, giving me the surrounding country, and pointed out the positions of the Confederate forces, and the known and supposed locations of the Federals, giving such additional information as to enable me to fully understand the actual condition of affairs. This was done rapidly. He then requested me to go at once and examine the extreme right of his line, as he considered it untenable for defence [*sic*].

1st. He desired for me to form an opinion if, by constructing a rifle pit, his line could be held against such an attack as might be reasonably, expected in the morning.

2nd. To carefully examine that part of the line enfiladed, to see if it was possible to construct traverses to enable him to hold the position on the defensive.

3rd. To examine the ground immediately in his front in reference to advancing, and to note in reference the positions then occupied by the Federal batteries in front and to the right of Lieutenant General Hood's line.

4th. If those batteries to the front and right of Hood's line could be taken by a special movement.[1]

These explanations, noting them down, and getting a tracing of the skeleton map, required about thirty minutes, and I started for that part of the line in question: General Polk impressing upon me the necessity of reaching that part of the line as soon as possible, as I would only have about two hours of daylight to make the examinations.

Furnishing me with a fresh horse, one of his own, and the necessary guides from his escort, I reached the ground in fifteen minutes. I was instructed to return as soon after dark as possible, for, if necessary, an invitation would be sent to General Johnston to come to his (Lieutenant General Polk's) headquarters. Lieutenant General Hood, I think, was with General Polk when I left.

Arriving upon the line of battle, I found Major General French's Division, Army of Mississippi, located on the extreme right of that Army, and occupying the part of the line in question. To his right was the line of Lieutenant General Hood's Corps, Army of Tennessee, forming the extreme right of the Confederate infantry forces.

The crest of the ridge occupied by French's Division was about one hundred and forty feet above the plain, or valley, in which the town of Cassville is located. This ridge is cut across by a ravine of about fifty feet deep, its sides rising from its bottom, on either side, at about 30 degrees. The location of this ravine on French's line was five or six hundred feet to the left of his extreme right. To the left of this ravine, for twelve or fifteen hundred feet, the crest of the ridge was entirely open, as was to the rear for eight hundred or one thousand feet. There were a few scattered trees of stunted growth in and about the ravine.

The remaining portion of General French's line to the left and to the rear was timbered, as also to the front for seven or eight hundred feet, increasing in depth towards the left. The ground to the front of the left half of his line descended about one hundred and forty feet for half a mile, continuing on to Cassville about one and a quarter miles to the northwest of his left. The ground in front of the right half of his line descended about a hundred feet on the left, and eighty feet on the right for a distance of half a mile on the left and a quarter of a mile on the extreme right. Then ascending to eighty feet on the left, and a hundred on the right to a ridge opposite, and due north.

---

[1] A few paragraph breaks have been added to make the letter easier to read.

This opposing ridge passed on a line about 23 degrees south of west, forming an angle with General Polk's line of defence [*sic*] of about 25 degrees, and forming something less of an angle with Lieutenant General Hood's line. This opposite ridge was occupied by the enemy, their left resting on a point about a mile and a quarter northeast on a prolongation of General Polk's line, and from half a mile to three-quarters of a mile in front of Lieutenant General Hood's, and passing on to the westward at a distance of about half a mile to one and a quarter miles north of General Polk, and in front of his extreme right.

The line occupied by the enemy on the opposite ridge was from twenty to forty feet higher than the position of General Hood's line, and from forty to sixty feet higher than General Polk's. The batteries of the enemy were posted on the most prominent and available points along their ridge, extending for a mile from their extreme left towards their right, reaching a point to the north and front of General Polk's extreme right, and directly in front of the ravine and open part of French's line. The batteries enfiladed and cross fired upon the entire open crest from 45 degrees to 60 degrees, and with a plunging fire of from twenty to sixty feet and sweeping through the ravine, and across the rear of the ridge to a distance of about a thousand feet. The rear fire being still more plunging than that on the crest.

There was no cover for the men within a reasonable distance to the crest, for from the extreme positions of the left batteries of the enemy, it would not be necessary for them to cease firing during the attack until their infantry had reached a line very close to the crest of the ridge occupied by General Polk's command.

The extreme left, or eastern batteries of the enemy, necessarily enfiladed a considerable portion of General Hood's line.

Having made these examinations and noted them down, I formed the following opinions:

1st. That the right of the line occupied by Lieutenant General Polk's command could not be held, as it then was, nor could it be held by constructing a rifle pit along the crest.

2nd. That traverses would be of no avail either for the rifle pits upon the crest or as a covered way to the rear, as such traverses would cover nearly the entire surface.

3rd. That it was extremely hazardous for Lieutenant General Polk to advance his line to make an attack upon the enemy while their batteries held the positions they then occupied.

4th. As to forming any opinion as to the taking of these left batteries of the enemy by a special flank movement, this I could not do, as I was unable to examine to the right of Lieutenant General Hood's line, as it had grown dark. But judging from the stream, as located on the skeleton map, there must have been a very narrow ridge to approach the enemy upon their left.

At the time I arrived about the centre of General Polk's right where the open crest of the ridge commenced, I found a very heavy enfilading and cross fire going on from the enemy's batteries. There were but a few sentinels remaining upon the crest, the main body of men, intended to occupy this part of the line, were compelled to withdraw to the right and left at the foot of the ridge, out of sight, but not out of range of the enemy's batteries.

I found that Major General French had one or two batteries in position upon the part [of] the line near the ravine, and while they were coming into their positions, and before the guns could be unlimbered, from one to two horses from each piece were killed. On my return over this part of the line, about dark, the fire from the enemy had nearly ceased.

Having completed the reconnaissance, I returned to Lieutenant General Polk's headquarters, just after dark.

I placed before him my sketches and notes, and explained to him substantially these facts. General Polk went at once to ask General Johnston to come to his headquarters. Lieutenant General Hood was already with General Polk. General Johnston arrived about 9 o'clock. I remained in the cabin during the conversation as to holding the position then occupied or advancing or retiring the Armies to the south of the Etowah river, about seven or eight miles to our rear.

Lieutenant General Polk expressed himself convinced that he could not hold his line against attack, and that Major General French, who occupied that part of his line in question, was of the same opinion as was his (General Polk's) engineer officer (myself), who had examined the position and reported that traverses would be of no avail.

Lieutenant General Hood stated that he was also convinced that neither he nor General Polk could hold their lines for an hour against such an attack as they might certainly expect in the morning—these Generals both advocating to the Commanding General to take the offensive, and advance on the enemy from these lines.

In reference to this proposed forward movement, General Johnston's attention was particularly called to the advantages of taking possession of the positions occupied by the batteries of the enemy on their extreme left, either by a special flank movement or by prompt action at the time when the

Confederate lines would be advanced. Lieutenant General Polk expressed himself entirely willing and ready to co-operate with General Hood to accomplish this object.

After some moments of silence, General Johnston decided to withdraw the Armies to the south of the Etowah. Soon after this, Lieutenant General Hardee arrived. General Johnston informed him of this decision to cross the river, stating that Generals Polk and Hood had informed him that they could not hold their lines.

Lieutenant General Hood then re-stated the reasons, and said that General Polk cold not hold his line an hour. Nor could he, Hood, hold his two hours if attacked in the morning. Lieutenant General Polk again explained the facts as existed in reference to his line, and stated his willingness to assume the offensive at any time, then or in the morning, rather than to await the attack of the enemy in his (Polk's) present position. Upon these points Lieutenant General Polk and Hood entirely agreed, urging the offensive rather than await the enemy.

Lieutenant General Hardee made but few, if any, remarks that I heard. After a few moments General Johnston gave the orders for the armies to move to the south side of the Etowah. Lieutenant General Polk called to his A. A. General to issue orders to his Division Commanders. This was about 10:30 or 11:00 o'clock.

The orders to Major General Loring, Army of Mississippi, were given [to] me to deliver; also one [another order] to him to order to report to me an officer with three hundred (300) men to occupy the exposed part of Major General French's line, as soon as his command was withdrawn.

I was introduced by General Polk to place this detail along that part of the line, and keep up such fires as would indicate the presence of the withdrawn command, and to cut timber and drive stakes to indicate that works were being thrown up, and to remain there until daylight and observe the movements of the enemy before leaving.

I went at once to General Loring's headquarters on the left of the Cassville road, saw that General, and delivered the orders; obtained the officer and detail, and arrived at General French's line about half-past eleven o'clock, and found that command ready to move; by twelve o'clock (mid-night), they had withdrawn and the detail was posted with a few men out in front.

It was a calm, clear starlight night, and the position of the enemy upon the opposite ridge was clearly seen, without their fires which could be traced along their line, and the cutting of timber could be distinctly heard and located. In addition to the enemy's location upon the crest of the ridge, and passing there or just in front of the town of Cassville and on to the southwest, there were also strong indications of an advance line upon the plane nearer to the foot of the ridge occupied by us, and their chopping and driving rails was very distinct, and their voices occasionally could be heard.

The work of the detail was kept up through the night. At daylight I instructed the officer to assemble his men to the rear. During this time of preparing to leave the line, I closely observed the enemy and his positions through a very strong field glass. I found that many of their batteries along the ridge had been advanced, and their principal and somewhat entrenched line appeared to leave the ridge at a point about a mile east of Cassville, and passing to the southwest fully a half-a-mile in front of their lines of the previous afternoon. It appeared that they enemy had been aware of the movement of the Confederate Armies, and their line advanced during the night, was now vacated and there were trains and artillery moving to the west upon the Kingston road, and solid bodies of infantry were moving in the same direction.

The detail having been assembled, I placed them upon a by-road to Cassville Station on the main road to Cartersville. I instructed the officer to proceed to the south side of the Etowah river by way of the Cartersville bridge, and to report back to his Division Commander. I passed on to cross the river at the same point, arriving there about half-past ten o'clock, and found the Army of the Mississippi nearly over to the south side, which was completed by noon.

Very truly yours,

Walter J. Morris,
Late Captain Engineer Corps, C. S. A.
Chief Engineers, Army of Mississippi

N.B.—Enclosed herewith you will find a map made by me from my notes taken at the time of reconnaissance.[2]

Yours, etc.
W. J. M.

[2] Map included as Exhibit 14.

Appendix F

Thomas Bennett (T. B.) Mackall Journal, "A," "B," and "O" Samples Comparison
Entries transcribed for 17–19 May 1864 while at Adairsville and Cassville

The entries, including brackets, parentheses, spelling, and abbreviations are shown exactly as they appear.

"A" Sample Swem Library, William & Mary College, Joseph E. Johnston Papers (Mss.39.1 J63) Item - Box: 3, Folder: 2 (Identifier: id112225)	**"B" Sample** Swem Library, William & Mary College, Joseph E. Johnston Papers (Mss.39.1 J63) Item - Box: 3, Folder: 2 (Identifier: id112227)	**"O" Sample** *OR*, ser. 1, vol. 38, pt. 3, 981–86
Discovered by McMurry, the "A" sample appeared to be T. B. Mackall's original diary. When compared with other known handwriting samples, it was determined that the author was, in fact, T. B. Mackall.	Discovered by McMurry, the "B" sample appeared to be written by the same person as a "rewrite," or more complete version, of the "A" sample. It contained fewer abbreviations and more complete sentences, yet still included many of the same terms as the "A" sample. When compared with other known handwriting samples, it was determined that the author was, in fact, T. B. Mackall.	The "N" sample was contributed to the War Department and published in the *Official Records*. This *Official Records* version is known as the "O" sample. See additional information below following the chart.
"May 17: Reached Adairsville Hdqrs in post near Church afterwards house. Enemy advance in afternoon Cav[alr]y & Cheatham engages. Army rapidly formed in line. Enemy reported turning our left	"May 17: Brig. Genl. Jackson with Miss. Cavalry met at Adairsville; also Sayre's [Sears] brigade. In afternoon advance of enemy encounters our	"May 17: Tuesday, May 17, 1864.—We reached Adairsville just before day, a little ahead of troops. Cultivated, rolling country from Resaca to Adairsville.

beyond Oothcaloga [Oothkallooga] C[ree]k. Report of raid on right Pontoons Ordered to Cartersville. Hood sleeps at Hd Qr. Leave A[dairsville] before 4 a.m. Genl Jackson div. of cavalry met here, with Armstrong, & ______[blank in ms] bgde [brigade]. Also Sayrs [Sears]bgde."	pickets; checked by Cheathan's divn, & cavalry. Enemy reported turning our left beyond Oothealoga Creek. Report of raid on right. Telegram from Rome states enemy were shelling the town. During night, army withdrawn to Cassville, Hardee's corps moved on Adairsville & Kingston road; Hood's & Polk's on Adairsville & Cassville road. French with Cockrell's brgde. In A.M. at Kingston—cars sent for Ector's [brigade]."	* * * * 9.45 p. m., this morning and forenoon guns heard at intervals at distance; Wheeler skirmishing; 2.30 p.m., dispatch received from Wheeler (2.10), saying enemy pressing rapidly two and a half miles from town, and he would have to fall back. General had ridden out to Hood's line; original sent to him and copies of to H. and H. [Hood and Hardee]. [Hardee] did not receive his until after his infantry informed him. At this time cavalry were coming in. General soon came in. by 5 p. m. Cheatham, who was one mile in advance, was skirmishing. Pack up and saddle. Troops who had not been in line, but massed in bivouac, quickly formed, while firing going on. Sent to Hardee to ask what dispositions he had made; found him on his left; Cheatham in advance of all infantry; Walker on his right, Cleburne next, part crossing Oothkaloga Creek; Bate in reserve. Returned soon, all the lieutenant-generals and Wheeler. Enemy reported on west of Oothkaloga Creek. Bate sent over; 6,000 cavalry reported six miles of

		Cartersville. pontoons at Cassville. Jackson's division cavalry ordered back. One brigade had no corn for three days. (Pontoons ordered to Etowah.) Firing heard at Rome, while all this going on. Telegram from Lieutenant-Colonel Steever, Rome, saying enemy in force, shelling town. I sent after General P[olk]. about 6 p. m. All in council. Can the army be withdrawn when so many roads into Calhoun? Carry a dispatch in room; General W. W. [Mackall] and J— looking at map. Latter traces road from here to Cassville; asks how long will it take all to go down one road? [Hoodl] says can't be done. [Hardee] said we will have to fight. [Hood] has been anxious to get from this place south of Etowah. 7.10 p. m., Roy and Cunningham have just been called for. In waiting. On 16th May received cipher from General S. D. Lee, Demopolis; not translatable. Repetition received on 17th, at night. Forrest will start on 20th from Corinth to cross Tennessee at Florence with 3,500 picked men and 2 batteries. Colonel Hill reported on authority of

		scout that enemy were moving down toward Rome, on Calhoun and Rome road, Palmer's corps in advance, wagon trains along, and one brigade cavalry. Did not learn whether any other force was behind."
"May 18: Cassville, Ga or Manassas. Wednesday, May 18, 1864. Reached Cassville 10 m from Adairsville. Get in camp about 7 A.M. Beautiful country. Army has good rest near fine stream."	"May 18: Cassville May 18, 1864, Wednesday [No other entry for this date.]"	"CASSVILLE. Wednesday, May 18.—Reached creek near Cassville about 7.30 a. m.; got into camp 9.30 a. m.; no firing so far (just after break-fast). Left headquarters just beyond Adairsville about 4 a.m. Hardee's corps moved on Adairsville and Kingston road, Hood's and Polk's on Adairsville and Cassville. Sears' brigade, French's division, reached Adairsville yesterday. French with Cockrell's this a.m. at Kingston; cars gone for Ector's. French had one brigade about starting from Rome to join this army when town was attacked. Cockrell's [should read Ector's] detained to aid in defense and protect the other brigade [Cockrell's]. 4 p.m., cipher from S. d. Lee, of 17th, Meridian, received. Forrest's move for 20th suspended on account of demonstrations from Memphis. Colonel

		Hannon just reports enemy's cavalry in force advancing on Fairmount road rapidly, and four miles from here. Armstrong ordered to support of Hannon. (Following written Thursday, 19th): Hood and Hardee and Polk at headquarters discussing over map plans for morning. Prisoner of Hooker's corps brought in; I questioned him. His command was behind Howard's; latter skirmished with Cheatham afternoon of 17th and all army was assembled close by. Next morning (on 18th) whole command in motion. Howard moved into Adairsville, halted, and cooked dinner. Prisoner got lost among Howard's men and was told Hooker had moved toward our right, and endeavoring to join his regiment was captured by our cavalry; was told that an additional corps was following behind Hooker; knew nothing of other commands. All appear in good spirits. Telegram received in afternoon from Thrasher reporting enemy acknowledge loss of 45,000 and 31 generals in Virginia. General J[ohnston] said Confederacy was as

		fixed an institution as England or France. Troops very much wearied by night marches; in good spirits and confident; press confident. Anxiety, however, to fight, particularly among officers, certain of whom thought good effect of Virginia and Louisiana news in raising gold in New York to 210 would be impaired by this retreat. Many thought Sherman would not fight—merely wanted to drive us across Etowah and to occupy territory acquired and send re-enforcements to Grant."
"May 19: "Heard first skirmishing on Adairsv[ille]. & Cassv[ille] rd. 10:20 AM. In ten minut[es], artillery on Sp[rin]g. Place road & on Ad[airsville] rd. After a few guns Genl. M[ackall] sent [word] more en[em]y close to H(oo)d on Canton rd. Lt. Genls sent for. Wagons moved [to] rear. Line changed 2:25 PM. Change going on. Artillery on Hardee's front. Change of line effected under fire. Report of column on Canton Road not afterwards confirmed. Battle expected next day. General Ross reports from Cartersville enemy across at Wooley's Bridge."	"May 19: "Line of battle formed to attack enemy. First skirmishing on Adairsville & Cassville road 10:20 AM. Ten minutes later artillery heard in direction of Spring Place road. After a few discharges report recd. from Genl. Hood that enemy was advancing on Canton road. Line of battle changed. At night army withdrawn."	"Thursday, May 19.— Moved out to attack enemy, but column reported advancing on Cartersville road; line changed; brisk skirmishing. General Ross reports enemy throwing pontoons across Etowah at Wooley's Bridge, and crossed a force-main force. *[Following written May 21 near Allatoona]*: Line changed under fire. Brisk skirmishing in afternoon and toward evening to effect the change. New line principally along a ridge running nearly north and south, covering Cassville and Cass

		Station road and facing westwardly. The signal corps and General Hardee reported in forenoon that enemy in front of Cassville were moving toward Kingston, all advantageous to the designed attack on his left flank. An order was written about 7 or 8 a. m. thanking troops for patience, and telling them they would be led against enemy. General J[ohnston] rode over to General Hood's and then passing by general headquarters rode out Spring Place road, north of creek, with Hood and Polk and Hardee to show former where he was to form his line for attack. General M[ackall] rode from headquarters east of town to join him; found Generals J[ohnston], P[olk], and Hardee returning (Sears' Mississippi brigade formed across road). Riding back, all passed Cockrell's Missouri brigade resting on road, and in town met Hindman's column, advance of Hood's corps, moving to take position on Polk's right. After a few moments in town rode rapidly back out Spring Place road; general saw Hood and returned to campground

		and dismounted; Hood's corps passing, Polk's troops shifting. About this time, 10.20 a.m., a few discharges of artillery on Adairsville and Cassville road, and in ten minutes report of artillery in easterly direction. General M[ackall], who had ridden out to Hood with directions "to make quick work," sent word back by courier, who reported to me that "enemy in heavy force close to Hood on Canton road." I tell general, who says it can't be. (Armstrong on that road reported none.) Called for map; said if that's so General Hood will have to fall back at once. Presently General M[ackal] rode up at a rapid rate, spoke with general, who sent him back in haste, riding one of his horses. Mason went off on another; still firing had ceased; confusion in passing backward and forward of Hood's and Polk's troops. At this time could be heard officers all around reading orders to regiments and cheers of troops. Some regiments in field where headquarters were. Polk detains two of Hood's brigades, as Hardee on his left had not closed up a gap. Headquarters

		wagons sent beyond Cassville. Corps commanders and Wheeler arrive. Instructions to change line. Generals J[ohnston] and M[ackall] and Polk ride on high hill overlooking town and back from original line. New line marked out, and troops rapidly formed on it and along a ridge. Late in afternoon considerable skirmishing and artillery. Enemy's skirmishers occupied town. At one time confusion; wagons, artillery; and cavalry hasten back; noise, dust, and heat. Disorder checked; wagons made to halt. Consternation of citizens; many flee, leaving all; some take away few effects, some remain between hostile fires. General M[ackall] and I remain several hours on roadside (Cassville and Cartersville road). Governor Harris brings lunch. General J[ohnston], about 5 p. m. in afternoon, rides down to Hardee's, leaving General M[ackall]; I remain. About 6 p. m. General M[ackall] sets out to find our camp; meets the general, and both go back to a field near road in rear of Polk,

		as skirmishing brisk. General J[ohnston] tells Governor Harris he will be ready for and happy to receive enemy next day. Wheeler comes up; cavalry falls back behind infantry. Dark ride to camp. By a muddy brook near General P[olk's] find supper ready and tents pitched. After supper, General J[ohnston] walks over to General P[olk]. General M[ackall] and rest turn in. Soon General J[ohnston] sends word by courier to send him two of inspectors-general mounted; then one of Polk's staff officers brings word that all the staff must report mounted; I was directed to remain. General Mackall returned to camping-place, where all staff waited until about 2 a. m., when they rode to Cartersville, passing trains and artillery parked in field; all hurried off without regard to order. Reach Cartersville before day, troops come in after day. General Johnston comes up—all hurried over bridges; great confusion, caused by mixing trains and by trains which crossed first parking at river's edge and others winding around wrong

		roads; about 2,000 wagons crowded on bank."

The "A" and "B" samples are from two unnamed diaries that Professor Richard McMurry discovered in the Johnston Papers at the Swem Library at William & Mary College. McMurray surmised that due to its many abbreviations, the "A" sample was the original diary, and the "B" sample, which contained more complete sentences and phrases, appeared to be a contemporaneous (or nearly contemporaneous) revision of the "A" sample.

The "O" sample is the version that was published in the *Official Records*. Two other examples, the "H" sample and the "N" sample, were also a part of McMurry's study. The "N" sample, a manuscript McMurry discovered in the National Archives, was determined to be in the handwriting of two different authors, neither of whom was Thomas Bennett Mackall. Sometime prior to 1891, General Joseph E. Johnston provided the "N" sample to the secretary of war and the Board of Publications staff of the War Department, who oversaw the publication of the 128-volume *Official Records*. The entry included the admonition, "Kept at headquarters Army of Tennessee by Lieut. T. B. Mackall, aide-de-camp to Brig. Gen. W.W. Mackall, chief of staff, and *furnished by General J. E. Johnston*." This "N" sample was duplicated almost verbatim in the *Official Records* and appears as the "O" sample in column 3 of the chart above. The "A" and "B" samples were perceptions and recollections of events that were written contemporaneously while the "N" and "O" samples were not. This fact must be taken into account for purposes of historical interpretation.

The "H" sample, also found by Dr. McMurry, is a detailed set of entries for 14–15 May 1864 and concerns the Confederate activities during the Battle of Resaca. It was also identified as being in T. B. Mackall's handwriting. It is located in the J. P. Nicholson Collection, Joseph E. Johnston papers, Henry E. Huntington Library, San Marino, California. Since this sample is located in the Huntington Library, McMurry labeled this sample as the "H" sample. Because the dates for the entries were 14–15 May, and thus outside the 17–19 May timeframe examined in this study, the "H" sample is not included in the chart above.

Abbreviations

ADAH	Alabama Department of Archives and History, Montgomery, Alabama
AHC	Atlanta History Center, Atlanta, Georgia
CMH	*Confederate Military History*
CSR	*Compiled Service Records of Confederate Soldiers Who Served in Organizations from the Union and Confederate States of America during the War of the Rebellion*
KRC, AHC	Kenan Research Center, Atlanta History Center, Atlanta, Georgia
MDAH	Mississippi Department of Archives and History, Jackson, Mississippi
MHSM	Military Historical Society of Massachusetts
MTSU	Middle Tennessee State University, Murfreesboro, Tennessee
NAID	National Archives Identifier
NARA	National Archives and Records Administration, Washington, DC
OR	*Official Records of the Union and Confederate Armies in the War of the Rebellion*
SHSP	*Southern Historical Society Papers*
TSLA	Tennessee State Library and Archives, Nashville, Tennessee

Bibliography

Primary Sources

Treatises and Official Records

Bartow County, Georgia. Land Records. Deed Book Q. Bartow County Superior Court Clerk's Office, State of Georgia. Robert Horrisburger, 24 February 1869, recorded 20 April 1869.

Brewer, Willis. *Alabama: Her History, Resources, War Record and Public Men, from 1540 to 1872*. Montgomery, AL: Barrett & Brown, Steam Printers, 1872.

Briant, Charles C. *History of the Sixth Regiment, Indiana Volunteer Infantry, of Both the Three Months' and Three Years' Services*. Indianapolis, IN: William E. Burford, Printer and Binder, 1891.

Cameron, Simon, Secretary of War. *U.S. Infantry Tactics, for the Instruction, Exercise, and Maneuvers of the United Sates Infantry*. 1861. Reprint, Philadelphia: J. B. Lippincott & Co., 1863.

Cassville Cemetery list. Transcribed by Raymond W. Watkins, Falls Church, VA. List donated to Bartow County Museum by Bob Crowe. RG 109, CSR. National Archives, Washington, DC.

Civil War Muster Rolls, 1861–1865, 19th Alabama Infantry, Company G, box 11, folder 8, images 3 and 6. ADAH, Montgomery, AL.

Civil War Muster Rolls, 1861–1865, 19th Alabama Infantry, Company A, box 11, folder 8, image 45. ADAH, Montgomery, AL.

Cockrell's Brigade Casualties. Microfilm 1045, roll 1 (old microfilm roll 22, box 15). TSLA.

Congress of the Confederate States of America. *Journal of the Congress of the Confederate States of America, 1861–1865*. 7 vols. Washington, D.C.: US Government Printing Office, 1904–1905.

Estabrook, Charles E. Adjutant General's Department. *Wisconsin Losses in the Civil War*. Madison: Democrat Printing Company, 1915.

Featherston, Winfield Scott. *Official Report of the Tennessee Campaign*. Subject File, Manuscript Division, TSLA.

Featherston's Brigade Casualties. Microfilm 1045, roll 2, TSLA.

Georgia Department of Natural Resources. Lonice C. Barrett, Commissioner, Historic Preservation Commission. *Report of Jackson Hill Historic District, Floyd County, GA* (17 April 1987). Courtesy Norman Dasinger.

Gilmore, Evangelist J. 96th Illinois Infantry. Database (contributed by Russell D. Gilmore), Illinois Civil War Detail Report, Illinois State Archives. Accessed 7 April 2023.

Haskell, Oliver C. Sixth Indiana Cavalry Regiment. Manuscript Department, Collection No. SC 0707, Folder CA. 1852–1943. William C. Smith Memorial Library. Indiana Historical Society, Indianapolis, Indiana.

Hewett, Janet B., et al. *Supplement to the Official Records of the Union and Confederate Armies*. 51 vols. Wilmington, NC: Broadfoot Publishing Co., 1994–2001.

———, and Joyce Lawrence, eds. *Georgia Confederate Soldiers 1861–1865*. Vol. 2, K–Z. Wilmington, NC: Broadfoot Publishing Co., 1998.

Hood Letters, Record group 9, roll 151, vol. 33. MDAH.

Inspection Reports and Related Records Received by the Inspection Branch in the Confederate Adjutant and Inspector General's Office, Featherston's Brigade, Loring's

Division, Stewart's Corps, Army of Tennessee, for 20 August 1864 and 22 September 1864. National Archives, microfilm publication M935, roll 1. Courtesy James Odgen, historian, Chickamauga and Chattanooga National Military Park, Fort Oglethorpe, GA.

Kesler, Thomas L. *Geology and Mineral Deposits of the Cartersville District Georgia, Geological Survey Professional Paper 224. A description of the mineral deposits and products from one of the oldest mining districts in the Southeastern States*. Washington, D.C.: US Government Printing Office, 1950. Courtesy James Odgen, Chickamauga and Chattanooga National Military Park, Fort Oglethorpe, GA.

Medical & Surgical History of the War of the Rebellion. In volume 2, part 3, *Surgical History*. Washington, D.C.: Government Printing Office, 1883. Available at http://resource.nlm.nih.gov/14121350R.

NARA, RG 109: Communications Received by Maj. Gen. P.R. Cleburne's Division, Armoy of Tennessee, 1862-1864, NAID 24468091, Local ID: Chapter II, vol. 265, p. 135.

Power, J. L. 1864 Scrapbook. Z 742v. MDAH.

Power, J. L. Family Papers. Z 0100.000S, box 8. MDAH.

Quarterly Report of Deceased Soldiers of the State of Mississippi. MDAH, C.S.R.-R.G. 269.

Quiner, E. B. *Military History of Wisconsin*. Chicago: Clark & Co. Publishers, 1866. Available at https://catalog.hathitrust.org/Record/006578836.

Record of Service of Connecticut Men in the Army and Navy of the United States during the War of the Rebellion. Hartford: Press of the Case, Lockwood & Brainard Company, 1889. Available at https://catalog.hathitrust.org/Record/100931069.

Record of Union Battlefield Burials, Atlanta Campaign. Courtesy of Bradley J. Quinlin, Chattanooga National Cemetery, and Marietta National Cemetery.

Rice, F. *Grand Summary of Casualties in Cheatham's Division*. B. F. Cheatham Papers, TSLA.

Robertson, John. *Michigan in the War*. Lansing: W. S. George & Co., State Printers and Binders, 1882. Available at https://catalog.hathitrust.org/Record/005579973.

Roster of Confederate Cemetery, Chattanooga, Tennessee. National Park Service.

Scott's Brigade Casualties. Microfilm 1045, roll 2, TSLA.

Toombs, Samuel. *Reminiscences of the Thirteenth Regiment New Jersey Volunteers*. 1878. Reprint. Hightstown, NJ: Longstreet House, 1994.

US War Department. *Atlas to Accompany the Official Records of the Union and Confederate Armies in the War of the Rebellion*. Washington, DC: Government Printing Office, 1895.

US Census Bureau. 1840, 1850, 1860, 1870, 1880, and 1890 censuses. 1860 US Census Records, Cass (now Bartow) County, GA, District 936, 892–98, enumerator W.W. Rich, transcribed by Susan M. Willis, Bartow County Genweb, Bartow History Museum.

US Geological Survey. "Facing Tomorrow's Challenges—U.S. Geological Survey Science in the Decade 2007–2017." Circular 13092007. Available at https://pubs.usgs.gov/publication/cir1309. Accessed 11 October 2023.

US Census Bureau. Eighth Census of the United States, 1860. M653. 1,438 rolls. NARA.

US Census Bureau. Seventh Census of the United States, 1850. M432. 1,009 rolls. NARA.

US Census Bureau. Sixth Census of the United States, 1840. M704. 580 rolls. NARA.

US War Department. *Compiled Service Records of Confederate Soldiers Who Served in Organizations from the Union and Confederate States of America during the War of the*

Rebellion. Record Group 109, National Archives, Washington, D.C.

US War Department. *The Official Military Atlas of the Civil War*. Washington D.C.: Government Printing Office, 1891.

US War Department. *The War of the Rebellion: A Compilation of the Official Records of the Union and Confederate Armies*. 128 vols. Washington, D.C.: Government Printing Office, 1880–1901. Available at https://ehistory.osu.edu/books/official-records. All citations are to *OR*, series 1, and by serial number, unless otherwise noted.

Maps

Blakeslee, G. H. "May 17 to 23 1864, Adairsville to Euharlee, GA, route of Harrison's Brigade." Library of Congress, Geography and Map Division, Washington, D.C. Available at https://www.loc.gov/item/2009582179/. Cited as Blakeslee Map.

Foster, Captain Wilbur S. "Map of Roads between Marietta and Dalton, Georgia." Image 4 of 5. NAID 70652905. RG 109, ser. Confederate Maps, file unit Georgia, NARA. Available at https://catalog.archives.gov/id/70652905?objectPage=4. Cited as Foster Map.

Johnston, Joseph E., to Charles G. Johnsen. 19 June 1874. *SHSP* 21 (1893): 319. Johnston's hand-drawn map was included with the letter when published in the *New Orleans Times Picayune*, 22 October 1893. Cited as Johnston Map.

Kurtz, Wilbur G. Map. In Lucy Josephine Cunyus, *History of Bartow County, Georgia, Formerly Cass [County]*, 233. Cited as Kurtz Map 1.

———. Hand-drawn map prepared for Colonel Thomas Spencer. 1949. In the *Cartersville [Georgia] Daily Tribune News*, 8 November 1949. Cited as Kurtz Map 2.

Martin, Major General William T. "Maps of Adairsville, Cassville, Cartersville and Vicinity, Prepared by John M. Stewart, Engineer, and J. S. Tyner, Assistant Engineer for Major General Will. T. Martin." Major General Henry D. Clayton Files, ADAH. Cited as Martin Map.

Merrill, W. E. "May 18th to 23rd." Plate 101, map 11, in *Atlas to Accompany the Official Records of the Union and Confederate Armies, 1891–1895*. Washington, DC: Government Printing Office, 1875–1877. Cited as Merrill Map.

Morris, Walter J. "Map Showing the Position of the Confederate Armies of Mississippi and Tennessee Under Command of Gen. J. E. Johnston, May 19th, 1864." Plate 62, map 7, in *Atlas to Accompany the Official Records of the Union and Confederate Armies, 1891–1895*. Washington, DC: Government Printing Office, 1875–1877. Cited as Morris Map.

Ruger, Edward, comp. "Map Illustrating the Second Epoch of the Atlanta Campaign." Plate 58, map 1, in *Atlas to Accompany the Official Records of the Union and Confederate Armies, 1891–1895*. Washington, DC: Government Printing Office, 1875–1877. Cited as Ruger Map.

Scaife, William R. "Affair at Cassville, Morning of May 19, 1864" and "Affair at Cassville, Evening of May 19, 1864." In vol. 2 of *The Campaign for Atlanta & Sherman's March to the Sea*, edited by Theodore P. Savas and David A. Woodbury, 278a and 284a. Campbell, CA: Savas Beatie, 1994. Cited as Scaife Map 1 (Morning Affair) and Scaife Map 2 (Evening Affair). In *The Campaign for Atlanta*. Atlanta, GA: W. R. Scaife, 1993. Maps also appear in Scaife, "Waltz between the Rivers: An Overview of the Atlanta Campaign from the Oostanaula to the Etowah."

US Geological Survey Department. "Georgia Adairsville quadrangle 15-minute series." 1891 topographical map. J. W. Powell (scale 1:125000). 1944. https://dlg.usg.edu/record/dlg_topos_usgs15-adairsville-1944#item. Accessed 11 October 2023.

Wheeler, Major General Jos. "Copy of a Rebel Map Received from War Department Showing Georgia." [1864.] Image 5 of 5. NAID 122206872. RG 77, ser. Civil Works Map File, file unit United States. https://catalog.archives.gov/id/122206872?objectPage=5. Cited as Wheeler Map.

Diaries, Journals, Personal Accounts, and Letters

Alexander, E. P. *Military Memoirs of a Confederate*. New York: Scribner's, 1907.

Anonymous letter to Miss Ginnie Thornton, 21 September 1864; Thornton Collection. Special Collections. Mitchell Memorial Library, Mississippi State University, Starkville.

Bainbury, Chester. *Bainbury's Civil War Diary*. Edited by Charles Wesley Lawrence. 1960. MSS-130, Kurtz Papers, KRC, AHC.

Baker, T. Otis. Co. B, 10th Mississippi Infantry. Papers. Subject files, MDAH.

Banks, Robert W. Letters. Courtesy Carter House Library and Museum, Franklin, TN.

———. *The Battle of Franklin, November 30, 1864: The Bloodiest Engagement of the War between the States*. New York: Neale Publishing Company, 1908.

Beattie, Taylor, diary, 25 July 1864, Southern Historical Collection, UNC Chapel Hill.

Belknap, Colonel William W. *History of the Fifteenth Regiment, Iowa Veteran Volunteer Infantry*. Keokuk, IA: R. B. Odgen & Son, 1887.

Bell, Rachael, to Mrs. Mollie J. Bell. July 1862. Thornton Collection, Special Collections, Mitchell Memorial Library, Mississippi State University, Starkville, MS.

Bender, Robert Patrick, ed. *Worthy of the Cause for Which They Fight, The Civil War Diary of Brigadier General Daniel Harris Reynolds, 1861–1865*. Fayetteville: University of Arkansas Press, 2011.

Berryhill, S. Newton. "Fresh Tidings from the Battlefield." *The Mississippi Poets*. Edited by Ernestine Clayton Deavors. Memphis: E. H. Clarke & Brother, 1922.

Berryhill, William Harvey. *The Gentle Rebel: The Civil War Letters of William Harvey Berryhill, First Lieutenant, Co. D, 43rd Regiment, Mississippi Volunteers*. Edited by Mary Miles Jones and Leslie Jones Martin. Yazoo City, MS: Sassafras Press, 1982.

Bevens, William E. *Reminiscences of a Private: William E. Bevens of the First Arkansas Infantry, C.S.A.* Edited by Daniel E. Sutherland. Fayetteville: University of Arkansas Press, 1992.

Biddle, James. Diary. Burton Historical Collection, Detroit Public Library.

Biggers, J. A. Diary. Subject files. MDAH.

Binford, James R. *Recollections of the Fifteenth Regiment of Mississippi Infantry, C.S.A.* Subject Files, Chickamauga and Chattanooga National Military Park, Fort Oglethorpe, GA.

Black, S. L., to Thomas Benton Roy. 31 May 1880. Quoted in Roy's "General Hardee and the Military Operations Around Atlanta." *Southern Historical Society Papers* 8 (August and September 1880): 347–50.

Brown, W. C. Diary of W. C. Brown [Barry's Lookout Battery (Darden's Battery)]. Special Collections, Chattanooga-Hamilton County Bicentennial Library, Chattanooga, TN.

Brown, William A., vertical files, Confederate MS-5, 166-67, Kennesaw Mountain NMP.

Buck, Captain I. A. *Cleburne's Division at Atlanta*. Subject File, PW-5, Kennesaw National

Battlefield Park, Kennesaw, GA.
Caldwell, Frank Hollis. *Reminiscences.* Special Collections, Chattanooga-Hamilton County Bicentennial Library, Chattanooga, TN.
Campbell, Henry. 18th Indiana Battery. *Three Years in the Saddle: A Diary of the Civil War.* Special Collections, Wabash College, Crawfordsville, IN.
Cannon, J. P. *"Bloody Banners and Barefoot Boys": A History of the 27th Regiment Alabama Infantry.* Edited by Noel Crowson and John V. Brogden. Shippensburg, PA: Burd Street Press, 1997.
Carpenter, Arthur B. Letters. Civil War Miscellaneous and Manuscripts Collection. Yale University, New Haven, CT.
Castle, Charles M. 102nd Illinois. Diary. 19 May 1864. Subject Files, Illinois State Archives, Springfield, IL. Cited as Castle Diary.
Cater, Alleen Williams. "The Civil War Papers of John Bell Hamilton and Thomas Hamilton Williams." Master's thesis, Jacksonville State University, 1972. Vertical files, Jacksonville State Library, Jacksonville, AL.
Chambers, William Pitt. *Blood and Sacrifice: The Civil War Journal of a Confederate Soldier.* Edited by Richard Baumgartner. Huntington, WV: Blue Acorn Press, 1994.
Champion, Sid. 28th Mississippi Cavalry, Armstrong's Brigade. Diary. Special Collections, MDAH. Cited as Champion Diary.
Clark, Edgar W. *History of "G" Company of the 1st Wisconsin Regiment of Volunteer Cavalry.* File 2225, folder 18. Special Collections. University of Wisconsin at Madison Library, Madison, WI.
Clark, Walter A. *Under the Stars and Bars: Memories of Four Years' Service with the Oglethorpes, of Augusta, Georgia.* Jonesboro, GA: Freedom Hill Press, 1987.
Cline, William. 73rd Ohio. Diary. Special Collections, University of Notre Dame Library, South Bend, IN.
Colville, Captain W. E., "Camp Near Etowah, May 22nd, 1864," vertical files, Confederate TN-1, Kennesaw Mountain NMP.
Conner, W. H., to Dunbar Rowland, State Historian. 20 October 1927. J. L. Power Collection. Box 8. MDAH.
Cooper, R. C. 6th Mississippi Infantry. Letters. Confederate file no. 37. Carter House Library and Museum, Franklin, TN.
Cooper, V. W. *Some Experiences of Dr. V. W. Cooper in the Confederate Army, 1861–1865.* Unpublished ms. Vertical files. Confederate NC-3. Kennesaw Mountain NMP.
Cox, Charles Harding. "'Gone for a Soldier': The Civil War Letters of Charles Harding Cox." Edited by Lorna Lutes Sylvester. *Indiana Magazine of History* 68/3 (September 1972): 181–239 (see letter of 30 July 1864 at 218).
Craig, R. A. B. 22nd Mississippi Infantry. Letters. Confederate file no. 35. Carter House Library and Museum, Franklin, TN.
Crenshaw, R. F., to Miss Ella Austin, 13 December 1860. Archives and Special Collections, J. D. Williams Library, University of Mississippi, Oxford.
Crittenden, John. Co. E, 34th Alabama. Letters dated 7, 9, and 18 July 1864. 2 Q491, vol. 2. Dolph Briscoe Center for American History, University of Texas, Austin. Typescript copy also available at Auburn University Library.
Crumpton, Washington Bryan. *A Book of Memories.* Montgomery, AL: Baptist Mission Board, 1921.
Cubbison, Douglas R. *Fireworks Were Plenty: The XV and XVI Army Corps at the Battle of*

Ruff's Mill, Georgia, July 3–5, 1864. KRC, AHC.
Cutter, Geo. H. 3rd Wisconsin. Diary. Hargrett Library Special Collections. University of Georgia, Athens.
Davis, Jefferson. *The Rise and Fall of the Confederate Government*. 2 vols. New York: D. Appleton & Co., 1881.
Day, D. L. *My Diary of Rambles with the 25th Massachusetts Volunteer Infantry*. Milford, MA: King and Billings, 1884.
Deavenport, Reverend Thomas, diary, vertical files, Confederate TN-13, 24, Kennesaw Mountain NMP.
Dickinson, Charles H. Diary. Wisconsin State Historical Society, Madison, WI.
Dillworth, Colonel W. S., to the editor. *Macon Daily Telegraph*, 20 June 1864. Washington Library, Macon, GA.
Dixon, Captain Mumford H., 3rd Confederate Regiment. Diary. Copy in Arkansas vertical files, Kennesaw Mountain NBP.
Dixon, Mumford H. Diary. 17 July 1864. William R. Perkins Library, Duke University, Durham, North Carolina.
Dobbs, Josephine Manning Austin. "Civil War Stories as Told to Her by Her Father, Joseph Manning Austin (1853–1931)." In vol. 3 of *Confederate Reminiscences and Letters 1861–1865*. Atlanta: Georgia United Daughters of the Confederacy, 1996–2000.
Dorr, Joseph B. Journal. Series no. 62, box no. 1, folders 4 and 5. Special Collections Department. Northwestern University Library, Evanston, IL. Cited as Dorr Journal.
Drake, Edwin L., ed. *The Annals of the Army of Tennessee, and Early Western History*. Jackson, TN: Guild Bindery Press, 1878.
Drane, James. Family Papers. Courtesy of James W. Drane Jr., Crossville, TN.
Drennan, William A. Diary of and Papers. Special Collections, Z-131, MDAH.
Dunn, Matthew A. Letters. Special Collections, Z-1792.00f; M I-11, MDAH.
Early, Jubal A., and Ruth H. Early. *Lieutenant General Jubal Anderson Early, C.S.A.: Autobiographical Sketch and Narrative of the War Between the States*. Philadelphia: J. B. Lippincott Company, 1912.
Elmore, Bruce, to Libbie Elmore. 29 July 1864, Manuscript Collection, MSS 673 F, KRC, AHC.
Faulkinbury, Henry Newton. Diary. MDAH. Courtesy special permission of Bob Lurate.
Featherston Collection. Archives and Special Collections, J.D. Williams Library, University of Mississippi, Oxford.
Fitch, Michael H. *Echoes of the Civil War as I Hear Them*. New York: R. F. Fenno and Co., 1905.
Fleming, L. H., to Lou. From Augusta, 3 July 1864. Moseley Family Letters, MDAH.
French, General Samuel G. *Two Wars*. Nashville: Confederate Veteran, 1901. Reprint, Huntington, WV: Blue Acorn Press, 1999.
Gale, Thomas. Diary. 17 May 1864. Gale and Polk Family Papers, 1815–1940. Collections no. 00266, Wilson Special Collections Library, University of North Carolina at Chapel Hill.
Gill, Maynard, to President Davis and General Bragg. June 1864. CSR, RG 269, roll 342, MDAH.
Gorgas, Josiah. *The Journals of Josiah Gorgas, 1857–1878*. Edited by Sarah Woolfolk Wiggins. Tuscaloosa: University of Alabama Press, 1995.
Grant, Ulysses S. *The Civil War Memoirs of Ulysses S. Grant*. New York: C.L. Webster & Co.,

1885.
Green, Johnny. *Johnny Green of the Orphan Brigade*. Edited by A. D. Kirwan. Lexington: University of Kentucky Press, 1956.
Greene, John W., to Mother. 18 May 1864, Cassville, Georgia. Greene Family Papers, mss. 6211. Albert and Shirley Small Special Collections Library, University of Virginia. Courtesy Dr. Keith S. Bohannon, University of West Georgia.
Hampton, Captain Thomas B., to Jestin C. Hampton (his wife). 26 June 1864 and 4 July 1864. File 2R30. Dolph Briscoe Center for American History, University of Texas at Austin.
Hargis, O. P. Journal. Typescript. Special Collections, Manuscript Division, University of North Carolina Library, Chapel Hill.
Harris, James Henry. 4th Indiana Cavalry. Diary. Special Collections, Indiana State History Museum, Indianapolis, IN. Cited as Harris Diary.
Hazen, William B. *A Narrative of Military Service*. Boston: Ticknor and Sons, 1885.
Henderson, Jesse L. Diary. Special Collections. Identifier MUM00226_Henderson_Diary. University of Mississippi Library, Oxford. https://egrove.olemiss.edu/ciwar_diaries/1/. Accessed 1 August 2023.
Hightower, William G. Co. C, 31st Mississippi. Diary. Courtesy Gloria S. Ramsaur, a descendant. Carter House Library and Museum, Franklin, TN.
Hood, John Bell. *Advance and Retreat: Personal Experiences in the United States & Confederate States Armies*. 1880. Reprinted with an introduction by Richard M. McMurry. New York: Da Capo Press, 1993.
Hoole, William Stanley. "Letters of Harden Perkins Cochrane" (to his mother, 6 June 1864 and 14 June 1864). *Alabama Review* 8/4 (October 1955): 285–287.
Howard, O. O. *Autobiography of Oliver Otis Howard*. 2 vols. New York: Baker & Taylor Co., 1907.
Hudson, William Spencer. *The Civil War Diary of William Spencer Hudson*. Edited by Weldon I. Hudson. St. Louis: Micro-Records Publishing Co., 1973. MDAH.
Huff, Sarah. *My 80 Years in Atlanta*. Subject files, AHC.
Ives, Washington. *Civil War Journal*. Transcribed and edited by Jim R. Cabaniss. Tallahassee: published by the editor, 1987. Unpublished copy of journal in vertical files, Chickamauga and Chattanooga National Battlefield Park Library, Fort Oglethorpe, GA.
Jennings, James Madison, to Martha Kimbrell Jennings. In *The History of Webster Co., Miss*. Webster County Historical Society, 1985.
Johnson, Joseph E., to General Johnson. 13 August 1863. Special Collections. Thornton Collection. Mitchell Memorial Library. Mississippi State University, Starkville.
Johnson, Dr. J. N. "Reminiscences." In *Confederate Reminiscences and Letters 1861–1865*. Vol. 15. Georgia Division, United Daughters of the Confederacy, 1996–2000. Chickamauga National Battlefield Park Library.
Johnson, R. W. *A Soldier's Reminiscences in Peace and War*. Philadelphia: J.B. Lippincott Co., 1886.
Johnston, Joseph E. *Narrative of Military Operations during the Late War between the States*, New York: D. Appleton & Co, 1874.
———, to Charles Johnsen. 19 June 1874. *Southern Historical Society Papers* 21 (1893): 319.
Karsten, Karl M. Company F, 26th Wisconsin. Diary. Microfilm 251. State Historical Society of Wisconsin, Madison.

Kean, Robert. *The Diary of Robert Garlick Hill Kean*. Edited by Edward Younger. New York: Oxford University Press, 1957.

Kellogg, Edgar Romney. Manuscript. US Army Military History Institute, Carlisle Barracks, PA.

Kennerly, James A., to sister. 8 August 1864. Vertical files, Kennerly Papers. Wilson's Creek National Park Library. John K. and Ruth Hulston Civil War Research Library, Wilson's Creek National Battlefield, Republic, MO.

Kern, John. Diary. Old Courthouse Museum, Vicksburg, MS.

Key, P. C. Family letters. Hargrett Rare Book and Manuscript Library. University of Georgia, Athens.

King, Green. Correspondence with Mary Jane King. Confederate file no. 102. Carter House Library and Museum, Franklin, TN.

Kirwan, A. D., ed. *Johnny Green of the Orphan Brigade: The Journal of a Confederate Soldier*. Lexington: University of Kentucky Press, 1956.

Kollock, Private Frederick N. Diary during the War 1864, Company B, 29th Pennsylvania, Ireland's 3rd Brigade, Geary's 2nd (White Star) Division. Transcribed by Charles S. Harris. Subject files. Chickamauga and Chattanooga National Military Park Library, Fort Oglethorpe, GA.

Landingham, Irenus Watson, to Mother. 14 July 1864. Landingham Papers. Folder 5, Special Collections. Auburn University Library, Auburn, AL.

Lane, Mills, ed. *"Dear Mother: Don't grieve about me. If I get killed, I'll only be dead": Letters from Georgia Soldiers in the Civil War*. Savannah: Beehive Press, 1977.

Lemmon, John G., "Memoirs," 1866, entry for May 19, 1864, Special Collections, The Huntington Library, San Marino, CA, Source, courtesy David A. Powell.

Little, Dr. George, and James R. Maxwell. *A History of Lumsden's Battery, C.S.A.* Tuskaloosa [sic], AL: R. E. Rhodes Chapter, United Daughters of the Confederacy, 1905.

Mackall, T. B. "The 'A' Sample, Journal of [Thomas B. Mackall] with the Army of Tennessee in Georgia, May 5–July 31, 1894." Box 3, folder 2, id112225. Joseph E. Johnston Papers (Mss. 39.1 J63). Special Collections Research Center, Swem Library, College of William & Mary, Williamsburg, VA.

Mackall, T. B. "The 'B' sample, Expanded Journal of [Thomas B. Mackall] with the Army of Tennessee in Georgia, and covering the period May 1–July 9, 1864." Box 3, folder 2, id112227. Joseph E. Johnston Papers (Mss. 39.1 J63). Special Collections Research Center, College of William & Mary, Williamsburg, VA.

Mackall, William W., Jr. *A Son's Recollections of His Father*. New York: E. P. Dutton & Co., 1930. (Original Mackall letters located in collection no. 01299, Special Collections. University of North Carolina at Chapel Hill Library.)

Mackall, William, to Minie Mackall. 18 and 21 May 1864. Joseph E. Johnston Papers (Mss. 39.1 J63). Special Collections Research Center, Swem Library, College of William & Mary, Williamsburg, VA.

Maddox, R. F. "Atlanta Battlefield Reunion." *Confederate Veteran* 8 (June 1900): 257.

Magill, Robert M. *Magill Family Record*. Richmond, VA: R. E. Magill, Publisher, 1907.

Markam, Thomas R. "Tribute to the Confederate Dead" *SHSP* 10 (April 1882): 175. Address delivered to veterans at New Orleans, 6 April 1882.

McCall, Phil, ed. Private Isaiah Crook Diary, 37th Ga., Smith's Brigade, Bate's Division, Hardee's Corps. Prepared for 1998 Crook Reunion. Vertical files. Kennesaw Mountain Battlefield Park Library, Kennesaw, GA.

McCuistion, Mitchell Henderson. Diary, Company K, 9th Texas. 20 July 1864. Special Collections, University of Texas at Austin Library. Dolph Briscoe Center for American History, University of Texas at Austin.
McElroy, Cyrus Decatur. *The Diary of a Confederate Volunteer*. San Antonio: Southern Literary Institute, 1935.
McKittrick, Samuel, to Mary McKittrick. 22 May 1864. South Carolina vertical files, Kennesaw Mountain National Military Park, Kennesaw, GA.
McMahon, John T. *John T. McMahon's Diary of the 136th New York 1861–1864*. Edited by John Michael Priest. Shippensburg, PA: White Mane Publishing Co., 1993.
McNeilly, James H. "A Day in the Life of a Confederate Chaplain." *Confederate Veteran* 26 (1918): 471.
Mead, Homer. *The Eighth Iowa Cavalry in the Civil War: Autobiography and Personal Recollections of Homer Mead, M.D., Augusta, Illinois*. Carthage, IL: S.C. Davidson, 1925.
Miller, J. M. *Recollections of "A Pine Knot" in "The Lost Cause."* Greenwood, MS: Greenwood Publishing Company, c. 1900.
Miller, James T. *Bound to Be a Soldier: The Letters of Private James T. Miller, 111th Pennsylvania Infantry 1861–1864*. Edited by Jedediah Mannis and Galen R. Wilson. Knoxville: University of Tennessee Press, 2001.
Montgomery, Frank Alexander. *Reminiscences of a Mississippian in Peace and War*. Cincinnati: Robert Clarke Company Press, 1901.
Mosman, Chesley A. *The Rough Side of War: The Civil War Journal of Chesley A. Mosman*. Edited by Arnold Gates. Garden City, NY: Basin Publishing Co., 1987.
Mothershead, W. I. Letter. Folder 5, SG024896. ADAH.
Murphy, Virgil S., to cousin. From Kennesaw Mountain, 21 June 1864. Vertical files. Kennesaw Mountain National Battlefield Park Library, Kennesaw, GA.
Neal, A. J., to father. 20 July 1864. *Letters from Georgia Soldiers*, 28–29. Vertical files, Kennesaw Mountain National Battlefield Park Library, Kennesaw, GA.
Nisbet, James Cooper. *4 Years on the Firing Line*. Edited by Bell Irvin Wiley. Jackson, TN: McCowat-Mercer Press, 1963.
Norton, Reuben S. Journal 1861. Special Collections. Rome/Floyd County Library, Rome, GA.
Norwell, William D. Diary. Georgia vertical files. Kennesaw Mountain NBP.
O.G.G., "Camp Near Calhoun, May 16," *The Daily Constitutionalist*, Augusta, GA, May 20, 1864, 2, NewspaperArchive.com.
Oldham, Van Buren. *Civil War Diaries of Van Buren Oldham, Company G, 9th Tennessee, 1863–1864*. Compiled and edited by Dieter C. Ullrich. Transcribed by Elizabeth Kitts. Martin, TN: D. Ullrich, [1999].
Opdycke, Emerson. *To Battle for God & the Right, The Civil War Letters of Emerson Opdycke*. Edited by Glenn V. Longacre and John E. Haas. Champaign: University of Illinois Press, 2007.
Ora, letter, "Army of Tennessee, Allatoona, GA, 6 miles south of the Etowah, Friday, May 20, 1864," *The Weekly Advertiser*, Montgomery, AL, May 23, 1864, 2.
Osborn, George C., ed. "Civil War Letters of Robert W. Banks: Atlanta Campaign." *Georgia Historical Quarterly* 27/2 (June 1943): 211.
Osceola, "Camp Dibrell's Brigade Cavalry," *Memphis Daily Appeal*, May 24, 1864, 3.
Otto, John Henry. *Memoirs of a Dutch Mudsill: The "War Memories" of John Henry Otto,*

Captain, Company D, 21st Regiment Wisconsin Volunteer Infantry. Edited by David Gould and James B. Kennedy. Kent, OH: Kent State University Press, 2004.

Palmer, Solomon. Diary. 19th Alabama. Subject file, PW-51. Kennesaw National Battlefield Park, Kennesaw, GA.

Phisterer, Frederick. Manuscript. Larew-Phisterer Family Papers. US Army Military History Institute, Carlisle Barracks, PA.

Pierson, Stephen. "From Chattanooga to Atlanta in 1864: A Personal Reminiscence." *Proceedings New Jersey Historical Society* 16 (1931): 324–56.

Porter, Albert Quincy. Diary. MDAH.

Power, J. L. *1864 Scrapbook*. MDAH.

Pressnall, James S. Memoirs. 63rd Illinois. Subject files. Carter House Library and Museum, Franklin, TN.

Rice, Ralsa C. *Yankee Tigers: Through the Civil War with the 125th Ohio*. Edited by Richard A. Baumgartner and Larry M. Strayer. Huntington, WV: Blue Acorn Press, 1992.

Rorer, Lt. Col. Walter A., to Cousin Susan. 31 March 1864 and 9 June 1864. 20th Mississippi. Transcribed by T. Glover Roberts. Carter House Library and Museum, Franklin, TN.

Roy, T. B. "General Hardee and the Military Operations Around Atlanta." *SHSP* 8 (1880): 382.

Sanders, J. B. (Co. H, 37th Mississippi) to his wife. 13 July 1864. Subject files. MDAH.

Schofield, John M. *Forty-Six Years in the Army*. New York: Century Co., 1887.

Sears, Claudius Wistar. Diary (copy). Vertical files, Confederate, MS-1. Kennesaw Mountain National Military Park, Kennesaw, GA.

Sherman, William T. *Marching through Georgia: William T. Sherman's Personal Narrative of His March through Georgia*. Edited by Mills Lane. New York: Arno Press, 1978.

———. *Memoirs of General William T. Sherman*. 1875. Reprint, Bloomington: Indiana University Press, 1957.

Shoupe, F. A. "Works at the Chattahoochee River." *Confederate Veteran* 3 (1895): 262–65.

Sloan, William E. Diary. Typescript. Special Collections. Chattanooga-Hamilton Bicentennial Library, Chattanooga, TN. Courtesy Chris Cash. Cited as Sloan Diary.

Smith, Benjamin L., Jr. Autobiography. Carnton Archives, Franklin, TN.

Smith, Elias, to Sydney Howard Gay. 31 May 1864. Gay Papers. Columbia University Libraries, New York, NY.

Smith, Robert Davis. *Diary of Captain Robert Davis Smith*. Special Collections. Chattanooga-Hamilton Bicentennial Library, Chattanooga, TN.

_____Robert Davis Smith, 1842-1910, *Confederate Diary of Robert D. Smith*. Columbia, TN: Capt. James Madison Sparkman Chapter, United Daughters of the Confederacy, 1975.

Steinmeyer, J. H. 24th South Carolina. Diary. South Carolina vertical files, Kennesaw Mountain National Military Park, Kennesaw, GA.

Stephens, M. D. L. "Narrative of the Battle of Franklin." In Ken Nail, *History of Calhoun County*, 41–48. Water Valley, MS: Calhoun County School District, 1975. Courtesy Thomas Cartwright, Carter House Library and Museum, Franklin, TN.

———. *A Brief History of the Stephens Family*. 14 February 1911. Courtesy of Allen Latimer, descendant, Water Valley, MS

———. *Recollections of 31st Mississippi*. RG 9, v. 136 R 151, B 20, S 3-289. Special Collections. MDAH.

Stevenson, T. A. Letter. 28 August 1885. Special Collections. Duke University Libraries,

Duke University, Durham, NC.
Sykes, Columbus. Letters to His Wife. Subject file, MI-4, p. 30A. Kennesaw National Battlefield Park Library, Kennesaw, GA.
Sykes, Edward T. *Walthall's Brigade: A Cursory Sketch, with Personal Experiences*. Columbus, MS: Edward T. Sykes [publ.], 1905.
Talley, William. Autobiography. Confederate GA-12. Vertical files. Kennesaw Mountain NBP.
Thatcher, M. P. *A Hundred Battles in the West*. Detroit: L. F. Kilroy, Printer, 1884.
Thompson, Col. J. C., to A. P. Stewart. 8 December 1867. Joseph E. Johnston Collection. Box 1, folder 5. Swem Library, College of William & Mary, Williamsburg, Virginia.
Thompson, W. C. "From the Defenses of Atlanta to a Federal Prison Camp." *Civil War Times Illustrated* 3/10 (February 1965): 40–44.
Thornton, Solomon M., to J. W. Starnes, Esq., 15 June 1862; Thornton Collection. Special Collections. Mitchell Memorial Library, Mississippi State University, Starkville.
———, to Mrs. S. F. Thornton, 15 May 1863. Hames H. Gardner Collection 1846–1948. Special Collections. Mitchell Memorial Library, Mississippi State University, Starkville.
———, to Mrs. S. F. Thornton, 18 November 1862, 1 May 1863, 27 August 1863, 7 March 1864, 25 April 1864. Special Collections. Mitchell Memorial Library, Mississippi State University, Starkville.
Thornton, William, letter to father, May 22, 1864, camp near Altonia [sic], Ga., vertical files, Confederate GA-26, Kennesaw Mountain NMP
Tower, Lockwood. *A Carolinian Goes to War: The Civil War Narrative of Arthur Middleton Manigault, Brigadier General*. Columbia: University of South Carolina Press, 1964.
Trask, W. L. Diary. Typescript. HM 48297. Special Collections. Huntington Library, San Marino, CA.
Trego, Alfred H. Diary. 3 July 1864. Chicago Historical Society, Chicago, IL.
Truman, W. L., Memoirs of the Civil War, vertical files, Confederate MO-4, Kennesaw Mountain NMP.
Tuttle, Miletus. Letters. University of Georgia Hargrett Rare Book and Manuscript Library.
Underwood, Adin B. *The Three Years' Service of the Thirty-Third Massachusetts Infantry Regiment 1862–1865*. Boston: A. Williams & Co., 1881.
Unknown, "From the Front," *Augusta Chronicle*, Augusta, GA, May 21, 1864.
Upson, Theodore F. *With Sherman to the Sea: The Civil War Letters, Diaries and Reminiscences of Theodore F. Upson*. Bloomington: Indiana University Press, 1958.
Vaughan, A. J. *Personal Record of the Thirteenth Regiment, Tennessee Infantry, by Its Old Commander*. Memphis, TN: Press of S. C. Toof & Co., 1897.
Walker, C. Irvine. *Historical Sketch of the Tenth Regiment South Carolina Volunteers*. Charleston: Walker, Evans & Cogswell, 1881.
Watkins, Sam R. *"Co. Aytch": A Side Show of the Big Show*. Edited by Bell Irvin Wiley. Wilmington, NC: Broadfoot Publishing Company, 1994.
Watson, James. "Private Watson Writes Home." *Webster Progress*. 15 July 1937. Subject files. Kennesaw Mountain National Military Park Library, Kennesaw, GA.
Watson, Joel Calvin. Diary. Special Collections. Grenada Public Library, Grenada, MS.
Wharton, John, vertical files, Confederate MO-5, 13, Kennesaw Mountain NMP.
Wilkes, Abner James. *A Short History of My Life in the Late War between the North and the South*. Wilson's Creek National Battlefield Park Library.

Willet, E. D., diary, vertical files, Confederate AL-4, 101, Kennesaw Mountain NMP.
Wilson, Thomas B. *Reminiscences of Thomas B. Wilson, 1904.* Special collections. University of North Carolina-Chapel Hill Library.
Winkler, Major Frederick C. *Civil War Letters of Major Frederick C. Winkler.* American Civil War Collection. Dakota State University, Madison, SD.
Womack, Lt. William A. Diary. Author's private collection.
Wood, Colonel James. *Report of the Operations of the 3rd Brigade, 3rd Division of the XX Army Corps, in the Atlanta Campaign of 1864.* Albany: Weed, Parsons & Co., Printers, 1889.
Worsham, Dr. J. W. "Reminiscences of the Battle Around Atlanta." In vol. 3 of *Confederate Reminiscences and Letters 1861–1865.* Georgia Division, United Daughters of the Confederacy, 1996–2000. Courtesy Chickamauga National Battlefield Park Library.
Wyatt, J. N., to J. B. Cunningham, 10 August 1864. *Confederate Veteran* 5 (1897): 521.

Newspapers and Periodicals:

Atlanta Appeal, July 20, 1864.
Augusta Daily Chronicle and Sentinel, July 26, 1864.
Binghamton Standard, August 1864.
The Chattanooga Daily Rebel, Griffin, Ga. July 27, 1864, TSLA, Microfilm 1045, Roll 1.
Chicago Daily *Tribune*, June 8, 12 & 16, 1864, MTSU Library and Archives.
Cincinnati *Daily Commercial*, June 7, 1864; July 26, 1864.
Cincinnati Daily Gazette, May 23, 1864.
Clarion-Ledger, June 9, 1864, Jackson, MS.
Clarion-Ledger Jackson Daily News, Carl McIntire, "Mississippi Soldiers Were Among the Dead at Rock Island Prison," Sunday, November 25, 1984.
Columbus Crisis, Aug. 3, 1864.
Columbus Sentential, quoted in the *Macon Daily Telegraph*, September 22, 1864, Washington Library, Macon City Library, Macon, Ga.
The *Daily Southern Crisis*, Jackson, Miss., M.S.U. Library.
The Daily Sun (Columbus, GA), Georgia Historic Newspapers, F.M.G, Company K, 37th Georgia, letter "In camp near Atlanta, May 22, 1864," May 28, 1864.
The Daily Tribune News, Cartersville, GA, November 8, 1949.
Georgia Journal & Messenger, Wednesday, July 20, 1864, July 27, 1864, Macon, Ga.
Harper's Weekly, Aug. 6, 1864, Aug. 13, 1864, & Oct. 29, 1864; KRC, AHC.
Ithaca Journal, Wednesday, August 24, 1864.
The *National Tribune*, Wash., D.C., 1900.
The New England Almanac for 1864, Nathan Daboll.
New York Herald, June 19. 1864; July 29, 1889.
New York Times, March 29, 1865.
New York Tribune, July 28, 1864.
New York Weekly Tribune, September 24, 1864.
(Macon) *Daily Intelligencer*, Aug. 6, 1864. Report of F. Rice, Chief Surgeon, Cheatham's Division, Benjamin F. Cheatham Papers, Atlanta, TSLA.
Macon Daily Telegraph, Thursday, July 21, 1864, & July 22-Sept. 22, 1864, Washington Library, Macon City Libraries, Macon, Ga.
Memphis Daily Appeal, May 24, 1864. Osceola, "Camp Dibbrell's [sic] Brigade Cavalry, Etowah River, May 23, 1864."
Meridian Star, February 1864: Emancipation in Meridian, by Greg Snowden, Feb. 15, 2004,

courtesy June Anderson.
Montgomery Weekly Advertiser, June 8, 1864, Tell, "Special Correspondence from Cantey's Brigade."
The Ottawa Illinois Republican, MTSU Library and Archives.
The *Richmond Enquirer*, March 25, 1865
Savannah Republican, July 25, 1864.
Southern Banner, Athens, GA: July 9, 1864.
The Pantagraph, Bloomington, Ill., MTSU Library and Archives.
Times Picayune, Sunday, October 22, 1893, New Orleans, LA. Johnston, Joseph E., letter to Charles Johnsen, June 19, 1874, letter and sketch map.
The *Tri-Weekly Citizen*, Canton, Miss.
Walker County Messenger, August 6, 1896.
The Weekly Advertiser, Montgomery, AL J.F. Gaines, letter to, Wednesday, June 8, 1864. *Yalobusha Pioneer*, Vol. XXI, Issue Three, Fall, 1996; Pension Application of Thomas J. Blackwell; and Diary of Dr. Thomas J. Blackwell, C.S.A.

Secondary Sources
Published Books and Articles

Adamson, A. P. *Brief History of the 30th Georgia Regiment*. Jonesboro, GA: Freedom Hill Press, 1987.
Aimone, Alan C. Essential *Civil War Curriculum: Official Records of the Union and Confederate Armies*, Virginia Center for Civil War Studies, Blacksburg, VA: Virginia Tech University, 2012.
Allendorf, Donald. *Long Road to Liberty: The Odyssey of a German Regiment in the Yankee Army*. Kent, OH: Kent State University Press, 2006.
Alexander, E. P., *Military Memoirs of a Confederate*, New York, 1907.
Anders, Leslie. *The Eighteenth Missouri*. Indianapolis: Bobbs-Merrill, 1968.
Andrews, J. Cutler. *The North Reports the Civil War*. Pittsburgh: University of Pittsburgh Press, 1955.
Aten, Henry J. *History of the Eighty-Fifth Regiment, Illinois Volunteer Infantry*. Hiawatha, KS: Regimental Association, 1901.
Avery, Isaac W., *The History of the State of Georgia, From 1850 to 1881, Embracing the Three Important Epochs: The Decade Before the War of 1861-5; The War; The Period of Reconstruction, with Portraits of the Leading Public Men of This Era*, New York, NY: Brown & Derby Publishers, 1881.
Aycock, Roger A. *All Roads to Rome*. Fernandina Beach, FL: Wolfe Publishing, 1981.
Bailey, Ronald H. *Battles for Atlanta: Sherman Moves East*. Civil War Series. Alexandria: Time-Life, 1985.
Banning, Leroy F. *Regimental History of the 35th Alabama Infantry, 1862–1865*. Bowie, MD: Heritage Books, 1999.
Barnard, George N. *Photographic Views of Sherman's Campaign*. New York: Dover, 1977.
Barnard, Harry V. *Tattered Volunteers, The Twenty-Seventh Alabama Regiment, C.S.A.* Northport, AL: Hermitage Press, 1965.
Bass, Ronald R. *History of the Thirty-first Arkansas Confederate Infantry*. Conway, AR: Arkansas Research Press, 1996.
Bates, Samuel Penniman. *History of Pennsylvania Volunteers, 1861–1865*. 5 vols. Philadelphia: T. H. Davis & Co., 1875.

Bearss, Edwin C. *The Campaign for Vicksburg*. 3 vols. Dayton: Morningside House, 1985.
Bearss, Margie Riddle. *Sherman's Forgotten Campaign: The Meridian Expedition*. Baltimore: Gateway Press, 1987.
Beaudot, William J. K. *The 24th Wisconsin Infantry in the Civil War: The Biography of a Regiment*. Mechanicsburg, PA: Stackpole Books, 2003.
Bender, Robert Patrick, ed., *Worthy of the Cause for Which They Fight, The Civil War Diary of Brigadier General Daniel Harris Reynolds, 1861-1865*, Fayetteville, AR: University of Arkansas Press, 2011.
Bennett, Lyman G., and William M. Haigh. *History of the 36th Regiment Illinois Volunteers during the War of the Rebellion*. Aurora, IL: Knickerbocker & Hodder, Printers, 1876.
Bettersworth, John K., ed. *Mississippi in the Confederacy*. Vol. 1, *As They Saw It*. Baton Rouge: Brepolis Publishers, 1961.
Bevier, R. S. *History of the First and Second Missouri Confederate Brigades, 1861–1865, and from Wakaruse to Appomattox: A Military Anagraph*. St. Louis: Bryan, Brand & Company, 1879.
Biggs, Gregg. "The 'Shoupade' Redoubts: Joseph E. Johnston's Chattahoochee River Line." *Civil War Regiments: A Journal of the American Civil War* 1/3 (1990): 82–93.
Blackburn, Theodore W. *Letters from the Front, A Union "Preacher" Regiment (74th Ohio) in the Civil War*. Dayton, OH: Press of Morningside House, 1981.
Bonds, Russell S. *War Like the Thunderbolt*. Yardley, PA: Westholme Publishing, 2009.
Bondurant, Sidney Wiggins, *The History of the 33rd Mississippi Infantry Regiment*, Toccoa, GA: Institute for Southern Historical Review, 2005.
Bonin, John Aubrey. "Lost Victories: Johnston & Sherman at Cassville." *Blue & Gray* 13/6 (August 1996): 28–37.
Bowers, John. *Chickamauga and Chattanooga, The Battles that Doomed the Confederacy*. New York: Harper Collins, 1994.
Bowman, John S., ed. *The Civil War Day by Day*. New York: Dorset, 1989.
Boyle, John Richards. *Soldiers True: The Story of the One Hundred and Eleventh Regiment Pennsylvania Veteran Volunteers and of its Campaigns in the War for the Union, 1861–1885*. New York: Eaton & Mains, 1903.
Bradford, Ned, ed. *Battles and Leaders of the Civil War*. New York: Fairfax Press, 1979.
Bradley, James. *The Confederate Mail Carrier*. Mexico, MO: James Bradley, 1894.
Brewer, Willis. *Alabama: Her History, Resources, War Record, and Public Men, from 1540 to 1872*. Montgomery, AL: Barrett & Brown, Steam Printers & Binders, 1872.
Briant, Charles C., *History of the Sixth Regiment, Indiana Volunteer Infantry, of Both The Three Months' and Three Years' Services*, Indianapolis, IN: William E. Burford, Printer and Binder, 1891.
Brown, Edmund R. *A History of the 27th Indiana*. Monticello, IN: Edmund R. Brown, 1899.
Brown, Joseph M. *The Mountain Campaigns in Georgia, or War Scenes on the Western & Atlantic Railroad*. Buffalo: Art-Printing Works of Matthews, Northrup & Co.: 1890.
Brown, Norman D., ed., *One of Cleburne's Command, The Civil War Reminiscences and Diary of Capt. Samuel T. Foster, Granbury's Texas Brigade, CSA*, Austin, TX: University of Texas Press, 1980.
Brown, Thaddeus C. S., Samuel J. Murphy, and William G. Putney. *Behind the Guns: The History of Battery I, 2nd Regiment, Illinois Light Artillery*. Carbondale: Southern Illinois University Press, 1965.

Bryant, Edwin E. *Third Wisconsin Veterans, 1861–1865.* Madison, WI: Democrat Printing Co., 1891.
Buell, Thomas B. *The Warrior Generals: Combat Leadership in the Civil War.* Pittsburgh: Three Rivers Press, 1997.
Busey, John W., and David G. Martin. *Regimental Strengths and Losses at Gettysburg.* 4th ed. Hightstown, NJ: Longstreet House, 2005.
Calkins, William Wirt. *The History of the One Hundred and Fourth Regiment of Illinois Volunteer Infantry, War of the Great Rebellion, 1862–1865.* Chicago: Donohue & Henneberry, Printer, 1895.
Cannan, John. *The Atlanta Campaign, May–November 1864.* Conshohocken, PA: Combined Publishing, 1991.
Capers, Walter B. *The Soldier-Bishop Ellison Capers.* New York: Neale Publishing Company, 1912.
Carlock, Chuck. *History of The Tenth Texas Cavalry (Dismounted) Regiment 1861–1865.* Richland Hills, TX: Bibal Press, 2001.
Carroon, Robert G., ed. *From Freeman's Ford to Bentonville, The 61st Ohio Volunteer Infantry.* Shippensburg, PA: Burd Street Press, 1998.
Carter, Samuel, III. *The Siege of Atlanta, 1864.* New York: St. Martin's Press, 1973.
Carter, W. R. *History of the First Regiment of Tennessee Volunteer Cavalry in the Great War of the Rebellion, With the Armies of the Ohio and Cumberland, under Generals Morgan, Rosecrans, Thomas, Stanley and Wilson, 1862–1865.* Knoxville, TN: Gaut-Ogden Co., Printers, 1902.
Cash, William M., and Lucy Somerville Howorth, eds. *My Dear Nellie, The Civil War Letters of William L. Nugent to Eleanor Smith Nugent.* Jackson: University Press of Mississippi, 1977.
Castel, Albert. *Decision in the West: The Atlanta Campaign of 1864.* Lawrence: University Press of Kansas, 1992.
Cate, Jean M., ed. *If I Live to Come Home: The Civil War Letters of Sergeant John March Cate.* Pittsburgh: Dorrance Publishing Co., 1995.
Catton, Bruce. *A Stillness at Appomattox.* Garden City, NY: Doubleday, 1954.
———. *The American Heritage New History of the Civil War.* Edited by James M. McPherson. New York: Penguin, 1996.
Charnley, Jeffrey. "Neglected Honor: The Life of General A. S. Williams of Michigan (1810–1878)." PhD diss., Michigan State University, 1983.
Cisco, Walter Brian. *States Rights Gist: A South Carolina General of the Civil War.* Shippensburg, PA: White Mane Publishing, 1991.
Clark, Charles T. *Opdycke Tigers, 125th Ohio Volunteer Infantry: A History of the Regiment and of the Campaigns and Battles of the Army of the Cumberland.* 1895. Reprint, Morgantown, PA: Higginson Book Company, 1998.
Clausewitz, Karl von. *On War.* Translated by J. J. Graham. London: Nicholas Trubner, 1873.
Clauss, Erol. *The Atlanta Campaign, July 18, 1864.* PhD diss., Emory University, 1965. Special Collections. Zach Henderson Library, Georgia Southern University.
Coffey, David. *John Bell Hood and the Struggle for Atlanta.* Abilene, TX: McWhiney Foundation Press, 1998.
Coggins, Jack. *Arms & Equipment of the Civil War.* Garden City, NY: Doubleday, 1962.
Coleman, Kenneth. *A History of Georgia.* Athens: Universfity of Georgia Press, 1977.

Collier, Major Calvin L., *"The War Child's Children," A Story of the Third Arkansas Cavalry*, Little Rock, AR: Pioneer Press, 1965.
Collins, Darrell L. *The Army of Tennessee, Organization, Strength, Casualties, 1862–1865*. Jefferson, NC: McFarland, 2017.
Commager, Henry Steele, ed. *The Blue & the Gray*. New York: Fairfax Press, 1982.
Conklin, Dennis Blair II. *Conflict and Controversy in the Confederate High Command: Johnston, Davis, Hood, and the Atlanta Campaign of 1864*. PhD diss., University of Southern Mississippi, 2013. Available at https://aquila.usm.edu/dissertations/574/.
Connelly, Thomas L. *Army of the Heartland: The Army of Tennessee 1861–1862*. Baton Rouge: Louisiana State University Press, 1967.
———. *Autumn of Glory: The Army of Tennessee, 1862–1865*. Baton Rouge: Louisiana State University Press, 1971.
———. *The Marble Man: Robert E. Lee and His Image in American Society*. Baton Rouge: Louisiana State University Press, 1977.
Connolly, James A. *Three Years in the Army of the Cumberland*. Bloomington: Indiana University Press, 1959.
Cope, Alexis. *The 15th Ohio and Its Campaigns, War of 1861–5*. Columbus, OH: Alexis Cope, 1916.
Corbin, William E. *A Star for Patriotism: Iowa's Outstanding Civil War College*. Monticello, IA: Corbin, 1972.
Cox, Jacob D. *Atlanta*. 1882. Reprint, Dayton, OH: Morningside Press, 1987.
Cozzens, Peter. *The Shipwreck of Their Hopes: The Battles for Chattanooga*. Civil War Trilogy. Champaign: University of Illinois Press, 1994.
———. *This Terrible Sound: The Battle of Chickamauga*. Civil War Trilogy. Champaign: University of Illinois Press, 1996.
Crabb, Martha L. *All Afire to Fight: The Untold Tale of the Civil War's Ninth Texas Cavalry*. New York: Avon, 2000.
Cram, George F. *Soldiering with Sherman: The Civil War Letters of George F. Cram*. Edited by Jennifer Cain Bornstedt. DeKalb: Northern Illinois University Press, 2000.
Crute, Joseph H., Jr. *Units of the Confederate States Army*. Midlothian, VA: Derwent Books, 1987.
Cunningham, H. H. *Doctors in Gray: The Confederate Medical Service*. Baton Rouge: Louisiana State University Press, 1958.
Cunningham, Sumner A., and John A. Simpson, ed. *Reminiscences of the 41st Tennessee: The Civil War in the West*. Shippensburg, PA: White Mane Books, 2001.
Cunyus, Lucy. *A History of Bartow County (Formerly Cass County)*. Greenville, SC: Southern Historical Press, 1933.
Daniel, Larry. "Adairsville." In vol. 3 of *A Series of Essays on the Atlanta Campaign*, edited by Steve Davis. El Dorado Hills, CA: Savas Beatie Press, forthcoming 2024.
———. *Cannoneers in Gray: The Field Artillery of the Army of Tennessee*. Tuscaloosa: University of Alabama Press, 2005.
Davis, Burke. *The Civil War, Strange and Fascinating Facts*. New York: Fairfax Press, 1982.
Davis, Stephen. "A Reappraisal of the Generalship of John Bell Hood in the Battles for Atlanta." In Savas and Woodbury, *Campaign for Atlanta and Sherman's March to the Sea*, 49–96.

———. *A Long and Bloody Task: The Atlanta Campaign from Dalton through Kennesaw Mountain to the Chattahoochee River, May 5–July 18, 1864*. Emerging Civil War Series. El Dorado Hills, CA: Savas Beatie Press, 2016.

———. *Atlanta Will Fall: Sherman, Joe Johnston, and the Yankee Heavy Battalions*. Number 3 in American Crisis Series. Wilmington, DE: Scholarly Resources, 2001.

———. *John Bell Hood: Texas Brigadier to the Fall of Atlanta*. Macon: Mercer University Press, 2019.

Davis, Stephen and Bill Hendrick, *The Atlanta Daily Intelligencer Covers the Civil War*, Knoxville, TN: The University of Tennessee Press, 2022.

Davis, William C. *The Commanders of the Civil War*. New York: Smithmark, 1991.

———, and Bell I. Wiley. *The Image of War, 1861–65*. 6 vols. New York: Doubleday, 1981–1983. Reprint in 2 vols., New York: Black Dog and Leventhal, 1994.

Dodge, Grenville M. "The Late Gen. J. M. Schofield." *Confederate Veteran* 15 (October 1907): 460–61.

———. *The Battle of Atlanta and Other Campaigns*. Council Bluff, IA: Monarch Printing Company, 1911.

Dodson, W. C. *Campaigns of Wheeler and His Cavalry 1862–1865*. Atlanta, GA: Hudgins Publishing Co., 1899.

Dubose, John Witherspoon. *General Joseph Wheeler and the Army of Tennessee*. New York: Neale Publishing Company, 1912.

Dwight, Captain Henry. "How We Fight at Atlanta." *The Blue and the Gray* 29/173 (15 August 1864): 939–43.

Dyer, John P. *The Gallant Hood*. Indianapolis: Bobbs-Merrill Company, 1950.

Eddy, Thomas Mears. *The Patriotism of Illinois*. 2 vols. Chicago: Clarke & Co., 1865–1866.

Elliott, Sam Davis. *Soldier of Tennessee: General Alexander P. Stewart and the Civil War in the West*. Baton Rouge: Louisiana State University Press, 1999.

Ellis, B.G., *The Moving Appeal, Mr. McClanahan, Mrs. Dill, and the Civil War's Great Newspaper Run*, Macon, GA: Mercer University Press, 2003.

Evans, Clement Anselm, ed. *Confederate Military History*. Vol. 7, *Atlanta*, Vol 13 *Louisiana*. 19 vols. Confederate Publishing Co., 1899. Reprint, Wilmington, NC: Broadfoot Publishing Co., 1987.

Evans, David. *Sherman's Horsemen: Union Cavalry Operations in the Atlanta Campaign*. Bloomington: Indiana University Press, 1996.

Fellman, Michael. *The Making of Robert E. Lee*. New York: Random House, 2000.

Fenton, E. B. "From the Rapidan to Atlanta: Leaves from the Diary of Companion E. B. Fenton, Late Twentieth Connecticut Volunteer Infantry. Read before the Commandery of the State of Michigan Military Order of the Loyal Legion of the United States, at Detroit, Mich., April 6th, 1893." In *War Papers Read before the Commandery of the State of Michigan Military Order of the Loyal Legion of the United States*. Volume 1, October 6, 1886, to April 6, 1893. Detroit: Winn & Hammond, Printers, 1893. Available at https://catalog.hathitrust.org/Record/004388831. Reprinted in Sydney C. Kerksis, comp., *The Atlanta Papers, No. 7*. Dayton: Morningside Press, 1980.

Ferguson, Edwin L. *Sumner County, Tennessee in the Civil War*. Edited by Diane Payne. Privately printed, 1972.

Ferguson, John Hill. *On to Atlanta: The Civil War Diaries of John Hill Ferguson, 10th Illinois Regiment of Volunteers*. Lincoln: University of Nebraska Press, 2001.

Fitch, John. *Annals of the Army of the Cumberland*. Philadelphia: J. B. Lippincott & Co., 1864.

Fleming, James R. *The Confederate Ninth Tennessee Infantry*. New Orleans: Pelican Publishing Company, 2006.

Foote, Shelby. *The Civil War: A Narrative*. Volume 1, *Fort Sumter to Perryville*. New York: Vintage Books, 1958.

Forbes, William, II. *Haulin' Brass, Captain Croft's Flying Artillery, Columbus, Georgia*. Dayton, OH: Morningside Press, 1993.

Foster, Captain Samuel T. *One of Cleburne's Command, The Civil War Reminiscences and Diary of Captain Samuel T. Foster, Granbury's Texas Brigade, C.S.A.* Edited by Norman D. Brown. Austin: University of Texas Press, 1980.

Foster, Wilbur F. "Battlefield Maps in Georgia." *Confederate Veteran* 20 (1912): 369.

Fox, Lt. Col. William F. *Regimental Losses in the American Civil War 1861–1865*. Albany, NY: Albany Publishing Company, 1889.

Fryman, Robert J. "Fortifying the Landscape: An Archaeological Study of Military Engineering and the Atlanta Campaign." In *Archaeological Perspectives on the American Civil War*, edited by Clarence R. Geier and Stephen R. Potter, 1–12. Gainesville: University Press of Florida, 2002.

Garrett, Franklin. *Atlanta & Environs*. Athens: University of Georgia Press, 1954.

Garrison, Web. *Atlanta and the War*. Nashville: Rutledge Hill Press, 1995.

Gillum, Jamie. *An Eyewitness History of the 16th Regiment Tennessee Volunteers May 1861–May 1865*. Privately printed, 2005.

Glass, F. M. *Long Creek Rifles: A Brief History*. Sallis, MS: Long Creek Rifles Chapter, United Daughters of the Confederacy, 1909.

Goodall, Barry D., Jr. *Glory Gone Forgotten: The Untold Story of the 12th Kentucky Cavalry*. Morgantown, KY: Goodall, 2004.

Goodson, Gary Ray, Sr. *Georgia Confederate 7,000, Army of Tennessee, Part II: Letters and Diaries*. Shawnee, CO: Goodson Enterprises, 2000.

Goodspeed, Wilbur. *Biographical and Historical Memoirs of Mississippi*. Chicago, Goodspeed Publishing Co., 1891.

Gottschalk, Phil. *In Deadly Earnest*. Columbia, MO: Missouri River Press, 1991.

Govan, Gilbert E., and James W. Livingood. *A Different Valor: The Story of General Joseph E. Johnston, C.S.A.* Indianapolis: Bobbs-Merrill, 1956.

Gresham, Matilda McGrain. *Life of Walter Quintin Gresham, 1832–1895*. 2 vols. Chicago: Rand, McNally & Co., 1919.

Groom, Winston. *Shrouds of Glory: From Atlanta to Nashville: The Last Great Campaign of the Civil War*. New York: Atlantic Monthly, 1995.

Haas, Garland A. *To the Mountain of Fire and Beyond: The Fifty-Third Indiana Regiment from Corinth to Glory*. Carmel: Guild Press of Indiana, 1997.

Hafendorfer, Kenneth A. *Mill Springs, Campaign and Battle of Mill Springs*. Louisville, KY: KH Press, 2001.

———, ed. *Civil War Journal of William L. Trask, Confederate Sailor and Soldier*. Louisville, KY: KH Press, 2003.

Hale, Douglas. *The Third Texas Cavalry in the Civil War*. Norman: University of Oklahoma Press, 1993.

Hall, Richard. *Patriots in Disguise*. New York: Marlowe & Company, 1994.

Hardy, Michael C. *The Fifty-Eighth North Carolina Troops, Tar Heels in the Army of Tennessee*. Jefferson, NC: McFarland & Company, 2010.

Hart, B. H. Liddell. *Sherman: Soldier, Realist, American*. New York: Frederick A. Praeger, 1958.

Haskell, Oliver C., 6th Indiana cavalry Regiment, Manuscript Department, Collection No. SC 0707, Folder CA. 1852-1943, William C. Smith Memorial Library, Indiana Historical Society, Indianapolis, IN..

Hatley, Allen G. *The First Texas Legion during the American Civil War*. Eagle Lake, TX: Centex Press, 2004.

Hay, Thomas Robson, "The Atlanta Campaign," *Georgia Historical Quarterly*, Savannah, GA: Georgia Historical Society, March 1923, vol. 7, no. 1, 18-43.

_____Hay, "The Davis-Hood-Johnston Controversy of 1864," *Mississippi Valley Historical Review*, Bloomington, IN: Journal of American History, formerly Mississippi Valley Historical Association, June 1924, vol. 11, no. 1, 54-84.

Head, Thomas A. *Campaigns and Battles of the Sixteenth Regiment, Tennessee Volunteers*. Nashville: Cumberland Presbyterian Publishing House, 1885.

Hebert, Keith S. *The Long Civil War in the North Georgia Mountains, Confederate Nationalism, Sectionalism, and White Supremacy in Bartow County, Georgia*. Knoxville: University of Tennessee Press, 2017.

Hebert, Walter H. *Fighting Joe Hooker*. Lincoln: University of Nebraska Press, 1999.

Henderson, Lillian, ed. *Roster of the Confederate Soldiers of Georgia 1861–1865*. 7 vols. Georgia Confederate Pension and Record Office. Hapeville, GA: Longino & Porter, 1955–1958.

Henry, Robert Selph. *"First with the Most" Forrest*. Indianapolis: Bobbs-Merrill Co., 1944.

Hess, Earl. *Civil War Infantry Tactics, Training, Combat, and Small-Unit Effectiveness*. Baton Rouge: Louisiana State University Press, 2015.

———. *Field Armies and Fortifications in the Civil War: The Eastern Campaigns, 1861–1864*. Chapel Hill: University of North Carolina Press, 2005.

Hewett, Janet B., ed. *The Roster of Confederate Soldiers, 1861–1865*. 16 vols. Wilmington, NC: Broadfoot Publishing Co., 1995.

Hinman, Wilbur F. *The Story of the Sherman Brigade*. Alliance, OH: Press of Daily Review, 1897.

Hoehling, A. A. *Last Train from Atlanta*. New York: Thomas Yoseloff, Printer, 1958.

Hood, John Bell. *Advance & Retreat*. 1880. New York: Da Capo Press, 1993.

Hood, Stephen. *John Bell Hood and the War for Southern Independence*. Lexington: University Press of Kentucky, 1982.

———. *John Bell Hood: The Rise, Fall, and Resurrection of a Confederate General*. El Dorado Hills, CA: Savas Beatie, 2013.

———. *The Lost Papers of Confederate General John Bell Hood*. El Dorado Hills, CA: Savas Beatie, 2015.

Horn, Robert C., *Men of the 45th Alabama Infantry Regiment, CSA*, Auburn AL: Horn, 1967.

Horn, Stanley F. *The Army of Tennessee*. Indianapolis, IN: Bobbs-Merrill, 1941.

Hornady, John R. *Atlanta: Yesterday, Today and Tomorrow*. Atlanta: American Cities Book Co., 1922.

Howell, H. Grady, Jr. *For Dixie Land I'll Take My Stand: A Muster Listing of All Known Mississippi Confederate Soldiers, Sailors and Marines*. 5 vols. Madison, MS: Chickasaw Bayou Press, 1998.

———. *Going to Meet the Yankees: A History of the "Bloody Sixth" Mississippi, C.S.A.* Jackson, MS: Chickasaw Bayou Press, 1981.

———. *To Live and Die in Dixie, A History of the Third Mississippi Infantry, C.S.A.* Jackson, MS: Chickasaw Bayou Press, 1991.

Hoyt, Bessie Willis. *Come When the Timber Turns.* Banner Elk, NC: Pudding Stone Press, Lees-McRae College, 1983.

Hughes, Nathaniel Cheairs, Jr., ed. *The Civil War Memoir of Philip Daingerfield Stephenson, D.D.*, Conway, AR: UCA Press, 1995.

———. *General William J. Hardee: Old Reliable.* Baton Rouge: Louisiana State University Press, 1965.

———. *The Pride of the Confederate Artillery: The Washington Artillery in the Army of Tennessee.* Baton Rouge: Louisiana State University Press, 1997.

Hurst, Samuel H. *Journal-History of the Seventy-Third Ohio Volunteer Infantry.* Chillicothe, OH: Hurst, 1866.

Jackman, John S., 1841-1912, *Diary of a Confederate Soldier: John S. Jackman of the Orphan Brigade*, Columbia, S.C.: University of South Carolina Press, 1990.

James, Alfred P. "General Joseph Eggleston Johnston, Storm Center of the Confederate Army." *Journal of American History* 14/3 (December 1927): 342–59. https://doi.org/10.2307/1891625.

Jenkins, Kirk, C. *The Battle Rages Higher: The Union's Fifteenth Kentucky Infantry.* Lexington: University Press of Kentucky, 2003.

Jenkins, Robert D., Sr. *The Battle of Peach Tree Creek, Hood's First Sortie.* Macon, GA: Mercer University Press, 2013.

———. *To the Gates of Atlanta, from Kennesaw Mountain, June 27, 1864 to Peach Tree Creek, July 20, 1864.* Macon, GA: Mercer University Press, 2015.

Johnson, Mark W. *That Body of Brave Men: The U. S. Regular Infantry and the Civil War in the West.* Cambridge, MA: Da Capo Press, 2003.

Johnson, Robert Underwood, and Clarence Clough Buell, eds. *Battles and Leaders of the Civil War.* 4 vols. New York: Century Company, 1887–1888.

Johnston, James Houston. *The Western and Atlantic Railroad of the State of Georgia.* Atlanta, GA: Georgia Public Service Commission, 1931.

Johnston, Joseph E. "Opposing Sherman's Advance to Atlanta." In Johnson and Buell, *Battles and Leaders of the Civil War*, 4:260–69.

———. "The Dalton-Atlanta Operations." In *The Annals of the Army of Tennessee and Early Western History*, edited by Edwin L. Drake, 1.1:1–13. Nashville, TN: A. D. Haynes, 1878.

Jones, Eugene W., Jr. *Enlisted for the War, The Struggles of the Gallant 24th Regiment, South Carolina Volunteers, Infantry, 1861–1865.* Hightstown, NJ: Longstreet House, 1997.

Jones, Terry L. "The Flash of Their Guns Was a Sure Guide." In Savas and Woodbury, *The Campaign for Atlanta & Sherman's March to the Sea*, 157–96.

Jordan, Weymouth T., Jr., ed. *North Carolina Troops, 1861–1865: A Roster.* 15 vols. Raleigh, NC: University Graphics, 1966–1999.

Kennett, Lee. *Marching through Georgia: The Story of Soldiers & Civilians during Sherman's Campaign.* New York: Harper-Collins Publishers, 1995.

Kerr, Homer L., ed. *Fighting with Ross' Texas Cavalry Brigade, C.S.A.: The Diary of Lieut. George L. Griscom, Adjutant, 9th Texas Cavalry Regiment.* Hillsboro, TX: Hill Junior College Press, 1976.

Key, Thomas J., Robert J. Campbell, and Wirt Armistead Cate, ed. *Two Soldiers: The Campaign Diaries of Thomas J. Key, C.S.A., and Robert J. Campbell, U.S.A.* Chapel Hill: University of North Carolina Press, 1938.

Key, William. *The Battle of Atlanta and the Georgia Campaign*. New York: Twayne Publishers, 1958.

Kimberly, Robert L., and Ephraim S. Holloway. *The 41st Ohio Veteran Volunteer Infantry in the War of the Rebellion, 1861–1865*. Huntington, WV: Blue Acorn Press, 1999.

Krick, Robert K. *The Gettysburg Death Roster: The Confederate Dead at Gettysburg*. 3rd ed. Dayton, OH: Morningside, 1981.

Lane, Mills, ed. *"Dear Mother: Don't grieve about me. If I get killed, I'll only be dead": Letters from Georgia Soldiers in the Civil War*. Savannah: Beehive Press, 1977.

Lanman, Charles. *The Red Book of Michigan: A Civil, Military, and Biographical History*. Detroit: E. B. Smith & Co., 1871.

Leeper, Wesley Thurman. *Rebels Valiant: Second Arkansas Mounted Rifles*. Little Rock: Pioneer Press, 1964.

Lewis, Lloyd. *Sherman: Fighting Prophet*. Lincoln: University of Nebraska Press, 1993.

Lindsley, John Berrien. *Military Annals of Tennessee, Confederate*. 2 vols. Wilmington, NC: Broadfoot Publishing Co., 1995.

Little, George, and James R. Maxwell. *A History of Lumsden's Battery, C.S.A.* Tuskaloosa [*sic*], AL: R. E. Rhodes Chapter, United Daughters of the Confederacy, 1905.

Livermore, Thomas L. *Numbers and Losses in the Civil War in America, 1861–65*. Boston: Houghton, Mifflin, 1900.

Longacre, Edward G. *Cavalry of the Heartland: The Mounted Forces of the Army of Tennessee*. Yardley, PA: Westholme Publishing, 2009.

Madaus, Howard Michael, and Robert D. Needham. *The Battle Flags of the Confederate Army of Tennessee*. Milwaukee: Milwaukee Public Museum, 1976.

Magee, B. F. *History of the 72nd Indiana Volunteer Infantry of the Mounted Lightning Brigade*. Lafayette, IN: S. Vater & Co., 1882.

Mahan, Joseph B., Jr. *A History of Old Cassville, 1833–1864*. Cassville, GA: Cass High School, 1956.

Manigault, Arthur Middleton, and Lockwood R. Tower, editor. *A Carolinian Goes to War: The Civil War Narrative of Arthur Middleton Manigault, Brigadier General, C. S. A.* Columbia: University of South Carolina Press, 1983.

Marcoot, Maurice. *Five Years in the Sunny South*. St. Louis: Missouri Historical Society, 1890.

Marvin, Captain E. E. *History of the Fifth Regiment C. V. Infantry, Record of Service of Connecticut Men in the Army and Navy of the United States during the War of the Rebellion*. Hartford, CT: Marvin, 1880.

———. *The Fifth Regiment Connecticut Volunteers: A History*. Hartford, CT: Press of Wiley, Waterman & Eaton 1889.

Massey, Steve. *Foremost: The 4th Mississippi Infantry in the Civil War*. Middleton, DE: Massey, 2023.

McBride, John R. *History of the 33rd Indiana Veteran Volunteer Infantry*. Indianapolis: Wm. B. Burford, Printer, 1900.

McDonough, James L. *Schofield: Union General in the Civil War and Reconstruction*. Tallahassee: Florida State University Press, 1972.

———, and James Pickett Jones. *War So Terrible: Sherman and Atlanta*. New York: W. W. Norton & Co., 1987.

———, and Thomas Connelly. *Five Tragic Hours: The Battle of Franklin*. Knoxville: University of Tennessee Press, 1983.

McKee, W. Reid, and M. E. Mason Jr. *Civil War Projectiles I: Small Arms & Field Artillery, with Supplement*. Orange, VA: Publisher's Press, 1980.

McLendon, Robert G., Jr. *History of the 53rd Regiment Alabama Volunteer Cavalry, and M. W. Hannon's Cavalry Brigade, Army of Tennessee, C.S.A.* Troy, AL: Black-Horse Publishing, 2007.

McMorries, Edward Young. *History of the First Regiment Alabama Volunteer Infantry, C.S.A.* Montgomery, AL: Brown Printing Co., 1904.

McMurray, W. J. *History of the Twentieth Tennessee Regiment Volunteer Infantry, C.S.A.* Nashville: Publication Committee, 1904.

McMurry, Richard M. *Atlanta 1864: Last Chance for the Confederacy*. Lincoln: University of Nebraska, 2000.

———. "Cassville." *Civil War Times Illustrated* 10/8 (December 1971): 4–9.

———. "The Mackall Journal and its Antecedents." *Civil War History: A Journal of the Middle Period* 20/4 (December 1974): 311–28.

______, ed., *An Uncompromising Secessionist, The Civil War of George Knox Miller, Eighth (Wade's) Confederate Cavalry*, Tuscaloosa, AL: The University of Alabama Press, 2007, 191).

_____. *The Civil Wars of General Joseph E. Johnston, Confederate States Army, Volume 1: Virginia and Mississippi, 1861–1863*, Savas Beatie Press, El Dorado Hills, CA: 2023.

McPherson, James M. *Battle Cry of Freedom: The Civil War Era*. New York: Ballantine, 1988.

McWhiney, Grady, and Perry D. Jamieson. *Attack and Die: Civil War Military Tactics and the Southern Heritage*. Tuscaloosa: University of Alabama Press, 1982.

Merrill, C. E. "Fearful Franklin." *Nashville World*, circa Dec. 1884.

Merrill, Catharine. *128th Indiana: The Soldier of Indiana in the War for the Union*. Indianapolis: Merrill & Company, 1869.

Merrill, Samuel. *The Seventieth Indiana Volunteer Infantry in the War of the Rebellion*. Indianapolis: Bowen-Merrill Company, 1900.

Miles, Jim. *Fields of Glory*. Nashville: Rutledge Hill Press, 1995.

Miller, John A. "A Memoir of the Days of '61." Manuscript. H. B. Simpson History Complex, Hillsboro, Texas.

Miller, Rex. *The Forgotten Regiment: A Day-by-Day Account of the 55th Alabama Infantry Regiment, C.S.A., 1861–1865*. Williamsville, NY: Patrex Press, 1984.

———. *Hundley's Ragged Volunteers: A Day-by-Day Account of the 31st Alabama Infantry Regiment, CSA, 1861–1865*. Round Rock, TX: Patrex Press, 1991.

Moe, Richard. "Narrative of the First Regiment of *Minnesota in the Civil and Indian Wars, 1861–1865*. St. Paul: Pioneer Press Co., 1891.

———. *The Last Full Measure: The Life and Death of the First Minnesota Volunteers*. New York: Henry Holt & Co., 1993.

Morris, Roy Sheridan, Jr. *The Life and Wars of General Phil Sheridan*. New York: Crown Publishing, 1992.

Neal, Diane, and Thomas Kremm. *The Lion of the South: General Thomas C. Hindman*. Macon: Mercer University Press, 1993.

Nenninger, Timothy K. *The Leavenworth Schools and the Old Army: Education, Professionalism, and the Officer Corps of the United State Army, 1881–1918.* Westport, CT: Greenwood Press, 1978.

Newlin, W. H. *The Preacher Regiment 1862–65: History of the 73rd Illinois Volunteer Infantry.* Springfield: Regimental Association of Survivors of the 73rd Illinois Volunteer Infantry, 1890.

Newton, Steven H. *Lost for the Cause: The Confederate Army in 1864.* New York: Da Capo Press, 2000.

O'Connor, Richard. *Thomas: Rock of Chickamauga.* New York: Prentice-Hall, 1948.

Obreiter, John. *The Seventy-Seventh Pennsylvania at Shiloh: History of the Regiment.* Harrisburg, PA: Harrisburg Publishing Co., 1908.

Overmyer, Jack K. *A Stupendous Effort: The 87th Indiana in the War of the Rebellion.* Bloomington: Indiana University Press, 1997.

Owen, Thomas McAdory. *History of Alabama and Dictionary of Alabama Biography.* Volume 3. Chicago: S. J. Clarke, 1921.

Palfrey, Francis W., *Military Historical Society of Massachusetts, Papers,* Cadet Armory, Boston, MA: 1918, vol. I.

Parks, Joseph H. *General Leonidas Polk, C.S.A.: The Fighting Bishop.* Baton Rouge: Louisiana State University Press, 1962.

Perry, Henry F. *History of the 38th Indiana Volunteer Infantry.* Palo Alto, CA: F. A. Stuart, Printer, 1906.

Polk, Dr. William M., *Leonidas Polk, Bishop and General,* vol. II, New York, NY: Longmans, Green, and Co., 1915.

Pollard, Edward A., *The Lost Cause; A New Southern History of the War of the Confederates,* New York, NY: E.B. Treat, Publisher, 1876, reprinted 1890.

Poole, John Randolph. *Cracker Cavaliers: The 2nd Georgia Cavalry Under Wheeler and Forrest.* Macon: Mercer University Press, 2000.

Porter, James D., ed. *Tennessee.* Vol. 10 of *Confederate Military History.* 1899. Reprint, Wilmington, NC: Broadfoot Publishing Company, 1987.

Priest, John Michael, ed. *John T. McMahon's Diary of the 136th New York 1861–1864.* Shippensburg, PA: White Mane Publishing Company, 1993.

Pula, James S. *The Sigel Regiment: A History of the 26th Wisconsin Volunteer Infantry, 1862–1865.* Campbell, CA: Savas Publishing Company, 1998.

Purdue, Howell, and Elizabeth Purdue. *Patrick Cleburne Confederate General.* Hillsboro, TX: Hill Junior College Press, 1973.

Quiner, E. B. *The Military History of Wisconsin: A Record of the Civil and Military Patriotism of the State, in the War for the Union.* Chicago: Clark & Co. Publishers, 1866.

Raab, Steven S., ed. *With the 3rd Wisconsin Badgers: The Living Experience of the Civil War through the Journals of Van R. Willard.* Mechanicsburg, PA: Stackpole Books, 1999.

Rabb, James W. *Loring: Florida's Forgotten General.* Manhattan, KS: Sunflower University Press, 1996.

Reed, Wallace Putnam. *History of Atlanta.* Syracuse, NY: D. Mason & Co., 1889.

Rennolds, Lieutenant Edwin H. *A History of the Henry County Commands which Served in the Confederate States Army.* Jacksonville, FL: Sun Publishing Co., 1904.

Ridley, Bromfield L. *Battles and Sketches of the Army of the Tennessee.* Mexico, MO: Missouri Printing & Publishing Co., 1906.

Rietti, J. C. *Military Annals of Mississippi.* Spartanburg, SC: The Reprint Co., 1976.

Robertson, John. *Michigan in the War*. Lansing, MI: W. S. George & Co., 1882.

Roddy, Ray. *The Georgia Volunteer Infantry 1861–1865*. Kearney, NE: Morris Publishing, 1998.

Roland, Dunbar. "The First Mississippi Cavalry." In *Publications of the Mississippi Historical Society*, Centenary Series. Vol. 2. Jackson, MS: Mississippi Historical Society, 1918.

Rollins, Richard, ed. *The Returned Battle Flags*. Redondo Beach, CA: Rank & File Publications, 1995.

Rowell, John W. *Yankee Artillerymen: Through the Civil War with Eli Lilly's Indiana Battery*. Knoxville: University of Tennessee Press, 1975.

Rowland, Dunbar. *The Official and Statistical Register of the State of Mississippi*. 1908. Reprinted as *Military History of Mississippi 1803–1898*, edited by H. Grady Howell Jr. Spartanburg, SC: The Reprint Company, Publishers, 1978.

Roy, Thomas Benton. "General Hardee and the Military Operations around Atlanta." *Southern Historical Society Papers* 8 (August and September 1880): 347–50.

Russell, James Michael. *Atlanta 1847–1890: City Building in the Old South and the New*. Baton Rouge: Louisiana State University Press, 1988.

Sandburg, Carl. *Abraham Lincoln: The Prairie Years & The War Years*. New York: Harcourt Brace & Co., 1954.

Savas, Theodore P., and David A. Woodbury, eds. *Campaign for Atlanta and Sherman's March to the Sea*. Essays of the American Civil War. 2 vols. Campbell, CA: Savas Woobury, 1994.

Scaife, William R. "Waltz between the Rivers: An Overview of the Atlanta Campaign from the Oostanaula to the Etowah." In volume 2 of *The Campaign for Atlanta & Sherman's March to the Sea*, edited by Theodore P. Savas and David A. Woodbury, 269–94. Campbell, CA: Savas Woodbury Publishers, 1994.

———. *The Campaign for Atlanta*. Atlanta, GA: Scaife, 1993.

Schuyler, Hartley & Graham. *Illustrated Catalog of Civil War Military Goods*. New York: Dover Publications, 1985.

Secrist, Philip L. *Sherman's 1864 Trail of Battle to Atlanta*. Macon: Mercer University Press, 2006.

———. "Resaca: For Sherman a Moment of Truth." *Atlanta Historical Journal* 22/1 (Spring 1978): 510–28.

Sesquicentennial Committee of the City of Rome. *Rome & Floyd County: An Illustrated History, 1834–1984*. Charlotte, NC: Delmar Company, 1986.

Shanahan, Edward P. *Atlanta Campaign Staff Ride Briefing Book*. Atlanta: Camp Creek Business Center, 1995.

Sherwood, G. L., and Jeffrey C. Weaver. *54th Virginia Infantry*. Lynchburg, VA: H. E. Howard, 1993.

Siegel, Alan A. *Beneath the Starry Flag: New Jersey's Civil War Experience*. New Brunswick: Rutgers University Press, 2001. Courtesy Gregg Biggs, MTSU Library and Archives.

Sifakis, Stewart. *Compendium of the Confederate Armies*. 10 vols. New York: Heritage, 1992–1995.

Skellie, Ron. *Lest We Forget: The Immortal Seventh Mississippi*. Volume 2. Birmingham, AL: Banner Digital Printing and Publishing, 2012.

Slay, David. "Playing a Sinking Piano: The Struggle for Position in Occupied Rome, Georgia." *Georgia Historical Quarterly* 90/4 (2006): 483–504.

Smith, G. W., *Confederate War Papers*, New York, 1884, Part I.

_____ *The Battle of Seven Pines* (New York, 1891).
Smith, Timothy B. *Champion Hill: Decisive Battle for Vicksburg*. El Dorado Hills, CA: Savas Beatie, 2004.
———. *This Great Battlefield of Shiloh: History, Memory, and the Establishment of a Civil War National Military Park*. Knoxville: University of Tennessee Press, 2004.
Steele, Matthew Forney, *American Campaigns, vol. I – Text*, Washington, D.C.: United States Infantry Association, 1922 [originally published 1909].
Stephens, Larry D. *Bound for Glory: A History of the 30th Alabama Infantry Regiment, Confederate States of America*. Ann Arbor: Sheridan Books, 2005.
Stewart, Bruce H., Jr. *Invisible Hero: Patrick R. Cleburne*. Macon: Mercer University Press, 2009.
Stewart, Nixon B. *Dan McCook's Regiment, the 52nd O.V.I.: A History of the Regiment, Its Campaigns and Battles, 1862–1865*. Alliance, OH: self-published, 1900.
Stone, Henry. "From the Oostanaula to the Chattahoochee." In vol. 8 of *Military Historical Society of Massachusetts Papers*. 1910. Reprint, Wilmington, NC: Broadfoot Press, 1990.
———. "1st Wisconsin Volunteer Infantry." Reprinted in *The Atlanta Papers*, No. 3, compiled by Sydney C. Kerksis. Dayton: Morningside Press, 1980.
Storrs, John W. *The Twentieth Connecticut: A Regimental History*. Ansonia, CT: Press of the Naugatuck Valley, 1886.
Strayer, Larry M., and Richard A. Baumgartner. *Echoes of Battle: The Atlanta Campaign*. Huntington, WV: Blue Acorn Press, 1991.
Strong, Robert Hale. *A Yankee Private's Civil War*. Edited by Ashley Halsey. Chicago: Henry Regnery Company, 1961.
Stroud, David V. *Ector's Texas Brigade and the Army of Tennessee 1862–1865*. Longview, TX: Ranger Publishing, 2004.
Sullivan, James R. *Chickamauga and Chattanooga Battlefields: National Park Service Historical Handbook*. Series No. 25. Washington, DC: National Park Service, 1956.
Sunderland, Glenn W. *Five Days to Glory*. Cranbury, NJ: A. S. Barnes and Company, 1970.
Sword, Wiley. *The Confederacy's Last Hurrah*. Lawrence: University Press of Kansas, 1992.
Sykes, Edward T. *Walthall's Brigade, A Cursory Sketch, with Personal Experiences*. Columbus, MS: Edward T. Sykes [publ.], 1905.
Symonds, Craig L. *Joseph E. Johnston: A Civil War Biography*. New York: W. W. Norton & Company, 1992.
———. *Stonewall of the West: Patrick Cleburne and the Civil War*. Lawrence: University of Kansas Press, 1997.
Tarrant, Sergeant E. *The Wild Riders of the First Kentucky Cavalry: A History of the Regiment in the Great War of the Rebellion 1861–1865*. Louisville, KY: R. H. Carothers Press, 1894.
Tennesseans in the Civil War, A Military History of Confederate and Union Units with Available Rosters of Personnel. 2 vols. Nashville: Civil War Centennial Commission, 1964–1965.
Thatcher, M. P. *A Hundred Battles in the West*. Detroit: L. F. Kilroy, Printer, 1884.
Thomas, Emory M. *The Confederate Nation: 1861–1865*. New York: Harper Collins Publishers, 1979.
Thomas, Wilbur D. *General George H. Thomas: The Indomitable Warrior*. New York: Exposition Press, 1964.
Thompson, Ed Porter. *History of the Orphan Brigade 1861–65*. Cincinnati: Caxton Publishing House, 1868.

Thompson, Illene D., and Wilbur E. Thompson. T*he Seventeenth Alabama Infantry: A Regimental History and Roster*. Bowie, MD: Heritage Books, 2001.

Toombs, Samuel, *Reminiscences of the Thirteenth Regiment New Jersey Volunteers*, Orange, NJ: The Journal Office, 1878, reprinted Hightston, NJ: Longstreet House, 1994.

Tucker, Glenn: *Chickamauga: Bloody Battle in the West*. 1961. Reprint, Dayton: Morningside House, 1984.

Van Horne, Thomas B. *History of the Army of the Cumberland*. 2 vols. Cincinnati: Robert Clarke & Co., 1876.

Walker, Scott. *Hell's Broke Loose in Georgia: A History of the 57th Georgia*. Athens: University of Georgia Press, 2005.

Warner, Ezra J. *Generals in Gray*. Baton Rouge: Louisiana State University Press, 1959.

Waters, Zack C. "The Partial Atlanta Reports of Confederate Maj[or] Gen[eral] William B. Bate." In *The Campaign for Atlanta & Sherman's March to the Sea*, edited by Theodore P. Savas & David A. Woodbury, 197–222. Campbell, CA: Savas Woodbury Publishers, 1994.

———, and Garry D. Fisher. *"The Damnedest Set of Fellows": A History of Georgia's Cherokee Artillery*. Macon, GA: Mercer University Press, 2010.

Watkins, Sam R. *Co. "Aytch": A Side Show of the Big Show*. Edited by Bell Irvin Wiley. Wilmington, NC: Broadfoot Publishing Company, 1994.

Weaver, Jeffrey C. *63rd Virginia Infantry*. Lynchburg, VA: H. E. Howard, 1991.

Weiss, Timothy F. "I lead you to battle: Joseph E. Johnston and the Controversy at Cassville," *Georgia Historical Quarterly* 91/4 (Winter 2007): 424–42.

Welcher, Frank J., and Larry G. Ligget. *Coburn's Brigade: The 85th Indiana, 33rd Indiana, 19th Michigan, and 22nd Wisconsin in the Western Civil War*. Carmel, IN: Guild Press of Indiana, 1999.

Wert, Jeffry D. *General James Longstreet: The Confederacy's Most Controversial Soldier*. New York: Simon & Schuster, 1993.

Wheeler, Lt. General Joseph. *Alabama*. Vol. 8 of *Confederate Military History*. Edited by General Clement A. Evans. Atlanta, GA: Confederate Publishing Company, 1899.

White, William Lee, and Charles Denny Runion, eds. *Great Things Are Expected of Us: The Letters of Colonel C. Irvine Walker, 10th South Carolina Infantry, C.S.A.* Knoxville: University of Tennessee Press, 2009.

Wiley, Bell Irvin. *Embattled Confederates: An Illustrated History of Southerners at War*. Illus. comp. Hirst D. Milhollen. New York: Harper & Row, 1964.

———. *The Life of Johnny Reb: The Common Soldier of the Confederacy*. Baton Rouge: Louisiana State University Press, 1943.

Willett, Elbert Decatur. *History of Company B (originally Pickens Planters), 40th Alabama Regiment, Confederate States Army, 1862–1865*. 1902. Reprint, Northport: Colonial Press, 1963.

Williams, Alpheus Starkey. *From the Cannon's Mouth: The Civil War Letters of General Alpheus S. Williams*. Edited by Milo M. Quaife. Detroit: Wayne State University Press, 1959.

Williams, T. Harry. *Lincoln and His Generals*. New York: Alfred A. Knopf, 1952.

Williamson, David. *The Third Battalion and the 45th Mississippi Regiment*. Jefferson, NC: McFarland & Company, 2004.

Willis, C. W. *Army Life of an Illinois Soldier in the One Hundred and Third Illinois*. Washington: Globe Publishing, 1906.

Willis, James. *Arkansas Confederates in the Western Theater*. Dayton: Morningside House, 1998.

Wood, Edwin Orin. *History of Genesee County, Michigan, Her People, Industries and Institutions*. Indianapolis: Federal Pub. Co., 1916.

Woodhead, Henry, ed. *Voices of the Civil War—Atlanta*. Richmond: Time Life Books, 1997.

Woodworth, Steven E. *Nothing but Victory: The Army of The Tennessee*. New York: Alfred A. Knopf, 2005.

———. "A Reassessment of Confederate Command Options during the Winter of 1863–1864," in *The Campaign for Atlanta & Sherman's March to the Sea: Essays of the American Civil War*, edited by Theodore P. Savas and David A. Woodbury, 1:1–22. Campbell, CA, Savas Woobury Publishers, 1994.

Wright, Henry H. *A History of the Sixth Iowa Infantry*. Iowa City: State Historical Society of Iowa, 1923.

Wynne, Ben. *A Hard Trip: A History of the 15th Mississippi Infantry, C.S.A.* Macon: Mercer University Press, 2003.

Wynne, Lewis N., and Robert A. Taylor, ed. *This War So Horrible: The Civil War Diary of Hiram Smith Williams, 40th Alabama Confederate Pioneer*. Tuscaloosa: University of Alabama Press, 1993.

Young, Lt. L. D. *Reminiscences of a Soldier of the Orphan Brigad*e. 1916. Reprint, Louisville, KY: Courier-Journal Job Printing Company, 1918.

Zinn, John G. *The Mutinous Regiment: The 33rd New Jersey in the Civil War*. Jefferson, NC: McFarland & Co., 2005.

Websites

6th Mississippi Infantry Regiment: "The Bloody Sixth." http://sixthmsinf.tripod.com/index.htm. Accessed 26 July 2023.

128th New York Infantry Regt. http://www.28thga.org/123ny_pictures_hq.html. Accessed 25 July 2023.

"Dewey Baptist Church Cemetery." Bartow County GenWeb. http://www.gabartow.org/Cem/cem.Dewey.shtml. Accessed 26 July 2023.

Ferguson, Edwin L. *Sumner County, Tennessee, in the Civil War*. Chapter 15. http://www.rootsweb.com/~tnsumner/sumnfg15.htm. Accessed 25 July 2023.

"Fort Attaway." RomeGeorgia.org. https://romegeorgia.org/civil-war/history/fort-attaway/. Accessed 24 April 2023.

Taylor, William Alexander. *Centennial History of Columbus and Franklin County, Ohio*. 2 vols. Chicago-Columbus: S. J. Clarke Publishing Co., 1909. Available at https://www.heritagepursuit.com/Franklin/FranklinIndex.htm.

"General Johnston's Address to the Army, May 20, Cassville, Ga.," *The Daily Sun*, Columbus, GA, May 24, 1864, 1, https://gahistoricnewspapers.galileo.usg.edu/lccn/sn82014939/1864-05-24/ed-1/seq-1/ (accessed July 24, 2023)

"Georgia Militia on Turner's Ferry Road." Historical Marker Database. http://www.hmdb.org/marker.asp?marker=17022. Accessed 26 July 2023.

Kennesaw Mountain National Battlefield Park. National Park Service. http://www.nps.gov/kemo/index.htm. Accessed 25 July 2023.

"The Letters and Papers of Captain Charles Manning Furman." http://batsonsm.tripod.com/letters/letters9.html. Accessed 25 July 2023.

Moore, Isaac V. "Diary of Isaac V. Moore." Our Confederate Ancestors. Edited by Ronald E. Jones. http://www.camp87scv.org/csa.htm. Accessed 23 July 2023.

"Special Correspondence to the Atlanta Intelligencer, May 18, 1864, Cartersville, Ga.," Columbus Times, Columbus, GA, May 21, 1864, https://gahistoricnewspapers.galileo.usg.edu/lccn/sn86053047/1864-05-21/ed-1/seq-2/ (accessed July 24, 2023).

Other

Atlanta History Center. Turning Point: The American Civil War. Permanent exhibit. See https://www.atlantahistorycenter.com/exhibitions/turning-point-the-american-civil-war/. Accessed 3 August 2023.

Bird, Frank. Childhood resident of Brookwood Hills subdivision. Phone interview with author, May 2008.

Brown, Chuck. "Map and Timeline, The Atlanta Campaign, May 7 through September 3, 1864, with a Focus on the Dallas Line in Relation to Pickett's Mill." Pickett's Mill State Historic Site Library, Dallas, GA.

Bunker, Robert M. Interview with author. July 2009. He also contributed photograph, letter, and biography of burial records for Thomas McCreary (1858) and Henry McCreary (1861) at Dewey Baptist Church Cemetery on Spring Place Road (author's field study, 28 August 2022).

Burns, Ken. *The Civil War*. Documentary. Interview with Shelby Foote. https://www.pbs.org/video/the-civil-war-ken-burns-interview-the-civil-war-shelby-foote/. Accessed 26 July 2023.

Correspondence with Stephen (Sam) Hood, 14 June 2023, copy of letter with signature of Francis M. Shoup confirming spelling without an "e;" original with Stephen Hood.

Calhoun County Mississippi: A Pictorial History. Special Collections. Calhoun County Library, Bruce, MS.

Georgia Historical Markers. Valdosta, GA: Bay Tree Grove Publishers, 1973. AHC.

Harrison, Patrick Morgan. "Confederate Dead at Canton, MS." January 1997. https://msgw.org/madison/Canton/index.htm. Accessed 3 August 2023.

Hunt, Patrick. "Quintus Fabius Maximus Verrucosus: Roman statesman and commander." *Encyclopedia Britannica*. https://www.britannica.com/biography/Quintus-Fabius-Maximus-Verrucosus. Accessed 3 August 2023.

Illinois Military and Naval Department. *Report of the Adjutant General of the State of Illinois*. Volume 5: *History of One Hundred and Fifth Infantry*. Springfield: Phillips Bros., State Printers, 1901.

Jones, Joseph. "Roster of the Medical Officers of the Army of Tennessee." *SHSP* 22 (1894): 165.

Julian, Col. Allen P. "Operations through the Present Ridgewood Community, July 1864." Mss 130, box 4, folder 4. Wilbur G. Kurtz Collection, KRC, AHC.

Kurtz, Wilbur G. Wilbur G. Kurtz Collection. Mss-130. KRC, AHC. Cited as Kurtz Papers.

Kurtz, Wilbur G., Sr. "General Joseph E. Johnston's Review of Sherman's *Memoirs*, published in Drake's Annals of the Army of Tennessee, Nashville, April 1878." Mss.

130, box 81, folder 3. Kurtz Papers. Special Collections. KRC, AHC.

Madry, Mrs. John Gray. "Battle of Peachtree Creek, July 20, 1864." Alfred Holt Colquitt Chapter, United Daughters of the Confederacy, MSS-130. Wilbur G. Kurtz Collection, KRC, AHC.

McCall, Phil. "Private Isaiah Crook, 37th Ga., Smith's Brigade." Typescript prepared for 1998 Crook Reunion. Vertical files. Kennesaw Mountain Battlefield Park Library.

McGavok Home and Cemetery records. Carnton Plantation Museum & Archives, Franklin, TN

McMurry, Richard M. *The Atlanta Campaign December 23, 1863, to July 18, 1864.* PhD diss., Emory University, 1967. Special Collections. Zach Henderson Library, Georgia Southern University.

Mitchell, Margaret. *Gone with the Wind.* New York: Macmillan, 1936.

Morris, Roy, Jr., and Phil Noblitt. *The History of a Failure, Spring 1864: A Federal Army Tries to Slip through Georgia's Snake Creek Gap.* Dalton, GA: Crown Gardens & Archives.

Murphree, T. M. *History of Calhoun County.* Special Collections. Calhoun Co. Library, Bruce, MS.

Nokes, Captain William N. Biographical information. Confederate file 134. Carter House Library and Museum, Franklin, TN. Contributed by Tim Burgess.

Popowski, Howard. "Battle of Dug Gap, May 8, 1864, Georgia Gilbraltar." Dalton, GA: Crown Gardens & Archives.

Powell, Dave. "Following Orders: From 'your Obd't Servant' to SMEAC and METT-T." Emerging Civil War. Blog. 30 March 2015. https://emergingcivilwar.com/2015/03/30/following-orders-from-your-obdt-servant-to-smeac-and-mett-t-2 (accessed April 25, 2023).

———. The Cassville Affair." In volume 1 of untitled book on the Atlanta Campaign. El Dorado Hills, CA: Savas Beatie Press, forthcoming 2024.

Quinlin, Bradley J. Historian, 21st Ohio Infantry, telephone and email conversations with author.

Rebellion Record, 1862–1869. Compiled by G. P. Putnam (1861–1863) and D. Van Nostrand, 1864–1868) consisting of a series of newspaper accounts and articles in 12 volumes; Frank Moore, editor, Vol. XI, p. 248, courtesy Special Collections, Rome/Floyd County, Ga. Library.

Resaca Confederate Cemetery Records. United Daughters of the Confederacy. Dalton, GA; Crown Gardens & Archives.

Simmons, Hugh. Historian and biographer of the 12th Louisiana. Correspondence with author.

Stone, Larry. *Snake Creek Gap—Resaca.* Dalton, GA: Crown Gardens & Archives.

———. *The Battle of Resaca (& Nance Springs).* Dalton, GA: Crown Gardens & Archives.

"Thrasherville: Where Atlanta Began." Georgia State Historical Marker no. 060–173. Erected 1992. Located at the Federal Reserve Bank, 105 Marietta Street, Atlanta. https://www.hmdb.org/m.asp?m=59670. Accessed 3 August 2023.

United Daughters of the Confederacy. Georgia Division. *Confederate Reminiscences and Letters 1861–1865.* Chickamauga National Battlefield Park Library.

WPA, Records for Calhoun Co., MS. R 139, B 11, S 4, 10654. MDAH.

WPA, Records for Choctaw Co., MS. R 139, B 11, S 5, 10661. MDAH.

INDEX